D0461410

STANDARDS AND GLOBAL TRADE: A VOICE FOR AFRICA

THE WORLD BANK
Washington, D.C.

This book was made possible through support provided by the Office of Sustainable Development, Bureau for Africa, U.S. Agency for International Development, under the terms of Grant No. AFR-G-00-00-00016-00. The opinions expressed herein are those of the author(s) and do not necessarily reflect the views of the U.S. Agency for International Development.

Library of Congress Cataloging-in-Publication Data

Standards and global trade: a voice for Africa / John S. Wilson, Victor O. Abiola (editors).
  p. cm.
Includes bibliographical references.
ISBN 0-8213-5473-6
  1. Africa—Foreign economic relations. 2. Exports—Africa. 3. Quality control—Africa. 4. Export marketing—Africa. I. Wilson, John S., 1956- II. Abiola, Victor O., 1975- III. World Bank.

HF1611.S73 2003
328'.3'096–dc21   2003045032

Cover Photo Credit: World Bank Photo Library / Illuminating Development Collection / Eric Miller

Contents

Foreword　v

Acknowledgments　vii

Contributors　ix

Abbreviations　xi

Executive Summary　xix

Introduction　xxv
John S. Wilson
Victor O. Abiola

**1　Improving Market Access Through Standards Compliance:
A Diagnostic and Road Map for Kenya**　1
Hezron Omare Nyangito
Tom Olielo
David Magwaro

**2　Bridging the Standards Divide: A Case Study and
Action Plan for Mozambique**　65
Gabriela Rebello da Silva
Lara da Silva Carrilho

**3　Standards, Technical Regulations, and Product Quality:
Institutional Evidence from Nigeria**　165
J. Adeboye Adeyemo
Abiodun S. Bankole

**4　Standards and Trade in South Africa: Paving Pathways for
Increased Market Access and Competitiveness**　235
André Jooste
Erik Kruger
Flip Kotzé

**5　Enhancing Uganda's Access to International Markets:
A Focus on Quality**　371
N. Rudaheranwa
F. Matovu
W. Musinguzi

Index　427

Foreword

TRADE IS A CRUCIAL DRIVER OF GROWTH, YET AFRICA WITH 10% OF WORLD population, represents less than 2% of world trade. Most African economies are small and provide limited national markets for local trade that can spur faster growth rates for development. As a result, the pursuit of better access to foreign markets is, therefore, a crucial component of Africa's development strategy. Yet, the erosion in the region's share of world trade between 1970s and 1990s represents approximately $70 billion, or about one-fifth of its gross domestic product (GDP).

Africa includes many of the world's poorest countries, with 300 million of its people living on less than 1$ a day. Simply halving the number of the continent's poor by 2015 will require an approximate annual growth of about 7% as well as more equitable distribution of income. Increasing its engagement in international trade and improving penetration of global markets can help achieve this pace of growth. While there are many complementary actions that are needed to improve the investment climate so as to allow a higher growth rate to be achieved, addressing the effect of product standards both as barriers to trade and opportunities to expand market access is likely to be one area where action will have a high rate of return.

In expanding trade, the link between standards, access to foreign markets, and development is at the forefront of policy debate. This is particularly true with regard to Africa. African countries face critical challenges in improving domestic capacity to meet production and quality standards that are required in foreign markets. As this volume documents, this process will include; (1) enhancing production practices, (2) improving quality assurance and management systems by firms, and (3) better monitoring, evaluation, product testing and packaging methods, to respond to changing technical requirements of trading partners. Institutional reforms, investment in human capital and infrastructure improvements in laboratories and facilities are also necessary.

However, Africa's investment in promoting exports in compliance with international norms will be more beneficial if its trading partners (particularly in Europe and the United States) advance complementary trade policies. These include reduction in agriculture subsidies that depress international product prices, reduction in high tariffs that restrict higher-end value imports, and elimination of non-tariff measures that limit trade, including restrictive standards and technical regulation, duplicative testing and certification procedures, rules of origin, and antidumping duties.

Non-compliance with international standards deprives African farmers access to key international markets, and may lead to a further reduction in global market share—especially in agricultural products like horticulture and fisheries, and light manufactures like textiles. Without addressing market access and international standards compliance issues, African firms and farmers will be unable to take full advantage of recent market opening initiatives such as the US African Growth and Opportunity Act and the EU's Everything But Arms initiative.

There is a strong need to support and strengthen effective programs and initiatives designed to improve the ability to comply with international standards and to support the harmonization of technical regulations regionally. The assessment and analyses contained in this book directly compliment related work on these issues. For example, the findings will serve to inform specific projects or programs that can be implemented through the new Standards and Trade Development Facility (STDF) established by the World Bank and partner agencies to strengthen international coordination in technical assistance on product standards. The Facility offers the opportunity to translate the results of the case studies contained in this book into concrete actions that can help African firms and farmers implement international standards to increase exports that will boost incomes of the poor.

The book provides in-depth case-by-case analysis of five African countries—Kenya, Mozambique, Nigeria, South Africa, and Uganda. It is intended to be a resource for information and guidance for policymakers, the development community, and others in a critical new "behind the border" barrier to trade. Each chapter discusses the economic context in which standards apply to each country and examines the mechanisms with which the country and its representatives have participated in the process of setting/revising standards and technical regulations at the local and international level. The analysis includes a review of existing laws and regulations and the extent to which they are consistent with current international norms. It examines each country's physical infrastructure and organizational capacities to design and implement standards and technical regulations. The authors also discuss and analyze the implementation processes and some estimated impact of various standards, technical regulations, and related production/marketing practices in about thirty specific industry segments.

Perhaps most important, the volume suggests concrete action plans on how African firms and farms can improve product quality and reach international markets in key commodity sectors. These recommendations directly complement Africa's market access development objectives, as outlined by the New Partnership for Africa's Development (NEPAD). By identifying concrete projects—including those that can be championed by development institutions and NGOs—to help African countries improve their trade capacity, the action plans can serve as a useful resource to inform decisions on practical ways to fulfill the commitment contained in the WTO's Doha Development Agenda to meet development and trade needs in the region.

Nicholas Stern
Senior Vice President and
Chief Economist
The World Bank

Acknowledgments

COMPLETION OF THIS BOOK WOULD NOT HAVE BEEN POSSIBLE WITHOUT THE participation, support, advice, and encouragement of many individuals who contributed directly to its publication.

Indeed the chapters included in this book reflect collaborative work among research teams consisting of trade specialists, economists, standards experts, and practitioners across several countries. The content in the volume also reflects input from colleagues at the World Bank, other institutions, research networks, universities, and private sector groups. In particular, we would like to acknowledge the Center for International Agricultural Marketing and Development (CIAMD), South Africa; The Development Policy Center, Department of Economics, University of Ibadan (DPC), Nigeria; Instituto Nacional de Normalização e Qualidade (INNOQ), Mozambique; Universidade Eduardo Mondlane (UEM), Mozambique; Kenya Institute for Public Policy Research and Analysis (KIPPRA); Institute of Economics, Makerere University, Uganda; Kenya Bureau of Standards (KEBS); Uganda National Bureau of Standards (UNBS); and other groups in Africa. The views and recommendations expressed in this volume, however, are of course entirely those of the authors. They do not necessarily reflect views of the World Bank Group, its Executive Directors, shareholder governments, or any other institution.

The book was produced as part of a project funded by the U.S. Agency for International Development, under the Africa Trade and Investment Policy Program (ATRIP). This financial support is gratefully acknowledged. Support for its completion was also drawn from work underway on trade and standards at the World Bank, supported by the United Kingdom, Department for International Development (DFID). Moreover, the content in this volume draws upon diagnostic work and country studies underway elsewhere, including work ongoing in international agencies including the World Trade Organization (WTO), Food and Agriculture Organization (FAO), and United Nations Conference on Trade and Development (UNCTAD), among others.

In particular, we wish to thank the World Bank country directors, country economists, and sector specialists for their valuable input as reviewers of each chapter, including Makhtar Diop, Fayez S. Omar, Robert R. Blake, Darius G. Mans, Delfin Sia Go, Peter G. Moll, Alberto D.K. Agbonyitor, and Dipac Jaiantilal. The encouragement and advice of Paul Collier and Bernard Hoekman throughout this project is especially acknowledged and very much appreciated. In addition, we would like to thank Steve Jaffee, who played an important role in providing assistance in the early stages of the project. We would also like to thank Lawrence Hinkle, Philip English, Keiko Kubota, Cornelis de Haan, Cornelis Van Der Meer, Victoria Kwakwa, Francis Ng, and especially Lolette Kritzinger-van Niekerk and staff in the Bank's country office in South Africa, among others. Special thanks also to Tsunehiro Otsuki and Baishali Majumdar in compiling the preliminary results of the World Bank TBT survey on standards referenced in several chapters of this book. We would also like to thank Rob Simms Jason Victor, and Michelle Chester,

Maria Kasilag, Rebecca Martin, and Maribel Flewitt for their support throughout the production of this book.

We would also like to acknowledge the participants in a seminar and videoconference in July 2001, as part of the work leading to this book. The U.S. Trade Representative Robert Zoellick, Trade Minister Biwott of Kenya, Director General Mike Moore of the World Trade Organization (WTO), Nicholas Stern, Senior Vice President of the World Bank, and members of the Africa Economic Research Consortium (AERC) were instrumental in launching this work. In particular we would like to thank Dominique Njinkeu and T. Ademola Oyeyide we would for their advice and assistance during the seminar. Furthermore, we are particularly grateful to Rosa Whitaker, William Jackson, Susan Troje, Lisa Ortiz, and other staff from the USTR and U.S. Agency for International Development; as well as staff from the U.K. Department for International Development for their encouragement, guidance, and support. Staff of the World Bank office of the publisher and others in the production of the book is also gratefully acknowledged.

Finally, the chapters included in this book also benefited from feedback and comments from numerous organizations, associations, and private sector representatives and participants in one-on-one interviews, focused group sessions, workshops, and seminars. We acknowledge the considerable time, effort, and valuable information these participants have devoted to the content of these chapters and hope readers will benefit from the collective efforts of many who contributed to the book's completion.

Contributors

Hezron Omare Nyangito	Kenya Institute for Public Policy Research and Analysis (KIPPRA)
Tom Olielo	Kenya Bureau of Standards (KEBS)
David Magwaro	Ministry of Trade and Industry
Dr. J. C. Kegode	Kenya Plant Health Inspectorate Service (KEPHIS)
Dr. W. Songa	KEPHIS
Esther Kimani	KEPHIS
Ann N. Kingori	KEPHIS
E. B. Manyara	Ministry of Trade and Industry (MTI), Kenya
Francis M. Warui	MTI
Janet Abilla	MTI
George Gachoka	MTI
J. Ombwori	Ministry of Agriculture and Rural Development (MA&RD), Kenya
Andama Mosoti	MA&RD
Caroline Outa	Kenya Bureau of Standards (KEBS)
J Mokaya	KEBS
Stephen J. Muli	Kenya Chamber of Commerce and Industry (KCCI)
Patrick Okoth	Attorney General Chambers
Rod Evans	Home Grown Ltd.
L.K. Mwona	MCFU Ltd.
John Njenga	Kenya Flower Council
Peter Gatonye	Kenya Flower Council
Dr. J.P. Nthuli	Department of Veterinary Services (DVS)
Cosmas Kyengo	Fresh Produce Export Association of Kenya (FPEAK)
Dr. Stephen Mwika	Association of Fish Processors and Exporters of Kenya
J. M. Nzuma	Kenya Institute for Public Policy Research and Analysis
J. Kamau	Kenya Association of Manufacturers (KAM)
Lydia Ndirangu	Kenya Institute for Public Policy Research and Analysis
	Sunripe Exporters of Vegetables and Fruits, Nairobi
	Suera Flowers, Nairobi
	Waridi Flowers, Nairobi
	Makindu Exporters, Nairobi
	Tea Board of Kenya, Nairobi
	Department of Fisheries, MA&RD
	Homegrown Ltd., Nairobi
	Cirio Del Monte Ltd., Nairobi

	Kenya Association of Manufacturers (KAM)
	Association of Fish Processors and Exporters of Kenya (AFIPEK)
	Fresh Produce Export Association of Kenya (FPEAK)
	Kenya Flower Council (KFC)
Gabriela Rebello da Silva	Instituto Nacional de Normalização e Qualidade—INNOQ
Lara da Silva Carrilho	Universidade Eduardo Mondlane (UEM)
J. Adeboye Adeyemo	University of Ibadan, Nigeria
Abiodun S. Bankole	University of Ibadan, Nigeria
André Jooste	The Centre for International Agricultural Marketing and Development (CIAMD)
Erik Kruger	InfoHarvest
Flip Kotzé	CIAMD
Hans Balyamujura	CIAMD
Ernst Idsardi	CIAMD
John le Roux	CIAMD
Stephan Hosking	UPE
Chris Ettmayer	UPE
N. Rudaheranwa	Makerere University Institute of Economics, Uganda
F. Matovu	Makerere University Institute of Economics, Uganda
W. Musinguzi	Uganda National Bureau of Standards

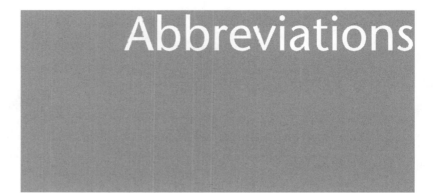

Abbreviations

AAM	Mozambique Cotton Association
ABT	Administrative Barrier to Trade
ABIODES	Association for Organic Agriculture, Biodiversity and Sustainable Development in Mozambique
ACE	Audit Control and Expertise
ACM	Mozambique Trade Association
AERC	African Economic Research Consortium
AGOA	African Growth and Opportunity Act
AGRARIUS	Association of Mozambican Farmers
AICAJU	Association of Cashew Producers
AIMO	Mozambican Industrial Association
AIOPA	Association of Edible Oil and Related Products Producers
AJAM	Young Farmers Association
AMAPIC	Mozambican Association of Industrial Prawn Fisheries
APAMO	Mozambican Association of Sugar Producers
APC—EC	Africa Caribbean, Pacific—European Union
APEC	Asia Pacific Economic Co-operation
APCER	Portuguese Association of Certification
APHIS	USDA Animal and Plant Health Inspection Service
APSSS	South of Save Salt Producers Association
ARC	Agricultural Research Council
ARSO	African Regional Organization for Standardization
ATRIP	Africa Trade and Investment Policy Project
BIPM	International Bureau for Weights and Measures
BM	Bank of Mozambique
BOP	Balance of Payment
BRC	British Retail Consortium
BSTM	Bank Standard Totta of Moçambique
BUDS/SSE	Business Uganda Development Scheme Support for Small Scale Enterprises
BVQI	Bureau Veritas Quality International
CAC	Codex Alimentarius Commission
CADI	Business Advisory Centre
CAIM	Manica Agro Industrial Company
CASCO	Committee on Conformity Assessment at ISO
CBI	Circuit Breakers Industry
CBS	Citrus Black Spot
CCA	Codex Coordinating Committee for Africa

CCP	Codex Contact Point
CCFFP	Codex Committee on Fish and Fishery Products
CCM	Mozambique Chamber of Commerce
CENELEC	European Committee for Electro technical Standardization
CEO	Chief Executive Officer
CFC	Common Fund for Commodities
CGA	Citrus Grower Association
CHAEM	Centre for Environmental Health and Medical Examinations
CIB	Coffee Industry Board
CIF	Cost Insurance and Freight
CKS	Coordinating Specifications
CLUSA	Cooperative League of the United States of America
CM	Council of Ministers
CM	Check Mate International Pty
CMB	Coffee Marketing Board
CMT	Committee of Ministers Responsible for Trade at SADC
CNPML	Mozambican National Cleaner Production Centre
Codex	Codex Alimentarius
COMESA	Common Market for Eastern and Southern Africa
COMPETE	The Competitive Private Enterprise and Trade Expansion
COPOLCO	Committee on Consumer Policy at ISO
CPAP	Comissão Permanente da Assembleia Popular
CPI	Investment Promotion Centre
CPLP	Community of Countries with Portuguese as the Official Language
CRI	Citrus Research International
CSIR	Council for Scientific and Industrial Research
CSTA	Customs Technical Council
CTA	Confederation of Mozambican Economic Associations
CTN	Technical Committees on Standardisation
CTNS	Sector Technical Committees on Standardisation
DANIDA	Danish International Development Agency
DDA	Dairy Development Authority
DECOM	Consumers Protection Association
DEVCO	Committee on Developing Country Matters at ISO
DF	Forestry Department-FAEF
DFID	Department for International Development UK
DFPT	Deciduous Fruit Producers Trust
DFR	Department of Fisheries Resources
DGR	Directorate of Genetic Resources
DHA	Department of Environmental Health at the Ministry of Health
DINA	National Directorate of Agriculture at Ministry of Agriculture and Rural Development
DINAP	National Directorate of Livestock at Ministry of Agriculture and Rural Development
DIP	Department of Fisheries Inspection at Ministry of Fisheries
DNCI	National Directorate of Domestic Market at Ministry of Industry and Commerce
DNE	National Directorate of Statistics
DNER	National Directorate for Rural Extension at Ministry of Agriculture and Rural Development
DNFFB	National Directorate of Forestry and Wildlife at Ministry of Agriculture and Rural Development
DNI	National Directorate of Industry at Ministry of Industry and Commerce
DNP	National Directorate of Fisheries at Ministry of Agriculture and Fisheries

DOH	Department Of Health
DPHQ	Department of Plant Health and Quality
DPIC	Provincial Directorate of Industry and Trade
DS (SNS)	Seed Department at Ministry of Agriculture and Rural Development
DSV	Department of Plant Protection at Ministry of Agriculture and Rural Development
DTI	Department of Trade and Industry
EAC	East African Community
EAP	Economically Active Population
EAN	Electronic Article Number
EBAS	Enterprise Business Assistance Scheme
EC	European Commission
EEC	European Directive Technical Regulation
EIA	Environment Impact Assessment
EMIA	Export Marketing Incentive Assistance
EPOPA	Export Promotion of Organic Products from Africa
ERP	Economic Recovery Program
ESLC	Electrical Supplies Liaison Committee
EU	European Union
EUREPGAP	Euro Retailers Produce Working Group Good Agricultural Practise
EVDLU	Essential Veterinary Drug List of Uganda
FAEF	Faculty of Agronomy and Forestry Engineering
FANR SDU	SADC Food Agriculture and Natural Resources Sector Development Unit
FAO	United Nations Food and Agriculture Organization
FDI	Foreign Direct Investments
FEMA	Business Forum for the Environment
FEWS	Famine Early Warning System
FLAG	Food Legislation Advisory Group
FPT	Fresh Produce Traceability
FRUTISUL	Southern Mozambique Fruit Growers Association
FSC	Forest Stewardship Council
FTA	Free Trade Area
GAP	Good Agricultural Practice
GATT	General Agreement on Tariffs and Trade
GDP	Gross Domestic Product
GLP	Good Laboratory Practice
GMO	Genetically Modified Organisms
GMP	Good Manufacturing Practice
GOM	Government of Mozambique
GPSCA	Office for the Promotion off Commercial Farming, Ministry of Agriculture and Rural Development
GSP	General System of Preference
GTM	Metrology Working Group at INNOQ
HACCP	Hazard Analysis of Critical Control Point
HAG	Hygiene Assessment System
IAF	International Accreditation Forum
IAFI	International Association of Fish Inspectors
HDI	Human Development Index
HORTEXA	Horticultural Exporters Association
HPI	Human Poverty Index
IAF	International Accreditation Forum
IAM	Mozambican Cotton Institute—Ministry of Agriculture and Rural Development

ICC	International Capital Corporation (Mozambique)
ICCIDD	International Council for the Control of Iodine Deficiency Disorders
ICM	Mozambique Cereals Institute at Ministry of Industry and Trade
IDD	Iodine Deficiency Disorders
IDEA	The Investment In Developing Export Agriculture
IDIL	Institute for the Development of Small-Scale Industry at Ministry of Industry and Trade
IDPPE	Institute for the Development of Small-Scale Fisheries at Ministry of Fisheries
IEC	International Electrotechnical Commission
IFIR	International Forestry Industry Round Table
IFOAM	International Federation of Organic Agriculture Movements
ILAC	International Laboratory Accreditation Co-operation
ILO	International Labour Organisation
IMF	International Monetary Fund
INA	National Sugar Institute—Ministry of Agriculture and Rural Development
INCAJU	Institute for the Promotion of Cashew at Ministry of Agriculture and Rural Development
INE	National Institute of Statistics
INFCO	Committee on Information Systems and Services at ISO
INIA	National Institute of Agronomic Research at Ministry of Agriculture and Rural Development
INIVE	National Institute of Veterinary Research at Ministry of Agriculture and Rural Development
INNOQ	National Institute of Standardisation and Quality at Ministry of Industry and Trade
IOLMF	Indian Ocean Legal Metrology Forum
IOR—ARC	Indian Ocean Rim Association for Regional Co-operation
IP	Integrated Programme for Industrial Development in Mozambique
IPA	Livestock Production Institute at Ministry of Agriculture and Rural Development
IPEX	Mozambican Institute of Export Promotion at Ministry of Industry and Trade
IPP	Fisheries Research Institute at Ministry of Fisher
IPPC	International Plant Protection Convention
IPQ	Portuguese Institute for Quality
IRLCO—CSA	International Red Locust Control Organisation
ISO	International Organisation for Standardisation
ISO 1400	Environmental Management Standard
ISO 17025	General requirements for the competence of test and calibration laboratories
ISO 9000	Management system standard
ISO 9001	Quality management system
ITC	International Trade Centre
ITS	Intertek Testing Services International Limited
ITU	International Telecommunications Union
JITAP	The Joint Integrated Assistance Program
KARI	Kawanda Research Institute
LBSC	Local Business Service Centre Agency
LDC	Least Developed Country
LINK	Forum of National and International NGOs in Mozambique
LMO	Living Modified Organisms
LNHAA	National Laboratory for Water and Food Hygiene
MA	Ministry of Agriculture
MAAIF	Ministry of Agriculture, Animal Industry and Fisheries
MADER	Ministry of Agriculture and Rural Development
MAC	Manufacturing Advisory Centre
MAP	Ministry of Agriculture and Fisheries
MD	Ministerial Diploma
MEC	Member of the Executive Council (Province)

MFPED	Ministry Of Finance, Planning and Economic Development
MIC	Ministry of Industry and Trade
MICOA	Ministry for the Co-ordination of Environmental Affairs
MICT	Ministry of Industry, Trade and Tourism
MISAU	Ministry of Health
MOA	Memorandum of Understanding
MOH	Ministry of Health
MOU	Memorandum of Understanding
MP	Ministry of Fisheries
MPF	Ministry of Planning and Finance
MRA	Mutual Recognition Agreement
MRL	Maximum Residue Level
MSC	Marine Stewardship Council
MSF—CIS	Doctors Without Borders
MTTI	Ministry of Tourism, Trade and Industry
NAFTA	North American Free Trade Agreement
NCC	National Codex Committee
NCD	New Castle Disease
NCS	National Calibration Service
NDA	National Department of Agriculture
NEDLAC	National Economic Development and Labour Council
NEMA	National Environment Management Authority
NEP	National Inquiry Point
NGO	Non-Governmental Organization
NMI	National Metrology Institute
NML	National Metrology Laboratory of South Africa
NOGAMU	National Organic Agricultural Movement of Uganda
NOSA	National Occupational Safety Association
NPPO	National Plant Protection Organisation
NSB	National Standards Body
NSC	National Standards Council
NSTIKA	Enterprise Promotion
NTB	Non-tariff Barrier
NTE	Non-traditional Exports
NYTIL	Nyanza Textile Limited
OAU	Organisation of African Unity
OECD	Organisation for Economic Development and Cooperation
OGL	Open General License
OIC	Orange International Certificate
OIE	International Office of Epizootics
OIE	World Organisation for Animal Health (Organisation International des Epizooties)
OIML	International Organisation of Legal Metrology
PAMM	Programme Against Micronutrient Malnutrition
PARPA	Plan of Action for the Reduction of Absolute Poverty
PDI	Previous Disadvantaged Individuals
PHA	Plant Health Auditing
PHC	Primary Health Care
PHP	Plant Health Promotion
PMB	Produce Marketing Board
PODE	Enterprise Development Project
PPECB	Perishable Products Export Board

PRA	Pest Risk Analyses
PROAGRI	Project for Agriculture and Rural Development
PSI	Pre-Shipment Inspection
PSF	Private Sector Foundation
PTB	German National Institute for Metrology
PWP	Protocols and Work Programmes
R&D	Research and Development
RDA	Recommended Dietary Allowance
RSPM	Regional Meeting of Salt Producers and Traders
SABS	South African Bureau of Standards
SACU	Southern African Customs Union
SADC	Southern African Development Community
SADCA	SADC Co-operation in Accreditation
SADCMEL	SADC Co-operation in Legal Metrology
SADCMET	SADC Co-operation in Measurement Traceability
SADCSTAN	SADC Co-operation in Standardisation
SAFTA	Southern African Free Trade Agreement
SALMA	South African Lumber Miller's Association
SAMIC	South African Meat Industry Company
SANAS	South African National Accreditation System
SAP	Structural Adjustment Program
SAPO	South African Plant improvement Organisation
SEILA	Secretary of State for Light and Food Industries
SEMOC	Mozambican Seed Company
SGS	Société Générale de Surveillance (Verification, testing and certification)
SI	International System for Units
SIDA	Swedish International Development Agency
SIMA	Agricultural Markets Information Systems
SIP	Special Import Program
SITCD	Industrial and Trade Sector Coordinating Division at SADC
SME	Small and Medium Enterprises
SMME	Small Medium and Micro Enterprises
SNS	National Seed Service
SOE	State Owned Enterprises
SPEED	Support for the Private Enterprise Expansion and Development
SPF	Sector Partnership Fund
SPIS	The Sanitary and Phytosanitary Inspection Services
SPS	Sanitary and Phytosanitary Measures
SQAM	Standardisation, Quality Assurance, Accreditation and Metrology
SQAMEG	Standardisation, Quality Assurance, Accreditation and Metrology Expert Group
SQMT	Standardization, Quality Assurance, Metrology and Testing
SSASI	World Bank Sub-Saharan Africa Seed Initiative
TAC	Tender Advice Centre Programme
TBT	Technical Barriers to Trade—WTO Agreement
TIPS	Trade and Investment Policy Secretariat
TC	Technical Committee
TCP	Technical Cooperation Programme
TDCA	SA-EU Trade, Development and Co-operation Agreement
TE	Traditional Exports
TEPU	Tropical Ecological Foods Uganda
TIDP	Trade and Investment Development Programme

TNF	Trade Negotiation Forum (SADC)
TQM	Total Quality Management
UCC	Uniform Code Council
UCDA	Uganda Coffee Development Authority
UCTF	Uganda Coffee Trade Federation
UEM	University Eduardo Mondlane
UEPB	Uganda Export Promotion Board
UFEA	Uganda Flower Exporters Association
UFPEA	Uganda Fish Processors and Exporters Association
UGIL	Uganda Garment Industries Limited
UIA	Uganda Investment Authority
UMA	Uganda Manufacturers Association
UN	United Nations
UNBS	Uganda National Bureau of Standards
UNCTAD	United Nation Conference on Trade and Development
UNDP	United Nations Development Programme
UNIDO	United Nations Industrial Development Organization
UNECE	United Nations Economic Commission for Europe
UNEP	United Nation Environmental Programme
UNICEF	United Nations Children's Fund
UNIDO	United Nations Industrial Development Organisation
URA	Uganda Revenue Authority
US $	United States Dollars
USA	United States of America
USAID	United States Agency for International Development
USFDA	United States Food and Drug Administration
USI	Universal Salt Iodisation
UTRA	Technical Unit for Customs Restructuring
UTRE	Technical Unit for Enterprises Restructuring
VAT	Value Added Tax
VAM	Vulnerability Assessment and Mapping
VC	SABS Compulsory Specification
WFP	United Nations World Food Programme
WHO	World Health Organisation
WTO	World Trade Organisation
WTO/SPS	World Trade Organisation, Sanitary and Phytosanitary Agreement
WTO/TBT	World Trade Organisation, Technical Barriers to Trade Agreement

Executive Summary

UNDERSTANDING THE LINK BETWEEN TRADE, STANDARDS, AND EXPORT COMPETITIVENESS is at the forefront of trade policy analysis and debate. This is particularly true in regard to enhancing pro-poor growth and employment opportunities in Africa. Global competition has become more intensified in terms of quality, price, supply chain management, and dependability of delivery systems. Consumer preferences (influenced by increased incomes, as well as, health and other social concerns) and demand for quality products are also changing the way suppliers and producers respond to market signals. Consumer demand in developed countries is also starting to reflect preferences for cultural values such as concern over child labor laws and environmentally friendly practices in product purchases.

This broadening of consumer demand (especially in the area of food safety) has intensified the development of new industry codes of practice and enforcement mechanisms. The development of standards is also becoming increasingly driven by the private sector as enforcement is moving toward primary production levels. Likewise, the burden of standards compliance appears to be shifting to producers. And, in concert with national regulatory agencies, monitoring compliance is increasingly becoming the function of retailers and other groups higher up in the distribution chain.

Changing consumer demand is not only influencing national and international market structures. It is also putting pressure on national and international standards development and regulatory agencies to become more effective in supporting the private sector and ensuring compliance. Consumer confidence in the regulatory capacity of national and international agencies is diminishing as a result of health-related product scares that have emerged in recent years (for example, foot-and-mouth disease and Bovine Spongiform Encephalopathy). Consumers are demanding more information about products, chemical content in foods, and production processes. For example, while many African countries, such as Kenya and Uganda, struggle with the challenge of restructuring the fishing industry after several product bans by Europe, some buyers in developed countries are insisting on eco-friendly fish harvesting and processing by suppliers.

Addressing these changes in international demand patterns, market structure, and enforcement requirements poses a real challenge to firms and farmers and their supporting organizations (particularly smallholders) in developing countries. This is particularly true in Africa. In this volume, we seek to identify the specific capacity constraints, opportunities, and institutional reform needed for market-access success in five African countries—Nigeria, Uganda, Mozambique, South Africa, and Kenya. We also seek to place trade facilitation measures and standards (both voluntary and mandatory technical standards) within a broader developmental context. Table 1 outlines the list of countries and commodity sectors included in our analysis.

The case studies in this volume reveal the existence of gaps in standards formulation, compliance, and enforcement capacity in Africa as compared to international norms. Such gaps appear to be even broader when a comparison is made between standards and industry codes of practice that are prevalent in specific industry sectors (in African countries and those of their trading partners in Europe and the United States).

Table 1: Specific Country and Sector Studies under the Africa Trade Standards Project

Country	Product Sector(s)
Kenya:	Coffee; Fruits & Vegetables; Flowers; Fish & Fishery Products; Cotton & Textiles
Mozambique:	Cashew; Sugar; Cotton; Peanuts; Seeds; Salt; Fruits & Vegetables; Flowers; Fish & Fishery Products
Nigeria:	Horticulture; Food & Beverages; Cocoa & Cocoa Products; Textiles and Clothing; Fish & Fishery Products
South Africa:	Electro-technical Products; Forestry; Textiles; Fisheries; Fruit Industries; Meat & Livestock
Uganda:	Flowers; Honey; Fish; Textiles; Horticulture (Flowers and Vegetables); Organic Coffee

Specifically, this analysis highlights the following common challenges facing the private sector in Africa:

(i) Differences in consumer preferences and demand for quality among consumers in African countries and those of their trading partners in developed countries (Europe, United States, etc.). Demand for product quality appears to be generally lower in African countries, and firms and farmers do not perceive quality issues as critical to domestic sales. There are a number of reasons for this. (a) The case study on Nigeria suggests, for example, that poverty forces local consumers to tolerate lower-quality products; (b) There appears to be a lack of consumer awareness about food safety and quality. Consumers are not aware of the impact of standards like Maximum Residue Levels (MRLs), animal diseases control procedures, etc.; (c) Unlike Europe, many African countries lack strong consumer organizations that pressure retailers and producer groups to provide higher quality goods; and (d) Differences in cultural preferences between consumer groups in many African countries and their counterparts abroad. For example, labor and environmental standards are not priorities for local consumer groups in Africa. To summarize, in meeting local demand, it appears that local business practices in many African countries tend to substitute quality for price—sometimes even in the procurement of intermediate goods.

(ii) Differences in the complexity of market structures, industry size, supply chain, and distribution systems facing local suppliers. In many cases, supplying the local market is less complicated and requires fewer middlemen (or none at all). Consumers rarely demand the use of traceability systems, relying more on local brand names and the reputations of product peddlers (which is not the case for non-local consumers). African firms (especially Small and Medium Enterprises [SMEs]) seeking to export have found the requirements of markets in developed countries (e.g., CE marking, Forestry Stewardship Council, United States Underwriters Laboratories Mark, EUREGAP, and packaging requirements) to be difficult to meet. Because local consumer expectations for product quality are much lower than international norms, national regulations are considerably "softer" than international ones. Therefore, local producers develop production systems that only meet these lower standards, thereby making it difficult for producers to "ramp up" to meet the stricter international standards should they choose to export. This leaves the bulk of the exporting market to the largest local firms and multinational companies who can afford to adjust their production systems to meet international regulations.

(iii) Most of the countries examined here have not replaced the quality functions of defunct commodity boards with appropriate quality control and enforcement mechanisms that will support more liberal access to markets. The Uganda study suggests, for example, that the depression in international prices of some commodities (e.g., coffee) is putting pressure on local coffee producers, in the absence of effective regulatory agencies, to substitute quality for price.

(iv) Participation in the formation of global standards, codes of practice, or regulations appears not to have been very effective in some African countries. National channels through which local private sector inputs are reflected in international standards debates appear to be ineffective because of low political priority inadequate government participation, and private sector representation. As a result, domestic codes of practice developed in these countries are neither recognized nor merged with similar codes in their export markets.

Moreover, standards development agencies and organizations offer few mechanisms to collect input from local African producers in the development of codes of practice. As a result, many domestic producers surveyed in this volume are standards-takers (forced to accept and try to meet international standards), reacting to ever-changing standards that do not accommodate unique constraints pre-existing in the local environments. Sometimes, as standards-takers, these domestic producers face harsh penalties (such as blanket industry bans) for non-compliance. This also affects their level of awareness and understanding of these standards, and their preparedness for compliance. Many firms have to rely on minimal interactions with importer agents, or on national standards development organizations in making such information available.

(v) Many of the industry sectors assessed here have directly benefited from foreign direct investment (FDI) in compliance with foreign standards. Multinational companies dominate most exports from these sectors. However, recent decline in FDI in the regoin, coupled with low technological capacity, and weak physical infrastructure and transport facilities are undermining the long-term competitiveness of these sectors.

(vi) While access to information about global industry best practices or standards does not appear to be a problem for most multinationals, in the five countries examined in this volume, the same cannot be said for local small- and medium-sized enterprises (SMEs)—particularly for small farmer groups. African SMEs do not to have the resources to invest in modern information systems. Government agencies and other organizations that provide extension services and assistance in standards often lack the necessary qualified staff, financial resources, and equipment to assist on a regular basis.

(vii) Compliance to international standards is also demanding a shift from manual and low-skilled labor practices in agriculture and light manufacturing to more sophisticated best practices comparable to those found in developed countries. For example, African farmers are now required to invest in Integrated Crop Management (ICM) practices and Euro Retailers Produce Working Group Good Agricultural Practise (EUREGAP) principles, Hazard Analysis of Critical Control Point (HACCP) protocols, and standards that require better enterprise-wide supply management techniques, record systems, and equipment, including detailed labeling and traceability systems. In implementing and managing these systems, private sector investment in human capital resources development is crucial.

Small- and medium-sized enterprises and farmer groups are particularly challenged by these requirements because (a) they lack the financial and human resources needed to upgrade their products and production/farming practices and processes to meet international norms, (b) industry players do not appear to be well organized in a manner that will facilitate cost-effective traceability of products, and (c) certification schemes and testing are mainly provided by foreign firms, and the costs of testing and certification for some industries (e.g., forestry) appear to be very high for SMEs. To summarize, simultaneous application of multiple standards and technical requirements the increasing costs and difficulties of testing and verification procedures; and rapidly changing consumer preferences of overseas markets raises the costs of entry into global markets for African SMEs. Many existing SMEs and smallholder farmers are also being forced to close as global competition raises the bar on the products and process standards that must be met before companies can export.

(viii) Some industry sectors in Africa have been successful in the adoption of internationally acceptable compliance systems, for example, the flower industry in Kenya and the fishing industry in Uganda. These industries have experienced improved product quality as well as increased revenues. However, the price paid for these improvements has been significant, and in many cases, was not attainable without increased foreign direct investments and donor assistance backed by political will and direct government support. For example, the fishing industry in Uganda and Kenya went through several costly European Union (EU) bans, and has not recovered its earlier production levels in Kenya. SMEs seeking to export needed to make significant investments in upgrading technology, equipment, and infrastructure, including the establishment of better quality control facilities before they could re-enter or expand their access to export markets. In some sectors, like textiles, firms may need to develop completely new product lines, overhaul spinning technology, develop a world class garment industry, etc. (as is shown in the case of Nigeria).

Finally, it is important to note that compliance with foreign and international standards does not necessarily secure global market share. Africa's deeper penetration of global markets ultimately depends on the ability of its farms and farmers to produce high-end value and quality products at internationally competitive prices. This task becomes more complicated as compliance to foreign and international standards in Africa is still fraught with many constraints and forthcoming challenges as the global standards development architecture evolves.

The case studies also highlight institutional challenges facing many of these countries. These include:

(i) A lack of consciousness about standards and technical regulations in policy-making. Trade liberalization has placed pressures on the entire policy-making apparatus and institutions dealing with export promotion in Africa, including those related to standards, quality management, and technical regulations. Many of the export promotion plans in these countries mention the need to develop competitive exportable products, yet, little attention is given to quality-related issues.

The assessment of the national standards development framework presented in this volume suggests that there are still numerous gaps in the national standards, metrology systems, quality laws, and codes of practices. It appears there are many national standards that need to be updated to conform to international norms (e.g., grading systems, agricultural practices, disease control, etc.). The Mozambique study, for example, points out that the local cotton grading system is below international standards. While this appears to benefit cotton farmers and traders, it causes technical problems in the ginneries, and affects cotton-seed separation and processing, ultimately resulting in low quality lint sold at discounted prices.

(ii) Many African standards development agencies and notification points lack well-functioning information management infrastructure to coordinate local standards-related activities and interest groups with their international counterparts. The mechanisms for consultations among national Sanitary and Phytosanitary Measures (SPS)/food safety authorities and other stakeholders, both internationally and locally, appear to be inadequate, slow, and sometimes inaccurate.

(iii) Representatives of key standards institutions cannot attend international meetings due to lack of funds. Even when they attend these meetings, the lack of capacity and infrastructure to develop scientific evidence to support negotiations at these meetings hinders them from influencing the outcomes significantly. For example, the capacity to undertake food safety risk assessments is very low in Africa—even in middle-income countries like South Africa—such that contesting or supporting standards for maximum residue levels, pest infection, etc., is very difficult for local producers.

(iv) Human and technological capacity is weak and there is Proliferation of regulatory roles and responsibilities across national agencies.

These create difficulties resource allocation and enforcement problems.

   a. Local regulations need to be updated and enforcement mechanisms need to be improved. The depth of required legal reforms necessary in each country depends on the development stage of its private sector, its Standardisation, Quality Assurance, Accreditation and Metrology (SQAM), etc.

   b. Essential facilities, such as testing laboratories, are not adequately staffed in many countries in the region and scientific equipment is outdated.

   c. Systematic collection and storage of records is not undertaken and local certification agencies are not internationally recognized. This situation is worsening given the declining levels of public expenditures in many countries.

   d. A lack of rural infrastructure, sufficient support services, technical information and credit; as well as, high transportation costs, constitute major problems for smallholders in the agricultural sector.

 (v) In supporting the private sector to invest in compliance, costs of compliance can be prohibitive for African governments, and Foreign Direct Investment (FDI) is low. Moreover, compliance with SPS measures and environmental requirements may become moving targets because standards often become more stringent once producers achieve compliance.

In addressing these private sector and institutional constraints, recommendations for a reform agenda are outlined in each chapter. In general, these include the following components:

 (i) Expand support for the integration of SMEs into the standards development system by designing programs and support schemes tailored to improve SME farming practices, develop extension services and support systems, leverage the use of technology, etc. Here, the focus should be on strengthening backward and forward linkages between SMEs and large export firms. Such programs should also include financial support, technology enhancement, and export support services components that would support SME investment in quality enhancement anchored on cost-effective upgrades of production and transaction processes.[1]

 (ii) Streamline the roles, responsibilities, and competencies of relevant standards monitoring, certification and enforcement agencies. Adequate financing; and investment in human, physical, and information assets for better co-ordination and participation in local, national, regional, and international standards should be provided to these agencies. Such support should be anchored on programs that induce active private sector participation.

 (iii) Strengthen the legal framework and harmonization process of national quality laws, standards, regulations, and policies to be consistent with international norms. This would involve reviewing national laws and updating them, and designing policies that create incentives and influence private sector investment in compliance.

 (iv) Establish integrated information management and reporting tools that can be shared among trade development organizations, their memberships and clients, and international counterparts. There is significant room for ICT-based projects that will enhance communication between stakeholders involved in making, monitoring, enforcing, and adopting standards in Africa.

 (v) Support projects that target better certification, accreditation schemes, and enforcement capacity. Monitoring and testing services could be provided through accredited local service providers to reduce costs and delays in

---

[1]These linkages should provide incentives to employ international standards and must be backed by adequate SME financing instruments. For example, a key strategy employed by South Africa was to develop an incentive scheme called "Competitiveness Fund" under its Department of Trade and Industry (DTI). The Fund offers grant fund assistance and comprehensive support of conformity assessment activities to its SMEs. DTI also hosts a "Sector Partnership Fund" that supports five or more firms and organizations in the development and execution of collaborative projects.

product shipment. Local/regional certification systems can be expanded and customized to meet the needs of SMEs (for example, group certification schemes have been effective in South Africa). In addition, this process should include developing programs to strengthen quality inspections at borders, ports, and production points. This may also extend to enhancing laboratory capabilities, deploying more effective monitoring equipment, etc.

(vi) Strengthen national and/or regional capacity to conduct risk analysis and other scientific and policy research. These analyses will provide critical evidence to boost negotiating capacity at international meetings and resolve disputes that may arise from enforcement either in exports or imports. This would help Africa better exercise rights within the context of the World Trade Organisation (WTO) agreements. This may also extend into strengthening research capacity for standards with a focus on the impact, benefits, and importance of compliance.

(vii) Develop high impact awareness campaigns to increase private and public sector awareness of standards and technical regulations. These awareness programs should include local consumer awareness campaigns on the impact of standards, the need for better product quality, and enforcement mechanisms through which violation of consumer quality concerns can be addressed.

(viii) Create better infrastructure for transportation, and other shared facilities (e.g., pack houses) that may help reduce costs of supply chain management and logistics, and improve delivery quality of export products.

A more detailed case-by-case set of recommendations are provided in subsequent chapters of this volume.

Introduction

John S. Wilson
Victor O. Abiola

TRADE FACILITATION AND STANDARDS IN SUB-SAHARAN AFRICA: AN OVERVIEW

O VER THE LAST DECADE, AFRICAN STATES HAVE INTENSIFIED, WITH VARYING DEGREES OF success, the implementation of export-led policy reforms that will spur economic growth. Yet, the continent's share of the world's output continues to decline. Progressive attempts at improving the region's involvement in the world economy appear to be marked by a simultaneous decline in its importance to the global economy. The continent's trade with the rest of the world is declining and foreign direct investment (FDI) has fallen. Income levels are among the lowest in the world, and the continent's debt overhang has further retarded growth over time. What role do non-tariff measures, product standards, and related capacity constraints play in this context?

In 1970, total world trade of goods and services were just US$1.5 trillion in current dollars, and made up about 13% of the Gross National Product (GDP). Today, the value of global trade in goods and services is approximately US$8 trillion. Trade in goods accounts for the largest share of global flows at US$6 trillion, followed by trade in commercial services, which represent another US$1.5 trillion (Stern, 2002). For Africa, the reverse is true. Ng and Yeats (1996) estimate a decline in Sub-Saharan Africa's (SSA) share of world exports between 1962 to 1964 and 1991 to 1993, equivalent to an over $11 billion reduction in annual exports. This trend is partly a consequence of a dependency on export products whose share of world trade is declining, as well as, a simultaneous decline in Africa's capacity to maintain its competitive advantage in the production and export of traditional export commodities. More recently, Ng and Yeats (2002) estimate that while global trade in Africa's traditional exports grew at an annual rate of below 2% between 1990 and 1999.

This loss in global market share of traditional commodities is attributable to several factors including: (1) the impact of agricultural production subsidies in developed country markets; (2) anti-export bias in the policies of SSA countries; (3) declining relative growth in global demand for Africa's specialized traditional exports; (4) dysfunctional government intervention, including regulatory policies and tax regimes; (5) high-risk and monopolistic market environments that have constrained the development of financial markets and ensured low returns on investment and capital flight; (6) a depreciation in physical infrastructure and human capital that has undermined cost-effective and competitive production of Africa's traditional exports (some of which relates directly to meeting standards for international market acceptance); and (7) external shocks and other constraints including those imposed by the continent's trading partners. Moreover, as noted in Ng and Yeats (2002), product price instability may be major problem for exporters. One half of traditional products experienced average price changes of 50% or more. Price changes are associated with collapse of traditional product prices.

The current problem with enhanced competitiveness for African exporters is also related to the fact that overall competitive changes over the past decade have had only a marginal impact on the environment that affects export success. There is no doubt that domestic policy reforms to remove measures of trade protection would contribute to African economic development and export expansion. This includes the type of regulatory and institutional reform outlined in subsequent chapters in this volume. Africa should also move to diversify away from traditional exports—removal of anti-export biases in domestic policy are critical. Increased emphasis on standards and quality, a major theme of this book, is one part of the overall context of reform. It is also important to recognize the compounding effect of physical environment and natural disasters on many of Africa's fragile economies. Many are landlocked, with poor infrastructure, and perilous diseases (including malaria and HIV) that undermine the development of human capital.

Reaping the benefits of reform, however, also depends on the successful engagement of African states with foreign national and regional institutions in the world economy. This engagement process becomes more beneficial as African states become more open to trade (Sachs and Warner, 1995, 1997); develop better institutional quality to promote change and manage external shocks (Fosu, 2000; Yilmaz and Gore, 2001); and secure access to global markets and investment opportunities. As African economies become more open and involved in international trade, compliance to foreign and international standards is also becoming more prominent an underlying factor driving export success, as the analysis in this book documents.

Economic development and trade expansion in Africa is also being shaped by policies external to African economies. Stern (2002) highlights some policy reforms that can and should be undertaken by high-income countries that will generate significant benefits for ordinary people in Africa and other developing countries. Some of these include (1) reducing agriculture subsidies;[2] (2) reducing the large number of high tariffs that restrict imports from developing countries, particularly where tariffs increase with the stage of production; (3) eliminating non-tariff measures that restrict trade including restrictive standards and technical regulation, rules of origin, and anti-dumping duties that too frequently target developing countries; and (4) removing restrictions on the temporary movement of natural persons supplying services.

In addition to these factors, Africa's debt burden further undermines its capacity for accelerated growth. The continent's debt burden is about US$200 billion, increasing from 62% of GNP in 1990 to about 66 per cent in 2000. Foreign direct investment has also been difficult to attract (Wohlmuth, K., et al—2000).

Considered together, these factors underline the uncertainty of Africa's current position and complicate policy reform initiatives. In this context, therefore, both foreign and local trade reforms are necessary for Africa to reap the full benefits of openness and trade liberalization. For these benefits to be sustainable, the empowerment of African public and private sector players to participate in international trade, foreign partnership, investment, and regional cooperation should be a fundamental part of Africa's development process. Included in this process is the need to improve global market penetration for Africa's agricultural commodities and light manufactures as a central defense against poverty. This is because most African countries are still primarily agricultural-based, with most states dependent on about two primary commodities for more than half of their export earnings. Here again, voluntary standards and mandatory technical requirements on food safety, animal, and plant health in importing countries play an important role. Additionally, Africa's

---

[2]In a speech delivered at the National Council of Applied Economic Research, New Delhi, November 28, 2002, Nicholas Stern, Senior Vice President and Chief Economist of the World Bank noted that the Organization for Economic Cooperation and Development (OECD) support for farmers is over US$300 billion—totaling almost one-third of all farm receipts. The potential impact of these policies on African exports has been highlighted in several New Partnership for Africa's Development (NEPAD) documents as well.

comparative advantage remains, in part, focused on the production of primary commodities (Wood and Mayer, 2001). Therefore, securing new and diversified agricultural markets that consolidate and increase Africa's trade position in agriculture products and light manufactures will have direct impact on the incomes of many Africans indirectly improving their poverty situation.

Seeking access to markets alone is, however, not enough. In addition, significant investment-based growth (financing and technology transfer) that will improve product quality and production practices, and help overcome supply-side constraints that hinder competitiveness of African products prospects for export diversification and other trade facilitation efforts, need to be improved. These constraints include good production infrastructure, better access to credit for technology-based expansion, reduction in subsidies in developed country markets, consistent policies that enable appropriate research, forecasting and competition, and private sector-led human capital development etc. These reforms need to be orchestrated in the context of more stable macroeconomic environments that are anchored in better fiscal discipline, high growth rates, and a greater degree of labor absorption.

African governments are conscious of these needs and are progressively prioritizing and stepping up efforts at widening intra-African market opportunities, as well as, trade with other developing and industrialized countries through trade liberalization. The most up-to-date attempt is subsumed in the "NEPAD Market Access Initiative" which underscores the need for effective participation of African countries in the World Trade Organization Doha agenda, anchored in successful regional integration, good governance, and increased productivity that would facilitate efficient exploitation of trading opportunities created by multilateral, regional, and bilateral trade agreements.

With a per capita GDP decline from about 1.3% per year in the 1980s to 1.8% per year between 1990 and 1994,[3] and real GDP falling from 3.2% in 2000 to 2.5% in 2002, Sub-Saharan Africa's development prospects hinge on its ability to create favorable conditions for growth and reduction in poverty (Rodrik, 1998; Collier and Gunning, 1999). Forecasts of growth estimates for 2003–2015 fall far short of the recommended growth target for a

major turnaround. According to the World Bank Global Economic Prospects (2003), real growth in Africa is estimated to rise to 3.2% in 2003 and to about 3.8% in 2004, with per capita growth averaging 1.5% over the 2005–2015 period. Thus, to meet development objectives outlined in the Millennium Development Goals (MDG) alone, rapid and sustained improvements in good, stable and productive governance processes, macro-economic stability, consistent deepening of regional and international trade and investment opportunities, and diversification of exports and markets are very urgent and vital in Africa.

The development of trade, in turn, requires deeper penetration into global markets, development of supply capacity and competitiveness, and the strengthening of the institutional, human, and regulatory capacity for trade and trade-related policy design. All of these must be implemented in line with global demand and standards. Central to this process is the recognition of the changing roles of international, regional, and local trade standards and technical regulations, and the impact they can have on the expected benefits from Africa's attempts at trade promotion and integration.

Why Standards Matter for Africa

Understanding the link between standards, technical regulations, and trade is crucial in the design of broader development programs that can create new opportunities for pro-poor growth. Standards and technical regulations define what can (or cannot) be exchanged, and outline the procedures under which such exchanges are or are not permissible. Wilson (2001) discusses two broad categories of standards—product and process standards. Product standards define quality, safety, authenticity, etc. that goods should possess (e.g., minimum nutrition content of a food item, maximum pesticide residues on an agricultural product, and performance requirements for pieces of furniture or machinery). Process standards refer to the conditions under which products are produced, packaged or refined. Examples include the use (or absence of use) of particular inputs into crop or livestock production, the technical processes used for fishing, traceability requirements required for meat, and some horticulture products, management practices used for

---

[3] About 5–6% below the average for all low-income developing nations.

tree-felling and forestry management, and the work conditions of laborers. These process and product standards provide the premise for various categories of standards including rules that define labor, food, health and environmental standards.

In this volume, the term "standards" is used to refer to both voluntary market-driven standards, as well as, technical regulations. These standards, in principle, should be based on scientific evidence, and are designed to facilitate information exchange, ensure product quality, and the provision of important objectives or goods that are otherwise neglected in the private market (e.g., public health and safety). Standards and regulations can, therefore, improve quality of life, create shared consumption benefits for the public, and solve common product and quality problems. Well-defined standards can facilitate trade by reducing transaction and other costs (including costs of information about the quality of goods or services and associated risks), and to improve linkages among firms across industries.

Standards as a Prerequisite for Access to Markets

The process for formulating standards (national or international) can be complex, as well as costly. This is increasingly so as globalization drives more intensive international competition between firms across nations. Changing global market conditions now require firms to meet more refined, diverse and sometimes unexpected and personalized customer tastes and societal preferences. Consumer demand is represented by a mix of informal rules reflected in industry practices (i.e., voluntary standards), as well as formal rules crafted within the context of national regulatory frameworks (i.e., technical regulations). Many times, regulations codify, replace, or underline pre-existing voluntary practices within an industry—and as such, can be private sector-driven.

For many voluntary standards driven by consumer demand, failure to comply with such standards may hinder consumer acceptance, but not necessarily block access to specific export markets. For standards that are mandatory in international or national law (mostly technical regulations), failure to comply prohibits a product or service from being sold in a given market. However, due to global or local weaknesses in enforcement, such products may still find their way into the marketplace at discounted prices. In some cases, voluntary standards may have stiffer requirements than is required by regulatory authorities. Also conformity assessments are made in compliance to the demands of the buyer. For example, in the horticulture industry, some buyers now demand descriptions of environmental circumstances and the location in which a product is grown. This is creating opportunities for differentiation among producers that adopt specific environmental standards and those who do not. The consequence, however, is that such requirements may add to production costs (especially for small- and medium-sized enterprises) of firms supplying these markets, or entering new ones.

Standards as Determinants of Competitive Advantage

In addition to the benefits standards can produce, there has been increasing concern about the use of standards and technical regulations as discriminatory non-tariff barriers to trade.

Meeting standards involves costs—investments in equipment and staff to ensure compliance and costs related to proving conformity to standards. Public welfare costs may include the systems needed to determine and certify that products meet legal requirements set in national technical regulations. These costs are generally referred to as costs of compliance. For the bearer of these costs, changes in costs of compliance directly influence production costs, and may alter the relative gains that accrue to producers and consumers. This is particularly true for agribusinesses and other firms in related industries experiencing falling revenues due to a decline in traditional African exports commodity prices.

Standards as Instruments of Commercial Policy

Standards designed to ensure food safety, animal, and plant health are critical. It is important to design standards and regulations, which consider risk, best practice international science, and trade. The standards development process can result in excessively stringent levels of protection in favor of a dominant interest group where the participation of diverse other interest and commercial stakeholders is limited, or where a dominant group has initial bargaining strengths. This is because such a process may be shaped by protectionist intents of a dominant interest group—such as a cartel or monopoly producer—which does not consider national welfare or consumer interests. When such standards form the basis for regulations, they may effectively block market entry, exclude competition, and consolidate and monopolize markets. Greater market power, in turn, may be used to influence the allocation of the benefits that may accrue from the use of these standards. Interest groups with less bargaining strength, and who are unable to participate in the rule-making process, become standards-takers. In many cases, they become bearers of the compliance costs associated with these standards.

Thus, when national government regulations and industry practices are designed to discriminate between sources of supply (e.g., through inefficient and duplicative national testing and certification requirements), they create secondary costs (or reduce gains from exchange) such that may restrict trade significantly. Furthermore, technical regulations that are not based on international norms (especially when they differ across countries) may limit trade by increasing costs of market entry. By extension, they can undermine global competition, shield local monopolies from foreign competition, divert trade, and impose severe costs on consumers. In addition, standards fragmentation may occur, where interest groups or countries tend to implement their own criteria even in the face of accepted international standards (e.g., CODEX) further complicates compliance costs and procedures for standards-takers.

Relative bargaining strengths and participation capacity are, therefore, two very crucial determinants of the outcomes of a standards development process. As a result, the improvement in effective participation and balancing of relative bargaining strengths among stakeholders involved in rules setting and enforcement is one of the central challenges facing current mechanisms governing the formulation and enforcement of trade rules today —including the World Trade Organization framework.

It is important to note however, that even when standards are universal and fair, compliance costs, especially those associated with upgrading production and infrastructure systems, and enforcement, may still differ significantly across countries. This is due to differences in institutional and financial capacity, infrastructure, human capital, consumer preferences and local conditions, and technological capacity, among other factors. This creates a gap between existing national standards and enforcement capacity in these countries, and those required internationally (termed "standards divide"). This is especially prevalent in many developing and low-income countries, and may alter the gains to compliance due to each country. Nevertheless, for firms and farmers in developing Africa to participate fully in the global marketplace, they must comply with acceptable international standards, and must therefore invest in compliance.

Standards and Trade in Africa: Some Prospects

In the case of sub-Saharan Africa, progress is undermined, in part, by trade barriers in the form of subsidies, tariffs, and other non-tariff barriers. These non-tariff barriers include rules of origin and increasingly stringent technical requirements imposed on traditional products (e.g., beef, aquaculture, banana, and peanuts) from developing countries including Africa. Some of these restrictions extend to manufactures (e.g., the European bans on the importation of electronically regulated earth leakage devices from countries like South Africa). There is increasing empirical evidence of the negative impact of these technical regulations and other non-tariff barriers to trade—especially in relation to phytosanitary and food safety rules.

Amjadi and Yeats (1995) have shown, for example, that the overall importance of pre-Uruguay Round non-tariff barriers is evident from the fact that approximately US$5.9 billion of OECD imports from Africa faced these measures. More recent empirical research at the World Bank also reviews the impact of standards on Africa's exports. In a case study of the trade effect of European food safety standards on African exports, Wilson and Otsuki (2001a) find that the new harmonized European standard on aflatoxin B1—a common contaminant affecting agricultural products—is estimated to cost African exporters over US$670 million per year in lost nut and grain exports.[4]

---

[4]"Saving Two in A Billion: A Case Study to Quantify the Trade Effect of Food Safety Standards," Tsunehiro Otsuki, John S. Wilson, and Mirvat Sewadeh, *Food Policy (26)* 2001.

In addition, (Wilson and Otsuki, 2002a) suggests that if governments followed international standards for pesticide residues in bananas, instead of national standards set by many developed countries, African banana exports would soar by about US$410 million a year. The same is true for beef. Research conducted at the Bankindicates that the adoption of science-based international standards for minimum residue levels of veterinary drugs could boost South Africa's beef exports by US$160 million a year. To summarize, by participating in international standards, and implementing acceptable international rules, it is estimated that Africa could gain up to US$1 billion a year from higher exports of nuts, dried fruits, and other agricultural commodities. These potential losses can be very costly to a continent with about 659 million inhabitants of which 300 million earn less than $1 a day.[5]

In further analysis of aflatoxin standards, Wilson and Otsuki show that the cost of not adopting a uniform international standard on aflatoxin (B1) is estimated at US$38.8 billion in lower global cereals and nuts trade. If the world were to adopt a standard (chlorpyrifos) at a level set in the European Union, instead of the one suggested by Codex—the body charged with setting global standards—there would be a US$5.3 billion loss in world banana exports. To summarize, there is evidence to suggest that losses associated with divergent national regulations may block African firms and farmers from entering new and diverse global product markets.

Furthermore, African firms and farmers have started to recognize and highlight the potential impact of technical barriers on their capacity to export. Preliminary results from a new survey of technical barriers to trade conducted by the World Bank, African firms confirmed that product quality and low demand are the most important factors that affect their firm's ability to export. See Box 1 on next page for a summary of these results.

The impact of standards and mandatory technical regulations to Africa's trade position can, therefore, not be overlooked. To participate effectively in global trade, African countries must develop the capacity to meet international standards. This in itself is a formidable challenge. Developing strategies to address these challenges requires targeted research to enhance understanding of the incentives, principles and constraints that influence production and trade in different products, economic sectors, and countries in Africa.

What about the WTO Disciplines?

The WTO Agreement on Sanitary and Phytosanitary Standards (SPS) was designed to help address some of the concerns that have been highlighted above. The Agreement seeks to promote transparency in the standards development process and promote principles of national treatment, non-discrimination, and use of sound science as the basis for standards. Moreover, standards should be applied only when necessary to protect human, plant, and animal health.

The Agreement aims to (1) encourage the adoption of measures of scientific principles in the application of standards; (2) prevent discrimination between members when identical or similar conditions prevail, and reduce restrictions to international trade; (3) promote SPS measures based on international guidelines and common risk assessment techniques; and (4) encourage standards based on broad-based participation and consensus.

The SPS Agreement also provides a mechanism for addressing issues related to developing country capacity to meet compliance costs. Members agreed to facilitate the provision of technical assistance to developing country members through bilateral or relevant international agreements. This includes encouraging technical assistance in processing technologies, research and infrastructure, advice, credits, donations and grants for the purpose of seeking technical expertise, training and equipment, and the establishment of national regulatory bodies so that countries are able to adjust to, and comply with, SPS measures in their export markets. In cases in which substantial investments are required to fulfill SPS requirements of an importing member, the latter is expected to consider such technical assistance to the extent of permitting the developing country members to maintain and expand its market access opportunities for the products involved.

---

[5]Moreover, Africa's trade and investment with the US still lags behind the rest of the world. Sub-Saharan Africa accounted for less than 1% of total US exports and less than 2% of total US imports in 2000. Likewise, the region accounts for 4% of total imports from the EU.

Box 1: The World Bank Global TBT Survey 2003

The World Bank Global TBT survey has generated data sets from a firm-level survey of 700 firms in 17 developing countries (including the five African countries reviewed under ATSP) on standards and technical barriers to trade. The database, still under construction, includes important information from firms exporting agricultural products and manufacturers in a wide range of industries. It details information on cost structures, production and exports, impediments to domestic sales and exports, and operations to comply with regulations. Particular efforts are made in the survey to elicit information on the relevant standards, government regulations, and technical barriers to trade (TBTs) confronting exporters from developing countries seeking to enter developed country markets. The database is planned for release in 2003. Preliminary results from African surveys are summarized below.

In Kenya, preliminary survey results from the TBT Database confirm that product quality; taxes and tariffs in export markets, and low demand were the most significant constraints to exports from Africa. Low demand ranked the highest. Other key factors highlighted include access to credit and foreign marketing costs. In Mozambique, the surveys highlight somewhat similar conclusions. The most important constraints to Mozambican exporters are product quality, low demand, and port charges and delays. Others include lack of skilled labor and access to credit. Unlike Kenya, Mozambican firms do not consider tariffs and quotas in export markets, and foreign marketing costs as significant constraints. In Nigeria, freight charges and product quality are ranked highest in the variety of factors that affect ability to export. Other important factors include port charges and delays, access to credit, tariff and quotas in export markets, and low demand. Foreign marketing costs and taxes on capital also seem to be very important to a majority of Nigerian firms. In South Africa, product quality, freight charges, port charges, and delays are the most important factors affecting exports while product quality, access to credit, and freight charges are the most important to Ugandan firms.

Over 70% of all firms surveyed in all five countries except Kenya indicate that compliance to technical regulations is important to increase export sales. In Kenya, about half of the respondents acknowledge this.

These SPS provisions—if fully implemented—would be particularly important for Africa. There is already a divide between local standards that are in place in many African countries and those of their major trading partners. As a result, there appears to be two main challenges facing the continent. First, there is the need to *invest in national standards development, monitoring and compliance consistent with international norms*. The development of these systems of standardization, quality assurance, accreditation and metrology is a crucial platform for sustained long-term competitiveness. Second, there is a need to *develop effective approaches for improving the continent's participation in the international standards development landscape and monitoring framework so as to minimize unfair use of standards that will restrict exports from the continent.*

Africans, in concert with the development community, are exploring ways to rationalize the costs of these regulations, reduce the tendency for trade diversion or restriction inherent in their use, improve participation in the standards development process, and facilitate the harmonization of standards. This process must involve strengthening the capacity of the private sector (and related regulatory institutions that support them) in the export of higher quality products at competitive prices.

In this context, measuring the current status and limitations to standards development in Africa, vis-à-vis prevailing international standards development processes could clarify a number of important concerns.

Based on work conducted as part of preparation for this volume there are several priorities for research in standards. First, gaps in African laws, policies, regulations, coordination, and monitoring systems governing quality of products and production processes need to be clearly identified, as a necessary step toward bridging the standards divide. Revealing these gaps should inform African governments as to whether their national technical regulations differ significantly from international standards. This would guide further empirical research on whether regulations depart significantly from the least-trade-restricting standards available for a given policy objective.

Second, identifying, assessing, and prioritizing the constraints to coordination and monitoring of standards-related activities at the country and sector level will facilitate the development of recommendations for reform. Developing actionable recommendations anchored in country-level and sector-specific analysis will serve very important purposes.

1. They will delineate activities African countries can embark on to ensure their firms and farmers take advantage of global trade opportunities by exporting products that meet internationally acceptable standards and quality.
2. These plans and underlying research evidence will provide concrete documentation of the needs of African countries and the challenges they face in exercising their rights—to inform the Doha Agenda of the WTO. Recommendations can then be crystallized into effective project ideas and policies that will pave the way for reform that can maximize trade-related aid to Africa.
3. Third, detailed analytical evidence can help to advance other objectives: (i) It can buttress Africa's position in trade panel meetings as well as dispute settlements, (ii) improve understanding of the various incentives and factors underlying Africa's capacity to participate effectively in global trade, and (iii) provide more information on how regulations operate in the African environment.

A critical evaluation of all these issues is best performed on a case-by-case basis. The analyses which follow adopt a country-by-country approach with an action plan for each country analyzed. Such a national agenda is important to

strengthen the competencies and the capabilities of each country in meeting international standards. This will help identify opportunities for deeper reforms and strengthen the foundations on which a regional and global framework can be further developed.

Methodology and Scope for Analysis

This volume contributes to ongoing search for creative ways of strengthening Africa's capacity to comply with international standards. It identifies opportunities for strengthening relative bargaining strengths and participation capacity of five[6] African countries in the global standards development framework. It also identifies key capacity constraints that may prevent them from complying with international standards. Though the primary focus is on SPS issues, the authors also discuss other standards and technical regulations applicable to specific industry sectors analyzed in each country. Finally, the authors provide recommendations for each sector and country based on their analysis. These recommendations highlight opportunities for intervention and assistance that could enhance the compliance and participation capacity of these countries.

This volume combines research efforts of teams of African scholars and professionals that included trade specialists, economists, and standards experts. Each chapter provides in-depth assessments of the current and anticipated use of international standards, and capacity for compliance on a case-by-case basis for five countries in the region—including Kenya, Mozambique, Nigeria, South Africa, and Mozambique. The analysis also includes a case-by-case study of specific industry and commodity sector of economic importance within each country. This work highlights, in detail, the main challenges and constraints facing the private sector and supporting organizations specific to each industry or commodity sector studied.

The country assessments were developed to meet the following objectives:

(i) Build awareness on the range, importance, and impact of international standards and technical regulations on the current and prospective trade of selected African countries,

---

[6]Kenya, Mozambique, Nigeria, South Africa, Uganda.

(ii) Document the challenges and opportunities faced by these countries in meeting their international agreement obligations and faced by African firms and farmers in complying with official regulations and private standards,

(iii) Document and assess the performance of countries and industries (including firms and farmers) in responding to these challenges and opportunities, and

(iv) Identify areas of priority attention and potential modalities for strengthening public and private capacities to utilize and apply internationally accepted and recognized standards and technical regulations.

Particular attention was given to the role of standards and technical regulations in areas of high export potential in each country (e.g., agricultural and food products and light manufacturing goods like textiles, wood products, leather/hides/skins and footwear), together with the standards/regulations associated with important material inputs needed by these industries (e.g., seeds, fertilizer, agrochemicals, animal feed and animal health products, farm and manufacturing machinery, etc.). See Table 1 for a list of commodity and industry sectors covered.

Primary attention was given to laws, rules, and practices which pertain to health and safety objectives, while secondary attention was given to a variety of environmental standards/regulations, including those which have been included within international agreements or national laws and those which have been adopted as private 'codes of practice'. O Labor and related standards were not included in the scope of analysis in this work.

The chapters in this volume highlight instances where products have been banned or restricted from traditional markets on grounds of quality or safety.[7] A discussion is provided as to whether these circumstances were caused by actual developments within the country (i.e., a disease) or due to changes in the overseas market rules/regulations or a hiatus in those regulations (which resulted in a de-facto ban on imports). Specific cases were identified, such

as where SPS measures have created compliance (and compliance cost) barriers for local producer/exporters; where overseas market standards (and testing procedures) are more stringent than those provided by international agencies (i.e., CODEX); and how this has materially affected the country's exports.

The authors also identify challenges these countries face in conforming to standards set by international industry-specific organizations (e.g., International Coffee Organization; forestry certification requirements, etc). The chapters include information on how problems can be addressed and estimates of compliance costs. Finally, the studies draw conclusions about the current status of legal frameworks related to standards and include recommendations on steps which should be taken by government, private organizations, and international development agencies to assist Africa. The authors in each chapter have drawn on broader economic analysis and other work ongoing at the World Bank and other organizations. Team-based research effort was also complemented by the use of national workshops, focus group sessions, and one-on-one interviews, and questionnaires which encouraged participation and input from key private and public sector stakeholders in each country.

An Overview of Challenges and Capacity Constraints

The focus on trade facilitation through standards in this volume is based on Africa's need to improve and secure access to world markets, which will in turn contribute to export-led growth. With domestic regulatory reform advancing in some African states,[8] the continent's potential for increased trade and investment with the developed world is growing. As the analyses in subsequent chapters demonstrates, capacity in the private and public sectors remains weak, even as globalization increases the need for innovative changes in the private sector and strengthened public sector institutions.

---

[7]For example, there might have been cases where fish exports were banned due to fear of listeria contamination; nuts/legumes/or spices banned for exceeding aflatoxin limits; or other cases.

[8]These reforms have not always been consistent. Collier 2000 points out several instances where policy reforms have been punctuated by disruptions and policy reversals.

Box 2: Liberalization, Commodity Prices, Coffee Standards

In Uganda, liberalization of the industry has been accompanied by increased involvement of inexperienced private sector players that compromise quality. This is exacerbated by the fact that compliance to codes of practices is voluntary, enforcement is weak, and penalties for non-compliance are not severe. Moreover, excess supply in international markets has depressed coffee prices such that there is little price incentives for investment in good quality coffee compliance practices.

Other industry constraints that must be overcome to spur growth in exports of high quality coffee include: (i) better treatment of aged coffee trees and prevalence of pests and diseases (e.g., coffee wilt); (ii) improvement in harvest handling methods at farm and primary processing levels; (iii) stronger enforcement at the production and primary processing levels (enforcement is weak due to unclear mandates among regulatory agencies); and (iv) decentralization of quality monitoring at the countryside to local authorities. This would require a new statute to be put in place to clarify the roles of various stakeholders in the process (ok)

In Kenya, with respect to monitoring quality, the previous quality monitoring functions of the Commodity Board in Kenya worked well, and as a result, Kenya coffee was sold at a premium in international markets. The main industry concern now concerns how liberalization of the sector will affect the efficacy of the transfer of responsibility of monitoring coffee quality standards from CBK to independent marketing agents, millers, and factory processors. KPCU is already taking the lead in soliciting and providing financial support to coffee farmers and factories to maintain quality. It is not clear how this new arrangement and regulatory framework will affect the coffee industry.

Realizing the potential for SME-based and export-led growth requires better and more systematic efforts to help African firms and farmers increase their capacity to export, produce internationally acceptable and competitive products, and overcome barriers to trade. African entrepreneurs, firms, and farmers may be successful at running small local businesses but many appear to be constrained from applying the same skills to challenges of dynamic global markets—especially in complying with international product and quality standards in a competitive manner. Moreover, for most African firms, the means of identifying, qualifying, and sustaining long-term export potential in international markets is difficult. Business support services are usually of relatively poor quality, lacking the timeliness and customization needed to support expansion in today's highly competitive global marketplace.

Just as African firms often lack the resources, links, and connections to effectively meet foreign and international product and process standards, so do African standards-setting organizations,

monitoring agencies, and business support associations often lack the capacity and breadth of networks and services necessary to mount high-impact development programs that will create and sustain better market access for their member firms and farmers. Collectively, for many African countries, the support services offered by trade and economic development agencies seem to be inconsistent in delivery, and shallow in foreign market penetration, to stimulate rapid expansion of private sector activities. Specifically, in many of the countries and sectors reviewed in this volume, they are limited in outreach and slack in direct connectivity to the standards of those of their trading partners.[9]

Several country-specific constraints and challenges that limit compliance to international standards in Africa are discussed in subsequent chapters. Among the most common include:

(a) Participation: Until recently, complaints about standards (especially SPS) from African countries to the WTO have been limited

---

[9]Excluding in many cases South Africa.

(Wilson, 2001). As can be drawn from the case studies in this book, this is partly due to the fact that African countries participate less effectively in WTO and other foreign standards-making processes. They also have very limited capacity and means to gather, analyze, absorb, and implement decisions that emanate from these processes.[10] Though there appears to be standard protocols for cooperation between local agencies and enquiry points in Africa and their international counterparts, this cooperation is typically not sustained in a way that is strategically significant to meet the policy or commercial objectives of producers and exporters in many African states. This is in part because, unlike in many developed countries, the mechanisms, agencies, and resources with which African states sustain international trade negotiations appear to be underdeveloped, under-financed, and sparingly inclusive of the private sector and the civil society groups. This is changing as African economies pursue more vigorous private sector-led growth strategies. The case study on South Africa, for example, highlights instances in which South Africa has influenced the formulation of international standards. However, for participation to be effective, more African states need to be actively involved in the process, on a selective basis, on standards of high relevance to export markets.

(b) **Standards-takers:** Lack of participation, coupled with limited capacity to provide credible information needed to articulate and defend their interests and/or complaints has transformed many developing countries (African firms and farmers in particular) into "standards-takers"—reactive, as opposed to proactive, players in the international trade system. This position raises three main concerns for African firms and farmers: (a) as standards-takers, they are vulnerable to sudden or frequent changes in foreign standards, especially when such changes are orchestrated with protectionist intent.[11] This vulnerability is more precarious when standards are defined ambiguously and the requirements associated with them are unclear, scientific evidence is unresolved, and compliance costs are high; (b) Many times, their situation is exacerbated by simultaneous exposure to divergent, multiple standards imposed by various trading partners. Servicing several markets with varying standards increases production costs,[12] complicates testing

---

[10]Africa's capacity to challenge or defend positions on exports of fruits and vegetables (especially regarding issues like maximum residue levels and pest risk analysis) for example is very weak. This is partly because there is lack of human capital, financial resources, and information infrastructure to maintain the required data, testing, and knowledge management for over long periods, necessary to develop credible pest risk analysis. Serious concerns already permeate the fastgrowing horticulture and flower industry in Kenya and Uganda. These concerns are based on threats arising from the industry's capacity to comply with maximum residue levels, labor and environmental standards, and pest risk analysis required by its export markets. For example, it is believed that the new EU requirement of inspections against nonindigenous harmful pests does not accommodate unique climatic conditions of producing African countries.

[11]The South African study outlines that Spain rejected a few consignments of South African white fish in 2001 due to the so-called "parasite infestation." Similarly, during the early 1990s, Italy banned imports from one or two South African suppliers due to mercury content problems. These acts were seen as an undesirable consequence of differing microbiological standards across countries, which have not yet been harmonized at CODEX level. However, South Africa experienced the most severe problems in early 1994 when France implemented EU Council Directive 91/493/EEC. This is the main EU legislation governing the health requirements of fishery products. Though other EU member states had given third countries time to prove compliance with the requirements of the Directive, the ban was implemented overnight in the French market. This step came as a shock to the South African Fishing industry, which believed the French government, was trying to appease fisherman who had protested in Brittany to protest difficult economic conditions and cheaper imports.

[12]Especially when such markets demand compliance to process standards that may require different production processes for the same export product, e.g., Members of South African Circuit Breakers Industry (CBI), for example, have pointed out that while Europeans suggest that IEC is the basis of all CENELEC standards, CBI are obliged to test according to EU standards. Alternatively, multiple process standards may limit trade by reducing the incentive for exporters to access more than one market, and benefit from economies of scale that may accrue from a uniform international standard that harmonizes production processes and allow for access to multiple markets, e.g., it was after Ugandan and Kenyan fish firms suffered a ban from the EU that they decided to try out the US market. The transition was easier because fish exports to EU must comply with HACCP standards which are not required in the US market.

and verification procedures;[13] and increases the burden of proof unnecessarily; (c) Foreign standards (e.g., packaging, testing, or environmental requirements) may become moving targets. Local consumer and producer groups and their supporting agencies abroad can influence (if not monopolize) the development of standards and codes of practice and make them more stringent once their competitors achieve compliance.[14] It is important to note, however, that some middle-income African countries, such as South Africa, have developed strong capacities to influence international standards-setting, and in some cases have become standards-setters (for example, the SABS Mark and the timber industry).

(c) *Information failure:* As standards-takers, the lack of firsthand participation in the development of international standards and voluntary codes of practice makes African firms and farmers overly dependent on local standards development agencies for relevant information. While the Internet is building tremendous connectivity, current management practices and access to timely information from these agencies are inadequate, and suffer from varied quality levels. In some countries, where information management infrastructure is still weak (e.g., Kenya, Nigeria, Uganda, etc.), there is a primary reliance on surface mail and postage services as a key mode of information transfer. Such countries experience further delays in coordinating key activities between international standards agencies to national contact points. Collaboration and exchange of ideas on standards with their private sector counterparts is also limited.

The combined effect of limited private sector participation, and information failure in part, explains why export and business development initiatives appear to be one-sided and do not foster effective representation of the interests of African businesses abroad. As a consequence, private sector awareness and investment in standards appear to be low across sectors – even in South Africa. This has created demand for high impact awareness campaigns and the need for information centers from which information about standards and quality is readily accessible. It should be noted however, that some of the information failure stems from inefficiencies in management and information flow from responsible international organizations, notification points, and foreign governments themselves.

(d) *Trade Limiting Impact of Standards:* The importance of understanding the impact of standards in Africa is also reflected in the rising incidence of technical regulations as instruments of commercial policy by governments. Africa's private sector and trade development agencies have increasingly voiced their concerns on issues relating to restrictive use of standards for protectionist intentions. These concerns were implicit in the review of Chapter VIII in "African Positive Agenda" summary of meeting co-sponsored by UNCTAD. They have also been explicitly outlined in the "NEPAD Market Access Initiative" document (2002), which outlines Africa's position on market access issues. According to this document, African leaders highlight two important concerns namely: the subsidies offered by OECD countries to farmers, and restrictive regulation through product standards.

Empirical evidence related to these concerns has been highlighted in the previous sections. Other specific examples of standards that can be trade-limiting are found in the case studies discussed in this book. In the case study on South African horticulture industry, for example, the authors point out that quality and packaging requirements imposed by importers on South African exports of fruits can be excessive. For most South African citrus growers, the packaging requirements are said to limit the

---

[13]As in Kenya, South African citrus exporters have to comply with two certification systems (EUREPGAP and HACCP) in order to export their produce, and do not have a say in the setting of these regulations (Grieb 2002).

[14]In Germany, local firms refuse to purchase foreign electrical components, as labor unions do not allow their members to install these products. Similarly, in 2001 in Kenya, for example, processed foods from Del Monte were restricted from European markets because of worker safety and environmental standards. Human rights associations were agitated that Del Monte did not provide adequate safety standards to its workers and that environmental health standards were not adhered to. This led to a boycott of Del Monte's products in most EU supermarkets.

proportion of their total crop that they may export to about 60 percent. Similar constraints with regard to packaging were confirmed in other country case studies. It appears, therefore, that packaging requirements are becoming an area of strict concern in meeting international standards.

Another concern is regulation that limits the importation of fruits infected with citrus black spot (CBS). It is believed that this requirement will seriously constrain South Africa's exports of citrus fruits to Europe.[15] Other rules of concern include EUREGAP requirements relating to services provided to workers (e.g., washing facilities and portable toilets for every 600 meters in the orchard).[16]

Pesticide residue requirements in EUREGAP are also critical areas of concern. To comply with this requirement, pesticides that are used must be registered in the country of origin. In many African countries, including South Africa, many pesticides are either not registered, or are registered for another crop or commodity. Registration requires two to three years of costly trials. The costs associated with this process are so high that only those crops that are of high national economic importance are selected for plant protection and residue analysis. As a result, where the range of plant protection products of importance to South Africa differs from those of its trading partners in Europe, the latter may not support calls for maximum residue levels for certain pesticide and crop combinations that are of importance to South African industries. This may lead to the loss of use of certain pesticides and activities vital to the pest management strategy of many South African farmers. The South African deciduous fruit industry is particularly concerned about this problem.

CE marking[17] to EU regulatory requirements is also becoming an important and binding constraint. Where the intervention of a notified body is required, African firms are paying high fees to have conformity assessment work carried out in the EU. Although many African countries have safety regulations governing the manufacture and distribution of products, the enforcement of these regulations is weak with mixed quality across sectors. This, in part, explains the lack of recognition by EU regulators of the local conformity assessment infrastructure (i.e., the absence of mutual recognition) that obliges exporters to test and certify overseas. As a result, many African firms pay conformity assessment fees in foreign currency that increases production costs and make their product prices less competitive.

The challenge of conformity assessment is further compounded by certification constraints. In the USA for example, large retailers, such as Home Depot, insist on FSC certification. South African Industry leaders in the timber industry, for instance, consider the US market as particularly difficult to do business because the US product quality requirements are exceptionally high. For example, in terms of visual quality, US importers are only interested in clear timber without any knots. They also insist on sliced veneer and do not accept rotary cut veneer. This is of great concern to South African timber exporters because it limits their US sales to only a relatively small number of carefully selected.

---

[15] CBS is perceived to be difficult to overcome because the fungus that causes black spots on the fruits can develop at any stage of production even after export processes have been concluded. These spots are said to merely detract from the appearance of the fruit and are harmless to consumers. The fungus does not occur in any winter rainfall areas and has never shown up in the Western Mediterranean climate. Moreover, South Africa has been exporting citrus fruits to Europe for over 70 years without any serious health issues.

[16] It is unclear to South African citrus producers why such worker services are relevant to the citrus export exchange and they feel that this is rather a matter for resolution between them, the workers, the labor unions and the South African government (Grieb, 2002). As a result, these growers feel that many of the regulations they are being forced to adhere to are out of line with domestic norms, enormously time-consuming and unrelated to the core production issue—the quality of the fruit they produce.

[17] The CE Marking is the manufacturer's declaration, showing compliance with all applicable EU directives. For most products sold in the EU, the use of the CE Marking and a Declaration of Conformity are mandatory. Source: Website TUV-Rheinland.

The role of some lobby groups and associations were also found to impact trade prospects, at least in the short term. There appears to be an increasing demand among international customers for "social audits". Some customers require reports from inspection bodies that confirm that suppliers comply with local labor laws. In Kenya, for example, processed foods from Del Monte were restricted from European markets in 2001 due to concerns over worker safety and environmental standards. Human rights associations argued that Del Monte did not provide adequate safety standards for workers and environmental health standards were not applied. This resulted in a boycott of Del Monte's products in most EU supermarkets. Similarly, while many African countries like Kenya and Uganda struggle with the challenge of restructuring the fishing industry after several bans, some buyers in developed countries are already insisting on eco-friendly fish harvesting and processing on the part of suppliers.

(e) *Costs and Financing of Compliance:* Not only are standards potentially trade limiting; the cost of complying with them can be prohibitive depending on the type of standards applied, the development stage of industry or country of interest, and the efficacy of support services available to the local private sector. Preliminary evidence from the World Bank global TBT survey suggests, for example, that over 30% of all firms surveyed in Africa believe that compliance with local labeling requirements costs less compared to compliance with foreign regulations. The same goes for testing and certification costs. In Mozambique, however, 50% of Mozambican firms indicate that certification costs for complying with foreign regulations are much more expensive than those for local certification requirements.

The results also show that African firms experience additional costs as a result of investments in new equipment, labor, and inspection activities related to compliance to international standards. A majority of the new investment costs range from 1–24% of total investments costs. Inspection and additional labor costs also fall within 1–24% of production costs. The data also suggests that Mozambican and South African firms experience costs associated more with *new equipment* and inspection services while firms in Uganda and Kenya face costs related more to *labor* and inspection services. This may have to do with the compliance strategies different countries adopt. These results however only show cost averages of all firms over a variety of industries.

Compliance costs differ across industries depending on the stage of production practices prevalent in the industry, and the level of support services available nationally to help the private sector adapt to changing global industry standards.

In the case of the Ugandan honey industry, for example, sunk costs associated with compliance are found to be very high. The Uganda study references a feasibility report, referenced from the study contained in Chapter 5 of this book which suggests that up to US$300 million, will be required for construction of processing facilities and the purchase of equipment necessary to upgrade a honey-processing center owned by Uganda Honey Association in Kampala. These purchases would allow the Uganda Honey Association to conform to ISO standards for food safety. This amount excludes the costs of airtight collection cans and protective gear needed by farmers, setting up of local centers to train farmers in apiary management systems, improving awareness, and upgrading production processes.

In the Ugandan coffee industry, the average firm's production costs are said to increase by about 200% if compliance costs for good quality coffee are included. In South Africa, The costs to comply with EUREPGAP (at two pack houses for example) have been estimated at R1, 290,000 (i.e., R1, 000,000 million for the new bar coding machine, R170 000 for a pack house upgrade and R120 000 for relocating the workshop to comply with EUREPGAP—Bakker, 2002). Similarly, the Department of Trade and Industry in South Africa, which currently receives only about US$3,154 million annually, has expended significant amounts of money to upgrade the national metrology laboratory over the past six years. This is done to ensure South Africa's measurement standards are at par with those of its trading partners.

Financing such investments in compliance can be extremely costly and problematic for

African countries, especially where aid flows have dropped by about 40% in the last decade, savings rates are low, foreign direct investment is limited, and access to local credit is costly and predominantly short-term. The textile industry in Kenya and Nigeria, for example, is seriously constrained by availability of financial resources to develop better cotton-seed development systems, plantations and farming practices, ginneries, and a garment industry that will enable the industry take full advantage of the Africa Growth and Opportunity Act launched by the United States to ease access for African products (including textiles) into the US market.

(f) *Constraints to SME performance:* Standards impose different cost structures and investment requirements that can undermine the ability of small- and medium-sized farmers in Africa to access developed country markets. For example, analysis of flower production in Kenya shows that the costs of flowers (e.g., Roses and Carnations) that are grown in high investment structures and green houses, and are required to meet the stringent standards of the importers/consumers, are ten times higher on average than costs of flowers (e.g., Carthamus and Solidago) grown under normal field conditions. However, the export price of Carthamus is said to be only 50% less than for Carnations. In South Africa, while compliance costs do not seem to constrain multinationals and large local companies from adherence to domestic or international standards, the government had to devise various finance and technical assistance schemes to help SMEs cope with the required upgrade of equipment and facilities, and related costs of conformity assessment requirements.

Strict adherence to the "analytical zero" pesticide residue requirement imposed by the EU may have serious cost implications for Kenyan and Ugandan firms, especially SMEs, if not backed by adequate technical and financial assistance to pursue compliance. If this results in another ban on Kenya's or Uganda's horticulture products, such a ban will have significant negative effects on the economy of these countries and greatly impact the livelihood of their citizens. Horticulture industry is the third most important source of foreign exchange US$180 million yearly for Kenya, and a major source of employment. Flowers contributed 53% of the annual earnings from the horticulture industry. Complying with standards intensifies competition and, along with constantly changing consumer demand for flowers, makes continual investments in upgrading skills and equipment critical to business success.

Awareness of SPS measures and access to information is problematic among SMEs in the countries studied. This is based, in part, on incentives and market structures prevalent in the specific industries examined. For example, the case study on the fruits and vegetables sector in Kenya confirms that: (1) Large producers with direct contacts with exporters have higher levels of awareness of standards required by export markets compared to small producers; (2) Market channels based on forward contracts with farmers create more awareness about standards as opposed to informal contracts. Production contracts also provide a higher level of awareness of standards to producers; (3) The presence of exporter agents creates more awareness about standards to producers as opposed to independent agents; and (4) Exporters who sell directly to consumers rather than importers provide more value-added services, are more aware of standards required by export markets, and demand that their producers meet these requirements.

To summarize, the lack of rural infrastructure, high transportation costs, insufficient support services, and limited access to technical information and credit, constitute major problems for smallholders in the agriculture sector. Installing the necessary traceability, labeling, and packaging systems is also important and have significant cost implications for SMEs in Africa.

(g) *Experience with standards-related product bans, and the difficulty of the adjustment process:* It appears from the case study evidence presented here that the susceptibility of African firms and farmers to bans, product rejections, and trade-limiting restrictions varies by country, industry size, and development stage. Fish exports from countries like Nigeria, for example, have not experienced industry-wide fish bans. Interviews with experts in the Nigerian fish industry suggest that this is because the industry focuses on minimally processed exports of frozen head-on shrimps, and have adopted good fishing practices. There are concerns that incidences of product rejections may increase as firms move up the production ladder into processed fish products. The experiences of fish farmers in Southern and Eastern Africa have been very different.

The case study on Uganda, for example, indicates that the loss in reduced revenue as a result of a fish ban from March to July 1999 alone is estimated at about US$36.9 million. This excludes the loss to fishermen due to reduced prices and fishing which could total approximately US$1 million per month. Out of 11 factories, which were operational before the ban, three closed down and the remaining factories operated at 20% capacity (Waniala, 2001). The decline in production resulted in about 60% to 70% of those directly employed in the industry losing their jobs. About 35,000 people involved in fish-related activities (e.g., fishermen, fish mongers and transporters) lost their jobs. Others indirectly employed through the industry had earnings reduced by one third of their pre-ban earnings. Related industries, such as packaging and transport were also negatively affected.

Individual firms have to make continual investments to comply with quality requirements. For example, over the last three years, additional cost in equipment has ranged from US$12,000 to US$13,500 for a representative fish firm in Uganda while the training of personnel on fish processing and handling cost from US$2,500 to US$5,000. The initial cost of certification was US$15,000 for each individual firm while the hired testing and certification services ranged from US$2,000 to US$4,000 over the same period. These costs were born by firms themselves apart from the training provided by development agencies such as UNIDO, USAID, and the World Bank.[18]

(h) *Potential limitations to intra-regional trade in Africa:* Overall, constraints to regional trade range from lack of infrastructure and credit, to restrictive trade policy, dysfunctional governments, political instability, and language barriers. There have also been instances where standards and technical regulations have been used to limit trade. Diverse and non-transparent national standards and implementation procedures may further limit cross-border trade, especially in Africa where the capacity to undertake risk assessments is very low—even in middle-income countries like South Africa. Lack of transparency creates potential avenues for trade-restrictive practices in the region. For example, an incident of a Kenyan ban on imports of one-day old chicks from Mauritius because of alleged detection of *Avian Encephalomyelitis* in two shipments was not backed by appropriate test evidence or detailed risk assessment. No notification of the action was made to the WTO by Kenya. The matter was settled before the case reached WTO's dispute settlement body.

Enforcement of standards within the region is also difficult, due in part to porous borders that support a significant volume of informal exchange of goods by small traders. While African firms seem to be indifferent about the extent of uncontrolled informal trade, this trend, if left unchecked, reduces the effectiveness of standards monitoring and traceability mechanisms (including quarantine and pest monitoring programs, surveillance and monitoring of data on disease spread, etc.). This increases the risk of the spread of product defects or diseases that can undermine industry reputation across countries. In Mozambique for example, there is the need to reduce aflatoxin and mycotoxin contamination (like hepatic diseases) that affect consumers of peanuts, but the volume of informal trade in peanuts that by-passes quality controls is very high. On the other hand, vaccination campaigns, coordination with neighboring agencies, and the introduction of geographic information systems have helped Mozambique to escape episodes of foot-and-mouth disease experienced by its neighbors.

---

[18]Note, however, that these investments have been beneficial since they played an important role in getting the ban lifted and increasing fish exports. For example, fish exports increased from 14,075 tons before the ban to 28,119 tons after the ban. This increase is partly attributed to the compliance to standards that enabled Ugandan fish and fishery products being upgraded from List II to List I. Kenya's fishing industry has also undergone similar changes, but has not been as successful as their Ugandan counterparts.

*(i) **Other Domestic Constraints:*** Four very important areas for capacity building are evident in all of the country case studies. First are institutional constraints. There is an increasing need to strengthen the capacity of institutions involved in monitoring compliance to national and international standards. This is particularly important in Africa where liberalization and subsequent dissolution of commodity boards (in the absence of strong monitoring institutions) appears to have undermined the quality of agricultural products.[19] Streamlining the roles of agencies creates better focal points of responsibility and competent authorities to implement and monitor standards critical for compliance. Proliferation of duplicative roles and responsibilities was found to be one important cause of declining quality systems in the countries reviewed.[20] Furthermore, many of the institutions examined in the studies still lack the necessary sophistication and equipment for making adequate assessments of compliance and certification is still largely performed externally. There is the need for technical assistance and physical infrastructure upgrades to promote public–private partnerships in transforming standards into production techniques and good agricultural practices.

Second, capacity to undertake Pest Risk Analysis (PRA) and develop adequate traceability systems needs to be strengthened. Almost all of the countries under review lack the personnel, financial resources and technical details necessary to undertake comprehensive PRAs required for exports of their horticulture products. PRAs are of particular concern to Uganda and Kenya, two countries with a high growth and dependence on horticulture and flower products. While technology and testing methods are becoming more complex facilities such as testing laboratories are not adequately staffed in many African countries. Scientific equipment is outdated. Systematic collection and storage of records is not undertaken. Moreover, local certification agencies are not internationally recognized. This situation is worsening given the declining levels of public expenditures in many countries. Middle-income countries, such as South Africa, have good facilities, but PRAs are done by a small group of personnel faced with a large backlog of work.

Third is transport and logistics. Packaging, marketing and distribution of agriculture products from the production point to the final consumer is a formidable challenge in Africa. As shown in Table 1, port charges, delays, and freight costs are significant constraints to exporting. The availability of adequate transport and logistics infrastructure and management greatly affects market delivery quality of products, especially where such products are perishable. The publication "List of Detentions", published by the Unites States Food and Drug Administration (USFDA), for example, reveals that the main reasons for detentions from Africa was that the food exports from the region were mostly rotten.[21]

*(i) **Limited Incentives for Investment in Compliance:*** Incentives for investing in compliance can be policy- or market-related. Though the case studies did not explore policy incentives for compliance in detail, some examples are provided. In certain instances, such as in Uganda's coffee industry, policies and incentives provided to farmers do not encourage investments in compliance, and may sometimes hinder it. The case study points out that coffee farmers

---

[19]The authors of the Nigeria case study, for example, argue that the absence of institutions that perform the quality functions of the defunct commodity boards was one of the main reasons for deterioration of the quality of cocoa and cocoa products. There are concerns about the impact recent liberalization of the Kenyan coffee industry will have on the quality of Kenyan coffee exports.

[20]In Kenya, for example, a lack of a unique focal point on fish quality monitoring and compliance was found to be one of the causes of the country's deteriorating fish export quality. The loose organization of farmers within associations also undermines their capacity for organization and deployment of technical assistance that can help these farmers comply with required good agricultural practices and standards. The quality of organizations and associations involved in standards monitoring is mixed.

[21]Veena, Jha, "Strengthening Developing Countries' Capacities to Respond to Health, Sanitary and Environmental Requirements." A Scoping Paper for Selected Developing Countries, April 2002.

have an incentive to invest in lesser quality coffee production processes because the regulatory penalty against low quality coffee suppliers are so small in magnitude compared to costs of investment in better processing facilities. Moreover, there appears to be little price incentive because the market price premium for higher quality coffee is minimal. However, in the flower and fish industry, in both Uganda and Kenya, investments in quality appear to be compensated through higher market prices. In the fish industry, investments in compliance have resulted in increased exports from Uganda to the EU (but not in the case of Kenya). The market in this case appears to have rewarded compliance with higher market share. It appears that these premiums, if any, accrue to producers of high-end value commodities or marketing agents closer to the retail end of the production process (i.e., retailers and supermarkets in Europe).

The low volume and quality of local demand in Africa may also diminish a firm's interest in investing in compliance, and may sometimes compel national agencies to develop standards that are lower than international norms. For many African firms, producing for the local market is a necessary first step in the export process. However, in meeting demand in the local market, the producer sacrifices quality for price that is affordable to the local consumers. This low local demand for quality is due, in part, to the poverty that pervades sub-Saharan Africa.

There are other issues to consider in regard to standards and enhanced market access. Some of the most prominent include: (1) intensifyied efforts to harmonize standards and technical regulations to reduce duplication of efforts that restrict trade. Underlying harmonization is a number of necessary first steps. These include harmonization of threshold limits across developed country markets, streamlining testing and certification requirements, improving transparency in the development and implementation of standards and technical regulations, and supporting a more balanced global standards development framework that encompasses the input and

participation of more developing countries; and (2) Until recently, most trade promotion programs and development assistance have not focused on the development of better quality systems needed to sustain trade. The ideas proposed in this volume suggest, supporting developing countries in their efforts to bridge existing standards divide deserves much more focused attention. This attention is already forthcoming. For example, G8 member countries, through the Africa Action Plan (2002)[22] have already pledged support in helping African states develop better capacity for trade, including in SPS and other issues related to technical regulations.

Section 3.4 of the G8 Africa Action Plan focuses on: Increasing the funding and improving the quality of support for trade-related technical assistance and capacity-building in Africa— including (a) supporting the establishment and expansion of trade-related technical assistance programs in Africa; (b) supporting the establishment of sub-regional market and trade information offices to support trade-related technical assistance and capacity-building in Africa; (c) assisting regional organizations in their efforts to integrate trade policy into member country development plans; (d) working to increase African participation in identifying WTO-related technical assistance needs, and providing technical assistance to African countries to implement international agreements, such as the WTO agreement; (e) assisting African producers in meeting product and health standards in export markets; and (f) providing technical assistance to help African countries engage in international negotiations, and in standards-setting systems. The continuous marginalization of Africa from global trade creates an unprecedented need to expedite the implementation of this action plan.

The action plans and ideas expressed in this volume provide concrete examples of the type of technical assistance and domestic reform measures needed to strengthen economic performance in Southern Africa. In addition, they can also serve to inform specific projects that might be implemented through the new Standards and Trade Development Facility (STDF)

---

[22]The Africa Action Plan was released at the G8 Summit in Kananaskis in 2002.

established by the World Bank, World Trade Organization, UN Food and Agriculture Organization, World Health Organization, and international standards organizations to strengthen coordination in technical assistance on standards. The work in this volume and through the project supported by the U.S. Government Trust Fund at the World Bank has contributed to the rationale and underpinnings of the facility's establishment. The activities of the STDF will complement ongoing trade facilitation efforts in each country towards greater access to global markets. Related work in other development agencies and African institutions has also been highlighted in the subsequent chapters of this book.

A Summary of the Country Case Studies and Action Plans

The subsequent chapters of this book discuss the challenges and opportunities Kenya, Mozambique, Nigeria, South Africa, and Uganda face in conforming to the standards set by international industry-specific organizations (e.g., International Coffee Organization; forestry certification requirements, etc.). They also draw conclusions about the current status of laws, regulations, capacities, and programs in relation to standards and technical regulations, and identify areas for priority attention and recommend key steps, which should be taken by government, private organizations, and international development agencies. A summary on each country is provided below:

1. Kenya

International standards are important for Kenya because merchandise trade contributes to about 40% of the total gross domestic product (GDP). The impact of international standards will be felt more in the agricultural sector, particularly if they have a negative impact on trade.

The mandate of coordinating standards development and implementation lies with the Kenya Bureau of Standards (KEBS), a public body set under an Act of Parliament. The KEBS is also the focal point for information on international standards development from bodies such as Codex Alimentarius Commission (CAC). Three other public bodies are also involved in standards development and

implementation. These are the Kenya Plant Inspectorate Services (KEPHIS) and Department of Veterinary Services (DVS) under the Ministry of Agriculture and Rural Development (MA&RD), and Ministry of Health (MOH).

The KEPHIS is responsible for standards related to health of plant and plant products and is the enquiry point for the International Plant Protection Convention (IPPC). The DVS is responsible for standards related to health of animals and animal products and is the enquiry point for the Office of International des Epizootes (OIE). The MOH is responsible for standards related to food safety and is an enquiry point for both CAC and OIE on matters related to food safety. There are also many other public and private organizations involved in standards implementation particularly in creating awareness about the required standards for various products. These organizations get involved in standards development through their membership in committees for standards development coordinated by KEBS.

Most standards for Kenyan products are set based on international standards or guidelines developed by CAC, OIE, and IPPC. This is possible through participation of Kenyan technical staff in some of the meetings held by these organizations or use of guidelines and procedures provided by the organizations. However, not all Kenyan standards conform to internationally accepted standards. This is partly because of constraints in financing attendance in international meetings by both the public and private sector officials involved in standards-setting. Failure to participate in international meetings inhibits institutional development, capacity building, sensitizing and educating both the public and private sector individuals and firms on standards implementation and conformity assessment schemes that guarantee acceptance of international standards.

Different bodies undertake different functions in the administration of standards and implementation of standards. The notifying agency of standards developed in Kenya to WTO is the Ministry of Trade and Industry (MTI). All the enquiry/focal points (KEBS, KEPHIS, DVS, and MOH) communicate the status of standards in the country to WTO through MTI. The government has also established a National WTO Committee to coordinate preparations for negotiations of WTO agreements. Within the national committee, specific sub-committees are established to deal with various WTO agreements such as the SPS and TBT Agreements. Besides the enquiry points, many public and private sector organizations are also involved in implementation of the standards. Some of the problems encountered in administration of standards are poor coordination among the various actors and weak information flow regarding international acceptable standards and practices among the various actors.

Capacity building efforts in standards particularly related to the SPS and TBT agreements of WTO have, in the past, focused on understanding these agreements. The government, through the National Subcommittee on SPS and TBT, implements these efforts. The focus has been to create awareness among stakeholders on the need for compliance with quality standards for products if they have to be competitive in the export markets. Some capacity has been developed at KEBS, KEPHIS, DVS, and MOH for standards development through formal training. However, this capacity is insufficient to deal with risk analysis (associated with food safety, and health of animals and plants and their products) in conformity with risk assessment methodologies promulgated by the relevant international organizations. Potential exports (e.g., beef, flowers, vegetables, and fruits) are restricted to markets because of significant disease or pests. In addition, the infrastructure for assessing required standards for animal and plant health is deficient.

Kenya faces constraints in implementation of standards and production of products that make it difficult for the country to comply fully with international obligations related to standards. Implementation constraints include: (a) alignment of domestic technical regulations with international standards. For example, standards for processed fruits and vegetables provided for by the KEBS Act are weaker than international standards; (b) weaknesses in export and import certification systems. Examples include weaknesses in certifying livestock products for export to European Union, Japan and USA markets and imports of textiles into the country; (c) inadequate testing capabilities including international accreditation for some laboratories involved in microbiology and chemical tests for foodstuffs; (d) risk analysis and surveillance programs for pests, diseases, chemical residues and food safety; (e) control and eradication of pests, which, for example, has restricted exports of beef products; and (f) production constraints including infrastructure weaknesses and different standards requirements for different markets, which make it difficult for producers and exporters to meet the required international standards.[23] Standards have had different impacts on Kenyan industries. Examples from coffee, horticulture (fruits, vegetables, and flowers), fish, and textiles industries are used to illustrate these differences.

The Coffee Industry. in Kenya has undergone major reforms with liberalization of the Kenyan economy in 1993. New entities (processing factories, marketing agents, and millers) have emerged from formerly government-controlled institutions that were charged with standards implementation. These organizations are adjusting to a new legal framework and they require technical support (financial and human capacity) to deliver better services to farmers. The costs of standards compliance for the coffee industry vary. At the production level, annual coffee production costs, which include methods that allow compliance to standards, range from US$600 to US$1000 per ha. Other costs are incurred at the processing levels and range from US$158 to US$770 per ton of coffee for factory processing and US$100 per ton for coffee milling.

The Horticultural Industry. (fruits, vegetables, and flowers) has expanded significantly in recent years. It is the second most important export industry for the country after tea. The industry is reasonably well organized with respect to production and marketing arrangements. Stakeholders (producers, exporters, and private sector organizations) coordinate the activities of the industry, which include advice on implementation of standards of the produce for the export markets. The major challenges in standards are the ability to meet the minimum residual levels (MRLs) in the export markets, pest

---

[23]For example, the poor transportation network which leads to long transportation periods for fresh horticultural products from production to exporting points necessitates investments in cooling vehicles for transportation of the produce and storage facilities at the ports of export to maintain standards for fresh produce required at the export markets.

risk analysis, and continually changing consumer preferences (e.g., adherence to socially and environmentally sound production methods).

Cost of Compliance Estimates Vary by Commodity. The compliance costs to meet these changing standards vary with the level of intervention and type of crop grown. At farm-level, farmers are required to invest in capacity, to advise, and to inspect the produce for good agricultural practices. This costs about US$2,000 per month for a production capacity of five tons of fruits or vegetables or ten tons of flowers daily. Investment for quality controls from the farm to port-of-export for the same tonnage of fruits/vegetables or flowers, respectively costs about US$123,000. This kind of investment is only affordable to large commercial farmers. Small growers are only able to achieve this through group investments or contracts with large-scale growers.

Fishing. is an emerging export industry for Kenya. The industry has faced problems with standards compliance, however, and fish exports have been banned to European Union markets in the past few years. This is because of weak hygiene and sanitary standards at fishing landing beaches and capacity (human and equipment) to examine and certify the quality of exported fish. The compliance costs vary with the level of intervention. However, the government has developed a new institutional framework to overcome these constraints. At the beach levels, about US$90,000 is required to develop the necessary infrastructure (clean water, drainage, insulated boxes, electricity and roads) per beach to maintain required health and sanitary standards. At the processing level, the costs of maintaining standards for management of Hazard Analysis Critical Control Point (HACCP) are estimated at about US$19,200 per fish processing firm.

Cotton and Textiles. The cotton–textile industry has undergone different phases of development since independence in 1963, starting with rapid growth in the 1960s to mid-1980 and a decline in the 1990s. The focus currently is to revive the industry to exploit emerging export market opportunities such as those offered by the United States through the African Growth and Opportunity Act (AGOA). Quality cotton production is hindered by lack of quality seed to farmers, sustainable disease and pests control methods and weak ginning facilities.

A good cottonseed development and distribution system that ensures provision of quality seed and other inputs to farmers, as well as, an efficient marketing system for cotton lint is required to solve these problems. Textile manufacturing is also constrained by use of obsolete technology, machinery and equipment. Another issue is the weak legislation to control imports of substandard textiles. The compliance costs for maintaining standards vary with each level of intervention. At farm level, the compliance costs relate to costs of production and vary from US$100 to US$200 per ha. At the ginning and manufacturing levels, costs of investing in ginning and manufacturing capacity varies depending on size of factory.

In conclusion, Kenya has the basic infrastructure for implementation of standards to facilitate international trade in agricultural commodities and agro-industrial products. The constraints in the system, however, include (1) lack of funds to attend international meetings for standards development; (2) capacity to define appropriate standards for the country and undertake risk analysis in food safety, and health of animals and plants and their products; and (3) implementation of standards. Thus, public programs are recommended to support public institutions in formulation, development and implementation of standards as well as making it possible for the country to comply with WTO SPS/TBT requirements.

The major constraints in implementation of standards are a lack of technical knowledge and limited funding to enable farmers, particularly small farmers, to maintain required standards. Thus, commodity support programs that could empower producers to meet the required standards in the production and marketing of different commodities are recommended. The focus is on small producers that are not able to invest in facilities to enable them to meet acceptable international standards. The recommended projects in the chapter on Kenya target the constraints faced by each industry such as accessing export markets or financing facilities required for achieving acceptable standards in the markets. The priorities in Kenya center on small-scale producers of horticulture, fish, cotton, and coffee, and associations for the production of these commodities. These projects could be useful in contributing toward poverty alleviation in rural areas, as identified in Kenya's recent Poverty Reduction Strategy paper (PRSP, 2002).

2. Mozambique

Mozambique's infrastructure, export performance, and quality standards development has been significantly affected by the country's civil war. As a result, the main objective of Mozambique's post-civil war national programs and policies is the rebuilding of its infrastructure and reduction of the level of absolute poverty. The government program for 2000–2004, as well as other national programs and policies in agriculture, industry and trade, recognize the need to increase the quality of domestic production and to assure consumer protection through the development and application of appropriate standards and technical regulations as a necessary step in alleviating poverty through trade.

Mozambique's industrial and commercial policies consider the importance of developing the national quality system according to international rules. However, though quality and standardization issues are reflected in several documents, they are not yet the subject of appropriate development programs, neither at government nor donor level. Quality is not yet prioritized by the private sector as a requirement for international market access, though the development of important projects like the Mozal project have encouraged some companies to invest in product quality and related issues.

National Standards System. The Mozambique study examines the challenges facing the country's producers of peanuts, salt, cotton, horticulture, and fish products. The need to take a more systematic approach to quality led to the establishment of the National Institute of Standardization and Quality (INNOQ) in 1993. The establishment of the institute followed the perceived need to monitor regional and international developments more closely and to support local firms in efforts to improve quality. The standards-setting system is coordinated by INNOQ. Various bodies participate on the development of standards either on a voluntary or a mandatory (technical regulations) basis. The national standardization program includes issues that are regional priorities (such as labeling of foodstuffs, fruit and juices) and products that are national priorities (such as copra, honey, sugar, tea, and cashew nuts, among others).

The Cotton Industry. Some major constraints identified in the cotton industry include: degeneration and low yields of cotton varieties used for more than a decade, influencing production yields and product quality, for example. Other capacity priority areas for improvement include public investment in roads and transportation systems, limited capacity to assist small farmers and immediate response to their needs; a low level of farmer education, reducing their capacity to work through associations and groups. Obsolete equipment in ginneries, with low productivity and frequent breakdowns are also significant problems. There are also clear financial constraints hampering the investment that private companies need to make to assure a more efficient and effective service to farmers and deterioration of public laboratory equipment and tools.

Peanut Industry. Peanuts are cultivated by small farmers in all provinces, and are part of the staple diet in several regions, particularly in the south of Mozambique. A significant volume of informal peanut production is not covered by quality controls. There are potential export markets for peanuts that require certification to aflatoxin limits that are often below the average content in local products. Reducing this and other mycotoxin contamination in peanuts is a significant challenge for Mozambique farmers. Progress in this area would not only impact opportunities for exports but also domestic sales, as individuals are more at risk with higher levels of contamination as if infected with hepatitis. Various extension services and research to support better varieties and production methods that may reduce aflatoxin contamination have been implemented with varying degrees of success, and there is increased demand for the use of better testing and decontamination methods, and improved storage facilities.

The Fish Industry. The fisheries sector is one of the most important contributors to the Mozambican economy, representing 27.7% of Mozambique's total exports in 2000. Prawn exports rose from 5,694 tons in 1994 to 9,729 tons in 2000. The total harvest of fish and seafood in 2000 was 39,065 tons and the estimate for 2001 is 32,781 tons (Ministry of Fisheries). Over the past 10 years, prawns account for 21%–38% of the total catch of fish and seafood. Investment opportunities in the fisheries sector lie primarily in the need for a gradual replacement of the fishing fleet and upgrading testing laboratories.

Training for middle- and senior-level staff of the various bodies and companies will also be necessary. Existing regulations also may need to be revised in some aspects.

Mozambique's legal and regulatory framework also needs to be updated and new legislation and regulations introduced. A brief analysis of the institutions responsible for the application of legislation shows that institutional capacity has increased in recent years. With regard to research institutions, the establishment of a Ministry of Science and Technology to develop programs that will enhance research capacity in the country is ongoing, and supervision activities in some other Ministries are being improved. MADER is also reorganizing its research institutions. There is limited capacity to enforce existing technical regulations. The quality inspections at the border and in shops are not efficient because of the lack of infrastructures and personnel. Laboratories are not well-equipped and they face the same problems as the other public institutions.

Mozambique has also participated in standardization activities in the SADC region. The business community, however, needs to be more involved in the development of Mozambican standards. Prioritizing standards-related activities is a major challenge for Mozambique. Consumers, in general, do not demand quality, volume of production is low, and the few export products are guided by specification requirements for different destination markets. Weights and measures inspection in Mozambique is virtually non-existent and the infrastructure that would create confidence in the accuracy of measurements in the country is only now being developed. There is no formal sub-system of certification except for some government bodies which carry out preliminary inspections.

Certification. In addressing certification constraints, INNOQ has established cooperation agreements with its Portuguese counterpart the Portuguese Association for Certification (APCER)—and with the South African Bureau of Standards (SABS), aimed at starting joint activities in certification. Private sector adoption of the ISO 9000 standard is also encouraged and under way. Three firms, in the service sector, have been by ISO 9000-certified standards, one by SABS and two by APCER. However, cement is the only Mozambican product certified by SABS. Certified companies utilize accredited laboratories and calibration services from South Africa, but costs are high. There are also serious attempts at securing approval for a national conformity mark. This will, however, require better service quality from national laboratories. Accreditation is being managed within a regional context, with national focal points designated to address regional accreditation issues.

Consumer Interests. Mozambique has three organizations representing consumers' interests: PRO-CONSUMERS, DECOM and the Consumer Protection Institute, the first two being very active. These consumer associations have seats on the various committees and working groups dealing with standardization and metrology. The associations are newly established and lack the technical capacity to become more active in this aspect. The government has selected Intertek Testing Services to carry out pre-shipment inspections, while SGS performs inspections of exports, which is contracted by a third party. It is believed that the growing need to follow international standards, the SADC Trade Protocol, and the process of state sector reform, will contribute to the improvement of public institutions involved in the standardization process.

Aligning Goals with the Southern African Development Community (SADC). Mozambique has a final draft quality policy (under consideration for approval) and a five-year strategic plan, which will be implemented when funding is identified from public budgets. The plan is intended to align with the SADC Trade Protocol goals, which emphasize the need for harmonization of standards and technical regulations as one of the ways to facilitate trade in the region. The need to properly manage programs related to quality, in general, and to standardization, in particular, has led the Ministries in charge of Industry and Trade in the region to adopt a Memorandum of Understanding on Standardization, Quality Assurance, Accreditation and Metrology (SQAM). Participation in regional and international standards-setting organizations is, however, limited to officials from various government organizations. Language barriers, inadequate financial and technical capacities, and a lack of awareness regarding SQAM issues are among the constraints that restrict effective participation in both regional and global standards-related activities.

Finally, the study highlights priority action items which require urgent attention. These include: (1) the development of an appropriate regulatory system including one for food safety protection; (2) effective control mechanisms for import and export goods; (3) development of an appropriate standards-setting system including facilities for training, metrology, accreditation, testing and certification; (4) strengthening of the country's participation on regional and international standards-setting bodies; and (5) support of the development of selected sectors in order to improve exports. Proposed projects to deliver these action points are highlighted in the concluding section of the case study.

3. Nigeria

The private sector in Nigeria is faced with crippling constraints such as high cost of production arising from devaluation of the local currency, high interest rates, increasing energy costs, inadequate infrastructure such as telecommunication, and transportation and domestic policy barriers. These factors are directly related to high costs of production and the failure of private enterprises. Even if these factors are removed, producing to meet the required international standards remains a challenge. Undoubtedly, if non-standard related constraints are removed, this will lower the cost of standards compliance. Yet, meeting quality standards still remains a problem to be solved if Nigerian firms are to derive full benefits from the market opportunities created through the WTO, AGOA, bilateral agreements, and regional market initiatives.

As in the Mozambique study, the chapter on Nigeria examines the awareness and impact of international standards and technical regulations on Nigeria's trade. It also assesses the current status of its laws, regulations, capacities and programs relating to standards and technical regulations. Additionally, the level of participation in international standards-setting processes is identified, and areas needing priority attention at the national level are listed. The chapter provides recommendations on key steps to be taken by government, private organizations, and relevant international development agencies to alleviate negative impacts and strengthen positive influences.

Unlike Mozambique and the other countries reviewed in this volume, the Nigerian economy is predominantly dependent on crude oil exports. Diversification of exports is a major challenge for Nigeria, and agricultural exports and output has declined. The dissolution of Commodity Boards, expected to stimulate the growth and diversity of non-oil exports by the private sector, has had a negative effect on the quality of agricultural products because the quality control functions of the commodity boards were not promptly reinstated.

Nigeria has skilled laborers, however, it lacks the resources and vintage infrastructure to conduct scientific research and properly harness inputs into standard development. For example, apart from the fact that standardization equipment is obsolete, modern communication equipment is lacking, including computers, which directly impacts Nigeria's ability to benefit from standards and related information information technology systems can provide.

In Nigeria, though local legislation relating to standards and technical regulations predate the WTO SPS Agreement, enforcement is weak, especially since the elimination of the Commodity Boards system in Nigeria. This has led to the rejection of Nigerian products in importing countries. The evidence shows that many of these rejections were due to the fact that commodities were not certified and were not subject to pre-shipment inspection. Through its standards regulatory agencies, SON, NAFDAC, and PQS, Nigeria has been involved in standardization; however, serious constraints are evident. These include; inadequate equipment and skilled technicians, lack of capacity to conduct risk assessment, and a limited laboratories accreditation program. These constraints suggest priority areas for technical assistance. Most programs in technical assistance since 1995 have been supported by multilateral institutions such as the UNDP, UNICEF, UNIDO, IAEA, and FAO, among others.

In Nigeria, the level of awareness by local firms and farmers with international standards is mixed. One reason for this is inadequate funding that limits outreach and communication activities of public and private sector groups. Public agencies have developed strategies to improve the dissemination of information including organizing workshops on food safety and quality focusing on hygienic practices, HACCP, and GMP; use of technical/news publications, informative press releases from the press and electronic media, advertisements, interviews, talk shows, consultative meetings with stakeholders, corporate briefs, paid advertise-ments, and interviews. Other recent programs have focused on the issuing of communiqués, dis-tribution of information and handbills, and at-tendance at commodity shows. Nonetheless, pub-lic awareness of quality and related standards is still very low.

The Nigerian study advances the following pri-ority actions: need for a 'Standards Campaign' in the six geopolitical zones of Nigeria to create and sustain awareness among consumers and produc-ers especially small scale producers; need to strengthen the National Codex Committee includ-ing its Secretariat to be able to modernize and in-tegrate properly into international standardization processes; equipment should be upgraded through procurement of new technology in conformity with assessment and risk analysis; staff knowledge re-quires upgrading, especially with regard to demon-strating equivalence of standards through regular scientific training of laboratory staff; and coopera-tion among regional (ECOWAS) members for at-tending international standards-setting meetings should be engendered; harmonization of standards through the ISO, ARSO, etc., should continue and be intensified by ensuring regular attendance of meetings; budgetary provisions from the Nigerian government to standards institutions should be improved; bilateral technical assistance needs to be introduced and sustained in line with the require-ments of the relevant articles of the SPS and TBT Agreements; formation of well-equipped private laboratories need to be facilitated by providing the enabling environment through relevant laws; and information and telecommunications facilities should be modernized to enhance good manage-ment of the standardization process. Some project ideas to facilitate the implementation of these rec-ommendations were also identified.

4. South Africa

During the 1990's, South Africa stabilized its macro-economic environment thereby laying the foundations for more rapid and sustainable growth. Trade liberalization played an indispensable part in this process and the economy is increasingly being drawn into the global economy while the overall economic growth rate is becoming even more de-pendant on export growth than ever before. The composition of the export basket changed substan-tially away from primary exports to processed and manufactured merchandise. While some progress was made to penetrate "new" (geographic) markets, the traditional markets of the developed countries remain particularly important. Ties with these mar-kets are believed to have become even stronger as the result of the SA-EU TDCA and the AGOA of the US. Deeper penetration into the more sophis-ticated domains of international trade, as suggested by these developments, increasingly requires South African producers to comply with applicable inter-national standards to reap the benefits inherent in standards compliance.

It remains important in South Africa to build on existing standards and compliance infrastructure, especially with regard to regulatory standards. Frag-mentation in a different sense, of the functions of standards-setting, compliance and dispute settle-ment, in the case of South Africa remains to be addressed. Furthermore, apart from regulatory requirements, standards that are being imple-mented in the procurement of merchandise by large developed country importers in the retail sector can, in fact, become barriers to trade.

While the SQAM initiative in South Africa ap-pears promising, problems are evident at several levels (See the full chapter in this volume for more complete details). These are briefly: There are idio-syncrasies in the budgeting system. While the NML and SANAS submit their budgets to the Ministry of Trade and Industry for approval, the SABS is allo-cated its core funding through Parliament's Science Vote for the Science Councils. This means that the SABS is forced to "compete" with research organi-zations for funding (which the SABS is not). The notification link to the WTO via the SABS works well. However, there is no effective mechanism of notifying South African industry of foreign techni-cal regulations. This means that industry is often not informed of draft regulations in other coun-tries. The process of standards harmonization within SADC has also been very slow. This is due, in part, to the fact that member states' delegates fail to participate in technical committee meetings due to financial constraints.

The interaction between government depart-ments in standards matters is limited. There are, for example, no regular meetings between government officials to discuss issues of common interest in stan-dards and technical regulations. The main obstacles to participating in the process of standards-setting are timely notification, capacity in dealing with standards-setting, language barriers, length of protocols and poor commercial understanding of those charged with negotiating on behalf of industry. The agencies that serve as national contact points for CODEX and IPPC have performed well, however, consultations with other departments needs to be strengthened.

Although the cost of compliance to standards, based on an initial review of results of the World Bank Technical Barriers to Trade Survey, appears not to be a primary obstacle to firms, problems are apparent in the following areas: (a) non-transparent international conformity assessment requirements that lead to lengthy intervals before information is received; (b) the foreign cost component for SMEs; and (c) the need to upgrade facilities, e.g., in plant equipment, hampers the ability of SMEs to participate in serving international markets.

The study shows that the South African government does provide significant assistance to SMEs in standards, quality assurance, accreditation and metrology. Most respondents interviewed in South Africa agreed that conformity assessment is important to export success and that SMEs had benefited from ISO 9000 certification, not only from a business point of view but also from a management point of view.

5. Uganda

Uganda has implemented a range of trade policy reforms since 1987. These reforms have aimed to reduce or eliminate policy biases against exports, while others have included direct export promotion measures. The significance of policy-induced barriers to trade has been substantially reduced. The foreign exchange market has been liberalized while domestic and external marketing of monopolies have been abolished. Producer and consumer prices have been deregulated. Tariff rates have either been reduced or rationalized and some non-tariff trade restrictions (e.g., quotas, import ban, etc.) have been converted into tariff equivalents, and taxes on exports have been abolished.

These policy initiatives have provided incentives, in the form of increased producer prices and prompt payment, to farmers resulting into increased growth and diversity of Ugandan exports. For example, the elimination of the monopoly by the Uganda Produce Marketing Board (PMB) has stimulated the growth and diversity of horticultural exports by the private sector. The share of non-traditional exports in total exports rose from about 14% in 1990 to just less than 40% in 2001. However, the diversity of Ugandan exports in terms of market destination is still lacking as the country's exports destined the European Union alone (about 69% in 1999) has been rising over the past decade.

Whereas policy-oriented constraints to external trade (e.g., tariffs, quotas, etc.) have reduced considerably over the past ten years, the role non-policy-induced constraints, including poor infrastructure, inefficient institutions and stringent standards, are increasing to significantly impact external trade. Much as the infrastructure and institutional constraints are important factors in limiting external trade, the Uganda analysis focused on the role and impact of standards and technical regulations on the competitiveness of Ugandan exports.

The responsibility of developing, monitoring and enforcing standards in Uganda falls under different ministries. Implementation of sanitary and phytosanitary requirements is the responsibility of the Crop Protection Department at Kawanda Agricultural Research Institute (KARI) and Fisheries Department under the MAAIF, while those in the manufacturing sector are implemented by the UNBS which falls under the Ministry of Tourism, Trade and Industry. Currently, these institutions have limited capacity (both personnel and infrastructure) to effect their mandate. For example, there are 28 government gazette custom entry/exit points that are supposed to have inspection units in Uganda, but presently SPIS, a department in the MAAIF based at KARI, serves only 11 points.

UNBS faces considerable constraints mainly regarding human capacity and infrastructure requirement to fulfill its obligations, (i.e., inspection, monitoring and enforcement of the compliance with the standards). It lacks equipment, sufficient technical staff and financial resources. UNBS requires about 130 technical staff but only 50 are in place currently. Four laboratories (located at Nakawa in Kampala) are still seeking international recognition. The constraints to accreditation are mainly both the lack of equipment to increase the capacity of these laboratories and the financial resources to commence the accreditation process. The overall estimated cost of restructuring the four laboratories for accreditation is US$12 million. In addition, UNBS lacks their own permanent office space which is expected to cost US$11.4 million.

At the regional level, a lot of progress has been attained in standardization programs since the revival of EAC in 1998. The work on harmonization of laws regarding legal metrology has started. Training needs in standardization, quality assurance, metrology and testing have been identified but they needed funding. About 207 standards for goods and some codes of practice have been harmonized and notification of harmonized standards to WTO has been made. An idea of establishing the East African Accreditation Body for Quality Systems has been mooted and consumer organization, in the region are slated to participate in the development of regional standards.

The sector-specific diagnostics on the Uganda study focuses on the coffee, fish, honey, floriculture, horticulture, and light manufacturing sub-sectors. These sub-sectors are very important export earners and employment providers in Uganda. Furthermore, the fish, flower and horticultural exports have experienced considerable improvements over the past decade and these are sectors where quality requirements have shown to be more stringent. There have been numerous private initiatives to develop, monitor, and enforce standards under producers/exporters' associations and codes of practice. Producers/exporters' associations undertake training to their members in matters relating to quality management.

The study also points out areas where incentives/penalties for producers to comply with standards are non-existent or weak. Enforcement of standards is also found to be weak, though with variation with different stages in production and distribution chains and across sectors. Fast growing but relatively new sectors (e.g., horticulture, honey, etc.) are poorly organized. Uganda's horticultural sector comprises of small, scattered and poorly financed producers and exporters, which makes it difficult to organize and regularize their standards on quality assurance, pest and sanitary control at the farm- or firm-level. Capacity to carry out pest risk analysis is also very weak and this undermines export market opportunities created by trade preferential agreements like AGOA that require such tests and standards.

Private institutions (e.g., SGS, ACE, TQM and producers/exporters' associations with voluntary standards, as specified in various codes of practice) have also played a role in standards development, monitoring and enforcement. For example, the TQM, which started operations in 1988 and is affiliated with International Quality Media AS (a Norwegian Company), trains corporate bodies and other organizations in the Total Quality Management process as per the ISO certification standards. The cost of training and certification tends to be prohibitive to small business establishments. Certification costs are about US$3,000 and training costs average US$7,000, which is done every 3 years. There are projects providing financial assistance to organizations to train for compliance with ISO standards. For example the BUDS-SSE project under PSF has assisted about 40 organizations while the USAID funded SPEED project is presently assisting the fish industry and will move to other sectors and a European Union project EBAS based in Nairobi.

Overall, there is considerable appreciation (both by public and private producers) of the need to develop and comply with standards but major problems in the setting, monitoring and enforcement of standards remain and include the following:

(a) There is limited capacity (both in infrastructure and technical personnel) in most institutions responsible for the setting, monitoring and enforcing of standards in the country. There are some efforts underway to harmonize standards across the region, mainly in the East African community (EAC) and COMESA, which may reduce costs of enforcement of standards compliance.

(b) Compliance to standards requirements is largely being spearheaded by producers mainly for export markets. Therefore, compliance applies to only a small portion of production. This limits producers from taking advantage of standards development and compliance, which would not be so if standards requirements were uniformly applied to output irrespective of the market.

(c) There is limited awareness of the nature and existence of standards (at varying levels) among producers, particularly international standards. However, some sectors have attempted to develop and enforce standards in the form of codes of practice, which demonstrates the willingness to comply with standards and appreciation of the importance of standards by producers and exporters.

(d) The enforcement of standards is more at the export level, yet the standards or quality control should start right from the first point of production through the production chain and distribution system.

(e) Inspecting, monitoring, and certifying local firms with international recognition are limited. Acquiring these services from foreign firms are very expensive for most producers. There are considerable cost savings if local firms are accredited for certification to the level of other international standards-setting bodies. UNBS and other government agencies responsible for developing and enforcing standards are inadequately funded and understaffed; therefore they do not perform to the expectations.

(f) Incentives for compliance with standards are still weak in some sectors, such as coffee, but strong in other sectors, for example in fish and flowers where no sales can be made without meeting the standards.

The subsequent sections of this book present a more detailed case-by-case analysis of the issues outlined above. Chapter 1 presents the case study and action plan for Kenya in greater detail. Chapter 2 discusses challenges and opportunities for bridging the standards divide in Mozambique. Chapter 3 examines evidence of Nigeria's participation in international standards development, and prospects for non-oil exports. Chapter 4 reviews South Africa's role in setting international standards and opportunities for advancement. Chapter 5 provides a detailed study of Uganda's standards development system.

References

Amjadi, A. and Yeats, A. (1995), "Non-tariff Barriers Africa Faces: What Did the Uruguay Round Accomplish, and What Remains to be Done?", Policy Research Working Paper No. 1439, Washington DC: World Bank

Akyuz, Y. and Gore, C. (2001), "African Economic Development in a Comparative Perspective", Cambridge Journal of Economics, 25:265–288

Callaghy, T.M. (1995), "Africa and the World Political Economy: Still Caught Between A Rock and A Hard Place", Africa in World Politics, 2nd edition, eds. John W. Harbeson and Donald Rothchild (Boulder: Westview Press, 1995), pp. 41–68.

Coe, D.T. and Hoffmaister, A.W. (1999), "North-South Trade: Is Africa Unusual?", Journal of African Economies, 8 (2): 228–256.

Collier, P. and Gunning, J. W. (1999), "Why Has Africa Grown Slowly?", Journal of American Perspectives 13, No. 3 (Summer 1999): 3–22

Collier, P. and Gunning, J. W. (1999), "Explaining African Economic Performance", Journal of Economic Literature, Vol. XXXVII (March): 64–111

Deardoff and Stern (1998), "Measurement of Non-tariff Barriers", University of Michigan Press.

Fafchamps, M. (2001), "Networks, Communities and Markets in Sub-Saharan Africa: Implications for Firm Growth and Investment", Journal of African Economies, 10 (2): 109–142.

Finger, J.M. (2002), "The Doha Agenda and Development: A View from the Uruguay Round", Paper prepared for presentation at the annual meetings of the Asian Development Bank, Shanghai, China, May 11, 2002.

Fischer, R. and Serra, P., (2000), "Standards and Protection", Journal of International Economics, 52, p. 377–400, 2000, FONDECYT 1950513.

Fouroutan, F. (1998), "Comments on "Why is Trade Reform so Difficult in Africa?" by Dani Rodrik", Journal of African Economies, 7 (1), AERC Supplement May 1997: pp 146–149.

Fosu, A.K., et al (2001), "Business Environment and Investment in Africa: An Overview", Journal of African Economies, 10 (2): 1–11

G8 Africa Action Plan, (2002), see http://www.state.gov/e/eb/rls/othr/11515.htm

Global Economic Prospects and the Developing Countries (2003), Washington D.C., World Bank.

Global Poverty Report (June 2002), "Achieving the Millennium Development Goals in Africa: Progress, Prospects, and Policy Implications", Washington D.C., World Bank.

Guillaumont, P. et al, "How Instability Lowers African Growth", Journal of African Economies, 8 (1): 87–107.

Gyimah-Brempong, K. and Traynor, T.L. (1999), "Political Instability, Investment and Economic Growth in Sub-Saharan Africa", Journal of African Economies, 8 (1): 52–86.

Helleiner, G.K. (Eds) (2002), "Non-Traditional Export Promotion in Africa: Experience and Issues", United Nations University

Hertel, T.W., Masters, W.A, and Elbehri, A. (1998), "The Uruguay Round and Africa: a Global, General Equilibrium Analysis", Journal of African Economies, 7 (2): 208–234.

Hoeffler, A. (2002), "Openness, Investment and Growth", Journal of African Economies, 10 (4): 470–497.

Hoekman, B. et al (Eds), (2002), "Envisioning Alternative Futures: Reshaping Global Trade Architecture for Development" in Development, Trade, and the WTO—A Handbook. Washington DC: World Bank

Hoekman, B. et al (2002), "Reducing Agricultural Tariffs versus Domestic Support: What's More Important for Developing Countries?" Policy Research Working Paper No. 2918, Washington DC, World Bank

Ianchovichina, E. et al (2002), "Unrestricted Market Access for Sub-Saharan Africa: How Much Is It Worth and Who Pays?" Journal of African Economies, 10 (4): 410–432.

Ingo, M. and Winters, L.A. (Eds), (2001), "Agricultural Trade Liberalization in a New Trade Round: Perspectives of Developing Countries and Transition Economies", Discussion Paper No. 418, Washington DC: World Bank

Lall, S. and Wangwe, S. (1998), "Industrial Policy and Industrialization in Sub-Saharan Africa", Journal of African Economies, 7 (1): AERC Supplement May 1997: 70–107.

Maskus, K and Wilson, J.S. (2001), "A Review of Past Attempts and New Policy Context", in "Quantifying the Impact of Technical Barriers to Trade: Can it be Done?" by Maskus, K. and Wilson, J.S. (Eds), University of Michigan Press.

McCarthy, C. "Opportunities and Challenges Facing Africa in the Development of Key Export Sectors Under the WTO Agreement—A Focus on Mining, Manufacturing, and Services", WTO Framework Papers (CRC-3-5), Collaborative Research Project.

Michalopoulos, C. (1998), "Developing Countries' Participation in the World Trade Organization", Policy Research Working Paper No. 1906, Washington DC, World Bank

NEPAD Initiative on Market Access (2002), see http://www1.worldbank.org/wbiep/trade/Standards/files/agr-init-mkt-access.pdf

Ng, F. and Yeats, A. (1996), "Open Economies Work Better! Did Africa's Protectionist Policies Cause its Marginalization in World Trade?", Policy Research Working Paper No. 1636, Washington DC, World Bank

Ng, F. and Yeats, A. (2002), "What Can Africa Expect from Its Traditional Exports?" Africa Region Working Paper Series, No. 26. Washington DC, World Bank

North, D.C. (1990), "Institutions, Institutional Change and Economic Performance", Cambridge University Press

Oramah, B.O. and Abou-Lehaf, C. (1998), "Commodity Composition of African Trade and Intra-African Trade Potential", Journal of African Economies, 7 (2): 263–300

Oyejide, A. et al, (2001), "Quantifying the Trade Impact of Sanitary and Phytosanitary Standards: What is Known and Issues of Importance for Sub-Saharan Africa" in "Quantifying the Impact of Technical Barriers to Trade: Can it be Done?", Maskus, K and Wilson, J.S. (Eds), University of Michigan Press.

Oyejide, A. (1998), "Using Trade and Industrial Policies to Foster African Development: Some perspectives on Issues and Modalities", Journal of African Economies, 7 (1): (AERC Supplement May 1997), pp 34–42.

Oyejide, A. (1998), "Trade Policy and Regional Integration in the Development Context: Emerging Patterns Issues and Lessons for Sub-Saharan Africa", Journal of African Economies, 7 (1): (AERC Supplement May 1997), pp. 108–145.

Rodrik, D. (1998), "Why Is Trade Reform So Difficult In Africa", Journal of African Economies v7, n0 (Supplement 1 June 1998): 43–69

Sachs, J. and Warner, A (1995), "Economic Reform and the Process of Global Integration", Brookings Papers on Economic Activity v0, n1 (1995): 1–95

Sachs, J. and Warner, A. (1997), "Sources of Slow Growth in African Economies", Journal of African Economies v6, n3 (October 1997): 335–76

Sachs, J. and Warner, A. (1997), "Fundamental Sources of Long-run Growth", American Economic Review v87, n2 (May 1997): 184–88

Shafaeddin S.M, (1996), "Risks of Future Marginalization of SSA in International Trade" Geneva, Switzerland: United Nations Conference on Trade and Development.

Standards and Trade Database (2003), "TBT Survey Results on Kenya, Mozambique, Nigeria, South Africa, and Uganda", Washington DC, World Bank

Wang, Z. K. and Winters, L.A. (1998), "Africa's Role in Multilateral Trade Negotiations: Past and Future", Journal of African Economies, 7 (1): 1–33

Waniala, N. (2001), "Impact of SPS Measures on Uganda Fish Exports", Paper presented at the UNCTAD-sponsored Workshop on Standards and Trade, Kampala.

Wilson, J.S. (2001), "Advancing the WTO Agenda on Trade and Standards: A Developing Country Voice in the Debate", Draft Paper Prepared for the African Economic Research Consortium Conference on Trade, Geneva, March 8–9, 2001.

Wilson, J.S. et al (2001), "A Race to the Top? A Case Study of Food Safety Standards on African Exports", Policy Research Working Paper No. 2563, Washington DC: World Bank

Wilson, J.S. et al (May 2001), "Agriculture in the WTO: The Role of Product Attributes in Agricultural Negotiations", The International Agricultural Trade Research Consortium Commissioned Paper Number 17

Wilson, J.S. and Otsuki, T., (2001), "To Spray or Not to Spray: Pesticides, Banana Exports, and Food Safety", Policy Research Working Paper No. 2805, Washington DC: World Bank

Wilson, J.S. and Otsuki, T., (2001), "Global Trade and Food Safety: Winners and Losers in a Fragmented System", Policy Research Working Paper No. 2689, Washington DC: World Bank

Wilson, J.S. (2002), "Standards, Regulation, and Trade: WTO Rules and Developing Country Concerns", in Development, Trade, and the WTO—A Handbook, Bernard Hoekman, Aaditya Mattoo, and Philip English, eds. Washington DC: World Bank

Wohlmuth, K. et al (Eds), (2000/1), "Africa's Reintegration into the World Economy: Part A: Basic Issues", African Development Perspectives Year Book

Wohlmuth, K. et al (Eds), (2000/1), "Africa's Reintegration into the World Economy: Part B: Country Case Studies", African Development Perspectives Year Book

Wood, A. and Mayer, J. (2001), "African's Export Structure in a Comparative Perspective", Cambridge Journal of Economics 2001, 25: 369–394.

World Development Report (2002): "Building Institutions for Markets", Washington DC: World Bank

Yeats, A. (1994), "What are OECD Trade Preferences Worth to Sub-Saharan Africa?", Policy Research Working Paper No. 1254, Washington DC: World Bank

Yeats, A. et al (1996), "Did External Barriers Cause the Marginalization of Sub-Saharan Africa in World Trade?", Policy Research Working Paper No. 1586, Washington DC: World Bank

Yilmaz, A. and Gore, C. (2001), "Africa Economic Development in a Comparative Perspective", Cambridge Journal of Economics v25, n3 (May 2001): 265–288

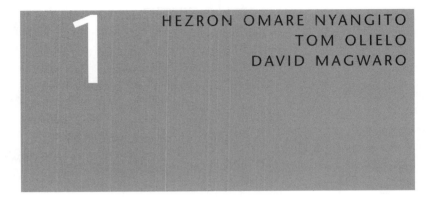

HEZRON OMARE NYANGITO
TOM OLIELO
DAVID MAGWARO

IMPROVING MARKET ACCESS THROUGH STANDARDS COMPLIANCE

A Diagnostic and Road Map for Kenya

K ENYA'S ECONOMY RELIES HEAVILY ON AGRI-CULTURE AND EXPORTS OF AGRICULTURAL commodities and agroprocessed products that dominate its international trade. The removal of restrictive trade policies by importing countries, particularly Europe under the ACP-EU Lome Agreement contributed to the good performance of the nontraditional exports in Kenya. This was further sustained by trade liberalization in the country.

This study focuses on the impact of international standards and technical regulations on the current and prospective trade of Kenya, and documents the challenges and opportunities faced by the country in meeting international agreement obligations.

International standards play an important role in international trade with the advent of reductions in tariff and nontariffs barriers to trade. This is because failure to meet international standards for goods and to comply with the WTO SPS Agreement can inhibit market access to export markets. For Kenya, international standards are important because trade is an important contributor to GDP with merchandise trade contributing about 40 percent of the total GDP. Agricultural commodities and agroprocessed products dominate this trade. Thus noncompliance with international standards for trade in goods affects the performance of the Kenyan economy because they have an impact on agriculture, which is the backbone of the economy.

In practice, however, standards and technical regulations may be strategically used to enhance the competitive position of countries or individual firms. Depending on industry or market circumstances, standards and technical regulations can raise or lower economic efficiency, promote or block competition, facilitate or constrain international trade, and enable or exclude the participation of the poor in remunerative economic activities.

The different integration organizations within Africa are expected to operate as building blocks toward the achievement of a single large market on the African continent. According to Kenya's Development Plans (1997–2000 and 2002–08), the country will work toward the continued reduction and eventual elimination of tariff and nontariff barriers to trade among members of a common trading bloc, while recognizing the need to implement changes at the institutional level to promote these regional initiatives.

Table 1.1 Kenya Social Indicators, 1992–2000

	1992	1993	1994	1995	1996	1997	1998	1999	2000[a]
GDP per capita at current prices (US$)	320.3	194.0	271.7	336.1	334.3	377.3	398.3	361.7	344.1
Population (million)	24.9	25.6	26.3	26.9	27.5	28.2	28.8	29.4	30.1
Growth of population (percentage change)	2.9	2.7	2.5	2.3	2.3	2.2	2.2	2.1	2.0
GDP (current prices) US$ million	8001.7	4977.4	7148.5	9046.7	9206.3	10625.0	11465.0	10638.0	10357.0
Exchange rate kshs/US$	32.2	58.0	56.1	51.4	57.1	58.7	60.4	70.3	76.2
Share in real GDP at factor cost (%)									
Agriculture, forestry, and fishing	27.6	26.6	26.6	26.6	26.6	26.2	26.3	26.2	25.7
Mining and quarrying	0.3	0.3	0.3	0.2	0.2	0.2	0.2	0.2	0.2
Manufacturing	13.6	13.8	13.6	13.5	13.4	13.3	13.3	13.2	13.0
Electricity and water	1.0	1.0	1.0	1.0	1.0	1.0	1.0	1.0	1.0
Construction	2.8	2.6	2.5	2.5	2.5	2.5	2.5	2.4	2.2
Services									
Trade, restaurants, and hotels	11.1	11.0	11.4	11.8	12.2	12.3	12.4	12.5	12.6
Transport, storage, and communication	6.1	6.1	6.1	6.1	6.0	6.0	6.0	6.0	6.0
Finance, insurance, and real estate	8.7	9.3	9.6	9.8	10.0	10.3	10.5	10.5	10.6
Ownership and dwelling	5.5	5.5	5.4	5.5	5.5	5.6	5.6	5.6	5.7
Other services	3.3	3.4	3.3	3.4	3.4	3.4	3.4	3.4	3.4
Nonmonetary economy	6.9	5.7	5.7	5.6	5.5	5.5	5.6	5.6	5.6
Private households	2.0	2.2	2.3	2.4	2.5	2.6	2.7	2.8	2.9
Government services	11.1	12.5	12.2	21.4	11.2	11.1	10.5	10.6	11.1
Share of employment (%)									
Agriculture, forestry, and fishing	—	—	18.7	18.9	18.7	18.6	18.5	18.6	18.5
Mining and quarrying	—	—	0.3	0.3	0.3	0.3	0.3	0.3	0.3
Manufacturing	—	—	13.1	13.2	13.0	13.0	13.0	13.1	13.0
Electricity and water	—	—	1.5	1.5	1.4	1.4	1.4	1.4	1.3
Construction	—	—	4.9	4.9	4.9	4.9	4.9	4.7	4.7
Services	—	—	61.5	61.3	61.7	61.9	62.0	61.9	62.1
Community, social, and personal services	—	—	43.0	42.5	42.5	42.6	42.8	42.7	42.9
Exports (f.o.b.) (US$ million)	1012.6	1103.1	1483.9	1923.8	1083.3	2059.5	2012.0	1754.6	1774.0
Imports (f.o.b.) (US$ million)	1608.4	1384.6	1761.3	2636.0	2512.2	2944.0	3028.1	2656.1	2965.0
Merchandise trade/GDP (%)	32.8	50.0	45.4	50.4	39.1	47.1	43.9	41.2	45.8

— Not Available.   a. Provisional.

Source: The World Bank Africa Database (2002a), World Bank (2002b) African Development Indicators, CBS, Economic Survey (various issues) and WTO (2000).

Kenya Economic Context

Kenya is situated on the east coast of Africa along the equator. It has a landmass of about 582,000 square kilometers. It has a coastline of about 600 kilometers along the Indian Ocean. The 1999 population census indicated that Kenya had 29.7 million people, of which more than 50 percent were less than 15 years old. Some 4.8 million Kenyans were unemployed, and more than four-fifths of the population lived in rural areas. Most of the population is concentrated in the high-potential agricultural areas of central and western Kenya.

Economic Conditions

Kenya is a developing country, with a per capita income of US$344 in 2000 (Table 1.1). This income declined from a high of US$398 in 1998, even though the population growth rate has been declining and was estimated only at 2.1 percent in 2000. The country's economic structure relies on three main activities: agriculture, services, and manufacturing.

Structure of the Economy. The services sector is dominated by tourism and includes financial services, communications services, and government services, and accounts for about 54 percent of Kenya's real gross domestic product (GDP). The services sector is also an important source of employment and a leading foreign exchange earner.

Agriculture is the second largest of all the economic sectors in Kenya and accounts for about 25.7 percent of Kenya's GDP About 80 percent of the population depends on it for its livelihood. Agriculture contributes to about 60 percent of the earnings are made from total merchandise export. However, only about 20 percent of the land can be described as suitable for agricultural production. The remaining 80 percent is arid and semi-arid and supports about 25 percent of the population (mostly pastoralists) and contains about 50 percent of the country's livestock herd. A wide variety of crops is grown in Kenya, including maize, rice, wheat, tea, coffee, horticultural products, sugar cane, and fibers. Kenya is the world's leading supplier of tea, pyrethrum, and bixa. Kenya's herd of livestock is also diversified. Most fishing activities take place in Lake Victoria. Adverse weather conditions, organizational problems, a weak infrastructure, and lack of financing have hampered further development of Kenyan agriculture (Kenya

2001). In addition, marketing problems (mismanagement of marketing boards) and insufficient supplies of inputs constrain the development of the sector such that it has registered poor performance since 1996 (Nyangito and others 2001). However, there has been high growth in the production and export earnings from tea and horticultural crops.

The manufacturing sector contributes about 13 percent of the GDP. Manufacturing activities that were relatively developed and diversified in the 1950s and 1970s have faltered in the second half of the 1990s and now agroprocessing industries and light industries dominate the activities (Kimuyu 1999; WTO 2000). The sector registered an average growth rate of 9.1 percent per year between 1964 (when the country attained independence) and 1979 whereas during 1980 to 1989 and 1990 to 1995, the annual average growth rates for manufacturing were 4.8 percent and 3.0 percent, respectively. The manufacturing sector's performance has declined over the last three decades even though it appears to be more resilient. Collapse of certain enterprises in the manufacturing sector has contributed to the rapid expansion of an informal sector, which employs about 3.3 million people. Mining activities in Kenya are mostly limited to exploitation of soda ash and fluorspar and the contribution of the sector to Kenya's real GDP is negligible.

Performance of the Economy. The economic indicators for the performance of the economy are shown in Table 1.2. The growth in GDP has been mixed because since 1990 there was a general increase from 0.2 percent in 1993 to a high of 4.8 percent in 1995. Then the growth in GDP declined to a low of 0.3 in 2000. A number of factors could explain the performance of Kenya's economy, but most of them are policy related (World Bank 1994; WTO 2000).

In the post-independence decade (1964–73), Kenya achieved a commendable economic growth rate comparable to other developing countries and its GDP grew at an average of 6.6 percent per year. The rapid growth rate during this decade was attributed to first, successful rural development policies (such as land redistribution from white settlers to Africans) that led to increased agricultural output; second, an import substitution industrialization policy that serviced the entire East African community (EAC) with goods; and third, good macroeconomic management policies (Kenya 1986; World Bank 1994; ILO 1999; WTO 2000).

Table 1.2 Kenya Economic Indicators, 1992–2000
(US$ million unless indicated otherwise)

	1992	1993	1994	1995	1996	1997	1998	1999	2000ᵃ
Real GDP (change)	−0.8	0.4	2.6	4.4	4.1	2.1	1.6	1.3	−0.2
Consumer prices (change)	27.1	46.1	28.9	1.5	9.0	11.2	10.6	15.0	8.4
Treasury bill rate (90-day rates)	16.5	49.8	23.3	18.3	21.6	26.4	12.6	20.4	11.7
Discount rate (end of period)	20.5	45.5	21.2	24.5	26.9	32.3	17.1	26.5	17.8
Nominal effective exchange rate (change)	−11.6	−41.2	49.3	−21.3	3.9	−4.0	—	—	—
Real effective exchange rate (change)ᵇ	11.7	−18.9	46.7	−18.4	12.6	0.2	—	—	—
Government budget (July–June)									
Current revenue and grants	2200.5	1642.5	2208.9	2777.2	2651.4	2826.3	3038.2	2702.1	2713.5
Current expenditure	2216.5	1179.6	1629.9	1954.1	1546.7	1870.0	2052.2	1808.5	1512.1
Government budget balance	408.0	438.0	593.3	660.4	570.8	510.0	550.3	521.3	300.4
Monetary sector (end period) (change)									
Narrow money (M1)	35.6	27.4	12.6	3.8	13.9	15.2	3.4	16.2	8.5
M2	33.6	25.7	−23.1	100.7	23.8	16.5	2.4	3.9	0.7
M3ᶜ	26.4	23.2	26.5	17.2	15.9	9.8	3.3	2.8	0.8
Percent of GDP									
Private consumption	69.7	63.1	62.4	69.3	67.9	72.6	74.5	81.0	80.9
Government consumption	16.1	16.7	15.2	14.8	16.0	16.2	16.4	17.0	18.0
Gross fixed capital formation	9.7	18.3	16.2	11.8	15.5	10.4	10.8	12.2	10.4
Exports of goods and nonfactor services	26.8	45.1	37.0	32.6	31.6	28.0	24.8	25.2	26.5
Imports of goods and nonfactor services	26.9	39.0	33.9	38.8	36.6	35.5	32.6	30.9	35.6
Public deficit	0	6.0	3.2	−6.2	−3.6	−7.5	−7.8	−5.7	−9.1
External sector									
International reserves (end of period)ᵈ	68.0	147.0	148.0	408.0	433.0	497.0	557.0	564.0	746.0
Foreign trade indices (1995=100)									
Exports	87.5	69.5	82.9	100.0	98.5	112.8	113.7	95.3	94.9
Imports	112.6	75.9	81.0	100.0	94.1	102.7	107.7	99.9	94.9
Terms of trade	77.7	91.5	102.4	100.0	104.6	109.8	105.6	94.5	94.5

— Not available.   a. Provisional.   b. The minus sign indicates depreciation.   c. Excludes local government deposits.   d. Excluding gold.

Source: African Development Indicators (2002), The World Bank Africa Database, WTO (2000), Central Bank of Kenya Statistical bulletin (various issues) (2000), Government of Kenya, Economic Survey (various issues) and Central Bureau of Statistics, Statistical Abstract (various issues).

The second decade after independence (1974–80) coincided with the first international oil and energy price crisis of 1973 that witnessed a decline in economic growth in the mid-1970s. The onset of the oil price crisis revealed serious structural constraints within the economy (World Bank 1994). Agricultural growth slowed as the forces that boosted its production during the 1960s weakened. In addition, the policies used favored the industrial sector at the expense of the agriculture sector (Nyangito 1999; Ikiara and others 1993). Industrial growth declined because of a weak incentive system that favored production for the domestic market over international market, and because of diminishing opportunities for efficient import substitution. These factors were exacerbated by the collapse in 1977 of the EAC, which was the traditional market outlet for Kenyan industry, and the growing inefficiency of public industrial investments. After the second international oil price crisis in 1977 and the severe drought in 1984, the structural constraints worsened leading to slower growth, high inflation, and deterioration in the balance of payments. The economy grew at an average of 5.2 percent per year during that period.

By mid-1980s, severe structural constraints emerged within the economy that prevented it from achieving the growth rates of the 1960s. Although indications pointed to the oil crisis, other countries that were at the same level of economic development as Kenya and that faced similar external forces, were able to emerge from the crisis unscathed because of sound macroeconomic and structural flexibilities (WTO 2000). It became evident that Kenya's internal policies and structural rigidities were constraining the country's economic growth and development. This led the government to adopt structural adjustments programs through the publication of the Sessional Paper No. 1 of 1986 on Economic Management for Renewed Growth (Kenya 1986).

The reforms, though effective in terms of reducing protection and encouraging manufactured exports, did not bring about any meaningful improvement in the performance of the economy. Indeed, if any thing, the economic growth rate continued to decline and registered an average growth of about 4.1 percent in 1990, 2.3 percent in 1991, 0.5 percent in 1992, and 0.2 percent in 1993 when the country was denied donor aid until it initiated significant economic and governance reforms. Thus in 1993, Kenya established significant structural and macroeconomic reforms to create a more conducive environment of economic growth (WTO 2001). These reforms included price decontrol on all commodities, removal of import licensing and foreign exchange controls, reforms in the financial sector and in investment incentives, abandonment of import substitution, adoption of outward-oriented policies and privatization of public enterprises. Kenya also dismantled its quantitative import restrictions and price controls on important products; tariffs remained the main trade policy instrument. The tariff structure was rationalized and incentive schemes were initiated. Several public enterprises were restructured and the influence of most agricultural boards reduced.

The policy reforms have had an important impact on the balance of payments, which in turn has affected the performance of the economy. The related financing needs, the pursuance of a tight monetary policy and the high level of nonperforming loans in commercial banks' portfolios contributed to the maintenance of high interest rates. The high level of interest rates, and the relative stability of interest rates and the Kenyan shilling favored short-term capital inflows. Through sales of treasury bills, the Central Bank of Kenya (CBK) sterilized the impact of its intervention in the foreign exchange market to contain the appreciation of the Kenya shilling that could result from large capital inflows. The sterilization policy fueled the increase in interest rates (WTO 2000; Ndungu and Ngugi 2000). Resumption of economic growth, which led to a higher increase in imports than exports, contributed to further deterioration of Kenya's trade deficit in 1995 and 1999; Kenya has run a current account deficit since then (see Table 1.3).

Foreign Direct Investments and Overseas Development Assistance. The evolution of foreign direct investments (FDI) has been somewhat erratic over the past decade, with a general downward trend (WTO 2000). FDI in Kenya was some US$20 million in 1997, up from US$13 million in 1996. The FDI inflows to Kenya averaged US$10 million per year during 1992–97, against an annual average US$35 million during 1986–91. FDI increased in 1994 as Kenya's economy recovered and reached US$33 million in 1995. A downward trend in FDI has been recorded since then. As a percentage of gross fixed capital

Table 1.3 Kenya Balance of Payments 1992–2000
(US$ million)

	1992	1993	1994	1995	1996	1997	1998	1999	2000
Current account balance	−290	88	14	−475	−124	−425	−467	−215	−243
Merchandise trade balance	−595	−282	−277	−712	−429	−884	−1016	−881	−1191
Exports	1013	1103	1484	1924	2083	2060	2012	1775	1774
Imports	1608	1385	1761	2636	2512	2944	3028	2656	2965
Services balance	564.6	554.2	476.6	189.2	115.7	104.7	134.4	143.4	202.6
Exports	1144	1152	1184	1050	974	955	872	964	1014
Travel	442.4	421.5	501.3	486.0	448.1	385.4	283.3	293.1	251.8
Freight and transportation	349.6	341.1	293.7	362.0	361.7	375.7	298.7	363.1	402.5
Other services	354.6	377.9	368.4	243.8	189.5	224.6	33.9	39.4	32.4
Imports	906	930	1041	1222	1101	989	880	841	903
Travel	28.6	47.9	113.8	144.8	167.1	194.4	185.5	110.5	128.8
Freight and transportation	359.7	355.9	381.7	537.8	515.9	442.9	301.8	227.7	334.4
Other services	193.7	182.5	191.1	219.9	200.6	243.8	130.4	149.0	188.2
Investment income—international	−354.3	−388.9	−362.7	−324.9	−220.8	200.9	−169.4	−153.6	−130.3
Exports	1.7	3.3	20.9	25.6	21.4	23.0	40.3	30.6	44.0
Imports	356.0	392.2	383.6	350.5	242.2	223.9	209.7	184.2	174.4
Unrequited transfers—government	0	0	0	0	0	0	0	0	91
Unrequited transfers—private	68	147	148	408	433	497	557	564	746
Capital and finance account balance	102.4	−102.3	−107.1	391.3	181.8	248.2	603.3	315.8	229.3
Government—long term	−64.8	152.7	−133.3	−5.7	5.0	−115.6	−227.0	−302.7	−218.4
Credit	−64.8	152.7	−113.3	346.1	369.1	203.4	238.6	123.5	208.7
Debit	—	—	—	351.8	364.2	319.0	465.5	426.3	427.1
Private long-term	−15.3	−8.8	−43.0	−8.0	−5.9	−7.2	11.1	13.3	108.6
Credit	−12.1	−8.8	−43.0	50.2	39.3	62.7	11.1	13.3	108.6
Debit	3.2	0.0	0.1	58.2	45.1	69.8	0	0	0

Government corporations	−82.0	−102.0	−57.2	−63.4	73.2	1.3	−7.7	−14.1
Credit	−82.0	−102.0	58.9	24.6	17.0	1.3	−7.7	−3.5
Debit	—	—	116.1	88.0	90.3	0	0	10.6
Short-term	−4.3	245.7	318.8	653.4	558.7	735.5	559.4	304.7
Credit	−4.3	245.7	318.8	653.4	602.9	778.9	631.1	309.9
Debit	—	—	—	—	44.2	43.3	71.7	5.2
Change in official gross reserves[a]	−149.1	−160.1	163.5	−378.7	−32.7	14.2	−122.9	—
Use of fund credit	25.9	16.6	−36.4	−41.8	−63.1	5.6	−71	−106.6
Change in other liabilities	392.0	49.0	16.4	13.3	−18.7	−24.6	99.0	—
Errors and omissions	−4.8	3.2	9.5	−107.9	129.1	−143.8	−215.8	109.8

a. Including Commercial banks foreign assets.

Source: CBK *Statistical bulletin* and African Development Indicators, World Bank.

formation, FDI to Kenya declined from an annual average of 2.2 percent during 1986–91 to 0.7 percent during 1992–96. The proportion of FDI to GDP for the period 1986–96 averaged at about 7.5 percent. FDI inward stock increased from US$626 million in 1990 to US$742 million in 1997. Outward FDI stock more than quintupled during the period 1980–97 (from US$18 million in 1980 to US$104 million in 1997). The European Union, notably the United Kingdom, Netherlands, Belgium, and Italy, and South Africa are the main sources of FDI into Kenya. The bulk of FDI in Kenya is in banking, tourism, horticulture, chemicals, and energy. The decline in FDI inflows into Kenya in the 1990s is attributed to the suspension of funding under the IMF's Enhanced Structural Adjustment Facility Arrangement in July 1997, the slowdown in economic growth since the second half of 1996, the implementation of the privatization program, and instability in some banking institutions.

Kenya encourages foreign investment and grants national treatment to foreign investors. Most business activities are open to foreigners, except those related to matters of security or health. To attract investment, Kenya offers tax incentives to local and foreign investors in the form of tax holidays, accelerated depreciation, investment allowance, lower duties on intermediate capital goods, and gradual reduction of corporate tax rates. Despite these incentives, Kenya has not been able to attract much investment.

Trade Performance

Net service exports and capital inflows have for years sustained deficits in Kenyan merchandise trade. Kenya's economy has become increasingly dependent on foreign trade, as shown in Table 1.1. As a result of trade reforms implemented since 1993, the share of merchandise trade in GDP increased from 37.4 percent in 1992 to more than 50 percent during 1993–96. Although it declined to about 40 percent in 2000, this is in line with the downward trend in the ratio of imports to exports since 1993.

Trends in Trade. Kenya's volume of trade for exports and imports since 1990 is shown in Table 1.4 and Appendixes A, B, and C. The volume of trade in exports has increased from US$1.07 billion in 1993, prior to Kenya's signing of the WTO agreement, to US$1.9 billion in 2001 while the volume of import trade increased from US$1.5 billion to US$3.7 billion during the same period. Agricultural commodities dominated the exports while manufactured goods dominated the imports.

The main destinations of Kenyan exports during 1994–99 have been the EAC, the EU, and the Common Market for Eastern and Southern Africa (COMESA) (Table 1.5). In 1994, the EU was the dominant market for Kenyan exports, but in 1997, EAC became, and still is, the main destination. This was possibly because of the regional trade agreement that was formed by the three East African countries. Kenya's trade with COMESA, excluding the EAC countries, has been declining. This is possibly because of the emergence of South Africa as a significant trading force in the region. The share of exports to the rest of the world has grown by 3 percent since 1994 and by about 10 percent for the rest of Africa.

Table 1.4 Total International Trade 1991–2001
(US$ million)

Type of Trade	1991	1992	1993	1994	1995	1996	1997	1998	1999	2000	2001
Exports											
Domestic	1148.0	943.2	1063.7	1860.3	1664.7	2070.6	1826.1	1848.6	1582.4	1534.6	1545.0
Re-exports	13.0	18.9	15.6	49.7	75.4	77.7	95.5	108.8	98.1	189.2	33.3
Total Imports	1161.0	962.1	1079.3	1910.0	1740.0	2148.3	1921.6	1957.4	1680.5	1723.8	1877.7
Commercial	1781.9	1562.0	1421.7	2478.2	2679.8	2960.5	2956.0	3077.7	2739.7	3081.4	3627.3
Government	103.3	69.6	62.0	88.2	94.0	101.8	86.0	117.1	90.4	93.9	63.6
Total	1885.2	1631.6	1483.7	2566.5	2773.8	3062.3	3042.0	3194.8	2830.1	3175.3	3690.9
Visible Balance	724.2	669.6	404.4	656.5	1033.8	914.0	1120.4	1237.4	1149.6	1451.5	1813.2
Total trade	3046.2	2593.7	2563.0	4476.4	4513.9	5210.6	4963.6	5152.1	4510.6	4899.2	5547.5

Sources: Central Bureau of Statistics, Statistical Abstract (2000) and Economic Survey (2002).

Table 1.5 Destination of Exports to Important Markets as a Percentage of Total Exports 1994–2001

Year	EAC	COMESA Less EAC	Rest of Africa	EU	United States	Japan	Middle East	Rest of World
1994	22.6	13.5	7	36.1	3.3	0.8	1.7	15.1
1995	28.5	10.1	9.9	32.2	2.7	0.7	2.3	13.6
1996	29.2	9.0	8.9	32.4	2.7	0.8	3.2	13.8
1997	29.2	8.9	8.6	31.6	2.9	0.8	3.2	14.8
1998	29.7	7.5	10.6	29.1	2.6	0.8	4.0	15.7
1999	30.5	2.3	16.9	27.4	2.3	0.9	4.4	15.3
2000	26.2	7.5	11.9	29.8	2.1	1.0	4.9	16.6
2001	29.5	7.2	12.4	27.1	2.3	0.9	6.1	14.5

Source: Kenya, Economic Surveys (various years).

Structure of Trade. The structure of Kenya's trade in exports (Table 1.6) indicates that there has been no marked difference in its composition since the country became a WTO member. Agricultural trade in food and beverages has not changed and it continues to dominate Kenyan exports constituting an average of 53 percent of the total exports during 1994–98. Kenya's exports can be divided into traditional and nontraditional exports. Kenya's traditional exports are those that account for more than 3 percent of total exports in the base year (1980) (Blackhurst and Lyakurwa),[1] and include industrial supplies, coffee, tea, and crude vegetable materials. Nontraditional exports include most of the horticultural products, and flowers.

Kenyan exports are dominated by agricultural commodities, particularly tea, coffee, pyrethrum, and horticultural products (flowers, fruits and vegetables). Other exports include mainly soda ash, petroleum products, cement, clothing, and leather products. Except for tea and crude vegetable materials, traditional exports performed poorly in the 1980s and 1990s; growth averaged 7.4 percent. Nontraditional exports performed better: in which growth was estimated at 20.1 percent (Mwega 2000). The good performance of the nontraditional exports is attributed to the removal of restrictive trade policies by importing countries, particularly Europe under the ACP-EU Lome Agreement. The good performance in 1992–96 overlaps with trade liberalization and is explained by the "removal of bureaucratic bottlenecks and availability of foreign exchange" (Kenya, Economic Survey 1996).

Imports. Industrial supplies dominate imports with a share of 36 percent of total imports into

Table 1.6 Composition of Kenyan Exports in Broad Categories 1994–2001
(percent)

Type of Commodities	1994	1995	1996	1997	1998	1999	2000	2001
Food and beverages	51.50	51.10	52.90	53.90	57.40	55.9	56.3	49.2
Industrial supplies	29.40	26.90	26.10	22.40	18.30	17.9	19.1	22.7
Fuel and lubricants	6.50	5.30	6.60	9.00	9.10	8.2	8.6	10.2
Machinery and capital equipment	0.90	1.40	0.90	0.60	0.90	1.3	0.5	0.6
Transport equipment	1.10	0.50	0.50	0.40	0.60	0.9	0.5	0.4
Consumer goods	13.60	14.80	13.10	13.90	13.70	15.9	15.1	16.8

Source: Kenya, Economic Surveys (various years).

---

[1] "Markets and market access for African exports: Past, present and future." Framework paper presented at the African Economic Research Consortium Workshop on Africa and World Trading System held at Novotel Hotel, Accra, Ghana, 24–25 October. Cited by Mwega (2000).

Table 1.7 Composition of Kenyan Imports in Broad Categories
(percent)

Type of Commodities	1994	1995	1996	1997	1998	1999	2000	2001
Food and beverages	10.04	4.53	7.69	6.62	8.60	7.3	7.7	10.5
Industrial supplies	39.37	39.22	36.60	39.75	33.83	32.6	27.4	29.5
Fuel and lubricants	16.15	12.98	16.09	15.50	16.13	16.4	25.6	20.1
Machinery and capital equipment	15.35	19.25	18.16	16.91	17.63	14.2	15.8	12.9
Transport equipment	12.27	17.00	14.42	14.43	15.67	8.7	6.4	19.6
Consumer goods	6.82	7.03	7.04	6.79	8.14	0.56	0.41	6.3

Source: Kenya, Economic Surveys (various years).

Kenya followed by machinery and capital equipment at about 15 percent. Food and beverages constitute an average of 8 percent. Imports into Kenya are less dispersed than exports (Table 1.7). The EU accounted for about 33 percent of Kenya's import in 1999 (down from 36 percent in 1994), while the other African countries accounted for about 10 percent, and the rest of the world accounted for 41 percent. Imports from the United States have also remained relatively constant, but imports from Japan have declined. Manufactured goods account for most of the imports from the EU, the United States, and Japan, whereas the African countries account for most of the agricultural products (e.g., processed goods and maize from South Africa; maize and beans from Uganda and Tanzania). However, most of Kenya's wheat exports come from Australia, Argentina, Canada, and the United States.

Summary of Tariffs

Tariffs have been Kenya's main trade policy instrument; however, since Kenya became a member of the World Trade Organization (WTO) in 1995, the overall level of protection of its economy has been reduced. The country has dismantled most nontariff restrictions, except for the moral, health, security, and environmental conventions to which it is a signatory. The tariff structure has been simplified through the reduction of the number of bands from eight in 1994 to five in 1990 (0 percent, 5 percent, 10 percent, 15 percent, and 25 percent on tariffs for imports) and the lowering of the maximum ad valorem rates from 60 percent in 1992 to 25 percent in 1999. Mixed duties apply to 10 percent of all tariffs lines and specific duties to 30 lines at the eight-digit

level of the Harmonized System; many, including mainly agricultural and petroleum products, are subject to a combination of specific duties.

In addition to tariffs, "suspended" (stand-by) duties, which were as high as 70 percent increased to 95 percent, the maximum ad valorem import duties are on wheat flour, meslin flour, and certain types of sugar. The suspended duties replaced the variable duties on food and currently apply to 17 percent of all tariff lines at the HS eight-digit level, in agriculture and manufacturing. The maximum suspended duty of 70 percent also applies to maize, rice, and milk. The simple average rate of Kenya's nonspecific imports duties (inclusive of applied suspended duties) is 18 percent (WTO 2000). Approximately 3.7 percent of all tariffs lines are duty free while 38 percent carry rates higher than 15 percent; except paper, paperboard, cards, and office stationery; and rates higher than 35 percent apply to agricultural products and their transformations. An import declaration fee (IDF) of 2.75 percent is collected on all imports including those not subject to the preshipment inspection that is required for all imports worth at least US$5,000. The inclusion of the fee raises to 20.75 percent the average rate of import duties. At an aggregate the positive escalation of Kenya's tariff (highly pronounced on products such as textiles, wearing apparel, leather, and metallic, rubber, petroleum, and chemical products) means that the effective protection provided to most industries is higher than the nominal rate. A value added tax of 15 percent and excise duties ranging up to 135 percent (the excise duties are mixed or specific in certain products) are levied both on imports and locally produced goods. Approximately 15 percent of Kenya's tariff lines are bound at ceiling rates ranging from 18 percent on pharmaceutical goods to 100 percent on all agricultural products. Other duties and charges on all these products are bound at a zero rate, notwithstanding the imposition of the IDF on all imports and a fee of 1 percent on agricultural imports.

Except for timber and fish, Kenya has abolished export duties and taxes on all products. In August 1993, Kenya abolished export subsidies granted under the export compensation scheme. Three main incentive schemes—the export processing zone, the manufacturing under bond, and the duty remission schemes—are currently available to export-oriented companies. The Minister for Finance may, on a discretionary basis, remit duties payable on imports: import duties are remitted on specific inputs or those used by specified firms and certain state-owned companies. However, certain agricultural products and food products are subject to special export licenses for self-sufficient purposes.

Trade Policy

Trade policy formulation is the responsibility of several ministries (Office of the President, Ministry of Trade and Industry, Ministry of Finance and Planning, Ministry of Foreign Affairs, and Ministry of Agriculture and Rural Development), which constitute the Cabinet's economic subcommittee, and the Central Bank. However, recommendations can be made by two interministerial and consultative communities, which include the private sector. Mainly the Ministry of Trade and Industry implements the trade policy.

Kenya is a founding member of the WTO and signed the treaty in 1995. It accords at least Most Favored Nation (MFN) treatment to all its trading partners. Provisions of the WTO Agreements cannot be invoked before Kenyan national courts. However, Kenya is reviewing its legislation, including laws on antidumping, countervailing, and intellectual property rights, to bring it into conformity with WTO Agreements. Kenya's commitment to WTO principles is integral to its economic policies. In addition to its participation in the multilateral trading system, Kenya also pursues preferential trade agreements as a means of increasing trade flows. The country is a member of the Common market of Eastern and Southern Africa (COMESA), the East African Community (EAC), the organization of African Unity (OAU), the Inter-governmental Authority on Development (IGAD), the African Caribbean, Pacific–European Union (ACP-EC), and the WTO.

The different integration organizations within Africa are expected to operate as building blocks toward the achievement of a single large market on the African continent. According to Kenya's Development Plans (1997–2000 and 2002–08), the country will work toward the continued reduction and eventual elimination of tariff and nontariff barriers to trade among members of a common trading bloc, while recognizing the need to implement changes at the institutional level to promote these regional initiatives. The plan also states the need for a shift in the government's role away from control and regulation toward the facilitation of private sector development, and the need for closure of the gap between policy objectives and their implementation. Sectoral policies are aimed at enhancing production and productivity, through a continuous process of economic reform and trade liberalization, as a way to promote a more efficient allocation of resources, while improving the environment for private domestic and foreign investment. Specific emphasis is placed on strengthening the agriculture sector, and promoting value-added activities through the processing of agricultural goods.

Administrative Structure for WTO Agreements

The government through the Ministry of Trade and Industry (MTI) handles all issues relating to the WTO agreements. The Ministry has devoted a large amount of resources over a number of years toward WTO issues. The Department of External Trade (DET) of the ministry is responsible for WTO matters. There are officers at the capital in Nairobi and in Geneva working specifically on WTO issues. Furthermore, there is a standing committee known as National Committee on World Trade Organization (NCWTO), which includes in its membership representatives from relevant government departments and agencies as well as private institutions, which prepares for WTO negotiations. Various subcommittees assist the NCWTO in its work; among them are the subcommittees on Sanitary and Phytosanitary (SPS) agreement and the Technical Barriers to Trade (TBT) agreement.

Administrative responsibility for issues related to standards agreements (SPS and TBT) with regard to trade is the responsibility of the Ministry of Trade and Industry (MTI). However, MTI delegates responsibilities of implementation to the Kenya Bureau of

Standards (KEBS), Kenya Plant Health Inspectorate Services (KEPHIS), and the Department of Veterinary Services (DVS) under the Ministry of Agriculture and Rural Development (MA&RD), and the Department of Public Health of the Ministry of Health.

Macroeconomy and Standards

Kenya's economy relies heavily on agriculture and exports of agricultural commodities and agroprocessed products that dominate its international trade. The standards required in the export markets can facilitate or constrain trade in these products and therefore affect the performance of the economy. For example, if Kenyan exporters of tea, coffee, horticulture, or fish cannot meet the standards required in the international markets, the country's competitiveness in these exports is affected and this is reflected in the poor performance of the economy.

In addition to the impact standards have on the traditional Kenyan exports, the country has a diverse range of agricultural products whose standards vary. However, the opportunities and challenges created by the international agreements on standards for Kenyan products have not been documented. This is important as export trade has an significant impact on the Kenyan economy.

Agricultural Subsectors of Focus

Kenya's exports are dominated by agricultural exports. Tea is currently the leading export, followed by horticulture and coffee. These commodities account for more than 50 percent of the country's export earnings and are the main sources of employment for many Kenyans.

Coffee, horticulture (fruits, vegetables, and flowers), fish, and cotton textiles are analyzed as case studies in this chapter. Coffee is chosen because it is an important export crop and represents the traditional exports, which together with tea has dominated Kenya's economy. An analysis of market access conditions for Kenyan exports indicates that the traditional exports for Kenya (tea and coffee) do not have a problem of accessing markets in industrial countries but there are issues on standards, particularly quality concerns, which affect export earnings. The horticultural subsector (fruits, vegetables, and flowers) is chosen because it has grown rapidly in recent years but a number of issues on standards, particularly concerns on SPS and

consequences on market access, which have implications for the future performance of this subsector, have become important. The fisheries industry is included for analysis because in addition to the horticultural sector, it provides a case in which the requirements of the SPS Agreement have affected exports from Kenya. The cotton textile industry is also selected to provide evidence of the impact of standards on the light manufacturing industries.

Kenya's Participation in International Standards

The WTO agreement on the application of Sanitary and Phytosanitary Measures (SPS) sets out the rights and obligations of WTO members in relation to certain requirements that may restrict international trade. Specifically, the agreement requires member countries to base their sanitary and phytosanitary measures on international standards and where they do not conform, to justify their measures on the basis of risk assessment, a consistent approach to risk management, and the adoption of the least trade restrictive means of achieving the appropriate level of protection for human, animal or plant life, or health. Such measures are presumed not to constitute arbitrary or unjustifiable barriers to trade. The Agreement recognizes three international standardizing bodies as the source of its international standards-setting mechanism: (a) International Plant Protection Convention (IPPC), (b) Codex Alimetarius Commission (CAC), and (c) The Office International des Epizooties (OIE).

The Codex Alimentarius (Food law or Code) commission is the international body responsible for the execution of the joint FAO/WHO food standards program. Started in 1962 by FAO and WHO, the program is aimed at protecting the health of consumers as well as facilitating international trade. Codex is a collection of international food standards adopted by the Commission and presented in a uniform manner. It includes standards for all principal foods whether processed, semi-processed, or raw. It also includes provisions in respect to the hygienic and nutritional quality of food, including microbiological norms, provisions of food additives, pesticide residues, contaminants, labeling, and presentations and methods of analysis and sampling.

The international organization for standards technical committee is made up of seven subcommittees and it is the ISO section that deals with the development of standards for environment guidance, environment audits, and ecolabeling. The Integrated Plant Protection Convention (IPPC) deals with integrated economic management of pests and rational use of pesticides, and gives guidelines on standards for plant and plant health protection. The Office International des Epizooties (OIE) deals with standards for animal health.

Kenya is a member of these international organizations and participates in the meetings of these organizations. The country has adopted some of the standards of these organizations and has in some cases adopted guidelines of these organizations to set its own standards. The country is also a member of the African Regional Standards Organization (ARSO), which is mandated to promote standardization activities in Africa, and to elaborate and harmonize regional standards.

Standards Development and Implementation in Kenya

The public organization responsible for development, setting, and implementing of standards in Kenya is the Kenya Bureau of Standards (KEBS). This organization works closely with three main public organizations in the development and implementation of health standards on animal and animal products, plant and plant products, and food safety. These are the Kenya Plant Health Inspectorate Services (KEPHIS) for standards on health of plants and plant products, the Department of Veterinary Services (DVS) for standards on health of animal and animal products, and the Fisheries Department is responsible for fisheries. The Ministry of Health (MoH) is responsible for food safety standards.

Kenya Bureau of Standards (KEBS). The KEBS is a national government body established under the Standards Act Cap 496 of the Laws of Kenya charged with standards development and implementation, certification of products and firms, testing, and metrology. The KEBS is the contact point for CODEX- and ISO-related standards. It coordinates Kenya's viewpoints on international standards developed by CAC and ISO for various products, particularly those that are important for local and export trade. These are mainly agricultural products and include tea, horticulture, coffee, pyrethrum, sisal, hides and skins, fish, and many others. The KEBS involves industry stakeholders in standards development through sector technical committee discussions and where possible, stakeholders are included as delegates to international standards-setting forums. The procedure used to develop standards is outlined in Box 1.1.

BOX 1.1 PROCEDURE OF SETTING KENYAN STANDARDS

All standards in Kenya are industry driven, or, in matters of health and safety, initiated by the relevant government authorities. The proposals for new standards are submitted through the Standards Industrial Council (SIC), an advisory body, which evaluates the proposals on the basis of studies or analyses made. The recommendations made by the SIC are forwarded to the National Standards Council who, after considering the facts presented, approve the proposals for the development of the standard by the technical committees. The technical committees consist of representatives from all interested parties and stakeholders who are guided by experts from KEBS. The technical committee drafts the standards and sends them back to the SIC for rec-

ommendations to the NSC for approval. Then, the standards are published and gazetted. The technical committees also advise on items of national interest following receipt of notification, and prepare comments to international technical committees. The KEBS establishes Kenyan standards for products in all industrial sectors focusing on specifications, codes of practice methods of test, and glossary of terms. KEBS has established about 1000 standards for processed and manufactured agricultural products. Most Kenyan standards are based on international standards, which are either adopted without change, or adopted to allow for local conditions, and in a few instances, Kenyan standards have been developed for a number of unique local products.

Legal notices provided for under the Standards Act declare all Kenyan standards compulsory. Inspectors appointed under the Act enforce the set standards. A product quality certification scheme (diamond mark), calibration mark scheme, safety mark scheme, and ISO quality management mark schemes have been declared and are operational. The Quality System Accreditation Committee has been established to accredit ISO to firms and laboratories. It is estimated that about 12 percent of the agricultural and food processing firms have a plant certified by ISO 9000 (World Bank 2002). The management standards for Hazard Analysis Critical Control Point (HACCP) and Codex Standard for risk analysis have also been adopted, particularly in the fruits, vegetables, and fisheries industries.

Kenya, through KEBS, is a member of international standards-setting bodies, namely, CAC and ISO. The country participates in some of the technical committees of these organizations and the choice is made from a project priority list for the country. For example, in the last two years KEBS staff participated in three ISO meetings (ISO TC 34SC 8 on tea held in Kenya; ISO TC 176 Working Groups (19 and 20) held in Nairobi; and ISO COPOLCO held in Trinidad). In addition, during the same period, KEBS participated in 5 Codex meetings of the 22 meetings planned. The KEBS technical committees for standards setting advise on items of interest and prepare comments for delegates attending various international meetings of these organizations. The country would like to attend all annual, biannual, and technical meetings each year, but financial constraints limit them to a few select meetings each year. The country is not a secretariat for any technical committee on international standards-setting but in the past it has hosted two ISO technical meetings as indicated above.

KEBS also participates in the development of regional Codex and ISO standards for Africa being a member of the African Regional Organization for Standardization (ARSO). During 2000–01, the country was the Chair holder of the main committee for the member states. The main function of ARSO is the development of regional standards, harmonization of technical regulations, and identification of new standards projects at national and international levels.

When enforcing standards, the KEBS officers visit production firms and supermarkets and collect samples for analysis. The fact that all national standards are compulsory allows for inspection to be carried out at the manufacturing stage. Samples are taken for testing during inspection. Occasionally, random samples are taken at the point of sale and tested. Imported products must comply with local standards or approved regional or international standards. New products entering Kenya must undergo inspection and testing prior to the first consignment being shipped into the country, and preinspection certificates of compliance are issued. KEBS inspectors thereafter take samples during random inspections of following consignments at the ports of entry into Kenya. The samples are tested in KEBS laboratories or other available facilities at KEPHIS or at the Government Chemist under the Ministry of Health. Provision is made for product certification by the exporting country either through mutual certification agreements or by prior investigation to confirm the competence of the certificator. However, KEBS inspectors must scrutinize all compliance certificates received for an imported consignment before customs are notified and a consignment is released.

Quality inspection of imports is carried out at the port of entry by KEBS on all imports into Kenya, covering food, beverages, vegetable oils and fats, chemicals, electric machinery, apparatus and appliances, and textiles. The quality inspection fee is 0.2 percent of the C&F value and is payable before issuance of a certificate of release. Imports that are tested by the KEBS and found not complying with the requirements of the relevant Kenyan standards cannot be sold in the Kenyan market. The importer will have to return them to the country of origin at the owner's cost.

All local manufacturers pay an annual product levy based on volume or value. This levy covers the cost of inspection and testing. The manufacturer or any person requesting additional tests, however, will pay for tests that are carried out. For all inspections, a quality inspection fee of 0.2 percent and 0.1 percent of the C&F value of the final products and raw materials, respectively is charged. Inspection and testing fees of import consignment samples are paid by the importer or the exporting agent, and are based on the actual cost for the work.

The KEBS assists Kenyan industries in promoting and developing organized in-plant standardization through training programs in the form of seminars, attachments, and factory visits. The focus is on standardization, industrial quality control, quality management, laboratory testing, and metrology. It also offers technical advice to manufacturers, exporters, importers, and others in the fields of quality assurance, formulation of standards, measurement and calibration, setting up in-plant testing facilities, setting ISO-9000 systems, quality standards for the country of exports, and quality of imported products.

The Bureau of Standards has about 800 staff members with half the number being technical staff. Most of the staff is based at the Nairobi Headquarters. Other staff members are in the regional branches and the export or import border ports. KEBS has testing facilities at Nairobi and the regional centers as well as at the main port of entry. It also uses laboratories owned by KEPHIS, the Government Chemist, and the Departments of Agriculture and Fisheries. Five KEBS laboratories have been accredited by UKAS in the past 10 years. Furthermore, KEBS is accredited as an ISO 9000 certificator by QSAC. However, there is no standards accrediting body in Kenya, which is internationally recognized, and the country has to rely on foreign bodies for this purpose. This restricts trade in most products as Kenyan recommendations and procedures such as on ISO 9001, ISO 14001, and HACCP are not recognized internationally unless accredited by an internationally recognized body. KEBS has recognized this problem and has started championing a program to establish an accrediting body that will be associated with an internationally recognized body.

The Bureau's funding comes from various sources including Standards Levy order, Import Quality inspection fees, annual Government Grants, sale of Bureau Products (Kenyan Standards, foreign standards, testing services, and so on), and grants from donors and well wishers. The annual budget is about US$1.5 million, most of which is generated internally (80 percent). The KEBS estimates that they require an additional US$280,000 annually to enable them undertake their functions effectively.

Although KEBS's mandate is well defined and it has some capacity to undertake its obligations, it faces constraints in terms of limited laboratory capacity and libraries in the branches required for effective implementation of its activities. With the adoption of WTO Agreement on SPS and TBT, there is more need for KBS staff to participate in the development of International Standards and their subsequent adoption as national standards.

For this reason, KEBS requires more funds to enable participation in more committees of Codex and ISO at the international level. The Codex contact point at KEBS needs communication equipment such as a computer to facilitate linkage between it and the stakeholders in the country and at the international level.

Kenya Plant Health Inspectorate Services (KEPHIS). KEPHIS is a government parastatal under the Ministry of Agriculture and Rural Development (MA&RD) and was established in 1997 to be in charge of plant health aspects including overseeing the health of plants and plant materials for import and export. The organization was established after the realization of the weakness in the previous fragmented regulatory mechanisms for sanitary and phytosanitary measures that existed in different government bodies. KEPHIS derives its regulatory powers from the Plant Protection Act Cap 324, Agriculture Produce (Export) Cap 319, Seed Act Cap 326, and Pest Control Products Act Cap 346 of the Laws of Kenya.

KEPHIS coordinates all viewpoints related to the health of plants and plant products and is the contact point for IPPC. KEPHIS works closely with KEBS to formulate standards related to plant and plant materials. The staff of KEPHIS regularly participates in international meetings of IPPC. The funds that enable the staff to attend the meetings are provided by FAO on request by KEPHIS. The managing director is a member of the Interim Commissions on Phytosanitary Measures and the Standards Committee. As a result of KEPHIS's participation it has developed guidelines for pest risk analysis based on IPPC procedures.

KEPHIS's mandate for the implementation of SPS focuses on plant protection services including quarantine of imported plants and plant products, phytosanitary certification of exports and export grading, and implementation of national policy on the introduction and use of genetically modified organisms.

The Plant Protection Act contains provisions to restrict the spread of insect pests and pathogens that occur in isolated areas of Kenya and to declare disease-free zones. Currently, there is a domestic quarantine on the following pests and diseases.

1. Larger grain borer (*Prostephanus truncates*) confined to south-eastern Kenya;

2. Serpentine leaf minor (*liriomyza trifolii*) confined to eastern Kenya;
3. Cassava bacterial blight (*Xanthomanas manihotisi*) confined to cassava-growing areas of Western Kenya;
4. Banana nematode (*Radophilus simulus*) confined to central Kenya; and
5. Ascochyta blight of cowpeas (*assochyta rabiei*) introduced in Kenya in 1990 and confined to Machakos District.

KEPHIS coordinates and regulates all matters relating to plant quarantine and restricts the entry of plants and plant products into the country without its permission and runs the Kenya Plant Quarantine Services (PQS) for this purpose. The PQS has made regulations and a list of plants specifying those that are prohibited and those that must be compulsorily imported upon obtaining import permits and issuing a Pythosanitary Certificate and, or, certificate of origin after having verified that the shipment meets the entry requirements (see Box 1.2).

KEPHIS has also developed arrangements for the certification of plants and plant products for export that is generally accepted by Kenya's trading partners. All plant and plant products for export are inspected and issued a phytosanitary export certification at the port of export. KEPHIS's export and import control activities are supported by a well-equipped laboratory facility at Nairobi. The strict application and observations of export standards are responsible for the expansion of a wide range of horticultural exports from Kenya. However, KEPHIS has not prepared a detailed pest analysis risk list covering a long period and a wide area and this is a hindrance in exporting to some countries (such as the United States, Japan, and South Africa).

KEPHIS has departments of Administrative Services, Plant Breeders Rights Services, Quality Control Services, and Plant Protection Services to aid in undertaking its mandate. It has headquarters in Nairobi and branches for other districts based in Nakuru, Kitale, and Mombasa and a plant quarantine station in Nairobi. It has offices at all ports of entry to check and ensure that export or import of plant or plant products is inspected and certified to be free from invasive plant species, noxious weeds, injurious foreign pests, and diseases.

KEPHIS has over 60 scientists, 100 technical officers, and 150 support staff. It collaborates with national and international organizations whose goals are to protect plant health, quality inputs, and plant produce. The estimated annual budget for KEPHIS is US$1.5 million, most of which is internally generated while the government provides the balance.

BOX 1.2 CERTIFICATION OF PLANT MATERIALS IN KENYA

Plants and plant products imported into Kenya must be inspected. The regulations stipulate pre- and postentry treatment to be undertaken upon arrival of plant products to eliminate disease and pest risks. A variety of facilities including a postentry plant quarantine facility supports controls at the borders. The plant pathology clinics provide diagnostic services on diseased plant parts. An entomology clinic provides similar services for pests. A copy of a permit issued by KEPHIS and an additional phytosanitary certificate or international equivalent must accompany all plants and plant materials entering the country. The phytosanitary certificate verifies that the competent authority in the exporting country has examined the plants for pests and diseases prior to their leaving the country and that the plants meet Kenya's requirements. The PQS is equipped with a tissue culture laboratory for in vitro rapid multiplication of imported plant materials for tests, studies, commercial propagation, and conservation of germplasm. Imported plants and plant materials may, if necessary, be detained in the quarantine station or special nurseries. Plants arriving without authority and accompanying documents may be destroyed or reshipped back at the owner's cost. An importer who contravenes or fails to comply with this Act is liable to a fine not exceeding US$250 equivalent in Kenya shillings or imprisonment for a period not exceeding six months or both.

Department of Veterinary Services (DVS) and Fisheries Department. The Department of Veterinary Services (DVS) is a department under the Ministry of Agriculture and Rural Development (MA&RD) and is charged with overseeing animal health services in the country. Its regulatory powers are derived from the Animal Diseases Act Cap 364, Fertilizer and Animal Foodstuff Act Cap 345, Dairy Industry Act Cap 336, Pest Control Act Cap 346, and the Meat Control Act Cap. The main functions of the DVS are:

a. Livestock disease control through monitoring the health status of livestock, regular vaccinations, vaccine production and distribution, and importation of suitable vaccines.
b. Implementation of meat hygiene through the supervision of slaughterhouses and meat-processing facilities, facilitating inspection and certification of meat imports and exports.
c. Implementation of milk hygiene.
d. Implementation and supervision of health and hygiene of all other livestock and livestock products and livestock feeds and use of drugs, vaccines and chemicals for animal use.

The DVS coordinates all viewpoints on standards related to animal health (livestock disease control, meat and milk hygiene) and is the focal point for OIE. The DVS is involved in the formulation of standards related to the health of animal and animal products and has the mandate to determine the existence of disease epidemic, quarantine, and disease-free zones. It also inspects and provides documents (no-objection permit for livestock imports and veterinary health and sanitary certificate for livestock exports) that facilitate trade in livestock and livestock products.

The Division of Veterinary Public Health of the DVS is the chair of the National Codex Committee and is responsible for attending international Codex and OIE meetings related to standards on health of animal and animal products. However, Kenya's attendance in the annual and biannual Codex and OIE meetings and also the technical committees is rare. Some of the meetings that DVS officials have attended include meetings on food hygiene, residues of veterinary drugs in foods and meat hygiene. The DVS considers measurers developed by OIE such as disease-free areas to be appropriate but the country has not been able to do so. This partly explains why beef products are restricted to EU, United States and Japan markets. The DVS also appreciates the need to implement the residue program to determine the safety of the use of drugs and pesticides in livestock products and risk analysis on various food-borne diseases but these activities are not performed adequately because of financial constraints (see Box 1.3).

The DVS has laboratories in Kabete and Nairobi for testing the disease status of imports and exports of animal and animal products, and has officers at other ports of entry. The Nairobi laboratory has

BOX 1.3 CERTIFICATION OF ANIMAL AND ANIMAL PRODUCTS IN KENYA

The Animal Diseases and Quarantine Act allow the DVS to enforce the SPS for livestock and livestock products. There is a specific veterinary import permit for each species (e.g., cattle, goats, sheep, pigs, and birds). All animals for export to Kenya must be held for 21 days in approved quarantine facilities that must be regularly inspected by the veterinary authorities of the exporting country subject to inspection by the Veterinary Officer from Kenya, where necessary. All the tests, clinical examinations, and treatment, which must be carried out during the quarantine period, must be stated in the veterinary certificate to confirm freedom from diseases. The animals may be held for 14 days in the quarantine facilities at the port of entry at the cost of the importer. All costs of post-arrival selection, testing, treatment, transport, quarantine, and service must be borne by the importer. The Veterinary Officer at the port or airport of entry issues a health clearance certificate if inspection shows the animals to be healthy and all accompanying health certificates are in order.

capacity (human and equipment) to undertake diagnostic and quality assurance work for most livestock and analysis of various livestock products. The DVS has a countrywide extension network of veterinarians who help in advising farmers on animal disease control and surveillance of disease. There are also five regional laboratories that are used for diagnostic tests by farmers. However, the Division of Veterinary Public Health, which is responsible for the implementation of the SPS aspect on the health of animal and animal products is understaffed. It has only 50 veterinarians and 700 meat inspectors countrywide. The staff is responsible for providing services on veterinary public health for the whole country and providing meat inspection services in all slaughterhouses including Kenya's only three operational export abbatoirs.

Improvements in animal husbandry are a major focus for the DVS and sanitation is an important issue. Accordingly, the DVS endeavors to apply most of the OIE norms, modified as appropriate for local circumstances, to domestic disease control and surveillance and control of imports of animals and animal products. However, exports are constrained by the presence of significant animal diseases such as foot and mouth disease, Rift Valley fever, contagious bovine pleuropneumonia, and African swine fever. Problems are also encountered with animal health infrastructure. For example, while the five regional laboratories in the country can diagnose animal diseases, there is no adequate capacity to test for residues in red meat, poultry, and dairy products. Similarly, implementation of risk analysis of various diseases to determine disease-free zones in the country is not undertaken. The government currently has not invested in these programs because of financial constraints. This is despite the potential the country has to export animals and animal products.

The Department of Fisheries is also a department under the MA&RD and is the competent authority for export certification for fish and fish products. The standards for fish were modified recently (Fisheries and Fish Quality Assurance Regulations 2000). The principal requirement of the regulation is that all fish products have to be inspected and thereafter a health certificate is issued to accompany exports. The procedure of issuing the health certificate involves ensuring that fish handling and processing meet the sanitary conditions laid out by the Fisheries Department. A fee of 0.5 percent of the FOB value of export is charged for the health certificate. The Department

has 20 fish inspectors responsible for the issuance of the inspection certificates. There are laboratories in Kisumu and Mombasa and one is under construction in Nairobi for use in the detection and diagnosis of diseases. However, they are inadequately equipped and in some cases, the Department uses KEBS and KEPHIS laboratories for diagnosis of fish diseases at a fee of US$100 per sample.

Ministry of Health (MoH). Food standards (other than those within the responsibility of the Department of Veterinary Services (DVS) and the Department of Fisheries within the MA&RD) are adopted via a procedure managed by the KEBS as indicated earlier and implemented by the Ministry of Health (MoH) under the provisions of the Public Health Act Cap 242 and the Food, Drugs, and Chemical Substances Act Cap 254.

The country has developed standards for food safety for most food products. Codex food standards are considered when developing food standards for application within Kenya (including standards for imported food). Cases in which no standards have been developed for imported foodstuffs, there is a requirement that the imported food comply with the standards of the exporting country. The main problem with implementation of standards is lack of information among the general public. The standards are not common knowledge for the business community because of weaknesses in information dissemination by the responsible authorities (MoH and KEBS) regarding the standards (see Box 1.4).

Relationships between Contact Points and National Authorities for Trade Policy

Overall, the Ministry of Trade and Industry (MTI) is responsible for trade agreements and it coordinates with all public agencies involved in standards setting and implementation at a ministerial level and at the National Committee on WTO (NCWTO) level. The MTI is the notifying authority for WTO issues. The KEBS, KEPHIS, and DVS are contact points for CAC, IPPC, and OIE, respectively, while MoH deals in food safety matters.

The KEBS is responsible for ensuring that all goods offered for trade in Kenya, whether imports or exports or for the domestic market, meet stipulated standards. KEPHIS coordinates all issues related to crop pests and disease control and is

BOX 1.4 FOOD SAFETY PROCEDURES

Ministry of Health officers stationed at recognized entry points into the country (Port Health Offices) are responsible for taking samples of foods imported and submit them to laboratories for analysis as appropriate. Microbiological analysis is carried out by the National Public Health Laboratories free of charge or by a similar facility maintained by the Kenya Bureau of Standards who charge a fee of 0.2 percent of the CIF value for the service. Food tests and chemical substances are subjected to inspection for the purposes of the prevention of any infectious or communicable diseases. It is a requirement that a health certificate accompany imports of these goods from the country of origin certifying that the products meet the sanitary standards. Besides, most food products are also subjected to radioactive tests. The Institute of Nuclear Sciences, University of Nairobi undertakes the tests but this is coordinated by the port health offices. A fee of US$40 is paid to the Institute by importers for the radioactive tests.

responsible for inspection, testing, certification, quarantine control, and variety testing and description of all planting materials. It is also responsible for grading and inspection of plants and plant produce at the ports of entry and exit and also approves all importation and exportation licenses for plants and seed. KEPHIS advises on relevant matters on plant and plant health in which the SPS and TBT Agreements are concerned. The DVS is responsible for animal disease control and advises on matters related to animal health. The Pest Control Products Board (PCPB), also under the Ministry of Agriculture and Rural Development (MOA&RD), is responsible for standards related to agricultural chemicals. The MoH is responsible for inspection of foods, drugs, and chemicals to ensure food safety. The enquiry points and the MTI are linked through the National Committee on WTO (NCWTO) so that the KEBS, KEPHIS, DVS, and MoH have representatives who advise on specific issues of trade and standards. Figure 1.1 outlines the linkages among the various bodies.

The three government ministries involved in standards setting and implementation are MTI, MOARD, and MoH. The MTI plays a leading role in standards setting and implementation through KEBS and in standards notification. The Ministry of Agriculture and Rural Development (MOARD), under which KEPHIS, DVS and PCPB fall, is in charge of standards setting and implementation for animal and animal products, and the health of plant and plant products in the country.

The Ministry of Health (MoH) plays a leading role in setting and implementing standards on food safety. Thus, a feature of the implementation of standards in Kenya is fragmentation of responsibilities. Fragmentation sometimes leads to overlaps and inefficiencies in implementation of the functions on different bodies. For example, KEBS

1.1 Coordinating Standards Development in Kenya

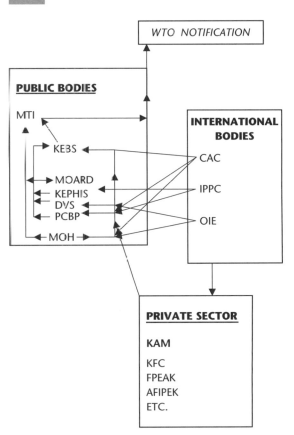

and port health offices duplicate each other in the inspection of foods for quality. DVS and the port health offices also duplicate roles in the inspection of animal products. There is need for better coordination to avoid overlaps that affect the enforcement of the standards in the country.

Notification of Standards

Kenyan standards relevant to TBT and SPS are notified to the World Trade Organisation (WTO) by KEBS through the Ministry of Trade and Industry. The KEBS is the Secretariat of the National Codex Committee, which reviews Codex draft standards and documents for the Codex Alimentarius. The Ministry of Agriculture and Rural Development through KEPHIS and the DVS notifies Kenyan standards on TBT and SPS measures on plant and animal health.

The KEBS, KEPHIS, and DVS also notify Kenyans (firms and farmers) about TBT and SPS standards using newsletters, letters, and meetings of stakeholders. The Export Promotion Council (EPC) also plays a leading role in notifying foreign investors and local producers on the SPS and TBT standards for all products traded in Kenya. The KEBS, KEPHIS, and EPC have online facilities for standards on TBT and SPS. The standards specifications under Kenyan laws and regulations are mandatory whereas codes and methods of tests are not mandatory. However, the NCWTO SPS and TBT committee has observed that the dissemination of information to stakeholders is not adequate. This is partly because of fragmentation of duties among the enquiry points and overlaps in functions among the authorities as well.

Participation in International Industry and Commodity Organization Meetings

Public agricultural commodity organizations such as the Coffee Board of Kenya (CBK) and the Kenya Planters Cooperative Union (KPCU) also get involved in standards setting by international organizations such as the International Coffee Organization (ICO). Representatives from these organizations occasionally attend meetings of ISO TC SC 15 for

Coffee. Similarly, the Tea Board and the Kenya Tea Development Agency (KTDA) have also attended meetings of ISO TC 34 SC for Tea.

Experiences of Private Sector Involvement

Private sector participation in standards setting is mixed. Codes of practice are the instruments private businesses commonly use to achieve standards including both classic quality standards such as taste, color, and size, as well as newer standards such as food safety, social justice, and environmental protection. Individual companies may develop them or draw from model codes, which are usually industry specific. The Codes of Conduct exist, for example, for fresh fruits and vegetables, flowers, and fish. These industry-specific codes are derived from international standards or requirements of export markets for these products.[2] However, the participation of Kenyan private business is not as strong as it should be. It rarely sends representatives to international meetings for standards setting. The World Bank Database on trade and standards (2002) indicates that only about 10 percent of Kenyan agricultural and food processing firms participate in international standards development meetings.

Another weakness in the participation of the private sector in international standards-setting is the failure to influence recognition of the domestic codes of conduct with similar codes in the export markets. For example, the Kenyan fruit and vegetable industry, although an important player in the European market, has had little input into, or participation in, the European discussions about codes of practice. Officials in the Kenyan fruit and vegetable industry has attempted, mainly through trade associations, to participate tried to take part in the European Union discussions about harmonization of codes of practice; but this has not been successful. For instance, the Fresh Produce Association of Kenya (FPEAK) and the Flower Label Program (FLP) of Germany unsuccessfully tried to "marry" their codes into a common label in 1998 (USAID 2001). FPEAK is also not an associate member of EUREP, a group of leading European food retailers whose objective is to raise standards for the production of fresh fruits and vegetables.

---

[2] The code of conduct for fresh horticultural producers takes into account EU technical and market standards while the code of conduct for fish is also derived from international and EU standards.

Producers and producer groups can become associate members and participate in the negotiation of the standards. However, the Kenya Flower Council (KFC) has been able to make progress through the Kenya Flower Day in London in the last two years. Despite this weakness, the efforts by COLEACP, an EU and ACP countries' initiative to support standards development and implementation in ACP countries will help in harmonization of standards for products targeted to the EU market.

The invitations from KEBS to the members of Kenya's delegations to technical meetings organized by international bodies are opportunities for the private sector in Kenya to influence international standards-setting. Their views during the meetings could influence standards setting internationally and in Kenya. However, it is rare for the private sector to attend these meetings. This lack of attendance is attributed to financial constraints. However, it could be that stakeholders fail to appreciate the role they can play in influencing international standards and the benefits that they can derive from it, because industry organizations can afford to sponsor participants in the international meetings.

Country's Strengths and Weaknesses in International Standards-Setting

Kenya is a full, paying member of international standards-setting organizations (Codex, IPPC, and OIE). Officers involved in standards development attend some of the meetings organized by the bodies. The benefits derived from the meetings include information used as a basis for Kenyan standards setting thereby making it easy for Kenyan standards to be easily accepted internationally. These include standards for many products such as coffee, tea, horticulture and fish, milk and milk products.

A major weakness in international standards-setting is the failure for the country to be represented in all meetings organized by international bodies. Kenyan participation in the setting and negotiation of international trading standards is limited due to lack of resources and organizational complications. More often than not, venues for such international meetings are in the industrial countries, and this limits the level and quality of participation because of administrative and financial constraints. The relevant actors are from different government ministries or departments or parastatals, each with specific interests and expertise, which may not necessarily be of technical standards. It is often difficult to organize harmonious and effective participation, given their special knowledge and experience in the agenda area. In most cases, only representatives from KEBS attend. One solution to this problem is for the government to increase funding to organizations involved in standards setting to participate more effectively. International development agencies can help the Government of Kenya to finance these efforts.

Failure to participate in the international meetings inhibits institutional development, capacity building, sensitizing, and educating the private sector on standards implementation and conformity assessment schemes such as quality schemes that guarantee acceptance of international standards. Currently, there is little proactive participation in the area by the private sector in Kenya. Most industry actors take a reactive position to international standards. This is exemplified, for example, by the adoption of European Union regulations on fish and horticultural produce unconditionally. Noncompliance with these regulations, as determined by the importing countries, automatically leads to trade penalties such as fines, destruction of produce, or total ban of exports from the affected countries. The paucity of expertise, resources, and technical capacity in many countries constrains their ability to play a significant role in the implementation of these laws and regulations.

Legislation or Regulations and Relationships to International Norms

This section outlines the important legislation that forms the basis for standards setting in Kenya and how the standards are related to international norms.

Standards Legislation

Legislation or regulations on standards in Kenya are established as Acts of Parliament, which empower various organizations to enforce the regulations. The laws serve the following functions:

- Ensure that agricultural inputs are safe to use
- Create control mechanisms to ensure quality of inputs and products

- Ensure that food consumed is produced and handled in a hygienic manner
- Standards are available
- Protect consumers from health hazards

The legislation can be grouped into five main groups according to the purposes of the legislations.

Standards Formulation and Implementation. The main legislation responsible for this is the Standards Act Cap 496. The Act provides for the establishment of the Kenya Bureau of Standards (1974) and specifies its functions, including promote standardization in industry. It also empowers the KEBS to prevail in cases of conflicts with standards under other Acts.

Public Health Safeguards. The legislation for these safeguards includes Public Health Act Cap 242: Foods, Drugs and Chemical Substances Cap. 254, Pharmacy and Poisons Act Cap. 244, and Radiation Protection Act cap. 243. The Acts provide for protection of human health and the prevention of the spread of diseases, and prevention and control of food adulteration.

Health of Animal and Animal Products. The Animal Health Act Cap 364 provides for the safeguard of Kenya's animals (livestock and wildlife). It confers the powers on the DVS to control imports and exports of animal and animal products, and other living organisms. This is also supplemented by the requirements of the Public Health Act Cap 242.

Protection of Plants and Plant Products. The Plant Protection Act (1937) and, the Seed and Varieties Act (1972) were the basis for the establishment of the Kenya Plant Health Inspectorate Service (KEPHIS) to regulate plant health and safety as well as the regulation of agricultural inputs (agrochemical, seeds, and so on) and produce. Thus, KEPHIS has the mandate to monitor for government, business sector, scientists, farmers, and other stakeholders all issues related to plant health and quality control of agricultural products. The Act is supplemented by the Pests Control Products Act Cap 346, which regulates and controls the use of products for the control of pests. The Act gives the mandate to the Pest Control Products Board

(PCPB) to assess pest control products for safety, efficacy, quality, and economic value and licenses various categories of pesticide traders and to generally advise the Kenyan government on the choice of pest control products in the country.

Quality of Agricultural Inputs and Produce. The Agricultural Produce Act Cap 319 provides for grading and inspection of produce, and its regulation, preparation, and manufacture. It also allows for the certification of horticulture exports through the Horticultural Inspection Services and establishes the Horticultural Crops Development Authority (HCDA) for the purpose of supervision and control of production. The Fertilizers and Animal Foodstuffs Act provides for the enforcement of technical standards for fertilizer use in Kenya and those for animal feeds.

Conformity of Laws to International Standards

Kenyan standards on food safety, and animal and plant health are based on various Acts of Parliament as indicated in the previous section. The matrix below shows the conformity of Kenya's standards to international standards for selected commodities. The matrix also shows that most Kenyan standards for many products are derived from internal standards and therefore conform to international norms.

Standards for Importation of Selected Products

This section reviews importation standards for milled sugar, maize, and wheat to illustrate the standards for selected products in Kenya. These three are important food imports into Kenya.

Milled Sugar. The international commission for internationally traded white sugar sets the quality standards referred as International Commission for Unified Methods of Sugar Analysis (ICUMSA) for sugar. Kenya has recognized the standards set by this organization for sugar and has incorporated the requirements in setting KEBS minimum quality standards of milled sugar to be manufactured and imported. The maximum value has been set at 400 ICUMSA units although sugar traded internationally should not register more than 150 ICUMSA units. The lower the unit, the whiter the color and the more costly it becomes.

Matrix on Comparative Kenyan and International Standards for Selected Commodities

Commodity	Kenyan Standard	International Standard
Tea	KSO1–65 Specification for Black Tea Chemical requirements for Black Tea (oven dried to constant mass at 103±2°C	ISO3720 Black Tea Basic requirements (Tea shall not have taint and be reasonably free from extraneous matter)
Coffee	KSO1–593 Specification for green coffee beans	ISO1–104760 Green coffee Defect reference
Fish	KSO5–1516 code of hygienic practice for the handling, processing, storage, and placing of fish on the market KSO5–1399pt1	European standards EU Directive 91/493/EEC CODEX STAN 165
Horticultural products	KS 1758 Code of practice for the Horticultural industry	Good agricultural practice MAAFF, UK; Integrated Crop Management, UK; and Environmental Protection Agency, USA CODEX ALIMENTARIUS VOL. 5B.
Fruits (Fresh fruits, e.g., avocado, pineapple, mango, papaya and pineapple)	KSO1–393: 1983 Kenya standard specification for fresh pineapples	CODEX STAN 182–188, 196–197
Flowers	KSO1–695 cut flowers	Reference UN/EEC standard H-1 on cut flowers

The KEBS standard KSO5–58:2000 defines and specifies chemical and microbiological requirements for refined sugar. The standard is derived from Codex Stan 4-198 for white sugar. The general requirements are that refined sugar shall have flavor and shall be free from any foreign materials and odor; shall be free from traces of pests, rodents, and any other contaminant; and shall be free from any objectionable extraneous matter.

Maize. Cap 319 of the laws of Kenya (Agriculture Produce Export) provides for the grading of maize rules to regulate the quality exported from Kenya, including its packaging method and assignment of grades. Rules for grading of wheat and beans are also provided.

The Kenya Bureau of Standards specifications have been set for dry shelled maize under title KSO1–42:1997, which recognizes all vital parameters geared toward ensuring the safety of the consumer. The National Cereals Produce Board (NCPB) specifications for dry shelled maize purchased from farmers are also set in line with the quality standards for shelled maize set by the Kenya Bureau of Standards under title KSO1–42:1997. The quality specification standards are shown in Table 1.8.

Table 1.8 Quality Specifications for Dry Shelled Maize

Factor	NCPB Specifications FAQ (%)	KSCO1–42:1997 Grade Requirements (% by wt) K1
Moisture content	13.5	13.5
Foreign matter	1	1
Broken grains	2	2
Pest damaged grains	3	3
Discoloured grains	2	2

Source: NCPB, Nairobi (2002).

NCPB, the main maize-purchasing agency, buys maize grains on the basis of Fair Average Quality (FAQ) criteria that effectively constitute a single average grade at intake. The grading factors constituting the FAQ grade are determined through surveys in the industry and are a compromise quality level designed to meet the requirements of the consumers. They also include quality factors, such as insect damage, rotten grains, and foreign extraneous matter levels, which are achieved when the farmer takes reasonable care in harvesting the produce.

Wheat. The wheat industry quality rules were first enacted under the Wheat Industry Ordinance of 1952, which prescribed conditions under which wheat, flour, and wheat feed were graded, inspected, distributed, imported and exported; ascertained the grades of wheat flour and wheat milled for sale; and identified the type and specification of machinery installed in mills. Kenyan wheat is rarely exported now but the Wheat Millers Association has defined its own standards for the wheat that they buy from farmers with a maximum defect of 10 percent. A well-cleaned mature grain will normally yield the higher specific weight that is necessary for dough forming during baking. Thus, the higher the specific weight, the better the grade. If any of the defects exceed the percentage given, then the wheat may be rejected or it will be at the discretion of the miller and may be subject to a financial penalty. The quality standards for wheat are shown in Table 1.9.

Labor Laws and International Norms

Kenya's laws on labor are outlined in a number of Acts of Parliament. They include the Employment Act Cap 226; Employment of Women, Young Persons, and Children's Act Cap 227; the Regulation of Wages and Conditions of Employment Act Cap 229; 234; the Trade Disputes Act Cap 234; and the Workmen's Compensation Act Cap 236.

The Employment Act, among other things, deals with issues regarding the employment of women and juveniles and issues such as keeping of records and penalty for failure to obey the law. It prohibits the employment of a child, whether gainfully or otherwise, in an industrial undertaking. Children may, however, be employed in family businesses, including agriculture. The Act also requires an employer to maintain a register indicating the date of entry and exit from employment and to ensure regular medical examination of employees. The Employment of Women, Young Persons and Children's Act provides for the enforcement officers to ensure the protection of these groups while in employment, prohibits the employment of women and young persons in certain economic sectors, and sets the minimum age for employment. It also provides for the maintenance of registers, issuance of permits, medical examination, and for necessary

Table 1.9 Quality Specifications for Wheat

Factor or Defect	NCPB Specifications FAQ (%)	KSCO1–42:1997 Grade Requirements (% by wt) K1
Moisture content	13.5	13.5
Infested wheat	0	0
Immature wheat	5	5
Foreign matter	1	1
Heat damaged wheat	3	3
Broken wheat	2	2
Germinated wheat	2	2
Insect/pest-damaged wheat	2	2
Weather-damaged or discolored wheat	5	5
Foreign seed excluding datura 2 seed per kg maximum	3	3
Total defects allowed	10	10

Source: NCPB, Nairobi (2002).

inspections to be carried out. The Regulation of Wages and Conditions of Employment Act sets the minimum wages payable to employees. The Workmen's Compensation Act covers workers in the event of injury out of or in the course of work.

In addition to the national legislation, Kenya is a signatory of the International Labor Organization (ILO) conventions on employment and labor. The conventions specify the standard minimum age a laborer must be, define conditions of night work, medical examination, and underground work. Since 1954, Kenya has ratified 47 ILO Conventions of which 41 are in force. Some of the main conventions ratified by Kenya include Convention No. 29 on Forced Labor, No. 98 on The Right to Organize Trade Unions and Collective Bargaining, No. 105 on Abolition of Forced Labor, and No. 138 on Minimum Age. The country has not, however, ratified three core conventions, namely No. 87 on Freedom of Association, No. 100 on Equal Remuneration, and No. 111 on Nondiscrimination in Employment and Occupations.

Influence of Regional Standards

An important area in which regional standards developments have influenced standards setting in Kenya is on sanitary and phytosanitary measures. The EAC Secretariat for the three east African countries, Kenya, Tanzania, and Uganda have developed a harmonized system of sanitary and phytosanitary measures to apply for the three countries. This work was spearheaded by the Association of Agricultural Research for Central and Eastern Africa (ASARECA). The harmonized measures focus on

- Requirements for importation of plant and plant products
- Requirements for exportation of plants and plant products
- Plant quarantine measures
- Importation and release of exotic biological control agents
- Importation of Living Organisms for research
- Standards of export or import of plant materials
- Communication mechanisms among partner states (vigilance)
- Breeding of seed and release of varieties

The measures that have been used to develop EAC standards are based on current standards applicable in the three East African countries and also take into account the recommended international standards and practices from organizations such as IPPC and OIE. They also take into account the principles of the WTO SPS Agreement. The basis for the EAC development of common standards is the ongoing regional integration effort to form one trading bloc under a customs union. Therefore, there is a need for common measures on standards and regulations on trade to be harmonized. This will make it easy for the three East African countries to comply with the SPS Agreement.

Standards and Regulations for Important Inputs

The regulations for the important inputs are also based on various Acts of Parliament. The main standards are for seeds and chemicals used in agricultural production.

Seed Quality and Standards. Kenya's regulations for seed certification and licensing are outlined under the Seed and Plant Varieties Act of 1972. KEPHIS regulates all seed that is intended for sale in Kenya to ensure that it is of the variety and quality named. The seed cannot be sold in Kenya unless it is certified by KEPHIS through a rigorous release procedure. The process of seed certification (from breeder to foundation to commercial seed) is mandatory before its local sale in Kenya. The trials in the country take one to three years before approval. KEPHIS is the only body that certifies any agricultural seed in Kenya and licenses dealers through District Agricultural Committees, which represent farmers' interests.

Agrochemicals. Kenya imports most of its agrochemicals. The importation is subject to prior authorization by the Pest Control Products Board (PCPB), which inspects and licenses all premises involved in the production, distribution, and sale of agrochemicals. It also registers all agrochemicals imported or distributed in Kenya. Local testing of the chemicals by an appointed research agency is required before their registration. The 1963 Fertilizers and Animal Foodstuffs Act, revised in 1977, provides for technical standards to be met by fertilizers for use in Kenya. A Code of Conduct, which was developed from the United Nations Food and Agriculture Organization Code, specifies the requirements for the manufacture, packaging, labeling, and distribution of agrochemicals in the country. There is a requirement that all persons involved in such activities must sign the Code of Conduct.

Although the standards for inputs are in place and are clear on quality and handling of the inputs, some problems have been encountered. Cases have been reported in the past in which substandard inputs (e.g., seed maize and pesticides for coffee disease control) were sold to farmers. This is an indication of weak enforcement of the laws that govern standards on agricultural inputs.

Imports for Research and Commercialization of Biotechnology Products

Kenya has laws that govern the importation of plant materials (e.g., seeds, cuttings, plantlets, and seedlings), and animals for research and commercialization in broad terms as discussed in earlier sections. However, no legislation has been enacted specifically to deal with research and commercialization of products derived from biotechnology and, in particular, genetically modified organisms (GMOs). Instead, the government developed regulations and guidelines for biosafety in biotechnology for the country in 1998 through the National Council for Science and Technology (NCST).

According to the guidelines, the NCST is the authority designated to oversee the implementation of the regulations and guidelines on the biosafety of biotechnology products. The functions for NCST include reviewing and ascertaining the suitability of both physical and biological procedures appropriate for research, and development of biotechnology products, reviewing the proposals on research and recommending those that can be implemented, and ensuring adequate testing of genetically transformed materials developed elsewhere before introducing them for local trials.

The NCST is mandated to form subcommittees to help in undertaking the outlined functions. The guidelines also provide safety measures (familiarity, risk assessment and management, control measures, and maintenance and dissemination of information) and regulatory procedures for research and commercialization of biotechnology products. The guidelines are aimed at providing minimum safety requirements, and those involved in biotechnology activities are encouraged to establish additional arrangements provided that they do not contradict the regulations and guidelines. The guidelines

recognize the potentially deleterious consequences of uncontrolled biotechnology activities and recommend that safety measures are the basis of penal sanctions. However, such penalties can be imposed only after the enactment of legislation or the establishment of ministerial rules and regulations but these have not yet been finalized. Therefore, the regulation of research and commercialization of biotechnology products is governed by the broad rules governing general research and commercialization of imported plants and plant materials as well as animal and animal materials. Enactment of regulations to govern biotechnology activities in the country is still missing and this is an area that needs to be addressed.

Conformity to International Requirements

Kenya has established and implemented the necessary structures and procedures to comply with the SPS Agreement. There exist contact points for international bodies involved in standards setting that are coordinated by the Ministry of Trade and Industry for the purposes of notifying the WTO. There is a SPS and TBT subcommittee of the WTO, which prepares Kenya's position on standards for deliberation by the NCWTO and whose recommendations Kenya's representatives send to the WTO. The country participates frequently in all meetings on SPS and TBT. However, members of the SPS and TBT subcommittee are not satisfied with the feedback on the information from the NCWTO secretariat to the industry actors. Stakeholders from some industries, particularly horticulture, complain of limited access to notifications of standards in export markets. Another concern by the SPS and TBT subcommittee relates to the delegations to the international meetings. The subcommittee considers some of the top managers, who represent the country, not to be the best qualified technically and therefore recommend that more technical staff be sent to the meetings.

The country has striven to develop standards that are based on international standards as indicated in section entitled Conformity of Laws to International Standards. However, standards for some products such as locally manufactured farm implements and equipment need to be adapted to the unique requirements of the country. The SPS Agreement obliges WTO members to base their standards measures on a risk assessment appropriate to the circumstances (in which import requirements are not based on specific relevant international norms). Kenya's capacity to carry out such risk analysis, which requires substantial empirical data and considerable professional expertise if it is to conform to the risk assessment methodologies promulgated by the relevant international organizations is constrained. This is an aspect that needs to be strengthened.

Organizations' Participation and Their Effectiveness

Other than the organizations that are directly involved in standards setting and implementation, discussed in the section "Kenya Economic Context," there are several government institutions and private organizations involved in standards implementation in some way. The functions include inspection and provision of advisory services to producers and firms. This section examines those public and private organizations, focusing on their functions and the services they provide to farmers and firms.

Public Organizations

The public organizations involved in providing services on standards include the Pest Control Products Board (PCPB), the Horticultural Crops Development Authority (HCDA), and the Ministry of Agriculture and Rural Development (MA&RD).

Pest Control Products Board (PCPB). The PCPB is a parastatal under the Ministry of Agriculture and Rural Development. Its mandate is to register all pesticides used in the country, license the premises that are used for storage of pesticides, monitor all dealers to ensure safe and proper use of pesticides, and coordinate the training of pesticide applicators to ensure the safety of all concerned. The PCPB was established under the Pest Control Products Act Cap 46. The PCPB is also a contact point for Codex and uses guidelines from international standards such as FAO and European Environmental Protection Agency Standards for Herbicides, Insecticides, Fungicides, and Acaricides to advise producers and firms on the required standards of use. It also advises on WHO standards for public health pests, for example, insecticides for mosquito, bilharzia, and malaria. The

PCPB's activities cover the whole country and it uses its own laboratories for analysis, and the laboratories of other research institutions for bioefficacy field trials. The PCPB also works closely with KEBS to ensure that appropriate authorization papers accompany all pesticide products entering or leaving the country.

The Horticultural Crops Development Authority (HCDA). The HCDA is a parastatal under the Ministry of Agriculture and Rural Development charged with the responsibility of supporting the production and marketing of horticultural crops in Kenya. Its specific functions include:

- Advising growers on the use of certified planting materials and helping them to identify both local and export market outlets for their produce;
- Dissemination of marketing information and export statistics to investors, exporters, and producers for planning purposes;
- Organizing groups of small growers for production and marketing purposes of export crops;
- Advising growers, exporters, and processors to plan production in relation to market demand;
- Training farmers in the proper use of inputs, particularly pesticides so that farmers adhere to the minimum residual levels (MRLs);
- Advising producers and exporters of appropriate post-harvest handling techniques;
- Licensing horticultural exporters and collecting government levies on exports (each exporter pays some fee on an annual basis to HCDA to be allowed to export).

The HCDA is mandated to implement and monitor grades and standards in the horticulture industry but it is not directly involved in the implementation of those standards. In most cases, it helps in promoting awareness of standards, particularly on horticulture exports among small and large growers. It also licenses exporters of horticultural produce and is paid about US$2.5 per ton of exported produce for its functions. The rationale for licensing exporters in an era of liberalized markets is questioned by stakeholders and particularly because exports have to meet the required markets standards.

Ministry of Agriculture and Rural Development (MA&RD). MA&RD is responsible for the implementation of standards for plants and animals. It is also responsible for all agricultural extension activities and therefore has a role of disseminating information regarding standards on plant and animal health. The ministry has different divisions charged with extension activities in specific groups of crops and animals. However, there are no serious efforts by the divisions to educate growers on grades and standards. MA&RD has also not recruited new staff for some time now (for most of the 1990s to date) and the extension staff to farmer ratio is quite low, approximately 1:1000. Additionally, liaison activities with research bodies are not adequately undertaken. This has created a situation in which farmers are not motivated to seek the advice of the extension staff on standards.

Private Organizations Participation in Standards Setting and Certification

A number of private-sector organizations are involved in the implementation of standards in Kenya. Most of these organizations are involved through participation in committees organized by KEBS, KEPHIS, PCPB, and DVS or by members of the Kenyan delegations to CODEX, IPPC, and OIE meetings. The organizations are also represented in the technical committees of the National Committee on WTO. Some of the organizations are involved in the implementation of standards and in the dissemination of information on the required standards for the products that are of interest to their members.

Fresh Produce Exporters Association of Kenya (FPEAK). FPEAK is a private association of about 200 exporters. Currently, it is the only association of exporters of fruits and vegetables. The objective of FPEAK is to undertake all those activities that increase the competitiveness of its members. These include:

- Provision of market information, organizing exhibitions and trade shows, and searching for new niche markets
- Implementation of FPEAK Code of Practice
- Implementation of an outgrower support scheme that aims at enabling their members to source produce from smallholders who meet the stringent market requirements
- Lobbying the government for better trading terms and other necessary support such as improvement of the infrastructure

- Liaison with other stakeholders such as research and regulatory bodies that can help in enhancing their members' competitiveness.

One of FPEAK's mandates is to link exporters with groups of small farmers to promote smallholder farm production and support exports from small farmers through technical assistance and training, small grants to invest in infrastructure such as grading sheds and charcoal coolers, and loans to purchase inputs. FPEAK also provides services to member exporters such as market intelligence, promotion of Kenyan products abroad, and government lobbying.

Without the technical and financial support of FPEAK, many farmers will not be able to meet the quality requirements of exporters. Similarly, without the help of FPEAK in organizing groups of farmers, many small exporters would not find it profitable to contract with small farmers because of high risk and transaction cost. FPEAK usually assigns exporters to specific groups of farmers.

The perception of both farmers and traders working with FPEAK is that they have both benefited from such an arrangement and that FPEAK provides a valuable service. However, the organization is still struggling with its financial and organizational sustainability in the long run. The outgrower scheme was supported by USAID-Kenya for a long time in the 1990s to support smallholders in horticulture production.

Agrochemicals Association of Kenya (AAK). The AAK is a private association of international and local companies involved in the agrochemical trade. The association mostly lobbies the government for a better business environment and trains retailers and end users in the use of the products manufactured by its member companies. AAK can play a larger role in ensuring that only legal chemicals are marketed in the country by being a watchdog for the industry and advising farmers accordingly. The association has a potential for industry self-regulation in marketing and use of pesticides, if effectively guided by national and international policies.

Kenya Flower Council (KFC). KFC, established in 1994, is a voluntary self-financing private organization. The council is made up of flower growers and exporters (small and large) but 32 members make up about 65 percent of the total flower production in Kenya. The main objective of the KFC is to provide a forum for flower growers for self-regulation and a forum for discussion and support of flower production and export. Some of its functions include:

- Ensuring implementation of code of practice for all growers
- Ensuring use of consistent standards
- Transferring best demonstration practices
- Fostering responsible and safe production of cut flowers
- Promoting a safe working environment for flowers production
- Ensuring the welfare of workers in accordance with the Kenyan law

Membership in KFC is only open to those producers, exporters, and propagators of cut flowers who comply within a 12-month period with a minimum set of labor and environmental standards. The labor standards relate to wage, work hours, housing, worker safety, and annual leave. The environmental standards relate to good practice guidelines on the use of locally registered agrochemicals, minimizing the use of WHO-classified "extremely" and "highly" hazardous pesticides and reducing pesticide use.

Kenya Association of Manufacturers (KAM). The KAM, which plays a leading role in lobbying for appropriate policies for manufacturers of various products, is an association of all manufacturers in Kenya. The KAM has various committees, which deal with service and policy-related issues for various sectors. The Association has a Standing Committee on SPS and TBT, which disseminates information regarding grades and standards for various products to its members.

The influence of KAM on standards setting and formulation is through its representatives in the standards formulation committees of KEBS and KEPHIS. The KAM is also represented in the National Committee on WTO under the Ministry of Trade and Industry.

Kenya Fish Processors and Exporters Association (AFIPEK). The Kenya Fish Processors and Exporters Association (AFIPEK) is the only fish processors' association recognized by the government as being the competent authority on fishery. The organization provides a vital link between the

fish processors, fish importers, the government, and development agencies. It was formally registered on 29 May 2000 as a company and is funded by the fish processing and exporting industries. The Association comprises membership drawn from fish processors in the Lake Victoria Basin involved in Nile Perch processing and export, and from the seafood processors of the coastal region of Kenya. There are 17 fish-processing factories based in Nairobi, Mombasa, Kisumu, Homabay, and Migori that cover 90 percent of the active fish processors and exporters in Kenya.

Within the industry, AFIPEK aims at specifically harmonizing the quality standards in all member industries and promoting the marketing of Kenyan fisheries products through:

- Establishing and maintaining an internationally recognized code of practise and HACCP across all member industries
- Facilitating marketing of Kenyan fish by, among others, organizing participation in international fish exhibitions, and trade negotiations with potential importers
- Liasing with the government, laboratories, development agencies, and other stakeholders to improve the fisheries industry in Kenya.
- Helping members in aspects such as value-adding, product development, packaging, and marketing
- Training members on quality control practises such as HACCP and GMP
- Research and dissemination of the latest technology and market information to the members

AFIPEK recognizes the positive role self-regulation can play within the industry. In 2000, the association with the help of UNIDO drafted a Code of Practice for all sectors in the fisheries industry. This code is based on the EU Code of Practice in the fisheries sector and the Fisheries Act requirements. Membership of the association implies that a particular establishment agrees to abide by the Code of Practice. All AFIPEK members have instituted HACCP practices in their establishments and comply with the Kenya Fisheries Act 2000 and EU Directive 91/493/EC.

Association of Better Land Husbandry (ABLH). The ABLH is an NGO funded by donors. ABLH promotes organic farming or use of minimal agrochemicals. The association is currently trying to institute a certification program for organically produced fruits and vegetables targeting the export market.

Kenya Institute of Organic Farming (KIOF). The KIOF is a local private body that promotes the concepts of organic farming in Kenya. KIOF focuses mainly on the production of organic produce with little, if any, interest in marketing. However, the members will benefit from a certification program being sought by ABLH as it will enable export of duly certified organic products.

SGS International. SGS is an international organization that operates a certification division under International Certification Services (SGS-ICS), whose role is to audit for certification under the ISO 9000X series, ISO 14000, HACCP, and the code of practice. The agency also undertakes preshipment inspection (PSI) for imports into Kenya. PSI involves verification of the quality, quantity, price (including currency exchange rate and financial terms), and the customs classification of goods to be exported. Such inspections assure importers that the goods they have ordered meet contractual specifications and quality standards, thereby reducing possibilities for disputes once the goods arrive in Kenya. The inspections also prevent the import of products that are considered health risks.

All imports with an f.o.b value exceeding US$5,000, except those exempted from preshipment, require preshipment inspection and a clean report of finding (CRF) must also accompany the imports into Kenya. An inspection agency in the country of importation issues an internal report containing details of transactions as well as a security label that is attached to the final invoice. The security label confirms that the goods have been inspected and a CRF has been issued by SGS.

Capacity Building for Standards and Regulations Development

Capacity-building efforts in standards have in the past focused on understanding the SPS and TBT agreement by the National SPS/TBT subcommittee and creating awareness among stakeholders on the need for maintaining quality standards for the products if they have to be competitive in the export market.

The SPS/TBT subcommittee comprises technical representatives, usually two each from the public agencies involved in standards development (KEBS, KEPHIS, DVS, and MoH), as well as those involved in the implementation of standards (e.g., HCDA, PCPB, etc.), and representatives from industry organizations (e.g., KAM, FPEAK, KFC, Chamber of Commerce and Industry, etc.). Some of the committee members have had opportunities of attending overseas meetings of the international standards-setting bodies. Furthermore, the members have also had the opportunity to attend and participate in local as well as overseas seminars and workshops organized by the World Trade organization (WTO), United National Conference on Trade and Development (UNCTAD), and the International Trade Center (ITC).

The government has also organized seminars and workshops on both SPS and TBT Agreements to sensitize the stakeholders and the business community in general to the importance of both sanitary and phytosanitary measures as well as on Technical Barriers to Trade. The government normally funds the local seminars and workshops and the resource persons are paid by the international donor agencies particularly the WTO, UNCTAD, and ITC. It is not possible to singularly tabulate the donor financial input toward the SPS Agreement because the same department implements all WTO agreements without singling out funding for specific agreements. The Commonwealth Secretariat recently conducted a study on SPS and TBT for the purpose of developing technical assistance programs for SPS and TBT, but the recommendations of the study are yet to be implemented.

Capacity building remains a top priority for Kenya if the country is going to participate effectively in meeting the WTO obligations and to undertake the increasingly complicated tasks of standardizing and regulating trade development. Currently, there is a paucity of local analytical skills and expertise, resources and technical capacity in several areas pertaining to trade negotiations and the preparation of proposals for negotiations at international organizations. The result is that Kenya is constrained from playing any significant role in the process. In the past, the country has received technical and financial assistance from a number of organizations and donor countries to help build her capacity in relation to trade-related standards and regulations. The matrix in Table 1.10 summarizes some of the organizations that have been funded to build capacity in areas of standards and regulations for trade in Kenya.

Table 1.10 Capacity Building Efforts in Kenya

Organization	Nature of Activities Funded	Donor	Status
Kenya Bureau of Standards (KEBS)	Promote standardization in industry and commerce Codes of practice Certification of products Quality control mark Training of personnel Provision of equipment	ISO ARSO CODEX WTO UNCTAD ITC	Complete
The Fresh Produce Exporters Association of Kenya (FPEAK)	Set up Kenyan horticultural industry standards Prepare code of practice Contract and train horticultural farmers Training of personnel Provision of equipment	USAID	Complete
Kenya Flower Council	Set up flowers industry standards Prepare code of practice Contract and train floriculture farmers Training of personnel Provision of equipment	DFID	Ongoing
MTI	Promote standardization in business and industry Codes of practice Certification of products Quality control mark Training of personnel Provision of equipment	ISO ARSO CODEX WTO UNCTAD ITC	Ongoing
Association of Better Land Husbandry	Set up organic farming standards Prepare code of practice Contract and train organic farming farmers Training of personnel Provision of equipment	DFID	
KEPHIS	Quality control laboratory services Testing MRLs Quality control of all plant materials imported and exported Training of personnel Provision of equipment	EEC	Ongoing
HCDA	Set-up preshipment cooling facilities and standards License horticultural exporters Prepare code of practice for horticultural exporters Training of personnel Provision of equipment	Japanese Government	Complete

Source: Authors' compilation from Ministry of Trade and Industry (2002).

The MTI has prepared a program that they would like to have implemented with respect to standards capacity building. The focus is on capacity building for institutions involved in standards development and implementation. In the public sector, the institutions identified include KEBS, MOTI, MOA, HCDA, KARI, KEPHIS, and EPC, while those in the private sector include production, manufacturing, and trade organizations such as FPEAK, KAM, and environmental and consumer lobby groups, as well as small and medium enterprises. The capacity of all the organizations to undertake their mandate with respect to standards and regulations, past and ongoing programs as well as training needs will have to be analyzed. This will be the basis for determining funding requirements, sources of funding, and time frame for implementing the standards and regulations. The logistical support needed to strengthen the organizations in terms of personnel will also need to be assessed. Recommendations from the MTI (NCWTO Secretariat) are included in the action plan.

Standards and Technical Regulations in Action and Compliance Costs

This section analyzes the application and estimated impact of standards, technical regulations, and related production practices. The main focus is on the analysis of five case studies of commodities to indicate the application of standards in the production and marketing of the commodities and the problems and opportunities faced.

Selected Commodity Cases

The cases of coffee, fruits and vegetables, flowers, fish, and textiles are used to illustrate the status of standards implementation in the country.

Coffee. Coffee is the third most important export commodity from Kenya after tea and horticulture. Farmers on both, small (cooperatives) and large holdings (estates or plantations) grow the crop. Small growers process and market their coffee through cooperative societies and account for about 75.4 percent of the total area under coffee and produce about 60 percent of the total output. Currently, Kenya produces about 55,000 metric tons of coffee but this is a decline from the high 128,000 metric tons produced in 1987. The decline in production is attributed to many factors, which

include low prices, high costs of production, weak management systems for cooperatives, and lack of credit for production. Approximately 95 percent of coffee produced in Kenya is exported.

Kenyan coffee plays a unique role in the world market. It is valued for its acidic blending and is used in small quantities by many international roasters to improve the quality of their standard blends (MA&RD 1997). The washed (wet processed) arabica coffee normally is more highly priced compared with unwashed or dry-processed arabicas or robustas. The main demand for Kenyan coffee comes from blenders, who use its strong flavor to improve the quality of bulk black robusta coffee. However, some Kenyan coffee is also used for gourmet consumer markets in which higher prices are available.

Coffee Grading. Kenya coffee standards are gazetted as KSO1–593 and are derived from ISO international standards as explained in section entitled "Capacity Building for Standards and Regulations Development. Nine separate grades are prepared for Kenyan coffee, namely,

1. AA consisting of largest size, normal shaped beans;
2. AB consisting of large, normal shaped beans;
3. C consisting of small size, normal shaped beans;
4. TT consisting of a light fraction from drawn from AA and AB;
5. PB consisting of peaberry or round beans;
6. T consisting of very small beans and brokens;
7. E consisting of extra large or elephant beans);
8. UG consisting of ungraded beans; and
9. Mbuni consisting of unwashed (dry processed) coffee, usually UG.

The best quality of washed coffee on the basis of the Kenyan classification is that belonging to the top six classes (AA to T). These usually comprise about 55 percent of the total crop. The remaining 45 percent is sold as Miscellaneous catalogue and includes the lower quality washed coffee and mbuni (dry processed coffee). The main determinants of coffee quality are the variety, environmental conditions, husbandry practices, and processing procedures.

Coffee Varieties and the Environment. The two coffee varieties, Robusta and Arabica, are qualitatively different. Robusta coffee usually has a neutral, uninteresting flavor, regardless of the cultivation or processing methods. Arabicas have such desirable qualities as aroma, flavor, and mild acidity. These qualities are affected, not only by the soil and climate, but also by the method of cultivation and processing. Favorable environmental conditions that ensure quality include reliable and well-distributed rainfall, and temperature, which provide long growing periods with little risk from frost.

Coffee Husbandry Practices. Crop husbandry practices affect the yields, disease losses, and the flavor of the beans. The main contributors are the levels of fertilizer use and selectivity in picking. Low fertilizer use tends to produce cleaner-tasting cherries, and hand picking only the ripest cherries ensures maximum cup quality. The highest quality of Kenyan coffee beans tends to come from low-input smallholders who hand pick the cherries. However, the use of fertilizer increases yields and reduces disease losses; therefore, higher input users tend to obtain better average quality and higher yields. Use of agrochemicals and pruning also has an impact on yields through control of disease loss, which also help improve average quality.

The estimated costs of coffee production according to the level of husbandry practices and management are shown in Table 1.11. Most estates achieve higher levels of husbandry practices while cooperative societies achieve low and medium levels of husbandry practices. The costs on estates estimated at US$897 per hectare are more than double those on low-management small farms estimated at about US$414 per hectare. However, on

tonnage basis, the costs are lower for highly managed farms estimated at US$598 per ton compared to US$1055 per ton for poorly managed farms. This is because the yields on better-managed farms are high, estimated at 1,500 kg of clean coffee compared to 400 kg per hectare on poorly managed small farms. The main reasons for the high yields on estates when compared with small farms are the high level of input use and the ability to irrigate coffee, which increases both coffee yields and coffee quality.

Processing. Primary processing is a critical factor in coffee quality. Coffee processing starts at the factory level. Most of the coffee from Kenya undergoes what is referred to as wet processing. This is a case in which the fresh fruits (cherry) are pulped to remove the outer skin and the beans are washed and soaked in water for 2–3 days to remove the pulp. This is an important stage because it ensures that the beans do not ferment together with the pulp that can ruin their flavor. Thereafter the beans are dried on open racks before they are sent for milling. An alternative procedure to wet processing is to dry the fruits in the sun, but this results in a much lower quality of beans when the coffee is finally milled. Small farmers use the factories built by cooperative societies for this purpose while estates have their own factories.

Estate factory processing costs average US$158 per ton of clean coffee with a conversion of 6.25:1 from cherry to clean coffee beans. The average factory processing costs for cooperative societies are about five times higher at about US$770 per ton, with an average conversion factor of 7:1. Because of

Table 1.11 Cost of Coffee Production in U.S. Dollars Per Hectare

Item	Low Management Level	Medium Management Level	High Management Level
Yield kg/ha	400	750	1500
Input costs (herbicides, fungicides, insecticides, fertilizers etc) Kshs/ton	325	472.3	392.9
Labor (weeding, pruning, picking, etc.) Kshs/ton	730.8	560.9	205.3
Total variable costs Kshs/ton	1055.8	905	598.2
Total variable costs per hectare	414.7	678.7	897.4

Source: Authors' compilation from Ministry of Agriculture and Rural Development.

weak management of many cooperative societies, factory processing of coffee from smallholders is not properly undertaken and this results in low quality of the coffee when compared with coffee from estates.

Milling. The basic function of coffee milling is to remove the hull to create green coffee. The wet-processed beans are also polished. The coffee millers also grade the coffee according to bean size, density separation, color, and remove defects. The milling of coffee and collection and transport of coffee beans, along with associated grading and sorting activities cost about US$100 per ton of clean coffee. The milled coffee is bagged according to the grades described earlier and sold at the auction markets for the export markets.

Implementing Standards in the Coffee Industry. The control on standards in the coffee industry has been for many years with the Coffee Board of Kenya (CBK). The CBK was established under the Coffee Act Cap 333 of the Laws of Kenya to play a regulatory role in the production, processing, marketing, and research in the coffee industry.

In production, the CBK had area managers and field inspectors in every coffee-growing region of the country, who, together with the extension staff of the Ministry of Agriculture, provided advisory services to farmers. The advice included better production husbandry practices including weeding, crop nutrition, disease and pest control, and harvesting time. Because of their close contact with farmers, the extension officers were able to solve the farmers' production problems.

The CBK also controlled licensing primary coffee-processing factories and milling and also monitored the performance of the factories and millers. The Coffee Act required smallholders to be members of a cooperative society to which they must deliver their coffee for pulping. Each society delivered the processed coffee to the miller and before liberalization of the coffee subsector, there was only one registered miller, the Kenya Planters Cooperative Union (KPCU). The KPCU was managed by farmers but was supervised by the government through the Cooperatives Act. With liberalization of the coffee industry in 1998, private millers (four) have entered the industry.

Marketing of coffee at the auction market was the responsibility of the CBK. The CBK appointed brokers to sell coffee in the auction market and had a roasting plant for roasting, grinding, and bagging coffee for the local market. The CBK did not sell coffee in international markets directly but used coffee dealers or exporters, who were registered for that purpose. The Kenya Coffee Auctions (KCA), an organization established by the CBK, operated the auction market.

The overall organization worked particularly well with respect to standards setting, implementation, and maintenance in the industry; however, problems related to low profitability and weak marketing arrangements under the monopoly of the CBK contributed to the poor performance of the coffee industry. This, together with the implementation of liberalized market policies in Kenya has led to changes in the management of the coffee industry. With liberalization of the coffee industry, the Coffee Act was revised in 2001 and the CBK retained only the regulatory functions for the industry. The commercial functions such as processing and marketing were left to the private sector. However, the coffee processors, marketing agents, and millers must still register with the CBK. Farmers are at liberty to select their own processors, either within the cooperative societies, marketing agents, and millers or from those who are registered with CBK. The marketing agents (to date only three have been registered) have the mandate to collect coffee from factories, and arrange for milling and marketing in the auction market.

The impact of quality on Kenyan coffee is reflected on the prices received. At the international market, arabica coffee fetches higher prices (50 percent higher) than robusta coffee. Furthermore, it has been seen that Kenyan coffee fetches premium prices (about 20 percent higher than unwashed arabica coffees) in the international market (CRF 1999). The same report also indicates that large coffee growers in Kenya receive higher payments for their coffee, partly because they are able to classify their coffee into the nine quality classes and sell it accordingly, while small growers who sell coffee through cooperatives in which it is classified into only two classes, cherry one and two, receive lower payments. Thus the quality of coffee sold by farmers has an important impact on the payments they receive.

Industry Concerns. Policy reforms in the coffee sector allow the CBK to continue playing a leading role in promoting Kenyan coffee in the world market but the marketing agents, millers, and factory processors now play a leading role in maintaining standards as required by the market. The impact of these arrangements is yet to be known because the industry is in a transitional stage from control by the CBK to a liberalized market system. However, the industry players interviewed believe that liberalization of the industry—particularly processing, milling, and marketing—is good for the industry. Quality control will be the responsibility of marketing agents who will be required to take a lead in advising farmers and factories on the quality requirements in the market and to provide financial support for the maintenance of quality and standards. The Kenya Planters Cooperative Union (KPCU), which is the largest coffee milling and marketing agency, has taken a lead in soliciting for credit locally and internationally to support farmers and factories. Because the organizations are adjusting to a new legal framework, they will require technical support (financial and human capacity) to deliver better services to farmers. This is necessary to help revive the coffee industry.

Fruit and Vegetables. The horticultural industry (including fresh-cut flowers as well as fruits and vegetables) is an important source of foreign exchange earnings and it is also an important source of domestic food with exports accounting for only 4 percent of the total production. In addition, it is an important source of employment with the industry employing about 2 million people directly

and another estimated 0.5 million indirectly. The quantities and value of exports of horticulture are shown in Table 1.12.

Production of Fruits and Vegetables. The most important export vegetables are French beans, canned beans, snow peas, and Asian vegetables (okra, baby corn, karella or bitter gourd, eggplant, chillies, and capsicums or peppers). Important fruit exports include avocados, mangos, passion fruit, and strawberries. Fruit and vegetable growers are grouped into small, medium, and large growers. The Horticultural Crops Development Authority (HCDA) estimates that 70 percent of production of vegetables and 40 percent of production of fruit for export is from the small producers.

The principal issue of standards in the production of fruits and vegetables is the use of chemicals for the control of pests and diseases, which attack the crops at any stage of production including post-harvest handling. Many disease-causing microorganisms and pests are favored by the tropical environmental conditions in Kenya. These microorganisms and pests infect plants and cause health damage of plants and plant products and therefore need to be controlled. The control of diseases and pests is achieved through a combination of factors such as good field sanitation and hygiene, use of chemicals, resistant varieties, cultural practices, and mechanical means.

Chemicals are usually the most effective means of controlling pests and disease, which leads to higher yields, but unfortunately the chemicals are a

Table 1.12 Exports of Horticultural Produce 1991–2000

Year	Value of Horticultural Exports (US$ million)			Volume of Horticultural Exports (tons)		
	Fruits	Vegetables	Cut Flowers	Fruits	Vegetables	Cut Flowers
1991	7.2	27.6	36.8	8367.8	25075.4	16405.0
1992	9.9	25.1	34.5	11233.0	23924.9	19806.0
1993	7.2	25.0	36.4	11608.1	38393.4	23645.7
1994	10.6	36.2	58.8	11591.0	26977.7	25121.1
1995	11.5	39.5	65.1	13866.0	27865.4	29373.5
1996	14.0	45.2	88.7	16869.4	31672.5	35212.2
1997	12.9	46.5	78.2	17454.7	29193.4	35853.0
1998	13.2	64.1	78.5	11352.1	35391.0	30221.4
1999	17.3	76.5	101.6	15595.2	44953.1	36919.3
2000	13.6	69.0	93.9	15415.8	43720.5	38756.7

Source: Authors' compilation from HCDA Export Statistics.

threat to human health (workers and consumers). As a result safe use of chemicals focusing on the protection of workers involved in the spray of the chemicals and control of chemical residues to protect consumers are important concerns. The use of the right chemicals, frequency of application and dosage applied for effective disease and pest control but avoiding being harmful to workers and with minimum residual levels that can affect consumers, are critical requirements in production of fruits and vegetables.

The cost of production of various crops that varies greatly among different farm categories for selected exports of vegetables and fruits is shown in Table 1.13. The costs of production are highest for large farms (level III), which use higher levels of inputs (chemicals and fertilizers) and better husbandry practices. The main cost elements are labor, which takes about 25–33 percent of total costs, irrigation averages about 16 percent of total costs (but is not incurred for rain-fed agriculture), and chemicals (fertilizers and pesticides), which account for 24–53 percent of the total costs. The cost components vary from crop to crop but the costs of chemicals usually account for the largest cost component (about 30 percent) because of the need to protect vegetables and fruits against diseases and pests.

Large companies produce vegetables and fruits on their farms using sophisticated production techniques. Production relies heavily on irrigated agriculture, use of approved chemicals and integrated pest management, and environmentally friendly practices such as water and soil conservation. The companies also contract outgrower farmers (small farmers) to produce fruits and vegetables for export. This is important to enable the large companies to maintain continuity of supply of the products to the markets. The companies provide the out-growers with seed and an assured market outlet at an agreed-on price in advance. The farmers are paid after one week of delivery of the produce to the companies. However, in some cases, contracted farmers default and fail to honor their contracts to exporters and instead sell their produce outside the contract resulting in huge losses to the contractors. This is a reflection of poor enforcement of contracts, which discourages the support provided by large growers to small farmers. The HCDA addresses this problem during its extension programs by way of educating small farmers of the importance and advantages of honoring contracts.

The HCDA has provided guidelines on the recommended levels of use of chemicals and frequencies of use to meet internationally accepted technical standards. The FPEAK has also a Code of Conduct of the production of fruits and vegetables to meet standards required in the market as indicated in Box 1.5.

Marketing of Fresh Vegetables and Fruits. The marketing of fruits and vegetables in Kenya falls under two categories, domestic marketing and export marketing. The focus here is on export marketing because of the impact of international standards associated with this marketing system.

The main export markets for fresh fruits and vegetables are Western Europe and the Middle East. The United Kingdom is the largest export market

Table 1.13 Average Cost of Production and Profits of Selected Vegetables and Fruits in the Main Producing Areas of Central Province, Kenya
(US$/ha)

Vegetable or Fruit	Level of Production for Small and Medium Farms					
	I Low Management		II Medium Management		III High Management	
	Cost	Profit	Cost	Profit	Cost	Profit
French beans	699.7	1223.3	826.7	1865.6	1005.9	2455.6
Snow peas	1291.3	1785.6	1410.4	2692.2	1684.0	4469.9
Onion	503.8	778.2	621.4	1301.7	749.5	1814.6
Avocados	897.4	1165.1	1346.2	2115.4	1794.9	2820.5
Passion fruits	456.4	365.4	687.2	523.1	911.5	716.7

Source: Authors' compilation from Ministry of Agriculture and Rural Development.

BOX 1.5 FPEAK CODE OF CONDUCT

FPEAK has developed a code of practice covering agricultural practices (including the use, handling, and storage of agrochemicals, traceability and environmental practice) to help its members in meeting the required standards in export markets on a voluntary basis. An external auditor, the International Certification Services (SGS), also conducts certification under the FPEAK code. An accredited exporter is allowed to use the FPEAK Eco-friendly logo on their letterheads, packaging material, and produce. The certification is a mark that the produce from grower or exporter meets the required standards in the export market. FPEAK Code is divided into two levels: namely, Silver and Gold.

Silver Level: Good agricultural practice (use of pesticides as recommended)

– Workers welfare (housing, health, wages, and so on).

– Environmental awareness and responsible pesticide use
– Mandatory audit within one year, which costs US$256 per year.
– Reaudit every six months, which costs US$256 per year.
– External audit every six months, which costs about US$10,000 per year.

Gold Level: is based on overall responsibilities as above and documentation in addition to:

– Land use impact assessment, minimum pesticide use and implement integrated pest management (IPM), minimum fertilizer use, and avoid contamination of water, soil conservation, water conservation, and non-pollution, protection of flora and fauna, control of waste products, and environmental policy.
– Labor standards—Occupational health and safety policy.

in Europe. France, Germany, the Netherlands, and Belgium are also significant markets. The marketing system for fresh fruits and vegetables for export is dominated by licensed exporters. They are more than 200 licensed fresh produce exporters in Kenya. However, only 50 are consistently operational while the other 150 exporters exploit favorable short-term market conditions, entering and exiting the industry sporadically during the October–April peak season. Among these 50 active export firms, 4 large firms dominate the export market. Exporters obtain produce from a variety of different types of producers using several types of transactions, namely, exporter–grower channel and exporter–agent or broker channel.

Large companies have integrated production, processing, prepackaging, exporting, and distribution of their products. The harvested produce is first held on houses or sheds on the farms (pack house). This is necessary to avoid destruction of the produce because of high temperatures and to also sort, clean, grade, and package the produce ready for export. Some of the companies also add value to the produce by washing, trimming, packaging, bar-coding,

and labeling. These activities are labor intensive and require high sanitary and hygiene standards. The size and sophistication of these activities depend on the exporter's ability to invest in the necessary equipment and management resources and its customer base. Export pack houses have varying degrees of quality control programs. Most supermarkets require that all exporters who sell to them must have a Hazard Analysis and Critical Control Point (HACCP) food safety management program. One company estimated that to invest in a pack house to meet these standards (HACCP management) costs US$375,000 dollars for a pack with a capacity of 20 tons. The exporters, who contract with small farmers, inspect the produce to enable them meet the required standards, particularly the use of approved chemicals and clean up of the produce when delivered to centrally placed pack houses.

Small farmers export their produce through exporters of different types, which include production contracts with large growers and exporter-brokers.

Production contracts (interlinked factor market contracts) are formal agreements to buy and sell produce to larger growers. They are often referred to as "outgrower schemes." This is most common for fresh exported vegetables. Farmers are usually organized into groups of 15 to 30 members to facilitate coordination of activities, technical assistance, and supervision by large companies. The buyers have field officers who visit the farmers' fields on a regular basis to ensure quality control and proper use of inputs.

Exporter–broker channels are either exporter agents or independent brokers. Exporter agents are paid a commission based on the volume of sales for providing certain services to exporters. These services include identifying and recruiting farmers, communicating short-term information to farmers regarding exporter quantity and timing requirements, communicating information about expected prices, informing the exporters about local supply and competitive conditions, distributing packaging materials to farmers, issuing payments to farmers, and providing a grading shed where farmers deliver their crops and the exporter collects them.

Direct exporters sell produce purchased from producers to importers. The importers may sell through two channels namely, wholesalers who service retail and food stores, and supermarkets and food service outlets. Most of the large exporters have a subsidiary for logistical services including cold storage, handling, and shipping. Independent logistics companies provide these services for small and medium exporters. Most of the medium and large exporters are involved in some types of value-added activities, which include washing, trimming, packaging, bar coding, and labeling. The size and sophistication of these activities depends on the exporter's ability to invest in the necessary equipment and management resources and its customer base.

Standards in Fruits and Vegetables. The Kenyan exporters have to meet quality standards demanded by the importing countries. The standards are divided into two groups, technical and market-demanded standards.

Technical Standards. Technical standards relate to the production and post-harvest handling of fruits and vegetables and have a direct impact on the food safety of fruits and vegetables as well as on the health of plants and plant products. The most important standards relate to chemical use and the risk of the spread of harmful insects to countries to which Kenya exports fresh fruits and vegetables. The importing countries have prepared a list of chemicals, which are considered harmful to food safety and should not be used on fruits and vegetables for disease and pest control. Furthermore, most importing countries have notified Kenya through the World Trade Organizations (WTO) of the minimum chemical residual levels allowed for various fresh vegetables exported from Kenya. The European Union has also imposed a Zero Analytic Level of chemical residues for fresh vegetables, fruits, and flowers.

The HCDA and the FPEAK provide information to farmers on the required technical standards on chemical use. The private sector through forward contract with farmers has also invested in supporting small farmers to meet the required standards through credit in inputs and extension services. The European Commission through the COLEACP started a project known as Pesticide Initiative program (PIP) to help ACP exporters comply with EU zero analytic MRL requirement. This program is implemented through FPEAK. The PIP focuses on information update and the database of EU regulations on MRLs, good practice with regulations on MRLs, import tolerances based on Good Agricultural Practices (GAP), and capacity building through farmer training programs on recommended pesticide use and crop production systems.

Another important technical standard requirement for the export of fruits and vegetables is the pest risk analysis. Most countries require to know the status of pest risk analysis to help control the spread of harmful pests from one country to another to protect plant and plant products' health. Pest risk analysis is undertaken by KEPHIS, which also advises growers and exporters accordingly. All importing countries have a list of pest risks, which must be adhered to before exports are made into their country. However, no comprehensive pest risk analysis over a longer period currently exists in Kenya. Besides, the country does have designated pest-free zones for fruits and vegetables and pest risk analysis is based on spot checks and controls during the production process. This is an area where the country needs support in terms of trained personnel and funding to undertake pest risk analysis.

Market-Driven Standards. The standards for fruits and vegetables for export from Kenya are determined by the requirements in the consumer markets. These standards include changing consumer tastes, and social and environmental concerns. Consumer tastes relate to the needs of consumers in the export market. For example, in response to consumer needs, supermarkets in Europe have shifted from packaging vegetables in homogeneous forms to diverse produce (e.g., onions, tomatoes, snow peas, and French beans in the same pack) as opposed to when the product is packaged individually. This has forced exporters to change the packaging styles and also forced growers to diversify into production of many products in small quantities. Other consumer tastes include the size, shape, and maturity of products. The social and environmental concerns relate to the production environment for various products. Some consumers require that labor standards such as protection of workers against harmful chemicals, nonuse of child labor, and environmentally friendly production methods be used.

Market-driven standards are usually communicated to growers through the exporters and are not notified through the WTO system. FPEAK also plays a leading role in communicating market standards to growers and exporters. According to the firms that were interviewed, market-driven standards are more stringent and costly to comply with when compared to technical standards. However, market-driven standards are associated with a price premium because producers who are unable to meet the standards cannot sell in such markets or receive lower prices. The producers or exporters, however, meet the costs of compliance.

Compliance Costs. The procedures for maintaining standards for vegetables and fruits include investing in personnel to advise and inspect on the level of use of pesticides, grading and precooling facilities at the production sites, refrigerated transportation, and cold storage at the port of export.

Growers employ agricultural specialists (agronomists) on their farms to inspect the produce and advise on quality including maintenance of zero level agrochemical residuals (MRLs). The cost of implementing this varies from grower to grower according to the size of the farm. However, on an average a farm of 50 hectares requires one agronomist and three technicians whose monthly cost is about US$2,100.

Pregrading and cooling of the produce at the production zones is an important measure on quality control. Most growers have adopted HACCP

management systems at the packaging centers to meet standards required in overseas markets. The produce is transported in refrigerated trucks to maintain low temperatures. At the airport, the produce is kept in cold store to avoid spoilage. The storage period can be up to two days depending on arrangements for freight. Most exporters have invested in their own cold storage facilities at the Cargo Village at Jomo Kenyatta International Airport (JKIA) while others lease from the larger growers or facilities owned by the Kenya Airports Authority. The large exporter growers have invested in their own airfreight planes while others charter freight aircraft for the purpose and others use general cargo aircraft.

The initial capital investment costs for facilities required to achieve international standards for export of vegetables and fruits from the farm to the airport are estimated at about US$1.2 million for a daily capacity of 10 tons as shown in Table 1.14. The operation costs per month for a 10-ton daily capacity to ensure that the product meets the required standards are estimated at about US$25,600. Given the costs of investing in standards for the export market, small farmers are not able to do it alone and are forced to rely on contracts with large growers or exporters.

Industry Concerns. The main concerns in the vegetable and fruits industry with respect to standards are the ability to meet the MRL requirements and undertake pest risk analysis. Good knowledge and the ability to test for the levels of MRLs are required to attain the required levels before the produce is harvested for export. Most of the recommended chemicals and safety use guidelines are quite expensive to use and implement. Furthermore, costs have to be incurred in employing qualified agronomists to advise on the use of pesticides and in the inspection of the levels of MRLs of the produce before harvest.

Pest risk analysis is another important concern. The failure for Kenya to have a pest risk analysis that covers a longer period is responsible for the restriction of Kenyan fresh produce of fruits, in particular to South Africa and the United States. Both countries require pest risk analysis over long periods of time before exports of fresh fruits and vegetables are made. The EU has also notified Kenya of the need for strict pest risk analysis for harmful pests, which are foreign in the EU and have

Table 1.14 Investment Costs of Maintaining Standards for Vegetables and Fruits for Export

Item	Dimensions	Cost (US$ million)
Precooling and grading shed at production center		
Building	70.4 m²	0.026
Refrigerator	4 units	0.031
Refrigerator diskettes	4 units	0.073
Suction chamber	4 units	0.100
Prefabricated pallets	28 m²	0.053
Standby generator	60 KVA	0.028
Fuel tank	1000 liters	0.032
Exhaust pipe		0.006
Trolley	60	0.022
Plastic crates	200	0.006
Working tables	650 m²	0.019
Subtotal		0.391
Refrigerated transport 2.5 ton trucks	5 trucks (2.5 ton)	0.436
Cold storage at airport		
Office block	325 m²	0.067
Cold store	704 m²	0.204
Chill room	260 m²	0.059
Work space and ablution	145	0.032
Perimeter fence		0.038
Generator	60 KVA	0.035
Subtotal		0.403
Grand total		1.229

Source: Authors' compilation from Exporter Surveys.

proposed a detailed inspection of pests on fresh produce to be undertaken before the produce is exported. Most growers consider this requirement to be too strict because growers do not know about the restricted pests. As a result, KEPHIS has requested the EU to send inspectors to Kenya to help in the inspection of the produce to identify the restricted pests and advise accordingly. KEPHIS are responsible for undertaking the pest risk analysis and they have reported that the main constraint is limited technical capacity and financial resources to undertake the analysis.[3]

Flowers. Flower growing is the leading horticulture export from Kenya. The flowers industry has three types of growers, namely large growers (companies), and medium and small growers. Presently, there are 5000 farmers or enterprises growing cut flowers for commercial purposes. However, export production is concentrated in only a few (about 75) large or medium flower operations. The 25 largest producers account for 75 percent of the total exports. The larger flower operations range in size from 20 to 100 hectares under production with a labor force of 250 to 6,000. Some of these enterprises supplement their own production with that purchased from small commercial growers.

Flower Production. Flower production on large farms is a highly sophisticated investment with facilities and quality assurance systems to meet supermarket requirements. Some of the flowers are annual crops that can be grown in open fields with relatively limited inputs (e.g., statice and alstrormeria); others require much more controlled growing conditions, more purchased inputs (especially agrochemicals) and more intensive field management (e.g., roses and chrysanthemum). Such

[3] Personal communication with the Managing Director of KEPHIS.

flowers are grown in high investment structures that require special production systems such as production in green houses, drip irrigation, high fertilization, safe use of chemicals and computer-controlled venting care. However, in all cases export markets require flowers to be produced according to the Good Agricultural Codes of Practice (GAP), which require that the use of chemicals should not pose any measurable hazards to the health of the consumer, farm workers, and the environment. So, flower growers are forced to produce flowers using environmentally sound practices. Most of the larger operations hire professional managers, including expatriates to manage the farms to meet these standards including MRLs standards as is the case of fruits and vegetables.

The Kenya flowers industry has always kept abreast with export requirements in production of flowers through the efforts of the Kenya Flower Council (KFC), which developed a Code of Practice that helps growers meet the required standards (see Box 1.6).

The KFC Code of Practice builds on international technical standards for flower production and market requirements such as those required by organizations in the EU market (e.g., EUREP, MPS, and British Retail Consortium). The Code of Practice has been revised five times, each time to take into account changing market conditions. Reputable companies such as Bureau Veritas of the United Kingdom and SGS undertake the external audits to ensure that firms meet the standards for each class. Those that pass the audit are permitted to display the KFC "Environmental Friendly" logo on all their products, packaging, and promotional material. Farm audits are repeated every six months, and those members that fail to maintain the necessary standards lose the right to use the KFC logo. The costs of being a member who adheres to the KFC Code of Practice is US$385 for joining and an annual subscription of US$8 per ton of flowers exported. The costs of implementation of the Code of Practice by growers vary but the costs of audits alone to attain a Silver or Gold standard are estimated at about US$25,640 per year.

The costs of flower production in Kenya are shown in Table 1.15. The analysis shows that the costs of production of various flowers vary greatly. The costs of flowers such as roses and carnations that are grown in high-investment structures and require special attention are high as opposed to flowers such as carthamus grown under field conditions. The average fixed costs are also shown in Table 1.16 and are estimated at about US$278,600 for a 5-hectare investment.

Below the large growers are several dozen small-to-medium commercial growers, each with between 5 and 20 hectares under production. Some of the medium growers have as many as 100 employees. The small and medium growers collectively

BOX 1.6 KFC CODE OF PRACTICE

Silver Level: Based on good agricultural practice

- Workers' welfare (abide by government labor requirements and Workers' Compensation Act Cap 236), housing, and protection against chemicals use
- Environmental awareness
- Responsible pesticide usage
- Mandatory audit within one year
- Reaudit every six months
- External audit of KFC every six months

Gold Level: Builds on Silver Standard

- Reporting: environmental matters and document at regular intervals

- Land use: environmental impact assessment prior to all main land use changes
- Pesticides: minimize uses and implement integrated pest management (IPM)
- Soil conservation: erosion control
- Water resources: pollution control
- Protection of flora and fauna: wildlife and indigenous plant life
- Waste products: safe disposal of chemical and organic waste
- Environmental policy
- Occupational health and safety policy

Table 1.15 Variable Costs for Cut Flower Production
(US$/season)

Cost (item/crop)	Roses	Statice	Carnation (spray)	Bupleurum	Solidago	Carthamus
Land preparation	1,400	160	160	160	160	160
Planting material[a]	53,250	702	43,860	1,600	20,880	526
Irrigation	500	1,053	1,580	526	1,053	526
Fertilizers	5,300	702	5,260	702	1,750	440
Pesticides	6,000	1,750	10,530	526	1,750	526
Labor	14,275	4,210	15,790	3,509	7,900	2,175
Electricity	—	—	—	—	1,750	—
Packaging material	3,500	9,650	7,020	1,842	5,260	2,403
Transportation	4,000	1,750	10,530	526	1,750	526
Total	100,825	199,77	94,730	9,391	42,253	7,282

a. Includes royalty where applicable.
Source: Thoen and others (2000).

Table 1.16 Average Fixed Costs for Kenyan Cut Flowers

Cost Item	Cost (US$)
Green house construction	50,000
Irrigation layout	5,000
Water pumps	2,500
Spray unit	1,300
Fertigation equipment	25,000
Cold storage[a]	90,000
Insulated truck[a]	105,000
Total costs	278,800

a. These costs cover five hectares of cut flower production.
Source: Authors' compilation from surveys.

account for 10–15 percent of Kenya's total exports. In some cases, the growers export directly but because of intensified competition in the export markets, many have shifted to supplying other firms (large growers) rather than shouldering the risks and transaction costs associated with exporting.

In general, smallholders face problems in the production and marketing of cut flowers. They lack credit, inputs, and technical capabilities and suffer from logistical constraints such as transport, haulage, and cold storage facilities. Sometimes, the growers organize themselves into groups to try and overcome the constraints they face while some grow flowers on contract for large growers. The large growers provide finance and technical support in the production and grading of the contracted flowers. Both HCDA and KFC support the smallholders through the provision of inputs, training on crop management, pesticide application, and quality control. Nevertheless, the requirements of the European market (product consistency, quality control, and compliance with health and safety requirements) pose problems for exporters wishing to source from smallholders.

Flower Marketing. Production and marketing of flowers is vertically integrated for large growers just as in the case with fruits and vegetable growers. The flowers are harvested and put in precooling houses on the farms for chilling, cleaning, sorting, grading, and packaging ready for export after inspection by KEPHIS officers at the airport for some growers. Other growers transport chilled flowers to cold stores at the airport where they are cleaned, sorted, graded, and packed for export after inspection by KEPHIS officers. Transportation from the farm to the airport is in all cases done using refrigerated vehicles unlike the case of vegetables or fruits in which it is not mandatory. A few firms that export flowers as well as vegetables and fruits use the same cold storage facilities for cooling the produce indicating an opportunity for shared facilities.

Several firms have formed linkages with freight firms, importers, and agents in Europe and most supply both the Dutch auctions and European supermarkets. These growers provide the range and volume required to fulfill their sales program. The international market for cut flowers is concentrated in the high-income countries of Northern America, Europe, and Asia. Europe is the largest market for Kenyan flowers.

The Kenyan flower trade operates on a counter-seasonal basis to the patterns of production in Western Europe. Kenya's exports are generally highest during the November to May period, with specific peaks in market demand associated with Valentine's Day (February), Easter (March and April), and Christmas (December). Kenya's exports are lowest between June and August because of the availability of low-cost supplies within Europe. Several Kenyan growers and exporters pursue alternative marketing arrangements—including direct supplies to supermarkets to achieve year-round sales.

Standards in the Flower Industry. Both technical and market-driven standards are factors that affect flower exports from Kenya.

Technical standards about flowers are similar to those for fruits and vegetables, namely; minimum residual levels (MRLs) for chemical use and pest risk analysis. The MRL is an important consideration in technical standards in the export market to ensure that the undesirable harmful chemical residues should not exceed the internationally accepted levels. Thus, pesticide residue analysis is necessary to determine the presence of MRLs before harvesting for export. To avoid this problem, a minimum number of days are recommended that a chemical can be applied before harvest. The number of days required vary with the type of chemical used. This requirement is achieved by Kenyan firms through investment in qualified agronomists who advise on the appropriate levels of the use of pesticides and harvesting periods.

Pest risk analysis is a particular problem for exports of flowers to Japan. One exporter indicated that they lost a consignment of flowers exported to Japan because it was fumigated against pests. The new EU requirement of inspection against (non-indigenous harmful pests in EU) is also considered a challenge to Kenyan growers. KEPHIS has made a request to EU to send inspectors to Kenya to help in the identification of such pests. A similar request is being made by Kenyan growers to the United States and Japan.

Market-driven standards are very important in the flowers industry. These include consumer preferences and social and labor standards. Important consumer preferences that affect the supplier of flowers from Kenya relate to product differentiation, life cycle of particular varieties, and environmental dimensions of production. Product differentiation is consumer desires encompassing greater variety both in terms of flower types and in terms of colors or other aspects of appearance. Product life cycle has become important because consumers are looking for new varieties with different colors, shapes, and fragrance. The Kenyan flowers industry has grown to keep pace with changing consumer preferences and standards in terms of flower varieties, assortments, and colors. Kenya currently produces more than 30 different types of flower varieties although the industry is dependent on a few varieties for its profitability and only three top varieties—roses, statice, and alstroemeria—to maintain market competitiveness.

Consumers have also taken an increased interest in environmental and social dimensions of flower production, which include intensity of use of agrochemicals, which raises concerns with respect to adverse effects on worker safety or water quality. The Netherlands has been on the forefront of a movement to reduce the environmental impact of floricultural production and a number of initiatives such MPS, which focuses on environmental care in floriculture, has an impact on flower production in Kenya. Kenyan flower growers have also responded to environmental and labor standards and the KFC Code of Conduct specifies the procedures to be followed in flower production to meet these social and environmental standards. The KFC allows firms to use their logo of certification on exports as verification that the firm has adhered to recommended production, environment, and labor standards.

Compliance Costs. Meeting international standards for flowers is a costly investment. It requires huge investments in irrigation, electricity, cold storage, precooling facilities, and refrigerated transport for the purposes of meeting the high-quality standards required in terms of consistency, reliability of supply, traceability, and environmental and social standards. The procedures for maintaining standards for flowers from the farm level to the export market are similar to those discussed for fruits and vegetables. The only difference is that flowers have to be chilled and kept at lower temperatures (3°C) than for fruits or vegetables.

Growers employ agronomists to inspect the produce and advise on quality including maintenance of zero-level agrochemical residuals (MRLs). The cost of implementing this varies from grower to grower according to the size of the farm. One expert alone can be paid up to US$6,000 per month. The cost for investing in facilities for a 5-ton capacity is the same as that required for a 10-ton capacity for fruits and vegetables shown in Table 1.14 or US$278,800 for a 5-hectare investment as shown in Table 1.16. The operating costs are estimated at about US$38,000 per month. As a result of the high expenses in investing in floriculture, only large growers benefit most from the industry. Small growers benefit from the industry through contracts with large growers; otherwise it is not possible for them to meet the standards required for exports.

Industry Concerns. Flowers contributed about 53 percent of the Kenya's estimated US$180 million annual earnings from the horticultural industry in 2001. The horticultural industry is the third most important foreign-exchange-earning industry for Kenya and it is also an important source of employment in the country. The threats to the industry are exports ban, which may arise from noncompliance to MRLs, environmental and labor standards, and pest risk analysis as required in the export markets. The large growers have made significant investments in the industry as part of the efforts to meet the required standards but small growers face problems because of the huge investments required. The alternative for small farmers is to produce flowers on contract for the large growers who provide them with the necessary support required for meeting the required standards. This, however, is not sustainable because the large growers tend to give priority to their own production because it is only possible to maintain high standards in production as a result of total control of management. This is not possible on contracted small farms because large growers do not have total control on the production practices on these farms. Thus small growers require support in production investments, which include equipment and machinery and technical capacity to enable them produce flowers that meet required standards in the export markets.

In general, the main concerns in the flowers industry focus on the ability to meet the MRL requirements and pest risk analysis. The ability for the growers to meet the ever-changing consumer preferences through investments in research or the ability to pay for royalties for new varieties developed by breeders are also significant.

Fish and Fishery Products. The fisheries industry is a vibrant part of the Kenya's economy earning US$96 million per annum. The industry is currently one of the fastest growing nontraditional export products in Kenya and generates both private and public benefits. Production has increased tremendously since independence. Growth in fish export revenue has risen from US$19 million in 1990 to about US$96 million in 2000. Besides, it is an important source of employment opportunities and food.

The main sources of fish and fishery products are divided into marine (saltwater) and freshwater (lakes and rivers). In the past years, aquaculture, especially of tilapia, has been growing. The main sources of fish are Lake Victoria and Lake Turkana, and the Indian Ocean.

Marketing Structure of the Fisheries Industry in Kenya. The marketing structure for fishery products in Kenya varies depending on whether the product is destined for export market or local consumption. At the production level fishing is mainly artisanal, especially in Lake Victoria. There are a few offshore trawlers off the coast of Mombasa dealing mainly with tuna and octopus. To encourage distribution of income to the local communities, fishing in the lakes is limited to artisanal. The middlemen who sell it directly to the large processing factories purchase Nile perch directly from the fishermen. Currently there are 17 export-oriented fish processing factories in Kenya. Fish destined to the local market (Tilapia, Omena) is purchased from the fishermen by small middlemen (mainly women) who process (drying) or sell it directly to the final consumers or to other middlemen. Large local processors (nonexport-oriented) mainly deal with the by-products such as *mgongo-wazi* (fish skeleton), which is transformed into a variety of products for human and animal consumption. There is little vertical integration in the industry.

Main Export Markets. The main export destinations of Kenya fisheries products (which are 90 percent Nile perch) are the European Union. This is mainly because the price offered is higher than that from other regions and transport cost to this destination is lower because of its close proximity to the African continent. Other destinations include

North America, and the Far East. In the past, Kenya has faced problems in fish exports to the main European market. There have been bans on fish exports to EU in 1997 and 1999 because of sanitary and health requirements. The 1997 ban was on account of the presence of salmonella cholera in Lake Victoria while the 1999 ban was because of the reported use of chemicals for harvesting fish in Lake Victoria and generally poor sanitary conditions along the fishing beaches. These experiences are elaborated in section entitled "Experience of Banned Products to Traditional Markets."

Sanitary and Health Requirements of the Export Markets. Because of health concerns, especially from consumers in the EU, fishery products from East Africa are among some of the heavily regulated food products on the market shelves today. This is because of concerns regarding sanitary and health practices for fisheries in the region, particularly on fisheries from Lake Victoria. The main sanitary requirements are to maintain high health standards at the beaches where the fish is landed for cleaning, sorting, and transport for processing and during processing at the factory plants. The practices before the ban of fish exports to EU in 2000 and those that were adopted subsequently are outlined in the following discussion to illustrate the standards required for the export markets.

Practices Before Ban on Fish Export in 2000. For a long time, facilities at the landing beaches were rudimentary and restricted to a covered area where fish were sold and in some cases a landing jetty was built where the fish were sold. Thus the beaches lacked basic facilities (sanitary containers with ice or water for cleaning or chilling fish). The fish were transported to processing plants for cleaning and packaging for the export markets. The sanitary conditions at the processing plants varied according to the capability of firms but most had a laboratory for chemical and microbiological analysis to ensure that sanitary and health standards required by the market were met.

The basis of standards to be met and procedures to be followed was outlined in the Fisheries Act Cap 378. The Ministry of Health was responsible for overseeing hygiene and sanitation in the industry, the Ministry of Trade and Industry was involved in trade issues while Ministry of Agriculture dealt with production aspects. This situation created confusion and conflict in the enforcement of regulations, especially when a particular market demanded some action to be taken. At the industry level, there was no organized group of actors (fishermen or processors); instead, fishermen and processors operated independently.

Practices After the Ban on Fish Export in 2000. The prevailing practices for the industry before 2000 did not ensure that the sanitary and health standards required for the export market were met adequately and this is what contributed to the fish ban. As a result of the export ban, Kenya has developed standards on fish based on Codex Stan 165 and EU Directive 91/493/EEC. The standards were legislated in 2000 under Legal Notice No. 10 as a supplement to the Fisheries Act Cap. 378. This move was especially aimed at responding to standards required in the EU market but they also apply for all fish products exported from Kenya.

According to the new regulations, the following requirements have been formulated.

At the production level, the following must be observed:

(a) The fishermen and fish handlers at the landing beaches should be trained in basic (level 1) hygiene and sanitary procedures.
(b) Fish at the landing beaches should be placed in sanitary containers with ice.
(c) Vehicles used for transporting fish to the markets or processing plants should be insulated (ice) and dust proof.
(d) Fish should be maintained at an unbroken cold chain from production to the market.

At the processing level, the following must be observed:

(a) A competent authority should inspect all establishments intending to export fish. The EU also requires its inspectors to approve the processors and issue them with an EU export number.
(b) The establishments should implement HACCP and GMP principles both in their construction and routine operating procedures.
(c) There should be regular and documented inspections of the establishments by the country competent authorities.
(d) All personnel are expected to have a certificate of health and training in hygiene and sanitation.

At the marketing level, the following should be observed:

(a) A Health Export certificate should accompany every consignment for export.
(b) There should be complete traceability of products right to the source. This is more important especially when tracing source of contamination in a particular batch.

The Government of Kenya has established a Competent Authority for the inspection of fish standards. The Competent Authority is the Fisheries Department in the Ministry of Agriculture and Rural Development. The Department is principally responsible for the development and conservation of fisheries, promotion and control of fish harvesting, trade on fish and fisheries products, fish quality control services, issuance of fishing licences and export certificates, and enforcing hygiene regulations within the industry.

At the industry level, fish processors formed AFIPEK, which is actively involved in a number of activities that have made significant contributions to the fish sector. These are, among others:

(a) Drafting and launch of the code of practice in the fisheries industry (in progress);
(b) Testing, compliance and verification of the quality control conditions at Lake Victoria;
(c) Rehabilitation of the fish landing beaches along the shores of Lake Victoria; and
(d) Organization and participation of members in international fish exhibitions and trade fairs.

The organization spends about US$2,500 annually for monitoring and supporting sanitary and health measures at the Lake Victoria beaches. It also spends US$3,800 annually on training and advising processors on better health standards in the processing of fish.

As a result of the recent health concerns on fish exports, the government has designated 10 landing beaches on Lake Victoria for development. The landing beaches are being developed through community and stakeholder participation. The developments include fencing; paved the reception area; improvement of drainage system; provisions of insulated fish boxes; improvement of the sorting sheds; provision of electricity and water; construction of landing jetties; modernization of fish reception; and improvement of access roads.

The new developments in the fisheries industry are expected to increase the exports in fish, particularly to the European Union (EU) market, which had shown a significant drop during the ban. For example, the ban had a significant impact on Nile perch exports to the EU causing a drop of 66 percent, a 24 percent drop in total fish exports from Kenya with a corresponding 32 percent decrease in value (Noor 2002). Although exports to other markets continued, the EU market is an important market because of its volumes and better prices offered for Kenyan fish.

Compliance Costs for Standards in the Fisheries Industry. Fishing on Lake Victoria, which is the main source of fish exports is largely undertaken using by wooden boats with a crew of between two and four fishermen. A small number of trawlers operate on the lake although this is illegal. Relatively few boats are motorized but the type and size of nets used vary. The average investment cost in the fishing gear (medium boats for four fishermen and nets) is about US$500.

An important investment in the fisheries industry, which is of concern in the standards for fish exports, is the landing beaches. The government has designated 10 landing beaches on Lake Victoria for development through community and stakeholder participation. The improvements on the beaches are divided into two phases. The first phase covering fencing to improvement of the sorting sheds has been done while the second phase covering the other elements will follow. The estimated cost of developing beaches to meet the required standards is US$90,000 per beach. Thus, the development of beaches on Lake Victoria alone will require US$900,000.

Fish processing is another area where high sanitary and health standards are required. All fish processors are required to invest in laboratories to undertake chemical and microbiological analysis as well as investing in processing facilities. With the new legislation on fisheries all processors are required to adhere to HACCP management systems. Currently, all the 17 processing factories have achieved the HACCP criteria. The costs of investing in a 10-ton fish processing factory are about US$962,800. Laboratory costs for achieving HACCP standards are US$19,200. The

Table 1.17 Average Costs (Fixed and Variable) for a 10 ton Daily Processing Capacity of Fish

Item	Average Cost (US$)
Fixed costs	
Factory buildings	350,000
Filleting equipment (stainless steels)	200,000
Temperature control equipment (Blaster and plate freezer and ice equipment)	180,000
Water treatment	12,000
Transportation trucks (6)	18,000
Subtotal	942,000
Variable costs/day	
Packaging materials	400
Labor	150
Other utilities	1,000
Subtotal	1,550
Laboratory costs	
Fixed lab equipment (weighing scales, autoclaves etc)	6,500
Equipment for microbiological test	3,200
Chemicals for microbiological tests	1,500
Equipment for physico-chemical tests	7,000
Chemical reagents for physico-chemical tests	1,000
Subtotal	19,200
Total	962,800

Source: Authors' compilation from surveys.

overall costs for fish processing are shown in Table 1.17.

Industry Needs. The main concern in the fisheries industry is on how the recommended standards can be met to avoid the bans on exports that were imposed earlier. According to industry players (processors that were interviewed, AFIPEK, and Department of Fisheries), the Kenyan fisheries industry still needs

- Better implementation of hygiene and sanitary standards especially at the production level (beach landings). This is currently a problem because there are no adequate funds to do so and the beaches have not been fully developed as planned.
- Increased awareness of hygienic practices especially on fish handling at the beaches during processing
- Infrastructural development especially the roads to the beaches for better access
- Capacity building of the Competent Authority and association to be able to perform the stipu-

lated activities, particularly with respect to testing and quality assurance and advising fishermen and processors.

Cotton Textile Industry. The cotton textile industry starts with cotton production and ends with textile manufacturing. Currently, the country produces only 2,000 tons of lint cotton annually but this is not adequate to meet domestic needs of the textile industry, which is estimated at 20,000 tons annually. As a result, the country imports cotton lint, yearn, and synthetics for use in the industry.

The cotton textile industry has gone through different phases of development since independence in 1963. Soon after independence, the government supported development of the subsector in many ways. Farmers were provided with support in form of seed, inputs, and advice to grow cotton. The government also helped farmers' cooperative societies to buy and invest in ginneries and instituted a marketing system through the Cotton Lint and Seed Marketing Board (CLSMB), subsequently renamed the Cotton Board of Kenya (CBK) to market lint cotton and cotton seed. In addition, the government invested in textile mills, which supplied the privately owned textile manufacturers.

In the above system of incentives, cotton production expanded gradually from about 13,600 tons in 1965 to about 39,300 tons in 1985. The textile industry also became the country's leading manufacturing activity in both size and employment. However, by 1986, government support to the subsector, which was dependent on donor assistance, dwindled and the local cotton industry became noncompetitive because of inefficiencies in cotton production, ginning, and distribution. As a result, cotton production started to decrease and reached its lowest levels of 2,000 tons per year in 1995 and to date the industry has not recovered.

The decline in cotton production and the shift from cotton to synthetics is explained by the inefficiencies in growing cotton, marketing, and ginning. Production constraints included delayed payments to farmers, poor extension service, poor infrastructure, low quality but highly priced pesticides, poor management of ginneries, late deliveries of inputs, use of poor varieties of cotton, and inadequate research on improved varieties of cotton. Marketing problems included the high price of domestic cotton in 1980s compared with those prevailing in the international markets. This made textile-exporting firms that used local cotton uncompetitive in world markets, hence the preference for either imported cotton or synthetics, which increased dependence on import of raw materials for the manufacture of textiles.

The textile industry still remains the second largest manufacturing activity in Kenya after food processing. There are about 60 textile mills producing a total of 83 million square meters of fabric, excluding blankets and knitted goods. All synthetic raw materials and dyes needed in the textile industry are imported while polyesters are imported as granules, which are heated and extruded into fine threads for the production of synthetic yarns. It is estimated that about 6,000 tons of dyestuff and 20,000 tons of plastic material are imported into the country annually. Capacity utilization in the textile industry is not uniform and ranges from 25 percent to 75 percent. Imports and shortage of cotton and high production costs in recent years have dramatically reduced the industry's output.

The garment industry, which uses the finished products of the textile industry is divided into formal and informal sectors and faces a number of external and internal problems. Key external problems include legal and illegal imports of substandard products. Internal problems include low quality of raw cotton, high costs of production, and consumer preferences for imported products. The most serious problem affecting the garment industry according to the industry actors is forward planning. Forward planning is vital for production, quality control, and keeping up with fashion trends. Few manufacturers seem to be doing comprehensive production or market research, which has led mills to use uncompetitive production techniques and technologies. Hardware technology used in Kenya's textile industry is a mixture of old obsolete machinery and modern state of art equipment. Poor market research has led to either overproduction or duplication of products or both, and inability to satisfy the dynamic consumer needs and preferences.

Domestic and External Marketing of Textiles and Garments. Before import liberalization in 1993, Kenya's textile industry was effectively protected. This led to a very successful domestic textile industry, which grew at a good pace. Concentrating on domestic markets, local manufacturers paid inadequate attention to quality and pricing. However, liberalization has enormously increased the importation of textiles, particularly apparel fabric from the Far East and readymade garments classified as "second hand or used." The manufacturers have therefore to compete with these imports in the domestic market resulting in the closure of some enterprises.

The introduction of export incentive schemes, such as Manufacturing under Bond (MUB) and Export Processing Zone (EPZ) has led to an increase in textile exports. The products from MUB and EPZ factories are exported mainly to the United States, United Kingdom, and COMESA countries. Exports to the U.S. market have increased particularly because of the African Growth Opportunity Act (AGOA). Kenya was among the first to meet the conditions required before obtaining market access to the United States in 2000. As a result, exports from the EPZ alone to the United States doubled from US$25 million in 1999 to US$55 million in 2001. Investments in garment production also rose five times from US$9 million to US$48 million during the same period.

Standards in Cotton Textile Industry. The Kenyan standards for the cotton industry are outlined in the Cotton Act Cap 335 of the Laws of Kenya while those for the textile and clothing industry are gazetted as KEBS standards. The required standards for textiles include resistance of textiles to attack by insects, resistance to microbiological deterioration, and length (span length) and uniformity of cotton fibers.

The cotton lint produced in Kenya is considered to be of low quality because of the use of poor-quality seed and poor husbandry practices. The cottonseed supply system has been poor since the liberalization of the cotton industry and the seed is not certified; therefore its storage period and germination level are not guaranteed according to Kenyan standards. Storage period of less than 5 months and maintenance of moisture content at less than 10 percent are important determinants of seed quality.

Weed and thinning are also important determinants of cotton yield and quality. Clean fields give quality cotton lint while timely harvesting is important to avoid competition between weed and cotton. Timely harvesting is also important for the preservation of fiber quality as field weathering weakens and discolors the fiber. In general, harvesting practices among farmers are poor, because there are delays in picking open cotton balls. Also, harvested cotton is stored in open piles on the ground, which increases the chances of contamination with foreign materials. The control of pests and disease is also an important factor that affects the quality of cotton.

The estimated costs of cotton production are shown in Table 1.18. Pest control costs are among the highest components of cotton production accounting for 29 percent of the total costs. Failure to control pests can lead to 80 percent loss in yields. Strategies to increase cotton yields and quality using available cotton varieties are to control pests with minimal pesticide use in line with the current worldwide trend of using fewer pesticides. Integrated pest management is the strategy recommended for this to happen but the level of use of these technologies Kenya is still low.

Farmers face problems and use sub-standard pesticides and seed because of unfavorable cotton-buying schedules and practices and lack of credit. Local input suppliers to farmers rarely advise farmers on the required standards for pesticide and input use. The government remains the main supplier of extension services to cotton farmers but only about 50 percent of the farmers are coverered and the remaining do not have access to information from the Ministry of Agriculture and Rural Development extension staff on better cotton production practices.

Ginning. Ginneries are the focal point of the cotton textile industry because the type of cotton fiber depends on ginning in addition to the quality of cotton lint. The ginning process can affect significantly the fiber length, uniformity and content of the seed fragments, trash, and short fibers. The minimum ginning technology required to give quality fiber is a dryer or moisture restoration device and a feeder to uniformly meter seed into a gin stand. Approximately 50 percent of the ginneries meet the minimum requirements but the remaining lack drying

Table 1.18 Average Cost for Cotton Production in Selected Provinces of Kenya
(US$ per hectare)

Item	Western Kenya	Nyanza	Rift Valley	Central Kenya	Eastern Kenya	Coast
Yield (kg/ha)	625	350	800	372.5	403.5	657.8
Land preparation	21.2	11.8	27.1	12.6	13.5	22.1
Seed	1.9	1.1	2.5	1.8	1.8	2.0
Labor	59.6	33.4	76.3	35.4	38.2	63.6
Pesticides	55.8	31.2	71.4	33.1	35.7	58.4
Equipment	53.8	30.2	68.9	31.9	34.5	56.4
Total cost	192.3	107.7	246.2	114.8	123.7	202.5

Source: Ikiara and Ndiranga (2002).

and moisture restoration devices. So, the lint they produce contains imperfections and lacks a smooth appearance, a quality that is required. The ginning outturn is also low and is estimated at about 33 percent. This leads to a loss in revenue and is attributed to the low-quality lint.

Textiles Manufacturing. The local textile manufacturing industry supplies only 45 percent of the Kenyan textile market while imported new and used clothes account for 37 percent of the market. Imported fabrics and clothing supplies take a large share of the market and this is attributed to the superior quality and style of the imported finished garments and fabrics relative to locally manufactured substitutes. However, local manufacturers indicate that the standards enforcement on imports is lax and that the quality of imported products is low compared with that of locally produced products.

This indicates that standards implementation in the cotton textile industry remains a main issue of concern in the country.

Textile manufacturers have quality control laboratories within their factories. These are used to ensure that the standards set by KEBs on the manufacture of textile materials are met. The garment factories manufacture garments according to the quality specifications (design and blending of materials) given by each buyer.

Maintaining Standards in Cotton Textile Industry. Both the public and private sectors manage the cotton textile, industry. The Ministry of Agriculture and Rural Development provides advisory service on cotton production through the Kenya Agricultural Research Institute (KARI) and the Cotton Board of Kenya (CBK). The Ministries of Trade and Industry (MTI) and Finance and Planning (MOFP) are involved in overseeing processing of raw materials and development of markets for finished products. The private sector is involved through many bodies. The Kenya Cotton Ginners Association (KCGA) supports ginners. The Kenya Association of Manufacturers (KAM) supports interests of textile manufactures. The Federation of Kenya Employers (FKE) supports various employers involved in the textile industry. The Kenya Apparel Manufacturers Exporters Association (KAMEA) supports exporters of apparels and textiles. The Kenya National Federation of Jua Kali Associations

(KNFJKA) supports the small and microtextile enterprises among others. These are the organizations that can be targeted to improve standards implementation to facilitate improved trade of textiles in Kenya. This would include targeting farmer groups for improving production of quality of cotton lint, ginners for processing quality of lint, and textile manufactures for quality of fabrics, yarns, and garments.

Currently, there is no national apex body that coordinates cotton production and ginning since the CBK is not operational and thus institutional enforcement of standards within the cotton industry is absent. The MA&RD is in the process of developing a regulatory framework for the cotton industry but this is yet to be established. Thus a vacuum exists in coordinating standards in the cotton production–ginning chain. The textile industry is well linked through KAM and the manufacturers are well informed about the standards needs of the industry, particularly for the export market. An important problem within the industry is the enforcement of standards of imported textiles by the government (Ministry of Trade and Industry and KBS). Large quantities of used and substandard textiles are imported into Kenya and stakeholders complain that this has hurt the development of the cotton textile industry because the imports create unfair competition with domestic products.

Industry Needs. Principal concerns in the cotton textile industry regarding standards relate to the provision of quality seed to farmers, sustainable disease and pests control methods for cotton production, investment in improved technology for spinning, and fabric manufacturing as well as for manufacture of garments.

Poor-quality cottonseed is a major constraint to increased cotton production. The main source of cottonseed to farmers is the Kenya Agricultural Research Institute (KARI), which provides the foundation seed. In most cases, farmers use the seed from the ginneries after the cotton has been ginned. This seed is often contaminated with disease and this affects cotton production. A good cottonseed development and distribution system that ensures provision of quality seed to farmers is required to solve this problem.

Disease and pests are an important problem in cotton production. Currently, there is heavy reliance on the use of chemicals to control pests and diseases but the costs of doing so are quite high. Furthermore, heavy use of pesticides results in environmental problems causing a problem for manufactured textiles from such cotton in facing market-driven standards. KARI has a program in developing disease- and pest-resistant varieties. The focus is on biotechnology research to help KARI achieve this but this has yet to be realized because of financial constraints.

The textile industry is characterized by the use of obsolete machinery and equipment. The concern is investments in new textile manufacturing technology for the production of quality textiles. This will require macroeconomic incentives such tax waivers to attract investments into the sector.

Imports of substandard textiles (low quality and used) into Kenya are an important problem. There is no adequate standards surveillance on such products by the government. Thus, there is need to enforce available standards to protect consumers and producers as well.

Adoption of International Quality Standard Systems

As outlined in section entitled "Kenya's Participation in International Standards," Kenya is a member of many international organizations involved in standards setting, namely, CODEX, ISO, OIE, and IPPC. The country has adopted many of the standards developed by these bodies. Some of the standards that have been adopted include ISO TC 34 SC for Tea, ISO TC 34 SC 15 for coffee, and ISO TC 120 for Hides and Skins and Leather. Others include:

- Code of Practice for hygiene in food and drinks manufacturing
- Labeling of prepackaged foods
- Code of Practice of handling, processing, and distribution of fish
- Methods for microbiological examination of foods
- Code of hygiene practice for handling, processing, storage, and placing on the market fish and fishery products

Firms in Kenya have also adopted the CODEX measures for Hazard Analysis Critical Control Point (HACCP) and IPPC measures for risk analysis. ISO 9000 has also been adopted by a few of the larger manufacturing firms.

Impact of the Adoption of Standards and Technical Regulations on Economic Opportunities of the Poor

The biggest challenge that has occurred in the adoption of standards on the economic status of the poor in Kenya is best reflected in the horticulture industry, particularly on smallholder producers. Many small growers of fruits, vegetables, and flowers face problems in meeting the standards required in the European markets because of the high costs in investing in production and marketing facilities to enable them to meet those standards. In general, smallholders lack adequate credit, input, and technical capabilities, and suffer from logistical constraints such as transport, airfreight, and cold storage facilities. This makes it difficult for them to meet the standards of the European market. As a result most of the small farmers have been shut out from the production of horticultural crops except where they are contracted by large growers. Otherwise, most small growers sell their produce in the domestic market where standards are not as stringent as those for the export market but the prices received in the domestic market are low.

Increasingly higher standards required by buyers in the export markets highlight the need for tight coordination of the production of horticultural crops and raise the question of what type of structure can meet these standards. The main concern is regarding access to export markets by small producers given their seemingly limited ability to meet those standards. Several actors in the industry assert that a vertically integrated production channel is the appropriate structure that can provide the performance necessary for the export markets. According to FPEAK, small farmers grow about 60 to 70 percent of the fruits and vegetables exported from Kenya. However, Dolan and Humphrey (2000) note that the share of small farm production in the fruits and vegetables export market declined throughout the 1990s.

The need to link smallholder farmers to the thriving horticultural producers cannot be overemphasized because the production and commercialization of the high-valued crops such as fruits, vegetables, and flowers can be beneficial to small farmers in several respects, namely increasing access to cash income; increasing access to inputs on credit, thereby improving their productivity; and increasing surpluses for household consumption, thus improving nutritional quality of their diet. However, Dolan and Humphrey (2000) have noted that to secure a continuous supply of commodities meeting high quality, environmental, and social standards, supermarket and their suppliers shy away from small exporters and smallholders and rely more on large firms and large producers because control over standards is more reliable and more costly. This means that the high standards required in export markets are marginalizing smallholders. This means that to promote the horticulture industry, more effort is needed to support small farmers in meeting the requirements of the market.

Experience shows that small farmers can meet the stringent standards of the export markets with assistance from exporters, trade associations such as FPEAK and KFC, NGOs, and donor organizations. Through the outgrower schemes exporters are able to closely control and direct the production of smallholder growers to ensure that they meet the codes of practices and standards required by the exporters. A new system being developed for the domestic market is to link local supermarkets with small growers for fruits and vegetables. This program, which is sponsored by USAID-Kenya, is in its trial phase and its success has yet to be ascertained.

On a positive note, the required standards at export markets have led to an improvement of the welfare workers in the horticulture industry. For example, the safety working conditions and environmental health requirements in the European markets have made the horticulture industry in Kenya through their organizations (e.g., FPEAK and KFC) to have codes on labor safety and working requirements, working hours, and environmental standards. This has led to improvements in the welfare of workers. Furthermore, the better horticultural production practices that are used reduce pollution of the environment. The large flower growers in particular are now investing more on farming methods that can reduce the use of pesticides and therefore a reduction in environmental pollution.

Small growers also benefit from contract farming with large growers with the latter helping the former in meeting technical (e.g., quality and pesticide free) and market (e.g., environmental and labor) standards through the provision of services such as machinery and equipment, technical capacity, and funds on credit. Contract farming is also practiced in the fruits and vegetables industries and is one of the practices that benefits small growers in meeting standards for export markets. The challenge in contract farming, however, is the enforcement of contracts, which when not implemented, leads to collapse in use of the practice and thus lack of support to small growers.

International Trade System and Meeting WTO Obligations

This section reviews experiences with the implementation of international trade system standards and meeting WTO obligations.

Experience of Banned Products to Traditional Markets

An example of products that have been restricted to traditional markets on grounds of quality and safety is fish. During the past 12 years continued business in the industry was hampered by bans imposed on it by the European Union market because of concerns for hygiene around the lake.

In 1994, there was repulsion of the East African fish following the Hutu massacre in Rwanda. In 1997, Spain and Italy imposed a ban on Kenyan fish exports on the basis of the presence of *Salmonella* bacteria, which causes cholera in human beings. As a result of this, a 13.1 percent drop in the foreign exchange from the sector was experienced. This was occasioned by a 33 percent drop in quantity of fish exported to the EU compared to 1996 with quantities exported to Spain declining by 86 percent. The 1996 export levels have not been attained to date.

In January 1998, the EU banned chilled fish imports from East Africa and Mozambique because of a cholera epidemic. The ban resulted in a 24 percent drop in the total quantity of fish exported from Kenya, accompanied by a 32 percent drop in value of foreign exchange earnings from the sector. The most recent ban on the market was imposed in March 1999. This was occasioned by the reported use of chemicals for fishing in Uganda. This ban resulted in a 68 percent drop in total quantity of fish exports compared to 1998. After extensive inspections and analysis of both fish and water samples from Lake Victoria, the ban was lifted in November 2000.

Following a DG SANCO inspection visit by EU in December 1998, Kenya was put on List II of third countries entitled to export to EU member states on the basis of bilateral agreement. This is a three-year agreement, which is now in its second year.

The Kenya fish processing sector is plagued by various changes in hygiene and quality control standards. The standards set by the authorities have been changing over the years: the term "shifting the goal post" best describes the changes. The "trigger" for these changes in standards has been the numerous health scares from fish from Lake Victoria in the last few years, namely Rwanda crisis effect,[4] *Salmonella* (cholera) scare mainly in Spain and Pesticide scare in Uganda.

These issues have put Lake Victoria on world focus resulting in fish from this lake being among the most scrutinized food items on the international market. The changing standards have resulted in significant overall improvement in quality control practices in factory operation.

Though the recent EU ban on fish from Lake Victoria was occasioned by use of pesticides for fishing in Uganda it was not immediately lifted in the three East African states even after the problem was contained. This is because the EU used this occasion to reorganize the entire industry to comply with the international standards. The lifting of the ban was made subject to a country meeting four principal requirements:

- Establishment of a Competent Authority to test and approve fish for export;
- Professional reorganization of the industry with respect to quality assurance;
- Adherence to hygiene and quality standards; and
- Enforcement of appropriate legislation.

Uganda and Tanzania had made significant progress with regard to these conditions prior to the last EU inspection of the sector. Subsequently, their fish ban was lifted and the countries were placed on list I of the DG SANCO of the EU, which means that there are no restrictions on their fishery products to EU. Kenya however, did not meet the stipulated standards, mainly because the industry structures were not in place at the time of inspection. Although the country had regulations to ensure the inspection of fish export, the mandate was scattered over two authorities—Department of Fisheries in MA&RD and Ministry of Health. The government of Kenya took more time to harmonize this into one competent authority (the Fisheries Department). Though the ban was temporarily lifted, Kenya is still on list II of the DG SANCO. This means that fishery products from Kenya to EU are subject to a bilateral agreement for 3 years during which the country's procedures of inspection and implementation of measures to improve standards on fish must be harmonized to continue exporting. This period ends in 2003.

Value-added Exports Issues

The case of processed fruits and vegetables shows the restrictions that can occur with value-added exports.

The main export markets for processed fruits and vegetables are Western Europe (Germany, United Kingdom, France, Belgium, and Italy) and to a lesser extent some African countries mainly belonging to COMESA and EAC. Important processed products are canned pineapple, pineapple juices, and concentrates. An important actor in the industry is the Del Monte Company now referred to as Cirio Del Monte, which exports canned pineapples, juices, and concentrates. Del Monte is a vertically integrated firm growing and processing pineapples on its plantation in Thika and is therefore in charge of maintaining standards from the production of fruits, through processing and exporting. However, most exporters mainly process fruits or vegetables and depend on the production of fruits from independent growers. Thus, these exporters are involved in maintaining the required standards at the processing level while the farmers themselves undertake quality and standards at the farm level. In this case, the scrutiny of standards at the farm level is not as stringent as it is at the processing level.

The product standards that processors are required to meet in the market relate to both technical and market-driven standards. Technical standards include food safety and food hygiene regulations. Market standards include ISO 9000 standards and HACCP management practices. Audit firms such as SGS, CMI of United Kingdom, and SGF of Germany certify the products. The KEBS also certifies the products. According to some

---

[4] This involved dumping of human dead bodies into Lake Victoria following massacre and killings in Rwanda.

processors the standards for canned fruits and vegetables, for example, required in the export markets are slightly higher than those required by KEBS for the domestic market.

SPS Compliance

As far as the transparency provisions of the SPS Agreement are concerned, Kenya has achieved a high level of compliance with its obligations. Enquiry and notification points are well established and are functioning effectively. So far, Kenya has made two notifications. One notification was in 1999 dealing with some 42 harmonized East African Standards, which included some aspects of the SPS obligations. The other is Kenya's ban on one-day chicks from Mauritius.

The case involving Kenya's ban on imports occurred in April 2001 and it involved restrictions on the import of day-old chicks from Mauritius because of the alleged detection of avian encephalomyelitis in two shipments. This ban was later lifted after thorough investigations were carried out and the two consignments found were isolated. The case is illustrated in Box 1.7.

Import prohibitions also apply to any plant-rooting medium that consists either wholly or in part of soil, whether or not it is attached to any plant, and fruit grown in, or consigned from, countries where the Mediterranean fruit fly is common. Imports of animals and animal products from countries with groups A and B diseases (according to the classification of the International Office of Epizootics), and with bovine spongiform encephalopathy (BSE) are also banned. Imports of timber from Tanzania are restricted because of

European aphid (*Cernaria cypress*); the timber must be treated before being allowed entry. A certificate issued by an authorized officer of the exporting country must accompany fruit grown in all countries. The certificate must indicate that a stated percentage of the packages in the consignment have been examined and found to be free from insect pests.

Constraints Encountered in the Implementation of SPS Measures

The most obvious problem associated with the SPS arrangements in Kenya for the implementation process with regard to animal and plant health is that there is not one but three enquiry points as the Agreement requires, as mentioned earlier. The Department of Health Services for food safety, the Department of Agriculture for plant health matters, and the Department of Veterinary Services for animal health issues are all under the Ministry of Agriculture and Rural Development. Kenya's notification point is the Ministry of Trade and Industry. The overlaps in implementation of the standards sometimes cause problems and there is need for better coordination of the process of standards development, setting, and notification among the three government bodies to avoid confusion and overlaps.

Some countries such as the European Union, Japan, and the United States have stringent sanitary and phytosanitary requirements, which require stringent pest risk analysis (PRA) information. PRA require personnel with adequate skills to undertake the analysis and regular upgrading, which is by itself very costly because of the numerous

---

BOX 1.7 BAN ON ONE-DAY-OLD CHICKS FROM MAURITIUS

Kenya imposed an emergency ban on the import of one-day old chicks from Mauritius ostensibly because of its concern about the avian encephalomyelitis disease. According to the Mauritian authorities, their documents showed that no risk assessment had been carried out, no testing had been conducted, and Kenya made no notification of the measure to the WTO. The Mauritian authorities therefore contemplated various options for obtaining redress, for example, (i) raising the matter with the SPS Committee (ii) seeking advice from the secretariat of the OIE concerning the status of avian encephalomyelitis. Before the case went too far (to the dispute settlement body of the WTO), the two countries settled the matter diplomatically and Kenya consequently withdrew the ban.

surveys that need to be carried out. Kenya has not been able to have an elaborate PRA because of these constraints. There is need to deal with issues urgently.

WTO members, (according to Article 4 on the equivalence of the WTO SPS Agreement), are required to accept the SPS measures of other countries as equivalent if the exporting country demonstrates to the importing country that its measures achieve the importing members' appropriate level of sanitary or phtosanitary protection. This means that there should be mutual recognition of the phytosanitary measures as long as they achieve an appropriate level of protection required by both importing and exporting countries. The challenge for Kenya usually is to demonstrate to most importing countries that the measures undertaken for Kenyan products, mainly flowers and fresh vegetables and fruits, achieve the levels required. In most cases, the importing countries are requested to send inspectors to Kenya to verify the SPS measures taken before the exports are made.

Opportunities for Differentiation

This section reviews examples of opportunities in which standards have been used by private firms to differentiate their products to achieve competitive advantage and experience with organic farming.

Differentiation of Products

The standard and technical requirements for horticultural products are a good case in which the standards have helped to differentiate the range of products' development in Kenya. In the fruits and vegetables industry, a wide range of products, which include avocados, mangoes, passion fruit, strawberries, pineapples, French beans, canned beans, okra, karella, snap beans, frozen beans, eggplant, and chillies are produced by various specialized methods targeting different consumer needs. Smallholder farmers, for example, have tended to focus on fruits and vegetables, which do not require intensive management practices such as tree fruit crops. Large farms have focused on high value crops such as snap beans and canned beans that require intensive field management practices. A new standard whereby supermarkets in Europe require a different mix of vegetables in a pack has made small farmers diversify into growing many vegetables in one farm at the same time rather than specializing in one vegetable type.

In the flowers industry, over 30 different types of flowers are grown because of consumer preferences and standards in terms of the varieties, assortments, and colors of flowers. Growers have also tended to specialize in different types of flowers depending on the ability to invest and the high value as a result of higher standards required. For example, large investors are putting emphasis on growing of roses and carnations and grow them under intensive management systems (green houses) as opposed to small growers who focus more on flowers that can easily be grown under open field management practices.

The high investments required in the flowers industry (machinery, equipment, inputs and packaging), as well as the high standards required by consumers and the associated high payoff, have led to many international companies to invest in Kenya in the industry and therefore bring in skills and techniques for quality assurance.

Experiences in Organic Farming and Marketing of Organic Products

Agricultural produce can only be described as an organic agricultural product after internationally recognized firms in the trade certify that no chemicals have been used in the crop at any stage of life from seed through processing to export. The firm will also certify that there was no genetic manipulation of the seed material and that the working conditions and environment were fair to workers and that no child labor (ILO standard) was used.

The International Federation of Organic Agriculture Movements (IFAOM) determines the international rules and standards of organic farming. The IFAOM is a federation of about 600 organizations in more than 110 countries. The membership is made up of producers, consumers, traders, research, and certification organizations. The accreditation system for organically grown products is administered by International Organic Accreditation Services, a subsidiary of IFOAM.

The EU legislation under EU Directive 2092/91 has since 1991 covered the marketing of agricultural products using the term organic ("biological" and "natural"). The directive names specific terms for the various languages and makes it mandatory. Directive 2092/91 means no products other than

55

those produced and inspected in accordance with the directive may be marketed as organic or similar ("biological" or "natural"). The directive imposes very extensive demands on regulations for dealing with imports or exporters from Kenya and other developing countries. The most important regulations include

(a) Countries that meet directive requirements must be included in a list determined by the commission. The production of goods imported shall be subject to the direction of inspection by the body that is specified in the list. Up to 1999, only five countries had been placed under this list: Argentina, Australia, Hungary, Israel, and Switzerland.

(b) The competent authority in the exporting country shall issue a certificate for each export consignment. The certificate shall state the method of production in accordance with a system, which is equivalent to that stipulated by the EU Directive.

(c) The country must have legislation covering the production and marketing of organic products. Importer Derogation or "the back door" is an exception rule that was introduced because third country imports were on the verge of totally stagnating. The rule implies that importers can be permitted to market organic products, which do not originate in the countries on the list, if they can provide competent authorities in the member state with evidence that the product was produced in accordance with a system that satisfies the demands of the EU directive.

The cost for external certification of organic products can be very high in developing countries. Local inspection bodies can help reduce these costs. However, local bodies must gain international recognition first, and this is a difficult process and often calls for assistance of expensive consultants. The development of partnerships between an accredited inspection body and a local body can be a possible route to facilitate the growth of domestic inspection bodies in developing countries. This initiative can be extended to incorporate a regional scheme such as one for the East African countries for accreditation and certification to expand opportunities in organic farming.

The Kenya Institute for Organic farming (KIOF) and Association for Land Husbandry (ABLH) are undertaking efforts for the certification of organic products from Kenya. An important problem for Kenyan producers who wish to export to the EU is that, to date, these organizations have not been able to obtain IFOAM accreditation. ABLH has developed standards for organic farming in Kenya and has requested accreditation from IFAOM. It is funded by DFID to develop standards for organic farming and to try to certify temporarily some products in Kenya.

Plan of Action

International standards play an important role in international trade with the advent of reductions in tariff and nontariffs barriers to trade. This is because failure to meet international standards for goods and to comply with the WTO SPS Agreement can inhibit market access to export markets. For Kenya, international standards are important because trade is an important contributor to GDP with merchandise trade contributing about 40 percent of the total GDP. Agricultural commodities and agroprocessed products dominate this trade. Thus noncompliance with international standards for trade in goods affects the performance of the Kenyan economy because they have an impact on agriculture, which is the backbone of the economy. The sector contributes to about 25 percent of the GDP, is the leading foreign exchange earner, and an important source of employment and food for the country.

Compliance with the provisions of the WTO SPS and technical barriers to trade (TBT) agreements can facilitate or constrain trade and therefore affect the performance of the economy. In Kenya, the impact will be felt more in the agricultural sector, particularly if they have a negative impact on trade of the traditional and nontraditional commodities. In addition, the country has a diverse range of agricultural products whose standards vary but can contribute significantly to economic growth if they can be compliant with international standards to increase trade of the products.

There are four main issues related to standards, which affect their role in international trade and in Kenya's economic development. These are (a) standards setting in Kenya and compatibility with international standards, (b) administration of the standards, (c) compliance with the standards, and (d) impact of standards in the development of different sectors.

Standards Setting in Kenya and Conformity to International Standards

The Kenya Bureau of Standards (KEBS) has the mandate of developing standards in Kenya. However, for conformity to international standards, the KEBS works closely with Kenya Plant Inspectorate Services (KEPHIS), Department of Veterinary Services (DVS), Ministry of Health (MoH), which are the contact or enquiry points for international standards for plant and animal health and food safety, respectively. The private sector is also involved in standards setting through participation in technical committees. Most Kenyan standards are based on international standards set by Codex Alimentarius Commission (CAC), Office of International des Epizootes (OIE), and International Plant Protection Convention (IPPC). This is possible through participation of Kenyan technical staff in some of the meetings held by these organizations or use of guidelines and procedures provided by the organizations for setting internationally acceptable standards.

Not all Kenyan standards conform to internationally accepted standards, partly because of constraints in financing attendance in international meetings by both the public and private sector officials involved in standards setting. Thus, there is need to build human capacity for Kenya to be able to develop and set standards that conform to international standards. Furthermore, although the country has some capacity to define appropriate SPS measures, it has little capacity to carry out risk analysis (associated with food safety, animals, plants and their products) in conformity with risk assessment methodologies proposed by the relevant international organizations. Potential exports (e.g., beef, flowers, vegetables, and fruits) are restricted to markets because of significant disease or pests. Additionally, because the plant and animal health infrastructure is deficient there is need for equipment and training to make international accreditation possible.

Administration of Standards

Different bodies undertake the administration and implementation of standards in Kenya. In the public sector, the notifying agency for the WTO is the Ministry of Industry and Trade (Director of External Trade), enquiry points are Ministry of Agriculture and Rural Development for animal health (DVS), plant health (KEPHIS and PCPB), and Ministry of Health for food safety. Many public and private sector organizations are also involved in the implementation of the standards. Some of the problems encountered in the administration of standards is poor coordination among the various actors and weak information flow regarding standards among the various actors. Thus, there is need to strengthen the administration and implementation of standards both at the public and private sector levels.

Compliance

Although Kenya has a reasonable institutional set-up for standards development and administration, it faces constraints that make it difficult to comply fully with international obligations. These include implementation and production constraints. Implementation constraints include:

(a) Compliance of some of the domestic legislation with international standards. For example, standards for processed fruits and vegetables provided for by KEBS Act are weaker than international standards.

(b) Weaknesses in export and import certification systems. Examples include weaknesses in certifying livestock products for export to European Union, Japanese, and U.S. markets and imports of textiles into the country.

(c) Inadequate testing capabilities including international accreditation for some laboratories involved in microbiology and chemical tests for foodstuffs.

(d) Risk analysis and surveillance programs for pests, diseases, chemical residues, food safety, and so on.

(e) Control and eradication of pests, which have restricted exports of beef products, for example.

Production constraints include infrastructure weaknesses and different standard requirements for different markets, which make it difficult for producers and exporters to meet the international standards requirements. For example, the poor transportation network, which leads to long transportation periods for fresh horticultural products from production to exporting points, necessitates investments in cooling vehicles for transportation of the produce and storage facilities at the ports of export to maintain standards for fresh produce required in the export markets.

Both implementation and production constraints need to be relaxed for standards to play an appropriate role in enhancing international trade.

Impact of Standards in Development of Different Sectors and Compliance Costs

Coffe Industry. The main concern in the coffee sector is the role that the new institutions (processing factories, marketing agents, and millers) that have developed as a result of liberalization of the industry, will play in maintaining standards as required by the market. Because the organizations are adjusting to a new legal framework, they will require technical support (financial and human capacity) to deliver better services to the farmers. This is necessary to help revive the coffee industry.

The costs of compliance for this industry vary with the level of activity. At the production level, farmers incur costs to improve coffee production. Annual coffee production costs, which include methods that allow compliance with standards, range from US$600 to US$1,000 per hectare. Other costs are incurred at the processing levels ranging from US$158 to US$770 per ton of coffee for processing and US$100 per ton for coffee milling.

Horticulture (Vegetables, Fruits, and Flowers). The main concerns in the horticultural sector are the ability to meet the MRL requirements, pest risk analysis, and the ever-changing consumer preferences. Attaining the MRLs required by producers requires implementation of good agricultural practices (GAP) and the ability to test for the levels before the produce is harvested for export. This requires investment in GAP and human capacity at the farm level. Pest risk analysis requires both human and capital capacity within the public sector to provide information to the export markets that is credible and to make producers aware of market requirements. The ever-changing consumer preferences require producers to invest in research or to pay for royalties for new varieties developed by the breeders.

The compliance costs required vary with the level of intervention and type of crop grown. At farm level, farmers will require to invest in capacity to advise and inspect the produce for good agricultural practices, which include recommended levels of chemicals use. An expert costs about US$2,000 per month for a production capacity of 5 tons of fruits and vegetables or 10 tons of flowers daily. Investment costs for quality controls from the farm up to port of export for the same tonnage of fruits and vegetables or flowers, respectively, costs about US$123,000. Only large commercial farmers can afford this kind of investment. For small growers to benefit, they will need to operate on a group basis or be contracted by large growers.

Fisheries. The main concern in the fisheries industry is how to meet the recommended standards so that bans on exports that have been experienced in the past can be avoided. The main concerns are:

- Better implementation of hygiene and sanitary standards, especially at the production level (beach landings);
- Increased awareness of hygienic practices, especially for fish handling at the beaches;
- Infrastructure development, especially the roads to the beaches for better access;
- Capacity building for the Competent Authority and Fish Processors Association to be able to perform its stipulated activities, particularly fisheries testing and quality assurance, and advising fishermen and processors.

Compliance costs vary with the level of intervention. At the beach level, about US$90,000 are required to develop the necessary infrastructure for each beach to maintain the required standards. However, since fishermen are spread out, funds will be required to develop the 10 designated beaches. This amounts to US$900,000. At the processing level, the costs of maintaining standards (HACCP) are estimated at about US$19,200 for each fish processing firm.

Cotton Textile. The main concerns in the cotton-textile industry are to improve cotton production at the farm level through the provision of quality seed to farmers and sustainable disease and pests control methods for cotton production; investment in improved technology for spinning and fabric manufacturing and the manufacture of garments. Poor cotton practices are a hindrance to quality cotton production. A good cottonseed development and distribution system that ensures provision of quality seed to farmers is required to solve this problem. Support is required by farmers to help in disease and pests control. This support can be extended to the ginneries for investments in better ginning technologies. Textile manufacturing technology is also constrained by use of obsolete machinery and equipment. The requirement is investment in new textile manufacturing technology for the production of quality textiles. Another issue of concern is legislation to control imports of substandard textiles. An adequate legal framework and enforcement of the laws is required.

The compliance costs for maintaining standards vary with each level of intervention. At the farm level, the compliance costs relate to costs of production and vary from US$100 to US$200 per hectare. At the ginning and manufacturing levels, costs of investing in ginning and manufacturing capacity varies depending on the size of the factory. Private investors are willing to invest if cotton production and supply are assured since there is a ready market for textiles made possible by AGOA and ACP-EU agreements and regional integration blocs such as COMESA.

Projects for Investment

Following on the issues arising form the analysis, three kinds of projects are possible, namely, commodity or product production support projects, private sector investments projects, and public sector support projects.

Commodity Support Programs. The main constraints in the production and marketing of agricultural commodities considered in this analysis are lack of technical knowledge and limited funding to enable farmers, particularly small farmers, maintain required standards during the production and marketing processes. Thus, commodity support programs should target empowerment of producers to meet the required standards in the production and marketing of different commodities. The focus should be on small producers who, on their own, are not able to invest in facilities to enable them meet international standards. The projects should be designed to support farmers as a group and on a regional basis, targeting the constraints faced by each industry such accessing export markets or financing facilities required for achieving standards required in the markets. The programs should be built on vertical linkages within the commodity

chains to facilitate better coordination of production and marketing of the products. The priority is the small producers of horticulture, cotton, and coffee, and fishermen, respectively, and associations for the production of the commodities. These projects will be useful in contributing toward poverty alleviation in the rural areas as identified in Kenya's Poverty Reduction Strategy paper (PRSP 2002).

Horticulture producers should be supported with credit for inputs and investments for centrally placed refrigerated pack houses for cooling, cleaning, and sorting out produce for both the domestic and export markets. Support is also required for personnel (extension) to advise on good agricultural production practices. The cost of the program will vary with the number of farmers considered in the group. Based on information that small farmers grow 5 hectares of horticultural crops on an average, about US$2,500 to US$6,500 can be earmarked for individual producers while US$123,000 can be earmarked for central facilities to serve farmers who produce at least 5 tons of vegetables and fruits or 10 tons of flowers daily. This program can be built on USAID-Kenya's planned programs on horticulture, which are aimed at linking small producers to domestic supermarkets. The total cost of the project will vary with the number of regions selected. Initially, it can be implemented as a pilot covering a few selected vegetable and fruits and flower growing areas. Funds can be channeled to producers through farmers' organizations such as FPEAK and KFC or any other farmers' groups that may be established for this purpose.

Fishing programs should focus on the development of landing beaches particularly along Lake Victoria. Ten beaches have been identified, which require about US$90,000 each, to enable fishermen to meet the required standards. Currently, the government of Kenya is involved in the development of the beaches but is constrained financially. This should be a project for all stakeholders (fishermen and processors) involved in the industry and can be built on the ongoing community-based activities to improve sanitary and hygiene standards at the landing beaches. The AFIPEK alone contributes about US$2,500 annually to the program. Hence, any additional assistance will support this initiative.

The cotton textile program should focus on supporting small farmers in cotton production through the provision of inputs for cotton production and on KARI for the development of better cotton varieties. This program should also focus on farmer organization or groups and develop a mechanism of providing credit to farmers for cotton production but this should be linked to ginning facilities. Based on information that most farmers grow 5 hectares of cotton, about US$2,500 to US$3,000 will be required by an individual farmer. Credit should be extended to farmers in Eastern, Coast, North Eastern, and Nyanza provinces where cotton is grown. Funds should also be made available for investing in ginneries to serve the groups or the private sector should be encouraged to invest in ginning capacity once increased cotton production is assured.

The *coffee* program should focus on strengthening the farmers' organization in coffee processing. This program can be built on the previous World Bank project, which focused on funding farmers through cooperative societies for small improvements in the coffee sector. The components should include funds for farmers as production credit, and for coffee societies for investment in processing factories.

Private Investment Projects. The growing of horticultural crops, particularly flowers, and processing of fish are capital-intensive activities, whose initial investments can be prohibitive. However, these activities offer good returns, which make them attractive to private investors. Thus, private investments can target financing horticulture production and fish processing on a large scale. The financial requirements vary but a minimum for new investments are about US$100,000 for horticultural crops and US$900,000 for fish processing.

Public Support Projects. Some of the constraints faced in bridging the standards gap in Kenya relate to standards development and implementation by public organizations. The constraints include lack of funds to attend international meetings for standards development, capacity to define appropriate standards for the country and undertake risk analysis in food safety, animals and plants and their products, and implementation of standards. Thus, public support programs should focus on supporting public institutions in formulation, development, and implementation of standards in Kenya as well as making it possible for the country to comply with WTO SPS and TBT requirements. The programs could be extended to providing information to producers and firms on international standards requirements. The Ministry of Trade and Industry has identified the required activities, which are outlined as follows.

The Commonwealth Secretariat has shown an interest in capacity building for standards and undertook a study to identify the needs for the country. However, the program has yet to be implemented. Other public programs funded by donors such as by UNCTAD under JITAP currently focus on human capacity building but on a short-term basis. These programs include training personnel capable of analyzing implications of various WTO agreements and how to effectively participate in the international negotiations of the agreements.

Item	US$ million
1. International standards-setting meetings and negotiation skills	0.49
2. Training 10 officers in risk analysis at KEPHIS	0.30
3. Risk analysis and research at KEPHIS	0.53
4. Upgrading laboratories at KEPHIS	0.85
5. Improve national SPS enquiry points	0.30
6. Preparation of standards—KEBS	0.13
7. Training officers on packaging—KEBS	0.03
8. Establish accreditation body for certification	0.25
9. Improve TBT enquiry point—KEBS	0.02
10. Improve metrology, radiation and other labs—KEBS	0.87
11. Training on standardization—KEBS	0.12
12. Upgrade testing and surveillance labs for DVS and fisheries	1.07
13. Information dissemination	0.16
Total	5.00

References

Central Bank of Kenya (CBK), 1990–2000. Statistical Bulletin, Nairobi, Kenya.

CRF. (Coffee Research Foundation). 1999. "Strategies to Enhance Coffee Production in Kenya." Unpublished Technical Report. Ruiru, Kenya.

Dolan, K., and J. Humphrey. 2000. "Who gains from the Boom in the African Fresh Vegetables Exports?" Norwich: University of East Anglia School of Development Studies.

Ikiara, G. K., M. A. Juma, and J. O. Amadi. 1993. "Agricultural Decline, Politics and Structural Adjustment in Kenya." In P. Gibbons ed. *Social Change and Economic Reform in Africa.* Nordiska Africainstitute, Uppsala.

Ikiara, M. and L. Ndiranga. 2002. Developing a Revival Strategy for Kenyan Cotton-Textile Industry: A Value Chain Approach. Unpublished Report. Kenya Institute for Public Policy Research and Analysis (KIPPRA). Nairobi.

ILO (International Labour Organization). 1999. "Kenya: Meeting the Employment Challenges of the 21st Century." ILO Regional Office, Addis Ababa, Ethiopia.

Kenya, Republic of, 1982–2000. *Economic Surveys.* Ministry of Planning and National Development. Central Bureau of Statistics. Nairobi.

Kenya, Republic of, 1982–2000. *Statistical Abstracts.* Ministry of Planning and National Development. Central Bureau of Statistics. Nairobi.

——— 1986. "Economic Management for Renewed Growth." *Sessional Paper* No. 1. Government Printer, Nairobi.

——— 1997 and 2002. *Eight Development Plan, 1997–2001 and 2002–2008.* Government Printer, Nairobi.

Kimuyu, P. 1999. "Structure and Perfromance of the Manufacturing Sector in Kenya." In Kimuyu P., M. Wagacha and O. Abagi (Eds.), *Kenya's Strategic Policies for 21st Century: Macroeconomic and Sectoral Choices.* Institute of Policy Analysis and Research (IPAR), Nairobi.

Mwega, F. M. 2000. "The GATT/WTO Agreements, Domestic Trade Policies and External Market Access: The Kenyan Case." Paper presented during AERC-KIPPRA Workshop on WTO Agreements. September 11–12, Nairobi.

National Cereals Produce Board (NCPB). 2002. Maize and Wheat Requirements. Unpublished Report. Nairobi.

Noor, H. 2002. "Sanitary and Phtosanitary Measures and Their Impact on Kenya." Unpublished Paper prepared for UNCTAD. Geneva.

Nyangito, H. 1999. "Agricultural Sector Performance in a Changing Policy Environment." In Kimuyu P., M. Wagacha and O. Abagi (Eds.), "Kenya's Strategic Policies for 21st Century: Macroeconomic and Sectoral Choices." Institute of Policy Analysis and Research (IPAR), Nairobi.

Nyangito, H. J. M. Omiti, G. A. Kodhek, and J. Nyoro. 2001. "Revitalizing Agricultural Productivity in Kenya: Paper presented during EAGER Workshop on Restarting Kenya's Economic Growth, Safari Park Hotel, Nairobi, March 2001.

Thoen, R. S. Jaffee, C. Dolan, and F. Ba. 2000. "Equatorial Rose: The Kenyan-European Cut Flower Supply Chain." Unpublished Report.

WTO. World Trade Organization. 2000. *Trade Policy Review, Kenya 2000.* WTO, Geneva.

World Bank. 1994. *Adjustment in Africa: Reforms, Results and Road to Ahead.* Washington D.C.: Oxford University Press.

——— 2002a. *World Bank Standards and Trade Database* Washington D.C.

——— 2002b. *African Development Indicators.* Washington D.C.

Appendix A Kenya's Exports by Destination 1990–2001
(US$ million)

Geographical Area and Country	1990	1991	1992	1993	1994	1995	1996	1997	1998	1999	2000	2001
European Union	479.4	476.3	429.2	415.5	646.7	560.3	605.1	626.5	585.9	523.0	512.9	508.6
Rest of western Europe	10.5	61.8	44.5	10.8	12.7	22.1	24.4	23.7	14.9	13.5	14.9	20.5
Eastern Europe	16.3	1.5	0.5	2.0	3.0	2.2	6.0	7.2	5.8	8.4	7.9	11.6
Canada	90.2	7.4	6.3	8.7	12.9	11.9	11.8	9.4	9.9	5.9	6.1	4.6
United States	35.4	41.0	35.0	40.1	65.5	47.1	57.7	53.8	49.3	37.9	36.0	43.4
Rest of America	0.2	1.6	0.3	0.8	1.6	1.7	1.4	1.4	1.7	1.3	4.0	6.2
COMESA	194.0	237.2	212.9	319.5	726.8	678.7	825.5	726.6	442.5	425.6	445.9	517.5
Rest of Africa	22.8	26.5	38.7	43.9	83.2	101.9	112.8	77.9	71.2	360.5	347.7	405.0
Middle East	40.1	33.3	27.9	30.8	33.3	41.6	72.0	62.9	77.3	74.5	84	113.7
Far East and Australia	130.3	125.6	131.1	137.7	217.5	190.2	222.8	201.0	253.2	293.5	292.9	333.7
Total exports	1023.6	1148.0	976.3	1063.7	1860.3	2036.5	2070.6	1826.1	1848.6	1680.5	1723.8	1777.7

Source: Kenya, Economic Surveys (various years).

Appendix B Kenya Imports by Country of Origin 1990–2001
(US$ million)

Geographical Area and Country	1990	1991	1992	1993	1994	1995	1996	1997	1998	1999	2000	2001
European Union	1033.0	835.1	591.0	543.2	908.0	1067.8	1153.9	979.7	1040.0	863.4	969.4	916.4
Rest of western Europe	346.0	37.5	32.3	21.1	51.7	36.7	70.4	52.8	566.0	48.9	45.5	69.1
Eastern Europe	13.0	17.1	10.0	8.2	29.2	39.7	38.0	35.4	36.9	45.2	65.1	27.1
Canada	13.0	17.4	11.8	11.8	11.4	12.4	32.6	25.4	22.5	23.8	12.6	20.3
United States	95.0	94.1	134.4	86.1	170.2	114.2	160.0	225.1	266.7	180.9	129.2	495.8
Rest of America	42.0	18.1	32.1	18.0	22.2	54.3	34.2	40.1	126.8	55.7	47.6	62.9
COMESA	57.8	49.5	47.0	34.9	66.7	32.6	38.4	108.4	40.4	4.2	6.6	8.7
Rest of Africa	5.1	6.8	5.0	1.7	286.7	198.5	255.7	353.0	239.6	301.5	284.9	395.2
Middle East	435.6	376.7	357.5	338.4	395.4	383.0	494.4	522.2	579.9	590.6	941.9	876.3
Far East and Australia	385.6	426.0	374.0	278.6	625.2	700.6	783.9	695.4	776.6	1287.2	1606.2	1694.6
Total imports	2114.8	1885.2	1631.6	1483.7	2567.1	2643.1	3062.3	3042.0	3194.8	2830.1	3175.3	3690.9

Source: Kenya, Economic Surveys (various years).

Appendix C Kenya Exports Value of Principal Commodities 1990–2001
(US$ million)

Commodities	1990	1991	1992	1993	1994	1995	1996	1997	1998	1999	2000	2001
Food, beverages, and tobacco	641.7	591.7	522.1	589.3	947.8	878.2	1107.3	972.0	1052.1	887.6	863.5	759.8
Basic materials: Minerals fuels and lubricants	210.9	279.7	219.5	192.1	310.8	277.8	372.2	355.8	343.6	129.3	131.2	158.0
Manufactured goods	172.2	255.8	237.1	269.7	600.3	507.7	575.5	470.1	293.0	281.2	293.7	350.4
Miscellaneous	0.3	221.8	16.8	12.7	1.3	1.0	5.4	7.1	5.4	284.3	246.2	276.8
Grand total	1023.6	1092.9	943.2	1063.7	1860.3	1664.7	2070.6	1826.1	1848.6	1582.4	1534.6	1545.0

Source: Kenya, Economic Surveys (various years).

GABRIELA REBELLO DA SILVA
LARA DA SILVA CARRILHO

BRIDGING THE STANDARDS DIVIDE

A Case Study and Action Plan for Mozambique

MOZAMBIQUE HAS UNEXPLOITED NATURAL RESOURCES AND ABUNDANT LABOR THAT give it enormous economic potential for overcoming the present state of underdevelopment. Its unexploited and underutilized water and energy resources could meet Mozambique's domestic consumption and development needs and still leave surpluses for other countries. The country's geographical location makes it an ideal gateway for the transport of products to and from neighboring countries, and facilitates the access of local importers and exporters to a large regional market of 200 million Southern African inhabitants. Indeed, its transport infrastructure has been developed to enable Mozambique to play a role as a supplier of services.

The lack of appropriate technology for small producers contributes to low yields, post-harvest losses, and low quality of the crop; these problems are associated with the lack of an appropriate trade network. Natural disasters strike the country almost every year and have caused destruction of crops, the death of livestock, and damage to factories in the affected areas. Natural disasters worsen the situation of food insecurity, both chronic and temporary, that prevails in some parts of the country.

The case studies show that, in general, that all the sectors of the economy need to improve to be competitive. This improvement requires not only the application of standards but also investments in technology and human resources. The analysis of the public institutions involved on the regulatory system and in the standards setting system, shows that they do not have appropriate infrastructure and they lack qualified personnel. Financing problems are also an important constraint. However, the Directive INNOQ 1, based on international rules, is a good basis for the development of the standardization subsystem. The legal framework is not adequate and needs to be updated or some new legislation and regulations need to be introduced. This has started through the revision of some laws and technical regulations related to animal and plant health.

The adoption of the ISO 9000 series of standard is under way. Currently few firms implement them because of a low level of awareness. APCER and SABS are providing certification services. Certified companies utilize accredited laboratories and calibration services from South Africa, but the costs are high. The HACCP system is being implemented in a systematic way only in the fisheries export subsector. The country has established an interministerial committee that deals with the implementation of the SADC Trade Protocol and other matters

related to trade policy. The country already has an inquiry point nominated for the implementation of the TBT Agreement and is in the process of nominating an enquiry point for the SPS Agreement.

To improve the standards and regulatory system and to ensure that it follows the internationally approved requirements and thus facilitates access to markets of Mozambican export products it needs develop an appropriate regulatory system including food safety issues, and effective control mechanisms for import and export goods; develop an appropriate standards setting system including facilities for training, metrology, accreditation, testing and certification; strengthen the country's participation in regional and international standards setting bodies; improve the response of the country on issues related to WTO, mainly SPS and TBT Agreement; support the development of selected sectors to improve exports.

Methodology and Overview

During the first phase of the project, the authors identified the institutions to be surveyed and prepared an interview checklist. At the same time, the sources of statistical data were selected and basic documentation for the development of the project was collected and reviewed.

In the second phase, the authors conducted several interviews in relevant institutions and visited Nampula province where they collected information relevant to this study. The list of interviewees, other contacts, and references, is attached as Annex C.

In a third phase, the authors analyzed the information and integrated it into this report, which is structured according to the country case study outline defined by the project coordination.

The outline of the study is as follows: An overview of macroeconomic conditions and performance is provided (in the section entitled "Economic Conditions and Performance") so as to contextualize the analysis of standards and technical regulations. This is followed by a summary on past, ongoing, and planned programs to refine legal arrangements and strengthen local capacities to implement trade promotion standards and technical regulations (in the section entitled "Provision of Development Assistance") and an analysis of trade performance (in the section entitled "Trade Performance and Outlook"), where specific case studies are developed. In the section entitled "Domestic Regulatory Structures and Policies: Internal Market Barriers," the study reviews and assesses existing laws and regulations and determines the extent to which they are consistent with current international norms. Finally, it determines the necessity of strengthening or reviewing the current legislation and the role of related institutions. In the section entitled "Domestic Standards Setting System," the study assesses the country's organizational capacities and physical infrastructure to design and implement standards. The section entitled "Involvement in Regional and International Standards Development" analyzes the ways in which the country and its representatives have participated in the process of setting or revising standards and technical regulations at the international level. The section entitled "Private Sector Perspectives" provides an analysis of the private sector followed by an analysis of the WTO and trade commitments (in the section entitled "WTO and Trade Commitments: Assessment of Implementation, Problems"). The report closes with an action plan based on the main conclusions (in the section entitled "Main Findings and Proposed Action Plan"). The list of contacts and the list of documentation reviewed are attached as annexes to the study. Other annexes consist of other references as mentioned in the text.

Economic Conditions and Performance

General Information about the Country

Mozambique has an area of 799,380 square kilometers and a population of about 17 million (2000); it is divided into 11 provinces. The country borders Tanzania, Malawi, Zambia, Zimbabwe, South Africa, and Swaziland, stretching 4,445 kilometers. The coastline is about 2,500 kilometers bordered by the Indian Ocean. The capital is Maputo and the official language is Portuguese. It is a member of the Southern African Development Community (SADC), the African Union (AU), the United Nations (UN), the World Trade Organisation (WTO), the World Bank (WB), and the International Monetary Fund (IMF).

Mozambique's population has grown by 42 percent during the past 20 years, to 17.2 million inhabitants in 2000, compared to the 12.1 million registered in the 1980 census. In 1997 the economically active population (EAP) was estimated to be 5.9 million, equivalent to 69.7 percent of citizens aged 15 years or more, with 81 percent active in agriculture. Women make up the majority of the EAP (52 percent). The average population growth rate is 2.26 percent per year (INE 1997). Agriculture is the main economic activity, contributing 25 percent of gross domestic product (GDP), while employing 80 percent of the labor force.

Mozambique is one of Africa's low-income and highly indebted countries—among the poorest in the world. The country has unexploited natural resources and abundant labor that give it enormous economic potential for overcoming this state of underdevelopment. Its unexploited and underutilized water and energy resources could meet Mozambique's domestic consumption and development needs and still leave surpluses for other countries.

The country's geographical location makes it an ideal gateway for the transport of products to and from neighboring countries, and facilitates the access of local importers and exporters to a large regional market of 200 million Southern African inhabitants. Indeed, its transport infrastructure has been developed to enable Mozambique to play a role as a supplier of services.

The principal markets for Mozambique's exports are Europe (mainly Spain and Portugal), North America (mainly the United States), and Asia (mainly India and Japan). In Africa, the principal destination is South Africa, which is Mozambique's second largest export market (Table 2.1). The country's main export products are primary agricultural commodities (cotton, cashew nuts, sugar, timber, and citrus) and fishery products.

Domestic agroindustry consists mainly of medium-scale processing of agricultural raw materials into primary commodities, and a small-scale food–processing subsector. The remaining industrial transformation is undertaken within small family units for their own consumption or local sales. Thus agroprocessing in Mozambique has not been able to absorb the agricultural produce that is currently grown in the country. This leads to the export of basic raw materials with little value added, and to the dependence of the country on imports of final consumer (and even intermediate) agricultural goods.

Natural disasters (floods, cyclones, and drought) strike the country almost every year and have caused destruction of crops, the death of livestock, and damage to factories in the affected areas. Natural disasters worsen the situation of food insecurity, both chronic and temporary, that prevails in some parts of the country.

Table 2.1 Values of Exports by Country of Destination
(thousand US$)

	1995	1996	1997	1998	1999	2000
Spain	36.4	47.6	42.6	36.6	34.5	39.1
Rep. South Africa	41	43.8	40.2	42.5	71	54.6
USA	9.5	25.8	26.5	14.8	12.6	17.3
Zimbabwe	7.9	9.8	9.5	47.3	40.2	64.6
Portugal	14.6	17.5	10.6	19.1	24.5	42.4
India	4.5	26.8	13.3	16.2	32	17.9
Japan	24.8	17.2	19.3	12.8	11.6	15.7
Others	35.6	37.5	68.2	56.8	44.5	112.4
Total	174.3	226	230.2	246.1	270.9	364

Source: INE (1996, 1999, 2000).

Human Development and Poverty Status

Mozambique is considered one of the poorest countries in the world. According to the United Nations Development Programme (UNDP) indicators, its Human Development Index (HDI) rating in 1998 was 0.341, putting it in 168th place in a list of 174 countries. Mozambique has the lowest HDI rating and the highest Human Poverty Index (HPI) rating in the SADC region. After the most recent update (2001) the UN HDI suggests that human development in Mozambique, in addition to being one of the worst, is declining. Thus, the international ranking of the country has worsened, after a slight recovery in previous years. Now Mozambique is categorized as the second poorest country in the world in terms of human development.

Aggregate and Sector Growth of Value-Added Output and Demand

Following almost two decades of failed economic development, Mozambique resumed growth in the early 1990s, thanks to the end of domestic and regional military conflicts and the pursuit (since the mid-1980s) of determined stabilization and structural adjustment policies. Thus, while in 1992 (the last year of war) the economy declined by 8.6 percent, in the subsequent years up to 2001, it has grown at an average annual rate of 8 percent. The year 2000 was a watershed year, as the economy was stricken by the worst floods of the century and growth faltered to less than 2 percent, implying a decline in real per capita GDP growth for the first time in the last 8–9 years (Table 2.2).

Most of this growth has come from the agricultural sector. It is estimated that during 1992–2001 the agricultural sector (including animal husbandry and forestry) has contributed, on average, 28 percent of value-added GDP (with a peak of 30.5 percent in 1996 and a low of 24.1 percent in 1992). Thus, its weighted contribution to aggregate value-added GDP during 1992–2001 is 2.4 percent, meaning that more than a quarter of the aggregate economic growth in Mozambique comes from the agricultural sector.

Table 2.2 1992 and Average (1993–2001) Sectoral Growth and Shares of Value-Added GDP

Items	Average Shares During 1992–2001	Average Growth During 1992–2001	Contribution to Total GDP Growth
Total gross domestic product	100.0	7.8	—
Total value added	99.6	7.9	7.91
Agriculture and forestry	28.2	8.5	2.39
Fishing	3.5	2.5	0.09
Mining	0.3	14.2	0.04
Manufacturing	10.3	14.1	1.45
Electricity and water	1.5	47.3	0.72
Construction	6.6	16.4	1.08
Commerce and repair services	23.6	4.4	1.03
Restaurants and hotels	0.9	11.5	0.10
Transports and communications	8.5	10.3	0.88
Financial services	3.6	5.5	0.20
Real State rentals	3.7	3.6	0.13
Public administration and defense	3.2	4.2	0.13
Education	1.4	7.8	0.11
Health	0.4	9.9	0.04
Other services	4.1	8.8	0.36
Import duties	2.2	1.4	0.03
Inputted financial intermediation services	−1.8	15.5	−0.3

Source: INE.

While this denotes a huge natural potential for development, it also points up the weaknesses and risks inherent in technologically backward agricultural activities, particularly when coupled with the vulnerability of the country to cyclical natural disasters. Thus, although producing only 28 percent of the value added GDP, the agriculture-based rural economy is source of income for 80 percent of the country's population, who make up the majority of the poorest and most vulnerable to hunger, endemic diseases, and failures of social delivery systems, and are out of reach of modern transportation and communication.

Among goods or commodity-producing sectors, the agriculture sector is followed in importance by the manufacturing and mining industries. However, because of its still low share in the economy, mining has made a relatively minor contribution to aggregate growth. On the other hand, during 1993–2001, manufacturing industry contributed 1.5 percent of the average aggregate value added GDP. Construction (1.1 percent), commerce and repair services (1.0 percent) also contributed to the average aggregate GDP value.

While representing a substantial share of total GDP, commerce and repair services are among the more slowly expanding sectors. This has critical implications for agricultural and rural development and poverty, as trade is a key service to link rural and urban economies that allow the movement of goods and services. Without such links with the industrial and final consumption sectors, agriculture faces constraints to the addition of value of its produce, further undermining the effort to reduce poverty and accelerate rural development.

It augurs well, however, that important infrastructure sectors such as electricity and water, construction, transportation and communications, as well as education and health, are expanding rapidly. It is expected that this, coupled with further structural reforms, should lower transaction costs more and allow the expansion of services into the countryside to support agriculture and rural development.

Despite the strong growth of the economy, there is still widespread poverty in Mozambique. Underlying the deterioration of the human development indicators and poverty there are various factors, including a steady and substantial trend away from private consumption. According to recent government and IMF data (IMF July 2002), the growth of private consumption in Mozambique has declined from 17.2 percent in 1996 to 4.6 percent in 1999 (Table 2.3). In 2000 and 2001 private consumption actually fell by 1.3 percent and 1.1 percent, respectively. While in the mid-1990s this trend was tilted in favor of public consumption, it has more recently been the basis for strong aggregate investment demand expenditures. This has increased its share of total demand GDP from an average of 21 percent

Table 2.3 Annual Changes in GDP by Demand
(percent)

Items	1996	1997	1998	1999	2000	2001
Private consumption	17.2	7.1	5.9	4.7	−1.3	−1.1
Public consumption	−6.3	21	21	9.7	17.4	−4.4
Total investment	−8.4	8.4	32.6	61.4	−9.5	10.3
Export of goods and nonfactor service	22.8	8.6	10.4	−1.4	30.9	65.2
Import of goods and nonfactor service	5	11.1	3.4	40.4	−3.1	−9.7
Gross domestic product	7.1	11.1	12.6	7.5	1.6	13.9
Deflators						
Private consumption	42.3	8.8	2.6	0.6	15.4	8.2
Public consumption	38.2	15.1	10.7	18.4	6.6	8.8
Investment	23.7	5.8	4.6	3.8	20.3	16.4
Export	20.1	4.3	−1.2	8.4	5.3	33.2
Import	26.6	4.4	−1.7	6.8	24.1	31.3
Gross domestic product	48.2	9.6	4.6	2.9	11.7	11.3

Source: IMF Statistical Appendix (July 2002).

in 1996–97 to 50 percent and 55 percent in 2000 and 2001, respectively. Government policy should ensure that this investment effort, which in recent years has been mostly toward mega-projects (in addition to infrastructure rehabilitation and expansion), reaches and helps to transform the agricultural production and marketing system on which the livelihood of most of the people depends. This also constitutes a substantial basis for the viability of the economy as it is still a source of most of its traditional exports (as well as, potentially, the nontraditional exports apart from the mega-project output).

Agricultural Production and Trade. Mozambique has high agriculture potential with 36 million hectares of arable land. Agricultural production is mainly represented by the family sector, with 2.5 million households cultivating 3.5 million hectares. There are small, medium, and large-scale commercial farmers.

The government program for 2000–2004 has identified agriculture as the basis for economic and social development. Mozambique's national agricultural policy objectives include food security, sustainable economic development, reduction of unemployment, and reduction of absolute poverty. Strategies designed to implement the agricultural policy include the sustainable use of natural resources, expansion of production capacity, improvement of productivity, and institutional and human resources development.

According to the national agriculture policy implementation strategy, quality improvement and the development of standards for products and production are among the main priorities.

Agricultural production of both food and export crops comes from the peasant family sector and small and medium commercial farms. The principal cash crops are cashew, sugarcane, tea, cotton, tobacco, and timber. Maize, rice, beans, groundnut, copra, sorghum, cassava, millet, and citrus are also among the more important products from agriculture. The total volume of food crops produced is higher than the total marketed, taking into account the amount that is kept for family consumption and

the amount of certain crops that is informally sold in neighboring countries. For example, maize is sold in Malawi and Zambia, rice in South Africa, and beans in Malawi.

Table 2.4 shows the evolution of the production of the primary marketed agricultural commodities, including export crops, basic food crops, and industrial inputs.[1] It becomes clear that marketed agricultural output of these commodities increased very rapidly up to 1998/99. In that year, the production of export crops and basic food crops was higher by 40 percent and 20 percent, respectively, than in 1996/97, while that of "industrial crops" remained stationary. The performance in the following year reflects the negative impact of the floods of 2000. Nonetheless, by 2000/01 all major crop groups had recovered strongly. The production of export crops in 2000/01 was higher by 72 percent than in 1996/97, while that of basic food crops was only 17 percent higher. The fastest growing subset in agricultural production since 1998/99 is that of "industrial inputs". In 2000/01, production of these commodities was more than ten times higher than its previous level, fueled by the recovery in the production of tobacco and sunflower.

In cases in which large companies are involved in the processing and trading of some primary commodity, for example, cotton, they provide farmers with materials, such as seeds, fertilizer and pesticides, and assure them a return on their crop.

Overall, agricultural production in Mozambique is recovering rapidly, particularly in regard to export crops and "industrial inputs". Food crop production does not seem to be recovering as fast, with the exception of beans and vegetables.

Factors hampering the steady recovery in production include lack of appropriate technology for small-scale producers who often lack farming materials and store their crops using local technology. This situation contributes to low yields, post-harvest losses, and low crop quality. Poor infrastructure, such as inadequate roads, grain stores, and warehouses affect agricultural output, reflected in high costs and frequent bottlenecks in the distribution of produce. Because natural disasters, floods, droughts, and cyclones destroy thousands of

---

[1] This classification is as given in IMF (July 2002). Note, however, that the distinction between "export crops" and "industrial inputs" is somewhat arbitrary and not accurate. Most export crops are industrial inputs and most agriculture-based industrial inputs are also exported.

Table 2.4 Mozambique Production of the Main Marketed Crops: 1996/97–2000/01

	Volume Indices					Three-year Average Volume Shares			Three-year Average Volume Growth	
	1996/97	1997/98	1998/99	1999/2000	2000/01	1996-99	1998-2000	1999-2001	1997-2000/ 1996-1999	1998-2001/ 1997-2000
Export crops	100.0	119.4	140.1	108.0	172.3	100.0	100.0	100.0	2.2	14.4
Cotton	100.0	123.0	144.2	43.6	105.1	44.2	38.6	35.1	-15.3	-5.7
Copra	100.0	101.1	124.7	123.6	179.8	10.6	11.6	13.6	7.2	22.5
Tea(leaf)	100.0	100.0	360.0	700.0	740.0	0.2	0.2	0.1	107.1	55.2
Sugarcane	100.0	132.2	168.3	142.4	352.6	8.2	9.3	13.6	10.6	49.7
Cashew nuts	100.0	119.4	135.6	119.9	134.2	32.7	35.6	32.8	5.6	3.9
Citrus	100.0	100.0	100.0	130.4	130.4	4.1	4.7	4.7	10.1	9.2
Basic food crops	100.0	103.2	121.5	103.0	117.6	100.0	100.0	100.0	0.9	4.4
Maize	100.0	105.4	118.7	97.1	112.2	38.1	37.5	36.8	-0.9	2.1
Rice	100.0	107.2	116.1	94.4	111.2	9.4	7.7	6.2	-1.7	1.3
Sorghum	100.0	93.2	129.5	100.0	125.0	1.0	1.0	1.0	0.0	9.9
Cassava	100.0	98.3	110.1	106.4	125.2	8.5	10.0	11.7	2.1	8.6
Peanuts	100.0	101.7	112.8	88.0	84.6	10.5	10.1	9.5	-3.8	-5.6
Beans	100.0	101.6	151.3	117.3	132.9	17.9	18.3	19.1	4.9	8.5
Vegetables	100.0	101.0	102.0	109.0	132.4	11.2	11.8	12.8	3.0	10.1
Onions	100.0	100.0	100.0	105.9	31.8	3.4	3.6	2.9	2.0	22.3
Industrial inputs	100.0	101.4	100.3	366.5	932.2	100.0	100.0	100.0	88.3	146.2
Sisal	100.0	100.0	100.0	0.0	0.0	2.0	1.0	0.3	-33.3	-50.0
Tobacco	100.0	100.0	100.0	600.0	1214.3	17.0	36.3	55.1	166.7	139.3
Maffura	100.0	214.3	100.0	42.9	71.4	0.9	0.5	0.1	-13.8	-40.0
Tomatoes	100.0	100.0	100.0	101.6	105.7	77.5	60.5	39.2	0.5	1.9
Sunflowers	100.0	100.0	120.0	80.0	1280.0	2.7	1.8	5.3	-6.3	393.3

Source: IMF Statistical Appendix (July 2002).

hectares of crops and stored food in the affected areas, the development and operation of an efficient early warning system and disaster management and mitigation system is a critical component of the agricultural development effort.

Some programs under way are aimed at improving the existing infrastructure and creating new infrastructure. The construction and rehabilitation programs for tertiary roads (third phase) and the Food Fund of World Food Programme (WFP), should be mentioned, in addition to research and extension projects in rural areas.

The main early warning structure is the Early Warning Department in MADER, which gathers information and publishes bulletins three times a month on the agro-meteorological situation, food balance sheets, crop areas planted, lost and harvested yields and projected production, and analyses of vulnerability and food security. Since its creation, this department has received funding from FAO, as well as from the state budget. The service currently relies on state funds, and the budget allocation in 2000 was less than half of its requirements. MADER has submitted a new funding proposal to FAO. Other systems for food security early warning include Famine Early Warning System (FEWS)—USAID; SIMA—Agricultural Markets Information Systems; Vulnerability Assessment and Mapping (VAM)—WFP; RESAL-EU; and the Market Management Assistance project (FAO and EU) in the MIC/National Directorate of Internal Trade. The MSF–CIS–Doctors Without Borders—Consolidated Information System currently assists MADER.

These developments have major implications for the issues of standards and quality. In particular, quality is not a determining factor in the marketing of products on the internal market, partly because of the levels of poverty and the need to satisfy basic requirements and partly because of lack of awareness. On the other hand, although traditional export products are well known and their market is secure, some appear to command lower foreign prices than would otherwise be the case, apparently because of poor quality. This has a negative impact on the income-generating potential of these crops for the farmers who grow them.

The Office for the Promotion of Commercial Farming in the Ministry of Agriculture and Rural Development (GPSCA) conducted a study to evaluate a group of preidentified agricultural products

with potential for generating a viable and promising rural agroindustry and exploring mechanisms to promote them (GPSCA 2002a).

One of the premises of this study was the assumption that small and medium rural agroindustries could supply semiprocessed raw materials to larger agroindustries, supplying and diversifying the local consumer and foreign market.

The study was based on the following products: maize, cassava, sweet potato, rice, cashew (especially the cashew apple), beans, fruit trees (particularly coconut palms), and oilseeds. Special attention was given to the following provinces: Cabo Delgado, Nampula, Niassa, Zambezia, Sofala, and Inhambane (GPSCA 2002b, Muendane, C. 2002).

This study identified 14 business plans (GPSCA 2002c), namely,

- Desiccated coconut factories to be installed in Zambezia and Inhambane;
- Production and promotion of charcoal from coconut husks in Zambezia and Inhambane;
- Products from coconut husks in Zambezia and Inhambane;
- Cashew apple spirit in Nampula, Zambezia, and Inhambane;
- Cashew processing in Nampula, Sofala, Zambezia, Inhambane, and Cabo Delgado (medium scale);
- Cashew processing in Nampula, Sofala, Zambezia, Inhambane, and Cabo Delgado (small scale);
- Dried fruit in Zambezia, Inhambane, and Sofala;
- Preparation of tangerine for export in Inhambane;
- Maize mills in Niassa and Zambezia;
- Packaging and export of pulses in Niassa;
- Processing of pigeon pea for export in Zambezia, Niassa, Nampula, and Cabo Delgado;
- Rice husking in Zambézia, Sofala, and Nampula;
- Processing of sunflower seed in Sofala, Zambezia, Niassa, Nampula, and Cabo Delgado; and
- Extraction of castor oil in Nampula and Cabo Delgado.

The study further concluded that some agricultural products (such as coconut, beans, banana, and tangerines) from the selected provinces could be sold on the local market and exported—as long as the products were cleaned, picked, and packaged—because there are external markets interested in these products. Some of these and other products could also be transformed into new products by using new technologies, as in the case of charcoal

Table 2.5 Production of Meat and Meat Products, Milk and Dairy Products, Eggs, and Animal Feed

	1995	1996	1997	1998	1999	2000
Cattle meat (ton)	877.5	843.7	1,012.6	1,140.4	1,350.4	1,554
Pork meat (ton)	300.5	297.1	300.6	295.9	331.5	250.4
Ruminants (ton)	90.1	94.2	110.3	209.9	264.1	302.2
Poultry meat (ton)	3,731.0	5,965.2	5,090.1	4,622.9	5,215.5	4,506.1
Milk (1000 liter)	953.9	880.7	931.6	743.9	1,000.9	1,302.9
Eggs (dozen)	603,407	362,272	854,306	429,197	548,237	299,127
Animal feed (ton)	7,290.0	23,053.1	26,472.7	23,515.5	21,608.3	24,936.9
Sausages (kg)		762.5	3,957.8	41,000.0	29,535.0	49,313.7
Fresh milk pasteurized (liter)	32,084	37,457	2,082,943	446,849	1,602,862	0
Condensed sweetened milk (ton)	0	0	1,777	1,786	1,840	1,712
Reconstituted milk (liter)	0	801	1,068,000	1,270,042	2,387,573	1,920,233
Flavored milk (liter)	0	0	0	0	353,787	456,939
Yogurt (liter)	20,136	48,692	27,509	31,767	472,572	292,283
Ice cream (kg)	0	0	0	623	154,250	42,220
Chocomilk (liter)	0	0	0	299,488	176,096	98,611
Butter (kg)	0	1,980	700	0	178,210	2,880
Cheese (kg)	0	1,825	1,200	17,517	83,330	19,540

Source: DINAP/MADER, 2000 report.

made from coconut husks and dahl made from pigeon pea. However, the study regarded most of these agroindustries as viable only if developed by self-financing entrepreneurs who already own infrastructure.

Livestock Production. Livestock production in Mozambique is characterized by rising numbers, except for pigs (owing to African swine fever) according to the annual report of the National Directorate of Livestock (DINAP) in 2000. Livestock promotion, particularly in the smallholder family sector, has contributed to this increase, despite the floods that killed many animals. The livestock census of 2000 showed 519,778 head of cattle compared to 292,826 in 1995; 1,655 dairy cows compared to 1,753 in 1995; 758,011 goats compared to 392,781 in 1995; and 188,462 pigs compared to 203,750 in 1995 (DINAP 2000).

The production of meat totaled 1,554 tons of beef, 250.4 tons of pork, 302.2 tons of mutton and goat, and 4,506 tons of chicken. This production represents an increase of 15 percent in beef, goat, and mutton, and a decrease of 13 percent and 24 percent in chicken and pork, respectively, compared to the output in 1999. Production of milk

and eggs remained very low in 2000—1,303.000 liters and 299,127 dozen, respectively, representing 30 percent and 45 percent of production in 1995 (Table 2.5).

With regard to animal health, there were outbreaks of foot and mouth disease in neighboring countries, but the disease was not found in Mozambique because of vaccination campaigns along the borders and the introduction of geographical information systems (GIS). When diseases are detected, the animal health authorities prohibit cross-border trade of the infected species (live animals, meat, or other products) in coordination with other national and regional authorities.

Beef, pork, mutton, chicken, turkey, fish, milk and dairy products, eggs, animal feeds, and their components were imported in 2000 (DINAP 2000).

Agroindustrial and Industrial Food Production. The agroindustry represented 18–29 percent of GDP during 1975–85. The main products of the food industry are beverages (notably beer and soft drinks), wheat flour and goods manufactured from wheat flour, brown sugar, vegetable oils, and soap. Other processed products are maize meal, condensed milk, liquid milk, and other dairy products.

Data for 1999 show that beer production is the largest food industry (74 × 106 liters), followed by wheat milling (114 × 103 tons), soft drinks (50 × 106 liters), raw sugar (42 × 103 tons) and oil products (15 × 103 tons) (MIC 2000).

The milk processing industry includes the production of fresh pasteurized milk (1,603,862 liters), condensed milk (1,840 tons), reconstituted milk (2,387,573 liters), flavored milk (472,572 liters), ice cream (154,250 tons), chocolate milk (176,096 liters), butter (178 tons), and cheese (983 tons). These figures show an increase in production in all products, compared to output in the last five years (DINAP 2000).

Most of the existing plants in the agroindustrial sector require rehabilitation. The factories located in the rural areas, such as the cotton ginneries, the sugar and tea factories, the rice husking plants, and the sawmills, were severely damaged during the war that ended in 1992.

Domestic production faces high costs because of such factors as high interest rates, customs tariffs, transport costs, and so on, and has to compete with lower priced imported products. The imported products are often smuggled into the country and some pose a threat to public health.

Some of the constraints in this sector are:

- obsolete technology and equipment;
- lack of skilled labor;
- inadequate fiscal and customs policies;
- lack of incentives to industry;
- poor state of roads, means of transportation and storage facilities;
- high prices and difficulty in acquiring quality packaging on the local market;
- inadequate procedures and lack of standards and technical regulations that allow improvements in the quality of production; and
- low quality and/or high costs of raw materials.

Foreign Trade and International Financial Relations

Table 2.6 shows the balance of payments of Mozambique. The overall balance of trade in goods has improved substantially in recent years, with the deficit declining from US$572.2 in 1998 to US$413.8 million in 2001. However, this improvement is mainly because of the exports of MOZAL (the aluminum smelter plant in Maputo). Without MOZAL exports, it shows a decline.

Services have traditionally been an important component of Mozambique's external trade. Until the early 1980s, Mozambique enjoyed a positive balance of trade in services (US$96.0 and US$56.0 million in 1980 and 1981, respectively). In 1980 transport revenue alone more than covered all external expenditure in tradeable services (including interest payments). By contrast, in 2001 the country had a severe imbalance in this category of trade, with a deficit of US$213.5 and US$363.1 million in 2000 and 2001, respectively. In those years, transport receipts could cover only 24.0 percent and 21.0 percent of total expenditures in foreign tradeable services excluding interest payments.

The deterioration of the balance of trade in services during the 1970s and the early 1980s was part of the overall economic decline as the command regime faltered and the civil war worsened. Nonetheless, beginning in the mid-1980s with the signing of the Nkomati Agreement that aimed at cooling tensions between Mozambique and the apartheid regime in South Africa, and as Zimbabwe became independent and the mandatory sanctions were lifted, the use of transport services started a slow but steady recovery. This was interrupted in the mid-1990s, but has more recently resumed strong growth. This has, however, been highly changeable, in large part because of problems affecting the neighboring countries using the services. In net terms, trade in transport services continues to improve while income from labor services declines.

The other traditional source of external income, namely workers' remittances, has not recovered as much. After showing significant instability over the years, receipts have declined in value since 1998, while payments increased sharply (certainly reflecting an outflow of resources through foreign technical assistance). In net terms, workers' remittances have fallen from an average surplus of US$35.0 million during the first half of the 1990s up to 1997, to a deficit of US$2.3 million in 2001.

Capital account transactions in Mozambique are simultaneously encouraged or restricted by law and policy depending on their nature. Nonetheless, financial liberalization and entry of foreign financial institutions appear to have substantially eroded the power of the controls, particularly of private capital (short, medium, and long term).

Foreign direct investment is encouraged and receives substantial fiscal incentives (border and

Table 2.6 Balance of Payments, 1980–2001: Five-Year Averages (1980–99) and Annual (1997–2001)

Description	1980–84	1985–89	1990–94	1995–99	1997	1998	1999	2000	2001
Trade balance	−519.0	−538.2	−779.0	−625.6	−530.0	−572.7	−916.0	−798.3	−413.8
Exports (f.o.b.)	203.6	92.1	141.9	231.8	230.0	244.6	283.8	364.0	703.7
Imports (c.i.f.)	722.7	630.3	920.9	857.3	760.0	817.3	1199.8	1162.3	1117.5
Service balance	−12.4	−129.4	−128.9	−140.0	−80.6	−171.7	−236.1	−213.5	−363.1
Receipts	159.3	137.3	216.9	327.2	342.3	332.5	355.5	405.1	349.0
Transportation	71.8	42.8	67.6	65.9	62.8	58.3	99.3	97.6	55.7
Workers remittances	61.9	58.3	59.7	53.6	63.6	46.3	38.0	36.8	29.9
Other receipts	25.6	36.2	89.6	207.7	215.9	227.9	218.2	270.7	263.4
Expenditure	171.7	266.7	345.8	467.2	422.9	504.2	591.6	618.6	712.1
Interest payment	54.3	141.3	157.5	159.8	147.3	158.7	197.7	204.7	224.7
Transportation	27.7	37.1	47.6	32.1	30.2	33.4	28.4	45.9	40.4
Workers remittances	24.8	25.2	24.5	24.3	22.9	31.1	31.3	35.5	32.2
Investment services	0.0	39.4	53.5	61.4	75.2	67.6	16.8	24.3	15.6
Other	64.8	23.8	62.8	189.6	147.3	213.4	311.6	307.9	378.9
Other services			88.3	97.8	65.4	119.3	96.4	108.2	105.7
Current account without unrequited transfers	−531.4	−667.7	−907.9	−765.6	−610.6	−744.4	−1152.1	−1011.8	−776.9
Unrequited official transfers	90.0	284.1	503.5	324.8	312.9	313.2	434.0	563.9	469.3
Private Transfers		32.6	115.5						
Current account with unrequited transfers	−441.4	−351.0	−288.9	−440.8	−297.7	−431.2	−718.1	−447.9	−307.6
Current account without unrequited transfers	−531.4	−667.7	−907.9	−765.6	−610.6	−744.4	1152.1	−1011.8	776.9
Unrequited official transfers	90.0	284.1	503.5	324.8	312.9	313.2	434.0	563.9	469.3
Private Transfers		32.6	115.5						
Current account with unrequited transfers	−441.4	−351.0	−288.9	−440.8	−297.7	−431.2	−718.1	−447.9	−307.6
Capital Account	414.7	−67.5	−110.9	268.5	179.7	287.7	582.4	150.7	1.2
Short term (Net)	187.0	2.0	0.0	−1.2	0.0	25.0	−31.0	−128.4	1.3

(continued)

Table 2.6 Continued

Description	1980–84	1985–89	1990–94	1995–99	1997	1998	1999	2000	2001
Medium and long term (Net)	227.7	−72.7	−135.7	114.4	115.3	50.0	231.7	139.9	−182.6
Loan receipts (Inflow)	510.0	265.6	202.2	343.5	316.3	299.5	472.0	483.9	209.7
Loan repayment (Outflow)	282.3	338.3	338.0	229.1	201.0	249.5	240.3	344.0	392.3
Direct investment	0.0	3.1	24.8	155.3	64.4	212.7	381.7	139.2	182.5
Errors and Omissions	−21.4	17.9	−248.9	0.8	20.4	−60.9	−100.3	−54.1	−112.3
Overall Balance	−192.7	−410.8	−396.8	−172.6	−97.6	−204.4	−236.0	−351.3	−418.7
Financing	192.7	410.8	396.9	172.6	97.6	204.4	235.9	351.3	418.7
Changes in foreign reserves and other liabilities (Net; increase −)	46.4	−16.7	−24.3	−98.1	−148.1	−77.2	−46.9	−98.0	−6.8
Net change in Arrears (+increase)	−2.5	1.4	33.5	−908.7	−3932.2	20.4	−761.5	0.0	0.0
Debt Relief	148.7	426.1	387.7	1179.4	4177.9	261.2	1044.3	449.3	425.5
Memo:									
Net Transport Receipts	44.1	5.7	20.0	33.8	32.6	24.9	70.9	51.7	15.3
Net Workers' Remittances	37.2	33.2	35.2	29.3	40.7	15.2	6.7	1.3	−2.3
Net Travel	—	—	—	—	—	−20.6	−33.2	−72.8	−33.4
Net Other services	−39.2	12.3	26.8	18.1	68.6	14.5	−93.4	−37.2	−115.5
Net Interest	−54.3	−141.3	−157.5	−150.8	−147.3	−133.8	−177.9	−162.2	−169.5

Source: Statistical Bulletin, DEE/Banco de Moçambique, Various issues (1996–2002); IMF Country Report No. 02/139 (July 2002): Statistical Appendix.

nonborder). This type of investment increased from an annual average of US$3.1 million in the five-year period 1985–89 to US$24.8 million in 1990–95. This then increased more than fivefold in 1995–99. During the last five-years, foreign direct investment (FDI) in Mozambique averaged US$200.0 million per year, with a high in 1999 of more than US$380.0 million, then falling to US$182.0 in 2001. Most of this was related to megaprojects, in particular MOZAL.

Unlike the steady growth of FDI, medium- and long-term borrowing has been very erratic. Net long- and medium-term outflows averaged US$72.7 million and US$135.7 million per year between 1985–89 and 1990–94, respectively. This was reversed between 1995 and 1999, when net inflows reached an average of US$114.4 million per year. However, this was only US$50.0 million in 1998. In 2000 net inflows were only 60 percent of the level in 1999, and in 2001 the country experienced a long- and medium-term net outflow of US$182.6 million. Compared to 1999 (and after experiencing a slight improvement in 2000), loan receipts in 2001 more than halved, while payments increased by more than 60 percent.

Net short-term capital flows became substantial in the late 1990s. They represented the principal form of external portfolio adjustment in 1999 and 2000, with outflows totaling US$31.0 million and US$128.4 million, respectively. This suggests that as the Mozambique financial system became more liberalized and open to foreign entry, capital account controls may have become increasingly ineffective.

During 1999–2001, long- and medium-term foreign borrowing, excluding that which was not related to big projects such as MOZAL, fell to around 50 percent of its level in 1997–98.

The country's development potential, its location as a gateway to the other countries of SADC, agreements facilitating trade, and incentives for foreign investment make Mozambique an attractive proposition for foreign investors.

In recent years, industry, agriculture, and tourism have been the sectors with the highest volumes of investment.

The Investment Promotion Centre (CPI), was established in 1984. CPI offers comprehensive service in support of foreign investors wishing to invest anywhere in the country.

Earlier, FDI came from South Africa, Britain, and Portugal, but now France, the Netherlands, China,

the United States, Mauritius, Spain, and Italy all appear on the lists of investors. Investments in food and beverages, such as Coca-Cola, beer, milk, and dairy products account for some of the foreign investment. Another example of recent foreign investment is in the Mozambican mobile phone service.

The role of South Africa and Britain as sources of investment increased because of their participation in MOZAL, an aluminum smelting company. MOZAL has annual production capacity of 250,000 tons of primary aluminum. The main shareholders in MOZAL are Billiton (Gencor), the Industrial Development Corporation (IDC) of South Africa, Mitsubishi, and the Mozambican government. MOZAL has been responsible for investing in such infrastructure as water and electricity supplies and a new wharf in the port of Matola. This project has served to attract other small- and medium-size projects to Mozambique.

Mozambican firms, mainly in construction and engineering, have been heavily influenced by the MOZAL project, which demanded higher quality of products and services than were not normally expected in Mozambique at that time. For example, the Mozambican cement company, Cimentos de Moçambique, saw the need to speed up certification of its products, making cement the first nationally certified product. A linkage program was begun in which 25 suppliers of the company were identified and given assistance to improve their quality.

The other main upcoming projects include the Temane and Pande Natural Gas Project, the Maputo Iron and Steel Project, the Corridor Sands Project, and the Mepanda Uncua Dam on the Zambezi River.

National policy is generally favorable to the development of the transport sector. In addition to the SADC Protocol on Transport, Communications, and Meteorology, Mozambique has bilateral transport agreements with neighboring countries. The most important feature of the agreements is the establishment of transport systems that offer efficient, economical, and fully integrated infrastructures and operations.

The most important surface transport system is the railway, which carries 77 percent of all freight (mainly working in the corridors linking to a neighboring country, not linking the north to the south of the country), followed by the road system with

13 percent and the maritime system with 10 percent. Growth in freight transport has been erratic during the past five years (1995–99), and is heavily influenced by events in neighboring countries.

Public Finance and Fiscal Policies

The tax system in Mozambique includes direct taxes levied on producers, indirect taxes levied on traders and consumers, and customs duties levied on the importers of goods and services. The direct taxes are corporation tax that is levied on the firm's profits at 35 percent (Decree 68/98), complementary tax that is levied on other values and dividends, and income tax that is levied on workers at rates of up to 30 percent (Decree 3/87). Indirect taxation consists of valued added tax (VAT) of 17 percent and consumption tax, from which all cereals and their by-products are exempt. Transport services provided inside the country are subject to VAT, while transport services to destinations outside the country and international transporters are exempt from VAT. The rate of customs duties is variable. For example, it is 2.5 percent on maize imports plus 1 percent for customs services levies. Maize exports are not taxed (Decree 30/99). The tax system increases the prices of agricultural and industrial products, to the detriment of domestic products that ends up with higher prices than imported products.

National Programs and Policies

The main objective of the national programs and policies is the reduction of the level of absolute poverty.

The government program for 2000–04, as well as the programs and policies in agriculture, industry, and trade refer to the need to increase the quality of domestic production and to assure consumer protection through the development and application of appropriate standards and technical regulations.

The promotion of agriculture and the resulting agroindustrial development are priorities on the various industrial and agricultural programs and policies. The promotion and diversification of exports and the reduction of imports are reflected in the commercial strategy and policy.

The industrial and commercial policies consider the importance of developing the national quality system according to international rules.

The development and implementation of the several programs and policies have had the support of donors and international development agencies. It is noticeable, however, that even though quality and standardization issues are reflected in several documents, these are not yet the subject of appropriate development programs, neither at government nor donor levels. This situation is related to low production levels, and the main priority of most interventions is the creation of conditions to increase production and lower costs.

To demonstrate the context of this study, we now present the programs and policies directly related to the topic under discussion. The details relating to agricultural and commercial policies are dealt with in the sections that specifically concern these subjects.

The Government Program for 2000–04. The government has identified agriculture as the basis of economic and social development, with industry as one of the determining factors for economic growth. With regard to science and technology, priority has been given to the development of a system for the generation and dissemination of science and technology not only as an input to teaching curricula, but also to finding solutions to the problems facing the country.

Government policy aims at achieving sustainable agriculture in order to reach five specific objectives: (a) poverty alleviation, (b) self reliance and security in basic foodstuffs, (c) supply of raw materials to domestic industry, (d) development of the cooperative and private smallholder family sector and the creation of jobs, and (e) improvement in the balance of payments.

The government specified the objectives in the development of industry as: (a) promoting the addition of value to agricultural, livestock, forestry, mineral, and energy products, (b) reduction in foreign trade imbalances, (c) increasing the supply of essential consumer goods to the population, and (d) helping to increase the supply of jobs. The programs further establish that industrial development should be associated with an improvement in the quality of products to make them competitive in foreign markets.

Assuming that trade is fundamental to the relationship between the urban and the rural economy, and between Mozambique and other countries, the activities to be undertaken are aimed at increasing agricultural and industrial production oriented toward internal supply, increasing exports and reducing imports, the diversification of domestic industry, the promotion of new industry and the development of small and micro firms. The development of appropriate standards and technical regulations that will promote consumer, health and protection of the environment, is one of the priorities.

The development of science and technology should be sustained by the expansion and improvement of education, with the aim of nurturing a scientific culture in society and a mentality directed toward development, direct participation in production, and the dissemination and utilization of knowledge.

Government Strategy and Plan of Action for Poverty Reduction in Mozambique. Eradicating poverty is a high priority for Mozambique's government. The first attempt to define specific policies resulted in the Poverty Reduction Strategy for Mozambique (1995). In 2000 the government approved its Plan of Action for the Reduction of Absolute Poverty (2001–05)—PARPA.

The PARPA is a medium-term programming tool in the public planning system related to the strategy and plan of action for the reduction of absolute poverty and the promotion of economic growth in Mozambique. Its preparation included consultations involving sectors active in the planning and programming process at central and district levels. This methodology has also been used to formulate government policies and strategies and to make them operational, such as the Economic and Social Plan (PES), Integrated Sector Programmes (PSI), Mid-Term Fiscal Scenario (CFMP) and the Three-year Public Investment Programme (PTIP).

The objective of PARPA 2001–05 is substantial reduction in the levels of absolute poverty in Mozambique, through measures to improve the skills and opportunities of all Mozambicans and the poor in particular. The specific objective is to reduce the incidence of absolute poverty from 70 percent in 1977 to below 60 percent in 2005 and less than 50 percent by the end of the decade.

With more than 70 percent of the population living in the rural areas and a greater proportion depending on agriculture for their livelihood, agricultural and rural development are obvious priorities in the poverty reduction strategy. Agriculture

accounts for 30 percent of the GDP, with the largest contribution from the family smallholder sector that includes more than three million households.

The main aim of rural development is to increase income-generating opportunities, particularly for the family smallholder sector, through the development of human capital and infrastructure. Agricultural extension programs will support the expansion of agricultural production. The policy of food security is fundamental for the implementation of PARPA.

PARPA also places a high priority on agroindustries and other types of manufacturing with labor-intensive processes directed toward exports. This should expand the market for agricultural products, and thus investment and jobs in agriculture and processing industries. Assuming that adequate macroeconomic and financial policies will create a suitable environment for private investment, development in these areas will require human resources and basic infrastructure services.

Financial services must be suitable to meet the needs of small producers. Simplification of legislation and administrative procedures will be undertaken. Good governance will be necessary to facilitate private initiative and investment.

Industrial Policy and Strategy. The objectives of the industrial policy and strategy approved in August 1997 (Resolution No. 23/97) are to support the process of adding value to natural resources, to help improve the balance of trade, to work to meet basic needs, and to promote the development of labor-intensive technologies to implement the government's program for 2000–04.

The food and agroindustries are the first priority in industrial policy, since they represent half of the value of industrial production in the country, and because of their export potential and the fact that they produce basic consumer goods.

The most important branches of industry are those that supply the internal and export markets, such as sugar and cotton; the export market, such as cashew nuts, copra, and tea; and those producing import substitutes, such as cereals, fruits, vegetables, beverages, mineral water, meat, and meat by-products.

Textile clothing and footwear industries are also among the priorities as they have a traditional position and weight within industry, employing a large number of people.

The industrial policy and strategy define the guiding principles of industrial development related to the role of the state and of the private sector, the reorganization of the business sector, the rehabilitation and modernization of industrial plants, the development of micro-, small- and medium-size firms, the role of the informal sector, the geographical decentralization of industry, the conservation of the environment, and regional integration.

Mozambique's industrial development strategy indicates the principal vectors that will contribute to the implementation of industrial policy. One of the main guidelines for the strategy is the promotion of quality to ensure the competitiveness of national production of goods and services both for internal and external markets.

The strategy refers, in particular, to the need to strengthen the National Institute for Standardization and Quality, under the Ministry of Industry and Commerce (INNOQ) and to develop a national quality system including the development of standards, the strengthening of laboratories, and metrology and accreditation activities.

Implications for Issues of Standards and Quality

The analyses of the data presented throughout this section show that Mozambique is a country with large agricultural and agroindustrial development capacities, with 70 percent of its population living in rural areas. However, in general, agricultural production is not enough for domestic consumption, and exports are based on traditionally exported products. Quality is not yet perceived by the private sector as a priority, as a facilitator to external market access.

It has been noticed, however, that in urban centers consumer awareness has increased, and the first consumer protection associations have been created in recent years and have been applying some pressure toward the improvement of product and service quality. By contrast, the economic environment has a tendency to change and the development of mega-projects associated with the application of the SADC Trade Protocol, has resulted in some companies becoming concerned with quality-related issues.

Therefore, the situation is changing, and issues related with quality improvement will become indispensable mechanisms for increasing competitiveness and access to markets, either from consumer pressure, or from the perspective of placing national products on external markets.

Provision of Development Assistance

Some projects with a foreign assistance component have been implemented and others are being executed that have an impact on the development of standardization and quality in the country. However, the assistance given until now did not focus on the development of the quality infrastructures, and so the support given to the private sector to improve quality is not matched with support to infrastructure development, as needed. Thus the new investments have to contract foreign services (for example, testing and calibration) sometimes at very high cost.

It has also been found that coordination among donors is not very efficient, as is the case among the institutions receiving support. The next section discusses some of the projects that relate to standards and quality improvement.

SIDA Agreement—Assistance to INNOQ

Between 1997 and 1999, SIDA supported INNOQ in its efforts to become a competent and sustainable institution and a new program to support quality infrastructure development was considered. A consortium composed of the Portuguese Institute for Quality (IPQ) and Resource, a Crown Agents subsidiary company, was the executing agency for the SIDA assistance. The project focused on Standards Development, Quality Systems for Companies, Standards and Quality Awareness, Information Services and Publications, Subscription Schemes and Management Systems.

This was the only foreign assistance project to Mozambique that had a specific component on standards, and it was developed with INNOQ. Its activities were completed successfully. The program included the following principal components: nine training courses with 580 participants, including technicians, representing state firms and institutions, and teaching and research institutions; awareness-raising activities involving some 400 participants; assistance to six firms to develop quality systems; strengthening of standardization activities through training for members of the technical committees; strengthening of the INNOQ documentation center and improvement of the INNOQ financial management system (SIDA 2000. Final Report. Assistance to the National Institute of Standardization and Quality).

However, there were some difficulties because human resources and physical infrastructure were not part of the project.

Following the previous project, a five-year program has been designed (National Quality System Objectives—Next Steps). This program has the following objectives:

- to create a sound legislative basis for Mozambique's standardization and certification systems;
- to develop programs and activities in support of these systems;
- to establish a quality control system through the integration of existing facilities;
- to provide basic training and upgrading of local staff in the field of standardization and quality assurance;
- to develop a national accreditation system within a network of other nationally recognized systems;
- to develop and implement a National Metrology Centre;
- to develop standards information and training centers to support the activities mentioned above.

This program will seek to develop and deliver the following:

- a stronger legislative framework;
- quality awareness in industry;
- implementation of quality management systems and certification;
- program of standards development/adoption;
- development of a standards-related business information center;
- development of a quality-related management training center;
- establishment of a National Focal Point for Accreditation;
- development of a national metrology center.

Based on the above-mentioned program, a strategic plan for quality has been developed. This plan, whose main objective is the improvement of the quality infrastructure, is estimated to cost US$12 million.

INNOQ is currently developing its quality policy with the participation of the main stakeholders in the country, SIDA and UNIDO.

Enterprise Development Project (PODE)

PODE is an enterprise development project that aims to increase private sector participation in economic growth. Its main objectives are to improve private company access to, and use of, external services, thereby encouraging competition; to facilitate access to finance; to increase possibilities for training, advice, capacity building and links with investors and buyers; and to build capacity in the Ministry of Industry and Commerce, the Investment Promotion Centre, and business and economic associations (PODE 2001. Project Brochure).

PODE has four components: the Technical Training Component (CAT), which has three subcomponents—the Business Competitiveness Office (GCE), the Training and Advice Office (GFA), and the Links Programme Office (GPL); the Finance Component; the Capacity Building Component; and the Social Component.

PODE provides technical assistance to businesses and offers training programs in financial and technical management. Under PODE some training has taken place and support has been given to enterprises in the development of their quality systems. For instance, PODE supported some companies that are suppliers of MOZAL to enable them to improve the quality of their goods and services.

UNIDO-Integrated Industrial Development Programme

The program aims at providing support to the government for the attainment of the country's industrial policy objectives and in facilitating private sector development. In this context, the program focuses on activities which (a) strengthen the capacity and capabilities of the public and private sectors for effective policy development and implementation, as well as in establishing strategic alliances between the two sectors; (b) reduce the regional imbalance of industry through the development of adequate institutional support services for SME; (c) promote investment and technology services for SME development, and (d) strengthen the capacity and capabilities for cleaner industrial production and effective urban waste management, quality management, and continuous performance improvement of industrial enterprises.

Institutions that are to be supported are SME support institutions, investment and technology institutions, environmental institutions, and quality management or standards institutions. At the sector level, the emphasis will be on food processing through the introduction of pilot demonstration plants or common production facilities, with corresponding training and entrepreneurship development programs (UNIDO 1999).

Under this program the following projects related to standards were developed:

- The "National Cleaner Production Centre" that provides environmental consultancy services to Mozambican enterprises to reduce pollution and increase productivity;
- The establishment of a Business Advisory Centre (CADI) in the AIMO (The Mozambican Industrial Association) building with INNOQ as one of the partners;
- Support to the development of the quality policy;
- Support to install a pilot laboratory on metrology under an SADCMET project (also financed by PTB, NML, and SABS and coordinated by the regional coordinator of SADCMET); and
- A food processing and safety development program providing technical and managerial support services to increase competitiveness and to establish a viable technical and entrepreneurial base.

As a result of this program, a proposal for "Assistance for a Food Action Plan for Improved Processing and Food Safety" was designed. The immediate work program proposed in the "Final Technical Report" includes (UNIDO 2001b):

- Establishing and strengthening national food control systems;
- Setting up a national food processing training center;
- Conducting workshops, seminars, and training courses;
- Strengthening laboratory analysis and food inspection capabilities;
- Providing training in all aspects of food control;
- Developing and publishing training manuals and texts;

- Helping with the establishment and strengthening of food control agencies; and
- Setting up a food safety inspection service.

UNIDO and the Ministry of Industry and Trade submitted the terms of reference for the implementation for funding.

National Agricultural Development Programme—(PROAGRI)

A five-year National Agricultural Development Programme (PROAGRI) was launched in 1998, with financial support from international organizations and governments. Its main goal was to ensure that public investment made in the agricultural sector was planned and implemented more efficiently. It was also intended to ensure that the mechanisms decided by the Ministry of Planning and Finance (MPF), for improved monitoring and evaluation of public expenditure, were effective, transparent, and well coordinated with donor procedures. The Agriculture Policy and the respective implementation strategies were drafted and approved before PROAGRI began (Programa Nacional de Desenvolvimento Agrário 1998a, 2003).

PROAGRI'S immediate objective is to establish the institutional mechanisms for funding and providing agricultural services to the family sector, and creating capacity in the Ministry of Agriculture and Rural Development (MADER) so that it can provide effective and efficient public services in three main areas—institutional reform; strengthening the capacity of, and developing, production support services; and sustainable natural resource management. The program operates on the basis of a set of fundamental principles, namely to contribute to poverty reduction; decentralize MADER functions; implement activities related to key functions; implement principles of good governance; give attention to crop producers' access to land, inputs, and markets; and take into account questions of gender, social and environmental sustainability.

The program has eight components: institutional development, agricultural research, extension, support for agricultural production, livestock, agricultural land, forests and wildlife, and irrigation. Each component has an action plan with targets, which is also based on specific basic principles (PROAGRI 2002).

Since it began, PROAGRI has been analyzed and reviewed both by MADER and with the donors, looking at basic principles, actions to be taken and the allocation of funding. Some components of PROAGRI include activities that relate to the development of standards, technical regulations, and codes of practice.

Trade Performance and Outlook

The country has taken various steps to promote and encourage exports. This activity is part of:

- The government's 2000–04 five-year Program, approved by Resolution No. 4/2000 of 22 March, which establishes that "in relation to foreign trade, one of the priority activities is to win and consolidate new markets for export products, with emphasis on nontraditional products, through better knowledge of foreign markets and the quality of the products" and
- The Trade Policy and Strategy, approved by the Council of Ministers in Resolution No. 25/98 of 1 July, that establishes the increase and diversification of exports, particularly nontraditional products and winning new markets for exports as priorities in foreign trade.

The Ministry of Industry and Trade is the body responsible for trade policy. The ministry relies on the National Directorate of Trade and the Export Promotion Institute (IPEX) to put this policy into practice.

Export Promotion

The Export Promotion Institute (IPEX). The Export Promotion Institute (IPEX) has administrative and financial autonomy. It was set up in November 1990 to spearhead the export promotion efforts of the Government of the Republic of Mozambique. IPEX began its activities in April 1991 with the objective of promoting and coordinating the execution of policies to develop national exports.

Currently, IPEX offers technical assistance, advice, and trade information to Mozambican exporters, promotes and publicizes the country's exports abroad, undertakes market research and studies on specific exportable products, assists foreign buyers and organizes and coordinates the participation of Mozambican exporters in international trade fairs, exhibitions and trade missions. It also identifies and recommends policies and other measures conducive to the promotion of exports from Mozambique.

The Institute also has a Trade and Market Information Centre and a current database, containing relevant information on Mozambican exporters, as well as on products that Mozambique can export.

The IPEX statutes are under review to bring the institution up to date in the new economic and business environment. It is thus expected that IPEX will take on a more active role in the advancement of production destined for the export market and in the creation of a business foundation for this purpose. IPEX participates in various activities for the development of exports, with emphasis on projects that have been mentioned elsewhere in this document (http://www.ipex.gov.mz and IPEX 1998. Directório dos exportadora moçambicanos).

Toward an Export Development Strategy in Mozambique. IPEX identified the need to formulate export strategies for pilot sectors identified as having export potential.

Thus the International Trade Centre of UNCTAD/WTO is providing assistance for the preparation of a project document for a study on "Wood Manufacturers with an Artisan Component."

The objective of the project is to stimulate the development of trade and the export of higher value goods to be sourced from the rural areas, thus contributing to income and employment generation, and ultimately to the reduction of poverty.

In the first phase, IPEX, together with relevant private and public sector stakeholders, will be assisted in the formulation of an export strategy for the pilot sector. During the second phase the project will support IPEX and the relevant partner institution in implementing the strategy.

Initiative for Development and Equity in African Agriculture (IDEAA)

The Initiative for Development and Equity in African Agriculture (IDEAA) is a program funded by the Rockefeller and Kellogg Foundations that operates in six SADC countries, namely South Africa, Botswana, Lesotho, Malawi, Swaziland, and Mozambique.

This program was designed to strengthen institutional transformation in the economic upstream and downstream of high-value cash crops, promoting these crops among smallholder farmers so that they could direct their production more to the market.

IDEAA Mozambique was created at a national conference held in Maputo in February 2002. The partners in this program are IPEX, IAC/CLUSA, AFRICARE, the Provincial Directorates of Agriculture, and some farmers in the provinces where implementation is to begin. The conference participants decided that the cash crop to receive IDEAA support should be oilseeds, with major emphasis on sesame and sunflower. The main oilseeds produced in the country have the following area distribution:

- Groundnut: Nampula, Inhambane, Manica
- Sesame: Nampula, Zambezia, Manica
- Copra: Nampula, Zambezia, Inhambane
- Sunflower: Nampula, Manica, Inhambane
- Castor oil plant: Nampula

Manica province was chosen for the start-up of the four-year program, with sunflower as the chosen crop, which will be followed by sesame.

The program to be developed will include activities to improve production, post-harvest management and processing, and technical assistance and technological support. The program is expected to expand to Nampula province in the second phase.

External Market Task Force. The National Directorate of Trade (DNC) in the Ministry of Industry and Trade (MIC), the Office for the Promotion of the Commercial Farming (GPSCA) of the Ministry of Agriculture and Rural Development (MADER), the Export Promotion Institute (IPEX), the National Institute for Standardisation and Quality (INNOQ) and the Confederation of Economic Associations of Mozambique (CTA), constitute the External Market Task Force. The EC-Food Security Unit (FSU-EC) and the MIC/FAO/EC Marketing Project, coordinated by MIC, support this group.

According to its terms of reference, the aim of the task force is to analyze the market potential for agricultural products in local and foreign markets.

The task force has identified seven products with potential for export: honey, beans, ginger, cassava, paprika, sweet corn, and banana. The South African market is working to determine what are the preferential tariffs and the size of the market for these products, and then identifying those where it is worth concentrating efforts.

At the same time, quality specifications are being identified, along with the sanitary and phytosanitary measures that could affect marketing of these products.

Concerns regarding the general situation in relation to the trade protocol include the customs system, aspects of the customs tariffs, high interest rates, and weak transport and communications infrastructure.

Preferential Mechanisms for Access to Markets. Among the various mechanisms for preferential market access the following were identified in this phase.

ACP (Africa, Caribbean, and Pacific) Group. Mozambique signed the third Lome Convention in 1984, and became a member of ACP (Africa, Caribbean, and Pacific) group. It benefited from favorable terms of commercial relations, namely the export of products to the EU markets with the exemption from customs duties.

Generalized System of Preferences (GSP). As a developing country, Mozambique also benefits from the Generalized System of Preferences (GSP) for industrial and agricultural products.

The African Growth Opportunity Act (AGOA). The African Growth Opportunity Act (AGOA) opens the American market to Mozambique in both textile and agricultural products. Textiles and fishery products were already approved for export (http://agoa.gov).

Zambia, Malawi, Mozambique Growth Triangle (ZMM-GT). As an initiative by the private sector in Malawi, Mozambique, and Zambia, supported by the United Nations Development Programme (UNDP), the Zambia, Malawi, Mozambique Growth Triangle (ZMM-GT) was inaugurated in

November 2000. It seeks to integrate market opportunities across transnational economic zones.

The SADC Trade Protocol. Among the various mechanisms for preferential market access is the SADC Trade Protocol detailed below. One of the main advantages of this Protocol is the establishment of a regional market that may attract foreign investment to Mozambique. It also represents a step toward liberalized international trade, through a phased reduction and elimination of barriers to trade within a timeframe of eight years. Special attention has been given to harmonization of standards and technical regulations.

The SADC Trade Protocol objectives are:

- To further liberalize intraregional trade in goods and services on the basis of fair, mutually equitable, and beneficial trade arrangements, complemented by Protocols in other areas;
- To ensure efficient production within SADC, reflecting the current and dynamic comparative advantages of its members;
- To contribute toward the improvement of the climate for domestic, cross-border, and foreign investment;
- To enhance economic development, diversification, and industrialization in the region;
- To establish a free trade area in the SADC Region.

This protocol was signed on 24 August 1996. Three countries in the region have not yet signed, namely Angola, Seychelles, and the Democratic Republic of Congo. Mozambique ratified the Protocol on 28 December 1999, and it went into force on 25 January 2000, with implementation beginning on 1 September 2000.

Each member state set up a task force to ensure the implementation of the protocol. A Protocol Implementation Unit was set up at the SADC headquarters in Gaborone, Botswana. In Mozambique, an interministerial working group functions in the Ministry of Industry and Trade to deal with implementation of the SADC Trade Protocol. The group has representatives from the private sector and INNOQ and began functioning in 1998.

This protocol includes special agreements on textiles, clothing and sugar, which are contentious areas in SADC. To facilitate trade, issues of standards and technical regulations are dealt with in detail in the Protocol (see Annex C).

Other Facilitation Mechanisms for Trade

Measures for the Protection of Intellectual Property Rights. The Department of Industrial Property at the Ministry of Industry and Trade was created in 1995 and is responsible for the industrial property rights including trademarks, service marks, patents, industrial designs, models, and so on. The Ministry of Culture is responsible for copyrights.

Mozambique joined the World Industrial Property Organisation (WIPO) in 1996, the Paris Convention in 1997, and the Madrid Agreement in 1998. In addition, Mozambique joined the Patent Cooperation Treaty (PCT) in May 2000. Mozambique is a member of the African Regional Industrial Property Organisation (ARIPO).

The Industrial Property Code was approved by Decree No. 18/99 in May 1999. This code establishes a special regime for industrial property rights and obligations on the basis of the concession of patents for inventions and utility models, the registration of trademarks, designs, industrial models, and business names, and the repression of the infringement of industrial property rights.

Major Markets Summary of Internal and External Barriers

The main export crops are sugarcane, cotton, cashew, tea, tobacco, and timber. These crops and their processed products are negatively affected by international prices. This is aggravated by the lack of subsidies, which could help during price reduction when production costs are higher for the same product from countries with protection policies for production and trade.

The import and export analysis shows that there was a reduction in the export of agrofood products from 52.1 percent in 1999 to 43 percent in 2000. Imports of the same group of products also decreased from 21.2 percent in 1999 to 14.4 percent. In 2000, citrus exports fell from 14.9 percent to 0.7 percent (Table 2.7). For instance, citrus plantations, mainly for exports, have been removed and replaced by other fruit species. Production from the family sector only supplies the domestic market.

In 1999, cereals were the main imported agriculture product representing 9.9 percent of total imports. In 2000, however, it had fallen to 5.2 percent.

In the last three years some nontraditional commodities have been exported, namely pigeon pea,

Table 2.7 Import and Export Values of Agro and Food Products Declared in 1999 and 2000
(thousand US$)

Description	Exports 1999	Imports 1999	Exports 2000	Imports 2000
Total products	270,893	685,234	363,962	1,162,270
Total agro food products	141,042	145,052	156,522	167,367
Subtotal live animals and their products	75,136	13,306	101,080	28,289
Fish, crustaceans,other seafood	74,768	7,243	100,652	7,647
Live animals, meat, eggs, milk and their products	368	6,063	428	20,642
Subtotal plant products	49,198	78,221	32,621	75,184
Live plants, edible vegetables, plants, roots and tubers	2,349	2,728	22,740	3,869
Fruits, coffee, tea and spices	40,481	578	2,666	3,538
Cereals	1,818	68,168	487	60,166
Milling products, malt, starches, oilseeds and seeds, gums and plant extracts	4,550	6,746	6,728	7,611
Subtotal animal fat and oils and waxes	5,492	21,602	3,747	12,407
Subtotal food, beverages and tobacco	11,216	31,923	19,074	51,487
Processed meat, seafood, cocoa, cereal, fruits and vegetable, and other food	60	7,737	15	17,388
Sugar and sugar products	5,506	14,628	4,324	12,233
Beverages, alcoholic drinks and vinegar	235	5,342	409	15,816
Food industry subproducts animal feed	2,828	2,024	6,504	2,987
Tobacco and tobacco products	2,587	2,192	7,822	3,063

Source: INE (1999, 2000).

sesame seed, groundnut, and castor oil seed. They are produced by the family sector and the traders receive support from some NGOs and firms to find foreign firms interested in these products. Years ago such crops were exported, but during the civil war, the abandonment of rural areas and access problems interrupted production and exports. Recovering the markets lost during that time, or conquering new markets is a challenge to producers.

Cashew kernels were a main export product for many years, but production fell during the 1980s. The largest factories invested in modernization and began to recover their production and export lev-

els, but were later forced into closure by the competion from higher prices offered for raw cashew nuts by Indian importers, putting thousands of people out of work. Other factors included obsolete machinery, aggravated by years of poor maintenance, and the increasing cost of operations. Today the main cashew product exported is raw cashew instead of processed cashew. However, Indian prices for this commodity have since fallen. The quality of the product has also decreased because of diseases of the cashew trees. Mozambican cashew kernels used to be well known in the U.S. and European markets, and although the quality of some factories' production fell, others maintained the international standards, as can be seen by the few complaints received.

Maize has been exported through the normal commercial system, but when the prices in neighboring countries are more attractive, rural farmers sell their maize directly, through cross-border trading, especially in the northern provinces of the country.

Cotton is also an important crop. During 1998 and 2000 the production volume reached about 100,000 tons, twice of the previous year because of favorable climatic conditions and the good financial situation of cotton ginneries, factors that declined in 2000. The quality of this product is usually not very high because its production system lacks irrigation and uses a quality of seed that produces a crop with short fibers. The classification departments in Mozambique have some organizational problems and the buyers complain that the product they receive does not match the classification given. This is apparently connected to the need for training and supervision in the classification offices (they are dependent on the Cotton Institute—IAM).

Major Problems in Standards for Market Access

We have decided to examine in more detail the fruits and vegetables, cashew, sugar, cotton, peanut, and seeds subsectors, because already there are plans for short-term action to increase and diversify output in these subsectors to meet demand on the domestic market and to increase exports.

The Case of Fruits and Vegetables in Mozambique. *General Information.* Mozambique's climate, soil, and topology allow the production of both tropical and temperate fruits and vegetables, for local consumption and for export. Long-term research on fruits and vegetables dates back many years, and gene banks were installed in agricultural research centers. Tested and approved cultivars were disseminated and fruit tree cultivation was promoted throughout the country. However, the research and fieldwork were interrupted because of the general situation in Mozambique, and the continuity of information as well as some cultivars were lost, on account of lack of maintenance of the gene banks.

Mozambique used to export fruit, mainly citrus and banana, but due to the war and population movements, the trees were abandoned, and the country began to import fruit, mainly from South Africa.

Most fruits and vegetables are produced by the commercial and family sectors. They can contribute to improving the national economy and also bring benefits to their producers, pickers and processors by generating income, health and nutrition. The private sector—individuals, companies, and associations—owns the organized plantations that are cultivated semi-intensively or intensively. Family sector production means fruit trees and vegetables are planted and sown on family plots around the home or in the fields, with minimal formal farming operations.

It must be stressed that citrus, cashew, and coconut are species that are usually dealt with individually, given the economic importance of the fruits and by-products as exports and their use for direct consumption and for processing as food or nonfood products. However, other fruit trees or other crops are replacing the large citrus plantations that once existed. Cashew is mainly grown in the family sector, with few organized plantations. The main coconut plantations belong to big agricultural companies, some of which also carry out industrial or commercial activities.

The other fruits, such as mango, banana, papaya, and pineapple, are also important domestically, with most production aimed at the local market for consumption as fresh fruit. They contribute to family income and to improving the general diet. Production is higher than consumption capacity as fresh fruit, and there is neither the knowledge nor tradition of home processing of by-products, which means that a significant proportion of the produce spoils.

Banana is an exception because although most production is for fresh consumption in the local market, interest and opportunities to turn it into an export product are increasing. But the lack of phytosanitary treatment may cause quality problems that some producers (mainly small) are experiencing when they try to export.

No real data on the quantity of plants or species and production of fruit and vegetables exist. An Agricultural and Livestock Census 1999–2000 was undertaken recently and some studies on fruit trees and agroindustry at the provincial and national levels and FAO data also provide indications of samples and estimates from different parts of the country. However, the figures vary, which may be

Table 2.8 Fruit Production in Mozambique
(thousand ton)

Fruit	1965	1970	1975	1980	1985	1990	1995	2000
Coconut *Cocus nucifera*	274	407	400	450	400	420	438	300
Cashew *Anacardium occidentale* L.	136	184	188	71	25	23	33	35
Citrus *Citrus spp.*	25	33.5	38.5	41.5	40.5	48.5	34.7	29.5
Orange *C. sinensis* (L) Osbeck	12.5	17	20	22	20	26	15	13
Grapefruit and shaddock *C. paradisi* Macf. e *C. grandis* (L) Osbeck	11	15	17	16	15	17	15	13
Lemon and lime *C. lemon* e *C. limetoides*	1	1	1	3	5	5	4.2	3.2
Mandarin *C. reticulata* Blanco	0.5	0.5	0.5	0.5	0.5	0.5	0.5	0.3
Banana *Musa* cvs	25	34	60	65	70	85	83	59
Mango *Mangifera indica* L.	33	35	30	30	30	34	30	24
Pawpaw *Carica papaya* L.	20	32	35	38	40	45	41	31
Pineaple *Ananas comosus* (L) Merr.	17	18	12	13	13	15	15	13

Source: FAO yearbooks.

because of the methodologies and criteria used and the areas covered by the surveys (Table 2.8).

Indigenous species of edible fruit and vegetables that grow naturally are much in demand by the rural population for consumption and for use in traditional medicine, becoming the main source of food in areas where drought prevents cultivation or destroys annual crops. Some of these products, such as paprika and mushrooms, are being promoted with a view to export. Mushroom picking has been encouraged and supported by NGOs in Manica and Nampula provinces, because they can be considered a biological product worth promoting, particularly for export.

Some of the existing processing plants were set up after the 1960s, when production overtook the capacity of the fresh food and export markets. These plants processed fruit and vegetables such as citrus, pineapple, papaya, tomato, pumpkin, and green beans, but ceased operations, mainly because of fall in production or lack of raw materials (in the case of citrus), and the high costs of raw materials and other components that made the products more expensive than similar imported products.

Most of the fruit and vegetable industrial processing units are currently closed, and some factories have been dismantled. The companies that are in operation prepare juices from concentrates or package imported juices and compotes, pickles, and chutneys. The fruit and vegetable products available in the Mozambican market are mostly imported.

In general, producers paid little attention to quality and the few laws and regulations that are in force in Mozambique related to food safety need to be updated. The process of developing standards and codes of practice for these products is still embryonic, and must be speeded up, because the lack of standards and codes of practice helping to guarantee quality and food safety in the different steps along the fruit and vegetable food chain could become a significant constraint in the development of agroindustry.

The local raw materials have quality problems because of the varieties chosen, which are not the most suitable for industrialization, their location in distant, scattered, and hard to reach areas, and the inadequate transport, cold storage, and handling conditions that contribute to product deterioration.

National production of raw materials has not benefited from incentives, either fiscal or credit, thus raising the costs of production and consequently the prices of the finished products.

The technologies used by the active industrial units for adding value to, and transforming, fruits and vegetables, are based on manual operations.

Packaging is usually imported and is a problem that needs to be addressed during the development of this sector.

As domestic production is not enough, products from South Africa, Portugal, other European countries, the United Arab Emirates and others supply the domestic market. Many of the imported products enter the country illegally and are put on the market with no control by the authorities responsible for inspection and quality control. Many of these products have no expiry dates shown, while others have already expired, a situation that worries both consumers and the local producers.

Food import policies do not differentiate between products, with the same taxes applied to local and imported products. Most imported products are thus sold at prices below those of the domestic products. The domestic producers consider the import system to be a barrier to the development of a national industry. Illegal products also constitute a threat to public health.

The analysis made by Technoserve in March 2001—"A Vision for the Fruit Industry in Mozambique—Building a Globally Competitive Tropical Fruit Industry"—shows that Mozambique could be a key actor in tropical fruit production and export at the global level within 10 years. The analysis considers the need to restart the production and export of high-quality bananas, and expand production geographically. It also considers the introduction of new products, namely mango, litchi and lime, for regional, Middle Eastern, and Indian markets, the latter two with seasonal advantages.

An earlier study done by Technoserve in January 2001 on "Species Selection for the Middle Eastern and Indian Markets for Mangoes and Citrus Fruits" concluded that India, Pakistan, and the Middle East could be potential markets for certain cultivars of mango (*Alphonso*) and citrus (easy peeling citrus), which are preferred by consumers in those countries, so long as they are available before or at the beginning of those countries' seasons for these fruits. The season for fruit in Mozambique is from September to March, while the fruit season in those countries is from March to August, depending on the species and variety. For example, mangoes are in short supply in the Indian market from September through to late February, while the season in Mozambique is from November to March.

In addition, the quality and packaging must be improved (for the Middle East), and there must be respect for local consumer habits (in India mangoes are considered a monsoon season fruit, and have a cooling effect). Mozambique could promote exports to these countries if it develops and produces the cultivars that are most in demand and have the highest consumer acceptance there

Development of cultivars forms part of the fruit tree project proposal made by MADER in 1995, which planned to install a fruit tree seedlings production center in Sofala province for distribution to the family sector. The 10–15-year strategy for developing citrus and other fruit crops that was prepared in November 1987 also gave priority to rehabilitating existing orchards and promoting citrus and other fruit trees nationally.

The AGOA Programme, offers producers an opportunity to develop the production and export of quality fruit and vegetables. Respect for the best practices to be defined will be essential, all the way from the field to the packing stage. The possibility of exporting dried fruit is also being considered within the AGOA framework.

The main constraint is probably the lack of awareness of the market forces by the Mozambican producers, who, for many years have supplied products for centralized institutions, like the Institute for Cereals. In addition, today the markets are much more demanding and they impose quality standards based on high-technology production and packaging. Because Mozambican producers have been absent from international markets for many years, they are less aware of the increasing demands for better quality. More important still is the low technological level of agriculture, usually rainfed, not mechanized, and with very little use of inputs, thus very little control of plant diseases that contribute to reducing the quality, especially of fruit. Usually the producers are not prepared, either because of the lack of funds or the conditions to guarantee essential agricultural practices, to buy the seeds of the varieties that the market wants. There should be a closer linkage between the buyer and the producer, even some credit facilities should be available to help improve Mozambican knowledge of the market and the quality control systems.

Institutions Involved. The Ministry of Agriculture and Rural Development (MADER) is the state body in charge of developing the fruit and vegetable subsector. The Production Department of the DINA, which has a fruit-farming sector, is directly responsible for overseeing its activities. Other departments of MADER, such as GPSCA, have promoted fruit and vegetable production and processing. A study of rural agroindustry, including fruit and vegetables, is currently under way with the aim of identifying the crops to be developed in some provinces and gathering information that could interest potential investors.

INIA is responsible for research, through its fruit tree sector, where work halted in 1992 but was recently reactivated. INIA is currently rehabilitating the gene bank containing around 100 varieties of mango at the Umbeluzi Agricultural Station, and plans to recuperate the collections of mango cultivars and organize gene banks for other fruit species in different parts of the country.

The Ministry of Health is responsible for establishing and enforcing legislation related to foodstuffs. The Ministry of Industry and Trade, through the National Directorate of Industry, controls some of the agroindustrial production.

The Eduardo Mondlane University Agronomy and Forestry Faculty has also carried out studies, written manuals, and organized training courses for fruit farmers.

INNOQ, the institution responsible for the development of Mozambican standards, defined fruit and juices as one of its priorities for the preparation of Mozambican standards, and is involved in developing harmonizing standards for them, particularly on fruits and juices at the regional level.

In 1995 the private sector created FRUTISUL—Southern Mozambique Fruit Growers Association—which is associated with FRUTIMEL Ltd. FRUTISUL, the first fruit farmers' association of Inhambane, Gaza, and Maputo provinces, has organized courses on fruit tree production and has conducted studies on the commercial production of some trees. Its priorities are to support the fruit farmers, encourage them to form associations at provincial and national levels, and seek partnerships for promoting and developing fruit trees and supporting the producers (Associaçâo de Fruticultores do Sul de Moçambique 1995).

Various NGOs are active in the sector, and have distributed fruit tree seedlings and vegetable seed as part of their rural development programs. These items have also been included in the emergency programs for agriculture, and are distributed to families affected by natural disasters.

Characterization of Some Mozambican Fruit Trees.
(a) Citrus cultivation in Mozambique dates from the 1920s, the most common species being oranges, tangerines, lemons, and grapefruit, grown in commercial orchards that are ordered and use grafted trees. Most production was destined for fresh fruit exports. These orchards are concentrated in Maputo and Manica provinces. There are also small informal orchards, using trees grown from seed, the production of which is destined for the domestic fresh fruit market in every province. These are mainly in Inhambane and Zambezia, with oranges and tangerines outnumbering (the tangerine species cultivated in Inhambane is well known, and is only produced in that area) shaddock (*Citrus grandis L*) or pomelo.

Orange production represents 40–50 percent of total citrus production in Mozambique in the period from 1965 to 2000, followed by grapefruit and pomelo (35–45 percent), and lemon and lime (3–12 percent). Though tangerine production is insignificant at the national level, it has considerable weight in Inhambane and also in the southern markets, particularly in Maputo City.

Documentation shows that 6,180 tons of citrus were produced in 1960, concentrated in the southern region (LOUMAR undated), rising to 144,000 tons in 1977 (MA 1997). In southern Mozambique the Citrinos de Maputo state enterprise owned around 2,000 hectares of citrus groves until the 1980s, but by 1995, it had only 301 hectares (UTRE 1995) following privatization and parts being sold off to different buyers, namely LOMACO, AGROFARM, and Citrinos de Umbeluzi. LOMACO and AGROFARM renewed part of their plantations and continued to produce and export citrus. The LOMACO area has now been sold, Citrinos de Umbeluzi has ceased production, and AGROFARM has replaced some of the citrus with other species. In central Mozambique citrus production reached 15,000 tons in Manica in 1984, of which 57 percent was oranges, 34 percent grapefruit, and 9 percent lemons (CAIM 1991). The Citrinos de Manica agricultural company was privatized and sold to the João Ferreira dos Santos group, which continues to produce and export citrus. In the early 1990s the Citrinos de Manica concession area was 4,500 hectares, with a total area planted with oranges and grapefruit of around 608 hectares (UTRE 1995). Parts of this area are currently abandoned.

Export accounted for 60 percent of the total production. Citrus exports grew from the 1950s to the early 1970s, growing from 4,000 to 10,000 tons. Oranges and grapefruit dominated exports, but tangerines and lemons also figured. The grapefruit surplus and some of the lemons that were unsuitable for export were distributed to social units and used for animal feed. Initially the importers were European countries, some Asian countries, and some Southern African countries, but from the late 1970s through the 1980s exports were mainly to the Eastern European countries. The joint enterprise LOMACO alone exported around 2,000 tons per year, selling its produce to Swaziland in its last years of activity.

Citrus processing includes fruit improvement and preservation, and also its transformation into by-products. In the 1960s and 1970s, 14 citrus-packing centers were established in Maputo and Manica, where the fruit was cleaned, selected, and packed—mostly for export. Only five centers are currently operational.

The ports of Maputo and Beira have cold storages owned by the Maputo Produce Terminal Company and managed by the South African company CAPESPAN (formerly OUTSPAN) and a Zimbabwean company respectively, where citrus and other perishable produce for export from South Africa (Maputo) and Zimbabwe (Beira) are stored. The Maputo Cargo Terminal (MCT) (formerly FRIGO), which is managed by CAPESPAN, has cold storages in Matola that were built in the 1980s for conserving export fruit and vegetables, because both Mozambican and the South African produce is exported through Maputo.

Mozambique has two citrus processing units located in Maputo and Chimoio, LOUMAR and SUMOVIT, respectively. Both their fruit processing lines are currently paralyzed for lack of raw materials. Until the early 1990s the production of these factories represented 90 percent of the national fruit juice consumption, particularly in the south; the remaining 10 percent was imported or came from small local producers.

LOUMAR Industries was established in 1964 to produce crystallized fruit, using orange peel and pulp from other fruits. The production line installed in 1995 had a capacity for transforming 14,000 tons of citrus into 6,000 liters of bottled juice. It also produced 500 tons of compote, 450 tons of crystallized fruit, and 1,145 tons of sweets and confectionery. Although national production capacity of 6,000 tons per year was available, the new line was expected to ensure continuous growth of citrus production. In 1992 a new bottling line for juices reconstituted from fruit concentrates was installed in response to national development and with the prospect of the emerging free market for citrus by-products. The citrus processing line was almost paralyzed for 10 years, processing a mere 50 tons of grapefruit per season so as to use the peel for crystallized fruit and jam. No use whatsoever was made of the grapefruit juice, because there was no local market for it. Orange production in the south fell every year and could not supply the industry. In 2000, the processing line only worked for 52 days. The best year was 1984, when the factory processed 4,300 tons of fruit, 3,000 tons of grapefruit, and 1,300 tons of oranges. The natural grapefruit juice was sold to SOVIM, a company producing wine and distilled drinks for the domestic market. But this company, state-owned at the time, was privatized, the equipment was dismantled, and the installations were turned into a supermarket for a South African company. LOUMAR is currently producing a small quantity of juice from imported orange concentrate.

SUMOVIT was established in Chimoio, Manica province, in 1968, and had the capacity to process around 4,000 tons of citrus a year (oranges and grapefruit), producing 178 tons of concentrates and 500,000 liters of juice in bulk. At the time the factory was of great importance to local agriculture, given that two-thirds of national citrus production came from there. The factory's production fell steadily until 1981, when it ceased production because of management difficulties and the obsolescence of its machinery. In 1982 a new bottling line was acquired, but was not immediately installed. In 1992 the state enterprise was privatized and bought by LOUMAR Industries, taking the name Agro-Industrial Company of Manica—CAIM, Ltd. At that time the factory was rehabilitated, and new equipment was installed to produce concentrates for export. The factory started production in 1997 with the new equipment, and only worked for three years (during one year it was managed by the João Ferreira dos Santos group). All the concentrates produced were wasted, because neither an external nor a domestic market was found. This factory is presently being handed over to Al Omran Agro Industrial Ltd., which is currently working from Beira.

Another company that should be mentioned is Palmar Ltd., which used to produce citrus syrups and tinned fruits and vegetables (compotes, jams), but currently only produces small quantities of jams, which are sold in bulk at the factory gate.

(b) Mango (*Mangifera indica L.*): There are some organized mango plantations in Manica province, with trees that were planted before 1975 but abandoned for many years. The mango is a fruit tree that grows throughout the country, scattered around the rural areas close to people's homes and fields. The fruit is eaten fresh, and much is wasted because consumption is lower than production.

In Mozambique most mango trees were planted from seed, which means that the quality of the fruit is extremely variable and often low. There are almost no organized orchards with grafted trees. The export of mangoes was tested in the 1970s, but did not last long.

There was no industrial use of mangoes until three years ago. At the family level only a few people know how to produce juice, jam, and other preserves. During 1999/2000 a mango processing unit was established in Beira, in the central region, with an installed capacity to process 12,000 tons of mango per year. The factory is owned by Al Omran Agro Industrial, Ltd. Around 100 tons of mangoes were processed in 2000 and around 4,500 tons in the first months of 2001, producing tinned pulp. It was all exported to Dubai, where the company has its headquarters and the main factory for producing mango, pineapple, and orange juice and nectar. The company is already engaged in the export market for mango and other fruit products, and is thus able to get the Mozambican products into the system. The concentrate produced in Mozambique is mixed with concentrate from other countries where the company has similar factories. With the aim of buying the CAIM factory in Chimoio, Al Omran Agro Industrial, Ltd. plans to transfer its production line from Beira to Chimoio, to produce mango pulp from November to February and orange pulp from June to September. It also aims to process litchis in November and December and pineapples when production is restarted in Manica. There is also an interest in producing tomato concentrate, taking advantage of an old concentrator in the factory that needs reconditioning.

(c) Pineapple (*Ananas comusus L.*): There are plantations of the ananas variety of pineapple in Zambezia province and pineapple plantations in Maputo province, representing around 115,000 tons of pineapple. Production is for fresh consumption, and there are no surpluses for supplying industrial units. The Maputo pineapple plantation was owned by the SOMOPAL Company, which also had a pineapple canning factory until the 1980s. It is now owned by Bonifica-Cabana Co., but the unit has been dismantled. There is considerable family sector production in Gaza, Inhambane, and Zambezia provinces.

SOMOPAL, located in Matola, was the only factory in Mozambique that processed pineapple, producing tinned pineapple rings and chunks, compote, and jam. It also produced vegetables, including tinned tomato puree, peeled tomatoes, and beans, and tropical fruit compotes and sweets. This unit was operational until the 1980s, and received new pineapple processing equipment in 1990, but this was never installed. Later the company was privatized and it never worked again.

The international market prefers pineapples to abacaxi for their flavor and because they are smaller. Frutisul believes there could be export possibilities.

(d) Coconut (*Cocus nucifera*): Coconuts grow along most of the Mozambican coastline, and particularly in the Zambezia and Inhambane provinces. They are grown by large agroindustrial units such as the Madal Group, the Zambezia Company, Boror and others, which have huge organized coconut plantations, and also by the family sector in small areas or with a few palms by their homes and in their fields. In Zambezia, family sector production is estimated to represent 57 percent of the total area occupied by coconut palms.

Coconut production grew steadily to reach 450,000 tons in 1980. The decrease in production since then is probably because of lower yields from aging trees, harvesting green coconuts for consumption, and crop diseases, such as the yellowing disease virus in the central and northern plantations.

The main export product is copra. Coconuts, both green and mature, are also widely used for food, for example, coconut water and the endocarp, which is eaten grated or used to extract coconut milk. Palm juice is extracted from the tree and used to produce vinegar and as a yeast and sweetener for breads and cakes. It can also be drunk fresh, fermented, or distilled. The copra is exported or processed to make coconut oil for soaps and other by-products. Coir is the commercial name for the fiber extracted from the coconut mesocarp, and has multiple uses, such as making matting, upholstery, paintbrushes, scrubbing brushes, and packing material. Charcoal is obtained from the slow burning of coconut shells. More recently, the trunks of coconut palms have been transformed into planks and logs for building. Coconut oil was once a big export but markets were lost during the war. Some factories buying copra to process oil have complaints about quality but there has been no systematic approach to this problem, only a case-by-case price discussion.

(e) Other fruit trees: There is considerable family and small-scale production of banana, papaya, guava (*Psidium guajava*), avocado (*Persea americana*), passion fruit (*Passiflora edulis*), and other fruits throughout Mozambique's ten provinces, which supplies the local markets.

Temperate fruits such as apples, peaches, damsons, plums, figs, and grapes are also grown and sold on the uplands of Niassa (north), Manica (center) and Namaacha (south). Litchi production (*Litchi chinensis*) takes place in Nampula (north), Manica (center) and Maputo (south).

Banana is produced throughout the country, in plantations in Manica, Zambezia, Gaza, and Maputo provinces, by companies (Inácio de Sousa) and other small- and medium-sized producers. There is an Association of Maputo Banana Producers. Production is essentially for one's own consumption and the local market, while there has also been some export from Manica and Maputo to neighboring countries. South Africa, which was the main buyer of Mozambican bananas, developed its own research and production and has transitioned from being an importer to an exporter. Most of the banana produced and preferred in Mozambique (Cavendish) have physical characteristics that do not meet the requirements of the international market, but have a flavor that makes them exportable. Annual banana production in Manica province is estimated at around 35,000 tons (Technoserve—Negrão, A. and Ruface, C. undated).

In addition to cultivated fruit, Mozambique has a tradition of gathering and eating fresh wild fruits, in particular the marula (*Sclerocarya caffra* SOND.), the "maçanica" (*Ziziphus mauritania* LAM.), the

"maçala," the "macuácua" (*Strychnos spinosa* LAM. e *Strychnos innocua* DEL.) and the "tinziva" (*Dialium schlechteri* HARMS).

Specific Features of Some Vegetables. Vegetable production is heavily conditioned by fresh consumption, given that the processing industry is quite small. Official statistics for vegetable production are based on a sampling of producers, which means that real production is higher than the figures provided in this report.

Out of 50,000–70,000 tons of vegetables per year, tomatoes represent 20–40 percent. Production grew regularly up to 1996/97, and has since stablized at around 70,000 tons per year despite tomato production having fallen from 1995/96 onward. Maputo and Gaza provinces are the largest producers of vegetables. Producer associations organized by the General Union of Cooperatives and the National Union of Farmers and Cooperatives have ensured production and supplied the markets in urban areas and consumption centers.

Commercial farmers produce vegetables in concentrated areas, whereas the family sector owns small plots in lowland areas together with other crops. Peasant associations also play a significant role in vegetable production and marketing. Vegetable production (tomato, onions, greens, and fresh maize) has always been an important source of income for peasants in the city green belts and in the Chókwè irrigation system.

In Gaza province the Chókwè area was a major producer both for immediate consumption and for the industrial units in the area and in Maputo City. The Chilembene area was part of the HORTIL Company that was created in 1983, which was taken over by LOMACO in 1986. The factory for processing tomatoes and other vegetables in Chilembene also has an area of 500 hectares for production, watered by a gravity-feed system. The factory and production area are currently up for sale. The floods of 2000 partially destroyed the factory, though some machinery has been recovered. This factory was established in 1960, and was rehabilitated by LOMACO in 1987. Before rehabilitation, its tomato concentrate production line had a capacity of 990 tons per year, which later rose to 2,500 tons per year. The maximum production actually achieved was 1,800 tons per year. Production capacity was 1,850 tons per year for peeled tomatoes, 2,800 tons per year for tomato conserve and 1,750 tons per year for other vegetable preserves (Mosca 1988). Of the 1,200 tons per year of tomatoes processed up to 1990, around 300 tons supplied the domestic market (local consumption capacity) and 850 tons were exported to Japan and Zimbabwe. LOMACO also has a production area in Chókwè. The two units (Choke and Chilembene) reached production levels of 14,000 tons per year of fresh tomatoes. LOMACO promoted tomato cultivation by the family sector, distributing seedlings to the peasants who were then contractually obliged to supply part of their produce back to the company. These contracts were not observed because the producers obtained bigger profits faster by selling their tomatoes on the market at the time of highest demand. When the market was saturated, the prices fell and the produce began to deteriorate, the peasants would start selling to the factory. Chókwè and Chilembene, in particular, have good growing conditions for tomato cultivation.

Conclusions. Fruit and vegetables are among the priority agricultural products for development. This food group is widely produced and consumed throughout the country, in both cities and the countryside, in addition to some items being on the list of export products.

The fruit growers' associations have given strong support to restarting fruit and vegetable production, providing information on the state of the sector in terms of production and marketing, and disseminating decisions and measures taken for product development.

The institutions related to fruit and vegetables believe that it is essential to prepare an updated master plan and strategy for fruit trees in general and some species in particular. They also want to improve the identification of potential markets at regional and international levels, and draw up investment plans for species that will be selected on the basis of these market studies.

There is no awareness about the need to apply good hygienic practices throughout the fruit and vegetable chains and the HACCP system is not known, with the result that the basic principles of quality are not applied. The institutions are not aware of the need to participate and collaborate more actively with INNOQ in drafting Mozambican standards and codes of practice on fruit and vegetables. This participation will certainly help speed up the development of standards, provide increased knowledge on the requirements of external markets, and improve the quality of produce.

AGOA provides an opportunity for exporting fruit and vegetables, particularly fresh fruit (and especially banana and citrus) and their by-products, in particular, juices, dried fruit, and essential oils, which is why investments must be made in the quality of these products.

Recommendations for an Action Plan. The priority actions identified for developing the fruit and vegetables subsector are the following:

- To update the policies and strategies for fruit and vegetables that were drawn up some years ago and draft plans for developing fruit production.
- To speed the process of drafting standards and codes of practice and revise or draft new laws and technical regulations to support the different actors in the fruit and vegetable food chain, namely producers, processors, traders, and consumers, with a view to obtaining and maintaining quality and safe products, both for the domestic market and for export. These measures will help reduce losses during production, post-harvest, and processing.
- To develop awareness campaigns and training courses in good hygienic practices, HACCP, and on the application of standards as a way to improve quality, protect consumers, and to export.
- To continue work on studying the markets for fruit, vegetables, and by-products in the region and internationally, prioritizing the most sought-after species, which have not yet been analyzed, and updating previous studies.
- To reactivate the gene collections or banks so that the most appropriate cultivars can be set up in the agricultural stations and subsequently disseminated and distributed for production.
- To support the organization of producers, processors, and other actors in fruit and vegetable producer associations, through which programs and activities are usually more successful, being more easily developed and implemented.
- To promote agricultural production and renew and replace plantations taking into account the species (including wild species), the seasonality of the species, product characteristics, and the most appropriate production conditions for obtaining quality products that are in demand on the international and domestic markets. Rehabilitating

and modernizing the fruit and vegetable industry in order to process domestic raw material is also a priority.

- To organize annual fruit trade fairs in the main fruit-growing cities and regions of the country, with the aim of promoting fruit cultivation by bringing together producers, consumers, researchers, equipment makers, agroindustries, and other interested parties;
- To promote the participation of Mozambican fruit in international fruit fairs and to make trade contacts and arrange technical visits for contacts, exchanges of experiences and collecting information on fruit production and processing techniques and technologies;
- To prepare a plan and give technical training to fruit producers and technicians.

The Case of the Cashew (*Anacardium occidentale L.*) Sector in Mozambique. Cashew is generally classified as a cash crop, instead of a fruit.

Cashew trees are distributed throughout the Mozambican coast, being more concentrated in the Nampula (main production area), Inhambane, and Zambézia provinces. Cashew production comes mainly from the peasant sector (95 percent of production), where it is mixed with other trees and crops. Cashew nut is one of the main export products from the agricultural sector.

Cashew nut processing in Mozambique includes the use of four components: the kernel (28–30 percent of the cashew nut's weight) for consumption and exportation; the cashew nut shell liquid (CNSL, which represents 48–50 percent of the cashew nut weight) used for a variety of industrial purposes such as brake lining, varnish, lacquer, insecticides, and medicine; the raw shell as a substitute for charcoal in some industrial plants (despite corrosion problems caused by CNSL); and the cashew apple or false fruit (90–92 percent of the total weight), which is consumed either as fruit itself or processed into juice and jams and into fermented and distilled drinks (cashew alcohol).

Tests were made in 1990 on juice extraction and concentration in one of the industrial plants, through a project financed by UNIDO, with positive results. However, it was observed that trees belonging to different people were spread out over great distances, and the distance between the trees and the factories was too vast to allow collection and processing of the fruit within 24 hours (before it started fermenting). The best alternative for using the fruit is the installation of simple processing units in rural areas for the production of juice, accompanied by training of the producers. Brazil's experiment in the production of clarified juice could be tried in Mozambique through the creation of small enterprises in cashew-growing areas, and the production of other fruit products, other than home-made fermented and distilled cashew juice. In this way there would be a better use of the fruit, through consumption by all ages and the waste products could be used in animal feed.

The nutshell was used in irrigation channels at an experimental level, in a health project, to reduce the prevalence of certain common diseases in irrigation areas.

Estimates indicate that the current tree population of the country is approximately 27.5 million trees, most of which are now in the smallholder sector: plantations accounted for roughly 6 million trees. Nampula province accounts for 37 percent of the total tree population, Inhambane has 26 percent, and Gaza province has 14 percent. Survey-based estimates of the total tree stock are somewhat different. These suggest a total tree stock close to 60 million (mature) trees, of which 38 percent is in Nampula, 30 percent in Inhambane, and 14 percent in Gaza (World Bank 2001).

There are some organized commercial cashew plantations in Maputo and Nampula. Since the 1980s there has been a decrease in the yields of cashew trees because of their aging and the occurrence of diseases, mainly powdery mildew (*Oidium anacardii* Noach) and pests (*Helopeltis* spp.) that attack the new leaves and flowers not allowing them to develop, rendering affected cashew trees as non-fruit-producing. Since the mid-1990s some activities have been undertaken to increase cashew production through phytosanitary programs to treat the trees, cashew renovation, and production of grafted seedlings resistant to *oidium*.

In 1972, Mozambique was listed as the first world producer of cashew nut and the second world kernel producer. According to the former Secretariat of State of Cashew (SEC), in 1972, 220,000 tons were marketed by Mozambique, which was 48 percent of the world cashew nut production. Gradually, the production decreased until the 1990s because of the civil war and the economic and political situation in Mozambique, with leadership

Table 2.9 Cashew Nut Marketing and Export

Year	Nut Marketing	Nut Export	Nut to Industry	Kernel Export	CNSL Export
1995/96	66,510	35,320	27,700	1,863.4	310
1996/97	43,325	16,680	25,283	4,500	1,384
1997/98	51,716	31,105	25,099	3,910	162
1998/99	58,721	30,391	16,300	4,888.3	108
1999/2000	52,608	28,537		2,401.99	200
2000/01	52,088	27,845	6,276	3,174.19	0
2001/02	65,000	24,400		946.06	0

Source: INCAJU.

passing to a group of other producers in the world ranking of cashew producers. The production and marketing has been increasing since 1990, particularly after 1995 (Table 2.9).

In 1972, there were 14 processing factories with a total capacity of 150,000 tons per year, representing one-third of the total exports. In 1991 only eight factories operated and processed 24,000 tons. A serious change in the cashew sector in recent years is the closure of processing plants, one of the most labor-intensive industries in the country, with about 20,000 people working in cashew factories. Now only small and medium plants, are in operation processing 5,000 tons per year.

Cashew production was always considered an important branch of agriculture, and there was always a specific state institution dealing with this crop, first the Secretariat of State of Cashew, and from 1997, the public Institute for the Promotion of Cashew (INCAJU). This Institute, under the Ministry of Agriculture and Rural Development, was set up in 1997 to promote the planting of cashew and other fruit trees and the cashew processing industry (see the section entitled "Institute for the Promotion of Cashew (INCAJU)".

The main legislation on cashew is the Cashew Act, establishing that the Council of Ministers must formulate a policy on the promotion of cashew production and processing, and make the regulations on cashew nut marketing, establishing the procedures and conditions for cashew nut marketing, and set the annual surcharge on the export of unprocessed cashew nuts.

There is a cashew processors' association at national level, the Cashew Industrial Association (AICAJU) and an exporters' association in Nampula province, the Commercial, Industrial and Agricultural Association of Nampula (ACIANA).

The major constraints for cashew production, processing, and exports in Mozambique as indicated by Bawden and others (2001) are:

- At the production level, insufficient expansion of output, low productivity and poor quality go hand in hand. This is the result of low productivity potential because of enforced neglect during the civil war, the declining health of the national cashew grove as trees age, and susceptibility to pests and diseases like *Oidium* anarcadium and *Helopeltis*.
- The unavailability of enough improved planting material to help improve yields and provide disease resistance, and the low rate of replacement of cashew trees in general which is insufficient for maintaining the national grove at its current size given the natural rate of tree death.
- Limited farmer investment in husbandry given unstable markets, inconsistent policy, and the fact that labor demands for cashew husbandry compete with the labor requirements for staple food crops.
- The low quality of harvested cashews because of the tendency for early harvesting from trees resulting in the sale of immature nuts, and inadequate drying which causes excessive humidity in cashew lots. This is caused in part by the heavy competition for cashew among traders, as well as in some cases by the fact that some cashew trees are owned communally (but whose harvest is not regulated) by villages, resulting in competition for the harvest and early harvesting and sale.

The processing industry has faced overwhelming challenges in recent years. Chief among these is the difficulty in acquiring sufficient raw material. Most of the cashew processing plants in Mozambique are currently closed. Those that are still operating use mostly manual technology, which produces the best quality kernel, and is able to process efficiently at relatively low scales of operation in spite of its labor intensity. The domestic industry has the capacity to process 80 thousand metric tons per year, but must compete with exporters of raw nuts to India because annual domestic production averages only 40–45 thousand metric tons. Other challenges facing the cashew processing industry include low quality of incoming raw material (it is estimated that between 12 percent and 36 percent of nuts processed are discarded as rotten, diseased, or immature) and difficulty in achieving the necessary volume for efficient production and marketing.

The exporters also face quality and quantity constraints that limit the expansion and value of their sales. In general, Mozambique's nut exports are graded with low quality, in mixed-quality batches, lowering the price.

Mozambique currently lacks a grading system for raw nuts at the domestic level. This is felt to be a major impediment to the development of the industry. Specifically, the lack of a grading system is felt to depress producer incentives to invest in producing quality nuts, to increase acquisition (transaction) costs for traders, processors and exporters, and to hurt the reputation and value of nuts exported from Mozambique.

Other problems to be taken into consideration relate to the climate changes in the last few years, causing changes in the production cycle, increase of pests and diseases, reduction of yields, and nut quality. For instance, in the present season, there was cashew fruit in some areas of the southern provinces as late as in March, which is quite unusual. The uncontrolled use of fire to burn vegetation and make hunting easier frequently destroys numerous cashew trees. Some cashew-growing areas were abandoned when the population moved because of war and natural disasters.

To overcome the main constraints on agricultural production, INCAJU is promoting the following activities, as set out in the Cashew Master Plan, to achieve 100,000 tons by 2004.

A program to control the *oidium* disease was started in the agricultural season of 1999/2000 for benefiting a large area and a large number of tree owners. For 2001/2002 it was intended to achieve 2,500,000 cashew trees under *cidium* control. The program has already assisted 53,644 households with 1,150,415 treated plants.

The *cidium* control program is included in the INCAJU budget, from state and several external funds, and is regarded as one of the main tasks of this institution. The program has been very successful because the trees in the areas where cashew trees were treated are growing better and producing more and better fruit. Cost recovery for the treatment from the owners of the trees is under study with a view to making the program self-sustaining. It will be necessary to train the cashew tree owners to identify the disease, maintain the treatment routine and take appropriate care with the chemicals.

A plant multiplication program aims to produce 1,200,000 grafted seedlings in 2001/02. The program produced 633,382 grafted seedlings in 1999/2000 and 1,106,317 in 2000/01. There is need to improve the distribution system before the planting season and broaden the education campaign in the family sector on the benefits and care of grafted seedlings.

Involvement of the private sector and NGOs in the cashew subsector is encouraged through outsourcing programs to improve assistance to cashew tree owners, to enhance production, and to increase cashew marketing.

It can already be observed that more producers are aware of the different problems that affect cashew trees, including pests and diseases, and therefore more trees are treated. Moreover, peasant farmers are prepared to accept changes to improve their situation. The yields have increased from 2–4 kilograms to 12–14 kilograms per tree in treated trees.

The marketing of cashew nuts starts every August in the north and later in the south. The total marketed cashew nut decreased from 58,721 tons in 1998/99 to 51,894 tons in 1999/00, because of low production and problems related to marketing and prices. The intervention of INCAJU contributed to the increase of marketed production to 53,613 in 2000/01, and an estimated 65,000 tons in 2001/02 (Table 2.9).

Cashew processing was replaced by exports of unprocessed cashew nuts. As mentioned above, there were 14 factories employing about 20,000 people. Most of the large factories have closed and the small and medium units process only 10,000 tons per year in five provinces, plus 5,000 tons that are manually processed in three of these provinces.

Regarding cashew processing and export, the importers set the price of exported cashews, based on their specifications and the international or their own country's grading system. Because Mozambique has only the rudiments of a grading system in place and no accredited laboratories, the exporters cannot negotiate with the importers on the quality of the export batches controlled by them or the low price offered.

In November 2000 INCAJÚ established a grading system for the 2000/01 season, differentiating producers and traders. For producers three sizes were set, using the number of nuts per kilogram. For traders, processors, and exporters four types were set, based on yield, moisture content, presence of impurities, immature and damaged nuts, number of nuts per kilogram. Marketing of natural immature nuts, mixed with other objects or cooked was not allowed. Moisture must be reduced to the set levels by a solar drying process and packaging has to use bags with a specific material. The specification includes the application of additional value as a bonus to higher grade nuts and penalizes low-grade nuts with a discount (Normas de Comercialização da Castanha de Caju para a Campanha 2001/2002).

The outcome of applying the specification may be considered positive. Many peasants offered better and more selected nuts, receiving better prices than they would for a mixed batch; the traders were also able to buy different grades at corresponding prices. It is an important improvement in product quality because there are more and more informal traders and processors that export nuts and kernels directly to neighboring countries, and are not dependent of the formal export system to India and other countries.

INNOQ is currently working with INCAJU, the private sector, and other stakeholders on the development of standards for cashew kernels and cashew nuts and a code of practice for cashew production.

Conclusions and Recommendations. The development of cashew production is important to the economic development in Mozambique. Cashew is one of the main export products and hundreds of thousands of people depend on it for their livelihoods.

The results of INCAJU efforts, with the collaboration of NGOs, producers, traders, processors, and exporters may be considered satisfactory, with increased production and marketing, more selected nuts and better product quality, trained producers, and more and better coordination among different players.

The specifications applied in 2001/02 were shown to be a useful tool for the recovery strategy of the cashew industry, by more careful selection of nuts according to the grades with benefits in marketing prices to the producers and traders. The application of specifications is the beginning of the learning process involving different cashew players in implementing them and improving selection procedures by grades.

More specific standards for the production and processing of cashew and the code of practice for the sector must be drafted as soon as possible. The main stakeholders should be involved in the discussion of the standards so that implementation is broad and successful, using public awareness campaigns and specific training programs. It represents an incentive to use better production and post-harvest technologies with a consequent reduction in losses.

The improvement of the grading system will contribute toward ensuring a better product for local cashew nut industry, reducing the processing losses and increasing the quality and quantity of cashew kernel exports. The supply of better raw material and the reduction of production costs may act as an incentive to more investment in the cashew industry.

The Case of the Sugar Sector in Mozambique. Mozambique's sugar sector comprises six sugar factories with sugarcane plantations covering a total of 52,800 hectares in the south and center of the country. There are two units in the south and four units in the center, with size ranging from 5,000 hectares at Buzi to 13,000 hectares in Marromeu. All the plantations have irrigation systems, mainly sprinkler systems, which cover 60 percent of the total area.

All the units have factories, with a total milling capacity of 23,760 tons per day of sugarcane, giving a maximum annual capacity of 428,000 tons of sugar. Cane processing began in Mozambique in 1908 (Buzi). The war that ended in 1992 halted agricultural and industrial production in four units, and caused it to fall in the other two units. Sugar production, which had reached 325,051 tons in

1972, fell to 16,289 tons in 1986. Production grew again to 31,700 tons in 1990, thanks to external funding, but dropped again to 13,224 tons because of the drought and the closure of one factory. Another consequence of the collapse in production was the reduction of the labor force from 45,000 workers at the beginning of the 1970s to 17,377 in 1999 (5,859 permanent and 11,518 seasonal workers).

Sugar exports fell and imports increased over the years, as shown in the Table 2.7.

The rehabilitation of the sugar sector forms part of the agriculture program, which considers sugarcane to be one of the priority crops. It has the advantages of lower prices than those of the international market, private foreign investment potential, knowledge and practice of production and processing, and being a crop that is hardly affected by climatic changes.

The sugar sector modernization and rehabilitation program is expected to bring domestic economic growth, job creation, improvement in the trade balance, and the creation of local entrepreneurs. The strategy includes restructuring and privatizing of the companies and protecting the internal market in relation to prices on the international market, as other producer countries have done. Given the fact that international prices are less than production costs and are variable, these protective measures are an attraction for investors and will enable national production to compete on the market. Measures will have to be implemented in conformity with the program of the World Trade Organization (WTO) to reduce imports and import levels, and by taking into account the European Union (EU) and the World Bank (WB) systems of quotas and subsidies.

Within the SADC, where many countries are sugar producers, production is generally higher than consumption. In 1998 production was 4,825 tons while 2,976 tons were consumed. By contrast, the sugar industry in the countries of the region is highly competitive and efficient by international standards. Mozambique has the advantage of geographical location, but the main disadvantage of being vulnerable to sugar imports.

With the rehabilitation program, sugar production has increased, going from 50.7 tons in 1999 to 136.7 tons in 2001. It is hoped that production will rise to 286.4 tons in 2002, and will increase to 400 tons by 2005.

The sugar sector's main problem is smuggling from Zimbabwe, Malawi, and Swaziland, estimated at 60,000–80,000 tons per year (a calculation based on the volume of sugar produced, imports inspected, estimates of domestic consumption, export volumes, and factory stocks). Considering that this sugar is sold at prices below the domestic costs of production, the factories are the main victims of this situation. Other problems are related to the shortage of specialized workers and the slowness of fiscal procedures (INA 2000).

The Mozambican Association of Sugar Producers (APAMO) has played a key role in presenting producer concerns and proposals for solutions to the government.

The agreements on sugar at the SADC level should be mentioned, in addition to the protective measures applied by the customs. At the February 2001 negotiating round the subcommittee on sugar decided to create a Committee Secretariat, working groups on cooperation, and a Federation of Sugar Producers to create mechanisms that will facilitate links among the members and harmonize decisions taken by each of the countries.

Raw sugar has been exported following the technical specifications requested by their importers There has been no rejection of sugar export because of lack of compliance with sanitary and phytosanitary (SPS) measures and other quality specifications. Sugar is a priority product in the Mozambican standardization program, given the importance of the export potential and the need to harmonize sugar standards in the SADC region.

The Case of Cotton in Mozambique. Cotton is important for the Mozambican economy, as it is one of the three main export products, along with fish and seafood and cashew nuts. It is the only fiber produced locally, while others are imported for textile manufacturing, and it is a raw material for the oil and soap industries.

This crop is grown mainly in the northern provinces of Nampula and Cabo Delgado but is also produced in the central and southern provinces, by about 250,000 households (family sector), representing 75 percent of the total production and, in some areas, by 10 companies with concessions given by the Mozambican government through contracts, employing about 25,000 workers. These economic operators are classified into six groups, namely family sector, nonautonomous producers,

Table 2.10 Cotton Production by Sector
(ton)

Season	Private Sector	Family Sector	Total
1991/92	19,481	15,154	34,635
1992/93	22,879	24,127	47,006
1993/94	17,080	29,244	46,324
1994/95	17,249	35,757	53,006
1995/96	17,837	32,670	50,507
1996/97	15,635	58,365	74,000
1997/98	11,600	79,488	91,088
1998/99	14,139	102,577	116,716
1999/2000	2,719	32,646	35,365
2000/2001	6,677	64,371	71,048
2001/2002	5,500	64,500	70,000

Source: IAM.

autonomous producers, concessionaires, ginners, local traders, and lint exporters (Tables 2.10, 2.11).

Peak cotton production occurred in 1973 with 144,000 tons and the worst season was in 1985, when only 5,000 tons were produced, because of the armed conflict that halted the production of cotton when the population was displaced from the cotton-growing regions and infrastructure was destroyed, and also because of management problems in the firms.

The cotton sector falls under the Mozambique Cotton Institute (IAM) of the Ministry of Agriculture and Rural Development, created in 1991. This Institute has a key role in cotton development, doing research and assisting the production and marketing systems. IAM maintains and improves the linkage between producers and processors, with government, national and international institutions, promoting awareness and dialogue among them so as to reduce their problems, setting minimum prices and assessing the export opportunities, assuring cotton classification in their laboratories and issuing origin and quality certificates.

There is also the Mozambican Cotton Association of producers, processors, and traders, working in coordination with IAM to improve the cotton subsector. NGOs are also important players in funding and giving technical assistance to extension and training programs and supporting the creation and strengthening of farmer organisations.

The companies have been replacing direct production in large areas by supplying inputs on credit to small farmers of their designated areas, giving technical assistance and buying their production.

Table 2.11 Cotton Production and Export
(ton)

Season	Seed Cotton Production	Lint Production	Lint Export
1991/92	34,635	15,426	11,815
1992/93	47,006	15,754	13,990
1993/94	46,324	15,700	13,990
1994/95	53,006	17,400	17,000
1995/96	50,507	16,311	13,759
1996/97	74,000	25,147	23,500
1997/98	91,088	31,007	28,204
1998/99	116,716	35,677	34,472
1999/2000	35,365	12,200	11,593
2000/2001	71,048	24,300	17,600
2001/2002	70,000	23,000	23,000

Source: IAM.

Farmers must pay back the assistance by selling the company their crop with subtraction of their debts (Coughlin 2001). Private cotton traders recently entered the business, purchasing seed cotton from farmers and selling it where it is more convenient.

Some major constraints of the cotton subsector that need mention are: degeneration and low yields of cotton varieties used for more than a decade, influencing production yields and product quality; poor road infrastructures and other resources, including inputs, production zones; reduction of production areas by companies that were using better and more advanced technology; limited capacity to assist small farmers and delivery of immediate response to their needs; low level of farmer education reducing their capacity to work through associations and groups, and increasing their needs in technical assistance; obsolete equipment in gins, most of them old, with low productivity, frequent breakdown, and using old technology; financial constraints that hamper investment by the private companies that would assure a more efficient and effective service to the farmers and to their own areas; deterioration and paralysis of classification rooms and laboratory equipment and tools (Bawden and others 2001; MADER 1998).

In addition, the agricultural and agroindustrial enterprises are facing financial problems, with negative influences from the international markets, particularly the policy of subsidies that protects the cotton producers in developed countries. Such subsidies do not exist in Mozambique. Local producers regard the recent U.S. farm bill as one of the constraints to Mozambican cotton exports. The low returns resulting from high production costs and the absence of subsidies, compared with the export prices, affects producer development and access to new and better technologies. The decline of international cotton fiber prices also negatively affects the Mozambican cotton subsector. Climate changes and natural disasters cause lower cotton production, yields, and quality.

Producers and purchasers want improvements in the quality of cotton. Harvesting and storage conditions at community level and conventional warehouses are controlled to avoid cotton deterioration.

A step forward is the fact that more and more producers and purchasers are taking into consideration the product quality and the requirements to get more production and better product quality.

There are only buying prices for two grades (first and second) of gross seed cotton to producers, applicable in mobile and fixed rural markets, set every year by MADER and the National Commission for Salaries and Prices. Second-grade cotton seed is often classified as first grade, benefiting the farmers and traders but causing technical problems in the ginneries, affecting cotton seed separation and cotton processing, resulting in poor quality lint.

There are 25 ginning mills, but only 14 are working (two of them new), and the other 11 are closed.

Grading of cotton lint for export is based on the quality of the cotton (color, cleanliness, strength) and the length of the lint. The grading system used in Mozambique dates back to the Portuguese colonial period. It classifies cotton lint into eight grades: extra, one, two, three, four, five, six and inferior, while cotton lint length varies between 1 5/32" and 1". This classification differs from the U.S. cotton grading with about 40 different grades. Grading has been done based on visual and manual inspection and the equipment that can automatically grade cotton is not available because of its high cost. Many buyers complain about the poor grading of Mozambican cotton and they often have to reclassify the cotton from Mozambique to reflect international standards (Bawden and others 2001).

The comparison of the classification in eight grades for Mozambican cotton fiber with the international grades is:

Mozambican Grades	American Standards According to Trash Content
Extra	Good middling
Type I	Strict middling
Type II	Middling
Type III	Between middling and strict low middling
Type IV	Strict low middling
Type V	Low middling
Type VI	Strict good ordinary
Type inferior	Good ordinary

The quality of Mozambican cotton fiber is still low and this is the main reason why it is sold at a lower price. The ginning outrun (cotton lint or seed cotton production) was 32–35 percent in the last decade, compared to an average of 42 percent in other African countries (Lemaitre P and CIRAD 2001).

Because of the general poor quality of Mozambican cotton and the absence of a better graded product, 75 percent of Mozambican cotton falls into Grades 3 to 4 with cotton length ranging between 1 1/8" and 1 1/16". Therefore, it usually fetches much lower prices than the Cotlook Index A price (Bawden and others 2001).

Grade	Lint Length							Total Production ('000 kg)	%
	1 5/32"	1 1/8"	1 3/32"	1 1/6"	1 1/32"	1"	S/C		
Extra		7.8	1.7					9.5	0
One		418.5	211.4	13.6				643.4	2
Two	18.4	1,251.6	3,543.9	774.7				5,588.6	18
Three	8.2	3,437.0	4,858.8	7,263.4				15,567.5	50
Four		1,727.6	922.3	4,689.5	1.7			7,341.0	24
Five		0.818	158.1	474.8	594.0	226.6		1,454.3	5
Six				321.2	30.0	50.2		401.4	1
Inferior							0.915	0.915	0
Total	26.6	6,843.3	9,696.3	13,537.0	625.8	276.8	0.915	31,006.6	100

The Cotton Institute has plans to increase the number of cotton grades to 11 instead of the 8 currently used.

The cotton subsector assessment (2001) refers to the challenge of updating the lint-classifying system to meet the market demand as one of the prospects for a better valuation of the cotton products. For lint classification the trash content, color, and lint characteristics (staple length, staple strength, maturity, and fineness) and micronaire readings are measured. However, features previously considered secondary are currently important and may result in a lower price, such as length uniformity, content of short fibers, contamination with organic and inorganic material, and others. These features are measurable. The modern method of lint classification with the high volume instrument (HVI) does not exist yet in Mozambique.

The Mozambique Cotton Institute is responsible for lint classification. However it lacks resources to fulfil the demand. Its four classification rooms are not enough and the laboratories lack instruments and reagents, with the result that the classification rooms and laboratories are unable to achieve a desirable quality control of cotton lint for domestic and international marketing (Bawden and others 2001).

The costs of compliance with quality standards for cotton lint are still insignificant and include only the cost of tests on cotton bales in the family sector (about 25 cents (US) per bale). The firms do not pay directly for the quality control done by IAM because they pay the institute 2 percent to 3.5 percent of the value of exports (the decree provides for a rate of 5 percent, but this was reduced because of the high costs the firms face for inputs).

Cotton cultivation, marketing, and export are better regulated than other crops. Besides the regulations on cotton (Ministerial Diploma No. 91/94 of 29 June, Ministry of Agriculture and its rectification of 27 July), other legislation deals with the establishment of the Mozambique Cotton Institute (Decree No. 7/91 of 23 April, Council of Ministers), the establishment of the principles for cotton production, marketing, and processing (Decree No. 8/91 of 23 April, Council of Ministers) and the internal regulations of the Mozambique Cotton Institute (Ministerial Diploma No. 77/2001 of 23 May, Ministry of Agriculture) and its legal framework, the Strategy for Cotton Development (Internal Resolution No. 15/98 of 22 September, Council of Ministers).

Conclusions

• There are good prospects for more cotton production for export and the local textile industry.

- Cotton quality is still poor and combined agricultural, industrial, and training and extension activities are required to improve it.
- Low prices offered for Mozambican lint may be overcome through improvements in cotton classification rooms and laboratories.
- The weakness of grading and lint classification hampers the evaluation of cotton in accordance with international standards, which would improve cotton prices.
- The Mozambican authorities are very keen to improve conditions and find mechanisms that increase the value of Mozambican cotton. IAM is interested in updating lint classification and the classification facilities, to meet the market demand, as recommended by Lemaitre P and CIRAD (2001).
- HVI probably is not the best short-term alternative, since the cotton laboratories may not have the necessary space, trained staff and maintenance systems (months ago IAM submitted a proposal for laboratory equipment, including HVI, but it was not accepted by the funding agency).

Recommendations for an Action Plan. For the development of the cotton subsector it is crucial to consider the following activities:

- Improvement of conditions and basic equipment and tools for the cotton classification rooms and laboratories;
- Review of the cotton grades and lint classification;
- Preparation and implementation of a training program for the new staff to be recruited for manual and visual lint classification, given that the more experienced workers are retiring or leaving the classification rooms and laboratories for other activities;
- Implementation of an extension or training program to train producers, traders, processors, extension workers, and technicians on cotton grades and lint classification, and the requirements for obtaining good-quality products and the benefits and losses of good and bad cotton quality.

The Case of Peanut (*Arachis hypogaea*) in Mozambique. Peanuts are cultivated in all provinces, by small farmers, and it is part of the staple diet in some regions, particularly in the south.

The crop area in the last five years is estimated to be between 150,000 and 440,000 hectares, with a production of 100,000–270,000 tons. The marketed peanut production during the same period was between 18,000 and 27,000 tons, which means that a considerable part of the harvest of small farmers is for their own consumption (roasted or cooked with or without the shell, peanut flour for baby food, peanut milk, other products), kept for seed, and processed into cooking oil.

The volume of unmonitored peanut export or import is estimated to be significant and held to specific quality standards. There are potential formal regional and international markets for peanut that require aflatoxin limits that are often below the average content in local products.

However, the mycotoxin problem is affecting peanut consumers and, therefore, export opportunities. Consumer's exposure is one of the main causes of hepatic diseases and the exports are rejected because of high aflatoxin contamination.

Through agriculture research and extension programs, some effort has been made with better varieties and production methods that may reduce the aflatoxin contamination. Very little has been done with regard to testing and using decontamination methods in storage facilities.

At the health level, some studies have shown that hepatic diseases are more often observed in areas where peanut is a staple food, such as in the Maputo province. Some medical researchers are studying this relationship, working with agronomists and nutritionists. Clinical data indicate that in Maputo there are fewer cases than before, raising the question of whether this is the result of better varieties, better agricultural practices, the consumption of better peanut, less peanut consumption or because infected consumers go to traditional doctors instead of hospitals.

Only a few laboratories in Mozambique analyze aflatoxins—LNHAA analyzes cereals and grains and their products and milk, mainly from the Maputo area. The INIVE laboratory analyzes aflatoxins only in animal feed produced in Maputo. The laboratories of the Faculties of Agronomy and Forestry Engineering, Veterinary Medicine, Medicine and Science (Biology Department) at the Eduardo Mondlane University study the microbiology of pests and diseases. The hospital laboratories perform blood and urine analysis. The INIA laboratories have the space and technicians to start mycotoxin analysis. The SGS company, at the request of potential exporters and importers, sends samples to its regional laboratory in South Africa. These three institutions analyze very few samples (less than 100 samples per year) of products from very specific areas. A representative sample from peanut fields and storage facilities may give a better picture of aflatoxin contamination, but such a sample does not exist at this time. Nevertheless, international researchers confirm that Mozambique is one of the countries with the highest rate of aflatoxin and other mycotoxin contamination.

In Mozambique, aflatoxins are the best or the only known mycotoxin and peanut the only contaminated commodity. Other mycotoxins in other products such as maize and oilseeds may be a primary concern, as it is in neighboring and other countries in the world.

There are no specific technical regulations on mycotoxins in Mozambique; international standards, mainly Codex Alimentarius is taken as a reference to evaluate food safety.

Conclusions. Peanut may be considered a common crop all over the country and in some regions it is a staple food.

There is the trend toward the increase of production and opportunities for exporting, local processing (packed roasted peanuts, cooking oil and other products—peanut butter is not a common product in Mozambique) and direct consumption as snacks and in cooked foods.

There is a need to control the results, in terms of aflatoxin contamination, of introducing new varieties and agronomic practices in the field and in storage facilities. This information is crucial to understand the degree of occurrence and the exposure of people and animals to mycotoxins, updating the health situation of peanut consumers and other products contaminated with aflatoxins. With this information, more adequate measures and programs may be prepared and implemented to improve food safety and human health.

There is a need to know the international standards better and adjust the quality of Mozambican products to required safety levels for the domestic market and exports.

Recommendations for an Action Plan. In order to update the existing information on the contamination of agriculture products and the exposure of

humans and animals to mycotoxins the following activities should be undertaken:

- To organize a mycotoxins working group to prepare a national program on mycotoxins;
- To promote meetings and seminars and training programs, mainly at the provincial and district level, to disseminate information and data on mycotoxins and preventive methods, oriented to producers, traders, processors, exporters, technicians, consumers, and decision makers;
- To prepare and carry out risk assessment, involving a multidisciplinary study to update and obtain information on the degree of occurrence, assessment of exposure to aflatoxins and other mycotoxins, particularly in peanuts and peanut products for consumption and for export;
- To understand the international standards and how they can be reached, while taking account of the SPS measures required by countries that might import Mozambican products;
- To organise the national laboratory network, planning the methods, areas to cover, and products to be analyzed by each of them. To equip the laboratories that will work on mycotoxins and train the laboratory technicians;
- To test and disseminate decontamination methods in conventional warehouses and traditional storage facilities;
- To develop partnerships with regional and international institutions, laboratories and, researchers to improve and develop specific assistance programs on mycotoxin issues.

The Case of Seed Production and Imports in Mozambique. Given that the availability and quality of seeds are fundamental to increasing agricultural and agroindustrial production, the description of this subsector is presented in more detail, including the studies and projects that have been developed in this area at the national and regional levels. Because of the important role of seeds in agriculture, several regulations regarding production, import, export, and trade are in force in Mozambique.

The National Seed Service of the National Directorate of Agriculture is the state body that regulates and monitors the importation, production, marketing, and export of seeds. This service has focused more on monitoring imported material and on the promotion of domestic seed production. Since there are no seed exports, its work in this area has been limited.

A consultative and advisory body, the "National Seed Committee" was created in MADER and should give its opinion on seed supply plans, the national list of varieties and legislation on seeds, among other subjects.

A medium-term Strategy of the Seed Subsector (1997–2001) was produced in December 1997 to assist the development of SNS activities, in the context of PROAGRI, and bringing up to date the strategy set out for 1987–1995. The aims of this government strategy were: improvement and strengthening of the public seed service in terms of coordination, agronomic research, and the improvement of plants, seed production, and the propagation of vegetative material for planting; the establishment of favorable conditions for the import and export of seeds; promotion of participation by the private sector in the production and distribution of farm inputs, including seeds; the informal production of seeds, the dissemination of information, with participation by NGOs; and certification and quality control. The priority areas for intervention in the seed subsector are indicated, with descriptions of subprograms and subcomponents, their activities and implementation mechanisms, and the estimated budgets.

The SNS prepared Procedures for the Evaluation and Registration of Varieties in the Official List (22 November 2000). For new seed varieties to be introduced and included in the National List of Varieties, whether they are produced in the country or abroad and are intended for use in Mozambique, from the public or private sector, they must be tested and submitted for the same type of evaluation. New varieties must be submitted to prerelease comparative testing of two types to be conducted by the SNS in at least two years or seasons. Widely used traditional and local varieties can be included in the national list by means of a very clear identification after they have been properly tested. The document contains the procedures for including new varieties and performing tests; the rights of the improver; provisional measures for the approval and registration of varieties; a model request for inclusion of a new variety; and information about the botanical characteristics and agronomic value of different species.

Seed importers are required to comply with the Seed Import Regulations, the objectives which are to ensure the importation of good quality seeds of varieties adapted to the different ecological zones, to discourage the imposition of seed imports when the country is producing sufficient quantities of acceptable quality, to coordinate and support the organizations that import seeds, and to establish the basis for a more effective control of seed imports. These regulations indicate the conditions, specifications of quality, licenses, and system of coordination for the importation of seeds. The Orange International Seed Lot Certificate, the Field Inspection Certificate, and the Phytosanitary Certificate must be presented.

The regulations on the production, trade, quality control, and certification of seeds cover licensing of producers, seed improvers, importers and exporters of seeds; quality control with the required documents, mechanisms of control, inspection and supervision of production, improvement, distribution, sale, import, and export of seeds; the duties and obligations of inspectors and supervisors; indication of tariffs; and penalties.

There are new provisions in the current regulations, particularly with regard to genetically modified varieties (GMO). Genetically modified varieties must not be imported and a declaration from the appropriate authorities of the exporting country to this effect is required to confirm that the seed is not a genetically modified variety.

Mozambique does not yet have the equipment to test if varieties are GMO. However, where necessary the country can use the existing facilities in South Africa or overseas services provided by firms such as SGS. The purpose of the declaration of origin is to ensure that suppliers do not send GMO if the seed is intended for agricultural production.

Seed exports require authorization, and for that purpose information is needed on the species and variety, quantities, where they may be inspected, their destination, and required certification. They must meet field and laboratory standards for certified seed and be properly packaged.

A list of 79 species and varieties, their common and botanical names, the weight of a lot, category of seed, field standards (isolation, percentage of atypical plants and number of inspections), and laboratory standards (percentage of purity, percentage of germination and percentage of humidity), is appended to these regulations.

Some studies related to legislation on seeds were carried out. They are:

(a) "Harmonization of Seed Policies and Regulations in Eastern Africa Project."

The Project was implemented in a pilot phase in Kenya, Tanzania, and Uganda from September 1999. This project was aimed at supporting countries in establishing a regional market, creating a seed industry in the region that would be viable and efficient, harmonizing policies and legislation on seeds in the countries involved, and establishing a fast and efficient regional quality control system.

(b) SADC "Regional Seed Security Network Project."

The idea of creating this seed security network emerged from a meeting on seeds at Mbabane in Swaziland in 1994 and was further developed at meetings in Maseru in Lesotho in 1997 and Kadoma in Zimbabwe in 1999. The project was launched in July 2001 in Pretoria and is in the first phase of year one. The purpose of the project is to create a database and develop activities related to training and harmonization of seed production, legislation, and marketing.

(c) "Assessment of the Requirements for Establishing a Seed Regulatory System in Mozambique Study."

Dr. D. Keetch conducted this study for the IFDC in March 2001, in the context of the "Mozambique Agricultural Input Market Strengthening Project," funded by USAID. Its objectives were to:

- Evaluate the current situation relating to seed legislation in Mozambique;
- Draft seed laws and regulations that are not included in the current seed regulatory system but which are necessary to complete implementation and make it function more efficiently;
- Submit a report on the implementation of the regulatory system that includes implementation methodology, recommendations on technical assistance, training and equipment needs, a schedule and budget and;
- Support the National Seed Organisation of South Africa.

The recommendations of the study are aimed at facilitating the development and distribution of new varieties among the countries of the southern African region, and seed legislation needs to be harmonized at the regional level. New laws and regulations were proposed, notably a national seed policy, a seed law, regulations on the classification of seeds, models for seed multiplication in a certification scheme, testing varieties and procedures for testing.

(d) "Status and Opportunity of Mozambique's Seed Sector Study."

In the context of the World Bank's Sub-Saharan Africa Seed Initiative (SSASI), a study was made of the status and opportunity of Mozambique's seed sector, a regional strategy was drawn up to improve the national seed distribution system and to facilitate the flow of seeds and varieties among the countries of the region, which measures have been shown to contribute toward better competition and an increase in the supply of good quality seed. Some recommendations were presented, including the strengthening of the supply of emergency seed.

(e) "Characterization of the Current Situation in the Seed Sector in Mozambique study."

This study, conducted by Freire and Banze (April 2001), describes the situation in the seed sector before and after independence, namely the existing infrastructure, its location and capacity, and who owned it. It presents statistical data on the production of certified seeds and seeds in general, both in total and by crop. It summarizes the strategies and legislation on seeds in Mozambique and describes the system of seed quality control and certification, the research and improvement program of new varieties, the formal and informal systems of production and distribution of seeds, imports and exports of seeds, with general and species-specific statistical data, and the actors in the seed chain. It gives a list of existing projects for the local production of seeds and the institutions that finance and operate locally with extension programs. It provides information on the production capacity of crops, seed security, and the conservation of phytogenetic resources. It does a SWOT (strengths, weaknesses, opportunities, and threats) analysis of the sector and presents the conclusions and recommendations at the national seed seminar held in March 2001.

The main findings and conclusions relate to problems of quality control of imported seeds and to seed distribution mechanisms.

Conclusions. The seed regulations have contributed to better seed supply from other countries, in terms of adequate varieties, good quality seeds that are free of pests and diseases. They positively influence seed production and multiplication, as well as crop production in general. While the regulations were being drawn up, some international and regional institutions gave their collaborative support, which facilitated the intended regional harmonisation of seed regulations. The seed control procedures should be specially designed for emergency situations to avoid delays of seed imports and distribution in affected areas.

Domestic Regulatory Structures and Policies: Internal Market Barriers

The Mozambican regulatory system includes several ministries and institutions that are responsible for different functions related to the development and application of laws and technical regulations.

It should be noted that Mozambican legislation relating to agricultural and food products, as well as hygiene and sanitary aspects, generally includes the procedures for importation, domestic consumption, and exportation. In general the legislation is not protective, giving the same treatment to domestically produced and imported goods.

Export products in general follow the standards and technical regulations requested by the importers. The fisheries sector is the only one that has an HACCP system to assure compliance with food safety requirements.

Introduction

The various main national policies (the Government Programme for 2000–2004, PARPA, the industrial policy and strategy, the trade policy and strategy, and the agriculture policy and strategy) have the common objective of creating an economic environment that will allow the development of agriculture so as to eradicate poverty, as well as to foster an environment for market-based agricultural development that will increase and diversify exports. Furthermore, these policies recognize the need to improve the quality of products

and to establish standards that will help producers to succeed in their efforts.

To allow the implementation of the above policies several consultation mechanisms between the private sector and government were established with the objective of permitting discussion of the main constraints and identifying ways to solve them. Offices to support the private sector and to allow the private sector to participate in the main decisions were created in the Ministry of Industry and Trade, and the Ministry of Agriculture and Rural Development; and the Higher Technical Council for Customs (CSTA) created as an advisory body. To allow discussions related to the labor and employment policies, an advisory body, the Labor Consultative Council (CCT), was created. Partnerships were also created among government, private sector organizations, NGOs, civil society and donors, with the aim of contributing to the sound development of the Mozambican economy.

A brief analysis of the institutions responsible for the application of the various pieces of legislation shows that institutional capacity has increased in recent years. With regard to research institutions, the establishment of a Ministry of Science and Technology will assist the development of research capacity in the country, while MADER is reorganizing its own research institutions, and supervision activities in some ministries are being improved.

However, in general, there is a lack of sufficient human, material, and financial resources, thereby preventing rapid institutional development.

Principal Institutions and Legislation

In Mozambique there are three types of legislative documents—laws, decrees, and ministerial diplomas (MD). Laws are passed by the parliament of Mozambique and typically address primary social and political issues, such as taxes, civil rights, public health, defense, and education. Decrees are passed by the Council of Ministers and typically address issues such as budgets, public security, social discipline, labor, or the details of a law. Ministerial Diplomas deal with specific issues that are the responsibility of a particular ministry or ministries. One or more ministries may approve an MD, depending on the extent of their mutual involvement. Regulations are drawn up and included in an

MD. An MD usually consists of only one or two paragraphs setting out what will be regulated, why, and by which ministry or ministries. Regulations within the MD are structured in chapters, sections, and articles and may include annexes and appendices.

There are few laws in force relating to hygiene, sanitary and phytosanitary standards, imports, production, commercial exploitation and export of foodstuffs and agricultural, livestock, forestry, and fishery by-products. What basically exist are technical regulations that are the responsibility of certain institutions, with regard to the preparation, execution, and control of their application, and which coordinate with other institutions linked to the relevant legislation.

Most of the laws how in force were enacted before the 1980s and are now being brought up-to-date in line with technical and technological developments, institutional changes, and variations in prices. This is happening mainly in what concerns regulations issued by the Ministry of Agriculture and Rural Development, namely related to cashew, seeds, pesticides, tobacco, and fertilizers. However, in most cases there is need to develop the standards that will support the regulations. Legislation related to food safety that was developed by the Ministry of Health, also needs to be updated.

However, the efforts being made are not yet enough, and awareness about quality issues in general is still quite rudimentary. The institutional infrastructure is weak, and there is a lack of trained people, while the legislation and the level of development of standards are not enough. Furthermore, there are very few standards and technical regulations related to specific products. The production level is low and there is a lack of awareness concerning how the application of standards and quality principles could benefit the producer. As producers also face the problems described in Section 4, the priority is to increase production: but improving quality is not yet among the priorities.

Some laws and technical regulations are described in more detail in Annex A because they have a strong link with the subject of this study, and can help toward a better understanding of the Mozambican legal framework.

This section presents in more detail the main institutions and related legislation. Strengths and weaknesses related to the subject of this section are also analyzed.

Ministry of Health (MISAU). The Ministry of Health (MISAU) is responsible for the establishment of specifications and for the control of most of the foodstuffs produced and imported into Mozambique.

The Department of Environmental Health (DHA) of the MISAU is the state body that regulates and monitors health and hygiene relating to food, water and sanitation, health relating to international borders, in industry and of workers, and conducts medical examinations.

With regard to health, there is only one law, the "Crimes Against Public Health in the Context of Food Hygiene, Act" (Law No. 8/82 of 23 June, Standing Commission of the People's Assembly). This is the basic law for the control of foodstuffs in the country, the application of which covers all sectors that directly or indirectly relate to foodstuffs, including the consumers.

The technical regulations and other legal provisions in force relate to hygiene and sanitary requirements for establishments dealing with food products, to workers' health and hygiene, to the sanitary control of imported food products, and to the list of additives.

The regulations on imported foodstuffs, (Ministerial Diploma No. 80/87 of 1 July, MISAU), specify the conditions and procedures for the importation of foodstuffs, namely specifications of the identity and quality of the foodstuff, inspection and quality testing, certificates, supervision, infestation, inorganic contaminants, and microtoxins. The regulations establish that the standards to be applied on the importation of foodstuffs must be according to those established by Codex Alimentarius. These regulations also indicate that the inspection and quality testing at the place of origin of all imported foodstuffs is mandatory, by entities with recognized capacities or accredited to carry out this work, at the expense of the buyer.

Legislation on food hygiene is compiled in a collection prepared by the DHA. The main legislation is described in Annex A. In general the legislation on health needs to be updated.

The DHA has prepared a Manual of Inspection on food hygiene, based on the Codex Alimentarius, which served as a working and training tool for health inspectors. This manual includes a profile and job description of the inspectors, procedures for sampling, and inspecting food and premises, some of the main cycles of food production, characteristics of some raw materials and of food-stuffs produced in the country, and the code of practice on food hygiene of the Codex.

The health inspectors are directly linked to the Centre for Environmental Health and Medical Examinations (CHAEM), which is the health body that conducts medical examinations, issues official health certificates, and inspects factories and shops.

The National Laboratory for Water and Food Hygiene (LNHAA) is the official national laboratory that tests the quality of water, food, and drugs, and issues test reports. LNHAA has regional and provincial laboratories. Work developed by LNHAA is based on Codex and WHO standards. Regarding water analysis a standard for drinking water was developed based on CODEX and WHO, and this standard is being utilized and analyzed in one of the Standardisation Technical Committees so that it is as updated and approved as a Mozambican Standard.

The DHA is the point of contact for the Codex Alimentarius. It has participated in the annual meetings of the organization and has contributed to the preparation of the technical specifications.

It has no financial resources to cover the production of publicity materials, or to organize meetings and other events to publicise information or raise awareness about the Codex Alimentarius. The department also has few technicians, which adds to the problems already mentioned.

Other difficulties relate to funds to replace broken or outdated equipment and machinery in the National Laboratory for Water and Food Hygiene to improve its capacity and rate of response to requests for laboratory tests.

Ministry of Agriculture and Rural Development (MADER). The Ministry of Agriculture and Rural Development (MADER) has several functions and responsibilities related to the setting and control of the application of technical regulations related to agricultural products. Under MADER there are several directorates, departments and institutions that are analyzed in this section together with the related legislation.

The Department of Plant Health (DSV). The Department of Plant Health (DSV) of the National Directorate of Agriculture (DINA) is the body that deals with the quality of seeds and vegetable matter for planting and multiplication, the quarantine of plants, and field inspections.

This DSV prepares the list of chemical products registered in this country and updates it every two years. The registration of each product is valid for five years. To date 553 products have been registered, including insecticides, herbicides, fungicides, acaricides, rodenticides, avicides, animal dips, molluscicides, and nematicides.

DSV supervises the application of the pesticide regulation (Ministerial Diploma No. 88/87 of 29 July. Ministry of Health and Ministry of Agriculture), aimed at disciplining and controlling the registration, importation, production, packaging, labeling, storage, marketing and sale, and transport and elimination of pesticides and related chemicals. In addition to a toxicological classification, the upper limits of residues tolerated in food, their inspection and penalties are specified.

New technical regulations on pesticides are being approved and these will repeal the regulations approved in 1987. These provide for a technical advisory committee on pesticides, seeds, and fertilizers to be created to make recommendations to the Ministry of Agriculture and Rural Development on questions relating to agricultural pesticides and related veterinary and public health chemicals, for normal and for emergency situations.

The DSV also supervises the application of the Regulations on Phytosanitary Inspections and Plant Quarantine (Ministerial Diploma No. 134/92 of 2 September, Ministry of Agriculture). The purpose of these regulations, covering plants, plant products, and agricultural products, and the means of cultivation, packaging, and transporting them, is to prevent the introduction and spread of harmful organisms, especially from things in quarantine, to control pests and diseases, to supervise and control fields, forestry plantations, nurseries and places for storing and selling plants, and plant health control of imports and exports.

A representative of the DSV has participated in International Plant Protection Convention (IPPC) meetings but has exercised no influence on the setting of standards.

National Seed Service (SNS). The National Seed Service (SNS) of the DINA is the state body that regulates and monitors the importation, production, marketing, and export of seeds. This service has focused more on monitoring imported material and on the promotion of domestic seed production. Since there are no seed exports, its work in this area has been limited.

Legislation on seeds in Mozambique has been under review since 1995 to bring it up to date in the concepts and procedures relating to production, improvement, trade, import and export, quality control of seeds, and for the creation of bodies to manage and monitor the seed system. In addition to the published legislation, there is a seed subsector strategy paper and other policy documents from the SNS.

The main legislation on seeds is "Norms for the Production and Trade of Seeds", (Decree No. 41/94 of 20 September, Council of Ministers). This decree is regarded as the basic law on seeds.

The "Regulations on the Production, Trade, Quality Control and Certification of Seeds," (Ministerial Diploma No. 184/2001 of 19 December, Ministry of Agriculture and Rural Development), complements the Norms on the Production and Trade of Seeds, approved by Decree No. 41/94 of 20 September, the Regulations on Seed Imports, Ministerial Diploma No. 95/91 of 7 August and the National List of Varieties, Dispatch from the Minister of Agriculture and Fisheries on 17 August 1995.

Seed imports are governed by the Regulations on Seed Imports, Ministerial Diploma No. 95/91 of 7 August and there are new provisions in the current regulations, particularly with regard to genetically modified varieties (GMO). Genetically modified varieties must not be imported and a declaration from the appropriate authorities of the exporting country to this effect is required to confirm that the seed is not a genetically modified variety.

Other documents required are the Orange International Seed Lot Certificate (or in authorized cases a certificate of integrity) and the plant health certificate. Seed exports require authorization and for that purpose information is needed on the species and variety, on the quantities, where they may be inspected, their destination, and certificates. They must meet field and laboratory standards for certified seed and be properly packaged.

National Directorate of Livestock (DINAP). The National Directorate of Livestock (DINAP) regulates and supervises the quality of production and the processing of animal products. DINAP is currently more focused on imports and domestic consump-

tion because there is no commercial export of animal products.

In 2001, DINAP prepared technical regulations on animal health, on livestock branding, and on industrial pig-farming zones, which are all in the process of being approved. Technical regulations are currently under preparation for meat inspection, the construction and licensing of abattoirs and slaughterhouses, on milk and dairy products, and for the Veterinary Medicines Act. Most of the legislation, regulations, and technical specifications in force were written between the 1960s and 1975. They need to be brought up to date, in line with technical and technological advances, institutional modifications, and changes in prices.

DINAP technicians may apply sanitary measures where these are justified. In the case of imports and the domestic market, sanitary control follows international standards.

This department is concerned with the welfare of live animals being imported or in transit to other countries in the region. Livestock inspectors at border posts or in police stations carry out health checks. DINAP representatives have participated in regional meetings of SADC, the Office International des Epizooties (OIE) and the World Trade Organization (WTO).

The National Directorate of Forestry and Wildlife (DNFFB). The National Directorate of Forestry and Wildlife (DNFFB), regulates and supervises subjects related to forestry and wildlife.

The Forestry and Wildlife Act (Law No. 10/99 of 7 July, Assembly of the Republic), establishes the principles and basic norms for the protection, conservation, and sustainable use of forestry and wildlife resources. This law contains the classification of the forestry and wildlife stock, the forms of protection of resources, the conditions and rules for forestry exploitation and hunting, for the replacement of these resources, forestry and wildlife management and supervision. For the export of forest and wildlife products, the law covers the promotion of the processing industry to increase the export of manufactured goods.

Regulations are currently being prepared for the application of the Forestry and Wildlife Act, and to harmonize it with the Land and the Environment Acts.

With regard to forests, a study was conducted recently on forestry certification that is based on the establishment of standards and codes of good practice. Forestry certification provides information on the management practices used in a given forestry unit and the attribution of a certificate to the forest or product gives the consumer assurance that it comes from a forest that is managed according to the established requirements.

Institute for the Promotion of Cashew (INCAJU). The public institute INCAJU, under the Ministry of Agriculture and Rural Development, was set up in 1997 (Decree No. 43/97 of 23 December) to promote the planting of cashew and other fruit trees and the cashew processing industry. INCAJU monitors the regulations for commercial and industrial licensing in force since 1998 (Decree Nos. 43/98 and 44/98 of 9 September) for the submission of proposals for commercial and industrial licensing of businesses in cashew.

INCAJU oversees the application and control of the Cashew Act passed in November 1999 (Law No. 13/99 of 1 November, Assembly of the Republic), which establishes that the Council of Ministers must formulate a policy on the promotion of cashew production and processing, with the aim of recovering the stock of cashew trees by providing incentives to organizations to become involved in the planting of and research into cashew trees, the technological development and economic and financial recovery of existing cashew processing firms, and the creation of industries to use cashew by-products.

INCAJU also oversees the application of the regulations on cashew nut marketing of 1999 (Decree No. 86/99 of 23 November, Council of Ministers). These regulations establish the procedures and conditions for cashew nut marketing and set the annual surcharge on the export of unprocessed cashew nuts.

Marketing specifications for cashew nuts in the 2000/2001 season were drawn up and published in August 2001, giving marketing procedures and parameters and ranges for the classification for producers, pickers, and traders of cashew nuts (primary level), and for traders, processing factories, and exporters (secondary level), and the influence of these on prices of the product.

The recommended prices for cashew nuts and cashew kernels are set and published by the customs service.

INCAJU participates in the Technical Committee on Standardisation that is currently developing national standards for cashew nuts and kernels and a code of best practice for the processing of nuts.

Mozambique Cotton Institute (IAM). The Mozambique Cotton Institute (IAM) was established in 1991 (Decree No. 7/91 of 23 April, Council of Ministers), to develop and supervise the cultivation, marketing, processing and export of cotton; to develop research and experimentation in cotton cultivation; promote compliance with technical standards for soil conservation, and the correct use of agricultural chemicals to protect the environment.

The IAM is responsible for the application of the Decree No. 8/91 of 23 April, Council of Ministers, which updates the legal framework for the cultivation, marketing, and industrialization of cotton in Mozambique and revokes Decree No. 45179 of 5 August 1963.

This decree gives the Mozambique Cotton Institute the responsibility for the promotion and supervision of cotton cultivation and technical and financial assistance to the growers. It specifies the procedures for marketing seed cotton, for the ginning and baling operations in cotton gins, for the marketing and export of baled cotton, as well as for penalties.

The IAM is also responsible for the application and control of the regulations on cotton cultivation (Ministerial Diploma No. 91/94 of 29 June, Ministry of Agriculture), which specify who are the economic operators and the concessions for cotton production, their registration, and the procedures for growing cotton and marketing seed cotton and cotton fiber. Some technical aspects regarding the characteristics of the soil, crop operations, ginning, and phytosanitary control are indicated.

Research Institutions Under MADER. There are other institutions under MADER that while not directly related to the regulatory system, play a role in research and also undertake some testing; a brief reference to these institutions is given below:

(a) Livestock Production Institute (IPA).

   The Livestock Production Institute was set up in 1988 to develop research in the areas of animal feeding (natural pasture, fodder, and by-products) and nutrition, reproduction, and artificial insemination, species improvement and selection, livestock production systems, and the production of meat, milk and other animal products.

(b) National Sugar Institute (INA).

The National Sugar Institute under the Ministry of Agriculture and Rural Development was set up in 1977 with the aim of promoting the production and processing of sugarcane.

(c) National Veterinary Research Institute (INIVE).

The National Veterinary Research Institute is a public institution that was created in 1987 (Ministerial Diploma 161/87 of 30 December) from institutions that had been set up in 1908 to work along similar lines. The functions of INIVE are to contribute to knowledge of Mozambique's nosological classification and provide the technical and scientific bases needed for the prevention and control of animal diseases, to make studies in the field of veterinary science and technology, to provide specialized services to guarantee the health of animals and public health, and to lead the application of research results to the benefit of national technical, scientific, and socioeconomic development. Its main areas are diagnosis and research, vaccine and biological reagents production, food quality control, and drug and biological product control.

INIVE has developed programs related to chicken, goat, cattle, and swine diseases, production systems, quality control of food of animal origin, and drug control.

Ministry of Fisheries. The standards and technical regulations followed by the fisheries sector are basically those from the Codex Alimentarius, which are required by clients of fish and seafood exports.

The Ministry of Fisheries, as indicated on the case of the fisheries sector in Mozambique in Section 4, is responsible for the application of the specific regulations, namely, The Regulations on Inspection and Guarantee of Quality of Fishing Products (Decree 17/01 of 12 June, Council of Ministers, BR no. 23, I Series), the basis for quality control of fishery products; the Fisheries Act (Law 3/90 of 26 September, People's Assembly, BR no. 39, I Series); the fisheries policy and implementation strategy (Resolution 11/96 of 28 May, Council of Ministers), and the Marine Fisheries Regulations (Decree 16 of 28 May, Council of Ministers, BR no. 21).

The responsibility for the control of the application of these laws falls under the Fisheries Inspection Department (DIP).

Under the Ministry of Fisheries there are research institutions described in the case of the fisheries sector in Mozambique. The Fisheries Research Institute (IIP) was established in 1988 (Ministerial Diploma No. 75/88 of 18 May, National Planning Commission) and restructured in 1998 (Decree No. 63/98 of 24 November, Council of Ministers) to make an inventory, evaluate and scientifically manage the fishery resources of the territorial waters. The Small-Scale Fisheries Development Institute (IDPPE) is a public institution established in 1998 (Decree No. 62/98 of 24 November, Council of Ministers) to promote development activity in small-scale fisheries production as an integral part of rural development. The objective of the Institute is to conduct studies so as to formulate development policies, strategies, plans, and programs.

Ministry of Industry and Trade (MIC)

The Ministry of Industry and Trade is responsible for the coordination and application of the policies related to industry and trade. One of the responsibilities of this Ministry is to support and promote actions with the objective of contributing to the quality assurance of products, processes, and services in the industrial sector, so as to allow them to satisfy the domestic market and to guarantee competitiveness on the external market. On trade its responsibilities are to support initiatives for the increase and diversification of exports and to protect consumers.

MIC supervises the quality services, at this time provided only by INNOQ.

MIC is also responsible for the inspection of industrial and commercial activity. The inspectors usually work with the Ministry of Health on issues concerning health regulations. As in other ministries, efforts are being developed to improve inspection services. However, there is a lack of appropriate human, material, and financial resources affecting inspection activities.

The main regulations issued and whose application is the responsibility of MIC and MISAU are:

- The MD that establishes the standards of quality for wheat and wheat flour and for maize and maize meal (Ministerial Diploma No. 120/87 of 21 October, State Secretariat for Food and Light Industries);

- The Dispatch that prohibits the importation of wheat flour containing potassium bromide (Dispatch of 05 October 1996, Ministry of Industry and Trade and Ministry of Health);
- The MD that enforces the iodination of salt and compliance with the Mozambican Standard on iodized salt. The MD mentioned sets the level of KIO_3 at between 25 and 55 ppm. Regarding the technical specifications it states that these must follow the Mozambican Standard on salt (Ministerial Diploma No. 7/2000 issued on 02 November 1999 by the Minister of Industry, Trade and Tourism and the Minister of Health). The application of this regulation is the responsibility of MIC, MISAU and Customs inspectors.

Mozambique's Customs System. Mozambique's customs system is made up of the existing bodies and legislation and others that may be created in the future. Its functions include proposing measures and changes in fiscal and customs policy relating to foreign trade, implementing them, punishing infringements, collecting customs duties and other taxes and tariffs, inspecting and controlling the entry and exit of goods to and from Mozambique, and giving opinions on international treaties and conventions (Presidential Decree 4/2000 of 17 March).

The Mozambican Government began the reform of its customs procedures in 1995. The Minister of Planning and Finance created the Technical Unit for Customs Restructuring (UTRA) in February 1995 with the objective of managing the customs reform process.

Under this restructuring, new legislation concerning preshipment inspection was enacted. Since 1996, preshipment inspection has been handled by Intertek Testing Services (ITS), a U.K. based company, chosen by international tender. Another private company, Crown Agents was contracted in January 1997 to implement the customs reform.

In 1998 the existing import and export procedures were simplified and a single document replaced the previous complicated paperwork requirements.

A joint government–private sector body, the Higher Technical Council for Customs, provides recommendations to the Government on tariff setting and changes to legislation related to rules of origin in the framework of SADC and the Cotonou Agreement.

According to the statutes, approved in March 2000, Mozambique Customs is a state body of a paramilitary nature, which operates throughout the territory of the Republic of Mozambique to inspect and police the customs, taking measures when necessary with regard to people and goods in frontier zones (Decree 3/2000 of 17 March, Council of Ministers).

The Tariff Code Book (*Pauta Aduaneira*) contains all relevant laws, regulations, and tariffs. Some of the main laws are indicated in Annex A.

Problems in Meeting Mandatory Technical Regulations. It has been noted that producers generally face problems in complying with technical regulations. These problems are related to the difficulties identified in the analysis (see the section entitled "agricultural Production and Trade") of the problems facing the agriculture and the agroindustrial sectors, mainly poor infrastructure, production technologies, knowledge, and qualified labor. The fact that the majority of the regulations on food refer to the Codex standards in general and these standards in particular are not yet among the group of Mozambican standards, sometimes leads to a situation where it is not known which standard to use.

In addition to the problems faced in the productive sector, the capacity to supervise the application of regulations is weak and the institutions responsible for inspection have problems in enforcing the law.

Even in the cases where the regulations are copied from the Codex standards and translated into Portuguese, as with maize and maize meal, and wheat and wheat flour, where the diplomas that specify their characteristics date from October 1987, these diplomas are not well known and are only referred to in exceptional circumstances. However, sometimes in commercial transactions other regulations are used, such as South African regulations.

The problems noted above can also be seen in relation to imports, where the supervision carried out is not always the most effective.

The case of salt will be used to illustrate this question. This product has an important role in nutrition and also has good potential for export. The case illustrates how embryonic is the process of developing standards and their associated regulations, and how great the difficulties faced in assuring

Table 2.12 Salt Production
(ton)

Product	1996	1997	1998	1999	2000	2001
Noniodized salt	32,500	41,200	41,200	45,500	20,700	29,400
Iodized salt	1,376	1,890	27,838	10,860	1,235	14,330
Percentage of iodized salt	4.2	4.6	67.6	23.9	6.0	48.7

compliance with them. Moreover, it is a typical process in which joint efforts have brought about some success.

The case of fisheries illustrates a success story in which, because of the importance of this production in the Mozambican economy, the system maintains the credibility of exports.

The Case of the Iodized Salt in Mozambique. Mozambique has excellent climatic conditions for salt production, encouraging the development of large modern salt production plants, making salt a major export and creating jobs for people living near the coast.

However, salt production is limited because of outdated technology used in production and a shortage of skilled technicians. The salt produced and placed on the domestic market, in general, is not of sufficiently good quality. Thus the salt on sale in the larger supermarkets (mainly in Maputo) is imported.

The salt industry is even more important for Mozambique because of its decisive role in nutrition in that it is the ideal way of introducing iodine into the diet. The iodination of salt has been mandatory in Mozambique since July 2000.

However, the salt production data available indicates that during the period from 1996 to 2001, output peaked in 1998. Of all the salt produced, 67.6 percent is iodized, whereas, 32.4 percent is not. The proportion of iodized salt fell to 6 percent in 2000, and rose again to 48.7 percent in 2001 (Table 2.12).

The Ministry of Industry and Trade is the state body in charge of developing the salt sector. UNICEF is giving support to the salt iodination program, and following the floods, UNIDO has also supported the recuperation of this sector.

With regard to exports, Malawi, Zimbabwe, and the Democratic Republic of Congo are the normal importers of salt produced in Mozambique. However, salt exports were very low in 2000, possibly because of the steep decline in exports to Malawi owing to the high costs of transport. Furthermore, it has been noted that large quantities of salt are exported in cross-border trade, without respecting the existing legal channels for exports. (Table 2.13).

It should be mentioned that salt produced in Nampula is exported to Malawi in bulk and receives the necessary treatment there to bring it up to standards for consumption.

Table 2.13 Salt Export
(ton)

Country	1986	1987	1988	1989	1990	2000	2001
Malawi	7,000	12,000	17,000	10,000	5,000	4,087	43
Zimbabwe	25,000	10,000	15,000	17,000	20,000		
RDC (formerly Zaire)		5,000	12,000	8,000	7,000	18	134
Swaziland				3,000	5,000		
Hong Kong[a]						39	
Malaysia[a]						21	
UK[a]						2	
Colombia[a]							23
Others							69

Nb. Between 1990 and 1995, the state enterprise Extrasal E.E. was closed and begun the privatization of the salt production.
a. Pure salt.
Source: EXTRASAL.E.E, INE.

Table 2.14 Salt Import
(ton)

Country	1999	2000	2001
África do sul		379	82
Namíbia		153	
Portugal		73	8
Espanha			13
Paises Baixos			1
Outros paises		98	24
Total (ton)		703	128
Thousand US$		151	55

Source: INE, DNA.

Salt imports to Mozambique come from South Africa, Namibia, and Portugal (Table 2.14).

Regional Harmonization of Standards and Regulations. Iodine deficiency is the most common cause of preventable mental retardation and brain damage in the world. A diet deficient in iodine can therefore lead to a wide range of abnormalities. Iodine Deficiency Disorders (IDD) is the general term used for all the complications that occur in populations with low iodine in their diets.

Salt is regarded as the ideal vehicle for ensuring iodine consumption and salt iodination is a vital factor in preventing IDD.

In July–August 1997, the Commonwealth Regional Community Health Secretariat (CRCHS) commissioned a consultancy to look at harmonization of salt iodination programs in Eastern, Central and Southern Africa (ECSA).

The recommendations made in the consultant's report included, among other issues:

- The need to facilitate and review harmonization of USI legislation and the relevant Standards Acts in the ECSA region.
- The need to conduct ECSA regional conferences on USI policy direction and review with regard to SADC and COMESA trade agreements that encompass salt as a basic and essential tradeable product for both human and animal consumption.

In 1999, Mozambique participated in the Inter-Country Workshop on Harmonization of Iodized Salt Regulations for Southern Africa where the following areas were identified as needing harmonization:

- Standards for salt quality;
- Method of analysis for salt iodine; and
- Sampling protocols.

For each of these areas, recommendations were formulated and adopted. On the basis of recommendations from the Botswana meeting and the Codex standards, INNOQ coordinated the formulation of a Mozambican standard in iodized salt. The standard became mandatory through technical regulations on iodized salt (Ministerial Diploma No. 7/2000 of 5 January). The regulation on iodized salt mainly establishes that all food salt must be iodized (iodine as KIO_3). The level of iodine must not be less than 25 ppm and not more than 55 ppm. This regulation applied to salt produced in Mozambique, as well as, imported salt. With regard to exports, the regulation states that exports must comply with the specifications of the importer.

This was the first experience that saw the successful formulation of a standard, with participation from various interested parties.

Efforts have been made to ensure that the salt available for public consumption complies with the standard and the existing legislation on the subject, with regard both to locally produced and imported salt.

The National Program of Salt Iodination. The salt iodination program has received support from UNICEF, and a national committee has been set up with representatives from the Ministries of Industry and Trade (MIC) and of Health (MISAU), the Institute for the Development of Small-Scale Industry (IDIL), the National Institute of Standardisation and Quality (INNOQ), and the South of Save Salt Producers Association (APSSS).

This program was carried out in two phases:

First phase: This consisted of the distribution of iodized salt capsules in Niassa province in 1991 and Tete province in 1992. The capsules were distributed to school-age children and to women of childbearing age in health units.

Second phase: This began in 1995 with the production of iodized salt, consisting of a mixture of iodized salt with normal salt and a little iodine.

As part of the effort to support salt producers who achieve the minimum quality standards in their salt products, the government has exempted them from value added tax (VAT), which was 17 percent.

The activities being carried out involve both state institutions and the private sector. Under the program, training is being given to salt producers, together with awareness campaigns. The objective is to provide them with technical regulations and information on the standard. Some work has also been done toward training inspectors.

However, there are various problems related to the production and the low purchasing power of the population, which result in the existing legislation being violated and the standard being ignored. The market continues to offer low-quality salt for human consumption, particularly in nonurban areas. Nevertheless, despite all these problems, studies conducted by the Ministry of Health show that the prevalence of goiter has fallen by 5 percent.

Conclusions and Recommendations. The work carried out to create awareness about the need to apply the regulations and the related standard has brought results: most of the salt producers know the regulations and the standard and some of them have improved the quality of this product.

There is a need to improve coordination between the work conducted through the National Committee together with UNICEF and that done by UNIDO.

The report of a visit held in November 2001, by members of the National Committee to the salt producers in the provinces of Zambezia, Cabo Delgado, and Nampula identified the main problems faced by salt producers such as high prices of railway transport, lack of packaging material, equipment in bad condition, or lack of equipment to iodize and improve salt quality.

The main recommendations from this visit, that we consider relevant, are the need to promote and

support the development of salt producers' associations and the need to set up laboratories near production areas.

The Case of the Fisheries Sector in Mozambique. The fisheries sector is one of the most important contributors to the Mozambican economy, representing 27.7 percent of Mozambique's total exports in 2000. Prawn exports rose from 5,694 tons in 1994 to 9,729 tons in 2000. Over the past 10 years, prawns account for 21 percent–38 percent of the total catch of fish and seafood (Tables 2.15 and 2.16).

The most abundant seafood resources are prawns, while, small pelagic fish and tuna are the main varieties of fish caught. In the large inland waters there still exists an unexplored potential of small pelagic fish.

In Mozambique, the small-scale fisheries are considered either semi-industrial or artisanal. Prawns are harvested mainly by industrial companies and by a large number of joint ventures between Mozambique, Japanese, Spanish, and South African companies.

Aquaculture in Mozambique is a priority for the government, especially prawn farming. The first major foreign investment in industrial-level prawn farming has been approved and is being implemented at Quelimane in Zambézia province. Opportunities also exist for farming fish, oysters, mussels, algae, and pearls.

Investment opportunities in the fisheries sector lie primarily in the need for a gradual substitution of industrial vessels by semi-industrial freezer boats that can discharge prawns for further on-shore processing.

Mozambique currently exports mainly raw materials. Government strategy is to promote processes that add value in this sector. Furthermore, Mozambique needs to improve its services to the fishing industry.

Prawns represent 90 percent of all exports of fish products, and can be found along almost the whole

Table 2.15 Catch by Type of Seafood

	1995	1996	1997	1998	1999	2000
Crustaceans	10,310	10,442	12,868	11,677	11,545	12,319
Fish	14,076	18,176	26,132	24,161	34,982	40,524
Calamari and others	526	672	705	779	754	688
Total catch	24,912	29,290	39,705	36,617	47,281	53,531

Source: INE (2000).

Table 2.16 Shrimp Capture and Export—Historical Evolution 1997–2002

Year	Shrimp Capture (ton)	Shrimp Export (ton)	Total Sea Products (ton)	Shrimp Capture/Total Sea Production (%)
1979	4,182		6,410	65
1980	6,984		14,413	48
1981	8,678		18,224	48
1982	6,220		15,831	39
1983	5,767		18,655	31
1984	5,847		17,555	33
1985	6,092		20,566	30
1986	5,863		25,686	23
1987	5,570		25,198	22
1988	7,436		32,131	23
1989	5,903		27,560	21
1990	6,863	6,353	32,919	21
1991	7,698	7,841	25,536	30
1992	6,760	8,680	27,808	24
1993	7,347	6,185	19,195	38
1994	6,645	5,694	23,058	29
1995	7,699	6,127	24,747	31
1996	8,123	6,525	35,621	23
1997	9,825	8,810	39,703	25
1998	8,559	9,159	36,677	23
1999	8,846	7,771	33,989	26
2000	9,460	9,729	39,065	24
2001[a]	9,489	9,331	32,781	29
2002[a]	9,500	9,300	35,090	27
Average				31

a. Estimated.
Source: Ministry of Fisheries.

length of the Mozambican coast. Prawn fishing boats use deep dragnets, and may be industrial, semi-industrial, or artisanal. Industrial fishing (notes on prawn fishing in Mozambique) is responsible for 87 percent of the registered catch, using modern, well-equipped boats.

Increased prawn fishing led to declining yields, and in 1990 the Ministry of Fisheries began to introduce prawn management measures, such as a closed season during which fishing was prohibited, increased size of the net mesh, and the establishment of acceptable catch quotas.

Most exports go to the European Union and Japan, as the largest fishing companies come from those regions. Within the SADC, South Africa, Mauritius, and Zimbabwe also import prawns. The AGOA program opens up opportunities for exporting to the United States on preferential terms.

Fish products are usually subject to restrictive quality requirements, given that their main destination is for direct human consumption. The high level of import requirements, particularly in the European Union, has meant that Mozambique's fisheries sector has gradually developed a system that enables it to meet the requirements and guarantee the exports. The system is primarily based on the European Union's quality requisites.

The Ministry of Fisheries is the government body in charge of developing the sector, through its Fisheries Inspection Department (DIP). This department classifies licenses, certifies, and audits the export-oriented fishing units; a total of 80 fishing boats and 6 companies on land, and carries out health controls of their export products, essentially following Codex standards.

The DIP guidelines for classifying fishing units are based on the HACCP system. Units are classified as regular, good, or excellent, and this defines the destination of their produce. Those with "regular" classification only produce for the domestic market, those with "good" classification export to South Africa and Japan, and the "excellent" export to the European Union and other countries.

The DIP has offices in six provinces, with inspectors and fish auditors, and has two inspection rooms and three laboratories for making sensory and chemical analyses. The laboratories on Beira and Maputo are also equipped to do microbiological analyses.

In addition to health control, the DIP draws up technical regulations and procedures with which all those wishing to set up fishing units or export units must comply. Its annual meeting discusses new proposals for regulations and procedures, and debates topics, which will enable its technicians to gain new knowledge.

The growth of DIP was mainly a consequence of the demands of the importers, the EU in particular, but an additional factor was that the National Laboratory for Water and Food Hygiene (LNHAA) in the Ministry of Health suffered a gradual reduction in capacity due to lack of funding, and was no longer able to provide the analyses requested with the necessary speed and quality. The DIP thus evolved from its initial inspection rooms for sensory analysis to establishing laboratories for chemical and microbiological analyses.

In addition to the DIP, the Ministry of Fisheries is responsible for the Fisheries Research Institute (IIP), the Small-Scale Fisheries Development Institute (IDPPE), and the Fisheries School (for training sailors).

The Fisheries Research Institute (IIP) was established in 1988 (Ministerial Diploma No. 75/88 of 18 May, National Planning Commission) and restructured in 1998 (Decree No. 63/98 of 24 November, Council of Ministers) to make an inventory, evaluate and scientifically manage the fisheries resources of the territorial waters. Furthermore, it collaborates in determining the most appropriate ways for the conservation and optimization of fisheries exploitation, conducts environmental studies needed for research into fishing resources, conducts studies and experimental research on the cultivation of aquatic species for the purpose of commercial production, and publishes technical and scientific information.

The research activities carried out by IIP influence and guide the formulation of policies and technical regulations in the Ministry of Fisheries.

The Small-Scale Fisheries Development Institute (IDPPE) is a public institution established in 1998 (Decree No. 62/98 of 24 November, Council of Ministers) to promote development activity in small-scale fisheries production as an integral part of rural development. The objective of the Institute is to conduct studies to formulate development policies, strategies, plans, and programs. It should carry out studies and promote development activities and projects related to socioeconomic aspects, fisheries technology, and complementary activities. It should also promote activities and projects to increase the skills of officials and fishermen.

The Ministry of Health is the body that controls the fishing units and their produce when it is destined for domestic consumption. The LNHAA also does laboratory analysis.

The National Institute for Standardisation and Quality (INNOQ) is the body that coordinates the development of standards at the national level. In this regard, as part of the program to harmonize SADC standards and technical regulations, which is being carried out by SADCSTAN, some fishery product standards, that the SADC members consider a priority, are already at the stage of final drafts for discussion—they are based on South African standards. The regional harmonization process plans for them to become mandatory once they have been approved. These standards are being analyzed by the Technical Committee on food, on which the Ministry of Fisheries is represented by the DIP.

The private sector involved in prawn fishing is organized into the Mozambican Association of Industrial Prawn Fisheries (AMAPIC), which has worked with the Ministry of Fisheries to improve the performance of the fishing units.

The SGS Company has done the certification of export prawns for some clients, but only with regard to the quantities prepared for shipping.

In terms of regulations, the Regulation on Inspection and Guarantee of Quality of Fishing Products (Decree 17/01 of 12 June, Council of Ministers, BR no. 23, I Series), is the basis for quality control, and was drafted to be equivalent to the European Union Directives 91/493/CEE and 92/48/CEE with regard to sanitary conditions in the productive units during operations and product quality. This regulation has many aims: to be a guiding instrument for the development of a processing industry; to update and modernize national legislation in accordance with the requirements of the international market; to set legal boundaries for the responsibilities of the fisheries inspectorate and the role of the processing industry; to serve, together with the marine fisheries regulations, as an instrument for fisheries management and administration; and to be a sectoral instrument that also has implications for other sectors such as health, customs, and commerce.

The main fisheries sector legislation currently in force also includes the Fisheries Act (Law 3/90 of 26 September, People's Assembly, BR no. 39, I Series), the fisheries policy and implementation strategy (Resolution 11/96 of 28 May, Council of Ministers), and the Marine Fisheries Regulations (Decree 16 of 28 May, Council of Ministers, BR no. 21). There is also a Master Plan for the Fisheries Sector, which was drawn up in 1994. A revised version is now awaiting approval.

Other technical regulations related to fisheries and public health in general are: Sanitary Control register (Order in Council No. 11/78 of 14 January, Ministry of Health and Ministry of Industry and Trade); health certificate (Dispatch of 13 November 1980 Ministry of Health); Decree No. 5/80 of 22 October Council Of Ministers and Ministerial Diploma No. 73/82 of 23 June, Ministry of Health, Ministry of Finance and Secretary of State for Labor); Crimes against Public Health in the Context of Food Hygiene Act (Law No. 8/82 of 23 June, Standing Commission of the People's Assembly); Hygiene and sanitary requirements in the production, transport and trade of foodstuffs (Decree No. 12/82 of 23 June, Council of Ministers); Regulations on the hygiene requirements of food establishments (Ministerial Diploma No. 51/84 Ministry of Health); Regulations on imported foodstuffs (Ministerial Diploma No. 80/87 of 1 July Ministry of Health); Regulations on food additives in respect of the importation, production, marketing, and use of food additives (Ministerial Diploma No. 100/87 of 23 September, Ministry of Health); Pesticide regulations (Ministerial Diploma No. 88/87 of 29 July, Ministry of Health and Ministry of Agriculture) Approval of new regulations on pesticides is in process and will revoke the regulations approved in 1987.

Mozambique has managed to comply with internationally acceptable levels of quality and with the requirements of importers, with the exception of one isolated case, when in January 1998 a ban restricted to fishery was imposed by the European Union, because of an outbreak of cholera. The decision was not applied to fishery products, which were caught, frozen, and packed in their final packaging at sea and exported directly to the EU.

Conclusions. In light of the challenges related to exports this sub-sector has an established system, based on HACCP, enabling the quality assurance of export products.

One of the subsector's largest needs is training for middle- and senior-level staff of the various bodies and companies involved. Another is upgrading of the laboratories.

Existing regulations need to be revised in one or another aspect. It is important to speed up the development of national standards and codes of good practice based on Codex Alimentarius and harmonize them at the regional level.

Constraints and Recommendations for an Action Plan. Notwithstanding the good performance of the fisheries sector, the planned short-term activities of the DIP need financial assistance in the following areas: licensing control and audit; certification; construction, equipping and operation of laboratories; revision of technical manuals for the laboratories; inspectors and other technicians; harmonization of the inspection activities with other institutions; dissemination of regulations; preparation of training materials and holding general staff training courses (English, IT skills, secretarial skills), and specific technical courses for industrial workers, sailors, inspectors, and other technicians on hygiene and good working practices, the HACCP system, and laboratory hygiene and techniques; participation in national and international events; and postgraduate training (DIF 2002).

AMAPIC feels the need to prepare private sector technicians for introducing the HACCP system. This subsector, like others, reflects the reality that activities around quality are still embryonic in Mozambique, with a consequent lack of infrastructures at different levels. Development of the national quality system and respective infrastructures will certainly be a contribution toward improving its performance.

The opening of the U.S. market to fish products is a new challenge for AGOA. In addition to the need to implement the standards, companies will have to demonstrate that they have implanted the HACCP system, which is already a precondition for exporting to other regions. Another requirement for the U.S. market is that the boats must have apparatus for detecting turtles and currently only one boat has it. The companies that process prawns and other products from artisanal fishing on land and prepare them for export, are not covered by this requirement.

One of the export companies has a technician who took a course in the United States on HACCP, and is registered at the FDA. INNOQ has a trainer of trainers and auditors of HACCP who is also registered at the FDA, and this will help to provide increased support to exports in this area. INNOQ plans to begin HACCP training courses in 2002, but technical and financial support may be necessary for the courses to be recognized.

Domestic Standards Setting System

The need to take a more systematic approach to some aspects of quality led to the establishment of the National Institute of Standardisation and Quality, INNOQ in 1993. The establishment of the institute followed the perceived need to keep up with regional and international developments and to support local firms in their efforts to improve the quality of their products.

The standards setting system is coordinated by INNOQ and various bodies participated in the development of standards either voluntary or mandatory (technical regulations). Some of the bodies that participated in this process have been analyzed in the previous section.

The Quality System

Currently Mozambique has only the rudiments of a system of standardization, quality assurance, accreditation, and metrology. Activities in standardization and quality assurance are not enough to meet domestic requirements and those arising from the importation of goods. There is at present no subsystem of certification. Most sectors have no standardized procedures, and there is no system of consultancy for industrial firms on issues relating to standardization and quality assurance. Factories in Mozambique use different systems of standardization at the same time (INNO © 2002. Plano estratégico para a qualidade).

The existing quality system generally possesses the following components.

Standardization. The development of Mozambican standards, based on international standards and harmonized in the region, would constitute an important factor in development since it would enable national production to be more competitive. These are also a basic requirement in quality certification for products. Furthermore, national standards could serve as an important tool in the control of imports, mainly in relation to such things as food, where poor quality could affect the health of consumers.

Broad consultation was held to determine the critical areas and priorities for the development of Mozambican standards, as the basis for the creation of a national subsystem of standardization. The consultation also served to identify the organizational structure to develop so as to ensure that the preparation of the standards represents national priorities, reflects the interests of the various stakeholders and above all, is suited to the current economic situation. Thus, a technical committee drafted the INNOQ 1 Directive, which was then approved at a meeting of the National Council on Quality. The Directive deals with how Mozambican standards will be drawn up, based on international procedures contained in Guides of the International Organisation for Standardisation (ISO) and establishes that the preparation of Mozambican standards should, in principle, be based on international standards.

Under the directive, four Sector Technical Committees on Standardisation (CTNS) were set up. These work with 11 Technical Committees on Standardisation (CTN), involving about 40 technicians from various institutions. Contact with various stakeholders led to the agro-food area being identified as one of the priorities. This subject was thus included in one of the sectoral technical committees on standardization, which is dealing with issues relating to food in general, as well as the environment and health.

The identification of specific subjects on which to develop national standards has meant that the standards on wheat and wheat flour, and maize and maize meal have already been ratified. However, no real steps have been taken to publicise and apply these standards, since the legislation in force on this issue dates from 1980 and needs to be revised.

A standard for iodized salt has also been written and approved, based on the Codex standard and in line with the SADC region. This standard is mandatory.

The national standardization program includes both subjects that are regional priorities, such as labeling of foodstuffs, fruit, and juices and others according to national priorities, such as copra, honey, sugar, tea, and cashew nuts among others. Some of these items may possibly be exported to the United States under the AGOA program. In general, the products mentioned above have significant consumption potential in the domestic and export markets.

One of the aims of standardization is to contribute toward the harmonization of standards and technical regulations in the region, with a view to implementing the SADC Trade Protocol. Mozambique has thus been active in the work going on in the region on these issues, which are discussed below. However, it is of prime importance that the various institutions and members of the business community become more involved in the development of Mozambican standards.

The process of developing standards is lengthy and the absence of specific standards for various products leads to problems in ensuring that imports and domestic products are checked and guaranteed as fit for consumption.

The main problem faced in the development of standardization is the fact that this activity is not considered as a priority. Consumers in general do not demand quality; the volume of production is low, as the few export products are guided by specification requirements of their different destination markets.

It is still necessary to convince the various sectors that the discussion, development, and application of national standards based on international demands, will determine access to foreign markets.

INNOQ does not have appropriate infrastructure (human resources, technical and financial means) to support the development of standardization.

Metrology. Quality control of food products, in particular those derived from agroindustries, is particularly important. The identification and correct measurement of the products is therefore essential and the use of harmonized procedures in this regard is one of the regional objectives.

Weights and measures inspection in Mozambique is almost nonexistent and infrastructure that would allow confidence in the accuracy of measurements in the country is only now being developed. Traceability is very important, since without this element it would be difficult to have calibration or test certificates accepted by trade partners.

The development of the metrology subsystem is especially importance, mainly because it will be decisive as one of the bases of the subsystem of certification and fundamental in guaranteeing the reliability of trade, including exports.

The absence of any appropriate infrastructure in the country that would allow effective development of activities related to metrology has led to priority being placed on the drafting of the first standards and preparing basic legislation, which is being done in conjunction with the countries in the region.

Regulations on the labeling of prepackaged products have been harmonized in SADC countries in 2002.

Metrology activities, mainly legal and industrial, are starting from scratch, on the basis of a development project prepared by UNIDO. Project implementation is dependent on the existence of financial and technical resources and physical infrastructures.

The first embryonic laboratories in this area developed under a regional project (SADCMET) were installed in 2001 and they have begun working in 2002, together with a mobile laboratory. Mass, volume, temperature, and length standards have been received and have allowed the start of some work in the south of the country. Efforts are under way to train appropriate personnel to run the laboratories.

A working group on metrology (GTM) involving the main stakeholders was created by INNOQ. This group is responsible for support to the development of standards and technical regulations in this area, and also for input on regional and international activities.

The absence of a subsystem on metrology to support the national quality system creates costs at industrial and commercial level. The enterprises that need calibration services are sending equipment to South Africa and other countries, even for simple operations that could be done in Mozambique. The costs are higher and it is time consuming, and there are problems because of the need to make temporary exports. With regard to scales and other equipment, it is often necessary to bring foreign technicians and equipment, to do the job, and it is not always possible to be certain about the efficiency and quality of the work. The needs of this area are growing and becoming more difficult, owing to the increase in the number of certified companies that need to prove that their equipment is calibrated by recognized entities.

Therefore, there are many needs regarding this subsystem whose main objective is to protect consumers and contribute toward the credibility to the whole quality system being created in the country.

Conformity Assessment. Quality assurance of food products is achieved in many countries by mandatory certification schemes or appropriate inspection infrastructures. Certification is thus designed to protect the consumers, putting products considered safe at their disposal. However, there is no formal subsystem of certification in Mozambique, and only state bodies mandated for that purpose carry out inspections.

The Ministry of Health, the Ministry of Fisheries, and the Ministry of Agriculture and Rural Development undertake inspections of the quality of food products, based on the Codex Alimentarius standards, which served as the basis for national legislation in this sphere.

The lack of specialized human resources and even of equipment and infrastructure means that the inspections carried out by the various state bodies are not enough to ensure the quality of products on the market, for both domestic and imported products. Also, these activities do not guarantee the application of the existing legislation, which in most cases results in the constant breach of the most basic standards of public health and safety.

Poor coordination among the various state institutions that deal with agroindustries also hampers the development and monitoring of programs that would support industrial development.

However, it should be noted that the quality of production does not improve the quality of the product alone, but also improves because of the existence, at the national level, of infrastructures that would support efforts by the local business community. This means, for example, that laboratories for testing, and research and other institutions need to be properly strengthened with the aim of ensuring that the internal system of support to business development and the improvement of quality is

transparent and allows similar quality standards to be required of imported goods.

Firms must have access to recognized certification schemes, till such time that national schemes are not developed. For this reason, INNOQ established cooperation agreements with its Portuguese counterpart—the Portuguese Association for Certification (APCER), aimed basically at starting joint activities in certification, and with the South African Bureau of Standards (SABS). This cooperation will allow INNOQ and other institutions to gain time to develop the standards institutionally and to establish required local infrastructure.

With regard to product certification, work is under way toward having a national conformity mark approved, since the creation of conditions to begin certifying the quality of products is regarded as a priority, which also requires better quality of service from national laboratories.

It is thought that a duly recognized national mark could play a very important role. This role could be, on the one hand to provide some guarantee to consumers regarding the safety of the product they are using, and on the other to oblige firms to pay more attention to the quality of their products to facilitate exports.

Creating a national quality system that is functional also implies dealing with questions of accreditation, either of certifying bodies, laboratories, inspection bodies, or the auditors themselves.

This issue is being considered in a regional context, and the national perspective is to create a focal point to deal with it, since the development of certification will become important in this process.

Organizations, Infrastructure and their Effectiveness

The public institutions that are responsible and participate in the process of preparing and developing standards and technical regulations are divided into two groups. Some institutions are the focal points for the international organizations for standardization and the others are collaborative research and extension institutions that are important in this process; the latter have been discussed in the previous section.

The role and participation of the private organizations will be described in the section entitled "Private Sector Perspectives".

Public Institutions. Institutions that are focal points for organizations on international standardization are the following:

National Institute of Standardization and Quality—INNOQ. The Mozambican Government on 24 March 1993 created the National Institute of Standardization and Quality (INNOQ), subordinated to the Ministry of Industry and Energy, now the Ministry of Industry and Trade. Its activities cover both goods and services produced in Mozambique and imported goods. INNOQ is a public institution at the national level, with administrative autonomy and a legal personality. On 30 April 2002 it had a total of 15 staff members for its various areas of work, including six technicians.

The objective of INNOQ is to set up a National Quality System, which will improve the quality of products and services through standardization, certification, metrology, and quality management. Some Activities are currently under way in the areas of standardization, metrology, and quality management.

(a) Standardization and metrology.

INNOQ is responsible for the development of Mozambican standards, which are drawn up by the Technical Standardization Committees (CTN) in line with INNOQ Directive 1. Five standards for the food sector have been approved (for maize, maize meal, wheat, wheat flour, and salt) and six for the construction sector. A further 100 Mozambican standards are in various stages of preparation.

INNOQ is the focal point for SADC work within the SQAM framework, and coordinates participation in the regional harmonization of sanitary and phytosanitary (SPS) measures and technical regulations.

INNOQ has been a correspondent member of the International Organization for Standardization (ISO) since 1994, and is the focal point for the SADC Expert Group Meeting on standardization, quality assurance, and metrology (see the section on involvement in regional and international standards development). It is also the enquiry point for the Agreement on Technical Barriers to Trade (TBT/WTO).

INNOQ is in the process of joining the Affiliate Program of the International Electro-Technical Commission (IEC), the aim of which is to facilitate increased participation by developing countries in international standardization.

With regard to metrology, INNOQ is a correspondent member of the International Organization for Legal Metrology (OIML). The work carried out by INNOQ on metrology was described in the section on metrology.

In addition to its SADC activities, INNOQ has participated actively in COMESA harmonization work, and is following the process now under way among the countries of the Indian Ocean Rim.

(b) Quality and environmental management, training and awareness-raising, and direct support for businesses and quality management.

Since its inception INNOQ has worked with companies in various sectors to support their efforts to improve quality. Direct support is provided for the drafting of procedures, through lectures and training courses.

From 1993 to 1996 the activities were carried out within the framework of a regional project implemented by DNV, a Norwegian company. From 1997 to 1999 they relied on support from the Portuguese Quality Institute/Resource consortium within the framework of an agreement with the Swedish International Development Agency (SIDA).

The program with SIDA began in 1997, with the participation of eight industrial and service companies. There were discussions in the companies to raise awareness about quality, enabling them to participate more fully. By the end of the program five companies had procedures drawn up and three had drafted quality manuals. The other companies dropped out for various reasons related to internal processes of reorganization or restructuring.

Nine training courses on Quality Management Systems and two on Standardization were held during this program, with an average participation of 40 people each.

A program to support improved quality in companies was launched in 2002 with backing from PODE. Its main objective was to help introduce quality systems and prepare the companies for certification. This training program is aimed at specific companies, to prepare them to apply ISO 9000 standards and to develop procedures and a quality manual, with a view to certification. The budget for this program is US$12,000, but the costs vary according to the size of the firm.

(c) Public awareness and training activities.

INNOQ organized courses and seminars for more than 1,000 participants during 1997 and 1999. Some of these activities took place in Beira and Nampula.

In 2002, PODE covered 50 percent of the costs of private enterprises participating in a training program administered in modules by INNOQ. The main objective of the training program, which began in July and extended to at least one province, was to equip the participants with the skills to introduce quality management systems based on the ISO 9000:2000 series of standards.

Jointly with the Mozambique–Portugal Chamber of Commerce, INNOQ drew up (in 2002) a broad program on various aspects related to quality and the environment, including the Hazard Analysis and Critical Control Point (HACCP).

Public awareness activities have taken various forms, including training courses; talks; seminars; the holding of quality weeks; making contact with institutions, businesses, intermediate and higher education institutions, and the press.

(d) Activities related to certification and accreditation.

Firms need to be aware and to prepare themselves for the new challenges ahead arising from the implementation of the SADC Trade Protocol. A priority was established to help them to improve quality directly through the implementation of quality systems. Work began in 1999 to raise awareness about the need to introduce systems of environmental management.

In the short term, certification should continue to be done only by firms or other institutions properly accredited for that purpose. However, INNOQ has established a cooperation agreement with the Portuguese Certification Association, aimed basically at opening the way to joint activities in this sphere, and in the first phase to the training of Mozambican auditors.

INNOQ technicians have observed the audits carried out on certified firms by the South African Bureau of Standards (SABS) in Mozambique and participated in audits conducted in South Africa so as to be registered as auditors.

With regard to the certification of products, INNOQ is working on the development of a national mark of conformity, to create the conditions to begin certifying the quality of products. INNOQ has established an agreement with SABS for the purpose of joint certification. The juxtaposition of the Mozambican mark of conformity to the South African mark as agreed, will help the Mozambican mark to become better known.

However, product certification requires the existence of laboratories recognized for competence, so that the mark of conformity attributed has some meaning and acceptance.

Certification is limited by the low level of awareness, expertise (consultants, auditors, and other qualified personnel) and accredited laboratories. Moreover, the lack of technical staff could become a bottleneck, if staff is not properly integrated for optimal use of their skills.

It should be noted that the subject of certification has become broader in Mozambique, including the discussion of schemes relating to the certification of forests and organic products.

While INNOQ has been working within the framework of SADCA (cooperation on accreditation within SADC), with the revision of INNOQ statutes, this activity should be handed over to a specific body that will handle this type of work in the country.

The national priority is to prepare laboratories for accreditation. The first training in a group of laboratories selected for this purpose was carried out in 2000.

(e) The INNOQ library.

A properly organized, equipped, and stocked library is the cornerstone of any national standards body, since it is thus appropriately endowed to satisfy the requirements of various clients.

The establishment of a documentation center that can respond to the requests it receives has long been a matter of concern. The INNOQ library currently has a large number of standards from the ISO, the Codex Alimentarius, the South African collection of standards, Portuguese standards, most from Malawi, Zambia, and the Seychelles, the OIML documents, and some others. Moreover, the library has reviews and journals from various other similar institutions and specialized books. The International Electrotechnical Commission (IEC) has supplied INNOQ with 200 standards in 2002, selected on the basis of national priorities, under the IEC Affiliate Programme.

Department of Environmental Health (DHA) of the Ministry of Health (MISAU).

The DHA is the point of contact for the Codex Alimentarius Commission. It has participated in the annual meetings of the organization and has contributed to the preparation of technical specifications. The analysis of this department may be found in section on the Ministry of Health.

Department of Plant Health (DSV) of the Ministry of Agriculture and Rural Development (MADER).

Mozambique is not a signatory of IPPC; however, a representative of the DSV has participated in IPPC meetings but has exercised no influence on the setting of standards. The analysis of this department may be found in the section on the Department of Plant Health.

National Directorate of Livestock (DINAP) of MADER.

The National Directorate of Livestock (DINAP) represents Mozambique at the OIE. The analysis of this department may be found in the section on the National Directorate of Livestock.

Consumers Associations. Mozambique currently has three organizations defending consumers' interests: PROCONSUMERS, DECOM, and the Consumer Protection Institute, with the first two being very active.

The consumers associations are associated the various committees and working groups dealing with standardization and metrology, although their participation is not always active. The associations are newly established and lack technical capacity to participate in these activities.

DECOM has drafted and proposed a consumer protection bill, which has already been discussed with a number of stakeholders. It includes proposals for the development of a series of specific technical regulations, and for the establishment of a Public Institute for Consumer Protection.

Other Organizations. Some economic associations are represented in the National Council for Quality and in other standardization and metrology committees. The number of participating associations is growing.

In relation to firms, some have taken part in the process, but their presence is generally insignificant.

The certification of firms according to the ISO 9000 series of standards is still in its infancy. Three firms, in the service sector, have been certified, one by SABS and two by APCER. Cement is the only Mozambican product to be certified by SABS.

The Government identified Intertek Testing Services as the firm to carry out preshipment inspections, while SGS normally carries out inspection of exports, contracted by a third party.

Strengths, Weaknesses, and Prospects

Quality and standardization are a new concept in Mozambique and the economic base of the country is very weak. However, a number of actions have been taken and some improvement may be observed both in very concrete aspects as well as in the attitude of managers and consumers toward the issue. Other strengths include:

- Five food standards have been approved.
- The standardization program in 2002 included standards for cotton, cashew, honey, tea, sugar, fruit, fish, water, milk, meat, vegetables and fertilizers, as well as the related sampling and testing methods.
- Standards for labeling are under preparation.
- The ISO 9000 series of standards (Quality Management) and the ISO 14000 (Environmental Management), have been adopted in 2002, while the standards related to HACCP (Hazard Analysis and Critical Control Point) are being analyzed.
- The certification process has improved and the first four companies have been certified in the last three years.
- The first metrology laboratories have become operational during 2002.
- Technical regulations are being revised, mainly in the agriculture sector.
- Foodstuff regulations, applied to domestic production and imported goods, generally mention the obligation to comply with the Codex standards.

Weaknesses of the system include:

- Lack of appropriate human, material, infrastructure, and financial resources.

- A low level of awareness about the importance of quality and standardization among government, private sector and donors.
- The process of developing national standards is in a very embryonic phase.
- The participation of most stakeholders in the drafting of technical regulations is limited because of the short notice given for their analysis.
- Coordination among institutions and stakeholders is deficient.
- Control of the compliance with technical regulations, is not effective, either with respect to imported or domestic products.
- Inspection of weights and measures is almost nonexistent.
- Inadequate legal framework. The revision of regulations should proceed and extend to other sectors more rapidly.
- Lack of trained technical staff and of mechanisms for retaining recruited staff;
- Laboratories with inadequate equipment;
- Inspectors with little and poor training;
- Poor means to circulate information;
- There is no culture of sharing information.

Prospects. There is growing need to follow international recommendations, the entry into the Trade Protocol and the whole process of state sector reform will contribute to the improvement of public institutions involved in the process, creating awareness about the need to develop a credible and transparent system aligned with international procedures.

The challenges that markets impose on companies make them change their attitude toward these activities, and this awareness is slowly improving. It is expected that the private sector needs will speed up the development of the appropriate infrastructures by government as well as the private sector.

It is expected that the quality policy now under preparation will be approved soon. The five-year strategic plan will be implemented when funds become available.

Involvement in Regional and International Standards Development

Mozambique is a member of various regional organizations that issue standards. However, it has placed priority on participation in the Southern African Development Community (SADC).

At multilateral level, Mozambique is a member of the International Organisation for Standardisation (ISO), the Codex Alimentarius, the International Office for Epizootics (OIE) and the International Organisation for Legal Metrology (OIML).

With regard to other international standards organizations, Mozambique is a member of the International Telecommunications Union (ITU) and is in the process of joining the International Electrotechnical Commission (IEC) Affiliate Programme that will allow the country to have access to some international standards in electro-technology.

Regional Standards Development

Among the regional organizations in which Mozambique participates, the following are notable.

African Regional Standardisation Organisation (ARSO). The African Regional Standardisation Organisation (ARSO) covers the whole of the continent. This is an intergovernmental organization created on 11 January 1977 with 23 members. It is open to all the members of the Organization of African Unity (OAU) and The United Nations Economic Commission for Africa. Its mandate includes the preparation and promotion of standards. Mozambique is not a member of ARSO for reasons related to limitations of technical staff and lack of financial resources. Nevertheless, the country has received assistance from the organization for the training of technical staff as well as a set of the principal ARSO standards.

Southern African Development Community (SADC). Questions relating to the trade of goods within SADC are covered in the SADC Trade Protocol.

However, besides the trade protocol, other protocols relating to other areas have also been signed, but a lack of coordination among the various institutions within the countries themselves and this is often reflected at regional level.

The coordination of activities related to standardization, quality assurance, accreditation, and metrology among SADC countries members would allow sharing of infrastructure, enabling countries such as Mozambique to benefit from the infrastructure existing in neighboring countries. This is happening in metrology, where the existence of advanced laboratories in South Africa will allow Mozambique to start with less developed infrastructures and in accreditation, where the facilities available in the region will be shared through SADCA. This will allow Mozambique to obtain accreditation services through the recognized bodies in the region while at the same time training auditors and preparing the national infrastructure.

Activities Related to the MOU on SQAM. With regard to the SADC Trade Protocol (summary appended in Annex C), many clauses mention the need for harmonization of standards and technical regulations as one of the ways to facilitate commercial exchanges in the region. The need to deal properly with questions related to quality in general and to standardization in particular led the ministries in charge of industry and trade in the region to adopt a Memorandum of Understanding on Standardization, Quality Assurance, Accreditation, and Metrology (SQAM), which is summarized in Annex C.

The objective of the MOU is to establish the formal framework in which the cooperation among the national institutions in standardization, quality assurance, accreditation, and metrology (SQAM) will take place in the region and this framework is referred to as the SADC SQAM Programme.

The objectives of the SADC SQAM Programme are the progressive elimination of Technical Barriers to Trade (TBT) among the member states and between SADC and other regional and international trading blocs, and the promotion of quality and an infrastructure for quality in the member states.

In the context of the activities covered by the MOU, a project was prepared in 2001, with UNIDO involvement, to develop these activities in the region. The cost of the project was €20 million (20 million euros).

To implement the SADC SQAM Programme, the following structures were created.

(a) SADC SQAM Expert Group (SQAMEG).

The objectives of SQAMEG are to coordinate regional activities of SQAM and provide a forum to deal with conformity assessment.

INNOQ has represented Mozambique at the meetings of this structure and has participated actively, although for reasons related to language and lack of technical capacity, INNOQ did not assume responsibility for any of the priority working areas of this structure, described in Annex C.

(b) SADC Cooperation in Measurement Traceability (SADCMET).

The objective of SADCMET is to coordinate metrology activities and services in the region to provide regional calibration and testing services, including regulatory bodies, with readily available traceability to the SI units of measurement, through legally defined and regionally and internationally recognized national measurement standards.

INNOQ represents Mozambique on this structure and participates in its meetings. Many subjects are dealt with, but Mozambique's participation has been limited because of the absence of any metrological infrastructure, lack of expertise and inadequate financial support. However, Mozambique has benefited from regional training activities and from a regional project, supported by NML, PTB, UNIDO, and SABS that installed the nucleus of a national metrology laboratory.

SADCMET is also involved in preparing projects to support the development of quality infrastructures, mainly related to metrology, in the member countries. Through SADCMET, awareness campaigns on metrology and SQAM in general are being prepared.

Internally, INNOQ has created a Metrology Working Group (GTM), which analyzes the issues arising in the regional meetings, as well as discussing questions related to the development of this subsystem in Mozambique. The group incorporates the various stakeholders, including ministries, research institutions, universities, economic associations, and consumers.

The network also permits information sharing to support the private sector, providing information that might enable firms to obtain the appropriate calibration services in neighboring countries.

(c) SADC Cooperation in Legal Metrology (SADCMEL)

The objective of SADCMEL is to facilitate the harmonization of the national legal metrology regulations of the member states and of SADC with other regional and international trading blocs.

INNOQ also participates in the meetings of this structure, where the main items on the agenda have been related to the harmonization of regulations as related to legal metrology in the region. For example, the final stage of discussion and harmonization has been reached of the recommendation from OIML on the labeling of prepackaged products, to be approved in the region. This will affect the labeling and packaging of some products in the context of this study with the aim of protecting consumers. A counter-scale document based on OIML recommendations was finalized for discussion by the private sector in member countries; requirements for beam scales are being discussed. A document on the minimum training requirements for metrologists in the region is being finalized.

Member countries representatives are attending training courses held under the auspices of SADCMEL and SADCMET.

The GTM mentioned above also deals with issues related to legal metrology, since one of its objectives is to ensure discussion and dissemination of information relating to this structure.

One of the main constraints to participation in SADCMEL is language, which creates problems for the dissemination and analysis of the information produced.

(d) SADC Cooperation in Standardisation (SADCSTAN).

The objective of SADCSTAN is to promote the coordination of standardization activities and services in the region, for the purpose of achieving harmonization of standards and technical regulations, with the exception of legal metrology regulations, in support of the objectives of the SADC Protocol on Trade.

INNOQ represents Mozambique in this structure. The priorities set for the region include the harmonization of standards, some of which relate to the areas of interest to this study, such as fish, fruit, and labeling.

The 2001 meeting of SADCSTAN approved the procedures for regional harmonization (harmonized SADC standards), which are based on international procedures. The first harmonized standards are now in final draft form.

The most serious obstacle to Mozambique's participation in this process is the language barrier and the impossibility of circulating the drafts of standards in Portuguese.

The last meeting of SADCSTAN redistributed the secretariats according to which countries volunteered. The secretariat for developing the various items for standardization is centered mainly in South Africa (South African Bureau of Standards—SABS), because of the lack of technical and financial capacity in the other countries in the region.

Mozambique assumed responsibility for the secretariat to develop the standard for salt, and an English translation by SABS of the draft has been circulated among the other countries in the region.

At national level, the Standardisation Technical Committees carry out the work and within the agreement with the National Standardisation Program, which includes the regional priorities.

One of the objectives of SADCSTAN is to be accepted by ISO as one of the standardization organizations of the region.

With regard to the harmonization of technical regulations, this matter has received special treatment and two meetings have been held to discuss regional integration. It was agreed that a Technical Regulation Framework would probably be the most appropriate policy framework that would link the requirements of the SADC Trade Protocol to the institutional infrastructure that make up the SADC SQAM environment. This framework will make it possible to ensure that technical regulations will be adopted and implemented according to the WTO TBT Agreement.

The SADC Secretariat arranged a workshop on a Technical Regulation Framework for SADC on 21 and 22 March 2002 in Gaborone. The workshop considered that there is a real need for a common regional approach; there is need for more detailed work to identify the pros and cons of the different approaches to the problem and member states need to carry out a stocktaking exercise to evaluate the current situation.

(e) SADC Cooperation in Accreditation (SADCA).

The objectives of SADCA are to facilitate the creation of a pool of internationally acceptable accredited laboratories and certification bodies (for personnel, products and systems, including quality and environmental management systems) in the region, and to provide member states with accreditation as a tool for the removal of TBT in both the voluntary and regulatory areas.

Mozambique has participated in this structure through INNOQ, which has circulated the principal conclusions that have been reached from the ongoing work. The various meetings of SADCA have made it possible to create a model for the development of accreditation in the region that is pioneering in the field. A project to implement this has been prepared and funding is being sought. The International Accreditation Forum, Inc. (IAF) has granted SADCA special recognition as a Regional Accreditation Group.

The prospect in Mozambique is to create an accreditation unit (focal point) that will coordinate its activities with what is going on in SADC and which will benefit from existing accreditation facilities in SADC.

Activities in the Context of SPS. The SADC Trade Protocol specifies that member states should base SPS measures on science, in accordance with the WTO Agreement.

Thus SADC created a Consultative Forum on SPS/Food Safety, which organized a workshop on sanitary and phytosanitary standards (SPS) and food safety issues in Windhoek, Namibia from 20–22 November 2000 to deliberate on specific actions and steps for harmonizing SPS measures in support of the implementation of the SADC Trade Protocol.

The workshop, was jointly organized by the SADC Food Agriculture and Natural Resources Sector Development Unit (FANR SDU) and the Trade Sector Coordinating Unit (TSCU), and was facilitated by the Food Security and Rural Development Hub. The SADC Workshop on SPS/Food Safety was organized to raise awareness among public officials, standards bodies, exporters, and the private sector on the importance of harmonizing SPS and food safety standards in support of the implementation of the Trade Protocol.

The key findings and recommendations of the workshop are: (a) there is need for clear institutional arrangements at both the regional and national levels to deal with issues of sanitary and phytosanitary measures and food safety so as to move more expeditiously in the implementation of the SADC Trade Protocol with specific regard to agricultural trade; (b) to move the regional trade agenda forward, closer coordination is needed both among the various agencies and players within the member states as well as between the states; (c) member states are hampered by an outdated legal and regulatory framework on SPS and food safety—some laws and regulations dating as far back as the colonial era. These outdated rules and regulations are inadequate to deal with current international standards and requirements; (d) member states often lack the appropriate technical and human resource capacity to deal with complex issues of SPS and food safety, to assess related risks, and to monitor policies and their outcomes; and (e) there is need to clarify the roles and responsibilities of the key stakeholders in both the public and private sectors in the implementation of the proposed SPS and food safety measures.

Mozambique has participated in some regional meetings on this subject and in the actions under way to follow up the recommendations of the seminar. Following the creation of the SADC Consultative Forum on SPS/Food Safety, a national working group was created to deal with this topic. INNOQ was given the responsibility by the Ministry of Industry and Trade to lead this group and coordinate activities in this sphere, incorporating representatives of the various related sectors, including ministries, institutions, and the private sector. However, this group suffers from a lack of resources and the specialists assigned to work with it are overloaded with work.

Mozambique is an active member of the plant protection organization within the SADC and is also an active member of International Red Locust Control Organisation (IRLCO)-CSA, the organization in charge of controlling migratory pests in the region, currently led by Mozambique's Ministry of Agriculture and Rural Development.

Participation in the activities mentioned above is through the Department of Plant Health in the Ministry of Agriculture and Rural Development. Mozambique also participates in meetings of the SADC Livestock subcommittee through the National Directorate of Livestock of the Ministry of Agriculture and Rural Development.

Community of Countries with Portuguese as the Official Language (CPLP). In the context of this community, Mozambique has coordinated its activities with Angola and Portugal. However, in

March 2002 the first meeting of SQAM representatives from the member countries of the CPLP, namely Angola, Brazil, Cape Verde, Guinea Bissau, Mozambique, Portugal, Sao Tome and Principe, and Timor was held. It was agreed to hold an annual meeting of standardization bodies and focal points from CPLP countries so as to discuss activities related to standardization.

Indian Ocean Rim Association for Regional Cooperation (IOR-ARC). This organization is composed of 14 countries (Australia, India, Indonesia, Kenya, Madagascar, Malaysia, Republic of Mauritius, Mozambique, Sultanate of Oman, Singapore, South Africa, Sri Lanka, Tanzania, and Yemen). In the context of this organization, Mozambique is a member of the Indian Ocean Legal Metrology Forum (IOLMF) of which the secretariat is with The National Standards Commission, Australia. Participation in the forum has been by correspondence and has produced information that is contained in the Directory of Legal Metrology in the Indian Ocean. There is almost no participation in other activities of the organization. Mozambique is also a member of the Committee that deals with SQAM in general.

International Standards Development

The following organizations are among the most notable in which Mozambique participates.

Codex Alimentarius Commission (CAC). The Department of Environmental Health of the Ministry of Health is the point of contact with the Codex Alimentarius. As the point of contact, it is responsible for coordinating activities relating to this organization in the country. Among other tasks, this includes maintaining Codex documentation and circulating information to interested parties, as well as coordinating the national position regarding the preparation and approval of Codex standards.

The point of contact should work with a national Codex committee, which does not exist in Mozambique.

Existing legislation in areas related to Codex activities generally refer to the standards that have become compulsory either in domestic production or in relation to imports.

The national program of standardization developed by the INNOQ has been identifying the priority areas for activity, including food, and Codex is used

as the basis for the development of Mozambican standards in this sphere. As in other areas, the preparation of the standards is by technical committees that involve ministries, technological and research institutions, including universities, economic, professional, consumer, and other interested associations.

So far Mozambican standards for iodized salt, wheat, wheat flour, maize, and maize meal have been developed in the context of Codex, and others are in various stages of development, for example, foodstuffs, sampling and testing methods, labeling, and pesticides. The Department of Environmental Health has also drawn up specifications based on the Codex, which are currently being used as the basis for the development of relevant national standards.

There have been problems, however, in obtaining the latest version of Codex standards, which often do not exist in hard copy. A summary on this organization is contained in the Annex C.

International Plant Protection Convention (IPPC). Mozambique is not a signatory of this convention, although the Department of Plant Health attends its meetings and the regulations written by the Ministry of Agriculture and Rural Development are in line with the recommendations of this organization. A summary of this organization is contained in the Annex C.

Office International des Epizooties (OIE). The Department of Animal Health of the Ministry of Agriculture and Rural Development represents Mozambique on this organization. However, it only participates in international meetings. A summary of this organization is contained in the Annex C.

International Organisation for Standardisation (ISO). Mozambique has been a correspondent member of the ISO since 1994, participating since then in the ISO General Assemblies and joining some of the policy development committees, notably the Committee on Conformity Assessment (CASCO), the Committee on Consumer Policy (COPOLCO), the Committee on Developing Country Matters (DEVCO), and the Committee on Information Systems and Services (INFCO).

Participation in ISO has helped Mozambique keep up to date with ISO standards, participate in the international network of standardization organizations, receive important information on various committees, and obtain support in specific training programs and other areas.

The most important information is circulated among INNOQ stakeholders. The standards and other documents are used as background for the development of Mozambican standards where possible and adopted as Mozambican standards whenever necessary. A stumbling block in the process of adopting standards is the fact that most of them have not been translated into Portuguese.

INNOQ has been active in representing Mozambique on DEVCO and through this has received support from the ISO, notably to attend courses and seminars outside the country and to hold courses inside the country. It was also through this committee that Mozambique took part in a project that allowed the first inventory to be taken of six laboratories with a view to their accreditation.

There is almost no participation in the other committees, where the main benefit from attendance is the receipt of information that is very useful in the work of standardization. Also, participation in the international process of developing standards and influence on this process is almost nonexistent. A summary of this organization is contained in the Annex C.

The International Organisation of Legal Metrology (OIML). Mozambique has been a corresponding member of the OIML since 1995 through INNOQ. The process of regional harmonization with regard to legal metrology is based on OIML recommendations and obtaining the documents of this organization is therefore particularly important.

Thus, while INNOQ does not participate directly in the activities of this organization, it has been given assistance through SADCMEL in the revision of some international recommendations. The recommendations are regarded as priorities and are under analysis in the region with a view to incorporating them into standards and regulations of each member country.

SADCMEL represents the countries of SADC in the OIML and in the International Bureau of Weights and Measures (BIPM).

The Country's Strengths and Weaknesses in Participating in Regional and International Standard Setting

Regional Standard Setting. As mentioned above, priority is given to participation in regional standardization activities in the context of SADC, where influence over decisions is sought. With regard to other regional organizations of which Mozambique is a member, it has sought to keep abreast of events and use the information where possible. Thus we will focus our analysis on SADC.

Mozambique benefits from participation in the SADC SQAM programme, mainly through sharing experience, regional training activities, and forming a common approach to specific subjects for dealings with donors. It also learns from the experience of other countries and is thus able to avoid some mistakes, while influencing the process of regional harmonization.

The main constraints to a more effective participation in the regional standards setting result mainly from the factors mentioned below:

Language: For harmonization of standards and regulations to take place it is required that all countries seek internal consensus. The fact that the working documents, draft standards or regulations, are written in English hampers discussion within Mozambique. The SADC Secretariat recently took some action to support translations. Priority, however, is given to translating finished documents. In technical areas such as this, that priority does not help much to resolve the problem. This situation has resulted in Mozambique being pushed to the sidelines in relation to some decisions on the adoption of standards and regulations. It also prevents the country from taking over the technical secretariat for the development of some standards and affects participation in some other activities.

Financial capacity: The situation described above is made even worse by the lack of financial resources that limits participation in the various meetings, given that the expenses involved are the responsibility of the member country. This affects, for example, translation capacity and the management of all the work of coordination and circulation of information.

Technical capacity: Scarcity of technicians and work overload of the existing technicians mean that they are often not available to take part in regional meetings. At the same time, the lack of infrastructure also affects participation.

The lack of incentives for the technicians: Despite the facts mentioned above, we have tried to circulate information and create specific groups such as the GTM, the group on SPS, and the technical standardization committees. This has helped discussion of these matters in the country, although participation in meetings has not always been adequate, because of the lack of incentives for the technicians and their work overload.

The lack of awareness: It should be mentioned that in the context of implementation of the SADC Trade Protocol, other matters have caught the attention of both the government and the business community, and quality is not yet a priority.

Strengths and Weaknesses of Participating in International Standards Setting. The benefit to be drawn from participation in international organizations, apart from the learning factor, is what results from the application of the available documentation as the basis for the development of national technical standards and regulations.

As mentioned in previous sections, while Mozambique is represented at some international meetings and is trying to base its standards on international standards, its participation in international standardization is very small. The very little that does exist is confined almost exclusively to the state sector.

Thus, many problems hamper effective participation in these organizations, most notably:

- Financial constraints for the payment of subscriptions that are normally high, and for the participation in meetings;
- The lack of awareness on the part of both the government and the business community of the importance of using standards, and ignorance of the consequences of not using them;
- The low production and the low levels of exports, which in most cases do not make failure to comply with standards a problem;
- The lack of consumer awareness of the quality or standards problem;
- The lack of technicians who would allow effective participation in the process;
- Technological questions.

It is thought that growing awareness of the World Trade Organization (WTO), implementation of the SADC trade protocol and the proximity of South Africa, a country with a very advanced economy will dictate a short-term reversal of the way of dealing with this problem.

The international organizations have given this matter some attention. The 24th General Assembly of the ISO in September 2001 discussed the matter and decided that regional seminars would be held in 2001 and 2002 to discuss this and propose ways of reducing the effects of weak participation by developing countries in international standardization.

The seminar for Africa was held in Nairobi, Kenya on 18 and 19 March 2002. Mozambique was represented by the Head of the Standardisation Department at INNOQ and by the chair of the Consumers Association. The conclusions of the seminar point to the design of a program of action for enhancing the participation of developing countries and economies in transition in international standardization, which will be on the agenda for discussion at the next ISO General Assembly and put for the consideration of donors.

Private Sector Perspectives

The private sector in Mozambique plays an important role in economic development in general and is one of the main actors in setting standards and quality systems.

Main Private Sector Associations

The Confederation of Business Associations of Mozambique (CTA), created three years ago, is an organization of more than 41 Mozambican business associations covering over 1,300 firms from almost all the productive and service sectors.

The mission of the CTA is to participate in and contribute to the economic growth and development in Mozambique by constructively engaging and lobbying with the government to ensure that the country's major macro- and micro-economic policies are not detrimental to domestic and foreign direct investment flows or to the development of small and medium enterprises (http://www.cta.org.m2).

The main objective of the CTA is to ensure that those government policies and programs are not detrimental to the economic development of the country and to the development of the local private sector.

CTA aims to strengthen and deepen a constructive policy dialogue between the government and the private sector; to improve the business and investment climate by reducing the cost of doing business in Mozambique; to promote the systematic reform of the legal framework of the country, including the reform of the Commercial Code; to encourage and stimulate business relations between national and foreign investors; and to develop and improve cross-border cooperation between the business sector in Mozambique and the business sector in neighboring countries.

CTA has worked closely with the government on a number of initiatives, including removing and simplifying administrative and procedural constraints to doing business, encouraging the reform of outdated legal instruments, providing comments on new laws such as labor and industrial laws, and presenting private sector views on policies in bilateral and multilateral trade agreements.

Mozambique has links with the business communities in several other countries through established associations. These include the Mozambique Chamber of Commerce (CCM), the Mozambique–USA Chamber of Commerce, the Portugal–Mozambique Chamber, and the Chamber of Commerce and Industry of Mozambique–South Africa (CCIMOSA).

The professional associations representing sectors and branches have been supporting their members in specific issues and representing them in sector associations or in CTA.

In the industry sector, the Mozambique Industrial Association (AIMO) was established in 1982. According to its statutes, the objectives of the association are to promote the participation of its members in the development of economic activities in the technical, financial, commercial, associative, and cultural spheres; to defend the interests of national industries and their shareholders; to disseminate professional ethical standards; to support and monitor best practice; and to promote, protect and coordinate the interests of its members.

Business associations representing producers of specific industrial branches include in salt, edible oil, sugar, cashew nuts and seafood.

In the trade sector there is the Mozambique Commercial Association (ACM) with the objectives of promoting the development and coordinating commercial and related activities to improve the situation of ACM members and to extend their participation in external trade.

In the agriculture sector there are business associations representing producers of sugar, cotton, fruits and vegetables. There are also specific associations representing farmers and peasants.

Non Governmental organisations (NGOs) play an important role in sectoral development, designing and implementing projects and activities in specific fields and locations. These organisations operate at national, provincial, and district levels, in coordination with the related government institutions. NGOs have the strong advantage of being linked with the international NGO networks, with faster and easier access to resources and information and with a more practical structure and working system.

Business Environment and the Situation of Firms

The private sector in general has been also affected by several problems that slow down the economy growth rate. Factories are being closed, unemployment is growing, and purchasing power is shrinking. In 1999, the net position of the largest 100 companies in Mozambique showed on average that they operate at break-even or at a loss, 23 percent of the total business volume involves six firms in the energy and fuel marketing sector, and the few firms making a net profit are in financial services and the trade sector. Among the largest companies, 52 operate in trade, banking, insurance, and other services although Mozambique is essentially an agricultural country. The banking, building, and hotel sectors depend mostly on foreign interests.

The small and medium firms, which dominate in Mozambique, do not fulfil their economic and social function and are unable to meet their fiscal responsibilities to the state.

The creation of branch commercial and industrial associations and their coalitions facilitate the relationship among the firms working in the same branch and related activities and help them to have better and easier access to information, to discuss and find solutions to members' problems, and achieve goals successfully.

The organisation of annual conferences of the private sector since 1995, considered a forum of reference on economic and business matters in Mozambique, has improved the dialogue between government and the private sector, facilitating the analysis of complex situations, programming concrete actions, and finding solutions to facilitate the economic growth.

A survey carried out in about 50 firms in 2001 shows that 62 percent were confident that their business would improve. In general, businesspersons are willing to find ways and means to overcome the problems and challenges that exist, such as the fact that the great majority of the population depends on subsistence farming and has practically no link to national and international consumer markets; the domestic economy is relatively small; the business environment in certain areas is dominated by monopolies and oligopolies, with foreigners predominating in vital sectors; Mozambican private capital is practically irrelevant; high operating and transaction costs reduce the competitiveness of small firms and serve as negative incentive to new investment, for example, the price of fuels, the costs of loading and unloading in the ports, the excessive costs of telecommunications, coastal shipping, banking services, air transport and the costs of energy.

During the 6th Annual Conference of the Private Sector in Mozambique, held in Maputo in March 2001, the following questions, considered central to ensure better functioning of the economy, were discussed in the thematic panels. The resulting matrix identified issues, proposed solutions, gave an indicative time scale, while comments showed that the participants in the agriculture, industry, and trade panels dealt with issues related to standards and quality. It was suggested that work should be undertaken to review and establish quality standards for farm produce to improve agricultural marketing and rural development. The need to strengthen INNOQ was recognized (CTA 2000. 6ª Conferência Anual do Sector Privado em Moçambique).

Quality Policy and the Role of the Private Sector

The quality policy currently under discussion in the country includes the development of a legal framework that will allow harmonious growth of state institutions and the participation of the private sector in specific activities. (INNO © 2001, 1 Conferência Nacional sobre a Politica da Qualidade (Proceedings)).

It prioritizes the following aspects for the private sector:

- Improve product and service quality assuring the introduction of international practices in what concerns quality, contributing to greater competitiveness;
- Participate through its representatives in governing bodies and technical committees with relevance to standardization and quality;

- Participate in and promote national events regarding quality, such as "Quality Weeks," "National Quality Awards" and others;
- Participate in and promote quality dissemination actions, such as meetings, workshops, and news in newspapers, magazines, and other media. Develop human resources, training the necessary technicians to improve quality of both on product and services;
- Invest in the development of quality infrastructures, taking advantage of business opportunities arising from the implementation of the quality policy;
- Participate in the financing of quality support activities.

Challenges

The private sector is represented in the National Council for Quality and in all the technical committees, including those formulating standards.

Representatives of private firms have, through INNOQ, taken training courses and participated in seminars outside the country. Several firms are currently taking part in activities that will help them to improve the quality of their services. A growing number of firms and technical staff are becoming interested in the training programs in this sphere.

However, the involvement of the private sector in both the formulation of standards and in other activities related to the provision of services to improve quality is very limited. There are no consultants or consulting firms specializing in assisting business development. Firms and business associations and their representatives need to regard activities related to quality assurance as priorities and must become more active in the production and implementation of activities planned jointly with INNOQ.

The development of important projects like the MOZAL aluminum smelter also demands extra effort from firms regarding the quality of their products. MOZAL's requirements of its suppliers are very high, both in the development phase of the project and during implementation. In that context, support projects were carried out for 25 firms to improve the quality of the service provided and the level of their performance as suppliers to MOZAL.

One of the targets in the development foreseen in agriculture and the efforts currently being made to diversify the export base is the improvement of quality and the establishment of good practice in production.

The private sector is facing various problems related to the high costs of production, problems of access to bank loans, unfair competition from imported goods, outdated customs tariffs and others with negative impact on performance. This is one of the reasons behind the low involvement of private firms in the development of standards or in other activities related to quality control.

The recent coming into force of the SADC Trade Protocol is a challenge. As the reform of the customs service advances and tariffs are consequently reduced and other trade barriers removed, the need to address questions related to quality becomes clear, not least because neighboring South Africa has a developed economy and a strong and well-defined quality assurance infrastructure.

WTO and Trade Commitments: Assessment of Implementation, Problems

The World Trade Organisation (WTO) was created by the Marrakech Accord of 15 April 1994 and began operating on 1 January 1995. Mozambique was a member of the WTO's predecessor, the General Agreement on Tariffs and Trade (GATT) from 27 July 1992 and deposited the documents of ratification of its membership of WTO on 26 August 1995.

As a member of the WTO, the Government has placed priority on activities that allow it to fulfil its obligations. Mozambique has coordinated its position taken at the WTO with the other members of SADC.

The Ministry of Industry and Trade is the focal point for the WTO.

The Agreement on Sanitary and Phytosanitary Measures (SPS)

This agreement reaffirms the right of any government to adopt measures to protect human, animal, and plant life or health, subject to the provision that these are not used in an improper way for protectionist purposes and that they do not give rise to unnecessary barriers to international trade.

The SPS measures include laws, decrees, regulations, requirements and procedures, covering, among other things, the criteria for finished products, production methods and processes, testing, inspection, certification and approved procedures, treatments, quarantine, statistical methods, sampling procedures, risk verification methods, and packaging and labeling requirements directly linked to food safety.

The agreement requires members to harmonize their SPS measures on the broadest possible base, using international standards and taking an active role in the relevant international organizations, such as the Codex Alimentarius, IOE, and the IPPC network.

The agreement contains provisions on the publication of regulations, enquiry points, and procedures for notification or new or modified SPS measures that deviate from international standards and recommendations. (APHIS and SPS Agreement: Rights and Obligations under WTO and NAFTA).

An SPS committee was created under the leadership of INNOQ to deal with matters of obligations arising from this agreement and because the members of SADC are taking steps toward harmonizing SPS measures. It includes representatives of the Ministries of Industry and Trade, Agriculture and Rural Development, Health, and Fisheries, and the private sector.

The appointment of persons to serve as enquiry points is under way and is expected to include INNOQ, the Ministry of Agriculture and Rural Development, and the Ministry of Health.

The Agreement on Technical Barriers to Trade (TBT)

The TBT agreement aimed at ensuring that technical regulations, standards, and procedures for conformity assessment applicable to international trade do not create unnecessary obstacles to such trade. The agreement further establishes that the compulsory standards for products will not create unnecessary barriers to trade if they are based on internationally accepted standards. If for geographical, climatic, or other reasons, it was not possible for the members to base the compulsory regulations on international regulations, they will be obliged to publish a draft of these regulations to allow producers in other countries the opportunity to comment.

The Code of Practice for the Preparation, Adoption and Application of Standards contained in Annexe 3 of the TBT agreement requests countries to apply their best efforts so that their national standardization bodies follow the same principles and rules in the preparation and adoption of voluntary standards as established for compulsory standards. (The Agreement on Technical Barriers to trade).

INNOQ notified the ISO of acceptance of Annexe 3 of the TBT Agreement. INNOQ Directive 1 that establishes the procedures for the preparation of Mozambican standards complies with the requirements of this Annexe. Compliance with this Annexe assures the international community that the signatories comply with the minimum rules established internationally.

The Mozambique Government, through the Ministry of Industry and Trade, which is the focal point for the WTO, appointed INNOQ as the enquiry point for the TBT Agreement.

General Analysis of the Main Problems

Strengthening internal organization and infrastructure is generally regarded as necessary to ensure that the country responds to the various requests in the context of the agreements, including the need to notify the existence of technical regulations and standards that affect trade. It also provides the capacity to analyze how much export products are affected by measures taken by other countries to which exports are made.

National standards are in the process of being developed and harmonized with the region on the basis of international standards. When these are in draft form, notification has been given of their existence in line with Annexe 3 mentioned above.

With regard to technical regulations in general, they need to be revised, some of them are out of date, and this revision is proceeding in various areas, including agriculture and fisheries. There is no exhaustive inventory of the technical regulations in force in the country. INNOQ has been working with the different sectors to identify priorities for standardization and the relevant international standard available to develop this work. The purpose is to ensure that basic standards for the implementation of these regulations are available.

The appointment of an enquiry point for the TBT Agreement was not accompanied by the availability of the necessary infrastructure to fulfil these functions. Ignorance of the contents of the agreement among several ministries and the business community affects the activities of the enquiry point.

Both the Ministry of Industry and Trade and INNOQ have organized a number of activities to raise awareness on these agreements and some continuity in these is regarded as necessary.

The enquiry point for the SPS Agreement has not been nominated yet. The SPS Committee under INNOQ needs appropriate support to develop its activities. The appointment of an enquiry point for the SPS Agreement should be accompanied by actions that will allow the conduct of its functions.

Main Findings and Proposed Action Plan

Main Findings

Mozambique is a country with great economic potential, mainly in the agriculture sector. Agriculture is the main economic activity, contributing around 25 percent to GDP and employing about 80 percent of the labor force. The lack of appropriate technology for small producers, who often lack farming inputs and store their crops using local technology, contributes to low yields, post-harvest losses, and low quality of the crop; these problems are associated with the lack of an appropriate trade network.

Agro-processing in Mozambique has been not been able to absorb the agricultural products, which leads to export of basic raw materials and to the dependence on imports of final consumer goods of agricultural origin.

Because of the level of poverty, the need to satisfy basic requirements and to be aware of quality is not a determining factor in trade for domestic consumption. Export markets are more and more rigorous with respect to quality, but Mozambican products have not yet faced export rejection because of lack of quality.

Studies have been conducted to evaluate agriculture products with potential for generating a viable and promising rural agroindustry and to explore mechanisms to promote them. Other studies are also being done to analyze the market potential for agriculture products in local and foreign markets. It is expected that results of the studies together with the other initiatives analyzed in this study will help solve some of the existing problems and develop agriculture and agroindustry.

The case studies show that, in general, that all the sectors of the economy need to improve to be competitive. This improvement requires not only the application of standards but also investments in technology and human resources.

The analysis of the public institutions involved on the regulatory system and in the standards setting system, shows that they do not have appropriate infrastructure and they lack qualified personnel. Financing problems are also an important constraint. However, the Directive INNOQ 1, based on international rules, is a good basis for the development of the standardization subsystem.

The legal framework is not adequate and needs to be updated or some new legislation and regulations need to be introduced. This has started through the revision of some laws and technical regulations related to animal and plant health.

There is limited capacity to enforce the existing technical regulations and the quality inspections at the border and in shops are not efficient because of the lack of infrastructure and personnel. Laboratories are not well equipped and they face the same problems as the other public institutions.

The adoption of the ISO 9000 series of standard is under way. Currently few firms implement them because of a low level of awareness. APCER and SABS are providing certification services. Certified companies utilize accredited laboratories and calibration services from South Africa, but the costs are high.

The HACCP system is being implemented in a systematic way only in the fisheries export subsector.

The Ministry of Industry and Trade is responsible for the implementation of trade policy. The country is member of bilateral, regional, and international organizations, in particular the SADC and the WTO.

The country has established an interministerial committee that deals with the implementation of the SADC Trade Protocol and other matters related to trade policy. This committee also has representatives of the private sector; which helps to achieve common approach to trade issues.

The country already has an inquiry point nominated for the implementation of the TBT Agreement and is in the process of nominating an enquiry point for the SPS Agreement. A committee is coordinating issues related to the SPS Agreement. Some awareness seminars were held to disseminate information about TBT and SPS Agreements. New technical regulations are not being notified to WTO.

There are several organizations participating in the process of developing standards and technical regulations. Public organizations have legal powers to enforce their obligation with respect to SPS requirements.

Mozambique is a member of some international organizations (ISO, CODEX, OIE, and OIML) that are involved in standards settings and SADC structures that work on standards settings and related activities.

The participation in regional and international standards setting organizations is limited to officials from various government organizations. Language, inadequate financial and technical capacities, and a lack of awareness regarding SQAM issues are among the constraints that affect the participation.

The private sector is organized into several business associations. The Confederation of Business Associations of Mozambique—CTA, is an organization covering more than 1,300 firms from almost all the productive and service sectors.

Nongovernmental organisations (NGOs) play an important role in sector development, designing, and implementing projects and activities in specific fields and locations.

The organization of annual conferences of the private sector since 1995, considered a forum of reference on economic and business issues in Mozambique, has improved the dialogue between government and the private sector. The matrix produced at the last annual conference mentioned standards and quality issues, suggesting that work should be undertaken to review and establish quality standards for farm produce to improve agricultural marketing and rural development. The need to strengthen INNOQ was recognized.

The need for the private sector in specific to participate in activities related to standardization and quality is addressed in the quality policy currently under discussion in the country.

The private sector is facing various problems related to the high costs of production, problems of access to bank loans, unfair competition from imported goods, outdated customs tariffs and others with a negative impact on performance.

The involvement of the private sector in both the formulation of standards and in other activities related to the provision of services to improve quality is very limited.

The development of important projects, such as the MOZAL aluminum smelter demands extra effort from firms regarding the quality of their products and influences their attitude toward quality.

In general, institutions do not possess information on the real costs associated with quality control of their products, nor on the possible costs of improving production processes. The existing legislation does not yet require producers and supervisors to demonstrate that they have complied with the requirements it establishes.

Action Plan

To improve the standards and regulatory system and to ensure that it follows the internationally approved requirements and thus facilitates access to markets of Mozambican export products, the following need to be done as a matter of priority:

- Develop an appropriate regulatory system including food safety issues, and effective control mechanisms for import and export goods;
- Develop an appropriate standards setting system including facilities for training, metrology, accreditation, testing and certification;
- Strengthen the country's participation in regional and international standards setting bodies;
- Improve the response of the country on issues related to WTO, mainly SPS and TBT Agreement;
- Support the development of selected sectors to improve exports.

The action plan to approach each of these objectives is described below in a table format. The costing of this plan at this stage is a very difficult task, as the actions are very general, and the main actors should develop a more detailed analysis of each.

Constraints to be Addressed	Justification	Projects	Activities	Inputs Needed	Main Actors	Estimated Costs/Potential Funder
Objective 1—Development of an appropriate regulatory system including food safety issues, and effective control mechanisms for import and export goods						
Inadequate legal framework	Standards and regulations in use are outdated, especially those related to health and safety.	Development of technical regulations and related standards for agriculture commodities and livestock production	• Revision of the technical regulations • Identification of the international standards that are their basis • Develop national standards • Training and awareness-raising programs for producers to follow regulations and standards	• Technical/financial assistance to MADER • Technical/Financial Assistance to INNOQ • Technical/financial assistance to MADER and INNOQ	MADER INNOQ Agricultural Producers	PROAGRI (ongoing project) SIDA (under discussion) PROAGRI
		Development of technical regulations and related standards for health and food safety	• Draft and Revise the Technical Regulations related to health and food safety • Update and develop standards and code of practices related to health and food safety	• Technical/financial assistance to INNOQ	INNOQ Food processors UNIDO	UNIDO (a specific project was developed)
Ineffective control of compliance	Lack of human, material, and financial resources; the few existing regulations are not applied. Appropriate performance of regulatory institutions is key for the implementation of standards and regulations	Strengthening regulatory and research institutions of MADER	• Strengthen DSV and DINAP (Focal point for OIE and IPPC) • Equip laboratories of MADER research institutions • Establish quality control systems (ISO 17025) in MADER laboratories	• Training/technical/financial assistance to DSV and DINAP (to be able to participate in IPPC and OIF and to disseminate information • Financial/training assistance to laboratories • Training/technical/financial assistance to MADER and INNOQ	DSV DINAP MADER INNOQ	PROAGRI (to be discussed)

(continued)

Constraints to be Addressed	Justification	Projects	Activities	Inputs needed	Main Actors	Estimated Costs/ Potential Funder
		Strengthening regulatory institutions of MIC and MISAU	• Train and upgrade staff of regulatory Departments of MIC and MISAU • Train and upgrade staff of CHAEM and LNHAA • Equip laboratories of CHAEM and LNHAA • Establish quality control systems in CHAEM and LNHAA laboratories	• Training/technical/ financial assistance to MIC and MISAU • Training/technical/ financial assistance to CHAEM and LNHAA • Financial/training assistance to laboratories • Training/technical/ financial assistance to CHAEM and LNHAA laboratories	MIC MISAU CHAEM LNHAA INNOQ Food processors	UNIDO (a specific project was developed)
Deficient institutional coordination	There is very little sharing of information, activities are often duplicated and some issues are never addressed. A quality control system should exist to rationalize the use of existing facilities.					
Objective 2—Development of an appropriate standard setting system including facilities for training, metrology, accreditation testing and certification							
Lack of Awareness on quality issues	Producers have to understand improving the	Quality awareness	• Seminars and workshops • Support for professional and economic associations	• Technical/Financial/ Material/training Assistance to INNOQ	INNOQ Producers	400 000 USD for 3 years

(continued)

	quality in products and services is to encourage and foster action within industry to improve international competitiveness.		• Preparation of quality publications and videos • Continuation and upgrading of the annual 'Quality Week' • Regular publication of the news broad-sheet, "Qualitema" • Participation of producers in international meetings • Dissemination of market requirements • Technical assistance to determine capacity and scope for utilization of existing facilities within the national system. • Advice on: equipment; personnel; training; marketing; management; quality systems needs. • Technical assistance to implement recommendations in strategy documents. • Training corses on "Quality management system for laboratories, according to the ISO 17025" for the INNOQ and personnel from laboratories.	INNOQ MIC	400 000 USD for 3 years

Outdated Legislative Framework	There is a need of strengthening the legislative frame-work; in order to create a sound legislative basis for Mozambique's standardization, metrology, accre-ditation, testing,	Development of a modern legislative framework standards, quality assurance, accreditation and metrology (SQAM)	• Review and propose updates and new legislation that concerns INNOQ's activities. Priority given to:
			  • National Quality System
			  • National Quality Advisory Council (if required)
			  • INNOQ updated statutes
			  • An internationally acceptable accreditation infrastructure		

Constraints to be Addressed	Justification	Projects	Activities	Inputs Needed	Main Actors	Estimated Costs/ Potential Funder
	certification and information sub systems		• Metrology legislation			
National Standards developing is only starting	INNOQ needs appropriate infrastructures and human, material and financial resources to better coordinate and speed up the process with	Standards development/ adoption program	• To give INNOQ appropriate infrastructures, human, material, and financial resources • To review and strengthen INNOQ's organizational skills and procedures for standardization activities • To train present INNOQ staff and Technical Committees members in the use of internationally accepted standardization procedures • To assist INNOQ in developing and enabling the adequacy and visibility of its standardization program • To create awareness on the need of the main stakeholders to participate on the process of developing standards and to create incentives for such participation • To support the translation to Portuguese of the international and regional standards		INNOQ and stakeholders participating on standards developing: Economical Associations, consumers, Ministries, research institutions, etc.	750 000 USD for 3 years

No Certification scheme	Urgent need to create the scheme and to develop appropriate infrastructures		• Training of national consultants and auditors • Accreditation of INNOQ and laboratories	INNOQ Laboratories	900 000 USD for 3 years
No accreditation infrastructures.	Mozambique is falling behind the other countries in the SADCA framework and this may affect the regional trade	Creation and setting up of a national focal point for accreditation	• To set up of a National Focal Point for Accreditation under SADCA framework (SADC cooperation on accreditation). • To develop the basis to implement a world-recognized National Accreditation Capabilities System designed to provide accreditation services to laboratories, certification bodies and inspection bodies operating in Mozambique. The accreditation function could also embrace the registration of certification bodies for quality and environmental management experts as well as training organizations working on these fields and other areas, as needed • Formal and in job training for accreditation auditors to work with partners accreditation bodies in SADC countries	MIC/INNOQ	500 000 USD for 3 years

(continued)

Constraints to be Addressed	Justification	Projects	Activities	Inputs Needed	Main Actors	Estimated Costs/ Potential Funder
		Capability survey of Mozambican testing facilities and support to laboratories accreditation	• To survey existing capabilities • To propose a strategy for development including a program for strengthening of testing capacity		Laboratories Consultancy	
Lack of appropriate knowledge of standardization, etc. certification, quality management, ISO 9000 and ISO 14000 and food safety issues including HACCP	To guarantee that the above projects succeed the technicians and all staff involved directly and indirectly, must have a better and deeper understanding of these issues and constantly update their knowledge with the international developments of the issue	Development of an information centre on standards, metrology and quality management	• To develop training programmes in issues related to standards • To design and Install an adequate information center • To strengthen INNOQ's standards library facilities, through the introduction of modern IT-based database and CD ROM facilities • To establish a modern and efficient database and to train INNOQ staff and staff from other institutions in the use of the database as a way to improve dissemination of information • To assist INNOQ in developing and enabling its information marketing services to "go public" • Enhance the collection of national and international standards and quality management related documents including video-training aids		INNOQ Economic Associations Research Institutions Consumers' Associations State Institutions Industry Business Community	350 000 USD

(continued)

		500 000 USD
	<ul><li>Improvement and extension of INNOQ's equipment such as computer network, copying equipment, SPS and TBT information technology needs</li><li>To create a network of clients of the information center</li></ul>	
Development of a quality related management training center	<ul><li>To train a pool of Mozambican trainers, consultants and auditors to be able to provide professional services to Mozambican companies and to the national or foreign certification bodies, on Management System Implementation and continual improvement, based on ISO 9000 and ISO 14000 series, or OHSAS 18001</li><li>To deliver short-term training courses on quality management system for laboratories, according to the ISO 17025</li><li>To deliver short-term training courses recognized by international or foreign professional organizations (e.g., standardization; quality principles; quality systems—ISO 9000; environmental management systems—ISO 14000; quality and environmental auditing; OH SAS 18001, HACCP, metrology/legal metrology etc.)</li></ul>	

145

Constraints to be Addressed	Justification	Projects	Activities	Inputs Needed	Main Actors	Estimated Costs/ Potential Funder
Objective 3—The strengthening of the country's participation on regional and international standards setting bodies						
Insignificant participation of Mozambique in regional and international standardization	Due mainly to: • Lack of financial resources • Lack of appropriate technical capacity • Lack of timely information about events The country needs to benefit from regional and international harmonization but for this it has to improve its participation.		• To identify mechanisms to support the country's participation on SADC SQAM meetings as well as on ISO, IPPC, OIE, CODEX, and OIML meetings, to ensure that Mozambique concerns are taken in consideration	• Financial Assistance • Improve network of in country and international contacts	INNOQ Focal Points	200 000 USD
Participation restricted to government	Private sector must be encouraged to participate in regional and international standards setting organizations					

146

Inappropriate coordination between Focal points				

Objective 4—The improvement of institutional capacity to deal with issues related to SPS and TBT Agreement

Constraint	Justification	Activities	Agency	Cost
Lack of awareness about the SPS and TB Agreements.	There is need to create awareness about SPS and TBT issues	• Delivery awareness seminars on SPS and TBT issues • Strength the TBT enquiry point and the national working group on SPS • Set up and strength the SPS enquiry point	MIC/ INNOQ MADER MIZAU	150 000 USD
Weak inquiry point on TBT.	There is need to strength the TBT inquiry point and to nominate the SPS enquiry point. There is need to identify mechanisms for better communication between stakeholders including public, private, consumers and others providing access to Internet and e-mail to facilitate the dissemination of information	• Develop the capacity for notify the existence of new technical regulations • Develop a database that will allow disseminating information		100 000 USD

(continued)

147

Constraints to be Addressed	Justification	Projects	Activities	Inputs Needed	Main Actors	Estimated Costs/Potential Funder
Weak national group on SPS.	There is need to strength the existing national group on SPS providing working conditions and to assist private sector operators in addressing SPS measures					US$ 100,000
Objective 5—Supporting of the development of selected sectors to improve exports						
Weak national group on SPS.	The case studies show that, in general, the sectors need to improve to be competitive		• Application of standards • Investments in technology and human resources.			To be studied per case

References

AGOA at: http://agoa.gov.

APHIS Trade Support Team. 1998. *APHIS and the SPS Agreement: Rights and Obligations under WTO and NAFTA.* Second edition.

Assembleia da República, 1999. Lei do Caju. Lei no. 13/99 de 1 de Novembro, BR no. 43, I série, 2° suplemento.

————. 2000. Programa Quinquenal do Governo 2000–2004. Resolução no. 4/2000.

Assembleia Popular. 1990. Lei das Pescas. Lei no. 3/90 de 26 de Setembro, BR no. 39, I série, 2° Suplemento.

Associação Comercial de Moçambique, no date. Estatutos da Associação Comercial de Moçambique.

Associação de Fruticultores do Sul de Moçambique. 1995, BR no. 25, III série de 21 de Junho. Criação da Associação de Fruticultores do Sul de Moçambique.

Banco Standard Totta de Moçambique. 2001. Relatório e Contas de 2001.

Bank of Mozambique a: http://www.bancomoc.mz.

———— b, Department of Economic Research and Statistics. Recent Macroeconomic Developments—Monthly Issues (1999, 2000, 2001, and 2002).

———— c, Department of Economic Research and Statistics. Statistical Bulletin—quarterly issue (1999, 2000, 2001, and 2002).

Banze, P. 1999. Regulamentação na área de Sementes.

Bawden, R., M. Kherallah, and D. Meinville. 2001. The Impact of Improved Grades and Standards on the Export Potential of Targeted Agricultural/Fishery Commodities in Mozambique: Phase one Report.

Biggs, T., J. Nasir, and R. Fisman, R. 1999. Structure and Performance of Manufacturing in Mozambique.

CAIM. 1991. Estudo de Viabilidade Técnico Económico—Projecto de Produção de Sumos, Concentrados e Segmentos. CAIM, Ltd.

Centro de Promoção de Investimentos. 2002. Projectos Aprovados por Sector.

Cerina Mussá, MIC, Memorando sobre o processo de negociação e implementação do Protocolo Comercial da SADC.

Comissão Permanente da Assembleia Popular. 1982. Lei sobre Crimes Contra a Saúde Pública no Âmbito da Higiene Alimentar. Lei no. 8/82 de 23 de Junho, BR no. 24, I série, 3° suplemento.

Confederação das Associações Económicas de Moçambique. 2001. 6ª Conferência Anual do Sector Privado em Moçambique.

Conselho de Ministros. 1982. Requisitos higiénico-sanitários de produção, transporte e comercialização de géneros alimentícios, regras gerais de inspecção e fiscalização e as infracções correspondentes que tenham a natureza de contravenção e respectivas punições. Decreto no. 12/82, BR no. 24 de 23 de Junho, I série, 3° suplemento.

————. 1995. Política Agrária e Estratégia de Implementação-Resolução no. 11/95 de 31 de Outubro.

————. 1996. Política pesqueira e respectivas estratégias, Resolução no. 11/96 de 28 de Maio.

————. 1997a. Política e estratégia industrial, Resolução no. 23/97 de 19 de Agosto.

————. 1997b. Estratégia para o Desenvolvimento do Cajú.

————. 1997c. Criação do Instituto de Fomento do Cajú—INCAJU. Decreto no. 43/97 de 23 de Dezembro, BR no. 52, I série, 2° suplemento.

————. 1998a. Política e estratégia comercial, Resolução no. 25/98 de 1 de Julho.

————. 1998b. Aprova o Regulamento do Licenciamento da Actividade Comercial Decreto no. 43/98 de 9 de Setembro, BR no. 36, I série, 4° suplemento

————. 1998c. Aprova o Regulamento do Licenciamento da Actividade Industrial Decreto no. 44/98 de 9 de Setembro, BR no. 36, I série, 4° suplemento.

————. 1999a. Aprova o Regulamento da Comercialização da Castanha de Cajú. Decreto no. 86/99 de 23 de Novembro, BR no. 46, I série, 2° suplemento.

————. 1999b. Linhas de Acção para Erradicação da Pobreza Absoluta.

————. 2001. Regulamento de Inspecção e Garantia de Qualidade dos Produtos de Pesca Decreto no. 17/2001 de 12 de Junho, BR no. 23, I série, suplemento.

Coughin, P. 2001. SADC Study of the Textile and Garment Industries—Mozambique.

CPI at: http://www.mozbusiness.gov.mz.

CTA. 1998. Sumário da Conferência final do sector privado para discussão do Protocolo Comercial da SADC.

CTA at: http://www.cta.org.mz.

Customs of Mozambique at http://www.alfandegas.org.mz/.

Departamento de Florestas-Faculdade de Agronomia e Engenharia Florestal-Universidade Eduardo Mondlane. 2002. Iniciativa para desenvolvimento de critérios e indicadores nacionais de maneio sustentável e certificação florestal.

Departamento de Higiene Ambiental. 1998. Manual de Inspecções no Âmbito da Higiene Alimentar. Projecto TCF/MOZ/6611 (Cooperação FAO—MISAU)

Departamento de Inspecção de Pescado. 2002. Proposta de Plano de Actividades do DIP—MP/2002.

Departamento de Sanidade Vegetal. 2001. Lista dos Produtos Registados.

Departamento de Sementes. 2000. Procedimentos para Avaliação e Registo de Variedades na Lista Oficial.

DFID—Department for International Developments. 2002. Ministerial Round Table: Closer cooperation between the EU and developing countries on product standards.

Direcção Nacional da Agricultura. 1987. Estratégia do Desenvolvimento de Citrinos (resumo).

————. 1993. Programa Nacional de Desenvolvimento de Fruteiras.

————. 1996. Estratégia de Desenvolvimento das culturas de Cereais e Leguminosas de Grão (Draft I).

————. 1996. Estratégia de Desenvolvimento das culturas de raízes e tubérculos.

————. 1997a. Estratégia de Apoio à Produção Agrícola.

————. 1997b. Estratégia de Apoio à Produção Agrícola (última versão).

————. 1997c. Estratégia do Subsector de Sementes.

————. 1997d. Estratégia do Subsector de Sementes.

————. 1999. Regulamento Interno do Sub-Commité de Registo e Libertação de Variedades.

————. 2001a. Regulamento sobre qualidade dos fertilizantes.

————. 2001b. Relatório Anual da DINA apresentado na V Reunião Anual.

————. 2001c. Relatório Final da Campanha Agrícola 2000/2001. Apresentado na V Reunião Anual da DINA.

————. 2001d. Síntese da V Reunião Anual da DINA, Bilene-Gaza de 7–10 de Agosto de 2001.

————. 2001e. Síntese final do Seminário Nacional sobre sementes em Bilene de 14 a 16 de Março de 2001.

————. 2002. Síntese do II Conselho Coordenador.

————. 2002. Regulamento de Pesticidas (nova versão).

Direcção Nacional de Estatística. 1987. Informação Estatística 1986.

Direcção Nacional de Estatística. 1988. Informação Estatística 1987.

Direcção Nacional de Florestas e Fauna Bravia. 1999. Lei de Florestas e Fauna Bravia.

Direcção Nacional de Pecuária. 2000. Relatório Anual.

Direcção Nacional de Pescas. 1996. Regulamento da Pesca Marítima—Decreto no. 16/96 de 28 de Maio, BR no. 2, I série de 28 de Maio

Direcção Nacional do Comércio Interno. 1995. Balanço Anual da Comercialização Agrícola 99.

Direcção Nacional do Comércio Interno. 1996. Balanço Anual da Comercialização Agrícola 95.

Direcção Nacional do Comércio Interno. 1997. Balanço Anual da Comercialização Agrícola 96.

Direcção Nacional do Comércio Interno. 1998. Balanço do Plano Económico e Social de 1997.

Direcção Nacional do Comércio Interno. 1999. Balanço Anual da Comercialização Agrícola 98.

Direcção Nacional do Comércio Interno. 2001. Balanço Anual da Comercialização Agrária 2000.

Direcção Nacional do Comércio Interno. 2001. Plano de Acção da Estratégia da Comercialização Agrícola para 2000/2004.

Dixie, G. (Accord Associates), for TechnoServe Mozambique. 2001. Species Selection for the Middle East and Indian Markets for Mangoes and Citrus.

FAO at: http://www.fao.org.

Food safety forum at: http://www.foodsafetyforum.org.

Freire, M and P. Banze. 2001. Caracterização da Situação Actual de Sector de Sementes em Moçambique.

Frutimel, Limitada, BR no. 1, III série de 7 de Janeiro. Criação da Frutimel, Ltda.

Gabinete de Promoção do Sector Comercial Agrário. 2002a. Identificação de Opções e viabilidade para a promoção da Agroindústria Rural em Moçambique—Termos de Referência.

————. 2002b. Criar uma agro-indústria rural viável: apresentação no Seminário de Disseminação dos Resultados da Primeira Fase do Estudo sobre a Agro-Indústria Rural em Moçambique.

————. 2002c. Recomendações Preliminares das Potenciais combinações de produtos/mercados (primeiro relatório/"Inception Report").

Henson, S., R. Loader, A. Swinank, M. Bredahl, and N. Lux. 2000. Impact of Sanitary and Phytosanitary Measures on Developing Countries—Report for the U.K. Department for International Development (DFID).

Henson, S., K. Preibisch, and O. Masakure. 2001. Review of Developing Country Needs and Involvement in International Standards-Setting Bodies. Centre for Food Economics research, Department of Agricultural and Food Economics, The University of Reading.

INCAJU. 2001. Normas de Comercialização da Castanha de Caju para a Campanha 2001/2002.

INCAJU. 2002a. Relatório Anual de Actividades do INCAJU-2001 apresentado no II Fórum Nacional do Cajú.

INCAJU. 2002b. Documentos do II Fórum Nacional do Cajú.

INIA. 2002. Relatório Anual de Investigação de Cajú em Moçambique (apresentado no II fórum Nacional do Cajú).

INNOQ. 2001a. 1ª Conferência Nacional sobre a Política de Qualidade (Procedings).

INNOQ. 2001b. Semana de Qualidade (Procedings).

INNOQ. 2002. Plano Estratégico para a Qualidade.

Instituto de Algodão de Moçambique. 2002a. Comparação de Tipos de Fibra de Algodão Nacionais com os Internacionais.

————. 2002b. Fábricas de Descaroçamento de Algodão.

————. 2002c. Ponto de Situação das Campanhas do Algodão 2000/2001 e 2001/02.

————. 1998. Estratégia para o Desenvolvimento do Algodão (proposta).

————. 2001. Cotton Subsector Assessment (volume 1, Draft report).

————. 2002d. Ponto de Situação das Campanhas do Algodão 2000/01 e 2001/02.

Instituto Nacional de Estatística—Moçambique. 1996a. Estatísticas Industriais.

————. 1999a. Estatísticas Industriais.

————. 1996b. Anuário Estatístico (Statistical Yearbook).

————. 1999b. Anuário Estatístico (Statistical Yearbook).

————. 2000. Anuário Estatístico (Statistical Yearbook).

Instituto Nacional de Estatística. 2001a. A Conjuntura Económica. no. 10, Fevereiro.

————. 2001b. Censo Agro pecuário 1999–2000—Apresentação Sumária dos resultados (quadros e gráficos).

Instituto Nacional do Açúcar. 2000a. O Sector do Açúcar em Moçambique: Situação Actual e Perspectivas Futuras.

————. 2000b. O Sector do Açúcar em Moçambique—Balanço do PES 2001 e Perspectivas para 2002.

————. 2001. O Subsector do Açúcar em Moçambique: Situação Actual e Perspectivas Futuras.

————. 2002. Balanço do PES 2001 e Perspectivas para 2002.

International Capital Corporation (Moçambique) LDA e ENTERPLAN. Identificação de Opções e Viabilidade para a Promoção de Agro-Indústria Rural: Proposta Técnica.

Intertek Testing Services International Limited. 2001. Directrizes para Exportadores, Programa de Inpecção Pré-Embarque para Moçambique.

IPEX. 1998. Directório dos exportadores moçambicanos.

IPEX at: http://www.ipex.gov.mz.

IPPC at http://sedac.ciesin.org/entri/register/reg-099.rrr.html.

ISO. 2001. Memento. ISO Publication.

Jaeger P. 1998a. The Indian Market for East African Pigeon Peas (Cajanus cajan). TechnoServe Mozambique.

————. 1998b. The Market in Europe for East African Pigeon Peas (Cajanus cajan). TechnoServe Mozambique.

————. 1999. Indian Pulse Buyer Visit to Mozambique. TechnoServe Mozambique.

Keyser, J. C. 1998. Cotton Subsector Analysis—Mozambique. TechnoServe, Moçambique.

KPMG, http://www.kpmg.co.mz/artigos-port/economia-Moç.htm. 2002. Desempenho Económico de Moçambique em 2000.

LOUMAR, undated. Economic Feasibility Study for a Citrus and Pineapple Industry.

Machungo, C. 2002. Perspectivas de Produção no Âmbito do Plano Director 2004 apresentado no II Fórum Nacional do Cajú.

Memorendum of Agreement on Co-operation in Standardization, Quality Assurance, Accreditation and Metrology, in the Southern African Development Community.

MIC. 2002. Rapid Market Appraisal—Terms of Reference.

MICTUR. 1999. Estratégia da assistência ao País 2001–2003.

MIC, Departamento de Planificação. 2000. Mapa de produções.

Ministério da Agricultura e Desenvolvimento Rural. 1997. Balanço da Campanha Agrícola 2000/01 e perspectivas da Campanha 2001/02.

————. 2001a. Regulamento sobre a Produção, Comércio, Controle de Qualidade e Certificação de Sementes—Diploma Ministerial no. 184/2001 de 19 de Dezembro. Boletim da República no. 51, I série de 19 de Dezembro de 2001.

————. 2001b. Regulamento sobre fomento, produção e Comercialização do Tabaco—Diploma Ministerial no. 176/2001 de 28 de Novembro, BR no. 48, I série.

Ministério da Agricultura e Desenvolvimento Rural, Direcção de Economia. 2000. Características dos Agregados Familiares Rurais nas Zonas Afectadas pelas Cheias do Ano 2000 no Centro e Sul de Moçambique. Relatório de Pesquisa No. 40 P, Março de 2000.

Ministério da Agricultura e Pescas. 1998. Regulamento Interno do Comité Nacional de Sementes—Diploma Ministerial no. 11/98 de 11 de Fevereiro. Boletim da República no. 6, I série de 11 de Fevereiro de 1998.

————. Lista Nacional de Variedades—Despacho. Boletim da República no. 38, I série de 20 de Setembro de 1995.

————. Programa Nacional de Desenvolvimento Agrário (PROAGRI) 1998a 2003.

Ministério da Agricultura. 1992. Regulamento da Inspecção Fitossanitária e de Quarentena Vegetal e seus Anexos, Diploma Ministerial no. 132/92 de 2 de Setembro, BR no. 36, I série.

Ministério da Indústria e Comércio. 2000. Estatuto Orgânico, Diploma Ministerial no. 161, A/2000.

Ministério da Saúde. 1998. Manual de Inspecções no Âmbito da Higiene Alimentar—Projecto TCP/MOC/6611 (Cooperação FAO–MISAU).

Ministério de Agricultura e Pescas. 1992. Regulamento de Inspecção Fitossanitária e de Quarentena Vegetal—Diploma Ministerial no. 134/92.

Ministério de Agricultura. 1977. Breve Monografia Agrária.

Ministérios da Agricultura e do Comércio. 1991. Regulamento de Importação de Sementes—Diploma Ministerial no. 95/91 de 07 de Agosto. BR no. 32, I série de 7 de Agosto de 1991.

Ministry of Fisheries at: http://www.mozpesca.org.

Ministérios da Saúde e da Agricultura. Regulamento de Pesticidas—Diploma Ministerial no. 88/87 de 29 de Julho. BR no. 39, I série de 30 de Setembro de 1987.

Ministérios da Saúde e da Indústria e Comércio. 1978. Caderneta do Controle Sanitário. Portaria no. 11/78, BR no. 6, I série de 14 de Janeiro.

Ministérios da Saúde, das Finanças e Secretaria de Estado do Trabalho. 1982. Processo de Emissão e Revalidação do Boletim de Sanidade Estabelecido pelo Decreto no. 5/80 de 25 de Outubro. Diploma Ministerial no. 73/82, BR no. 37, I série de 22 de Setembro.

Mozambique Official Home Page: http://www.mozambique.mz.

Mucavele, F. 2000. Analysis of Comparative Advantage and Agricultural Trade in Mozambique. SD Publication Series, Office of Sustainable Development Bureau for Africa, Technical Paper no. 107, November 2000.

Muendane, C., Ministério da Agricultura e Desenvolvimento Rural, Gabinete de Promoção do Sector Comercial Agrário. 2002. Identificação de Opções e Viabilidade para a Promoção da Agro—Industria Rural em Moçambique—1ª fase: Relatório Preliminar.

National Institute of Statistics: http://www.ine.gov.mz.

Negrão, A.S., TechnoServe. Projecto de Comercialização de Banana de Manica.

OIE: http://www.oie.int/eng/oie.

Otsuki T., J. S. Wilson, and M. Sewadeh. 2001. A Race to the Top? A Case Study of Food Safety Standards and African Exports. World Bank Research Paper. www.worldbank.org/whiep/trade/standards/html

Patrick Lemaitre Consultant and CIRAD. 2001. Cotton Subsector Assessment, Volume 1 Draft Report.

Patrocínio M. L. Q. M. 1997. Compilação da Legislação Pecuária desde 1913 até a Presente Data.

Pereira, C. R., M. Michaque, and F. Kanji, UEM-FAEF-GNRB. 2002. Estratégia e Capacitação na Área de Certificação Florestal.

PODE, 2001. Project Brochure.

Presidência da República. 2000. Atribuições e competências do Ministério da Indústria e Comércio, Decreto Presidencial no. 15/2000.

Rebello da Silva, G., L. S. Carrilho, and R. Tibana. 2001. Mozambique country paper presented at the Nairobi workshop for the preparation of the study "Bridging the Standards Divide: Challenges for Improving Africa's International Market Access."

SADC, Protocol on Trade.

SADC SQAM at: http://www.sadc-sqam.org.

SIDA. 2000. Final report. Assistance to the National Institute of Standardisation and Quality (INNOQ)—project number 2104 0040 01 001.

Singh Y. K. 1995. Proposta do Projecto de Fruteira.

Snikars, F. H. 2002. Propose programme of action for enhancing the participation of developing countries and economies in transition in international standardisation—Africa of action (draft). SIS Forum A B.

TechnoServe, Inc. 1998. PIGEON PEA Subsector Report.

———. 2001. A Vision for the Fruit Industry in Mozambique—Building a Globally Competitive Tropical Fruit Industry.

Technoserve, Inc. Moçambique. 1998a. Análise do Subsector do Amendoim.

———. 1998b. Análise do Subsector do Cajú—USAID Grant no. 656-G-00-98-0011-00.

———. 1998c. Análise do Subsector do Milho.

———. 1998d. Sunflower Subsector Report.

TSG Inc.—The Services Group/Sociedade Austral de Desenvolvimento, SARL. 1999. Avaliando os custos e benefícios da zona de comércio livre da SADC, Moçambique.

UNDP. 2000. Human Development Report 2000.

UNICEF/ICCIDDD. 2000. Harmonisation of Policies and Standards for Salt—Background Information for SADC, COMESA, ARSO.

UNIDO. 1999. Programme Document Integrated Industrial Development Programme to Facilitate Private Sector Development in Mozambique.

———. 2001b. Assistance for Food Action Plan for Improved Processing and Food Safety—Final Technical Report (based on the work of Ravi Awashi).

UTRE. 1995. Informação sobre Citrinos de Maputo.

Wilson, J. S. and T. Otsuki. 2001. Global Trade and Food Safety: Winners and Losers in a Fragmented System.

World Bank, 2001. Cashew production and marketing in the smallholder sector in Mozambique.

———. 2001. Mozambique country economic memo.

———. 2001. Mozambique country economic memorandum growth prospects and reform agenda. Report no. 20601-MZ.

———. 2001. Africa's integration into the world Trading System: challenges in market access, standards and regulatory reform. Project action plans and country study. Terms of reference.

———. 2001. Bridging the Standards Divide: Challenges for Improving Africa's International Market Access. Draft Terms of Reference for Country Action Plans and Studies. Case study and action plan for Mozambique.

World Bank at: http://www.worldbank.org.

WTO. 2001. Trade Policy Review.

http://www.mol.co.mz/economia

http://www.africapolicy.org

List of Relevant Contacted Persons

Alexandre Carreira	SGS Moçambique, Lda
Amélia Mondlane	National Sugar Institute—Ministry of Agriculture and Rural Development
Ana Machalela	Institute for the Promotion of Cashew at Ministry of Agriculture and Rural Development
Bonifácio Saulosse	Provincial Directorate of Industry and Trade, Nampula
Cardoso Muendane	Consultant SORGAZA Company
Carmen Ramos	Consultant Verde Azul Company
Egídio Paulo	Directorate of Commerce, Ministry of Industry and Trade
Felisberto Ferrão	Mozambican Institute of Export Promotion
Felisberto Manuel	AMAPIC
Fernando Rodrigues	National Directorate of Livestock at Ministry of Agriculture and Rural Development
Gabriel Paposseco	Mozambican Cotton Institute—Ministry of Agriculture and Rural Development
Issufo Nurmamade	Sanam—Sociedade Algodoeira de Namialo, Lda
João Aragão	AGT, Nampula

Joaquim Santos	National Directorate for Rural Extension at Ministry of Agriculture and Rural Development
Jorge Salvador	Technical Unit for Trade at Ministry of Industry and Trade
Jorge Tinga	Clusa, Nampula
José Alcobia	Association of Fruit Producers From South of Mozambique
José Varimelo	Department of Plant protection at Ministry of Agriculture and Rural Development
Luisa Ribeiro Arthur	Department of Fisheries Inspection at Ministry of Fisheries
Luisa Santos	Faculty of Agronomy and Forestry Engineering
Maria dos Anjos Hauengue	Department of Environmental Health at the Ministry of Health
Nordino Ticongolo	ABIODES
Rita Freitas	Mozambican Institute of Export Promotion
Roberto Tibana	Consultant
Rodrigues	National Directorate of Livestock at Ministry of Agriculture and Rural Development
Salvador Jorge	Technical Unit for Trade at Ministry of Industry and Trade
Sérgio Chitará	Confederation of Mozambican Economic Associations
Setina Titosse	National Directorate of Agriculture at Ministry of Agriculture and Rural Development
Ventura Macamo	National Directorate of Livestock at Ministry of Agriculture and Rural Development

Annex A Main Legislation

In this annex some laws and technical regulations are presented and the institutions responsible for the application and control of the legislation are indicated.

Legislation Related to the Health

Crimes against public health in the context of food hygiene, Act—Law No. 8/82 of 23 June, Standing Commission of the People's Assembly. This is the basic law for the control of foodstuffs in the country, the application of which covers all sectors that directly or indirectly relate to foodstuffs, including the consumers. The law rests essentially on the possibility that offences might produce danger or harm and not in the effective production of the said danger or harm to the health of the consumer.

The following are regarded as crimes against public health: to produce, sell or display for sale, purchase, transport or store for commercial purposes imitation, spoiled or corrupt foodstuffs; to produce, sell or display for sale, purchase, transport or store for commercial purposes, kitchen utensils or tableware, containers, any other equipment or object that come into contact with foodstuffs in their normal course of use and from this contact may

transmit toxic substances in quantities larger than the legally fixed limits; it is presumed that the transport of imitation, spoiled and corrupt foodstuffs is done for the purpose of commerce whenever these foodstuffs are those traded by the recipient.

The DHA of the Ministry of Health is the institution responsible for the application of this law.

Decree No. 5/80 of 22 October, Council of Ministers. This decree makes it compulsory for all workers of different professional categories who are involved in the preparation, handling and trade of foodstuffs, as well as workers who deal regularly with children, to obtain a health certificate.

The DHA of the Ministry of Health is the institution responsible for the application of this law.

Hygiene and sanitary requirements in the production, transport and trade of foodstuffs, Decree No. 12/82 of 23 June, Council of Ministers. This document contains the hygiene and sanitary requirements for the production, transport and trade of foodstuffs, as well general rules on inspection and supervision and the corresponding offences that have the nature of contravention, and their respective penalties.

The decree assigns to the Ministry of Health the task of establishing hygiene and sanitary quality requirements for import and commerce of food-stuffs in Mozambique as well as to establish the physical and chemical characteristics, criteria of purity and maximum permitted dosage of chemical additives.

The DHA of the Ministry of Health is the institution responsible for the application of this law.

Regulations on the hygiene requirements of food establishments, Ministerial Diploma No. 51/84 Ministry of Health.

These regulations establish the minimum and compulsory hygiene requirements of food establishments used for the production, transport and marketing of food-stuffs. These regulations cover food establishments, means of transport, equipment, utensils, storage of foodstuffs, establishments for food consumption, restaurants and similar establishments, establishments for the sale of foodstuffs, means of transport for transporting foodstuffs, places and installations, bars, cafés and bakeries. They include the minimum compulsory requirements for establishments producing and packaging foodstuffs. The regulations also specify the health personnel with competence to carry out inspections and the hygiene standards for staff.

The Ministry of Health is the institution responsible for the application of this law.

Regulations on Imported Foodstuffs, Ministerial Diploma No. 80/87 of 1 July, Ministry of Health.

These regulations specify the conditions and procedures for the importation of foodstuffs, namely specifications of the identity and quality of the foodstuff, inspection and quality testing, certificates, supervision, infestation, inorganic contaminants and micro toxins. The regulations establish that the standards to be applied on the importation of foodstuffs must be according to those established by Codex Alimentarius. These regulations indicate also that it is mandatory the inspection and quality testing on origin of all imported foodstuffs, by entities with recognized capacities or accredited to realize this work, the expenses of this are of the buyer's responsibility.

Furthermore, these regulations indicate that foodstuffs for export must be manufactured according to the standards in force in the country of destination, and the manufacturing firm can consult the Codex point of contact regarding the said standards.

The DHA of the Ministry of Health is the institution responsible for the application of this law.

Regulations on food additives in respect of the importation, production, marketing and use of food additives, Ministerial Diploma No. 100/87 of 23 September, Ministry of Health.

According to these regulations, all additives and technological aids in the preparation of foodstuffs must comply with the physical and chemical characteristics set out in Codex Alimentarius specifications. The list of authorized food additives and their maximum dosage in the foodstuffs in which their use is authorized is appended.

Order in Council No. 11/78 of 14 January, Ministry of Health and Ministry of Industry and Trade.

This order determines that all establishments where foodstuffs are manufactured, handled or sold must possess a "sanitary control" register.

Dispatch. 13 November 1980, Ministry of Health.

Determines which workers in the different branches of professional activity listed in the dispatch must carry a health certificate, and this became compulsory in Decree No. 5/80, of 22 October, for the exercise of certain professional activities.

Issue and renewal of the health certificate, Ministerial Diploma No. 73/82 of 23 June. Ministry of Health, Ministry of Finance and Secretary of State for Labour.

This document establishes who regulates and supervises the mechanisms for conducting the medical examinations and of inspection of compliance with the regulatory standards in this matter, at the same time attributing responsibility to the competent authority.

Pesticide Regulations. Ministerial Diploma No. 88/87 of 29 July. Ministry of Health and Ministry of Agriculture.

The pesticide regulations are aimed at disciplining and controlling the registration, importation, production, packaging, labelling, storage, marketing and sale, transport and elimination of pesticides and related chemicals. In addition to a toxicological classification, the upper limits of residues tolerated in food, inspection and penalties are specified.

Approval of new regulations on pesticides is in process and will revoke the regulations approved in 1987. These provide for a technical advisory committee on pesticides, seeds and fertilisers to be created to make recommendations to the Ministry of Agriculture and Rural Development on questions relating to agricultural pesticides and related veterinary and public health chemicals, for normal and for emergency situations.

The DHA of the Ministry of Health together with DINA of the Ministry of Agriculture and Rural Development are the institutions responsible for the application of this law.

Dispatch of 05 October 1996—Ministry of Industry and Trade and Ministry of Health. This prohibits the importation of wheat flour containing potassium bromate.

Legislation Related to Cereals and Iodised Salt

Ministerial Diploma No. 120/87 of 21 October. State Secretariat for Food and Light Industries. This MD establishes technical regulations where the standards of quality for wheat and wheat flour and for maize and maize meal are stated.

Ministerial Diploma No. 7/2000 of 02 November 1999. Minister of Industry, Trade and Tourism and the Minister of Health. This MD enforces the iodisation of salt and compliance with the Mozambican Standard on iodised salt. The referred MD fixed the level of KIO3 between 25 and 55 PPM and, with regards to the technical specifications it refers that they need to follow the Mozambican Standard on salt.

Legislation Related to Forestry and Agriculture Production

The Forestry and Wildlife Act—Law No. 10/99 of 7 July. Assembly of the Republic. The Forestry and Wildlife Act establishes the principles and basic norms for the protection, conservation and sustainable use of forestry and wildlife resources. This law contains the classification of the forestry and wildlife stock, the forms of protection of resources, the conditions and rules for forestry exploitation and hunting, for the replacement of these resources, forestry and wildlife management and supervision. For the export of forest and wildlife products, the law covers the promotion of the processing industry to increase the export of manufactured goods.

Regulations are currently being prepared for the application of the Forestry and Wildlife Act, and to harmonise it with the Land and the Environment Acts.

With regard to forests, a study was conducted recently on forestry certification that is based on the establishment of standards and codes of good practice. Forestry certification provides information on the management practices used in a given forestry unit and the attribution of a certificate to the forest or product gives the consumer assurance that it comes from a forest that is managed according to the established requirements.

The National Directorate of Forestry and Wildlife (DNFFB) of the Ministry of Agriculture and Rural Development (MADER) is the institution responsible for the application of this law.

The Cashew Act—Law No. 13/99 of 1 November, Assembly of the Republic. The Cashew Act passed in November 1999 establishes that the Council of Ministers must formulate a policy on the promotion of cashew production and processing, with the aim of recovering the stock of cashew trees by providing incentives to organisations to become involved in the planting of and research into cashew trees, and the technological development and economic and financial recovery of existing cashew processing firms and the creation of industries to use cashew by-products.

The Ministry of Agriculture and Rural Development—INCAJU is the institution responsible for the application of this law.

Regulations on cashew nut marketing, Decree No. 86/99 of 23 November, Council of Ministers. In line with the Cashew Act, the regulations on cashew nut marketing of 1999 (Decree No. 86/99 of 23 November) establish the procedures and conditions for cashew nut marketing and set the annual surcharge on the export of unprocessed cashew nuts.

The Ministry of Agriculture and Rural Development—INCAJU is the institution responsible for the application of this law.

Decree No. 8/91 of 23 April—Council of Ministers updates the legal framework of the cultivation, marketing and industrialisation of cotton in Mozambique and revokes Decree law No. 45179 of 5 August 1963. This decree gives the Mozambique Cotton Institute the responsibility for the promotion and supervision of cotton cultivation and technical and financial assistance to the growers. It specifies the procedures for marketing seed cotton, for the ginning and baling operations in cotton gins, for the marketing and export of baled cotton, as well as penalties.

Regulations on Cotton Cultivation, Ministerial Diploma No. 91/94 of 29 June, Ministry of Agriculture. The Mozambique Cotton Institute (IAM) is responsible for the application and control of the regulations on cotton cultivation, which specify who are the economic operators and the concessions for cotton production, their registration and the procedures for growing cotton and marketing seed cotton and cotton fibre. Some technical aspects regarding the characteristics of the soil, crop operations, ginning and phytosanitary control are indicated. These regulations require cotton fibre destined for the domestic market to be accompanied by a certificate of origin and classification, whereas in the case of exports, there should be a national certificate of origin issued by the classification laboratories in the Mozambique Cotton Institute (IAM). For this purpose, the seller must present documentation with information on the ginnery, the variety, the sector of production, the year of production and other data that identify the provenance of the product and its packaging.

Regulations on the Promotion, Production and Marketing of Tobacco, Ministerial Diploma No. 176/2001 of 28 November, Ministry of Agriculture and Rural Development. These regulations include the classification of operators and the requirements for their registration in the Provincial Directorate of Agriculture and Rural Development, and indicate the procedures and tariffs for the production, marketing, inspection and supervision of tobacco. For the export of leaf tobacco, the regulations require that a certificate of origin and a plant health certificate issued within a given schedule accompany the product. The preparation of technical standards for the cultivation, curing and storage of tobacco and the type of seed is planned.

Norms for the production and trade of seeds, Decree No. 41/94 of 20 September, Council of Ministers. This decree is regarded as the basic law on seeds. It contains definitions of seed and its classification, and procedures and obligations for the production, improvement and trade in seeds, and the system of quality control and certification of seeds. This decree announces the creation of the National Seed Committee as the body to monitor and advise the Ministry of Agriculture on matters relating to seeds.

The Ministry of Agriculture and Rural Development—National Directorate for Agriculture is the institution responsible for the application of this law.

Regulations on seed imports. Ministerial Diploma No. 95/91 OF 7 August. Ministry of Agriculture and Ministry of Trade. These regulations derive from the then significant quantities of seeds being imported to meet the country's needs, since domestic seed production was not sufficient, was of inferior quality, without standard certificates and was of nonadapted varieties. The objectives of these regulations were to ensure the importation of good quality seeds of varieties adapted to the different ecological zones; to discourage the imposition of seed imports when the country is producing sufficient quantities of acceptable quality; to coordinate and support the organisations that import seeds; to establish the basis for a more effective control of seed imports. These regulations indicate the conditions, specifications of quality, licenses and system of coordination for the importation of seeds. The specifications required in the seed order, the characteristics of the seed from a list of 30 species, the wording of a request for a license of plant health by the importer and the wording of the seed import authorisation from the Ministry of Agriculture's National Seed Service are contained in an annexe. The Orange International Seed Lot Certificate, the Field Inspection Certificate and the Phytosanitary Certificate must be presented.

National list of varieties, Dispatch of 17 August 1995—Ministry of Agriculture and Fisheries. The list includes the names of the varieties, the user and the growing cycle of 27 varieties of maize, 12 of rice, 12 of sorghum, 4 of wheat, 26 of cowpea, 20 of common beans, 1 of pigeon peas, 8 of Soya, 16 of groundnut and 6 of sunflower.

Internal Regulations for the National Seed Committee, Ministerial Diploma No. 11/98 of 11 February—Ministry of Agriculture and Fisheries. These regulations describe the organization, functioning and responsibilities of the Committee and its bodies. From its nature and responsibilities, the Committee is a consultative and advisory body in the Ministry of Agriculture and Fisheries and should give its opinion on seed supply plans, the national list of varieties and legislation on seeds, among other subjects.

Regulations on the production, trade, quality control and certification of seeds, Ministerial Diploma No. 184/2001 of 19 December— Ministry of Agriculture and Rural Development. These regulations complement the Norms on the Production and Trade of Seeds, approved by Decree No. 41/94 of 20 September, the Regulations on Seed Imports—Ministerial Diploma No. 95/91 of 7 August and the National List of Varieties—Dispatch from the Minister of Agriculture and Fisheries on 17 August 1995. These regulations contain definitions of words and expressions related to seeds, the classification of seeds, procedures for the recognition, registration, introduction, dissemination and marketing of new varieties and seed certification. They also cover licensing of producers, seed improvers, importers and exporters of seeds; quality control with the required documents, control mechanisms, production inspection and supervision, improvement, distribution, sale, import and export of seeds; the duties and obligations of inspectors and supervisors; indication of tariffs; and penalties.

Seed imports are governed by the Regulations on Seed Imports—Ministerial Diploma No. 95/91 of 7 August and there are new provisions in the current regulations, particularly with regard to genetically modified varieties (GMO). Genetically modified varieties must not be imported and a declaration from the appropriate authorities of the exporting country to this effect is required to confirm that the seed is not a genetically modified variety.

Other documents required are the Orange International Seed Lot Certificate (or in authorised cases a certificate of integrity) and the plant health certificate. Seed exports require authorisation and for that purpose information is needed on the species and variety, on the quantities, where they may be inspected, their destination and certificates. They must meet field and laboratory standards for certified seed and be properly packaged.

A list is appended to these regulations of 79 species and varieties, their common and botanical names, the weight of a lot, category of seed, field standards (isolation, percentage of atypical plants and number of inspections) and laboratory standards (percentage of purity, percentage of germination and percentage of humidity).

Legislation Related to Phytosanitary Inspections and Plant Quarantine

Regulations on Phytosanitary Inspections and Plant Quarantine, Ministerial Diploma No. 134/92 of 2 September, Ministry of Agriculture. The purpose of these regulations, covering plants, plant products and agricultural products, and the means of cultivation, packaging and transporting them, is to prevent the introduction and spread of harmful organisms, especially from things in quarantine, to control pests and diseases, to supervise and control fields, forestry plantations, nurseries and places for storing and selling plants, and plant health control of imports and exports.

The importation of plants covered by these regulations requires a Plant Health Import Permit, a plant health certificate of origin or provenance in accordance with the International Plant Protection Convention (IPPC) standards. For the export of plant material for commercial purposes, the DSV checks the production site of this material in order to issue a plant health certificate. Where plants are to be exported for personal use, they are inspected before a certificate is issued. The regulations include the conditions/type of plant material to enter the country, lists of harmful organisms and their hosts and the requirements for quarantine of whole grain maize to be imported or in transit from countries with the Large Grain Borer (LGB) *Prostephanus truncatus*.

The application of these regulations is the responsibility of the Department of Plant Health (DSV) in the Ministry of Agriculture and Rural Development.

Legislation Related to Fisheries

Regulation on Inspection and Guarantee of Quality of Fishing Products (Decree 17/01 of 12 June, Council of Ministers, BR no. 23, I Series). This regulation is the basis for quality control, and was drafted to be equivalent to the European Union Directives 91/493/CEE and 92/48/CEE with regard to sanitary conditions in the productive units during operations and product quality. This regulation has a number of aims: to be a guiding instrument for

157

the development of a processing industry; to update and modernise national legislation in accordance with the requirements of the international market; to set legal boundaries for the responsibilities of the fisheries inspectorate and the role of the processing industry; to serve, together with the maritime fishing regulation, as an instrument for fisheries management and administration; and to be a sectoral instrument that also has implications for other sectors such as health, customs and commerce.

Law on Fishing (Law 3/90 of 26 September, People's Assembly, BR no. 39, I Series).

Fisheries policy and implementation strategy (Resolution 11/96 of 28 May, Council of Ministers).

Maritime Fishing Regulation (Decree 16 of 28 May, Council of Ministers, BR no. 21).

Technical Regulations in the Process of Approval

Internal Regulations for the Sub-Committee for the Registration and Release of Varieties Prepared in September 1999. These regulations cover the organisation, functioning and responsibilities of the Sub-Committee on the Registration and Release of Varieties, a consultative and advisory body to the National Seed Committee, with responsibilities for offering opinions on the registration and release of varieties.

Regulations on Fertiliser quality prepared in September 2001. The aim of these regulations is to protect the consumers and vendors of fertilisers, making sure that they comply with certain requirements, namely the registration of producers, importers and vendors, labelling, limits of nutrients and harmful substances. It is thought that the specification of methods of inspection and sampling will be based on Mozambican manuals of fertiliser inspection and analysis.

The regulations propose the creation of a Mozambican unit responsible for the application of the regulations. It would be in charge of the administration of and compliance with the provisions of the Regulations on fertiliser quality.

These regulations also foresee the creation of a Mozambican advisory fertiliser committee, composed of representatives of different institutions and the private sector.

Legislation Related to Custom

Presidential Decree 4/2000 of 17 March Mozambique's Customs System. Mozambique's customs system is made up of the existing bodies and legislation and others that may be created in the future. Its functions include the following: propose measures and changes in fiscal and customs policy relating to foreign trade, implement them, punish infringements, collect customs duties and other taxes and tariffs, inspect and control the entry and exit of goods to and from Mozambique, and give opinions on international treaties and conventions.

Decree 3/2000 of 17 March—Council of Ministers. According to its statutes, approved in March 2000, Mozambique Customs is a state body of a paramilitary nature, which operates throughout the territory of the Republic of Mozambique to inspect and police the customs, taking measures when necessary with regard to people and goods in frontier zones.

Decree 4/2000 of 17 March. Council of Ministers. This Decree refers to the Customs Staff Statute.

Decree 56/98 of 11 November. Council of Ministers. The licensing of foreign trade operations to and from Mozambique and respective instruments, namely the Import and Export Registration Forms, are abolished.

The forms used by the Customs at the date of publication of this Decree for customs clearance, permits and other documents related to clearing goods through customs are also abolished.

The Single Document is created as the form to be used for customs clearance of all goods entering or leaving Mozambique, regardless of the customs schedule to which they are subject, with the exception of goods in transit.

Decree 59/98 of 24 November. Council of Ministers. The introduction of the Single Document by Decree 56/98 of 11 November overtakes various articles on stamp duty contained in Decree 31883 of 12 February 1942.

Decree 61/98 of 24 November. Council of Ministers, Pre-shipping inspection of imported goods—Amendment to the text of Article 1 of Decree 21/90 of 18 September. The pre-shipping inspection of imported goods is designed to assist customs activities. At the same time, as capacity is built in the customs, systematically submitting all goods to pre-shipping inspection loses relevance. This practice is therefore limited to imports that are at higher risk from evasion of duties. This decree establishes that all imports under the definitive import or bonded warehouse customs regimes, and that do not fall within the norms of the simplified regime laid down in Decree 56/98 of 11 November, are subject to pre-shipping inspection. The selection of goods for pre-shipping inspection and the type of intervention will be decided randomly from among the imports that offer greatest risk of evasion of duties. Pre-shipping inspection includes analysis of price, quality, quantity, packaging, specifications and other conditions set out and agreed between the contracting parties and in accordance with current domestic legislation.

Ministerial Diploma 206/98 of 25 November. Ministry of Planning and Finance, Goods Clearance Regulation. Updates the norms regulating goods clearance, following the introduction of the Single Document and the Simplified Single Document, through Decree 56/98 of 11 November.

Ministerial Diploma 207/98 of 25 November. Ministry of Planning and Finance, Pre-Shipping Inspection Regulation. Specifies the types of intervention in pre-shipping inspections, namely Simple Inspection, Basic Inspection and Full Inspection.

Decree 62/99 of 21 September. Industrial Free Zones Regulation. Industrial Free Zones represent a regime in which the goods that are in or circulate within these zones, and which are exclusively destined to produce for export, as well as the resulting export goods themselves, are exempted from all customs, fiscal and para-fiscal obligations.

Ministerial Diploma 14/2002 of 30 January, Office of the Minister. Industrial Free Zones Customs Regime Regulation. Specifies the customs regime, contains the customs control norms that must be observed by operators and companies in the Industrial Free Zones.

Ministerial Diploma 12/2002 of 30 January, Office of the Minister. Bonded Warehouses Regulation.

Dispatch. Ministry of Planning and Finance, Office of the Minister. On international fairs: common general procedures for imports for international fairs and exhibitions.

Dispatch. Ministry of Planning and Finance, Office of the Minister. Considering the importance of the rehabilitation the sugar factories for national development, and the specific nature of imports for this productive activity, it was determined that the system defined in this dispatch applies exclusively to goods that are exempted for investment projects to rehabilitate the sugar factories, in the terms of Decree 74/99 of 12 October. The importer must request exemption from the Customs Regimes Department of the National Directorate of Customs, and obtain the form that grants exemption. Goods with this status will also be exempted from pre-shipping inspection. In order to clear the goods through customs the importer must present the Single Document, appropriately filled in, and the I.2. authorisation form.

Special counters to deal with customs clearances under this regime will be created—one in the Maputo International Road Terminal and the other in the Beira Customs.

The Customs may request a post-disembarkation inspection should doubts arise about the declared value of the goods or their customs classification, and in such cases the cost of the services will be paid by the importer. If the post-disembarkation inspection and the Customs agree that the goods have been under-valued a fine will be charged in the terms of Article 13 of Ministerial Diploma 207/98 of 25 November.

In addition to the customs legislation in force, the Customs have drawn up specific regulations to facilitate the implementation of international agreements and conventions, such as:

Ministerial Diploma 170/2001. Regulation on the issuance of certificates of origin and validation of invoices for textiles and garments to be exported to the USA within the framework of African Growth and Opportunity Act—AGOA

Ministerial Diploma 2/2002-06-02. Amendment of Article 15 of the regulation on the issuance of certificates of origin and validating invoices for textiles and garments to be exported to the USA within the framework of AGOA.

Annex C Résumé of the Main International and Regional Standards Organizations in which Mozambique Participates

Codex Alimentarius Commission (CAC)

Codex Alimentarius Commission was established on 1962, to implement the joint FAO/WHO Food Standards Programme. The purpose of the Programme is:

- Protecting the health of the consumers and ensuring fair practices in the food trade;
- Promoting coordination of all food standards work undertaken by international governmental and nongovernmental organisations;
- Determining priorities and initiating and guiding the preparation of draft standards through and with the aid of appropriate organisations;
- finalising standards elaborated under c) above and, after acceptance by governments, publishing them in a Codex Alimentarius either as regional or world wide standards, together with international standards already finalised by other bodies under b) above, wherever this is practicable;
- Amending published standards, after appropriate survey in the light of developments.

The Codex Alimentarius is a collection of internationally adopted food standards presented in a uniform manner.

The publication of the Codex Alimentarius is intended to guide and promote the elaboration and establishment of definitions and requirements for foods to assist in their harmonization and in doing so to facilitate international trade.

International Organisation for Standardisation (ISO)

ISO (International Organization for Standardization) is a world-wide federation of national standards bodies, at present comprising 138 members, one in each country. The object of ISO is to promote the development of standardization and related activities in the world with a view to facilitating international exchange of goods and services, and to developing cooperation in the spheres of intellectual, scientific, technological and economic activity. The results of ISO technical work are published as international standards.

The scope of ISO covers standardization in all fields except electrical and electronic engineering standards, which are the responsibility of the International Electrotechnical Commission (IEC).

ISO brings together the interests of producers, users (including consumers), governments and the scientific community, in the preparation of International Standards.

ISO work is carried on through 2,858 technical bodies. More than 30,000 experts from all parts of the world participate each year in the ISO technical work which, to date, has resulted in the publication of 13,025 ISO standards. (ISO Memento 2001)

International Plant Protection Convention (IPPC)

The objectives of the International Plant Protection Convention (IPPC) are to maintain and increase international cooperation in controlling pests and diseases of plants and plant products, and in preventing their introduction and spread across national boundaries.

Summary of provisions:

a) *Parties undertake to adopt the legislative, technical and administrative measures specified in the Convention;*
b) *Specific and regional agreements to be made in conjunction with the Food and Agriculture Organisation of the United Nations (FAO);*
c) *Each Party to set up an official plant protection organisation to:*

- *Inspect areas under cultivation and consignments of plants in international traffic for existence or outbreak of plant pests or diseases;*
- *Issue certificates relating to the phytosanitary condition and origin of plants and plant products;*
- *Carry out research on the field of plant protection.*

d) Parties to regulate very strictly the import and export of plants and plant products, by means, where necessary, of prohibitions, inspections and destruction of consignments.

International Office des Epizooties

The OIE is an intergovernmental organisation created by the International Agreement of 25 January 1924, signed by 28 countries.

Objectives

a) *Transparency—To guarantee the transparency of animal disease status world wide;*

b) *Scientific Information—To collect, analyse and disseminate veterinary scientific information;*

c) *International Solidarity—To provide expertise and promote international solidarity for the control of animal diseases;*

Sanitary safety—To guarantee the sanitary safety of world trade by developing sanitary rules for international trade in animals and animal products.

Southern African Development Community (SADC)

Originally known as the Southern African Development Coordination Conference (SADCC), the Organisation was formed in Lusaka, Zambia, on April 1, 1980, by Governments of the nine Southern African countries of Angola, Botswana, Lesotho, Malawi, Mozambique, Swaziland, Tanzania, Zambia and Zimbabwe.

The Declaration and Treaty establishing the Southern African Development Community (SADC) was signed at the summit of Heads of State or Government on August 17, 1992, in Windhoek Namibia. SADC Headquarters in Gaborone, Botswana and the working languages are English and Portuguese.

Current member states are Angola, Botswana, Democratic Republic of Congo (DRC), Lesotho, Malawi, Mauritius, Mozambique, Namibia, Seychelles, South Africa, Swaziland, Tanzania, Zambia and Zimbabwe.

The SADC Treaty commits member states to the fundamental principles of:

- Sovereign equality of member States;
- Solidarity, peace and security;
- Human rights, democracy and rule of law;
- Equity, balance and mutual benefit.

Over the past two years SADC has undertaken an exercise to restructure its institutions and an Extra-Ordinary Summit adopted a report on this on March 9, 2001 in Windhoek, Namibia.

SADC Aims

1. Harmonise political and socio-economic policies and plans of member States;

2. Mobilise the people of the region and their institutions to take initiatives to develop economic, social and cultural ties across the region, and to participate fully in the implementations of the programmes and projects of the SADC;

3. Create appropriate institutions and mechanisms for the mobilisation of requisite resources for the implementation of the programmes and the operations of the SADC and its institutions;

4. Develop policies aimed at the progressive elimination of obstacles to free movement of capital and labor, goods and services, and of the peoples of the region generally among member States;

5. Promote the development of human resources;

6. Promote the development, transfer and mastery of technology;

7. Improve economic management and performance through regional cooperation;

8. Promote the coordination Promote the coordination and harmonisation of the international relations of member States;

9. Secure international understanding, cooperation and support, mobilise the inflow of public and private resources in the region; and

10. Develop such other activities as member States may decide in furtherance of the objectives of SADC (http://www.sadc_squam.org).

SADC Protocol on Trade

The signatories of the SADC Trade Protocol considered that trade in goods and services and the enhancement of cross-border investments was major areas of cooperation among the Member States of the Community and recognized that the development of trade and investment is essential to the economic integration of the Community. With the implementation of the SADC Trade Protocol was also expected that new opportunities will be create for a dynamic business sector, the customs cooperation and combat illicit trade within the Community would be strengthen.

The signatories of the Trade Protocol also noted the provisions of the Abuja Treaty calling for the establishment of regional and sub-regional economic groupings as building blocs for the creation of the African Economic Community; was mindful of the results of the Uruguay Round of Multilateral Trade Negotiations on global trade liberalization and recognized the obligations of Member States in terms of existing regional trade arrangements and bilateral trade agreements.

The objectives of the SADC Trade Protocol are:

1. *To further liberalize intra-regional trade in goods and services on the basis of fair, mutually equitable and beneficial trade arrangements, complemented by Protocols in other areas.*
2. *To ensure efficient production within SADC reflecting the current and dynamic comparative advantages of its Members.*
3. *To contribute towards the improvement of the climate for domestic, cross-border and foreign investment.*
4. *To enhance the economic development, diversification and industrialisation of the Region.*
5. *To establish a Free Trade Area in the SADC Region.*

Main articles under the SADC Trade Protocol related to standards and related activities are:

Part four

Article 16
Sanitary and Phytosanitary Measures

1. *Member States shall base their sanitary and phytosanitary measures on international standards, guidelines and recommendations, so as to harmonize sanitary and phytosanitary measures for agricultural and livestock production.*
2. *Member States shall, upon request, enter into consultation with the aim of achieving agreements on recognition of the equivalence of specific sanitary and phytosanitary measures, in accordance with the WTO Agreement on the Application of Sanitary and Phytosanitary Measures.*

Article 17
Standards and Technical Regulations on Trade

1. *Each Member State shall use relevant international standards as a basis for its standards-related measures, except where such standards would be an ineffective or inappropriate means to fulfil its legitimate objectives.*
2. *Member State's standards-related measures that conform to an international standard shall be presumed not to create an unnecessary obstacle to trade.*
3. *Without reducing the level of safety, or of protection of human, animal or plant life or health, of the environment or of consumers, without prejudice to the rights of any Member State and taking into account international standardisation activities, Member States shall, to the greatest extent practicable, make compatible their respective standards-related measures, so as to facilitate trade in goods and services within the Community.*
4. *Member States accept as equivalent technical regulations of other Member States, even if these regulations differ from their own, provided that they adequately fulfil the objectives of their regulations.*
5. *A Member State, shall upon request of another Member State, seek through appropriate measures, to promote the compatibility of specific standards or conformity assessment procedures that are maintained in its territory, with the standards or conformity assessment procedures maintained in the territory of other Member States.*

Annex V

Concerning Trade Development
Article 6
Harmonization of standards and quality assurance

1. *In order to improve quality and competitiveness of SADC products and achieve the diversification of the market for such products, Member States shall promote harmonized standards and appropriate quality assurance systems within the Community, in accordance with the provisions of this protocol.*
2. *Members States and the private sector shall take measures to ensure that SADC exports meet the quality and standards, in accordance with specifications set by International Standards Organisation (SADC, Protocol on Trade).*

Memorandum of Understanding (MOU) in Standardisation, Quality Assurance, Accreditation and Metrology (SQAM)

The Ministers responsible for the Industry and Trade Sector in the Southern African Development Community (SADC), agreed in 1998 on the implementation of a Memorandum of Understanding in Standardisation, Quality Assurance, Accreditation and Metrology (SQAM).

The decision to implement this Memorandum came from the following:

SADC Treaty has set objectives such as achieving development and economic growth (Article 5(1)(a)), achieving complementarity between national and regional strategies and programmes (Article 5(1)(e)) and promoting and maximising productive employment and utilisation of resources in the Region (Article 5(1)(f));

SADC Treaty has also set actions to achieve its objectives, such as creating appropriate institutions and mechanisms for the mobilisation of requisite resources for the implementation of programmes and operations of SADC and its institutions (Article 5(2)(c)), to develop policies aimed at the progressive elimination of obstacles to the free movement of capital and labor, goods and services, and of the peoples of the Region in general, among Member States (Article 5(2)(d)) and to improve economic management and performance through regional cooperation (Article 5(2)(g));

SADC Protocol on Trade, on Article 33 calls upon Member States to take all appropriate measures to ensure the carrying out of the obligations stipulated therein;

The SADC Protocol on Trade has set specific provisions on Non-Tariff Barriers to Trade (NTBs, Article 6) and on Standards and Technical Regulations on Trade (Article 17);

The Ministers were aware also about the importance of cooperation in the areas of Standardisation, Quality Assurance, Accreditation and Metrology (SQAM) for the elimination of NTBs, both in terms of the SADC Protocol on Trade and in terms of the commitments by Member States with respect to the World Trade Organisation (WTO) Technical Barriers to Trade (TBT) Agreement;

Identified also that cooperation in SQAM is not just essential in the Industry and Trade Sector, where it is mainly driven by the provisions of the SADC Protocol on Trade and the WTO TBT commitments, but in all SADC Sectors;

And they also took in consideration the role SQAM can play in enhancing the quality of life of the citizens of the Member States through the assurance of the quality of the goods and services being produced.

The objective of the MOU is to establish the formal framework in which the cooperation amongst the national institutions in Standardisation, Quality Assurance, Accreditation and Metrology (SQAM) shall take place in the Region and this framework is referred to as the SADC SQAM Programme.

The SADC SQAM Programme encompasses standardisation, accreditation, certification, conformity assessment, testing, inspection, metrology and related matters.

The objectives of the SADC SQAM Programme are the progressive elimination of Technical Barriers to Trade (TBTs) amongst the Member States and between SADC and other Regional and International Trading Blocks, and the promotion of quality and of an infrastructure for quality in the Member States.

In order To implement the SADC SQAM Programme, the following structures were created:

a) SADC SQAM Expert Group (SQAMEG)
b) SADC Cooperation in Measurement Traceability (SADCMET)
c) SADC Cooperation in Legal Metrology (SADCMEL)
d) SADC Cooperation in Standardisation (SADCSTAN)
e) SADC Cooperation in Accreditation (SADCA)

SQAMEG

The objectives of SQAMEG are to coordinate regional activities of SQAM and provide a forum where conformity assessment can be dealt with.

SADCMET

The objective of SADCMET is to coordinate metrology activities and services in the Region, in order to provide regional calibration and testing services, including regulatory bodies, with readily available traceability to the SI units of measurement, through legally defined and regionally and internationally recognized national measurement standards.

SADCMEL

The objective of SADCMEL is to facilitate the harmonization of the national Legal Metrology regulations of the Member States and between SADC and other regional and international trading blocks.

SADCSTAN

The objective of SADCSTAN is to promote the co-ordination of standardisation activities and services in the Region, with the purpose of achieving harmonization of standards and technical regulations, with the exception of Legal Metrology regulations, in support of the objectives of the SADC Protocol on Trade.

SADCA

The objective of SADCA is to facilitate the creation of a pool of internationally acceptable accredited laboratories and certification bodies (for personnel, products and systems, including quality and environmental management systems) in the Region, and provide Member States with accreditation as a tool for the removal of TBTs in both the voluntary and regulatory areas.

Membership

The national SQAM member organisations, one per Structure per Member State, shall be designated by the Minister responsible for industry and trade. (SADC Protocol on Trade, Memorandum of Understanding and SADC web page.)

3

J. ADEBOYE ADEYEMO
ABIODUN S. BANKOLE

STANDARDS, TECHNICAL REGULATIONS, AND PRODUCT QUALITY

Institutional Evidence from Nigeria

SINCE EARLY 1960S, NIGERIA'S TRADE POLICY HAS BEEN AND CONTINUES TO BE INFLUENCED by several factors with domestic concerns and objectives, globalization trends, and its involvement in regional and multilateral trade agreements playing an prominent role. Between the early 1960s and the mid-1980s, the trade policy in Nigeria was basically inward looking with particular focus on the development of an industrial base through a series of protectionist frameworks. The economic depression of the early 1980s coupled with the widespread structural changes within the economy necessitated a shift in trade policy outlook that accompanied the structural adjustment program (SAP) of 1986. From an exclusive inward-looking posture, Nigeria's trade policy became more outward-oriented, mainly as a means of diversifying Nigeria's productive base to reduce the exclusive dependence on the oil sector and on imports. Nigeria was one of the 118 countries that were signatories to the Uruguay Round Agreement (URA) after the protracted negotiations that began in 1986 was finally concluded in 1994 at Marrakesh in Morocco.

The World Trade Organization (WTO) recognizes and gives credence to the standards, codes, and guidelines of the Codex Alimentarius Commission (CAC) as adequate for the protection of human life and health related to the application of Sanitary and Phytosanitary (SPS) measures. The Federal Government of Nigeria established the codex contact point (CCP) through a decision of the then Federal Executive Council. The country, thus, already had a CCP and a National Codex Committee (NCC) prior to the beginning of the WTO in 1995. The emergence of the democratic system of administration in April 1999 further marked a major change in the structure of the policy-making process (including trade policy) in Nigeria.

The level of Nigeria's participation in international standards development and the impact that such participation generates for the process of setting international product norms are, to a large extent, a function of the interests and involvement of public and private sector representatives in the activities of the National Codex Committee. Compliance with international standards is an important challenge for Nigerian firms (producers and exporters) if they are to take advantage of the market access opportunities of the WTO and AGOA. The current administration's efforts to make the private sector lead the economy can be seriously jeopardized if quality standards are not strictly adhered to. Thus, the issue of conformity with international standards in the production and export of non-oil commodities poses a serious concern to both the public and private sectors. If the private sector were to jump-start the economy to move on the path of sustainable growth, the sector must be equipped and empowered to face the challenges of international competitiveness.

The study draws conclusions about the current status of laws, regulations, capacities and programs relating to standards and technical regulations in Nigeria. It also identifies areas needing priority attention at the national level, and provides recommendations on key steps to be taken by government and private organizations and relevant international development agencies to alleviate the negative impact, and to strengthen the positive influences so as to face the challenges to trade facilitation posed by SPS measures and technical barriers to trade.

Economic Context: Economic and Trade Profile of Nigeria (1970–2000)

Introduction

This section broadly describes the overall economic conditions and recent economic performance of Nigeria using an array of macroeconomic and trade indicators. In addition, it provides the changing pattern of the structure of the economy, including imports and exports, their structure and the main sources and directions of trade, the tariffs applicable to the country's main exports in its primary external markets, as well as Nigeria's position in regional trade agreements and preferential access agreements. Finally, the section summarizes the locus and responsibilities for trade policy in the country, the main structures for interaction between the country and the World Trade Organization (WTO), and the coordination systems to deal with trade matters as they relate to issues both within government, and between government and the private sector.

Nigeria's Economic Performance and Trade Structure

Nigeria's Macroeconomic Performance. The last three decades in Nigeria can be described as a period of relative macroeconomic instability characterized by a few years of fair output performance and a long period of price instability, unemployment, and economic recession.[1] As shown by the annual growth rate of the real GDP (Appendix A (Table 3.28)), Nigeria suffered stagnating and declining output in the 1980s relative to the other decades. While Nigeria experienced negative output growth in only two of the years in the 1970s and positive growth throughout the 1990s, a large part of the 1980s was characterized by large negative output growth. Specifically, from an impressive level of 24.5 percent and 21.4 percent in 1970 and 1971, respectively, the real GDP growth rate decreased (though still positive) to 5.5 percent in 1973. Except for 1975 when a slight decrease occurred in the real GDP growth rate, the entire mid-1970s show an impressive output growth rate performance largely because of the commercial exploitation of crude oil and the global oil boom of the period.

The largest output contraction in Nigeria was experienced in 1981 when the real GDP decreased by an unprecedented magnitude of 26.8 percent from its 1980 level. The output decrease in the next three years of this great recession was fairly reduced by adopting various fiscal measures and restraints. An important exception to the poor output performance in the mid-1980s is the annual growth rate in real GDP of 9.4 percent recorded in 1985. Following the adoption of the structural adjustment program (SAP) in 1986, the real GDP grew by 9.9 percent, 7.4 percent, and 8.2 percent in 1988, 1989, 1990, respectively, only to decrease to 4.7 percent, 3.0 percent, and 1.3 percent in the years 1991, 1992, and 1994, respectively, largely because of political instability and uncoordinated and lopsided implementation of the economic reform process. Since 1995, the growth rate of the real GDP has leveled off at the lower level. From 2.2 percent in 1995, it grew slightly to 3.4 percent and 3.2 percent in 1996 and 1997, respectively, only to decrease slightly to 2.4 percent and 2.7 percent in 1998 and 1999.

As expected, Nigeria's poor output growth performance is replicated by a relatively stagnant real GDP per capita. From an average of ₦1,320 in 1970s, the real GDP per capita decreased to an average of ₦945 in the 1980s only to improve slightly in the 1990s when it averaged ₦1,050. While the plummeting real GDP per capita can be attributed to poor output growth, other factors also account

---

[1] Most of the discussions in this section are based on data contained in the Appendix.

for its stagnant posture. Of particular significance among these factors is Nigeria's population increase. It should be noted that taking the effects of the Naira depreciation on the real GDP per capita into consideration would show a deteriorating and unpalatable income per head situation.

Basing the price stability assessment on the reported inflation rate, the performance of the Nigerian economy has been mixed, though mostly unimpressive. Of the 31 observed series (years), 10 (about 32 percent) were characterized by single-digit inflation rates. The periods during which there was single-digit inflation 1982 (7.7 percent), 1985 (5.5 percent), 1986 (5.4 percent), 1990 (7.5 percent), 1997 (8.5 percent) and 2000 (6.9 percent). High inflation rates were recorded in 1993 (57.2 percent), 1994 (57.0 percent), and 1995 (72.8 percent). While some attempts can be made to provide causal explanations for a few episodes of price increases; to do justice to others becomes very difficult. The price increase in the mid-1970s is attributable mainly to the monetization of the windfall from the oil boom of the period. Such monetization includes general increases in both private and public salaries and other emoluments, and the award of several projects. While the high rates of inflation recorded in the late 1980s are due to the large depreciation of the domestic currency associated with the economic reforms of the period, the price increases from the early 1990s to 1996 can be described as resulting from cost-push and depreciation factors, augmented by other supply constraints that resulted from infrastructural inadequacy and political instability.

Capacity utilization of the Nigerian manufacturing subsector for 1970–2000 is also shown in Appendix A (Table 3.28). From an average of 75 percent in the 1970s, the manufacturing capacity utilization deteriorated to 50 percent, 40 percent, and 38 percent in 1983, 1987, and 1992, respectively. Throughout the 1990s, this important statistic fluctuated between 29 and 42 percent giving an average of 35 percent. While the low capacity utilization in the manufacturing subsector can be attributed to a large variety of domestic factors, a school of thought (mostly comprising manufacturers) has continued to hold the Nigerian liberal trade policy posture as being responsible. This school maintains that the influx of a variety of household goods and consumables poses an enormous challenge to, and unwarranted depletion of demand for domestically produced goods. Some of the domestic factors that have contributed to low capacity utilization in the manufacturing sector include inadequate infrastructural facilities, for example, electricity, water supply, telecommunication, and so on; high cost of inputs because of domestic currency depreciation; unstable and unpredictable government fiscal policy prescriptions; depleted production capacities of installed equipment because of poor maintenance and servicing culture; and inadequate support by government for its production boosting incentives, and so on.

Another important dimension for assessing the overall performance of the Nigerian economy is its fiscal operations. Throughout the period under consideration, the fiscal operation of the federal government was persistently in deficit except in a few periods. From ₦2 billion in 1980, the deficit in the federal fiscal operations grew steadily to ₦8 billion in 1986 and to ₦107 billion and ₦285 billion in 1993 and 1999, respectively. Measured as a proportion of the GDP, the deficits are 8 percent, 12 percent, 11 percent, and 16 percent of the GDP in 1978, 1982, 1986 and 1993, respectively. While the fiscal surplus recorded in the 1970s is a clear case of improved financial fortunes (mainly from crude oil exploitation), the ₦1 billion and ₦32 billion fiscal surpluses recorded in 1995 and 1996 (Appendix A Table 3.29) are controversial because payments for a large number of projects executed by local contractors and certified as satisfactory by the appropriate authorities were not made during the two years, thereby not showing a true and fair view of the actual performance of the federal fiscal operations.

To finance the fiscal deficits, the federal government of Nigeria in most cases resorted to borrowing from both internal and external sources. Nigeria's external debt that averaged 2.5 percent of GDP in the 1970s became overbearing in the late 1980s to the extent of outstripping the overall GDP by 7 percent and 15 percent in 1989 and 1990, respectively (Appendix A Table 3.29). To service its external debt stocks of US$27.5 billion and US$28.5 billion in 1992 and 2000, respectively, Nigeria requires 65.4 percent and 35.0 percent of its earnings from export of goods and nonfactor services. Overcoming the debt overdues and sustaining its external debt-servicing capabilities constitute major challenges to the Nigeria's balance of payments and its trade policy formulation and implementation processes.

Nigeria's Trade Performance. Appendix A (Table 3.30) shows some indicators of Nigeria's trade performance. Nigeria's total exports of merchandise increased steadily in the 1970s up to 1980 when it started to experience a slight decline. Specifically, from a level of about ₦2 billion in 1973, Nigeria's total exports increased to ₦14 billion in 1980 only to decline to ₦11 billion in 1981 and further to ₦7.5 billion in 1983. The resuscitated increasing trend in export that started in 1984 was short-lived by another slight decline in 1986. Except in 1998, when total exports fell to ₦752 billion from ₦1,242 billion in 1997, they continued to increase up to 2000. As a ratio of GDP, the export performance becomes diluted. Except in a few instances, the export GDP ratio was less than 30 percent until 1995. Between 1995 and 2000, the ratio of exports to GDP averages 48.7 percent, though it stood at only 27.6 percent in 1998. Despite the need for caution in the interpretation these exports figures because of the effects of currency depreciation, the sudden increase in the ratio of exports to GDP in 1995 and thereafter suggests some causal linkage with the emergence of the WTO and the embedded Uruguay Round of agreements of which Nigeria is a signatory.

The total value of Nigeria's merchandise imports follows almost a similar pattern of growth as exports. Specifically, both exports and imports moved in tandem up to 1980, though with exports persistently outstripping imports. Between 1981 and 1983, imports actually exceeded export. In particular, the value of total imports increased from ₦5 billion in 1976 to ₦10.8 billion and ₦8.9 billion in 1982 and 1983, respectively, from ₦12.8 billion recorded in 1981. Because of the stringent measures adopted by the new military administration, imports decreased by about 19 percent to ₦7.2 billion in 1984, stagnated at almost the same level in 1985 and fell again by another 15 percent to ₦6.0 billion in 1986. From 1986 onward, the value of imports increased steadily except in 1996. For instance, imports that stood at around ₦18 billion in 1987, increased to ₦30.9 billion, ₦87 billion and ₦755.1 billion in 1989, 1991 and 1995, respectively. In 2000, the total value of imports was ₦963.0 billion. As a ratio of GDP, excessive importation constituted a serious threat to the economy in general and to the balance of payments in particular between 1977 and 1982 and since 1991. For these periods, it ranged between 20 percent and 38 percent. For other periods, ratio of imports to GDP could be described as relatively reasonable, ranging between 8.3 percent and 19 percent. Measured as a ratio of GDP, the worst periods of excessive importations are 25 percent in 1981, 39 percent in 1995, 37 percent in 1999, and 36.5 percent in 2000.

Using the ratio of total trade to GDP as a measure of the degree of openness, the Nigerian economy could be described as relatively open, with the 1990s being characterized by a higher degree of openness than the earlier decades. Specifically, while the degree of openness for the entire period (1970–2000) averaged 49 percent, the decade (1990–99) recorded an average of 66 percent (Appendix A Table 3.30). While the year 2000 recorded the highest degree of openness of 110 percent, the lowest value of 21 percent was recorded in 1986. The spectacular performance of the Nigerian economy in terms of openness during the 1990s must also be viewed in relation to Nigeria's involvement in regional and multilateral trade agreements and the market access that is associated with those agreements.

The Changing Structure of the Nigerian Economy. The Nigerian economy experienced radical structural changes during the 1970s and 1980s. These changes were particularly significant in the external sector of the economy. For instance, agriculture was the most important sector of the Nigerian economy in the 1960s. It provided the largest share of the country's gross domestic product (GDP), employment, and export earnings. This picture changed dramatically in the 1970s, as crude petroleum became the economy's leading exports sector. The resulting heavy reliance on crude petroleum exports made the economy highly vulnerable to external shocks, which were periodically transmitted through sharp changes in the world demand for and prices of petroleum products. In other words, the agricultural-based Nigerian economy of the 1960s was considerably less vulnerable to external shocks than the petroleum-dominated economy of the 1970s and beyond (Oyejide 2001).

Table 3.1 shows the share of the major sectors in real GDP for selected years. From 16.3 percent in 1982, the share of oil in real GDP increased to 33.4 percent in 1990 and declined to 24.8 percent in 1994. Between 1981 and 1998, the share of oil in real GDP was an average of 28 percent. This value is in sharp contrast with the near 0 percent contribution of oil to the real GDP in the 1960s.

As shown in Table 3.1, the fortune of agriculture (including livestock, forestry, and fishing) in real GDP that suffered significant setbacks in the

Table 3.1 Composition of Nigeria's Real GDP for Selected Years
(percent)

Activity Sector	1982	1986	1990	1994	1998	Average (1981–1998)
1. Agriculture (including crops, livestock, forestry and fishing)	30.9	38.6	32.6	38.2	38.9	33.8
2. Crude petroleum	16.3	13.6	33.4	24.8	27.9	28.1
3. Mining and quarrying	1.7	0.3	0.3	0.2	0.1	0.5
4. Manufacturing	9.6	8.7	5.5	6.9	5.4	6.8
5. Building and construction	4.8	2.7	1.7	1.1	0.9	2.1
6. Transportation	4.8	5.2	2.0	3.4	2.9	3.3
7. Wholesale and retail trade	12.8	13.2	13.9	17.4	16.1	13.9
8. Others	19.1	17.7	10.6	8.0	7.8	11.5
Total real GDP (percent)	100	100	100	100	100	100
Share of oil in real GDP	16.3	13.6	33.4	24.8	27.9	28.1
Share of non-oil	83.7	86.4	66.6	75.2	72.1	71.9

Source: Derived from Appendix A (Table 3.31).

1970s because of crude oil exploitation, improved relatively in the late 1980s, mainly as a result of the economic reforms, which attempted to diversify the productive base of the economy. From 30.9 percent in 1982, the share of agriculture in real GDP increased to 38.6 percent in 1986, declining slightly to 32.6 percent in 1990, and continued its increasing trend from 1994. The share of manufacturing in real GDP declined continuously during the period under consideration from 9.6 percent in 1982, and fell to 8.7 percent and 5.5 percent in 1986 and 1990, and increased slightly to 6.9 percent in 1994. There was a similar declining trend in the building, construction, and transportation sectors.

Another important structure of the Nigerian economy that underwent change was the increasing share of wholesale and retail trade in real GDP. From 12.8 percent in 1994, the share of wholesale and retail trade in real GDP increased steadily to 17.4 percent and declined slightly to 16.1 percent in 1998.

Composition of Nigerian Exports and Imports. An important contributor to the radical shift in the structure of the Nigerian economy that commenced in the 1970s was the changing structure of its exports. In the 1960s, agricultural products constituted the bulk of Nigeria's commodity exports. With the advent of oil in commercial quantity

in the 1970s, the share of agriculture in export earnings has depleted to incredibly low levels. From 30 percent in 1970, the share of agricultural products in export earnings decreased steadily to 4.7 percent and 2.2 percent in 1975 and 1990, respectively. In fact, since the mid-1970s, the share of agricultural products in export earnings has stagnated at around 2.0 percent. The share of mineral products (mostly crude oil) in export earnings, on the other hand, improved extraordinarily from the early 1970s. The share of mineral products in total exports that stood at 57.7 percent in 1970 increased sharply to 92.7 percent in 1975. Since 1980, it has continued to fluctuate within the range of 96 percent and 98 percent, thereby rendering other commodities highly insignificant in the items to be exported.

The fact that the structure of Nigerian exports has remained at the 0 percent level of manufactured exports between 1970 and 2000 is of great interest. In other words, Nigerian exports have been dominantly in the primary sector. This primary-products-oriented export base has major implications for both the value added of such exports and the vulnerability of the entire economy to external shocks. The SAP package of the late 1980s was a significant attempt aimed at arresting the undesirable situation. Also of special importance to Nigeria's trading relation with the rest of the world and particularly, its involvement in regional and multilateral trade agreements, is the contribution of textile and clothing to Nigeria's total exports. Trade in the textile and clothing sector has come to constitute the most controversial of all the issues in multilateral trade negotiations. Nigeria's share of this sector, and the global market accessibility, are of great significance to its overall development. Throughout the period under consideration, the share of textiles in total exports stood at almost 0 percent.

The composition of Nigerian imports between 1970 and 2000 remained almost the stagnant except for a few changes that are incomparable with those of exports. As shown in Appendix A. (Table 3.33), four product lines jointly constitute the bulk of Nigeria's total imports. These are food (including live animals), chemicals, manufactured goods, and machinery and transportation equipment.

Together, these four product lines were responsible for 86.6 percent, 89.7 percent, and 87.6 percent of Nigeria's total imports in 1970, 1985, and 2000, respectively. Within these major product lines themselves, some fairly remarkable changes can be identified over the historical period. From a level of 7.6 percent and 8.0 percent in 1970 and 1975, respectively, the share of food and live animals in total imports increased to 15.8 percent and 17.0 percent in 1980 and 1985, respectively, only to decrease sharply to 7.6 percent in 1990, largely because of the protectionist policies in the form of the outright ban on some food items. The share of chemicals in total imports that was 7.0 percent in 1975 increased steadily to 19.7 percent in 1990 and to 22.9 percent in 1999. A significant contributor to the increasing share of chemicals in imports is the importation of refined petroleum products since the late 1980s largely because of underutilization of the installed capacities of the refineries in the country and their closure in some instances. The share of manufactures in total imports remained almost the same between 1970 and 2000, ranging between 22 percent and 30 percent.

Directions of Nigeria's Trade. Questions regarding the destinations of a country's exports and the sources of its imports matter for the country's trade policy, especially as they relate to regional and multilateral trade agreements whose negotiations are usually influenced by such questions (Oyejide 2001). Data on the direction of Nigerian exports and imports during 1971–98 are shown in Appendix A. (Table 3.34).

Even though there was a relative improvement in Nigeria's trade with the rest of Africa especially in the 1990s, Europe (European Union), and North America (particularly the United States) dominated both as the destination of Nigerian exports and the source of its imports. Together, Europe and the United States accounted for 80 percent, 77 percent, and 73 percent of Nigerian exports in 1971, 1980, and 1995, respectively, while Nigerian exports to the rest of Africa stood at 2.2 percent, 3.0 percent, and 9.2 percent during the same years. As shown in Appendix A (Table 3.34), the trend of the United States' share of Nigerian exports contrasts sharply with that of Europe's share. While the United States' share increased from 29 percent in 1975 to 39 percent and 54 percent in 1980 and 1990, respectively, EU's share declined from 62 percent in 1971 to 38 percent, 36 percent, and 34 percent in 1980, 1990, and 1995, respectively. Nigerian exports to the Asian countries improved relatively in the 1990s. From its near 0 percent share in the 1970s and 1980s, Nigerian exports to Asian countries increased to 6.3 percent and 14 percent in 1995 and 1998.

The relatively steady improvement in Nigerian exports to the rest of Africa and Asia, especially in the late 1990s, also applies to its imports from the two regions. From nearly 1 percent in between 1971 and early 1990s, Nigerian imports from the rest of Africa increased to 2.8 percent and 3.7 percent in 1995 ad 1998, respectively. From 5.4 percent and 7.5 percent in 1971 and 1985, respectively, the share of Asian countries in Nigerian imports improved remarkably to 17.4 percent and 22.3 percent in 1995 and 1998, respectively. Together, the countries of the European Union (EU) contributed 60 percent, 58 percent and 51 percent of Nigerian imports in 1975, 1990, and 1995, respectively, while the United States accounted for 11 percent, 6.3 percent and 12 percent during the same period.

In general, Nigeria's trade with the Middle East and the former Communist States (especially Russia) has been highly insignificant.

Structure of Tariffs Applicable to Nigeria's Main Exports

Given that the United States and the European Union (EU) jointly account for three-quarters of Nigerian exports, the analysis of the structure of

Table 3.2 Structure of Applied MFN Tariffs in the United States
(percent)

Indicators	1996	1998	1999	Full Implementation of UR
1. Bound tariff lines[a]	100.0	100.0	100.0	100.0
2. Duty-free tariff lines	21.4	13.8	29.7	36.4
3. Specific tariffs/all tariffs	24.4	14.3	12.9	11.2
4. Simple average bound tariff rate	n.a.	5.9	5.7	4.7
5. Simple average applied tariff rate	6.4	5.9	5.7	4.7
- Agricultural products	10.0	10.3	10.7	8.2
- Industrial products	5.7	5.0	4.7	4.0
6. Domestic tariff "peaks"[b]	4.0	4.9	5.0	6.9
7. International tariff "peaks"[c]	8.9	7.7	7.4	5.2

a. Two tariff lines, applying to crude petroleum, are not bound.
b. Domestic tariff "peaks" are defined as those exceeding three times the overall simple average MFN rate.
c. International tariff "peaks" are defined as those exceeding 15 percent.
Source: WTO (1999): *Trade Policy Review: United States—1999* (p. 47).

tariffs applicable to Nigerian major exports, which is the focus of this section, is directed mainly at these two economic blocs.

United States' Tariffs Structure (1996–99). Table 3.2 provides a few summary indicators of the overall structure of tariffs applicable in the United States. Based on the 1999 tariffs schedule, there are 10,173 tariff lines (at the HS 8-digit level) in the United States, with different tariff rates applicable to the same tariff lines depending on whether MFN or preferential rates are involved. Following the Uruguay Round, all U.S. tariff lines, except two, are bound and all applied MFN rates coincide with bound rates, thereby guaranteeing a high degree of tariff predictability. Of particular significance to Nigerian exports is the exclusion of two of the 10,173 tariff lines from the MFN tariff bindings. Coincidentally, the two unbound tariff lines cover crude petroleum, a product of which the United States is actually the largest importer from Nigeria. An important implication of the exclusion of crude petroleum products in the MFN tariff bindings is to weaken the degree of tariff predictability on these items.

As shown in Table 3.2, 29.7 percent of tariff lines in the United States are duty free, considerably more than in 1998 (13.8 percent) and 1996 (21.4 percent). With the full implementation of the UR agreements, this ratio is expected to rise to 36.4 percent. As noted earlier, the overall simple average bound tariff rates of 5.9 percent and 5.7 percent in 1998 and 1999, respectively, coincide with the average applied tariff rate. It is expected that this rate will decline to 4.7 percent with the full implementation of the UR agreements. However, while the applied MFN tariff average for industrial products is slightly lower than the overall average, the applied MFN tariffs average for agricultural products is almost double the overall average between 1996 and 1999. A major trade policy implication of this disparity between applied rates on industrial and agricultural products is that a higher tariff protection is granted to the latter, which by implication imposes some market restraints on Nigerian agricultural products.

Also of importance to the degree of protection granted to the domestic production of Nigeria's main exports in the United States, is the imposition of specific (and compound) duties, which are a common feature of the U.S. tariffs. In 1999, these forms of tariffs accounted for 12.9 percent of all tariffs in contrast to the proportion of 24.4 percent in 1996 (Table 3.2). Specific tariffs are imposed mainly on agricultural products, footwear and headgear, a number of textile materials, and a few other items. Even the application of ad valorem equivalents (AVEs) of specific duties such as quotas in an attempt to ensure their transparency, they nevertheless tend to increase the effective tariff protection while at the same time being regressive. Overall, specific duties tend to impose a greater impact on exports from developing countries than those of

Table 3.3 Protection in Selected Agricultural and Textile Sectors in the United States, 1999
(percent)

HS	Chapter/Description	Ave. Tariff	Max. Tariff	Dom. Tariff Peaks	Specific Tariff
	Agriculture				
04	Dairy produce, etc.	22.3	232.2	42.2	50.2
17	Sugar and sugar confectionery	15.7	168.7	18.2	51.5
18	Cocoa and preparations	14.7	191.5	19.2	43.6
19	Preparations of cereals, etc.	19.0	151.7	30.9	26.5
21	Miscellaneous edible	14.9	109.8	22.7	44.3
24	Preparations	53.3	350.0	25.0	51.8
	Tobacco, etc.				
54	Textile	13.3	n.a.	n.a.	n.a.
55	Man-made filaments	13.2	n.a.	n.a.	n.a.
61	Staple fiber	13.7	n.a.	n.a.	n.a.
	Clothing				

Source: WTO (1999): Trade Policy Review: United States—1999 (pp. 159, 164).

industrial countries since developing countries export relatively low-priced products (WTO 1999).

The incidence of increasing tariff protection for agricultural products also applies to the clothing and textile materials. Table 3.3 shows the level of tariff protection in the agricultural and textile sectors in the United States for 1999. The MFN tariff on cocoa and cocoa preparations, one of Nigeria's main agricultural products, exceeded the overall average of 5.7 percent to 9 percent. On textile and clothing materials, the average applied tariff was 13.5 percent, also far in excess of the overall average. Related to the high average applied tariff rates on agricultural and textile products is the use of tariff quotas on some broad categories of agricultural products. Between 1996 and 1999, the use of tariff quotas covered 1.9 percent (some 198) of all the tariff lines in the United States. The unprecedented higher protection made possible by the use of tariff quotas is best evident when compared the simple average in-quota MFN tariff rate of 9.5 percent, the corresponding average out-of-quota MFN tariff is 55.8 percent (WTO 1999).

In spite of the disparity between the overall average applied tariff of 5.7 percent and the average nominal MFN tariff for agriculture of 10.8 percent in 1999, some 42 percent of the duties on agricultural goods are non-ad valorem.

Tariffs Structure in the European Union. Compared to 10,173 in the United States, the 1999 EU tariff schedule consists of 10,428 tariff lines of which 2,132 (20.4 percent) belong to agriculture, 8,257 (79.2 percent) to nonagriculture, and the balance of 39 (0.4 percent) lines belong to petroleum. As shown in Table 3.4, the overall simple average applied MFN tariff rate for 1999 in the EU was 6.9 percent, just slightly below 7 percent for the bound tariff rate. As was the case with the United States, the simple average applied rate for agricultural products exceeds the overall average by a wide margin of 10.4 percent. Specifically, while the simple average applied tariff rate for agricultural products was 17.3 percent, it was just 4.5 percent for nonagricultural products and in fact only 2.9 percent for petroleum products. The range of applied tariffs, in terms of the minimum and maximum rates, is also more important on agricultural products (from 0 to 236.4 percent) than on nonagricultural products (from 0 to 26 percent).

Table 3.4 further shows the MFN bound and applied tariffs on selected products in the EU in 1999. The structure of the simple average tariffs on these products has some specific implications for Nigerian exports. For instance, the low simple average tariff of 2.9 percent on petroleum products coupled with its low dispersion (from 0 to 4.7 percent) indicates weak effective tariff protection for the EU's petroleum sector, thereby constituting a source of market access for Nigerian crude oil, which incidentally is the largest source of foreign exchange earnings for the country. Another main implication for Nigerian exports is the wide disparity between the simple average tariff on cocoa

Table 3.4 MFN Bound and Applied Tariffs in the EU on Selected Products by HS Chapter, 1999

HS Code	No. of 8-Digit HS Lines	Description	MFN Bound Rate	MFN 1999 Simple Average	Maximum
	10,428	Total	7.0	6.9	236.4
	2,132	WTO Agriculture		17.3	236.4
	8,257	WTO Nonagriculture (excluding petroleum)		4.5	26.0
	39	Petroleum		2.9	4.7
10	55	Cereals	47.3	47.3	179.7
17	47	Sugars and sugar confectionery	17.6	17.6	72.2
18	27	Cocoa and cocoa preparations	12.3	12.3	76.2
1801	1	Cocoa beans		0.5	0.5
52	162	Cotton	7.4	7.4	9.0
54	88	Man-made filaments	7.8	7.8	9.5
55	168	Man-made staple fibers	8.1	8.1	9.5
61	171	Apparel and clothing accessories, knitted or crocheted	12.3	12.3	13.0
97	7	Works of art, collectors' pieces, and antiques	0.0	0.0	0.0

Source: WTO (2000): Trade Policy Review: European Union—2000 Vol. 1 (pp. 44, 173–8).

beans, which is 0.5 percent and on its derivatives (cocoa and cocoa products), which is 12.3 percent. On account of this wide margin, the export of raw cocoa beans to the EU is given greater market access whereas the export of its derivatives, which could generate higher added value, is strongly discouraged with a high tariff protection.

The duty-free access granted to the works of art, collectors' pieces, and antiques could be interpreted from two perspectives. One is to grant greater market access for these items and encourage their production, especially by African countries. The other perspective is to consider this duty-free access as an avenue for stimulating the depletion and extradition of works of arts and antiques accumulated by Africans across centuries. Therefore, the zero tariff on works of art and antiques could be described as damaging for the Africans, particularly in the long run.

On the structure and average tariffs imposed on agricultural products by the EU, a few implications for Nigerian exports exist. The first is that the EU's non-ad valorem duties, which constitute about 10 percent of the tariff lines, apply mostly to agricultural products. As the EU applies non-tariff barriers such as quantitative restrictions (QRs) alone or in combination with ad valorem creates confusion in estimating tariff on such products because of the need to convert the duties to ad valorem

equivalents (AVEs). Another important trade policy implication of the EU's tariff on agricultural products arises from the nature of the duty regime itself, in which a band of entry prices is established for each period of importation during the year, increasing in the peak European harvesting period (WTO 2000).

Table 3.5 shows the applied MFN tariffs of selected sectors in the EU in 1999. As shown by the reported simple average tariffs and the associated ranges, the mining and quarrying, and electricity, gas, and water sectors were heavily liberalized with either zero or close to zero average tariffs. The tariff protection for the manufacturing sector and agricultural manufactures was exceedingly high, whereas basic agricultural products were less protected.

Nigeria's Preferential Access Agreements and Its Status in International and Regional Groupings. Nigeria is involved, in varying ways in the full range of formal trade relations with other countries in the framework of bilateral, regional, and multilateral trade cooperation arrangements and agreements. Embedded in some of these frameworks are agreements for Nigeria's preferential access to participating countries. Even though Nigeria has maintained bilateral trade agreements with a number of African, European, and Caribbean countries, these

Table 3.5 Applied MFN Tariffs in the EU by ISIC Rev. 2 Category, 1999

ISIC Code	No. of Lines	Description	Applied Rate	
			Simple Average	Range
1	653	Agriculture, hunting, forestry and fishing	9.1	0–179.7
11	475	Agriculture and hunting	10.0	0–179.7
111	475	Agriculture and livestock production	10.0	0–179.7
2	137	Mining and quarrying	0.2	0–8
220	9	Crude petroleum and natural gas production	1.0	0–8
3	9637	Manufacturing	6.9	0–236.4
311	1438	Food products	21.4	0–236.4
3112	156	Dairy products	41.6	0.3–146.1
3116	116	Grain mill products	36.5	2.7–212.3
3119	46	Cocoa and cocoa confectionery	13.9	0–76.2
321	1059	Textiles	8.5	0–13
3212	98	Made-up textile goods except wearing apparel	10.3	2–13
3213	226	Knitted and crocheted fabrics	11.7	6.5–13
3311	133	Saw mills and woodmills	2.6	0–10
35	1795	Chemicals, petroleum, coal, rubber, plastics	4.7	0–41.7
353	62	Petroleum refineries	2.1	0–6.5
355	105	Rubber products	5.5	0–17
4	1	Electricity, gas, and water	0.0	0–0

Source: WTO (2000): *Trade Policy Review: European Union—2000 Vol. 1*, pp. 182–4

arrangements have not included trade preferences and therefore, have had no significant impact on Nigeria's direction of trade or its trade policy (Oyejide 2001).

Regional and multilateral trade alignments have, by contrast, offered Nigeria the opportunity for preferential access to markets of participating countries. The first in this category is the Nigeria's participation and membership of the Economic Community of West African States (ECOWAS), which was set up primarily as a preferential trade arrangement within the context of a series of trade and investment liberalization commitments. Despite the lopsided and lackluster attitude of the member nations in the implementation of the trade liberalization scheme (TLS) contained in the ECOWAS treaty, the regional grouping has nevertheless created both preferential and wider market access for Nigeria and other member nations. An assessment of whether Nigeria has actually utilized this opportunity of preferential access, which has remained a contentious issue in its trade policy trend.

Another important agreement that has granted Nigeria preferential access to other developing countries (African and non-African) is the Global System of Trade Preferences (GSTP). As noted by Oyejide (2001), the benefits that would have accrued to Nigeria with the tariff preference arrangement within the GSTP have been substantially eroded by the reduction in its applied tariffs, which began after the mid-1980s.

The establishment of the African Economic Community (AEC) by the OAU member nations in 1991, which provides for the creation of a pan-African economic and monetary union over time is another arrangement that would have offered a preferential and free access opportunity for Nigeria to African countries. With no concrete measures taken so far to implement the trade component of the AEC Agreement, utilizing the preferential access opportunity will remain elusive for Nigeria for some time.

The Lome Convention between the EU and the African-Caribbean Pacific States (EU-ACP), and the succeeding Cotonou Economic Partnership Agreement, which granted the ACP countries including Nigeria nonreciprocal duty-free access to EU, are the most significant opportunity of preferential access to the industrial countries that Nigeria has had. For a variety of reasons, there has been great difficulty for Nigeria to take full advantage of the benefits offered by the EU-ACP preferences.

Nigeria's preferential access to the United States has been constrained in the past for two main reasons. One is its exclusion from the beneficiaries of the U.S. generalized system of preferences (GSP), a program that grants preferential duty-free entry to some 4,468 products (as of July, 1998) from specified countries and territories, because of its membership of the Organization of Petroleum Exporting Countries (OPEC). The other factor that has limited Nigeria's access is the restriction imposed on its export of textiles and clothing products to the United States since 1990. With the recently enacted African Growth and Opportunity Act (AGOA) the preferential access opportunity that a number of African countries (especially South Africa) have started to enjoy, Nigeria's access to the U.S. market is expected to improve remarkably.

Locus and Responsibilities for Trade Policy and Nigeria's Interaction with the WTO

Since early 1960s, Nigeria's trade policy has been and continues to be influenced by several factors with domestic concerns and objectives, globalization trends, and its involvement in regional and multilateral trade agreements playing an prominent role. Between the early 1960s and the mid-1980s, the trade policy in Nigeria was basically inward looking with particular focus on the development of an industrial base through a series of protectionist frameworks. The economic depression of the early 1980s coupled with the widespread structural changes within the economy necessitated a shift in trade policy outlook that accompanied the structural adjustment program (SAP) of 1986. From an exclusive inward-looking posture, Nigeria's trade policy became more outward-oriented, mainly as a means of diversifying Nigeria's productive base to reduce the exclusive dependence on the oil sector and on imports.

With the broad objective of promoting economic efficiency in the process of expanding non-oil exports and reducing the import content of locally manufactured products, it is useful to distinguish among several sectoral components. In relation to imports, the primary objectives were to protect existing domestic industries and reduce the country's dependence on imports, by ensuring the availability of intermediate inputs and capital goods that could not be obtained from domestic sources. In relation to the export sector, the central objective of trade policy was the expansion and diversification of non-oil, and particularly manufactured exports. The industrial focus of the trade policy with respect to exports included the desire to increase the local content of manufactured products on the assumption that an increase in the level of locally sourced raw materials and intermediate products is important for raising capacity utilization of domestic industries. By comparison, the focus of trade policy with respect to agriculture was to discourage food imports and encourage local production of agricultural raw materials for local industry (Oyejide 2001).

The emergence of the democratic system of administration in April 1999 marked a major change in the structure of the policy-making process (including trade policy) in Nigeria. Based on suggestions and submissions of the relevant ministries and agencies, the National Assembly approves proposals that become law after presidential assent. Changes in trade and investment policies, including changes in tariff levels and import prohibitions that are generally formulated in the context of the annual budget, also undergo the same legislative procedure before their implementation. Overall, the principal ministries and agencies responsible for the administration of trade and investment policies in Nigeria are the presidency, the Federal Ministry of Finance, the Nigerian Customs Service, the Federal Ministry of Commerce (FMC), the Federal Ministry of Industry, and the Central Bank of Nigeria.

Regarding its interaction with the WTO, the Federal Ministry of Commerce (FMC) is the main coordinating agency. The FMC is the main channel through which trade issues and legislation are discussed between Nigeria and the WTO. Also, the minister of Commerce and Tourism represents and leads the country's delegations at WTO meetings, particularly at the periodic trade policy review meetings. There are other agencies that coordinate trade policy matters in Nigeria with the FMC at the apex. For instance, interministerial meetings are periodically held on a case-by-case basis when required to harmonize trade issues that cut across ministries. Also, the National Council on Trade and Tourism, which meets annually, coordinates intergovernmental trade issues that affect federal, state, and local governments. Between government and the private sector, trade issues are coordinated through various "umbrella" bodies collectively identified as the organized private sectors (OPS). The Nigeria Economic Summit Group, the Nigerian Association of Chambers of Commerce, Industries, Mines, and Agriculture (NACCIMA), Manufacturers Association of Nigeria (MAN), the Association of Nigerian Exporters, the Nigerian Association of Small-Scale Industrialists, and Export Commodity Associations comprise the OPS. Through the OPS, these various groups give advice on policies, and in some instances, pressurize for change in particular trade policy legislation and the position considered detrimental to their primary interest.

In addition, the private sector through the OPS is represented at various levels for the purpose of initiating, formulating, and in a few instances administering trade policies. The OPS performs these roles through its interaction with the FMC.

Nigeria's Participation in International Standard Development

Nigeria's Participation and Influence in International Standards Setting Processes

The World Trade Organization (WTO) recognizes and gives credence to the standards, codes, and guidelines of the Codex Alimentarius Commission (CAC) as adequate for the protection of human life and health related to the application of Sanitary and Phytosanitary (SPS) measures. The implication of such recognition is that national governments need to harmonize their regulations with those of CAC, as its final texts will apply in cases of trade disputes involving SPS measures. The Codex Alimentarius Commission is the standards setting agency for the WTO agreement on sanitary and phytosanitary measures (SPS) and it advises developing countries in setting up codex contact points and national codex committees for ease of coordination of SPS-related issues. The codex contact point (CCP) is the focal point for codex activities in a member country. However, the focal point of WTO issues in Nigeria is the Federal Ministry of Commerce.

The Federal Government of Nigeria established the codex contact point (CCP) through a decision of the then Federal Executive Council. The country,

thus, already had a CCP and a National Codex Committee (NCC) prior to the beginning of the WTO in 1995. The Standards Organization of Nigeria is the secretariat of the National Codex Committee while another regulatory agency, the National Agency for Food, Drugs Administration, and Control (NAFDAC) currently holds the chairmanship. The Standards Organization of Nigeria, which represents Nigeria in its obligation as a member of the International Standards Organisation (ISO), is the CCP that serves as the secretariat of the National Codex Committee and arranges the meetings of that committee. Its functions include the receipt and dissemination of documentation and information on codex and related issues. In addition to the communication function, it is the main repository of Codex documents distributed to relevant persons and organizations, acts as the link between the public and private sectors as well as between ministries in the public sector, coordinates all Codex activities, and maintains a library of codex standards, codes of practice, and other documents.

The National Codex Committee advises the government on food standards and related issues, particularly in the context of its CAC work and formulates national position papers on codex texts circulated by Codex circular letters. The Committee is also expected to educate ministers of various ministries, which have influence on food safety and consumer protection policy with regard to its Codex related work. The National Codex Committee has four technical committees to deliberate on and arrive at informed positions on Codex issues. These include the General Purpose Committee, Animal and Animal Product Committee, Plant and Plant Product Committee, and Miscellaneous Committee.

The National Codex Committee participates in Codex work in three ways. These include organizing and attending local and regional workshops and seminars; regional cooperation on codex issues; attending Codex meetings at the international level to present Nigeria's position on deliberated Codex issues; sending written views to the Codex Secretariat when national representatives cannot attend meetings; and organizing quarterly meetings to consider and approve submissions by the Technical Committees of the National Codex Committee. It is expected that the NCC convenes and approves responses to Codex circular letters and reviews government positions on the provisional agenda.

The level of Nigeria's participation in international standards development and the impact that such participation generates for the process of setting international product norms are, to a large extent, a function of the interests and involvement of public and private sector representatives in the activities of the National Codex Committee. The NCC is composed of the Ministries of Health, Agriculture and Rural Development, Commerce, Foreign Affairs, and Science and Technology; Standards Organization of Nigeria, NAFDAC, the academia and research institutes such as National Institute for Food Science and Technology (NIFST), as well as the private sector represented by Manufacturers Association of Nigeria, NACCIMA, the National Association of Small Scale Industrialists (NASSI), and the Consumer Protection Council. Table 3.6 shows the proportion of representation of the different relevant agencies and ministries. On the average, a typical NCC meeting has 25 percent representation from the Standards Organization of Nigeria followed closely by the academia and research institutes (24 percent), NAFDAC (22 percent) and the private sector (18 percent). Government ministries' representation averaged only 9 percent at NCC meetings while agencies involved in law enforcement constituted 3 percent. The structure of representation thus indicates irregular attendance of government ministry officials at NCC meetings with the probable implication of inadequate commitment to resolutions and budgetary issues.

The low rate of participation of government officials has a constraining influence on the degree of commitment of the private sector to NCC and CAC work. For example, an individual firm's participation in CAC meetings is limited to multinational organizations, which sponsor their personnel to meetings of their interest. At the CAC level, private sector participation in the absence of government officials generates limited impact as the private sector representatives attend as observers.

Issues on the agenda of a characteristic NCC meeting include a report from the Secretariat of the NCC; a delegate's report of the Codex Alimentarius Committee meetings, and a discussion of Nigeria's participation in and delegation to any forthcoming Codex Committee meeting. As required by the CAC, the NCC considers CAC agenda items and accordingly passes resolutions in the form of Nigeria's positions. For example, the NCC considered the supplementary Agenda 7 (a) of the 16th session of the Codex Committee on General Principles scheduled in Paris for 23–27 April 2001, which sought the amendment of Rule 1 of the Rules of Procedure of the CAC to permit the entry of the European Commission as a member of the CAC. Another instance is the consideration of agenda item 5 (b) of the 29th session of the Codex Committee on Food Labeling scheduled in Ottawa, Canada for 1–4 May 2001, on the labeling of foods and food ingredients obtained through certain techniques of genetic modification or genetic engineering.

In the first example, the NCC resolved that Nigeria should not support any amendment to the specific rules of the procedure, especially as it is merely to allow the EC to become a voting member of the CAC. Such a position was taken because the views of the EC, even as an observer, were often

Table 3.6 Participation at National Codex Committee Meetings

Institutions Represented	Number of Representation (Persons)[a]			Average Representation (percent)
	April 2001		August 2001	
Government ministries	1	1	3	9
Standards Organization of Nigeria	5	3	5	25
NAFDAC	4	4	3	22
Academia and research institutes	5	4	3	24
Private sector	2	2	6	18
Law enforcement agencies (e.g., police, customs, etc.)	—	—	2	3
Total	17	14	22	100

a. There were two meetings in April.
Source: Standards Organization of Nigeria.

respected and accommodated and that such amendment could set off similar demands from other sources in the future. In the second case, the NCC resolved that "all foods and food ingredients obtained through certain techniques of genetic modification/genetic engineering shall be labeled to comprehensively inform the consumer on such genetic modification and/or engineering that has taken place on the food or food ingredient." This resolution was circulated at the meeting as Nigeria's comments on the proposed draft amendment to the general standard for the labeling of prepackaged foods (FAO-WHO 2001a).

The CCP (i.e., Standards Organization of Nigeria) in line with the requirements of the CAC organizes and provides training for its staff through local and international workshops and seminars to fulfil its obligation to Nigeria's membership of the CAC in particular, and to ensuring product standards in general. Tables 3.7 and 3.8 show that the staff of the NCC Secretariat attended Codex-related programs thrice in 1994 and twice in 1997. NCC activities are entrenched in a monitoring mechanism established by the CAC, which enjoins the NCC to hold quarterly meetings to consider Codex-related issues, discuss and approve Nigeria's position, and review government positions on the provisional agenda. Accordingly, the Nigerian NCC meets quarterly as shown by the dates on NCC reports. For example, the NCC met in April and August 2001 as well as in January 2002. The CCP has also created a Codex Library as a unit in SON where Codex materials are stored and a library staff is assigned to monitor the unit.

Usually, the CAC sends requests for comments on draft standards to Codex Contact Points. For example, a Codex Committee, say, on Fresh Fruits and Vegetables, may adopt a proposed standard in

Table 3.7 Staff Training in 1994

Rank of Trained Staff	Program	Sponsor	Venue
Director General	International seminar on implementation of ISO 9000 standards in NAM countries	UNIDO	Colombo, Srilanka
Director General	Executive Committee of UN Codex Alimentarius Commission	SON	Rome
Chief Standard Officer	Standardization management and techniques	Swedish Govt./SON	Stockholm, Sweden
Senior Technical Officer	Field of textiles processing and finishing of cotton textiles	Turkish Govt./SON	Turkey
Internal Auditor II	International Auditing Accounting Govt. Establishments	SON	University of Ibadan, Nigeria
Higher Technical Officer 1	Laboratory methods for the analysis of non-grain starch Staple food crops	National Resources Institute, UK	Ghana
Higher Technical Officer 1	Laboratory methods for the analysis of non-grain starch staple food crops	National Resources Institute, UK	Ghana

Source: Bankole (2001).

Table 3.8 Staff Training in 1997

Rank	Program	Sponsor	Venue
Director General	ISO General Assembly Meeting, September	SON	Geneva
Director General	Codex Alimentarius Committee Meeting, 19–29 July	SON	Geneva
Director General	Group Meeting of Experts on Standardization and its Implication on Trade in Developing Countries under, ITC 27–31 October	SON	n.a.
Deputy Director	Workshop on management of Pension Schemes of Parastatals and other Organizations funded by FGN, May	SON	n.a.
Chief Technical Officer	ISO 14000 Standards Workshop	SON	South Africa
Chief Technical Officer	ISO General Assembly Meeting, September	SON	Geneva
Assist. Chief Personnel Officer	Workshop on Gender Sensitization and Awareness 27–28 August	SON	CMD, Lagos
Assist. Chief Personnel Officer	Codex Alimentarius Committee, 19–29 July	SON	Geneva
Assist. Chief Personnel Officer	ISO General Assembly Meeting, September	SON	Geneva
Principal Standards Officer	Nationwide Training on ISO 9000 Standards	SON	n.a.
Principal Standards Officer	Workshop on Gender Sensitization and Awareness, 27–28th August	SON	CMD, Lagos
Standards Engineer	Training course in OES Technology July/August	SON	Switzerland
Standards Officer	Workshop on Spectrophotometer in Industrial Measurement for Quality Assurance, 5–7 August	SON	n.a.
Standards Officer	Seminar on Volume of/Flow chart Course, 23–27 June	SON/PTB	Nairobi, Kenya
Standards Officer	NIFST National Workshop, 2–3 July	SON	Lagos
Standards Officer	NIFST National Workshop, 2–3 July	SON	Lagos
Principal Standards Officer	DGQ Quality Management Course, August/September	SON	Pretoria, South Africa
Senior Standards Officer	Nationwide Training on ISO 9000 Standards	SON	n.a.
Senior Standards Officer	Nationwide Training on ISO 9000 Standards	SON	n.a.
Senior Standards Officer	Nationwide Training on ISO 9000 Standards	SON	n.a.

Source: Bankole (2001).

respect of a particular product. It then sends a request for comments from the CCP of member countries. Such requests elicit reactions in the form of replies that may be as short as two lines. Nigeria's reply through its CCP to a request for comments on the draft codex standards for cassava (at Step 6) indicated that it was satisfied with the proposed draft standard for cassava in its current level (at Step 6) and had no objection regarding the standard (FAO-WHO 2001b).

There have been cases where Nigeria's reactions to a proposed draft standard were accommodated in the process of developing international standards. In particular, the Nigerian delegation to the 24th session of CAC in July 2001, in Geneva, Switzerland, expressed the view that the reduction of the lead content in cocoa butter, from 0.5 mg per kilogram to 0.1 mg kilogram was not justified. The CAC therefore adopted 0.5 mg per kilogram as the maximum level for lead in cocoa butter. Apart from this, the Nigerian delegation participated in the CAC meetings where certain draft standards were adopted (Table 3.9).

Thus, while Nigeria's participation arguably appears notable in international standards development, yet there are many constraints on the country's more effective and fuller participation in Codex work. Haphazard attendance at Codex meetings and nonavailability of meeting reports make

follow-up actions almost impossible. Currently, the NCC secretariat coordinates the attendance of national delegates at Codex meetings and expects participants to submit meeting reports to the national secretariat for further follow-up action, a missing requirement in the past. Hitherto, representatives of government from ministries sent to attend meetings did so on their own, without recourse to the national secretariat, creating problems of nonaccreditation and refusal of entry visas. Haphazard attendance can be attributed to funding problems generated by the frequency of these international meetings. For instance, there was at least one meeting every month from July to December 2001 at different locations (Table 3.10).

Nigeria sends a maximum of six persons to any one of the meetings that it wishes to attend. The funding implication is enormous for a country that is experiencing slow growth. Therefore, regional cooperation appears to be an attractive option to deal with the funding of participation at international Codex meetings to maximize the benefit of involvement and commitment to the work of the commission. Another dimension to the funding problem is the source of funding of NCC operations in Nigeria. Funding is required to circulate Codex documents among members of the NCC who are widely dispersed, for the day-to-day running of the Secretariat, to pay sitting allowances to

Table 3.9 Nigeria's Participation in International Standards Development

Draft Codes/Standards	Nigerian Delegate's Action
Draft code of practice for bottled/packaged drinking waters	Supported
Draft revised standard for honey	Supported
Draft maximum levels for lead:	
0.1 mg/kg for cocoa butter	Not supported; CAC reverted to 0.5 mg/kg
0.1 mg/kg for vegetable oils	Supported
0.02 mg/kg for milk	Supported
0.1 mg/kg for milk fat	Supported
Draft maximum level for aflatoxin in milk—0.5 µg/kg	Supported
Draft recommendation for the labeling of foods obtained through certain techniques of genetic modification	Objected to the term "modern biotechnology." CAC returned draft to step 6 for further country comments
Draft Revised Codex Standard for Cocoa Butter—exclusion of the use of n-hexane as processing aid	Supported

Source: National Codex Committee, 2001.

Table 3.10 Frequency of Codex Alimentarius Commission Meetings

Meeting	Date	Venue
24th session of the CAC	2–7 July 2001	Geneva, Switzerland
34th session of the Food Hygiene Committee	8–13 October 2001	Bangkok, Thailand
19th session of the Cocoa Products and Chocolate Committee	3–5 October 2001	Switzerland
23rd Session of the Committee on Nutrition and Foods for Special Dietary Uses	26–30 November 2001	Berlin, Germany
13th session of Committee on Residues of Veterinary Drugs in Food	4–17 December 2001	Charleston, South Carolina

Source: NCC Reports.

NCC members during meetings, to transport and accommodate members during quarterly meetings, and to procure and maintain equipment. Funds can be obtained locally from the private sector and governmental budgetary allocations but the magnitude of funds required needs assistance from international organizations. Inadequate flow of information among NCC members is quite problematic for the work of the NCC on the one hand and its ability to take informed official positions on Codex matters on the other. Late receipt of documents and letters is an important constraint in this regard. Nigeria depends on surface mails from FAO, WHO, and Codex and this creates problems associated with late receipt of documents. Adequate funding of NCC operations will go a long way in redressing the situation and make the CCP or NCC functional.

While the above analysis shows a modest contribution by Nigeria to Codex work, much of it appears to be based on limited scientific evaluation as a result of the quality and operationalization of the laboratories. For example, was Nigeria's claim (that a maximum level of 0.5 mg per kilogram of lead in cocoa butter is adequate) based on scientific research or on expert opinion? According to responses elicited from the CCP, Nigeria needs to carry out scientific research to find out why the lead content of cocoa is as high as manifested in the cocoa butter content in the country. The ability of Nigeria to conduct appropriate risk analysis and assessment before responding to Codex request for comments is suspect and thus poses a serious constraint on its effective participation in Codex work. Lack of adequate preparations, such as scientific

risk assessment, before attending these meetings puts Nigeria in a disadvantageous position as the ability to confidently justify national positions in deliberations and comments are severely constrained. In addition, lack of awareness among policy makers of the importance of Codex work impinges on their commitment. High level of advocacy is thus required for policymakers to appreciate the roles that safe and good quality food and agricultural products play in the development, health, and economic well-being of a nation as this would then stimulate their interest in the funding of Codex work.

Experiences of Local Private Sector in the Formation of Industry "Codes of Practice" at the National, International, or Regional Level

The Nigerian private sector does not appear to fully understand the relevance of standardization in the enhancement and advancement of their businesses. Most have only complied with official regulations to avoid punitive actions and sanctions. According to a senior staff member of SON, "companies have been closed down due to persistent noncompliance with product standard specification and regulations in line with laid down guidelines." Indeed, some companies are not aware of available national standards and do not make enquiries because of their preoccupation with profitability and consumers' complicity in terms of their complacency regarding product standards. Some companies adhere to their own private/company standards, which in comparison, are below national standards. An example was cited in discussions with a senior staff member of SON about a multinational company, which did not comply with certain regulatory aspects of a product standard. The company was prevented from further production of the product in 1994 and advised to upgrade the product standard to the national standard. Because the company did not positively respond to the advice it was stopped from producing the product. Many firms and farmers have only come to terms with the need to comply with internationally accepted and recognized standards and technical regulations consequent on the unpalatable experience arising from the rejection of their products in the export market.

Despite such negative experiences, especially of exporters, the local private sector has also invested resources by getting involved in the formation of industry "codes of practice" directly at the national level and indirectly at the international level. Apart from their active participation in the formation of codes of practice through membership of the NCC, most Nigerian industrial standards have the private sector as technical product committee members. A case in point is the standard for milk powder whose technical committee comprises, among others, UAC Foods Limited, Fan Milk, Carnco Foods (Nig.) Limited, and Foremost Dairies Limited (NIS 287, 1992), constituting about 30 percent of the technical committee membership. These are large companies in Nigeria. While at the national-level private sector participation is substantial it is not the case with international development of industry codes of practice for two reasons. Many large companies are multinational companies, which have foreign affiliation and technical assistance arrangements. Two, when private companies attend international meetings relating to standards setting they do so haphazardly, perhaps because of their observer status as only public officials are recognized and lead delegates to these meetings.

Nigeria's Strengths and Weaknesses in Participating in the International Standards Setting Process

Nigeria's strengths and weaknesses in participation in the international standards setting process can be assessed through its current level of participation in Codex work and the infrastructure on ground to do so effectively. First, the country's main strength consists in its participation experi-ence, which provides it with the opportunity of fine-tuning its strategy to benefit fully from the global standards arrangement. Already, Nigeria has the National Codex Committee and the Codex Contact Point, which analyze Codex-related issues for most effective and beneficial participation. Nigeria's performance is hampered by its incapacity for risk analysis and assessment that is required to justify national positions and technical comments on proposed draft standards. Usually, these comments depend on background papers and information from research institutes and universities in the country. Inadequate funding and noncommercialization of research findings from these institutions greatly impinge on their work because of obsolescence of equipment, which severely constrain the extent of risk assessment required in modern scientific enquiry into product or process standards.

One of Nigeria's main strengths is the certification of the NAFDAC laboratory by the World Health Organization to test shrimps for export (NCC Report 2001). Given the observed export potential of fish and shrimps and the existence of other laboratories in the country, the certification should enhance the ability of the NCC to ensure that export products are subject to official standards conformity tests as well as to convince export destination countries of Nigeria's preparedness in the area of demonstrating equivalence for particular standards. The attendant weakness that it is not obligatory for exporters to apply for tests. In January 2002, SON advertised in a newspaper that "Prospective exporters *wishing* to have their products certified, shall send applications to SON not later than two weeks before shipment, with information on name and address of exporter and importer, product and importer's specification, and an indication of the standard to which the product is manufactured (NIS, British standard, or company standard)." Since it is not mandatory to apply for certification, some category of exports said to experience a high incidence of rejection may actually have not been certified. Secondly, the timing of application by exporters is often too short that goods, especially fish and shrimps, may have been exported before test results are released. Finally, there are private laboratories whose operations should enhance that of official laboratories but lack of modern equipment is their limitation.

Domestic Legislation or Regulations and their Relation to International Norms

Introduction

A review of the laws of the Federation of Nigeria shows that it contains a number of legislation that affects standards requirements in food safety, animal health, and plant protection. There are those pertaining to importation. Specifically, the following standards-related legislation is found in the Federation: Agriculture (control of importation) Act Cap 12 of 31 March, 1964; Export of Nigerian Produce Act Cap 119 and Export Produce (Federal Powers) Act Cap 120 of 5 October 1961; Import (Prohibition) Act Cap 172 of 7 December 1989; Produce (Enforcement of Export Standards) Act Cap 371 of 1 December 1959; Live fish (Control of Importation) Act Cap 209 of 1 February 1965; Quarantine Act Cap 384 of 27 May 1926; and Animal Diseases (Control) Cap 18 of 24 February 1988. Besides this legislation, there were two decrees setting up the Standards Organisation of Nigeria (SON) and National Agency for Food and Drug Administration and Control (NAFDAC). The decrees are No. 56 of 1971 and No. 15 of 1993 amended by decree No. 20 of 1999, respectively.

Nature and Status of Local Laws, Regulations, and Standards

Food Safety. The law regulating and standardizing food production for export and import is Decree No. 15 of 1993 as amended by Decree No. 20 of 1999 setting up NAFDAC. The decree provides that no processed food, drug, drug products, cosmetics, medical device, or packaged water shall be manufactured, imported, exported, advertised, sold, or distributed in Nigeria unless it has been registered in accordance with the provisions of the decree or regulations made under it. The purpose of NAFDAC's control on export of regulated products is to ensure that products exported from Nigeria are wholesome, safe, and of good quality so that the image of the country is not tarnished in the international trade arena. It is in this way that the country's foreign exchange earnings can be enhanced. Only registered regulated products can be lawfully exported from Nigeria. Therefore, whether the product is locally manufactured or imported, it is expected to have satisfactorily undergone the registration processes.

To export regulated produce, a prospective exporter writes to the Director General (NAFDAC) an application accompanied with the stipulated fee per consignment of intended export attaching evidence of registration of the regulated product with NAFDAC. In the case of fish and fishery products, the evidence that is required is registration as an exporter of seafood together with a registration certificate granted by the Nigerian Export Promotion Council. Other details of the product required include name and full address of the manufacturer; batch numbers; date of manufacture; expiry date or best before date; destination of intended export; and certificate of analysis of the product batch by batch.

The agency issues an export certificate with the full details of the product(s) batch by batch to be exported if the company involved maintains the standards requirements of good manufacturing practice (GMP) and the regulated produce passes NAFDAC laboratory tests. It is important to note that for fish and fishery products, the report on their status, and the results of the NAFDAC laboratory tests on the products are forwarded to the Federal Department of Fisheries and Federal Ministry of Agriculture and Natural Resources for further action and issuance of export certificate.

There are other guidelines and procedures for the registration of locally manufactured processed foods. Application for registration of processed foods should be accompanied with a bank draft payable to NAFDAC covering the prescribed fee for preproduction inspection. Preproduction inspection is carried out to assess whether manufacturing facilities, personnel, and location of the plant are satisfactory. The registration procedure is halted at this stage if the facilities are not satisfactory. If successful, a certificate of recognition as a producer of the product is issued to the company. This enables the producer get the product registered. Preregistration inspection and sampling of the product for NAFDAC laboratory analysis are also undertaken. Final vetting of reports and preparation of briefs for consideration by the Food and Drug Registration Committee are carried out by the agency.

A processed food, for instance (regulated product), will not be manufactured in Nigeria, unless the factory is inspected, and a certificate of recognition is issued by NAFDAC. In the case of imported products, there must be evidence of registration of such a product by the competent health authority of the country of manufacture, that is, product license or certificate of registration; and there must be evidence from the competent health authority that the sale of the product does not constitute a contravention of the cosmetics laws in the country, that is, free sale certificate.

Animal Health. The Animal Disease (Control) Act Cap 18 of 1988 provides for the control and prevention of animal diseases with the object of preventing the introduction and spread of infections and contagious diseases among animals, hatcheries, and poultries in Nigeria. To achieve the above objectives, the Act prohibits the importation of any animal hatching eggs or poultry into the country except where there is a permit issued by the Director who shall state the conditions under which the animals may be imported. Such an imported animal, may be examined, disinfected, or inoculated and quarantined, at the risk and expense of the owners as instructed by the Director. The law also provides that any importation into Nigeria of any animal product, for example, semen, or egg or biologics, is prohibited unless a permit has been granted by the Director who may attach conditions, as he deems fit. Punitive measures including seizure or destruction, or any other form of penalty will be applied by the Director or by an authorized officer. However, it is expected that any punitive actions taken must be reported immediately to the Magistrates having jurisdiction. The legislation goes further to provide specific sanctions that may be imposed on an offender.

Plant Protection. The appropriate legislation for protecting plants in Nigeria is the Agriculture (Control of importation) Act Cap 12 of 31 March 1964. The Act provides for the regulations of the importation of articles for the purpose of controlling plant diseases and pests. The Act empowers the Minister for Agriculture to designate any officer in the public service of the Federation as an authorized officer for the purposes of this Act. The Act empowers the Minister to make regulations prohibiting restriction or laying down of conditions for the importation from any or all countries of plants, seeds, oil, containers, straw and other packing materials, artificial fertilizers, and any other similar goods or things. Any person found guilty will be liable for conviction.

Nigeria's Standards and Regulations Pertaining to Export and Import Trade

Export Trade. There are four major acts that govern export trade in Nigeria. These are: Export of Nigerian Produce Act Cap 119, Export Produce (Federal Powers) Act Cap 120 of 5 October 1961, Export (Incentives and Miscellaneous Provisions) Act Cap 118 of 11 July 1986, and Export (Prohibition) Act Cap 121 of 16 February 1989.

The first two acts on export of produce were enacted shortly after independence. At this time, produce like cocoa, groundnut, and palm oil were the main trading commodities, which earned foreign exchange for the country. Therefore, ensuring that quality of produce conformed to standards in the international markets was a major concern to policymakers. The Export of Nigeria Produce Act repealed the Nigerian Central Marketing Board Act, which empowers the Minister to prescribe grades and standards of quality for produce purchased by the commodity boards for exports; grant, withhold or cancel licenses in his discretion and can acquire subject to the provision of any state marketing law and produce for exports, and require any holder of a license for the export of produce and any commodity board and the servants or agents of any such holder or board to furnish him with such statistics, estimates, returns, or other information relating to produce as in his opinion are necessary for the discharge of his functions under the Act. The Act prohibits the export of any produce without license. Any attempt to contravene or in the case of contravention, the offender will be liable to a term of imprisonment.

The Export Produce (Federal Powers) Act Cap 120 was to further strengthen the powers of the minister in relation to certain produce intended for export. The Act empowers the minister for the purpose of external trade to prescribe grades and standards of quality of any produce intended for export. The Act contains provisions that specifically prescribed grades and standards for rubber and sundry produce regulation.

The beginning of the structural adjustment program (SAP) in 1986 provided the platform to encourage the diversification of exports culminating in the promulgation of the Export (Incentives and Miscellaneous Provisions) Act Cap 118 of 11 July 1986. The Act provides incentives to exporters such as the establishment of the Export Development Fund, Export Expansion Grant Fund, and the Export Adjustment Scheme Fund. The Export Development Fund is to be used to provide financial assistance to private sector exporting companies to cover expenses in respect of export promotion activities. The Export Expansion Grant Fund is to be used to provide cash inducement for exporters who have exported a minimum of ₦50,000 worth of semimanufactured or manufactured products to enable them to increase the volume of export and diversify export products and market coverage. The Export Adjustment Scheme Fund is expected to serve as a supplementary export subsidy or as an additional fund dealing with the huge costs of production arising mainly from infrastructural deficiencies and other factors beyond the exporter. To ensure that produce conforms to international standards and regulations, the Act authorizes the exportation of all raw or unprocessed commodities whether mineral or agricultural, to be covered by the export license issued by the Export Licensing Authority. The Act repealed the monopoly of exportation granted to the commodity boards. Since the operation of the Act, there have been several complaints about substandard produce exported from the country. The blame has been in the scrapping of the marketing Commodity Boards.

In 1989, as a result of the shortage of basic foodstuffs in the country, the Export (Prohibition) Act was promulgated to prohibit the exportation of certain foodstuffs from the country and to make provisions for the trial of offenders by the tribunal established under the Special Tribunal (Miscellaneous Offences) Act. The prohibited foodstuffs include beans, cassava, tuber, maize, rice, yam tuber among 57 items, as well as their derivatives. The ban is also extended to include imported food items.

Import Trade. The import trade is governed by Import (Prohibition) Act Cap 172 of 7th December 1989. The Act provides for the prohibition of importation into Nigeria of certain foodstuffs, especially those contaminated by toxic substances, and the penalty for the contravention of the Act. The importation of the following goods into Nigeria was prohibited either by way of trade or otherwise: meat (whether frozen or fresh); chicken (whether frozen or fresh); fish (whether frozen or fresh; except those caught and landed by vessels licensed and authorized by the appropriate Nigerian authority; expired food products (whether in cans or any other packages); all imported foodstuff items (including fruits and vegetables), for which the Minister of Health or the Director and Chief Executive of the Federal Environmental Agency has issued a certificate of contamination with any toxic or nuclear substance or any other harmful waste.

Industry-Specific Standards Governing Agricultural Produce and Trade. The importance of agricultural produce to the country's economy is responsible for the passage of the Act permitting trade in agricultural produce as early as 1 December 1959. The Produce (Enforcement of Export Standards) Act Cap 371 of 1959 provides for the inspection of commodities for export from Nigeria at ports of shipment, for the purpose of enforcement of grades and standards of quality in respect of such commodities, and for issues incidental to the execution of the powers conferred by this Act. The Act provides for various punitive measures for attempts to contravene or the contravention of the provisions of the Act. The Act repeals the provisions of the Produce Inspection Act 1950 as it applies to ports or shipment of produce and to the port of Lagos. It contains subsidiary legislation, which is specific to cotton lint and cotton seed, copra, and coffee for export and regulations. It also established produce inspection boards for benniseed, capsicums, cassava, starch, cocoa, copra, cotton seed, cotton lint, fruit, fruit produce (other than oils), ginger, groundnut, groundnut cake, palm kernels, palm oil, rubber, and soy beans—products to which the Act applies.

Nature and Status of Mandatory Technical Regulations on Nigeria's Main Light Manufacturing Industries

All standards and other mandatory technical regulations that affect Nigeria's light manufacturing industries are under the purview of the Standards Organization of Nigeria (SON) Act Cap 412 of 1 January, 1970, and the National Agency for Food and Drug Administration and Control (NAFDAC) Decree No. 15 of 1993, amended by Decree No. 20 of 1999. Both the SON and NAFDAC are the enquiry points regarding standards and technical regulations in Nigeria. The country is a member of ISO through the SON that sets standards for processed food, beverages, medical devices, drugs, and other chemicals (including raw materials). Nigerian standards specify production process, quality characteristics, and mandatory testing procedures. The SON adapted the ISO 9000 series of standards (9001, 9002, 9003) in 1993 after six years of implementation of the series by the ISO. The SON formulates, enforces, and monitors various food standards and provides technical advice to industries. New companies are required to lodge copies of product standards with the SON for clearance for importation of machinery.

SON's quality standards appear to arise from a series of structural analysis and organization. The establishment has ten steps in the certification of products:

- Setting up management quality steering committee
  - Appointment of a management representative and quality assurance manager
  - Establishing quality system coordinating committee
- Training Quality auditors and other employees handling quality-related jobs
  - Appointment of lead auditor
- Development of
  - Quality Manual (QM)
  - Quality Assurance Procedure Guides (QPG); and
  - Obtaining approval and Implementation
- Submission of application, QM, and QPG to SON
- Conducting internal quality audit
- Conduct awareness session and training
- Preassessment audit by SON
- Complete implementation of corrective actions and recommendations
- Final assessment by SON
- Granting ISO Certification

Regulated products comprising processed food, beverages, tobacco, cosmetics, drugs, drug products, and chemicals must be registered with NAFDAC to protect and promote public health. NAFDAC recognizes testing and certification procedures of most conformity assessment bodies in foreign countries.

Enforcement and Conformity with International Norms

The following observations can be generated about the enforcement and conformity of standards to international norms.

(a) All local legislation relating to standards or technical regulations predates the SPS Agreement and is aimed at conforming to international norms; otherwise the export would be rejected. In some cases, exporters impose stiffer standards or are self-regulated.

(b) Enforcement seems weak, which has led to the rejection of Nigeria's produce and products abroad (see below).

(c) Through Nigeria's participation in international standards-setting all efforts are made to ensure that the country complies with the dictates of international norms. The detail was provided in the section on participation in international standards development.

SPS Organizations, Infrastructure, and Their Effectiveness

Nigeria's Organizations Involved in Assuring SPS Standards

Nigeria's drive for accelerated growth and development impels it toward envisaging and ensuring adequate diversification of its export base into non-traditional export commodities. Its manufacturing sector through which this diversification dream is expected to be actualized strives to imbibe and adopt best manufacturing practices (BMP) to increase the country's foreign exchange earnings and to improve the quality of life of Nigeria's citizens by increasingly recognizing the importance of industrial standards. The expectation that increasing consumer income will generally lead to a higher demand for foods, drugs, and other essential health-related commodities makes standard measures to ensure safe and wholesome food and drug a necessity. Both technical competence and an effective food control management system are necessary to ensure that regulatory measures keep pace with the continuously changing socioeconomic situations to provide vital means by which the food system is optimally maintained. An efficient regulatory system increases consumer protection from health hazards and commercial fraud arising from information asymmetry. It is thus imperative that Nigeria's sanitary and phytosanitary (SPS) measures are based not only on international standards and Codex guidelines in which they exist but also they should be consistent with the key principles of the SPS Agreement.

Nigeria's challenges in meeting the crucial obligations of the need to institute a regulatory standards regime have remained the responsibility of the various regulatory agencies set up by the government. These agencies include the Standard Organization of Nigeria (SON), the National Agency for Food, Drug Administration, and Control (NAFDAC), the Plant Quarantine Service (PQS) of the Ministry of Agriculture, and the Livestock Health Department of the Federal Ministry of Agriculture, as well as the Federal Department of Fisheries, and Ministry of Health.

The SON since its inception in 1971 has remained the fulcrum of standardization, quality assurance, and testing in Nigeria for ensuring compliance with government policy on the quality and safety of both locally produced and imported products. As the Codex Contact Point for Codex Alimentarius Commission in Nigeria, the SON has been involved in activities relating to food standardization with emphasis on the application of sanitary and phytosanitary measures to facilitate trade and ensure a satisfactory health status among the population. Also, as the secretariat of the National Codex Commission (NCC) comprising representatives from organized private sector such as the Association of Food, Beverages, and Tobacco Employees (ATBTE), Consumer Protection Agency, National Agency for Food, Drug Administration and Control (NAFDAC), Ministry of Commerce, and other relevant government agencies, SON coordinates with other stakeholders in the NCC, the implementing committee of Codex provides guidelines relating to information dissemination on new regulations or requirements and other issues. The committee also coordinates the National position for presentation at every Codex Alimentarius Commission meetings, and NCC quarterly meetings as well as NCC delegates' meeting in preparation for the scheduled Codex Alimentarius Commission meetings. Thus, the responsibility for preparing food standards in Nigeria lies with SON in consultation with the food industry, relevant ministries, consumer organizations, academic and research institutions, and other interested parties.

NAFDAC was established as a parastatal of the Federal Ministry of Health by Decree No. 15 of 1993 and as amended by Decree No. 19 of 1999. The mandate of the agency is to promote and protect public health by ensuring that regulated products are of good quality, safe, and adequate for their intended use. This function is carried out through the various laws and regulations that govern the manufacture, importation, exportation, advertisement, distribution, sale, and use of regulated products. These laws, regulations, and guidelines, among others constitute the core of Nigeria's sanitary and phytosanitary standards harmonized with those of the Codex Alimentarius Commission and other relevant and recognized international bodies, and are applied and enforced by NAFDAC. NAFDAC adopts the Codex standards where a national standard does not exist for a particular product.

The application and enforcement mechanism of SPS standards by NAFDAC includes an inspection and monitoring procedure covering food production and consumption. This is done by applying the Hazard Analysis Critical Control Point (HACCP) principle and the code of practice and general principles of food hygiene to manufacturing processes in Nigeria. The packaging and labeling provisions are also an integral part of the control mechanism to ensure compliance with laboratory analysis results and advertisement requirements enumerated in the appropriate guidelines.

Effectiveness and Constraints facing National Contact or Enquiry Point

NAFDAC and SON are linked to the WTO through the Codex Alimentarius Commission. They are both member agencies of the National Focal Point (NFP) on Multilateral Trade anchored in the Federal Ministry of Commerce (FMC). This focal point is responsible for WTO issues in addition to other trade-related issues. Both NAFDAC and SON are the enquiry points for WTO in Nigeria while the FMC is the notification authority. The WTO expects the enquiry points to provide relevant documents or adopted or proposed SPS regulations, procedures for control and inspection, quarantine treatment, pesticide residues, and food additive approval.

The effectiveness of a particular regulating agency can be viewed in light of its inputs into a broader policy framework arrangement and its ability to initiate, formulate, and implement rules and measures in accordance with its statutory mandates. NAFDAC's communications with the WTO through the FMC can be described as quite effective with the agency's participation in the Trade Policy Review Mechanism (TPRM) of the WTO conducted in

1998. The Agency continues to articulate its concerns through the FMC about the complex WTO procedures for establishing dumping. The procedures to establish dumping are sufficiently complicated and sophisticated that it has been difficult for Nigeria to establish dumping according to WTO principles and disciplines. Not only this, NAFDAC agrees with most developing countries that implementation difficulties of some of the WTO Agreements limit their effective participation in world trade negotiations and their simplification should be the focus of future rounds of negotiations.

As a WTO enquiry point, NAFDAC is accessible to investors and other interested parties through the notifications it sends to the notification authority as its laws are reviewed or changed. SON is the Codex Contact Point and the secretary of the NCC, while NAFDAC chairs the meetings. The CCP receives and circulates all Codex working documents and circular letters for comments. The CCP is the link between the country and the CAC in Rome. All correspondence to the CAC is routed through the CCP and vice versa. While the CCP generally strives to perform its roles, it needs to be more effective: circulation of codex documents is not efficient and NCC meetings are irregular. Not only can the constraints be traced to lack of political will or generally low commitment to the standards issue, but lack of infrastructure also limits the effectiveness of the NCC. The NCC has no adequately furnished and equipped secretariat, which also requires competent staff and facilities such as fax machines, telephones, computers, email, Internet facilities, and so on, for it to be functional and effective.

The predominant constraint is nonavailability of funds and the main culprit in this financial constraint that the CCP and NCC face is the absence of separate budgetary vote to run the national codex secretariat to conduct necessary codex work. The budget constraint also prevents relevant members of staff of NAFDAC, SON, and other government agencies such as the CCP and NCC from attending most of the codex meetings scheduled in foreign countries. Table 3.11 shows budgeted and actual recurrent and capital expenditures of SON over 1992 to 1997. For most years, budgeted figures are not available and the actual figures are discontinuous. This makes comparison difficult. However, for years that data are available, both the recurrent and capital expenditures grew over those years. The ratio of budgeted to actual expenditure is particularly low in 1997, less than 10 percent for recurrent expenditure and about 15 percent for capital expenditure, a situation suspected to have been the case in the pre-1997 period.

In spite of budgetary inadequacies, SON and NAFDAC have progressed in the direction of strict enforcement of their regulatory powers through investigation, seizure, and destruction of substandard domestically produced and imported goods. The recent thrust of rules enforcement has indeed been bolstered in the democratic regime whose anticorruption stance seems to have generated the political will and support for the work of SON and NAFDAC. Instances of destruction of substandard and fake pharmaceuticals and other imported goods and arrests were widely reported along with paid advertisements on new rules and fake goods. Table 3.12 presents a list of imported substandard food and drugs, which were advertised and destroyed in 2001 and 2002.

Risk Assessment. Risk assessment is an integral part of risk analysis of food safety and the CAC is in the process of producing necessary guidelines as

Table 3.11 Budgeted and Actual Recurrent and Capital Expenditure

Year	Recurrent Expenditure			Capital Expenditure		
	Budget	Actual (₦ million)	Ratio of Actual to Budget (percent)	Budget	Actual (₦ million)	Ratio of Actual to Budget (percent)
1992	n.a.	10.6	n.a.	n.a.	6.7	n.a.
1993	n.a.	12.5	n.a.	n.a.	8	n.a.
1994	n.a.	20.0	n.a.	n.a.	9	n.a.
1995	n.a.	n.a.	n.a.	n.a.	n.a.	n.a.
1996	n.a.	n.a.	n.a.	n.a.	n.a.	n.a.
1997	379.8	37.6	9.9	1307	183	14

Note: n.a. is Not available.
Source: Bankole (2001).

Table 3.12 Summary of Fake and Substandard Goods Advertised and Destroyed

Period	Commodity Type	Source	Registration Status with NAFDAC
2002	Pharmaceuticals	Incomplete manufacturer's address; imported	Not registered
2002	Ditto	Imported	Not registered
2002	Food: table salt	Unknown	Not registered
2002	Pharmaceuticals	Unknown	Not registered
2002	Pharmaceuticals	Imported	Not registered
2002	Pharmaceuticals	Imported	Not registered
2001	Food: Instant noodles	Imported	Not registered

Source: The Guardian (2001, 2002).

part of Codex requirements for internationally traded foods. Risk analysis involves three elements namely, risk assessment, risk management, and risk communication. Under the risk analysis framework, CAC is the risk manager while advisory expert committees such as the Joint Export Committee on Food Additives and Contamination (JECFA) and the Joint Meeting on Pesticide Residues (JMPR) are the risk assessors. Neither NAFDAC nor SON have started conducting risk assessment for lack of adequate training in the area. However, their interests in training programs on risk assessment have been notified to the NCC through the CCP for a possible FAO or WHO training assistance. Such capacity building in risk assessment as an integral part of risk analysis is envisaged as a component of CAC's training assistance.

Both the SON and NAFDAC are not aware of risk assessment guidelines by the International Plant Protection Convention (IPPC) and the International Office of Epizootics (OIE). Codex standards are the benchmark for food safety issues recognized by the WTO while the IPPC and OIE standards are recognized by WTO for plant and animal health respectively, which are used in WTO's dispute settlement. NAFDAC hardly deals with unprocessed plant or animal products though all three organizations are relevant to the SPS Agreement of the WTO.

Relationship Between "Contact Points" and the Main National Authorities for Trade Policy and Negotiation. Both SON and NAFDAC work closely with the Federal Ministries of Commerce and Foreign Affairs. Imported products into Nigeria must have a Manufacturer's Certificate and a Free Sale Certificate issued by Nigerian Foreign Missions having

authenticated the license to manufacture the product in the exporting country to qualify for NAFDAC's registration. A Certificate of Analysis showing evidence of registration by the competent health authority in the exporting country is also required. Samples and data of potential import products must be sent to NAFDAC's laboratories at least three months before the product arrives in Nigeria. This aids in the achievement of the objective of identifying and blacklisting companies engaged in the exportation of fake and counterfeit drugs and substandard goods to Nigeria. The established mechanism to coordinate standards–related work of the various notification, certification, and regulatory agencies locally include the NCC and NFP on multilateral trade.

In terms of the effectiveness of SON, NAFDAC, Federal Ministry of Commerce, and the NFP on multilateral trade in the dissemination of information to local stakeholders, both SON and NAFDAC have adequate email and online facilities for importers and exporters to obtain information on SPS standards and other compliance issues and also obtain forms from their web sites, which are updated regularly. Both also engage the print and electronic media to pass information to local stakeholders through jingles and prime time advertisements educating the members of the public of the hazardous implications of substandard drugs and other goods.

Functions, Capabilities, Infrastructure and Overall Effectiveness of National Standard Agencies

Functions, Capabilities, and Infrastructure. These issues are concerned with the mandates and enforcement capacities of national standards agencies

189

including the possession of tangible and intangible infrastructure. The physical infrastructure available in and outside government regulatory agencies reflects the level of understanding, development, and importance attached to the standardization and food quality control system in the country. This has an influence on the magnitude of investment to procure adequate scientific equipment and instruments, and well-trained and technically competent staff to undertake tests related to standards and technical regulations in food control agencies, research institutions, and universities. Because of the inadequate concern of the government and the private sector, their involvement in standardization thus seems of lowest priority. However, NAFDAC, the food control agency is sufficiently equipped to meet the challenges of setting safety and quality standards for food and can request for support from other the scientific community like the Institute for Public Analysts of Nigeria (IPAN).

The functions of SON as entrenched in the enabling decree No. 56 of 1971 and its subsequent amendments include, among others, the organization of test and other necessary activities to ensure compliance with standards designed and approved by the council; investigation into the quality of facilities, materials, and products in Nigeria; and the establishment of a quality assurance system including certification of factories, products, and laboratories. SON's others functions include fostering interest in the recommendation and maintenance of acceptable standards by industries and the general public; registration and regulation of standards marks; specifications, development, and distribution of standards samples; the coordination of all activities relative to its functions throughout Nigeria; and cooperation with corresponding national or international organizations in such fields of activity as it considers necessary with a view to securing uniformity in standards specifications.

The broad function of NAFDAC is the control and regulation of food, drugs, cosmetics, chemicals, and packed water. The specific functions of the agency, according to its enabling Decree No. 15 of 1993, include the regulation and control of the importation, exportation, manufacture, advertisement, distribution, sale, and use of food, drugs, cosmetics, medical devices, bottled water, and chemicals; conducting appropriate tests and ensuring compliance with standard specifications desig-

nated and approved by its council for the effective control of quality of food, drugs, cosmetics, medical devices, bottled water, and chemicals and their raw materials as well as their production processes in factories and other establishments; and registration of food, drugs, cosmetics, medical devices, bottled water, and chemicals. In addition, NAFDAC is expected to control the exportation and issue quality certification of food, drugs, cosmetics, medical devices, bottled water, and chemicals intended for export; pronounce on the quality and safety of food, drugs, cosmetics, medical devices, bottled water, and chemicals after appropriate analysis; and advise Federal, State and Local Governments, the private sector, and other interested bodies regarding the quality, safety, and regulatory provisions on food, drugs, cosmetics, medical devices, bottled water, and chemicals.

The SON has a Standards Directorate comprising six main departments namely, Chemical Technology; Civil Engineering; Electrical Engineering; Mechanical Engineering; Food Technology; and Textile and Leather Technology departments. Technical committees are set up to coordinate the activities of each of these departments and set, approve, and review standards concerning the departments. SON's Directorate of Quality Assurance is fashioned into six subject areas covering Chemical Technology, Food or Codex, Mechanical Engineering, Electrical or Electronics Engineering, Civil or Building Engineering, and Textiles and Leather to ensure quality control. The Directorate embarks on routine factory inspection and surveillance to enforce compliance with set standards and established quality control practices. Regular market surveys are also undertaken whereby samples of locally produced and imported goods are taken and are subjected to laboratory tests.

SON has three laboratories across the country, namely the Food and Chemical Laboratory, Ikoyi, Lagos; Engineering Laboratory, Emene, Enugu; and Textile and Leather Laboratory, Kawo, Kaduna. The laboratories conduct third-party conformity assessment tests of products using statutory approved quality control standards. SON also embarks on port and border operations to ensure that imported and exported goods meet the required local and international standards. Imported and export products are made to carry labels showing producer name, country of origin, ingredients, and manufacture and expiry dates. Samples of these goods are also taken and subject to laboratory tests and substandard products are seized and destroyed. A certificate of standardization—the Nigerian Industrial Standard (NIS) certificates—are issued to locally produced goods to indicate that such products have met approved and recognized standards by SON. SON is active in the work of the African Regional Organization for Standardization (ARSO), Codex Almentarius Commission, International Organization of Standards (ISO), and other international agencies.

NAFDAC, on its part, is well equipped to perform its regulatory functions as it has both competent and specialized manpower to carry out inspections at the port of entry, and in local and foreign manufacturing outfits. It has the physical infrastructure, equipment, facilities, and competent technical manpower to conduct tests related to standards and technical regulations. There are four functional NAFDAC laboratories in Oshodi and Yaba in Lagos, Kuduan and Maiduguri adequately staffed and equipped with modern laboratory equipment such as HPLCs, GC-MS and so on. The vaccine laboratory in Yaba is well equipped and adequately staffed. NAFDAC also has an ongoing arrangement for international certification of its laboratories.

NAFDAC's inspection function is carried out by the Inspectorate Directorate, with the Ports Inspection Division (PID) and the Establishment Inspection Division (EID) having responsibility for ports inspection and establishment inspection, respectively. The EID guides manufacturers toward adherence to SPS standards.

The Division advises on the location of factories that must not be near a refuse dump, cement factories, sewage treatment and oxidation ponds, abattoirs, smoky and dusty areas and so on. It ensures that the HACCP system, a food safety management system that identifies critical points where control is essential to prevent food safety problems that may otherwise arise, has been established. This system is applied from the beginning to the end of the production process. In addition to the HACCP concept, the general principles of the code of practice of food hygiene are applied to ensure the maintenance of the appropriate degree of personal cleanliness, behavior, and operation in an appropriate manner during the food handling and manufacturing processes.

The PID monitors regulated products at the ports of entry into the country. It checks for the appropriate certificates required for importation, in addition to compliance with labeling requirements such as batch numbering, manufacturing date, expiry date, location address, manufacturer and so on. When the products comply, they are inspected and released if the product is registered. A new product must undergo the process of registration before importation is allowed into the country. This is where the work of the Registration and Regulations (R&R) Directorate begins.

This R&R Directorate gives approval for importation of registration samples on receipt of an application requesting approval. The imported registration samples undergo laboratory analysis in NAFDAC laboratories while the results in addition to meeting the labeling requirements, and so on, determine the registrability of the product. The R&R Directorate anchors all the activities required for product registration. It organizes consultative meetings with manufacturers including clinical trials committee meetings and formulates all the regulations enforced by NAFDAC.

The Food, Drug, and Related Products Approval Committee (FDRPAC) considers the results of analysis and other requirements and scrutinizes the products after the R&R Directorate and the Subcommittee of the FDRPAC must have considered and recommended them for approval. Membership of this committee is drawn from the R&R Directorate including the Advertisement Unit, EID, PID, Laboratory Directorate, Planning Research and Statistics (PRS) Directorate, the Director General's office, Legal Unit, Food and Drug Information Center (FDIC), and the Codex Office.

The laboratory services directorate analyzes all products for registration, compliance routine, and research purposes, among others. The laboratories, located in Oshodi and Yaba in Lagos, Kaduna and Maiduguri have appropriate infrastructure, equipment, facilities, and staff to carry out its functions adequately. The Food and Drug Information Center (FDIC) is a computerized (with email and internet facilities) and adequately staffed technical unit responsible for the monitoring of adverse drug reactions and for circulating related information to health care providers, staff, and clients.

The Codex Office is also the technical arm of the NAFDAC, which serves as the link between the Codex Alimentarius Commission (CAC) in Rome, Codex Contact Point (CCP) in Nigeria, and NAFDAC. There is a National Codex Committee (NCC), which has NAFDAC as the chairman and SON as the secretary of the NCC.

The four technical committees of the National Codex Committee that deal with Codex issues include the General Purpose Committee; Animal and Animal Product committee; Plant and Plant Product committee; and the Miscellaneous committee. The scope of work of the Animal and Animal Product committee covers carrying out effective deliberations, providing technical inputs, and reviewing issues arising from Codex standards, code of practice, guidelines, and other advisory texts with respect to meat hygiene, fish and fishery products, milk and milk products; and meat and poultry products. It examines these issues in relation to the global concern for growing health problems. The scope of work of the plant and plant products committee covers deliberations and provision of technical inputs as well as reviewing issues arising from codex statements, codes of practice, guidelines, and other advisory tests concerning cereals, pulse and legumes; vegetable proteins; fats and oils; cocoa products and chocolate; sugars and honey; fresh fruits and vegetables; processed fruits and vegetables; and soups, broths, and bouillon cubes. Specifically, it is mandated to examine critical issues involved in fats and oils of animal, vegetable, and marine origin including margarine and olive oil; the high lead content in cocoa as well as the inclusion of bitter varieties of cassava in the draft Codex standard for cassava under fresh fruits and vegetable committee of Codex Alimentarius.

The Miscellaneous committee is charged with the responsibility of ensuring standards, guidelines, or other principles, as appropriate for foods derived from biotechnology or traits introduced into food by biotechnology; examine, amend if necessary, and endorse provisions on nutritional aspects proposed for inclusion in Codex standards, guidelines, and related texts; elaborate comments on regional standards for national mineral waters; and examine guidelines as appropriate on good animal feeding practices to ensure safety and quality of foods of animal origin.

Overall Effectiveness of National Standard Agencies. The broad concept of food control, which covers the elements of compliance with mandatory requirements, quality control procedures, monitoring, and surveillance activities, has considerable influence on critical socioeconomic indicators of development. The Food or Codex Department of the SON has established over 100 standards on food and related products as well as a good number of Codex of hygienic practices for food and food products (SON 1997). These standards and codes specify the essential quality requirements for nutritional, health, and safety, and for labeling.

Standardization is made complete with the enforcement of set standards. Consequently, the SON amendment Act of 1990 empowers it to punish manufacturers or importers whose products do not conform to established standards. Apart from various fines, SON, on satisfactory establishment of product defectiveness considered hazardous to life and safety, will apply its powers of seizure or destruction or prohibition of any person offering such products for sale. It is empowered to seal premises where such products are manufactured, or direct the manufacturer or importer to rectify the deficiency where possible.

There are basically four types of inspections undertaken by SON. These include routine, certification, consumer complaints, and port inspections with the objective of ensuring that locally produced or imported food is safe, unadulterated, and properly labeled to meet the essential quality characteristics stipulated in the standards.

NAFDAC as a regulatory agency functions effectively and has the capability and infrastructure as a national standard agency though it has sufficient room for improvement. The agency has offices in the 36 state capitals of the Federation in addition to "special" offices located in Onitsha, Kano, and Aba that have peculiar problems related to substandard goods and other violations. There are ongoing concerted efforts to augment staff strength in all departments to strengthen NAFDAC's regulatory and enforcement functions. The agency currently has an enforcement arm specifically geared toward enforcing laws on fake and counterfeit drugs; and violations of food, drug, and related products registration.

Both SON and NAFDAC have a number of local and international research cooperation projects. NAFDAC have such projects in collaboration with the International Atomic Energy Agency (IAEA) aimed at certification of NAFDAC laboratories and standards-related work. Also, laboratory and inspectorate staff and others are provided with training programs abroad.

NAFDAC's new guidelines released in the first week of April 2002 require mandatory preshipment inspection for every pharmaceutical products whether registered with NAFDAC or not, by its approved agencies in the country of origin, which will issue a certificate. In addition, foreign producers of drugs and beverages should affix NAFDAC registration numbers on the packaging while importers ensure that production plants of their foreign partners are WHO-certified for good manufacturing practice. Failure to comply will result in impounding and destruction of goods at the port of entry.

From July 2002, NAFDAC inspectors have commenced inspection of foreign producers' plants, fruit orchards, and the production process to ensure that they satisfy NAFDAC's standards to safeguard public health. There were more than 15 brands of unregistered MSG food seasoning products in Nigeria in 2001. Despite NAFDAC's invitation, producers never came forward for registration. As part of its enforcement strategies, NAFDAC published the list of registered and unregistered brands of MSG in Nigeria.

Private Individuals and Organizations in Certification Services, Standardization and Codes of Practice in Nigeria

NAFDAC has some government-designated food and drug analysts who are recognized private analysts and whose certification services for the analysis of regulated products are accepted by NAFDAC. The private analysts are active in the packaged water, food, drugs, and cosmetics sectors. Most of the analysts are members of the Institute of Public Analysts of Nigeria (IPAN). The role of private organizations and companies in formulating standards and codes of practice is usually through their contributions at meetings of the NCC and other standards-setting bodies such as SON. In addition, NAFDAC holds consultative meetings where private sector inputs are included during the making or review of regulations as the need arises.

NAFDAC also encourages the formation of product associations to contribute to self-regulation to conform to international standards. Such associations also make NAFDAC's functions of regulatory control easier as the group can easily be reached and depended on to disseminate relevant information on SPS standards to its members, which would have been slower and more difficult if communicated on a one-on-one basis. The product associations also ensure compliance to self-regulation, which usually conforms to international standards. This structure has proven to be an effective self-regulating tool to NAFDAC in its regulatory functions.

There are a couple of preshipment inspection agencies, namely Swede Control Intertek, Bureau Veritas, Cotecna International Ltd, and Societe General de Surveillance (SGS) that the Nigerian government engages to verify the quality, quantity, the price and financial terms, and the customs classification of goods imported into Nigeria under the Comprehensive Import Supervision Scheme (CISS). Apart from this mandate and agreements, the SGS complements the SON and Produce Inspectorate division of the Ministry of Commerce as recognized agencies to carry out test, preshipment inspection, and certification of goods for export.

The relationship between the private organizations and regulatory agencies goes beyond paying attention to factors which impinge on food safety or quality and fraudulent trade practices and extends to joint sponsorship of training and workshop activities as a means of solving common food quality problems within a given industry. This is the avenue through which industry partakes in the overall implementation of the food standard control strategy.

Participation of consumer organizations in the formation of standards and codes of practices creates a strong consumer lobby system that can be an effective means of withstanding undue pressure from the industry and vice versa. Education of consumers about the hygiene and sanitation, food hazards, and improved food labeling practices should be an equally important element of the strategy to build up demand for improved food quality control by the industry. This area has not been thoroughly developed.

Relationship Between Legislation and Implementation Capacity and Key Principles Underpinning the SPS Agreement

Though the SPS agreement allows members to adopt or enforce measures necessary to protect human, animal or plant life, or health, it strives to ensure transparency in the formulation and application of standards and regulation and thus encourages reduction of compliance costs related to inspection, testing, and certification from multiple standards that may arise in the absence of the agreement. In addition, the agreement endeavors to guarantee socially optimal standards by ensuring that they are not excessive and costly to consumers and producers through their restrictive influence on trade flows. It thus aims to achieve a measure of standard that is least restrictive to trade. Thus, the SPS Agreement supports member countries' activities in the area of generating improvements to their human health, animal health, and phytosanitary conditions by the establishment, adoption, and application of SPS measures but such measures should not be used to restrict trade. The likely negative effects on trade of SPS measures are thus attenuated through the harmonization of SPS measures via standards, guidelines, and recommendations developed by the relevant international organizations, such as the Codex Alimentarius Commission, the International Office of Epizootics, and the International Plant Protection Convention.

The key underpinning principles of the SPS Agreement are as follows. First, there is need to base measures on scientific principles and apply them only to the extent necessary to protect human, animal or plant life, or health. Second, SPS measures will not arbitrarily or unjustifiably discriminate between members when identical or similar conditions prevail, and will not be applied to constitute a disguised restriction on international trade. Third, members will base their SPS measures on international standards, guidelines, or recommendations, where they exist and base such measures on risk assessment techniques developed by the relevant international organizations. In this regard, members are obliged to fully participate in the work of CAC, IOE, and IPPC within the limits of their resources.

From the analysis and assessment of the regulatory and implementation frameworks of Nigeria's standardization process and procedures through SON and NAFDAC, legislation and supporting implementation capacity are based on the key principles of the SPS Agreement enumerated above. First, apart from the fact that Nigeria's regulatory standards are not discriminatory as they apply equally to both imported and domestically produced goods, to that extent they avoid any unnecessary barriers to Nigeria's trade flows. Second, many standards are harmonized with Codex standards, which are internationally accepted as required by the SPS Agreement. This is indeed ensured through the link of Nigeria's regulatory agencies with, and participation in, the Codex Alimentarius Commission's work. The SPS Agreement suggests that national regulations that are consistent with those of Codex meet its requirements in this regard. Finally, though capacity remains weak, standards development agencies in Nigeria endeavor to set standards that are based on scientific principles and evidence confirmed by laboratory analysis.

Capacity Building for Standards and Regulations Development

Introduction

Both the SPS and TBT Agreements obligate industrial WTO member countries to aid developing countries through the provision of technical assistance. The TBT Agreement specifically requires members to advise developing country members in terms of the preparation of technical regulations, the establishment of national standardizing bodies and participation in international standardizing bodies; and in the establishment of conformity assessment bodies, institutions, and legal framework that would enable them to fulfil the obligations of membership or participation. In the SPS Agreement, members agree to facilitate the provision of technical assistance to developing country members, through bilateral or relevant international arrangements, in the area of processing technologies, research and infrastructure; advice, credits, donations and grants for the purpose of seeking technical expertise, training and equipment; and the establishment of national regulatory bodies so that countries are able to adjust to, and comply with, SPS measures in their export markets. In addition, in cases in which substantial investments are required for an exporting developing country member to fulfil the SPS requirements of an importing member, the latter is expected to consider providing such technical assistance to the extent of permitting the developing country member to maintain and expand its market access opportunities for the product involved. It is in the context of these that donor-supported programs are evaluated below.

Table 3.13 Donor-Supported Program for Standards Capacity in SON

Donor Agency	Period	Focal Area	Implementing Agency	Committed Resources	Main Accomplishments
UNIDO	1994	Implementation of ISO 9000 standards	SON	Cost of staff training abroad	Exposed officers to the implementation of ISO 9000 standards
Swedish Govt./SON	1994	Standardization management and techniques	SON	–ditto–	Exposed officers to standardization management and techniques
Turkish Govt./SON	1994	Field of textiles processing and finishing of cotton textiles	SON	–ditto–	Exposed officers to textiles processing and finishing of cotton textiles
National Resources Institute, UK	1994	Laboratory methods for the analysis of nongrain starch staple food crops	SON	–ditto–	Exposed officers to analysis of nongrain starch staple food crops
SON/PTB	1997	Seminar on volume flow chart course	SON	–ditto–	Exposed officers to volume/flow chart
UNIDO	1972–1998	Establishment of laboratories and supply of laboratory equipment	SON	n.a.	Establishment of laboratories, supply of laboratory equipment
ISO/Swiss Government	1998	Awareness lecture for stakeholders from Nigeria, Senegal, Côte d'Ivoire, Guinea, Cameroon, and Liberia	SON	n.a.	ISO 14000 training and certification, exposed officers to the use of facilities on ground
UNDP/BSI	1998	Training of staff	SON	n.a.	Exposed officers to the use of facilities on ground
UNICEF	Ongoing	Vitamin A fortification	NAFDAC, SON, Manufacturers	Equipment used, clean up, sampling, HPLC	Exposed officers to the use of facilities on ground

Source: Standards Organisation of Nigeria, 2002.

Donor-Supported Programs for Standards Capacity in SON

Table 3.13 shows donor-supported programs for capacity building in regulatory standards in Nigeria. In SON, capacity building programs were commenced in 1972 by UNIDO, which provided assistance that comprised laboratory establishment and supply of laboratory equipment. This lasted up to 1998. Most of the other components of assistance are related to staff training. Thus, in 1994, selected members of staff were exposed to standardization management and techniques, textiles processing

and finishing of cotton textiles, analysis of nongrain starch staple food crops, and the implementation of ISO 9000 standards. In 1998, selected members of staff were further exposed to the use of facilities on ground as well as ISO 14000 training and certification. The assistance in the areas of implementation of ISO 9000 and ISO 14000 has enhanced Nigeria's capacity, as more firms in the country have been ISO certified since 1994. Available data, however, did not indicate that these firms are export firms, implying that more efforts need to be directed toward encouraging export-oriented small firms in food processing, textiles and garment industries, chemicals, plastics, bottles or glasses, among others to apply for ISO certification. There is also an ongoing program with the UNICEF in conjunction with NAFDAC under which equipment is being supplied for vitamin A fortification.

Donor-Supported Programs for Standards Capacity in NAFDAC

Donor-supported programs for resource and capacity building in NAFDAC are mainly from the International Atomic Energy Agency (IAEA) and UNICEF, both of which are sponsoring activities in the area of equipment supply (e.g., High Pressure Liquid Chromatography, HPLC), teaching analytical methods for the formulation of pesticides and determining pesticide residues as well as conducting mycotoxin research. UNICEF is currently facilitating a program of vitamin A fortification with SON, NAFDAC, and manufacturers as implementing units. NAFDAC is also discussing the possibility of collaborating with the United States Food and Drug Administration, Tuskegee University, USA, and the USAID to strengthen its activities. An important issue of note is that through the assistance from IAEA and UNICEF or Roche, NAFDAC is empowered to determine pesticide residues for exports. This is significant for many processed foods such as cocoa butter, cocoa paste, and yam powder, among others. It is also noteworthy that many of these assistance efforts

are provided by multilateral institutions while little or no assistance is given by trading partner countries as required by the SPS and TBT Agreements (see Table 3.14).

Donor-Supported Programs for Standards Capacity in PQS

The Food and Agricultural Organization, United Nations Development Program (UNDP), and the World Bank have been involved in the provision of post-entry facilities; establishment of PQS Training School for personnel development; procurement of laboratory equipment, vehicles, and office and residential buildings. An on-going program in the PQS, though sponsored through its annual allocation, and which will certainly fortify private capacities in implementing agricultural products standards, includes compilation of a checklist of plant pest in Nigeria, revision of current legislation, and evaluation and administration of phytosanitary capacity. The FOA or TCP program that is currently on ground is geared toward strengthening of PQS through the provision of modern technical equipment, computers, and accessories for Internet, insectary, and phytosanitary standards training (see Table 3.15).

The World Bank assistance that lasted between 1991 and 1997 is instructive. The assistance appears to have been packaged long before the SPS Agreement, though it extended beyond 1995. This suggests that the SPS Agreement was not part of World

Table 3.14 Donor-Supported Program for Standards Capacity in NAFDAC

Donor Agency	Period	Focal Area	Implementing Agency	Committed Resources	Main Accomplishments
IAEA	Ongoing	Capacity building, equipment	NAFDAC	HPLC, GC, Glass ware	Exposed officers to the use of facilities on ground
UNICEF	Ongoing	Vitamin A fortification	NAFDAC, SON, Manufacturers	Equipment used, clean up, sampling, HPLC	–ditto–
IAEA	1997 onward	Pesticide residues, exports (seafoods), pesticide formulation	NAFDAC	Equipment and cash	Research presentations aimed at validation of analytical methods
UNICEF/ Roche	n.a.	Mycotoxin research	NAFDAC	–ditto–	n.a.

Source: NAFDAC (2002).

Table 3.15 Donor-Supported Program for Standards Capacity in
Plant Quarantine Service (PQS).

Donor	Period	Focal Area	Implementing Agency	Resource Commitment	Main Accomplishment
FAO/ UNDP	1970–80	PQS Post-entry facilities set up; personnel development; establishment of PQS Training School	FMA/FDA	n.a.	Glass House, Phytotron, laboratories, office building, regional training school, training PQS personnel, training for OAU member countries
IBRD/ World Bank	1991–97	Personnel development; procurement of lab./G.H. equipment; vehicles and buildings (office/lab., and residence)	FDA/PQS supervised by World Bank/FMA	US$5.2 million	Staff development, provision of staff quarters and laboratories; purchase of vehicles; various equipment and institutional reform
FAO/TCP	2002 onward	Strengthening of PQS; computer and accessories for internet, insectary, and phytosanitary standards training	FAO/FMA	US$220,000	Expected to provide modern technical equipment, staff training on phytosanitary standards measures and insectary

Source: Plant Quarantine Service (2002).

Bank assistance. There was no new assistance package until 2002, seven years after the signing of the agreement.

Standards and Technical Regulations in Action in Nigeria under the WTO Obligations

Level of Awareness with International Standards

In Nigeria, the level of awareness of local firms and farmers with international standards can be described as inadequate though some elements of mixed results of awareness can be discerned. First, interactions with officers of SON, NAFDAC, and PQS provided the impression that there is little or no awareness of international standards among local

firms and farmers. In the case of PQS, publicity regarding its activities is at a very low level because of inadequate funding of its activities while there is also a very weak linkage between the agency and the Agricultural Development Programs (ADPs) in the country, which have direct contact with local farmers. In addition, there have been import rejections or refusals in destination countries without adequate explanation. The lack of full understanding of the relevance of standardization in business enhancement and market creation and sustainability as well as ignorance of national standards even in some cases account for the low level of awareness of local firms and farmers.

All the three organizations are gearing up toward imprinting indelibly on the consciousness of businesses about standards generally in Nigeria with many information- and communication-related activities to improve the status quo. The measures that have been taken and are currently adopted to improve the dissemination of information on these standards have emphasized creating awareness on national standards and good manufacturing practice. NAFDAC organized a series of workshops on food safety and quality focusing on hygienic practices, HACCP, and GMP. The agency collaborated with reputable drug companies to organize GMP seminars on drugs and with the WTO, whose staff were used as resource persons, to organize workshops and seminars on SPS and TBT.

NAFDAC enhances its information dissemination through technical or news publication, the print and electronic media using press releases, advertisements, interviews, talk shows, and consultative meetings with stakeholders, among others. SON, on its part, has generally improved its information dissemination also through technical or news publication including corporate briefs, paid advertisements, and interviews. In particular, many large firms that won SON's NIS Quality award generally advertise such an occasion but with a view to appealing to their clientele. This avenue generates some awareness about SON's activities but the reach of its impact is limited to the literate urban population. A related issue is the communique released at the end of the Stakeholder's Forum on "Product Competitiveness—the Way Forward" on 9 October 2001 during SON's Quality Week. The communique states, among others that (a) standards can be used to drive markets; (b) improving quality and the management of technological changes are the major vehicles of industrial growth with standardization as the driving force; and (c) standards being consensus based are subject to reviews based on stakeholders' inputs. In other words, SON has generally increased awareness about the need to consider standardization as a paramount requirement for industrialization. What is missing still is the need to accept standardization among the general population who purchase products and bear the health risks of substandard products.

According to the PQS, though inadequate funding has tended to critically hamper its drive to create public awareness of its activities, it is taking the cheapest route to advertise its activities. This route includes distribution of PQS information service and handbills, attendance of World Food Day and Agricultural Shows where information on its

activities is disseminated, and participation of PQS officials in seminars and workshops organized by other agencies. To buttress the negative impact of inadequate funding on its publicity drive, the last national workshop or seminar that the agency organized was as far back as 1994 during its PQS week, while an ambitious national workshop on IPPC and ISPM planned for 1999 to involve farmers, importers, exporters, and other stakeholders was not held.

Adoption of HACCP and ISO 9000

The status of the adoption of the Hazard Analysis and Critical Control Points (HACCP) and ISO 9000 in Nigeria is moderately impressive. For example, NAFDAC is quite comfortable with the application of HACCP and has assisted firms that are aware of its advantages to draw up their HACCP plans and continues to offer assistance when problems arise in the process of its implementation. SON on its part has continued to certify firms based on the ISO 9000 standards quality system. The first training program on ISO 9000 was held in November 1994 with 23 participants from large and reputable industries. By the end of 1994, only one company was able to obtain ISO 9000 Standards Certificate while the applications of three other companies were under processing and three firms were at the enquiries stage. According to SON (1997, p. 17), "the implementation of NIS ISO 9000 series of standards went smoothly within the year as many companies approached SON for assistance to certify the conformity of their quality management systems to the relevant requirements...."

Table 3.16 indicates that at the end of 1997 seven companies were ISO 9000 certified. The status of adoption of the ISO 9000 series across firms in Nigeria is also shown. Because the adoption is still very recent and had been slow, no adequate data can be used to compare the status and adoption patterns in different industries by size, market orientation, and ownership structure. While it has been more possible for large firms such as those shown in Table 3.16 to adopt the ISO 9000 standards quality system, small and medium companies face particular problems related to funding as well as the voluntary nature of the certification process. These problems are related to the degree of the awareness of the benefits that the adoption can generate in terms of efficient utilization of scarce resources,

Table 3.16 Status of Adoption of the ISO 9000 Series in Nigeria

Name of Company	Scope of Certification	Standard Type	Year of Award
International Computer (Nig.) Ltd.	Companywide	NIS ISO 9001	1994
NCR (Nig.) Plc.	Customer support services	NIS ISO 9002	1995
Mobil Oil Nig. Plc.	Manufacture and distribution of PJ and insecticides	NIS ISO 9002	1996
Agip Nigeria Plc.	Blending plants, Kaduna	NIS ISO 9002	1997
Mobil Oil Nig. Plc.	Manufacture and distribution of lubrication	NIS ISO 9002	1997
Lucky Fibres Nig. Ltd.	Manufacture and sale, Nobel carpet and rug	NIS ISO 9001	1997
Dunlop Nig. Plc.	Companywide	NIS ISO 9002	1997

Source: SON, *Annual Report* (1997).

reduction in materials waste arising from better production design, ensured international market access, and the enhancement of the company's image and credibility.

Adoption of ISO 9000 Standards and Economic Opportunities for the Poor

In principle, if the adoption of particular standards raises the cost of production and price then the economic opportunities of the poor may be hampered. Empirically, the scope of certification of companies in Table 3.16 shows that consumer products are not directly affected and by extension the poor as consumers are not affected. However, outputs of the oil firms and the tyre-manufacturing firm may affect consumers if the prices of those goods rose substantially post-ISO certification. Since prices of these commodities have been on the rise generally, a part of the increase can be attributed to certification and thus could have resulted in loss of consumer surplus. These products are also used as production inputs and the price rise noted would also contribute to a rise in the price of the final product for which they are purchased. Thus, for small firms whose main problem is working and investment capital, such input price increases can only lead to a decline in sales as demand drops as a result of the increased price of the final product.

Quality and Safety-Related Restricted Exports

There have been documented cases of bans and restrictions of export products from Nigeria in traditional markets, particularly the United Kingdom and United States. Investigations revealed, however, that the refusal at the destination points is because the exports do not carry evidence of certification from NAFDAC, SON, or PQS. This suggests that the refused consignments may not have met national and international standards in the first place before the exporters embarked on exporting them. Apart from goods that are injurious to human health, which require mandatory conformity assessment, presentation of other types of goods for conformity assessment is voluntary. Analysis of the types of goods involved in importing country refusals shows that a substantial proportion is in the food category but which do not have evidence of preshipment testing, which is supposed to be mandatory. Table 3.17 shows a list of plant interception notices sent from the United Kingdom in 2001/2002 on Nigeria's export. According to the table, there is no evidence of inspection at the point of departure, which was Lagos. Thus, the interceptions were because of the presence of pests in the consignments, which could have been detected during preshipment inspection, rather than the presence of a disease in the exporting country or changes in the overseas market rules or regulations.

Table 3.17 Plant Interception Notices from the United Kingdom in 2001/2002 on Export Plants from Nigeria Infested with Various Pests

S. No.	Date of Notice	Plant/Quantity	Pest Found	Exporter Address	Consignee Address	Evidence Inspection
1.	19/02/2001	Amaranthus sp. (14 boxes)	Helicoverpa armigera and Spoladea recurvalis	Seglarola (Nig.) Ltd. (No address)	Not stated	None
2.	17/04/2001	Cassava Manihot esculenta (20 kg)	Bemisia tabaci	Fresh Veg. Co. (No address)	Not stated	None
3.	20/04/2001	Chrysophyllum (5 kg)	Ceratitis anonae	Victor Onuekwusi, Lagos	Not stated	None
4.	24/04/2001	Chrysophyllum sp. (10 kg)	Pryalidae, Tortricidae and Stictococcus sjostedti	Mrs. Oregubo (No address)	Not stated	None
5.	2/01/2002	Amaranthus sp. (17 NMB boxes)	Spodoptera Littoralis	Kiverlin Coy (No address)	Not stated	None
6.	24/01/2002	Amaranthus sp. (5 boxes)	Spoladea recurvalis	President Cargo Ltd. (No address)	Not stated	None
7.	31/01/2002	Cassava Manihot esculenta (3 boxes)	Bemisia tabaci	Millanivic Ent. NG. (No address)	Mrs. Clark	None
8.	25/02/2001	Amaranthus sp. (30 boxes)	Sapentine leaf miner Liriomyza sativae	Kilverlyn Co. Ltd., 19 Isolo Way, Ajao Estate, Lagos	Not stated	None
9.	7/03/2002	(Soko/Green) Celosia argentea Amaranthus sp. (39 baskets)	Spoladea recurvalis	Kiverlin Co. Ltd. (No address)	Not stated	None
		(Ugu) Telfairia occidentalis (1 basket)	Bemisia tabaci and Trialeurodes ricini	–do–	Not stated	None
		(Ewedu) Corchorus olitorius (1 basket)	Bemisia tabaci	–do–	Not stated	None
10.	15/03/2002	(Ewedu) Corchorus sp. (10 kg)	Bemisia tabaci	Kiverlyn Co. Ltd. (No address)	Not stated	None
		(Soko/Green) Celosia (10 kg, 1 box)	Spoladea recurvalis	–do–	–do–	–do–
		(Ugu) Telfairia occidentalis (66 boxes)	Trialeurodes vicini and Bemisia tabaci	–do–	–do–	–do–
11.	27/03/2002	Amaranthus sp. Celosia sp. Telfairia sp. Unknown leaves Vernonia sp. (80 kg)	Aleurodes disperses, Bemisia tabaci, Spoladea recurvalis, Trialeurodes ricini, Phenococcus sp., Aleurodicinae whitefly and another non-indigenous whitefly	V. Iroagbu, Harry Agency, Lagos, (No address)	–do–	–do–
		(Ewedu) Corchorus sp. Ugu Telfairia sp. (110 kg)	Bemisia tabaci and Trialeurodes ricini	Fibodis Nig. Ltd., Hajj Camp, Ikeja, Nigeria	–do–	–do–

Source: PQS (2002).

No exporter's address was given though the consignment was exported from Lagos through MMIA. Many of the consignments refused entry into the United Kingdom shown in the above table were agricultural goods. At least 15 kg of *Chrysophyllum*, 66 boxes of *Amaranthus sp.*, 20 kg of cassava *Manihot esculenta*, 39 baskets of *Celosia*, 66 boxes, apart from 110 kg, of *Telfairia sp*, among others, were refused entry into the United Kingdom in 2001/2002. These appear to be small but have had a large negative impact on the expected incomes of the plant exporters.

The United States Food and Drug Administration refused entry into the United States of both agricultural or raw and value-added products on standard or quality or safety grounds though there is no evidence that these restrictions have helped to confine the concerned industry to the exports of raw materials. This is because of the fact that refusals were in respect of small exporters. The range of products and the reason for refusal into the United States are shown in Table 3.18. Recall that SPS measures are designed to protect (a) humans or animals from risks arising from additives, contaminants, toxins, or disease-causing organisms in food, or disease carried by plants and animals; (b) plant and animal life from pests, diseases, or disease-causing organisms; and an importing country from the entry, establishment, or spread of pests; whereas technical regulations are measures designed to promote the provision of information to aid the control of human diseases, and the protection from human diseases, and the protection of human, animal, and plant life. Then, analyzing the structure of refusals in Table 3.18 revealed that 15 of the measures are technical regulations while 10 are SPS measures.

In all, there were 80 refusals between July 2001 and May 2002. Table 3.19 also lists the reasons for the refusals of these export products. They range from filth, misleading labeling, to preparation and packaging under unsanitary conditions, unsafe color additive, among others. About 47.4 percent of refusals involved new drugs without approved new drug application while 5.2 percent of refusals were based on the reason that product label did not contain accurate statements of contents such as weight, measure, or numerical count. Many export products were refused entry because they were either prescription drugs manufactured in the United States and reimported without authorization; misbranded; did not bear name and place of business of manufacturer, packer or distributor; or their

manufacturer did not file information on the scheduled process. In addition, 22.3 percent of refusals relate to enforcing SPS measures including failure of manufacturer to file information on the scheduled process, unsanitary manufacturing, processing, and packing, among others.

SPS-Induced Import Bans in Nigeria

Cases of explicit import ban informed by government policy statements are uncommon, perhaps because there are agencies established to implement SPS and TBT-related work in the country. These agencies have imposed bans and indeed meted out punishments in terms of the destruction of the concerned consignments. Table 3.20 shows substandard or nonconforming articles intercepted at the Nigerian ports between 1994 and 1997. Some of these imports were intercepted for not conforming to either SPS measures or technical regulations. The characteristic process of interception is preceded by categorization of such goods into those that meet noncritical conformity parameters and those that do not. The latter are seized and destroyed while for the former the importers are usually notified of the corrective measures that can be undertaken and issued warning to desist from such future importation. For these kinds of products, a notification in terms of time required to comply does not arise because the refusals simply did not meet existing international standards.

According to the TBT Agreement, members will ensure that technical regulations will be based on relevant international standards, which if not in existence, will be published as a notice in a publication at an early appropriate stage in a manner that enables interested members to become acquainted with it, and allows reasonable time for other members to comment on it. Furthermore, except in cases of safety, health, environmental protection, or national security urgencies, members are allowed a reasonable interval between the publication and entry into force of technical regulations for producers in exporting member countries, particularly developing country members, to adapt their product or methods of production to these requirements. Thus, given that about six months lapsed before the implementation of the bans, a reasonable time is deemed to have been allowed for the exporting country to adjust to the regulations though there is no evidence that Nigeria informed the TBT Committee of the regulations. While this is true, it is

Table 3.18 Nigerian Exports Refused Entry into the United States

S. No.	No. of Refusals	Refusal Date	Product Description	Reason for Refusal	Source/ Exporter
1.	4	July 2001	Smoked fish; virgin anti-spot cream; virgin hair fertilizer; mild flower hair medicine	MFR INSAN, NOT LISTED UNAPPROVED, NOT LISTED UNAPPROVED, NOT LISTED UNAPPROVED	Lagos, Lagos, Lagos Lagos
2.	2	August 2001	Bean flour; Amoxil	FILTHY; AGR RX	Lagos, Enugu
3.	5	September 2001	Pharmaceutical drugs; herbal medicine; herbal soap	UNAPPROVED; UNAPPROVED; DIRECTIONS; SCTIC LBLG; AGR RX	Lagos, Lagos Lagos Lagos Lagos
4.	1	November 2001	Vitamins	FALSE	Lagos
5.	2	December 2001	Woodward's Gripe Water; herbs	UNAPPROVED LACKS FIRM	Ogun state Ogun state
6.	38	January 2002	35 refusals for cosmetics; unknown product (beige powdery cubes); unknown product (leafy dried); whole bulb with roots	UNAPPROVED (35); LIST INGRE, LACKS FIRM, USUAL NAME, LABELING; FALSE, LACKS FIRM, USUAL NAME, LABELING; FALSE, LACKS FIRM, USUAL NAME, LABELING	
7.	5	February 2002	Pharm. Drugs; sardines; beans; zennat; pharm. Drug	AGR RX UNAPPROVED; NO PROCESS NEEDS FCE NO PROCESS; UNAPPROVED; AGR RX	Lagos Lagos Lagos Lagos Lagos
8.	6	March 2002	Palm juice; Maggi cube broth; skin toning cream; Top gel cream, fashion fair cream; dry cray fish;	LIST INGRE; FILTHY; LACKS N/C; JUICE percent; NUTRIT LBL; LACKS N/C; NUTRIT LBL; NOT LISTED;...; INSANITARY, LABELING.	Lagos Lagos Lagos Lagos Lagos Lagos
9.	10	April 2002	Soap; sardines; pharm. drugs	UNAPPROVED; NEEDS FCE; UNAPPROVED	Lagos; Lagos; Benin
10.	7	May 2002	Malt drinks; Emu Nigerian palm juice; Crevette–shrimp seasoning; tomato puree and peppers; Full cream powdered milk; methyl salicylate; glucose D with calcium and vitamin D	LACKS N/C, NUTRIT LBL; LIST INGR, NO PROCESS; UNSAFE COL, LACKS N/C; LACKS N/C, NO PROCESS; NO PERMIT, LIST INGR; DR QUALITC; POISON PKG, DR QUALITC	Lagos; Lagos; Lagos; Lagos; Lagos; Lagos

Source: http://www.fda.gov/ora/oasis/5/ora/ora_oasis_c_ng.html
Key to reasons: see Table 3.19.

Table 3.19 Structure of Regulatory Standards

Refusal Reasons Decoded	Types of Standard
AGR RX: prescription drug manufactured in the United States reimported without authorization	TBT
DIRECTIONS: Lack adequate directions for use	TBT
DR QUALITY: Adulteration—Quality declines below recognized or purported standard	TBT, SPS
FALSE: False or misleading labeling	TBT
FILTHY: Consists of filthy, putrid, or decomposed substance and unfit for food	SPS
INSANITARY: Article prepared, packed, or held under insanitary conditions and injurious to health	SPS
JUICE percent: Beverage not containing information on the percentage of fruit or vegetable juice	TBT
LABELING: Misbranding regarding placement, form, and contents statement	TBT
LACKS FIRM: Package does not bear name and place of business of manufacturer, packer, or distributor	TBT
LACKS N/C: Label does not contain accurate statements of quantity of contents such as weight, measure, or numerical count	TBT
LIST INGRE: Food derived from two or more ingredients, the common names of which the label does not show	TBT, SPS
MFR INSAN: Insanitary manufacturing, processing, and packing	SPS
NEEDS FCE: Manufacturer not registered as low-acid canned food or acidified food manufacturer	SPS
NO PERMIT: Article is milk or cream not subject to a valid permit	SPS
NO PROCESS: Manufacturer did not file information on scheduled process	SPS
NOT LISTED: Drug or device not included in list required	TBT
NUTRIT LBL: Labeling fails to bear required nutrition information	TBT
POISON PKG: Drug whose packaging and labeling is in violation of an applicable regulation	TBT
SCTIC LBLG: labeling failed to comply with cosmetics labeling requirements	TBT
UNAPPROVED: New drug without an approved new drug application	TBT
UNSAFE COL: Article is or contains a color additive that is unsafe according to requirements	SPS
USUAL NAME: Label does not bear the common or usual name of the food	TBT

Source: Derived from Table 3.22.

Table 3.20 Interceptions at Nigerian Ports by SON

	1994			1997		
Article	Amount (₦ million)	Type of Measure	Article	Amount (₦ million)	Type of Measure
4 containers of electric cables	7	TBT	2 containers of filament lamps	n.a.	TBT
4 containers of used car tyres	4.2	TBT	2 containers of used tyres	n.a.	TBT
3 containers of Geisha canned fish	1.8	SPS	1 container of fruit drink	n.a.	SPS
			1 container of electric cables	n.a.	TBT
			1 container of electric pressing iron	n.a.	TBT
			2 containers of biscuits	n.a.	SPS

Source: SON *Annual Report* (1994, 1997).

noteworthy that since most of the imported articles have been scientifically certified as environmentally unfriendly and obsolete in exporting countries, such regulations in Nigeria may not be viewed as restrictions to international trade that do not meet international norms and may not require notification to the TBT committee.

Problems and Opportunities of Implementing TBT and SPS Agreements

There are many problems associated with the implementation of WTO obligations in the TBT and SPS Agreements. The first of these is the level of poverty in the country. In principle, high-income countries tend to consume high-standard goods because quality products are normal goods. The higher the income, the higher the quantity of quality goods that will be demanded. Therefore, it is difficult to insist on a high level of standards for many goods in Nigeria because of the pervasive poverty in the country. Second, with the theoretical prediction of a positive association between costs and increase in quality, low-income countries like Nigeria trade off quality for low-priced goods. Third, the generally low level of standards of uncertified products implies that they cannot be exported to high-income industrial countries unless they are upgraded, a compliance task that requires more resources in terms of variable and fixed costs.

Given an adequate awareness and assistance program, however, Nigeria's small producers in particular can meet international standards and create and maintain market access in industrial countries. The opportunity to do so is enhanced by the recognition of such international standards as the ISO, Codex, IPPC, and IEC by the WTO with whom Nigeria, through SON, NAFDAC, and PQS, actively collaborates. Indeed, the regulatory agencies in Nigeria are certain that products certified by them easily access the markets in industrial countries. The aspect of the SPS and TBT Agreements that continues to pose problems is the requirement that national standards can be higher than international standards if it is scientifically justifiable and notified promptly to all parties concerned. This is problematic because of an inadequate number of scientific personnel and obsolete scientific equipment in the standards agencies as the country cannot realistically demonstrate, based on scientific evaluation, the need for higher-than-normal standards, even

when it has the opportunity to comment on the new standards as stipulated by the agreements.

It is in light of this that an assessment of the programs to assist in the implementation of WTO obligations and exercise of rights in Nigeria is attempted here. The agreements obligate trading partner countries, in particular, to strengthen developing exporting partner countries such as Nigeria in areas of capacity and resources to be able to maintain or even increase their exports to the industrial countries. The industrial trading partner countries are obliged to provide assistance in the area of processing technologies, research and infrastructure; advice, credits, donations; and grants for seeking technical expertise, training, and equipment; and the establishment of national regulatory bodies. Many of the programs to assist in implementation of WTO obligations and exercise of rights in Nigeria, especially since 1995, have been supported by multilateral institutions such as the UNDP, UNICEF, UNIDO, IAEA, FAO and so on Trading partner countries have been minimally involved in technical assistance, a clear negation of their obligation under the SPS and TBT Agreements. Furthermore, the issue of funding is a serious constraint in the implementation of SPS and TBT Agreements in Nigeria given the number of activities required to effectively participate in the standards setting process.

Opportunities for Differentiation

Differentiation of products to achieve competitive advantage by Nigerian exporters is not a common occurrence in Nigeria. Rather, this development is widespread in the importation business where product differentiation, albeit negative in terms of their substandard nature, is well developed. Such a phenomenon is easily established in Nigeria, especially in respect of importation and sale of electronic and electrical goods. Many of these goods carry deceptive labeling about their worth and carry lower but not necessarily cheap prices. Indeed, many substandard goods have been imported as imitations of the original: Dhilips pressing irons instead of Phillips; SUNNY Radios instead of SONY, among others. The phenomenon is also widespread in the pharmaceutical market where many drugs carry deceptive labels or whose purported contents are about 10 percent of the requirements. NAFDAC is currently ensuring that overseas manufacturers are inspected to establish their integrity based on GMP.

Relevance of SPS to the Private Sector

Introduction

In spite of the sustained drive toward a global free trade economy in which all trade barriers across countries would be eliminated, the general concern for the health and well-being of plants, animals and humans has made sanitary and phytosanitary standards (SPS) an important issue in global trade. More so, because it is capable of inhibiting free trade flows among trading countries. Thus, through the negotiation framework of the WTO, an agreement on what should constitute international standards by all member countries so as to avoid duplication of standard rules has been adopted. The need to assess and conform to these international standards by African firms, industries, and farmers has posed a stringent challenge. In enforcing international standards, firms, industries, and farmers are expected to comply through assessment, audits, certification, and traceability. This is a major challenge for Africa's continued market access in terms of its prohibitive cost implications for the new or small exporter.

This section documents the experience of firms' and farmers' efforts at complying with standards requirements in the process of accessing export markets on commodity sector basis. The commodity sectors covered are horticulture; food and beverages; cocoa and cocoa products; textiles and clothing, as well as fish and fishery products.

Commodity Case Study

The commodity sectors selected for analysis in this study was informed by their importance as export products. In 1998, crude petroleum contributed about 96.1 percent of the country's export. In the same year, the main agricultural products contributed 2.2 percent, manufactured exports contributed 0.1 percent, processed agricultural products 1.6 percent, while textiles contributed nothing.

Though crude petroleum is the leading export commodity, the country remains one of the richly blessed countries in agriculture in sub-Saharan Africa with great potential for exports. In fact, agricultural and agroprocessed products together contributed 3.8 percent to export, making it the second largest leading export sector. This is followed by manufactured exports. The agricultural sector has the potential of overtaking the oil sector as the largest export commodity if the sector is properly developed. Crude oil was not explicitly considered because it was not part of the TOR, even though the issue of standards compliance in the sector has been a "hot" political and environmental issue in the country. In the agricultural sector, we considered cocoa and cocoa products, which are the main agricultural exports. Horticulture, and fish and fishery products were selected because of their vast export potential. Food and beverages, and textiles and clothing subsectors were selected in the manufacturing sector for a similar reason of potential export importance.

Horticulture. Horticulture has three subcommodities, namely floriculture (covering flowers), phonology (fruits and medicinal plants), and honorenculture (vegetable plants). Floriculture and cut flowers are increasingly becoming an important commodity sector in the international market. Important developing country exporters include Columbia, Kenya, Ecuador, Thailand, Zimbabwe, Costa Rica, and South Africa. The world market for this product is valued at about US$8 billion. Flowers account for about half this trade and indoor plants have a share of 35 percent, while foliage and bulbs contributes about 7.5 percent. The main market is the EU, while the growing market includes United States, Japan, and Switzerland. In West Africa, Cote d'Ivoire, Ghana, and Cameroon are known to be exporting between 3 and 10 percent to the European Union (see Table 3.21).

From the preceding table, total floriculture export from Cote d'Ivoire and Cameroon to the EU

Table 3.21 Floricultural Exports from Cote d'Ivoire and Cameroon to EU Markets

Products	Values (in thousands)	
	Cote d'Ivoire	Cameroon
Cut flowers	2,182	724
Cut foliage	229	320
Cuttings	923	0
Total floriculture	3,334	1,024

Source: COLE ACP.

market accounts for US$4.4 million. Nigeria has yet to break into this market in West Africa, even though it has fertile soil to grow the best species in the temperate region of Jos Plateau. Indeed, there have been at least three export-oriented floricultural enterprises in Nigeria that have failed. The chrysanthemums and palm plants experiment from around Lagos and a Rose Nursery in Jos also failed. The failure was attributed to dearth of skilled operators who are able to adopt new crop production techniques and grow export quality products. Production was also affected by the lack of adequate packinghouse facilities for post-harvest handling, treatment, and packing for export. Some of the producers also complained of the inability to comply with processing standards because of lack of technical expertise and financial resources.

The market for medicinal plants is rapidly growing around the world. In 1999, the market was worth US$19.4 billion and comprised markets in North America (US$4.0 billion), Europe (US$6.7 billion), Asia (US$5.1 billion), Japan (US$2.2 billion), and the rest of the world (US$1.4 billion). The common sub-Saharan medicinal plant used as a source of natural medicine is *Prunus africana*. Several others include Griffonia, Vocanga, and the various Aloes. The *Prunus african's* bark is commonly sought after by Italian companies from Madagascar. Some other European companies import processed or unprocessed bark from Cameroon, Kenya, Uganda, and Zaire. Extracts in tablets or capsules are marketed under two main trade names: "Tradman" produced by Laboratories Debat in France and "Pygenie" produced by Indena Spa in Italy.

In West Africa, the export market for medicinal plants is dominated by Cameroon. As importers seek larger quantities of bark, they put pressure on the harvesters and ignore sustainable practices of harvesting it. Thus, it has been reported that in Cameroon alone, close to 80 percent of mature trees die as result of poor harvesting techniques. This provides an opportunity for Nigeria, which has the product in abundance, though it is owned by small holders around the Mambilla Plateau. Given the versatility of this product and its high demand, establishment of an industry involving propagating elite cultivars with a high content of active ingredients in the bark and the establishment of plantations of *Prunus africana* in the Mambilla Plateau would certainly provide export opportunities in this commodity sector. According to the Chemonics/USAID report (2002), a number of constraints have to be overcome to meet the needs of the industry. These constraints are standards-related. They are the need to move away from wild harvesting to managed cultivation for neat products, delivery of full traceability on raw material from origin, improvement of post-harvest system through introduction and implementation of simple but important improved technologies (drying, storage, handling, sampling procedure and so on), and the development and implementation of quality standards for the industry.

The production and processing of vegetables for export is not well developed in Nigeria as in Israel, North Africa, East Africa, South Africa, and Ghana from West Africa which export mostly to European markets. In Nigeria, an attempt was made in the early 1980s and early 1990s by a farm in the South of Kano to grow Mange tout pees for export. The farm also diversified into a range of other products, including baby corn, papaya, passion fruit, chilli peppers, and okra. The weather conditions in the area did not allow for more than three months of production in a year. Thus the venture was discontinued. The Jos Plateau area offers a veritable opportunity for vegetable production as the weather condition is regarded as superior because of its high altitude. It is believed that the weather at Jos area can support a wider range of products such as beans and other exotic vegetables (Asian vegetables, melons such as *galia* and *chanretaris*) over a longer period. Table 3.22 shows a list of exportable horticultural crops grown in Nigeria.

Table 3.22 Exportable Horticultural Crops Grown in Nigeria

Fruits	Vegetables	Spices	Ornamental
Banana	Okra	Occium	Heliconia sp
Mango	Roselle	Xylopia	Orchids
Pawpaw	Fluted pumpkin	Parkia	Cycads
Shaddock	Bitter leaf	Garlic	Roses
Pineapple	Onion	Pipermgrum	Aloe

Source: One-day Stakeholder Workshop, September 2002.

The vegetable subsector faces problems with post-harvest handling facilities such as cold storage, rollabeds, forklifts, trucks, and transportation. These problems affect the quality and standards of vegetables produced for exports.

The horticulture sector generally faces certain standards-related constraints, which have hindered small holders and large farmers from meeting international standards. These include nonavailability of packing houses, which is a basic requirement for moving, handling, processing, quality maintenance, and providing the required temperature for the product between inter-land harvest point and the port; nonavailability of required technical information needed to upgrade products to international standards; and a general lack of awareness of specific or required international standards to be met by producers. These constraints are, however, largely because of the existing gap between the government and private regulatory agencies and the farmers. Another important constraint is the nature of the products in the commodity subsector, which are highly perishable within a short period of time. The limited time between harvest and delivery to the final consumer at the export destination often greatly affects the quality of the product. Maintaining the right quality that meets international standards requires modern processing techniques, which are presently not available in the country.

The report of the One-Day Stakeholder Workshop (2002) indicates that the cost of compliance by producers in this commodity subsector is highly prohibitive. It was estimated that at least ₦682.5 million would be required to set up a modern processing unit to handle post-harvest activities and delivery at export destination. This amounts to more than 75 percent of the cost outlay for a 50-acre plantation.

To improve the method of production to meet international standards, participants at the One-Day Stakeholder Workshop recommend that the horticultural sector would require technical assistance from relevant agencies and regulatory bodies within the country in the area of up-to-date information on international standards requirement; capacity building through training and workshops; building of laboratories; and adopting relevant technologies to upgrade the current state of art in the commodity sector.

It was suggested at the workshop that to close the standards gap in the commodity sector, foreign partnership through joint ventures should be encouraged. There should be participation in international trade fairs to enhance their knowledge about how foreign counterparts handle such products meant for international markets and in international meetings, especially those that serve as the forum for setting international standards. Such participation, it was suggested, will provide opportunities to influence decisions in setting international standards as well as raising the level of awareness. Provision of legislative support is also necessary ensure proper coding of products and minimal delays of consignments in transit by customs and produce inspectors.

It was, however, difficult to identify specific cost for the suggested actions as the participants at the workshop felt that most of these activities fell directly under government and private agencies with possible support from relevant international agencies. About 30 percent of the production cost was suggested as the cost of compliance to bridge the standards gap in this commodity sector.

Food and Beverages. That the private sector's response to international standards is closely associated with the firm or farm's size, entrepreneurial skills, prominence of foreign ownership or long-standing strategic business ties and historical exposure of market or consumer pressures are true in the food and beverages sector. The summary statistics of the export survey on Nigeria and the One-Day Stakeholder Workshop (2002) on standards and quality of exports clearly demonstrate this. In Nigeria, the main players in the food and beverages sector are the multinational corporations such as the Unilever Nigeria Ltd. and Cadbury Nigeria Plc. The only indigenous company operating at a scale close to the first two giants mentioned earlier is the Doying Group of Companies. All other firms in the sector are small and medium producers. Unilever Nigeria Ltd. controls more than 65 percent of the export to neighboring West African countries, followed by Cadbury and the Doying Group. The first two companies, being multinationals, do not have the problem of complying with product standards as they simply ensure conformity with their parent companies in Europe. Interestingly, the only indigenous company operating close to the scale of the multinationals also does not have problem with standards with regards to product quality because it makes use of foreign technical expertise. However, the three companies face problems with product packaging standards.

From the summary statistics on Nigeria's export survey on standards compliance, the processed food

Table 3.23 Technical Requirements and Exports to EU and U.S. Markets

Processed Food and Food Products	European Union					United States				
	NI	SI	I	VI	NA	NI	SI	I	VI	NA
Performance	0	0	0	1	0	0	0	0	1	0
Product quality	0	0	0	1	0	0	0	0	1	0
Testing and certification	0	0	0	1	0	0	0	0	1	0
Consumer safety	0	0	0	1	0	0	0	0	1	0
Labeling	0	0	0	1	0	0	0	0	1	0
Health and environment	0	0	0	1	0	0	0	0	1	0

NI = Not important,　VI = Very important,
SI = Somehow important,　NA = Not available,
I = Important.
Source: World Bank Export Survey for Nigeria (2002).

and food products showed that compliance with technical requirements in the area of performance, product quality, testing and certification, consumer safety, labeling, and health and environment, is crucial for their ability to increase exports to the EU and U.S. markets (see Table 3.23).

To improve the quality of exports firms in the food and food products according to the World Bank export survey would require about 1–10 percent of the total investment to acquire additional plant or equipment and a one-time product redesign. No further investment is required for product redesign for each export market, no additional labor for production, no additional labor for certification and testing, and decreased labor. The processed food sector does not face rejection because of conformity certificates issued in Nigeria by the customs authorities of their export destinations. This is largely because of their compliance with the standards of operation through their parent companies. In meeting both domestic and foreign tech-

nical requirements, operators in the processed food and beverages sector observed minor duplication, which leads to an average of 5 percent increase in overall testing costs. In the export markets, the food and beverages sector also witnesses minor duplication in testing for multiple foreign requirements. So far, the domestic regulations in the food and beverages sector remain aligned with recognized international standards, which are mostly accepted in the EU, U.S., and Japanese markets (see Table 3.24).

However, as it has been noted, the food and beverages sector in Nigeria faces constraints in packaging because there are insufficient packaging companies in Nigeria that meet international packaging standards. This is the main problem for Unilever Nigeria Ltd. It was observed at the One-Day Stakeholder's Workshop that the cost outlay for meeting international standards in this sector is very high leading to high product price. This also creates difficulties for domestic consumers because meeting international standards leads to high product price,

Table 3.24 Approximate Cost of Compliance as a Percentage of Total Investment

Processed Food and Food Products	1–10%	11–25%	26–50%	51–75%	76–100%	>100%
Additional plant or equipment	1	0	0	0	0	0
One-time product redesign	1	0	0	0	0	0
Product redesign for each export market	0	0	0	0	0	0
Additional labor for production	0	0	0	0	0	0
Additional labor for certification and testing	0	0	0	0	0	0
Decreased labor	0	0	0	0	0	0

Source: World Bank Export Survey for Nigeria (2002).

which domestic consumers cannot afford because of low income. Producing to meeting international standards for export markets and satisfying domestic consumers pose a serious challenge to operators in this sector. A related problem is the need to harmonize international standards with the culture of the people. For instance, most domestic consumers prefer a salty margarine, which does not meet international standards.

It was estimated that to meet the packaging required by international standards would cost about ₦150 million. The level of awareness of technical assistance to bridge the standards gap is low among the small and medium enterprises in the sector. However, this level is high for multinationals, such as Unilever, and they rely more on the technical assistance from their parent companies located mostly in Europe and the United States. Other operators in the sector reported that international technical assistance to close the standards gap comes mostly from UNIDO, UNICEF, and the World Bank, among others. The Standards Organization of Nigeria provides local technical assistance. At the workshop, it was suggested that to bridge the standards gap in the sector there is the need for awareness workshops for stakeholders, most especially, the quality control officers in the various organizations; retraining of quality control officers; and financial assistance from the government for procuring necessary equipment and machines. On the cost of implementing compliance process, it was agreed that putting a value for the implementation of compliance, process by process, is very difficult without a detailed process evaluation because of its multifaceted nature. An estimate of ₦750 million

is suggested to be modest for the food and beverages industry to comply with international standards.

Cocoa and Cocoa Products. The figures of the Federal Office of Statistics on Nigerian exports show that cocoa and cocoa products are the leading export commodities and the largest foreign exchange earner for the country after crude oil (see Table 3.25).

It is evident from the table that crude petroleum has consistently maintained the lead, contributing between 95 and 98 percent to the country's exports between 1993 and 1997. This is followed by cocoa and cocoa products, though they are far behind petroleum and have a fluctuating performance. The dwindling fortune of cocoa and cocoa products is the result of the "Dutch disease syndrome" being witnessed in the oil sector. This notwithstanding, the cocoa and cocoa products sector still has a high potential as a major commodity export.

In the cocoa and cocoa products sector, the key constraints were induced by the economic policy reforms of 1986, generally know as the Structural Adjustment Program (SAP). The liberalization component of the program had serious adverse effects on the quality and standard compliance by cocoa producers and exporters. The general consensus during the workshop was that before the liberalization of 1986, there was the Cocoa Commodity Board that ensured that all the cocoa produced conformed to the specified international standards. There were various standard control measures to ensure better quality for export. Such controls include inspection by a produce warden, supervised store keeping, thorough examination of various levels from the farm to the ports, and certification was made in such a

Table 3.25 Percentage Contribution of Major Nigerian Commodity Export

Commodity	1993	1994	1995	1996	1997
Cocoa and cocoa products	2.08	6.59	1.40	9.83	0.08
Coffee	0.01	0.20	0.002	0.01	n.a.
Palm and palm products	0.01	0.23	0.03	0.16	0.02
Rubber and rubber products	0.93	1.24	0.61	1.32	0.03
Crustaceans and Molluses fresh and frozen	0.31	2.82	0.31	0.16	0.02
Crude petroleum oil	96.65	88.34	97.65	96.29	98.29
Automative gas oil	n.a.	n.a.	n.a.	0.91	1.52
Tin ore and Cumlatraty	0.04	n.a.	n.a.	0.00	0.01
Hide and skin	0.01	0.45	0.00	0.07	0.03

Source: Computed from FOS Annual Abstract of Statistics (1998).

manner that references could be made to whoever approved the product at different stages. Shortly after the liberalization policy was introduced in 1986, the Cocoa Commodity Board that guaranteed quality and standard compliance by farmers and marketers was scrapped. This was done without a replacement with any effective mechanism to assume the role of the commodity board to ensure quality and standard of cocoa products for the international market. The export of cocoa was taken over by unscrupulous private exporters who cared little for quality. Thus, for the first time, Nigerian cocoa, which always competed with Brazilian cocoa for the first position in the international market, was routinely rejected because of low quality. The factors that were responsible for low quality were the preliberalization standard and quality control system were no longer strictly adhered to by the private exporters that invaded the market, the rising cost of chemicals as a result of exchange rate depreciation and deregulation of the exchange rate as part of SAP; the removal of subsidy on chemical inputs; nonavailability of high-quality seedlings, and where they were available, they were very expensive unlike the preliberalization period when there was easy access to improved seedlings; and team grading, the pre-port and postinspection process is no longer well supervised and is regularly by-passed. The current poor quality and standard compliance in the cocoa commodity sector can be largely blamed on the liberalization policy component of the International Monetary Fund imposed Structural Adjustment Program. The policy largely disrupted the chance for cocoa production from which it has not recovered till now.

Some cocoa-producing states of the Federation reacted to the unpleasant development by enacting produce laws or edicts to streamline the operations of the private entrepreneurs in the produce trade and to prescribe legal sanctions for noncompliance with the quality standards. For instance, Oyo State, which is one of the leading producer of cocoa, took the following initiatives: introduced the Inspection Edict (1987); established three commodity companies in 1999; organized a conference of commissioners of 13 cocoa-producing states to fashion out control systems; adopted a standard and universal grading system; formed a universal marketing system, and registered produce stores and merchants. Officials of the State Produce Inspection Service continue to perform the functions of primary grading and evacuation check-testing. With the removal of what was

known as "Port Organization," which was established before 1986, the officials of the Federal Produce Inspection Service (FPIS) took over such other quality control and certification functions, arrival check-test, supervision of private warehouse operators at the ports, and preshipment tests.

In recent times, the Federal Ministry of Commerce, with which the Federal Produce Inspection Service is associated, has been making renewed efforts at ensuring that items of produce entering the export market and those meant for domestic industrial processing comply with acceptable quality standards. The Federal authorities have continued to enlist the participation and cooperation of the State Produce Inspection Services in this crusade of presenting the best quality produce to the export market.

The workshop could not provide an estimate for what it would cost to comply, but listed the areas requiring inputs to meet international quality standards. The main item of expenditure is fumigation. The fumigation exercise required for standard or quality is very expensive and mostly unaffordable for small holders and processors, who provide the bulk of the output in the cocoa and cocoa product commodity sector. Under the defunct Marketing Board there was a kind of assistance to reduce farmers' cost of fumigation. Other assistance includes grading, clearing, storage tools, and store maintenance; appropriate modern farm implements such as sprayers, harvesters, dryers, weighing and storage equipment; high-quality seedling: and training of inspection officers at the different stages of cocoa processing.

It was strongly suggested that to ensure better compliance with international standards in the cocoa commodity sector, there is need for the reintroduction of the pre-1986 practice in which the commodity board maintained control over the cocoa exports. Indeed, the Nigerian government has initiated steps in this direction. The state, in conjunction with the federal government plan to raise ₦1.5 billion to establish a three-commodity board in each state, which will be managed by the farmers themselves.

Textile and Clothing. The textile and clothing industry in Nigeria has been a vibrant sector in the manufacturing industry. There were 46 firms in the sector that engage in spinning, weaving, and finishing, eight engaged in made-up textiles except apparel, and nine knitting mills in 1989. In 1994, the sector accounted for about 15.4 percent of manufacturing value added, 42 percent of the total employment in manufacturing industry, and ₦ 14.3 billion in output. The sector did well in the 1960s with a cumulative average growth rate of 12.5 percent in the 1970s. The sector began to witness a decline in growth rate in the 1980s largely because of the general neglect of the agricultural sector with the ascendancy of crude petroleum exploration as the leading export commodity. This affected cotton production, which is an important input in textile production. When the economic recession of the early 1980s, induced by the collapse of the international crude oil price, occurred, the attendant foreign exchange scarcity leading to import licensing greatly affected the textile sector as it could not obtain foreign exchange to import cotton yarn and this resulted in capacity under utilization in the industry. The cumulative textile production index, which was 100 in 1972, declined from 427.1 in 1982 to 171.1 in 1984, using the 1985 production index as base year. The index declined further to 118.0 percent in 1990, 92.1 percent in 1994, rose marginally to 94.5 percent in 1998, and declined again to 92.3 percent in 2000. The dwindling fortune of the textile and clothing industry since the early 1980s was aggravated by the trade liberalization policy of the Structural Adjustment Program (SAP). The sector is generally acknowledged as the most affected by the liberalization policy and inconsistent government policies toward processed exports. In addition to the general problems that the manufacturing industry faces, such as dumping, devaluation of the Naira, high cost of production (wages, transportation, energy), irregular electricity supply, poor communication, high interest rates, and multiple taxation, there is an acute supply problem of quality cotton yarn and fiber supply from the upstream cotton production to the downstream garment manufacture subsector of the industry.

The sector is dominated by two players: the large producers and small producers with different specialties. The large producers make use of modern production equipment with large factories and specialize in printed fabrics. Many of them produce for the domestic market with few finding their way to the ECOWAS market through informal traders. There is little or no record of official export of textile to the ECOWAS market. The sector is dominated by Asian producers who take advantage of the large domestic market and relatively cheap labor to produce in the country. The production plants are mostly established around Lagos in the South, and Kano and Kaduna in the North took advantage of the abundance of local cotton production in that part of the country in the 1960s and 1970s.

The small producers are scattered all over the country and produce mainly traditional clothes and tie and dye. The tie and dye clothes have been modernized and generally have great appeal for a large segment of the population both as a simple and formal wear. While the technology for production by small holders remains rudimentary and simple, the demand for their products has grown. Tie and dye products are even finding their way to the export markets in Europe and the United States. The unrecorded nature of the business makes it difficult to have a figure of volume or value of exports.

The Nigerian market has a strong demand for African prints, as well as for satin and brocade. In the early 1990s, most of the local needs were met by local industry, the balance being made up by high-quality fabrics entering through unofficial sources from the Netherlands, Austria, China, and Japan. In spite of all the difficulties faced by the textile and clothing subsector, it has grown over the years and diversified into fiber production, spinning, weaving, knitting, lace and embroidery making, dyeing, printing, and finishing. The official statistics published by the Central Bank of Nigeria in 1995 show that of the 13 subsectors in the manufacturing sector, the textile sector continued to account for a significant proportion of the overall growth of manufacturing production. The subsector also contributes 25 to 30 percent of the manufactured export. Its contribution to total exports is, however, negligible. For instance, CBN statistics show 0 percent level for 1970 through 1985 and 0.2 percent during 1990 and 1995, and which declined again to 0 percent in 1998. This is, however, not to say that it is not potentially a viable export commodity.

To demonstrate the challenges that textile firms face in Nigeria, the experience of the Nigerian Textile Mills (NTM) and ENPEE Industries is very illustrative.

NTM is a joint venture domestic enterprise, which produces wax prints, hollandis, super prints, drills, and bleached cloth. The company has been in business for more than four years, but only started producing bleached cloth in 2002. As many other textile mills, NTM has just resumed exports after a long break since the import-substitution era of the 1970s. It now derives about 0.6 percent of its total revenue (i.e., US$60,000) from export of Africa Print to the Republic of Benin and Togo and the company looks set to expand exports significantly to other African countries through the ECOWAS trade liberalization scheme. Gross revenue from sales in 2000 was about US$9.35 million, of which, 46 percent (US$.32 million) represents the cost of raw materials. About 50 percent of its raw materials are sourced locally (mostly cotton), while the rest (mostly intermediate products like dyes and other chemicals, worth US$2.17 million in 2000) is imported. NTM employs 1546 full-time monthly workers and its expenditure on payroll is about 20 percent of revenue (i.e., US$1.96 million in 2000).

ENPEE Industries is also a domestic enterprise, which sources 90 percent of its input locally. ENPEE has no export division though its products are sold in other West African countries like Republic of Benin, Togo, and Ghana. While it produces other products, African Print is believed to be the product in which it has comparative advantage for exports. The African Print market is consumer regulated, and there are no specific international standards to which compliance is required (though some voluntary standards on usage of dyes and chemicals may apply).

NTM's management highlighted both policy and market-related issues that affect their product quality and capacity to access larger markets. Supply of skilled labor, taxes on capital, access to credit, import tariffs and charges, port charges and delays, product quality, and freight charges were found to be the critical success factors that influence the capacity of NTM to expand exports. The first four were found to be most important.

Furthermore, technical regulations governing textiles (particularly garments) were found to be more important for NTM to sell in export markets than in the local market. In fact, the company is in the process of applying for ISO 9000 and ISO 14000 certification. Testing equipment, accounts for about 2.5 percent of NTM's investment costs, and the cost of testing done within the firm are about 0.15 percent of the total production cost. The firm's test results are generally accepted by customs authorities in Republic of Benin and Togo (its major export markets), hence there seems to be no duplication, However, compliance with performance standards, product quality, and testing certification at the international level is said to be more expensive than compliance at the local level—particularly the standard for health and environment. This is largely as a result of weak enforcement of local standards.

For Enpee Industries, apart from basic voluntary standards, most technical standards on textiles are seen as irrelevant to its ability to export. Certification schemes like ISO 9000 and 14000 are seen as generating little or no business value. Ensuring formal distribution networks to other countries is not of paramount interest to the company. This is because Enpee is so focused on the local market for African Prints (and its informal channels to other West African countries) which have completely different standards from international standards for clothing, textiles, and apparel. Enpee however identifies with the need for better quality cotton input. The firm currently uses low quality cotton between 12 single count (used for printed furnishings) and 20 count cotton (used for short staple designs). Enpee also finds the lack of business development services to be very crucial to its ability to export.

For both Enpee and NTM, product standards are derived from customer/importer specifications, trade fairs, and some government agencies like the Nigeria Export Promotion Council. NTM managers acknowledge that they have difficulty obtaining information about applicable regulations in EU, US, Canada and other countries. However, this is probably due to their mild engagement in exports since exports only account for 0.6 percent of its revenues.

Other constraints highlighted are the availability of good quality cotton that feeds directly into NTM's final products. This is one of the key constraints to product quality as identified by the company. Current cotton production in Nigeria is described as unorganized, with little or no monitoring, and no grading system that conforms to international standards. Hence, cotton production in Nigeria is said to be inefficient, small in production scale, and the quality is poor compared to that of Benin or Cote d'Ivoire. The few good quality cotton produced in this environment are often exported at the expense of the needs of the local industry. Thus, many companies like NTM and Enpee have adopted products (e.g., Africa Prints) that require lower grade cotton inputs (about 20–25 counts compared to 35–100 count quality used in the garment industry in developed markets). This focus on the production of African Print is self-limiting because the market for African Prints is limited to Africa, and its Diaspora, and African Print does not compete effectively with other imported garments and textile products in Africa and internationally.

Therefore, for NTM, designing a cotton production and development program to improve the quality and availability of Nigerian cotton from the upstream sector, both for local consumption as well as exports is a necessary first step for improving quality of textile products in Nigeria. Such a program must also reintroduce appropriate cotton grading systems consistent with international ranking to facilitate better cotton pricing and selection, and to avoid unfair discounting of Nigerian cotton at the international markets.

As an alternative, NTM could import its cotton. However, this is not a desirable option since the international price of better quality cotton is higher than the price of the low count cotton required to manufacture African Print. So as long as NTM constraints itself to the export of African Print, the firm will not need higher quality international cotton inputs. However, if NTM were to access other markets like the United States or Europe, it will need to diversify its export base toward higher quality textile products like yarn, synthetic products, and garments, the current availability and quality of cotton production in Nigeria will increasingly become bigger constraints, and importation of cotton will become more attractive.

In diversifying their export base to take advantage of market opportunities like AGOA, textile companies like NTM face other constraints. Many of the textile mills in Nigeria would need to develop complete new production lines and capacities to integrate into the global garment industry. NTM, for example, estimates that it would need up to ₦1 billion for refurbishment of its machines and production processes to position itself for the U.S. and EU market for garments and other textile products. Moreover, this level of corporate investment will only be justified if a better organized garment industry is available to leverage such investment.

One can conclude from NTM's experience that market opportunities created by schemes like AGOA became available to textile companies like NTM when cotton production and quality were in the gloomiest condition, capacity was under utilized and in less competitive product ranges, and the local garment industry was too premature and unorganized to compete internationally. Furthermore, textile firms like NTM have never been able to achieve optimum capacity utilization, and exploit opportunities for economies of scale inherent in Nigeria's large domestic market for clothing and textiles, which will precipitate exports. By contrast, increasing capacity utilization by exporting abroad has been unattainable because of all the factors discussed above—mainly lack of high-quality and large quantity of cotton inputs, diversification of product design, long-term investment capital, and high production costs that undermine price competitiveness of Nigerian textile products.

Fish and Fishery Products. Fish and fishery products are not yet an important export commodity in Nigeria, but it is a highly promising sector because of the richness and vastness of Nigeria's marine, coastal, and inland waters. Most catches are consumed locally, which are mainly sourced from natural waters, both inland and offshore, from 7 maritime states and 14 inland states. Nigeria's total fish production comes from artisanal and industrial production with fish farming accounting for the lowest production (see Table 3.26).

Table 3.26 Nigeria's Fish Production by Sectors
(thousands of tons)

Sector	1986	1988	1990	1993	1995	1997
Artisanal						
Coastal and brackish water	160,169	185,181	170,459	106,276	142,279	152,213
Inland river and lakes	106,967	112,443	115,044	94,876	26,642	185,327
Fish farm: agriculture	14,881	15,764	7,297	18,703	20,753	18,537
Industrial: Commercial trawlers						
Fish	22,419	32,740	21,120	22,464	1,473	14,742
Shrimps	2,623	2,868	3,666	8,956	9,024	10,664
Eel	—	941	743	4,224	823	1,570
Distant (imports)	65,242	113,603	118,219	363,688	265,882	449,410
Total	372,301	463,540	436,548	619,187	466,876	832,463

Source: Department of Fisheries, Federal Ministry of Agriculture, Nigeria.

The commercial production is effectively controlled by large trawler fleets, which are mostly owned by foreign companies. However, as there are numerous small fishermen and women, particularly in coastal areas, catches from coastal brackish water and inland rivers and lakes presently dominate the total fish catches in Nigeria. While most small fishermen produce for domestic consumption, large trawlers use the deep sea to catch for the export market, mainly in Europe. Generally, there has been slow growth in all sectors, but easily the most important of the markets is frozen shrimps. According available statistics, the most important sector is frozen, cooked "penaens" prawns (see Table 3.27). Most tropical prawns are sold either headed or de-headed, green, and after blest-freezing.

From Table 3.27 export of Nigeria's frozen fish fillets, frozen shrimps, frozen crabs and cuttle fish shows an increasing trend between 1995 and 1999. For frozen cooked "penaeus" prawn, its export increased at a rate of more than 10 percent per year, while that of sepiola cuttle fish remained unchanged. The total EU market is 280,000 tons of prawns and is valued at 2 billion euros, that is, US$1.75 billion. Nigeria's exports were valued at 57 million euros in 2000, that is, US$50 million. Nigeria, in effect, holds about 2 percent of the European market. Important markets are Spain (25 percent of sales), France, Belgium, and the United Kingdom.

Fish products, being perishable, raise important health concerns, especially from consumers in Europe and the United States. Thus, the National Agency for Food and Drug Administration and Control, (NAFDAC) enforces stringent rules to ensure that fish products exported from Nigeria comply with international standards. NAFDAC does this for the purpose of ensuring that products exported from Nigeria are wholesome, safe, and of good quality so that the image of the country is not tarnished in the international market. In the case of fish and fishery products, the evidence required for participation in fish exports is registration as an exporter of seafood with a registration certificate granted by the Nigerian Export Promotion Council (NEPC). The product to be exported must have the following particulars: name and full address of the manufacturer; batch numbers; date of manufacture; expiry date or best before date; destination of intended export; and certificate of analysis of the product batch by batch. Before the agency issues an

Table 3.27 Trend of Nigeria's Export of Marine Products to the EU (1995 = 100)

Code	Product	1995	1996	1997	1998	1999
030420	Frozen fish fillets	100	49	121	169	343
030613	Frozen shrimps	100	113	121	118	112
030614	Frozen Crabs	100	134	140	177	224
030749	Cuttle fish	100	137	165	193	195
Frozen Shrimps and Prawn						
03061350	Frozen cooked "Penaeus" Prawn (1997 = 100)	—	—	100	129	123
0306138	Frozen other cooked prawns (1997 = 100)	—	—	100	62	57
03061390	Frozen cooked prawns	100	113	—	—	—
Frozen Crabs						
03061490	Frozen cooked crabs	100	132	140	168	221
Frozen Cuttle Fish						
03074911	Frozen "Sepiola" cuttle fish (1996 = 100)	—	100	209	496	321
03074918	Sepolia Offinalis + Rossia Macrocosma	100	123	136	126	136

Source: Computed from Chemonic/USAID Report (2002).

export certificate, the product most conform to the standard requirements of good manufacturing practice (GMP) and the regulated product must pass NAFDAC laboratory tests.

It is important to note that for fish and fishery products, the report on the status of good manufacturing practice in the establishment and results of NAFDAC laboratory test on the products, is forwarded to the Federal Department of Fisheries and Federal Ministry of Agriculture and Natural Resources for their action and issuance of an export certificate. Before the Department of Fisheries issues an export certificate, the following standard practice must be observed at the production, processing, and marketing level. The fishermen and fish handlers at the landing beaches must be trained in basic hygienic and sanitary procedures. Fish at the landing beaches must be placed in sanitary containers with ice; vehicles used for transporting fish to the markets or processing plants must be ice-cold and dust proof; and fish must be maintained in an unbroken cold chain from production to the market. At the processing level the following must be observed: a competent authority should inspect all establishments intending to export fish. The EU also requires that its inspectors approve the processors and issue EU export numbers; the establishments should implement HACCP and GMP principles, both in their construction and in routine operating procedures; there should be regular and documented inspections of the establishments by the country competent authorities; and all personnel should to have a certificate of health and training in hygiene and sanitation. At the marketing level, a health export certificate should accompany every consignment for export, and there should be complete traceability of products right to the source. This is made more important especially when tracing the source of contamination in a particular batch.

To improve on the standard practice in the commodity sector, there is need for increased awareness on hygienic practices in the area of processing and packaging at the beach; construction of modern beach landings; and improving the skills of inspection officers in the area of testing and quality assurance. According to the Chemonic/USAID report on marine products, it was noted that Nigerian prawn farming offers the potential for a new industry with a strong demand. It must be noted that prawn farming does have difficulties, such as unfavorable environmental condition.

There is a large demand for prawns. Europe is predicted to have particularly strong expanding demand. Aquaculture provides the only realistic opportunity for satisfying the increasing world demand. Some experts are projecting that farmed prawn output could double to 1.4 million tons over the next decade, which would generate about US$7 billion income for developing countries. The shrimp farming industry is currently looking for new locations to expand production. New production industries are being considered on the east coast of Africa and in Brazil. Correctly planned and designed shrimp farms could provide additional income for the artisanal fishermen of the Niger Delta. Developing an environmentally sound, sustainable and socially responsible prawn industry in Nigeria would be challenging, but this industry would provide an opportunity for Nigeria to participate in this projected, very significant increase in trade from the tropics to the industrial markets.

So far only one prawn commercial farming is known to have operated in Lagos and has folded up. There could be very important lessons for a future industry to be learned here. It is also believed that some of the oil companies, that is, Shell and AGIP have been considering investments in this area. There is then an opportunity for a project in Nigeria to pull together the disparate elements of this future industry, so that they share information and work together, and that responsibilities are sensibly divided. Much has been learned about best practices on both the environmental and social sides, in recent time which any new industry needs to embrace. We have assumed that the farmed prawn industry would grow at 40 percent per year. Nigeria could take as much as 14 percent of this projected growth. This could lead to an industry worth US$200 million over the next decade and require some 5000–6000 hectares of prawn ponds. There may also be opportunities to link tilapia farming with the prawn industry.

Summary of the Private Sector Experience

The private sector operators in the manufacturing and agricultural export in Nigeria are standard takers. They have been largely unable to influence the content and direction of international standards and technical regulations. However, most exporting firms and industries in the country are sufficiently aware of basic standard rules and regulations but are usually not abreast of new developments and changes in standards practice. Therefore, the awareness that noncompliance with required quality standards may and often lead to sanctions ranging from fines, seizures, rejection and confiscation of noncompliant consignments at the port of export or import has often led to self-imposed privately determined standards and conformity assessment requirements, which are more stringent than official standards. These self-imposed standards are sometimes beyond the requirement for international negotiations and regulations. This practice is very common among large and multinational firms. Compliance with required standards is not a problem for large and multinational firms.

Thus, for small firms and farms, they are highly disadvantaged in the process of accessing information and adopting measures to conform to international standards. Many of them lack the technical expertise and financial resources to comply with such requirements. Thus, it can be concluded, given the experience of the private sector in Nigeria, that the sector's response to international standards is closely associated with the following factors, namely, the firm's size, the size of foreign ownership or long-standing strategic business ties, and historical exposure to the export market. Thus conformity assessment, and its certification and traceability are an important challenge for Nigeria's private sector's continued access to the international market and can be very prohibitively expensive for a new or small export industry in the country.

Ongoing Public and Private Initiatives Related to Regulatory Standards

The agreements that emanated from the Uruguay Round were signed by the Nigerian military government in 1995, though there were no concerted efforts to integrate the provisions of the Round into Nigerian laws throughout the period of military rule. The democratic government has quickened the pace of fulfiling Nigeria's obligations to multilateral rules by initiating landmark measures including restructuring the National Focal Point on WTO issues, reviewing its trade policy stance in 2000, and generally introducing sector-specific reforms in line with the WTO rules. However, the Nigerian legislature has also been interested in reviewing Nigeria's membership of the WTO. It is the view of the legislature, particularly the Lower House, that the country's membership of the multilateral rules-making body is disadvantageous to Nigeria's interest, contrary to the position of the Executive arm of government.

Nonetheless, both the private and public sectors individually and jointly are initiating bold steps in the form of policies, programs, and even intentions to ensure the deeper integration of Nigeria's economy into the world trading arrangement. Indeed, the thrust of Nigeria's draft trade policy released in 2000 was to use domestic policies to encourage production and distribution of goods and services to foster, among other things, international competitiveness. Furthermore, sustained rise in trade will be encouraged through the establishment of an open, rules-based market-oriented economy, while the role of the government would be constrained to that of a facilitator of a favorable business environment to generate higher exports and strengthen the country's structural competitiveness through the improvement of physical infrastructure, promotion of exporter–supplier relations, maintenance of continuous dialogue with the private sector, and the generation of pro-export growth policies. The draft document further asserts "the aim of Nigeria's trade policy is to ensure that Nigeria derives maximum benefits from participating in international trade negotiations through the creation of favorable market access conditions for its export products at the bilateral, regional and multilateral levels. Government would take advantage of opportunities provided by programs such as the African Growth and Opportunity Act (AGOA) ... and the new ACP-EU Agreement" (Trade Policy of Nigeria, 2000, p. 2).

The Federal Ministry of Commerce continues to be the organ responsible for commercial relations between Nigeria and other countries in areas involving trade negotiations, implementation of trade agreements, collection and dissemination of trade related information, and the formulation and administration of import and export policies and measures. In effect, certain new institutions were slated for establishment, such as the National trade Policy Advisory Council, Sectoral Subcommittees of the Council, Nigerian International Trade Commission, Foreign Commercial Service, Foreign Trade Institute, Intellectual Property Commission, Bankruptcy Commission, Export Trading Companies/ Houses, and Commodity Exchange and Futures market. Of the 16 trade institutions already established, SON, NAFDAC, and the Federal Produce

Inspection Unit (FPIS) are related to the regulatory standards while there is also the Consumer Protection Council that functions to a lesser extent to implement some standards-related issues. In contrast to the regulatory conditions of the past, the draft trade policy envisages a regulatory environment characterized by inter-sectoral linkages, effectiveness, and coordination of the implementation of trade-related laws as well as a situation in which regulations would be in line with Nigeria's obligations under the international agreements. In terms of the strategy to implement regulatory standards, the government plans to strengthen and enforce the intellectual property rights regimes, including copyrights, patents, trademarks and designs; evolve guidelines and standards for exports and import procedures that facilitate smooth trading systems; as well as initiate inspection and monitoring arrangements to ensure that goods meet the requirements of national and international standards.

Prior to the new policy, there were no sectoral standards implementation agencies but apex institutions that are charged with the responsibility of regulating standards in general. This condition was maintained in the new policy, but which recognizes the need to strengthen and equip SON, NAFDAC, FPIS, and PQS to effectively perform their functions. Accordingly, it is also a crime to export any scheduled agricultural commodity without grading, a crime that is punishable by a fine, imprisonment, or both. The envisaged quality certification and control mechanism requires all processed and manufactured export products to have quality certification as well as to exhibit evidence of agreed product specification between importer and exporter. Importers of Nigerian products will also have access to the inspection facilities available for quality control in the country.

According to the policy's implementation strategy and Action Plan for the regulatory environment, policy process, export promotion, industrialization, trade support infrastructure, and agricultural production, all problems related to regulatory standards are planned to be resolved in the short to medium term, with the Federal Ministry of Finance, Central bank of Nigeria, SON, FPIS, Federal Ministry of Commerce, Federal Ministry of Agriculture, PQS, NAFDAC, Federal Ministry of

Industry, Nigeria Police Force, and NEPC remaining the implementation agencies for the various strategic solutions to the international standardization problem for Nigerian goods. The SON has resolved to work in accordance with the ISO General Assembly directive on quality system certification and conversion. In effect, the agency directed all certified organizations to convert from the Nigeria Industrial Standard NIS 9600 1994 series to NIS ISO 9001 2000 standards by December 15, 2002.

The private sector, on its part, has generally becoming more proactive to WTO issues especially those that relate to increasing import liberalization of the Nigerian economy. For example, in the week prior to the Seattle meeting of 30 November–3 December 1999, Nigerian Textile Manufacturers,[2] in a paid newspaper advertisement captioned "a punching bag for the whole world," explained that the industry had suffered job loss to the tune of 196,000 in two years with projected job losses of an additional 50,000 and a capacity utilization of only 30 percent. The manufacturers implored the Nigerian government, in view of the WTO Agreement on safeguards, infrastructure deficiencies, high interest rates, low capacity utilization, and the closure of 24 textile mills with an additional 11 in distress, to ban textile imports so as to develop the country's textile industry. In addition, NACCIMA, the Nigerian Marketing Association (NIMARK), MAN, and the Nigerian Employers' Consultative Association (NECA) have variously advocated for the review of the WTO agreements as they are perceived as being inimical to Nigeria's industrialization process. According to NECA, products adversely affected by a rise in import include textiles, shoes, tyres, dry cell batteries, matches, vegetable oil, biscuits and confectioneries, cement and aluminum extrusions products. The association sought that the Nigerian government should request through the WTO negotiating mechanism for a 5–10-year grace period to prepare industries producing these goods to face the challenges of global competition.[3]

The various influences of the Organized Private Sector (OPS) can be said to be yielding results as the Federal government has announced a ban on the import of some items including textiles, secondhand clothing, outdated refrigerators, vehicles older than five years, frozen chicken, and so on. Import

---

[2] The Guardian, November 26, 1999, p. 24

[3] The Guardian, November 29, 1999

prohibitions related to the age of products in question such as refrigerators, second-hand clothing, and vehicles older than five years border on regulatory standards. In the case of textiles, a committee comprising SON, MAN, and Nigeria Customs Service (NCS) is expected to establish the specifications of the different categories of textiles that could be imported after which the temporary ban will be lifted.[4] The Federal government has also adopted new measures to revive the textiles industry, including introduction of incentives for the NCS officials for any seizure of contraband textiles; reduction of import duties on textile raw materials, machinery and spare parts; compulsory patronage of locally manufactured textiles by the armed forces, paramilitary forces, government agencies and schools; and the stipulation of internationally accepted quality guidelines. A landmark initiative is the establishment of two ministerial committees each mandated to make Nigeria self-reliant in rice and textiles production by 2006.

In deference to the demands of commodity producers and exporters, the federal and state governments are planning to pool ₦1.5 billion to establish three commodity boards in each state of the federation to strengthen the quality and standards of Nigerian cash crops. In addition, the federal government has approved ₦420 million for NAFDAC to acquire a new head office after the destruction of its Lagos laboratory whose resuscitation is valued at ₦250 million. To curtail the importation and sale of substandard drugs, NAFDAC has initiated a bill in the National Assembly for the establishment of one drug mart in each of the six geopolitical zones of the federation.

The law that established the SON made it the only body responsible for all standardization issues in Nigeria, including the implementation and application of international standards. However, private organizations, which SON considered unaccredited and illegal, have been engaged in training, system certification, and the award of ISO 9000 quality management and ISO 14000 Environmental Management Standards certificates. These private organizations include Federation International Des Demanageurs Internationaux (FIDI), KPMG, BUREAU VERITAS Quality International, SGS, and Trithel International Consulting. With the credibil-

ity crisis that is being generated, there is an explicit need for a new body of laws recognizing the private certification systems in Nigeria. As a temporary measure, the SON advertised the process of registration with it for private training and certification companies as a sequel to serious disagreement about their accreditation and legality.

A complete private sector initiative is the introduction of product labeling and coding system against faking and counterfeiting Nigerian manufactured goods by a Nigerian private marketing company, Flurex Limited, for Willet Coding and Labeling Company. The initiative is said to be capable of creating better market access opportunities for Nigerian products, through enhanced product standardization, labeling and coding, in the international market.

Action Plan

Introduction

Compliance with international standards is an important challenge for Nigerian firms (producers and exporters) if they are to take advantage of the market access opportunities of the WTO and AGOA. The current administration's efforts to make the private sector lead the economy can be seriously jeopardized if quality standards are not strictly adhered to. Thus, the issue of conformity with international standards in the production and export of non-oil commodities poses a serious concern to both the public and private sectors. If the private sector were to jump-start the economy to move on the path of sustainable growth, the sector must be equipped and empowered to face the challenges of international competitiveness.

The private sector in Nigeria generally faces some crippling constraints such as high cost of production arising from devaluation of the local currency, high interest rate, increasing energy cost, inadequate infrastructure such as telecommunication, and transportation, and domestic policy inadequacy. These factors have a negative impact on the cost of production leading to under utilization of capacity in the sector and sometimes, total closure of some private enterprises. Even if these factors are removed, producing to meet the required

---

[4] Press briefing by the Minister of Information at the end of the weekly Federal Executive Council Meeting of October 2, 2002.

international standards still remains a challenge to operators. Undoubtedly, if non-standard-related constraints are removed, it would translate to lower cost of compliance. Yet meeting quality standards still remain a problem to be solved if Nigerian firms are to derive full benefits from the market opportunities created through WTO, AGOA, bilateral agreements, and regional market initiatives.

As has been noted in the previous section, Nigerian producers and exporting firms are to some extent standard takers. This is because they have been largely unable to influence the content and direction of international standards and regulations. Efforts must be made at the local level to become active participants in standards and technical regulations setting in collaboration with the main players in the world market so as to ensure adequate compliance by the Nigerian exporting firms. Therefore, this action plan is being put together to summarize the constraints that the Nigerian firms and exporters face in the five commodities studied. It is a probable solution together with the identification of projects that can assist in bridging the standards divide between Nigerian producers and exporting firms, and the importers in the rest of the world.

Standard and Related Constraints

From the study, there are industry-wide constraints that have been established. This section will focus on standards-related constraints in the five-commodity case studies. The standards-related constraints are inadequate awareness, insufficient and ineffective administration and enforcement, high compliance cost, and evasion of conformity tests.

(a) *Awareness*. From the main study, it can be seen that there is a low level of awareness about quality standards among small producers across the five commodities. They all lack modern equipment in production as they rely on traditional method of production. The traditional method of production often fails to produce quality goods. However, this is not the case among the large producers and exporting firms. Some of these firms sometimes even impose self-determined standard requirements that are generally more stringent than official standards. This is very true of multinational corporations in the food and beverages sector because the adopted standards are those of

their parent companies in Europe and the United States. This is also true of the big trawler fish sector, which is largely dominated by foreign owners. In the cocoa and cocoa products sector, both the large and small farmers are quite aware of the applicable standards and strictly adhere to them. However, because of the adoption of the trade liberalization policy in the country at the wake of the Structural Adjustment Program in 1986, the Cocoa Commodity Board responsible for final quality control before exports was scrapped. The private entrepreneurs that forayed into the cocoa export market demonstrated less concern about standards, leading to subsequent rejection or discounting of Nigerian cocoa, which had competed favorably with Brazilian cocoa in the international market. Small producers who hardly export any produce largely dominate the horticulture sector though the country has an abundance of flora and medicinal plants. In effect, generating sufficient awareness among the small producers about export markets and their requirements for standards will certainly leverage the opportunity of the high potential for foreign exchange earning from the sector.

In Nigeria, SON and NAFDAC are the two main public institutions that are responsible for standards development and implementation. In recent times, NAFDAC has been organizing a series of workshops to inform the producers and exporters. This was largely influenced by the SPS Agreement of the WTO. SON is engaged in similar activities with the manufacturing sector. The general assessment is that they have to do more by strengthening their activities and also collaborate with other government agencies that are responsible for standards enforcement. These include the federal and state produce inspection facilities located in the Ministry of Commerce and Trade, and the various departments and agencies in the Ministry of Agriculture such as the Fisheries and Livestock Departments that issue final certification to exporters of fish and fishery products, and the Plant Quarantine Service, which issues certificates for varied plant exports and imports.

(b) *Administration and Enforcement*. Though the two main agencies responsible for standards development, implementation and enforcement are the SON and NAFDAC, some private sector organizations, such as the Societe Generale du Surveillance (now SGS Inspection Services), are engaged in standards certification and quality control. Most Nigerian standards are based on international standards set by Codex Alimentarius Commission (CAC), Office of International des Epizootes (OIE), International Organization of Standards (ISO), and International Plant Protection Convention (IPPC). Both SON and NAFDAC are members of these international standard bodies and participate in some of their meetings. While most Nigerian standards conform to the international standards using guidelines and procedures provided by these international standards-setting organizations, implementation and enforcement are weak partly because of the huge costs involved in effective participation, monitoring, and enforcement. Most technical officers of SON and NAFDAC are not adequately exposed to international practices because of poor attendance in international standards meetings, a result of severe financial constraints. Thus, there is need to upgrade the skills of the officers in the two agencies to adequately administer standards rules and technical regulations in the country. Given the fact that many agencies in the public and private sectors are involved in the administration of standards, there is the need to harmonize operations to give room for proper coordination for better and effective administration of standards in the country.

(c) *Compliance Costs.* One issue that became clear from the study is that the cost of compliance with international standards is prohibitive. This is the case for both the agencies responsible for standards development, administration, and enforcement, and the private firms and farmers producing and exporting. The heavy costs involved in complying with international standards mainly constrain the standards agencies and private producers and exporters from minimally implementing and sustaining quality control in production. For instance, because of cost constraints, the standards agencies found it difficult to ensure that some domestic standards and regulations are developed, revised, and implemented in compliance with international standards; overcome the weaknesses in export and import certification systems; and provide adequate testing capabilities including international accreditation. For the private producing and exporting firms, cost constraints prevent them from carrying out risk analysis and surveillance programs for pests, diseases, chemical residues, food safety, and control. This is the general experience of operators in the five commodity sectors studied. The cost of compliance at the private level is indeed very prohibitive.

Suggested Solutions

One critical success factor arising from the study for bridging the standards gap being experienced in Nigeria is information dissemination. All the actors and stakeholders in standard development, implementation, enforcement, and users must be ready to make available the latest discovery, in terms of the practice and production of standards. Information sharing and networking through formal training and workshops would help upgrade the relevant skills and knowledge of standards and about recent developments in the field of standards. For instance, NAFDAC has organized workshops and seminars for stakeholders in the past on Sanitary and Phytosanitary (SPS) measures and Technical Barriers to Trade (TBT) in collaboration with WTO, which sent experts from Geneva. Besides, NAFDAC routinely organizes workshops on food safety and quality, that is, hygienic practices, HACCP, and GMP locally. GMP seminars on drugs have also been organized in collaboration with reputable drug companies. There is also continuous public enlightenment through technical or news publications, press releases, advertisements, interviews, and talk shows. The NAFDAC efforts can be emulated by other agencies involved in the promotion of standards development.

There is also the need to strengthen the public and private agencies that are involved in standards development. The two most prominent are the SON and NAFDAC. For instance, NAFDAC requires capacity building in the area of analytical procedures, food safety issues, risk assessment, HACCP, GMP and so on, for food, drugs, and cosmetics. It also requires training in the area of the maintenance of analytical instruments. For NAFDAC to carry out its functions effectively, it would require well-equipped laboratories and adequate information management systems. The following is a list of what NAFDAC would require to have well-equipped laboratories, given what is currently on ground in their laboratories.

List of Equipment Needed by NAFDAC

S. No.	Equipment	Use
1.	UV/Visible spectrophotometer (Unicam/Phillips) Thermo Helios Gama with 7 positions and printer	Analysis of organic compounds
2.	Thermo Matteson IR 300 spectrophotometer	Determination of different functional groups
3.	Thermo (Unicam/Phillips) AAS Solar M Series	Trace metals analysis
4.	Capillary GC/FID	Pesticide formulation analysis
5.	Upgrading of Perkin Elmer GC/ECD	Upgrading of the integrator
6.	Moisture analyzers	Rapid analysis of moisture in food
7.	pH meters	Hydrogen ion concentration
8.	Electronic Toploading balance 60 kg (min.)	Weighing of samples 50 kg and above
9.	Analytical balances	Weight determination
10.	Coring Cherwood flame photometers	Sodium/potassium analysis in fruit juice
11.	Handled refractometers	Determination of sugar
12.	Ultrasonic bath	HPLC analysis
13.	Casometer	Determination of carbon dioxide in drinks
14.	Multisoxhlet extractors	Extraction
15.	Polarimeter	Optical rotation
16.	Binocular microscope	Cell examination
17.	Electronic digital colony counter	Plate count
18.	Rapid milk analyzers	Analysis of milk
19.	Heating mantles	Heating
20.	Multisocket heating mantles	Heating
21.	6 Hole water baths	Heating
22.	Heating block	Heating
23.	Vortex mixers	Mixing
24.	Automatic pipettes	Accurate pipetting
25.	Membrane filters and pumps	Microbiological analysis
26.	Bucket autoclave	Microbiological analysis
27.	Incubators	Microbiological analysis
28.	Hot plates	Microbiological analysis
29.	Anaerobic jars	Microbiological analysis
30.	Binocular microscopes	Microbiological analysis
31.	Khedjal apparatus	Microbiological analysis
32.	Ovens	Microbiological analysis
33.	Electronic colony counters	Microbiological analysis
34.	Cold rooms	Storage of perishable meat/sea foods etc
35.	Capillary gas chromatograph/FID	For pesticide formulation
36.	Autosampler GC Varian Workstar 3800	To compliment existing GC
37.	Atomic absorbance spectrophotometer with graphic furnace and mercury hydride generating accessories	To include lamps
38.	Rotary evaporators	
39.	GC column HP 1 (30 m $\times$ 0.53 mm $\times$ 1 μm)	
40.	GC column HP 17 (30 m $\times$ 0.25 mm $\times$ 1 μm)	
41.	GC column HP 5 (30 m $\times$ 0.25 mm $\times$ 1 μm) (30 m $\times$ 0.25 mm $\times$ 1 μm)	
42.	GC column HP 5 (30 m $\times$ 0.53 mm $\times$ 4.6 mm)	
43.	HPLC column C18 ODS (150 mm $\times$ 4.6 mm) ODS (150 mm $\times$ 4.6 mm)	
44.	Ion exchange column (150 mm $\times$ 4.6 mm) (150 mm $\times$ 4.6 mm)	
45.	Ultrasonic bath	
46.	Workstation for GC	Upgradation of the existing Perkin Elmer XL

Source: NAFDAC Office, Lagos.

In Nigeria, there are several commodity sector business groups. They all came together under the umbrella of the Manufacturing Association of Nigeria (MAN) and the National Association of Chamber of Commerce, Industry, Manufacturing, and Agriculture (NACCIMA). MAN and NACCIMA do not currently have capacities to resolve issues of standards at the level of their secretariats. However, the two business associations are well placed to instruct their members with the need to comply with standards. Thus, strengthening these associations can assist in providing the necessary impetus in bridging the standards gap in Nigeria.

The prohibitive cost of compliance at the level of private and public agencies calls for donor support intervention. This is more important for agencies that are responsible for standards development and the provision of support for business association in carrying out information programs and activities. NAFDAC and SON already enjoy such support from UNIDO, UNICEF, CODEX, and so on.

Projects

The following are specific projects requiring investments, which when undertaken can assist in bridging the standards gap in Nigeria. The benefits of these projects cut across all the five commodity sectors studied.

1. *Information Exchange Center:* The Information Exchange Center serves the source of accessing and disseminating standards and technical regulations that may be relevant to the different commodity sectors. This project can be located in the MAN and NACCIMA secretariats in the six geopolitical zones, each secretariat specializing in the product in which that zone has comparative advantage in production. A list of equipment that would be required in one zone include:

a. 10 sets of desktop computers	₦900,000
b. Internet connectivity	₦1,000,000
c. Personnel cost (for 2 years)	₦500,000
d. Contingency (10 %) of total cost	₦240,000
Total cost	₦2,640,000

To make the project sustainable, after a year in operation, user fees should be charged.

2. *Upgrading of Facilities in Public Standards Agencies:* SON and NAFDAC need to strengthen their standards-oriented activities. To perform their regulatory functions effectively, their facilities require upgrading to meet modern standardization requirements including conformity assessment, and testing and certification procedures, so that they can even serve the West African markets. As a matter of priority, NAFDAC in particular has identified the provision of modern laboratories. The project would cost about ₦50 million to supply the laboratory equipment for the seafood laboratory, food compliance laboratories, radiation laboratory, and drug laboratory.

The breakdown is as follows.

	₦
a. Seafood laboratory	4,296,790
b. Food compliance laboratory	24,212,984
c. Radiation laboratory	2,630,000
d. Drug laboratory	8,350,000
e. Miscellaneous	200,000
Total	50,000,000

Other expenditures include the cost of giving appropriate training to staff on laboratory analysis, food quality, and safety and training on drugs, cosmetics, and other regulated products. This expenditure, however, cannot be fixed now but it was estimated by NAFDAC to be ₦25 million for a period of two years.

3. *Skill Development for Small Holders:* The skills development program for small holders to produce to meet the required international standards will involve training of small producers through extension and field officers by SON, NAFDAC, and other standards-related agencies in the federal and state Ministry of Agriculture and Health. It is, however, difficult to put a fixed cost on this program but it is estimated to be ₦250 million a five-year period for the five commodity sectors studied.

Summary of Major Findings and Recommendations

Summary of Major Findings

The Uruguay Round Agreement (URA) of 1994 and the establishment of the World Trade Organization (WTO) in January 1995 reinforced the philosophy that "free trade is better than restricted trade," culminating, since then, in a general decline in tariffs and quotas. However, the application of SPS and TBT as a disguise to restrict trade flows is threatening this free-trade philosophy. Though enforcement of standards and regulations is necessary for responsible governments, these standards especially in relation to agricultural, food, and health products can negatively impinge firm- and country-level competitiveness through cost raising incidences that also result in export market share loss. In Nigeria's case, the agricultural sector employs 70 percent of its total labor force indicating the vulnerability of the Nigerian economy through its agricultural sector, and whose performance is second only to the oil sector, to externally imposed measures with a grave potential impact. Thus, the SPS and TBT issues are viewed seriously as they border on restricting market access of Nigeria's agricultural products into importing countries.

This study examines the awareness and impact of international standards and technical regulations on Nigeria's trade, and assesses the current status of laws, regulations, capacities, and programs relating to standards and technical regulations in Nigeria. It also identifies the level of participation in the international standards setting process and the areas needing priority attention at the national level. It also provides recommendations on key steps to be taken by government and private organizations and relevant international development agencies to alleviate the negative impact and strengthen the positive influences to face the challenges in trade facilitation posed by SPS measures and technical barriers to trade.

In effect, a critical examination of the trade and economic profile of Nigeria shows that the real GDP per capita stagnated at a low level between 1970 and 2000 while the growth rate of real GDP improved relatively in the few years following the introduction of the Structural Adjustment Program (SAP) in 1986 only to fluctuate between 2.1 percent and 3.8 percent in the post-UR period. The inflation rate reached 72.8 percent in 1995 only to decrease continuously thereafter with the period 1997–2000 recording low levels of price level increases. The study also observes that in spite of the increasing openness of the Nigerian economy, its total exports as a proportion of the GDP were unimpressive until around 1995. The federal fiscal balance that was found to be perpetually in deficit

further complicates the economic situation through its effect on the country's indebtedness. Both domestic and foreign debts accumulated to unprecedented levels and their servicing became cumbersome and almost unbearable.

In terms of the direction of trade, the United States and the European Union jointly account for three-quarters of Nigerian exports, the bulk of which is crude petroleum. Even though Nigeria's trade with developing countries (Africa in particular) has improved relatively in the recent period, it nevertheless remained highly insignificant. A review of the tariffs applicable to Nigerian exports in its main external markets indicates that its major export, crude oil, is excluded among the U.S. market tariff-bound products and that it enjoys a low tariff in the EU implying that its effective tariff protection in the EU is low. Basic agricultural products are highly protected, both in the United States and the EU as high tariffs, mostly in addition to the overall simple rate, are applied coupled with a spectrum of other restrictions and specific duties, which are applicable to the agricultural products as well as the textile and clothing products. Overall, Nigeria's increased involvement in regional and multilateral trade agreements should bring about an improved trade position with the rest of the world.

For Nigeria, giving priority to regulatory standards is a key to its effective participation in the rapidly integrating world, especially because its economic growth not only fully depends on the external sector but also because Codex, IOE, and IPPC standards have been accorded greater prominence and recognition in the Uruguay Round of Multilateral Trade Negotiations and this will likely be the case in future rounds. Nigeria seems to have the relevant manpower but lacks the resources and necessary infrastructure to conduct scientific research and properly harness inputs into standards development. Thus, though it is desirable to be an important player in the global trading arrangement, the lack of adequate resources and necessary infrastructure to conduct scientific research to integrate properly into the global standardization process, as found in this study, even where there is the requisite manpower, is a binding constraint for Nigeria. For example, apart from the fact that the standardization equipment is obsolete, communication equipment is generally nonexistent and coupled with inadequate computerization, all of them aggravate the problem of ineffective participation in the international standards-setting process.

In Nigeria, though local legislation relating to standards and technical regulations predate the SPS Agreement, enforcement is weak. This has led to the rejection of Nigerian products in importing countries. Evidence shows that many of these rejections were not certified, having evaded preshipment inspection, but the fact remains that the products were shipped from Nigerian ports.

Through its standards regulatory agencies, SON, NAFDAC, and PQS, Nigeria has been modestly involved in standardization but its effective participation is limited in the world standards arrangement because of such constraints as inadequate equipment, chemicals, highly skilled technicians and limited funds, lack of private capacities, acute capacity problem in risk assessment, and a limited laboratories accreditation program. These constraints suggest a vital role for technical assistance through bilateral and multilateral arrangements. However, an important finding is that trading partner countries have been minimally involved in technical assistance in negation of their obligation under the SPS and TBT Agreements as many of the programs since 1995 have been supported by multilateral institutions such as the UNDP, UNICEF, UNIDO, IAEA, FAO, among others.

In Nigeria, the level of awareness among local firms and farmers of international standards is mixed. One reason for this is inadequate funding that limits the publicity work of the standards agencies. However, the agencies have developed coping strategies to improve the dissemination of information including organizing series of workshops on food safety and quality focusing on hygienic practices, HACCP, and GMP; use of technical or news publications, the press and electronic media for press releases, advertisements, interviews, talk shows; consultative meetings with stakeholders, corporate briefs, and paid advertisements, and interviews. Others include issuing of communiqués, distribution of information through handbills, and attendance at relevant commodity shows. Nonetheless, public awareness is still very low. Another reason is the poverty level in the country that allows consumers to be satisfied with low-priced but not necessarily cheap substandard products.

The status of the adoption of the Hazard Analysis and Critical Control Points (HACCP) and ISO 9000 in Nigeria is moderately impressive, especially since 1994 in the case of ISO 9000. It has also been more possible for large firms to adopt the ISO 9000 standards quality system than for small and medium companies that face particular problems of funding. The study finds that though the adoption of ISO 9000 standards has not directly affected the economic opportunities of the poor, they nevertheless affect them indirectly as many ISO certified firms produce commodities that serve as inputs into the production of goods that the poor purchase.

In addition, there are documented cases of restrictions of export products in Nigeria's traditional markets. These include raw agricultural goods, plants, processed agricultural goods, and cosmetics. By contrast, statutory agencies such as SON and NAFDAC have tended to enforce regulatory standards on imports such as electric cables, used tires, canned fish, and pharmaceutical drugs and beverages.

Finally, the sort of product differentiation to achieve competitive advantage experienced in Nigeria is widespread in the importation business where substandard products, labeled to deceive the consumers are imported for sale at lower but not necessarily cheap prices.

Recommendations

The summary contains issues related to opportunities and challenges for bridging the standards gap in Nigeria. In effect, it is recommended that:

- there should be a "Standards Campaign" in the six geopolitical zones of Nigeria to create and sustain awareness among consumers and producers, especially small producers of exportable commodities;
- there is an urgent need to strengthen the National Codex Committee including its Secretariat to be able to modernize and integrate properly into the international standardization process;
- equipment should be upgraded through procurement of new technology in conformity with assessment and risk analysis;
- staff knowledge requires upgrading, especially with regard to demonstrating equivalence of standards through regular scientific training of laboratory staff;
- cooperation among regional (ECOWAS) members for attending international standards-setting meetings should be encouraged. This is a result of the high costs involved in attending all Codex

and other international standards institutions' meetings;

- regional harmonization of standards through the ISO, ARSO, and so on, should continue and be intensified by ensuring regular attendance of meetings;
- budgetary provisions from the Nigerian government to the standards institutions should be improved;
- bilateral technical assistance needs to be introduced and sustained in line with the requirements of the relevant articles of the SPS and TBT Agreements;
- the formation of well-equipped private laboratories need to be facilitated by providing the enabling environment through relevant laws; and
- information and telecommunications facilities should be modernized to enhance good management of the standardization process.

References

Bankole, A. S. 2001. "Sanitary and Phytosanitary Standards and Processed Agricultural and Food Products Exports: Evidence from Nigerian Firms." Presented at the African Economic Research Consortium (AERC) biannual research workshop, December, Nairobi, Kenya.

Central Bank of Nigeria. *CBN Annual Reports and Statement of Accounts* (Various Issues)

———. 1998. *Statistical Bulletin*, December.

FAO. 1999. *Importance of Food Quality and Safety for Developing Countries*, Committee on World Food Security, 25th Session, FAO, Rome

FAO-WHO. 2001a. Agenda Item No. 5 (b), XC/FL 01/07-CRD.45

———. 2001b. Document CL 2001/39-FFV, November

National Codex Committee, 2001. Report of the National Codex Committee Meeting of 29th August.

Ogunkola, E. O. and Y. F. Agah. 1998. "Nigeria and the World Trading System." Draft final research report submitted to the African Economic Research Consortium (AERC) Collaborative Project on Africa and the World Trading System.

Oyejide, T. A. 2001. "Nigerian Trade Policy in the Context of Regional and Multilateral Trade Agreements." DPC Research Report, No. 27.

Oyejide T. A., E. O. Ogunkola, and A. S. Bankole. 2000. "Quantifying the Trade Impact of Sanitary and Phytosanitary Standards: What is Known and Issues of Importance for Sub-Saharan Africa." Paper presented at the workshop on "Quantifying the Trade Effect of Standards and Regulatory Barriers: Is It Possible?" World Bank, Washington, D.C., 27 April 2000.

Standards Organisation of Nigeria. 1992. "Nigeria Industrial Standards—Standards for Milk Powder." First edition.

Standards Organisation of Nigeria. 1997. Annual Report.

World Bank. 2000. "Africa's Integration into the World Trading System: Challenges in Trade Facilitation, Regulatory Reform, and Standards Tariff Project Action Plans."

WTO (World Trade Organization). 1998. *Trade Policy Review: Nigeria*. Geneva: WTO.

———. 1999. *Trade Policy Review: United States*. Geneva: WTO.

———. 2000. *Trade Policy Review: European Union*. Geneva: WTO.

Appendix A

Table 3.28 Macroeconomic Indicators

Year	Real GDP Growth Rate (percent)	Real GDP per Capita (₦)	Nominal GDP per Capita (₦)	Inflation Rate (percent)	Industrial Production Index (1985 = 100)			Manufacturing Capacity Utilization (percent)	External Reserve (₦ billion)
					All Sectors	Manufacturing	Mining		
1970	24.50	957	92	13.8	41.3	24.1	72.2	n.a.	0.105
1971	21.35	1,186	119	15.6	54.8	27.3	104.9	n.a.	0.132
1972	5.48	1,193	124	3.2	62.3	29.7	122.5	n.a.	0.191
1973	6.42	1,238	184	5.4	72.4	36.6	138.0	n.a.	0.241
1974	11.74	1,369	304	13.4	76.2	35.5	151.2	n.a.	3.11
1975	−2.96	1,274	334	33.9	71.8	43.9	119.9	76.6	3.38
1976	11.08	1,514	454	21.2	85.5	54.1	139.0	77.4	3.06
1977	8.15	1,596	524	15.4	88.6	57.5	140.3	78.7	2.52
1978	−7.36	1,452	563	16.6	90.4	65.8	127.0	72.9	1.25
1979	2.44	1,445	665	11.8	120.3	97.3	154.4	71.5	3.04
1980	5.48	1,487	767	9.9	119.0	102.4	138.5	70.1	5.45
1981	−26.81	1,054	755	20.9	115.6	117.4	96.2	73.3	2.04
1982	−0.34	1,026	754	7.7	122.9	132.8	86.2	63.6	1.02
1983	−5.37	939	802	23.2	96.4	94.8	82.5	49.7	0.78
1984	−5.10	863	863	39.6	91.6	83.4	93.0	43.0	1.14
1985	9.38	913	945	5.5	100.0	100.0	100.0	38.3	1.64
1986	3.13	912	926	5.4	103.5	96.1	97.8	38.8	3.59
1987	−0.47	879	1,328	10.2	122.1	128.4	88.4	40.4	4.64
1988	9.91	935	1,715	38.3	108.8	135.2	95.3	42.4	3.27
1989	7.39	983	2,620	40.9	125.0	154.3	109.2	43.8	13.46
1990	8.20	1,042	2,974	7.5	130.6	162.9	115.1	40.3	34.95
1991	4.73	1,063	3,598	13.0	138.8	178.1	120.1	42.0	44.25
1992	2.98	1,065	5,949	44.5	136.2	169.5	119.9	38.1	13.99
1993	2.65	1,063	7,350	57.2	131.7	145.5	124.6	37.2	67.25
1994	1.31	1,047	9,412	57.0	129.2	144.2	121.1	30.4	30.46
1995	2.15	1,040	19,705	72.8	128.8	136.2	124.2	29.3	40.33
1996	3.39	1,052	26,788	29.3	132.5	138.7	129.0	32.5	174.31
1997	3.16	1,056	26,947	8.5	133.7	138.4	141.5	30.4	262.20
1998	2.36	1,051	25,153	10.0	133.9	133.1	134.1	34.9	226.70
1999	2.72	1,076	20,886	6.6	129.1	137.7	124.5	36.0	503.25
2000	3.80	1,066	22,889	6.9	139.0	138.2	139.2	34.5	1007.40

Sources: CBN Annual Reports and Statements of Accounts (various issues); CBN Statistical Bulletin, December, 1998.

226

Table 3.29 Economic Indicators and Selected Ratios

Year	Federal Fiscal Balance (₦ billion)	Total Domestic Debt (₦ billion)	Total External Debt (₦ billion)	Fiscal Balance/ GDP (percent)	Domestic Debt/ GDP (percent)	External Debt/ GDP (percent)	Actual Debt SS Payments/Export (percent)	Debt SS Due/ Exports (percent)
1970	−0.455	1.112	0.175	−8.8	21.38	3.37	3.5	
1971	0.172	1.245	0.179	2.6	18.95	2.72	2.3	
1972	−0.059	1.001	0.266	−0.8	13.88	3.69	2.1	
1973	0.166	1.061	0.277	1.5	9.65	2.52	1.3	
1974	1.796	1.267	0.322	9.8	6.92	1.76	0.5	
1975	−0.428	1.679	0.35	−2.0	7.79	1.62	0.7	
1976	−1.09	2.63	0.375	−4.0	9.63	1.37	0.5	
1977	−0.781	4.636	0.365	−2.4	14.16	1.11	1.0	
1978	−2.822	5.983	1.252	7.8	16.58	3.47	2.7	
1979	1.462	7.231	1.612	3.4	16.76	3.74	1.7	
1980	−1.975	8.232	1.867	−3.9	16.19	3.67	2.0	
1981	−3.902	11.196	2.331	−7.7	22.06	4.59	6.1	
1982	−6.104	15.01	8.819	−11.8	29.03	17.05	10.0	
1983	−3.365	22.224	10.578	−5.9	38.89	18.51	17.8	
1984	−2.66	25.675	14.809	−4.2	40.36	23.28	29.1	
1985	−3.04	27.952	17.301	−4.2	38.63	23.91	33.2	
1986	−8.25	28.44	41.452	−11.3	38.93	56.74	29.4	79.5
1987	−5.80	36.79	100.79	−3.4	33.79	92.56	11.8	75.9
1988	−12.16	47.031	133.96	−8.4	32.38	92.23	10.0	81.5
1989	−15.13	47.051	240.39	−6.7	20.93	106.94	26.9	73.5
1990	−22.12	84.125	298.61	−8.5	32.28	114.57	28.1	46.4
1991	−35.76	116.2	328.05	−11.0	35.86	101.25	29.0	43.9
1992	−39.53	161.9	544.26	−7.2	29.45	98.99	19.8	65.4
1993	−107.74	261.09	633.14	−15.5	37.45	90.82	16.6	37.7
1994	−70.27	341.27	648.81	−7.7	37.30	70.91	15.2	40.9
1995	1.00	248.77	716.87	0.1	12.58	74.70	13.8	37.6
1996	37.05	343.67	617.32	1.3	12.17	80.50	11.6	32.7
1997	−5.00	355.06	595.93	−0.2	12.21	70.70	9.8	32.8
1998	−133.39	537.49	633.02	−4.7	18.94	87.20	14.2	40.2
1999	−285.11	794.81	2,575.0	−8.4	23.53	76.24		26.4
2000	−103.77	898.25	3,121.73	−2.9	24.90	84.20		35.0

Sources: CBN Annual Reports and Statements of Accounts (various issues); CBN Statistical Bulletin, December, 1998.

Table 3.30 Trade Performance Indicators

Year	Export (₦ billion)	Import (₦ billion)	Current A/c Balance (₦ million)	Export/ GDP (percent)	Import/ GDP (percent)	Degree of Openness (percent)
1970	0.885	0.756	−50	16.99	14.51	31.5
1971	1.29	1.079	−229.4	19.63	16.42	36.0
1972	1.43	0.99	−322.7	19.83	13.73	33.5
1973	2.28	1.22	52.7	20.75	11.10	31.9
1974	5.79	1.74	4,671.5	31.64	9.51	41.2
1975	4.93	3.72	42.6	23.52	17.75	41.3
1976	6.75	5.15	−258.4	25.32	19.32	44.6
1977	7.63	7.09	−647.5	24.21	22.49	46.7
1978	6.06	8.21	−1,157.4	17.54	23.77	41.3
1979	10.84	7.47	9,427.3	25.84	17.81	43.7
1980	14.19	9.1	13,057.9	30.43	19.52	49.9
1981	11.02	12.84	10,070.3	21.84	25.45	47.3
1982	8.21	10.77	7,980.9	15.92	20.88	36.8
1983	7.5	8.9	6,752.3	13.23	15.69	29.0
1984	9.09	7.18	8,234.3	14.43	11.40	25.8
1985	11.72	7.06	10,738.9	16.42	9.89	26.3
1986	8.92	5.98	8,006.6	12.37	8.29	20.6
1987	30.36	17.86	17,138.2	28.41	16.71	45.1
1988	31.19	21.45	31,586.1	21.86	15.03	36.9
1989	57.97	30.86	59,112.0	26.06	13.87	39.9
1990	109.89	45.72	79,810.1	42.61	17.73	60.3
1991	121.54	87.02	51,969.8	37.95	27.17	65.1
1992	207.27	145.91	93,680.5	38.08	26.81	64.9
1993	218.77	166.1	−34,414.7	31.63	24.02	55.6
1994	206.06	162.79	−52,304.3	22.62	17.87	40.5
1995	950.66	755.13	−186,084.6	48.49	38.51	87.0
1996	1309.54	562.63	376.02	47.79	20.53	68.3
1997	1241.66	845.72	268,899.3	43.80	29.83	73.6
1998	751.86	837.42	−331,429.5	27.63	30.77	58.4
1999	1,189.01	862.53	41,074.1	50.85	36.89	87.7
2000	1,945.76	962.97	706,977.0	73.79	36.52	110.3

Note: The degree of openness is measured using the ratio of total trade (exports + imports) to GDP.
Sources: CBN Annual Reports and Statements of Accounts, (various issues); CBN Statistical Bulletin, December, 1998.

Table 3.31 Sectoral Share of Nigeria's Real GDP for Selected Years
(percent)

Activity Sector	1981	1982	1984	1986	1988	1990	1992	1994	1996	1998	Average
1. Agriculture (crops)	20.0	21.9	26.9	28.3	34.1	26.5	22.2	32.5	26.0	32.9	26.9
2. Livestock	3.4	5.2	7.1	6.9	4.2	3.7	2.9	4.0	3.2	3.9	4.5
3. Forestry	2.1	2.1	2.0	2.0	1.2	0.8	0.5	0.6	0.3	0.5	1.1
4. Fishing	1.4	1.7	1.8	1.4	1.0	1.6	1.1	1.1	1.1	1.6	1.3
5. Crude petroleum	20.3	16.3	15.2	13.6	21.0	33.4	46.8	24.8	43.6	27.9	28.1
6. Mining and quarrying	1.8	1.7	0.5	0.3	0.2	0.3	0.2	0.2	0.1	0.1	0.5
7. Manufacturing	9.2	9.6	7.8	8.7	7.5	5.5	4.8	6.9	4.8	5.4	6.8
8. Utilities	0.9	0.9	0.8	0.6	0.4	0.5	0.3	0.2	0.1	0.1	0.5
9. Building and construction	5.5	4.8	3.0	2.7	1.7	1.7	1.1	1.1	0.6	0.9	2.1
10. Transportation	5.5	4.8	4.2	5.2	3.0	2.0	1.6	3.4	2.3	2.9	3.3
11. Communication	0.5	0.5	0.4	0.4	0.2	0.2	0.1	0.1	0.1	0.1	0.2
12. Wholesale and retail trade	12.8	12.8	13.6	13.2	14.5	13.9	11.4	17.4	13.0	16.1	13.9
13. Hotel and restaurant	0.8	0.8	0.8	0.7	0.3	0.2	0.1	0.2	0.1	0.2	0.4
14. Finance and insurance	3.2	3.7	3.8	4.6	3.5	4.5	2.8	1.4	1.0	1.3	2.9
15. Real estate	0.3	0.4	0.3	0.3	0.2	0.2	0.1	0.1	0.1	0.1	0.3
16. Housing	3.1	3.2	3.0	3.0	1.7	1.5	1.1	3.0	2.2	3.6	2.4
17. Producer of govt. services	8.4	8.5	7.3	7.0	4.5	3.1	2.6	2.3	0.8	1.3	4.3
18. Communication, social and personnel services	0.9	1.0	1.0	0.9	0.5	0.4	0.2	0.6	0.6	1.0	0.6
Total real GDP (percent)	100	100	100	100	100	100	100	100	100	100	100
Share of oil in real GDP	20.3	16.3	15.2	13.6	21.0	33.4	46.8	24.8	43.6	27.9	28.1
Share of non-oil	79.7	83.7	84.8	86.4	79.0	66.6	53.2	75.2	56.4	72.1	71.9

Sources: CBN Annual Reports and Statements of Accounts (various issues); CBN Statistical Bulletin, December, 1998.

Table 3.32 Imports by Product
(N' million and percent)

		1970	1975	1980	1985	1990	1995	1999	2000
0	Food and live animals	57.7 (7.6)	298.8 (8.0)	1,437.5 (15.8)	1,199.0 (17.0)	3,474.5 (7.6)	88,349.9 (11.5)	103,489.8 (12.0)	113,630.5 (11.8)
1	Beverages and tobacco	4.0 (0.5)	48.1 (1.3)	12.1 (0.1)	9.4 (0.1)	228.7 (0.5)	3,020.5 (0.4)	4,312.1 (0.5)	6,740.8 (0.7)
2	Crude materials inedible except fuel	16.6 (2.2)	74.4 (2.0)	156.7 (1.7)	350.5 (5.0)	1,417.2 (3.1)	31,715.4 (4.2)	38,808.7 (4.5)	44,296.6 (4.6)
3	Mineral fuels, lubricants and related materials	22.0 (3.0)	100.4 (2.7)	154.8 (1.7)	61.1 (0.9)	274.2 (0.6)	9,061.5 (1.2)	12,073.8 (1.4)	12,518.6 (1.3)
4	Animal and vegetable oil and fats	0.8 (0.1)	8.9 (0.2)	115.0 (1.3)	71.0 (1.0)	228.7 (0.5)	8,306.4 (1.1)	12,073.8 (1.4)	14,444.6 (1.5)
5	Chemicals	88.5 (11.5)	333.2 (9.0)	913.5 (10.0)	1,108.2 (15.7)	9,006.4 (19.7)	199,353.7 (26.4)	196,630.6 (22.8)	218,594.2 (22.7)
6	Manufactured goods classified by materials	227.0 (30)	1,007.4 (27)	1,981.5 (21.8)	1,611.8 (22.8)	10,240.8 (22)	175,944.8 (23.3)	253,550.0 (29.4)	279,261.3 (29.0)
7	Machinery and transportation Equipment Miscellaneous	285.3 (38)	1,561.0 (42)	3,650.4 (40.1)	2,414.4 (34.2)	18,515.8 (41)	206,905.0 (27.4)	204,392.3 (23.7)	232,075.8 (24.1)
8	Manufactured articles Miscellaneous	39.5 (5.2)	278.7 (7.5)	645.1 (7.1)	224.5 (3.2)	2,194.5 (4.8)	30,960.2 (4.1)	35,359.0 (4.1)	38,518.8 (4.0)
9	Transactions unclassified	15.0 (2.0)	10.6 (0.3)	29.0 (0.3)	12.7 (0.2)	137.1 (0.3)	1,510.3 (0.2)	1,835.2 (0.2)	2,888.8 (0.3)
	Total	756.4 (100)	3,721.5 (100)	9,095.6 (100)	7,062.5 (100)	45,717.9 (100)	755,127.7 (100)	862,525.3 (100)	962,970.0 (100)

Sources: CBN Annual Reports and Statements of Accounts (various issues); CBN Statistical Bulletin, December, 1998.

Table 3.33 Exports of Major Commodities by Economic Sectors
(₦' million and percent)

	1970	1975	1980	1985	1990	1995	1998
Major agricultural products	265.2 (30.0)	230.6 (4.7)	340.1 (2.4)	258.8 (2.3)	2,429.3 (2.2)	15,512.0 (1.6)	16,338.9 (2.2)
Manufactures and semi manufactures of agricultural products	65.8 (7.4)	53.8 (1.1)	39.0 (0.3)	65.4 (0.6)	224.8 (0.2)	1,570.8 (0.2)	11,899.8 (1.6)
Textiles	—	—	—	—	172.0 (0.2)	1,638.3 (0.2)	332.4 (0.0)
Mineral products	512.0 (57.7)	4,565.3 (92.7)	13,524.0 (96.1)	10,890.6 (97.1)	106,641.4 (97.0)	928,007.3 (97.6)	722,684.3 (96.1)
Manufactured exports	—	—	—	—	334.0 (0.3)	3,792.7 (0.4)	601.3 (0.1)
Other exports	34.8 (3.8)	70.2 (1.4)	147.0 (1.1)	n.a.	84.6 (0.1)	140.3 (0.0)	—
Total domestic exports	877.0 (99.0)	4,920.2 (99.9)	14,050.1 (99.8)	11,214.8 (100)	109,886.1 (100)	950,661.4 (100)	751,856.7 (100)
Re-exports	8.4 (0.9)	5.3 (0.1)	26.9 (0.2)	n.a.	n.a.	n.a.	n.a.
Total	885.4 (100.0)	4,925.5 (100)	14,077.0 (100.0)	11,214.8 (100.0)	109,886.1 (100)	950,661.4 (100)	751,856.7 (100)

Sources: CBN Annual Reports and Statements of Accounts (various Issues).

Table 3.34 Direction of Nigeria's Trade
($' million and percent)

	Exports (Destinations)						
	1971	1975	1980	1985	1990	1995	1998
Total	1810 (100)	7995 (100)	26,958 (100)	14,289 (100)	10,273 (100)	11,664 (100)	11,791 (100)
Industrial countries	85.6	82.1	80.4	79.1	92.0	79.4	64.5
Developing countries	7.8	15.8	19.1	20.8	7.9	20.6	35.5
Africa	2.2	2.0	2.0	2.4	6.5	9.2	10.7
Asia	0.4	—	—	0.5	0.3	6.3	14.0
Others			17.1	17.9	1.0	5.1	
EU	1125 (62)	3704 (46)	10246(38)	7974 (56)	3662 (35.6)	3951 (33.9)	n.a.
US	320 (17.7)	2316 (29.0)	10471 (39)	2826 (19.8)	5569 (54.2)	4595 (39.4)	4135 (35.1)
Canada	31 (1.7)	51 (0.6)	36 (0.1)	171 (1.2)	122 (1.2)	426 (3.7)	209 (1.8)
Japan	25 (1.4)	280 (3.5)	110 (0.4)	5 (0.0)	3 (0.0)	122 (1.0)	78 (0.7)
France	267 (14.8)	872 (10.9)	2728 (10.1)	1533 (10.7)	294 (2.9)	734 (6.3)	673 (5.7)
Germany	99 (5.5)	543 (6.8)	2756 (10.2)	1950 (13.6)	593 (5.8)	567 (4.9)	289 (2.5)
Italy	79 (4.4)	96 (1.2)	859 (3.2)	1461 (10.2)	299 (2.9)	242 (2.1)	340 (2.9)
Netherlands	247 (13.6)	899 (11.2)	2639 (9.8)	594 (4.2)	936 (9.1)	367 (3.1)	116 (1.0)
Spain	49 (2.7)	8 (0.1)	235 (0.9)	707 (4.9)	942 (9.2)	1036 (8.9)	876 (7.4)
UK	392 (21.7)	1130 (14.1)	320 (1.2)	745 (5.2)	300 (2.9)	259 (2.2)	211 (1.8)
Africa	40 (2.2)	163 (2.0)	548 (2.0)	349 (2.4)	670 (6.5)	1072 (9.2)	1267 (10.7)
Cameroon	—	—	4 (0.0)	2 (0.0)	74 (0.7)	95 (0.8)	88 (0.7)
Cote d'Ivoire	7 (0.4)	48 (0.6)	53 (0.2)	174 (1.2)	225 (2.2)	417 (3.6)	290 (2.5)
Ghana	16 (0.9)	54 (0.7)	208 (0.8)	42 (0.3)	255 (2.5)	352 (3.0)	424 (3.6)
Senegal	2 (0.1)	23 (0.3)	70 (0.3)	86 (0.6)	43 (0.4)	21 (0.2)	84 (0.7)
S/Leone	5 (0.3)	19 (0.2)	45 (0.2)	24 (0.2)	16 (0.2)	8 (0.1)	10 (0.1)
China	—	—	5 (0.0)	3 (0.0)	9 (0.1)	54 (0.5)	25 (0.2)
Hong Kong	6 (0.3)	—	—	—	2 (0.0)	4 (0.0)	4 (0.0)
India	—	2 (0.0)	1 (0.0)	—	4 (0.0)	572 (4.9)	1014 (8.6)
Korea	—	—	—	62 (0.4)	—	—	240 (2.0)
Other Europe	59 (2.7)	20 (0.3)	934 (3.5)	263 (1.8)	23 (0.2)	41 (0.4)	61 (0.5)
Romania	—	—	313 (1.2)	—	—	17 (0.1)	1 (0.0)
USSR	49 (2.7)	122 (1.5)	4 (0.0)	10 (0.1)	14 (0.1)	—	7 (0.1)
M/East	1 (0.1)	1 (0.0)	4 (0.0)	2 (0.0)	3 (0.0)	4 (0.0)	6 (0.1)
Western Hemisphere	95 (5.2)	1100 (13.8)	3662 (13.6)	2290 (16.0)	80 (0.8)	549 (4.7)	1202 (10.2)
Argentina	2 (0.1)	—	34 (0.1)	—	—	45 (0.4)	5 (0.0)
Brazil	28 (1.5)	—	82 (0.3)	1293 (9.0)	9 (0.1)	258 (2.2)	630 (5.3)

Source: Direction of Trade Statistics Yearbook (various issues).

Imports (Sources)						
1971	1975	1980	1985	1990	1995	1998
1510 (100)	6032 (100)	16,478 (100)	7577 (100)	4317 (100)	5588 (100)	7446 (100)
84.5	86.5	81.9	69.5	78.1	68.6	52.2
7.4	6.7	15.2	25.3	21.6	31.2	36.0
0.5	0.9	1.4	1.0	0.7	2.8	3.7
5.4	3.3	8.7	7.5	11.7	17.4	22.3
		5.5	20.4	9.2	10.9	
878 (58)	3617 (60.0)	9553 (58.0)	3746 (49.4)	2497 (58)	2841 (51)	n.a.
212 (14.0)	663 (11.0)	1265 (7.7)	743 (9.8)	274 (6.3)	662 (11.8)	902 (12)
8 (0.5)	39 (0.6)	96 (0.6)	57 (0.8)	18 (0.4)	21 (0.4)	18 (0.2)
128 (8.5)	595 (9.9)	1651 (10.0)	379 (5.0)	257 (6.0)	193 (3.5)	252 (3.4)
61 (4.0)	501 (8.3)	1483 (9.0)	627 (8.3)	394 (9.1)	461 (8.2)	624 (8.4)
184 (12.2)	882 (14.6)	2010 (12.2)	714 (9.4)	647 (15.0)	597 (10.7)	714 (9.6)
57 (3.8)	369 (6.1)	752 (4.6)	379 (5.0)	194 (4.5)	240 (4.3)	360 (4.8)
52 (3.4)	257 (4.3)	1027 (6.2)	240 (3.2)	207 (4.8)	316 (5.77)	371 (5.0)
11 (0.7)	86 (1.4)	299 (1.8)	113 (1.5)	59 (1.4)	88 (1.6)	136 (1.8)
482 (31.9)	1389 (23.0)	3079 (18.7)	1338 (17.7)	739 (17.1)	749 (13.4)	854 (11.5)
8 (0.5)	55 (0.9)	227 (1.4)	73 (1.0)	31 (0.7)	156 (2.8)	276 (3.7)
—	3 (0.0)	5 (0.0)	18 (0.2)	1 (0.0)	10 (0.2)	8 (0.1)
1 (0.1)	7 (0.1)	39 (0.2)	19 (0.3)	5 (0.1)	7 (0.1)	69 (0.9)
—	3 (0.0)	1 (0.0)	—	1 (0.0)	52 (0.9)	71 (1.0)
1 (0.1)	2 (0.0)	8 (0.0)	12 (0.2)	1 (0.0)	9 (0.2)	6 (0.1)
—	—	—	—	—	—	—
—	—	57 (0.3)	5 (0.1)	128 (3.0)	168 (3.0)	393 (5.3)
24 (1.6)	95 (1.6)	411 (2.5)	58 (0.8)	96 (2.2)	262 (4.7)	180 (2.4)
19 (1.3)	39 (0.6)	75 (0.5)	71 (0.9)	67 (1.6)	152 (2.7)	217 (2.9)
—	—	137 (0.8)	43 (0.6)	54 (1.3)	—	169 (2.3)
38 (2.5)	216 (3.6)	374 (2.3)	254 (3.4)	163 (3.8)	174 (3.1)	297 (4.0)
5 (0.3)	10 (0.2)	47 (0.3)	93 (1.2)	10 (0.2)	30 (0.5)	32 (0.4)
16 (1.1)	24 (0.4)	13 (0.1)	195 (2.6)	13 (0.3)	—	36 (0.5)
19 (1.3)	37 (0.6)	62 (0.4)	23 (0.3)	44 (1.0)	125 (2.2)	47 (0.6)
3 (0.2)	110 (1.8)	409 (2.5)	997 (13.2)	189 (4.4)	313 (5.6)	404 (5.4)
—	6 (0.1)	19 (0.1)	37 (0.5)	6 (0.1)	4 (0.1)	36 (0.5)
1 (0.1)	58 (1.0)	299 (1.8)	926 (12.2)	176 (4.1)	268 (4.8)	361 (4.8)

233

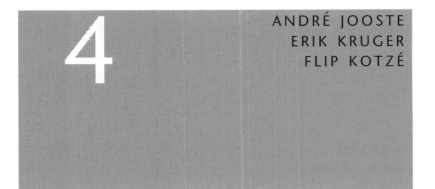

4

ANDRÉ JOOSTE
ERIK KRUGER
FLIP KOTZÉ

STANDARDS AND TRADE IN SOUTH AFRICA

Paving Pathways for Increased Market Access and Competitiveness

CONSUMERS WORLDWIDE ARE BECOMING MORE DEMANDING WITH REGARD TO WHAT they want. This is clearly evident from the shift from "quantity" to "quality" issues (Howells 2000). The ability of price movements and people's per capita income alone to explain problems associated with food demand and trade is increasingly questioned. In this regard, two broad classifications for factors that influence the demand for goods are important, namely

- Economic: These factors include income and price. For example, consumers will generally increase their consumption of goods when real income increases, while consumption falls when price relative to other goods rises.
- Noneconomic: These factors include issues pertaining to health and safety, convenience, quality, animal welfare, and the environment.

The latter is becoming more and more important with respect to consumer buying patterns and trade in general, thus the importance of standards (voluntary and mandatory) and technical regulations. In many instances, standards and regulations are considered vital to the maintenance or improvement of international market access, but there is also an increasing concern that these measures are being used unjustly to restrict access to important markets. In South Africa, the feeling is no different.

The purpose of this chapter is, therefore, to provide insight into the South African standards and regulations landscape, South Africa's international participation in setting standards and regulations; and how such standards and regulations are applied and policed: to identify the role and importance of different stakeholders, and to find out to what extent stakeholders comply, as well as identify the problems associated with such compliance.

The outline of the chapter is as follows. We provide an overview of the macroeconomic conditions and trade in South Africa in the first section. In the section entitled "Domestic Regulatory Structures and Policies," different regulatory bodies and structures are investigated. Another section investigates domestic regulations and standards, cost of compliance, and problems associated with compliance with regard to regulations and standards in specific industries. South Africa's international involvement in standards development is discussed in the section after that. In the next section, private sector perspectives and development assistance to Small, Medium, and Micro Enterprises (SMMEs) are discussed. The chapter concludes with action plans.

Macroeconomic Conditions and Trade in South Africa

The advent of complete democracy in South Africa in 1994 created the opportunity to undertake urgent changes in the management of the economy. Three areas were singled out in this respect:

• Stabilization of the macroeconomy to serve as a sound platform for future growth;
• Normalization of the international financial relations that included the phasing-out of controls on foreign exchange transactions; and
• Liberalization of the international trade of the country and the globalization of the economic activities.

The primary objective of these changes was to rectify the many structural deficiencies apparent in the economy at that stage.

Progress with the objective of liberalizing the trade is of particular importance within the context of this study. Growth and diversification of exports are the main objectives of trade liberalization and globalization of the economy. Growing demand for

compliance with standards by customers is an implicit challenge to producers in the course of trade liberalization. This challenge is more acute to exporters. Sales on the local market also require improved standards and quality, as tariff and other forms of protection are reduced.

This section begins with a review of South African economic conditions and performance, the sector structure of the economy, and the structure of imports and exports. Bilateral and multilateral trade agreements, as well as the institutional framework for trade negotiations are reviewed. The chapter concludes by discussing the relevance of quality and standards in sustaining export growth and some public policy responses in this respect.

This serves as the broad framework against which the analysis of standards is undertaken for the preselected sectors. A short description of the performance of these sectors in international trade is given. Emphasis is placed on progress over the period 1994–2001, as this is the period that followed the lifting of trade sanctions and liberalization of trade.

Economic Conditions and Performance

Although success had been achieved with many of the above-mentioned objectives, it happened at a cost, mainly in terms of low growth in output and the shedding of employment as the result of the economy responding to international competition

Table 4.1 South African Macroeconomic Indicators

Subject	Unit	1991	1994	2001
GDP at current prices	Rand billion	332	482.1	975.2
Percentage growth in real GDP	1995 prices	−1	3.2	2.2
GDP per capita at current prices	Rand	9,168	12,504	21,889
GDP per capita in real terms	1995 prices	14,352	13,786	14,321
Fiscal deficit before borrowing	Percent	4.7	5.7	1.4
GDFI: General government	1995 Rand billion	15.7	12.4	14.4
Savings: General government	Rand billion	−6.8	−28.6	−5.1
Prime overdraft rate	Percent	23.5	17.81	13
Yield: Government loan stock 10 years +	Percent	16.66	16.8	11.63
Consumer prices 2000 = 100	Percent	16.2	10.1	4.5
Balance current account/GDP	Percent	−1.9	−0.1	−0.2
Real effective exchange rate	1995 = 100	102	101.52	74.6
Household savings/disposable income	Ratio	2.7	2.8	0.3
GFI/GDP	Ratio	17.2	15.2	14.8
Nonagricultural employment	1995 = 100	105.4	101.3	88.3
Nonagricultural labor productivity	1995 = 100	88.4	96.4	131.7

Source: Quarterly Bulletin June 2002, South African Reserve Bank.

after a long period of economic isolation. Growth improved to some extent, growth in real gross domestic product averaged 2.6 percent per year in the period 1995–2001 as opposed to 0.6 percent per year between 1991 and 1995.

The most noticeable success in rectifying structural deficiencies was achieved in public sector finances (Table 4.1). The budget deficit before borrowing had been reduced from a high of 9.5 percent in 1993 to 1.4 percent in 2001. In addition, the negative savings ratio of government had been nearly eradicated by 2001. These improvements were accompanied by reductions in the corporate tax rate as well as the personal income tax rates. Disciplined public sector expenditure and vastly improved tax collection supported these improvements.

Inflation, as measured by the consumer price index, was brought down significantly and the Reserve Bank adopted a policy of inflation targets. According to that, core inflation is to remain within a band of 3–6 percent per year. Because of the sharp depreciation in the value of the rand, inflationary pressure started to build up by the end of 2001. As a result, the Reserve Bank raised interest rates in the first half of 2002 to ensure the achievement of its inflation targets.

The real effective exchange rate of the rand declined over the past decade making imported goods more expensive and exports cheaper. This development supports trade liberalization to compensate for the reduction in import tariffs and the scrapping of export subsidies. Thus, significant growth in exports contributed to the current account of the balance of payments, showing only small deficits in relation to the gross domestic product.

Given the favorable developments with regard to a number of fundamental macroeconomic aggregates, the low levels of real economic activity remain a major cause of concern. Although the investment ratio increased somewhat after 1994, it has fallen back in the past three years. Furthermore, the low savings rate remains a persistent structural deficiency.

Labor productivity improved and has been consistently spurred by the forces of progressive globalization of the South African economy. However, the labor absorption capacity of the economy suffered substantially less than before with nonagricultural employment.

Having achieved a great measure of success in the macroeconomic and financial environments, the performance of the real economy remains below expectations. Government is thus starting to place more emphasis on micro policies to activate various sectors, primarily in the development of agro-industries, tourism, labor-intensive and resource-based manufacturing, and the technology economy.

To summarize, success had been achieved in stabilizing the macroeconomy and consolidation of sound public finances. The challenge now is to direct the economy to a higher growth path and a greater degree of labor absorption. The remaining structural deficiencies of great importance are the low savings and investment rate.

Sector Structure of the Economy

Main Sectors. The tertiary sectors achieved higher growth than the primary sectors (agriculture and mining) as well as the secondary sectors (manufacturing electricity, gas, water, and construction) in the period 1990–2001 (Table 4.2). Among the latter, the electricity, gas, and water sectors achieved a growth equal to the national average.

As a consequence, the share of the services' sector increased from 58.8 percent in 1990 to 63.4 percent in 2001. Robust growth occurred in the supply of transport, storage, and communication services. This, among others, is the result of strong expansion in the market for mobile communication. Like elsewhere in the world, the sector for financial services expanded significantly along with the supply of other services.

The investment in fixed assets (Table 4.3) showed a corresponding trend to that in production, i.e., in favor of the services' sectors. However, fixed investment in mining and manufacturing recovered in the period 1994–2001 after significant declines between 1990 and 1994. In the case of manufacturing, the increase in investment relates to technology upgrades that were prompted by the need for improved competitiveness because of trade liberalization.

Growth in aggregate demand (Table 4.4) saw consistent growth in real household expenditure between 1990 and 2001. Real growth in government consumption expenditure became marginal after 1994 but growth in real gross capital formation picked up. Real growth in exports was double the rate in expenditure on gross domestic product over the period 1995 to 2001 signaling a rise in the export intensiveness with the advent of trade liberalization. Real imports of goods and services rose equally and the economy thus tended to be more open.

Sector changes can be summarized in that the production structure transformed in favor of the

Table 4.2 Percentage Change in Sectoral GDP

Sector	1990–1994	1995–2001	1990–2001
Agriculture, forestry, and fishing	0.39	1.05	0.78
Mining and quarrying	0.29	−0.84	−0.37
Manufacturing	−1.52	2.34	0.73
Electricity, gas, and water	2.80	2.44	2.59
Construction	−2.78	2.27	0.17
Trade, catering, and accommodation	−0.06	2.43	1.39
Transport, storage, and communication	1.34	6.70	4.47
Financial services	1.27	5.38	3.67
General government	1.25	0.18	0.62
Other services	3.02	3.18	3.11
Other producers	0.55	1.95	1.36
Gross domestic product	0.21	2.65	1.64

Source: Annex D as calculated from data in Annex A.

Table 4.3 Average Annual Real Gross Fixed Capital Formation Growth
(percent)

Sector	1990–1994	1995–2001	1990–2001
Agriculture, forestry, and fishing	−1.02	−0.73	−0.85
Mining and quarrying	−7.66	5.03	−0.26
Manufacturing	1.87	4.76	3.56
Electricity, gas, and water	−4.07	−5.84	−5.10
Construction	−2.69	3.15	0.71
Trade, catering, and accommodation	3.15	5.30	4.40
Transport, storage, and communication	6.64	10.70	9.01
Financial services	−2.05	3.34	1.09
Community, social, and personal services	−2.56	2.80	0.57
Total fixed capital formation	−1.39	3.75	1.61

Source: Annex D calculated from data in Annex B.

Table 4.4 Expenditure on GDP: Real Annual Growth
(percent)

Description	1990–1994	1995–2001	1990–2001
Final consumption expenditure by households	1.37	3.22	2.44
Final consumption expenditure by general government	1.67	−0.12	0.63
Gross fixed capital formation	−1.46	3.75	1.58
Change in inventories	−96.45	−86.67	−90.75
Residual items	−29.31	−5.58	−15.47
Exports of goods and services	2.64	5.65	4.40
Imports of goods and services	5.11	4.66	4.85
Expenditure on gross domestic product	0.20	2.65	1.63

Source: Annex D as calculated from data in Annex E.

services sectors over the period 1990–2001. This trend is replicated in the sector pattern of gross fixed capital formation. However, gross fixed capital formation in manufacturing expanded significantly over the period 1995–2001, among others, as the result of modernization of technology due to the competitive forces of globalization and trade liberalization. For the same reason the economy tended to be more open to the outside world with both exports and imports of goods and nonfactor services outstripping the growth in aggregate expenditure.

Primary Sectors and Subsectors of the Manufacturing Sector

Output. Trade liberalization that started in 1994 was bound to have a differential impact on growth especially with regard to the subsectors of the manufacturing sector. Outcomes in this respect are discussed in the following paragraphs with reference to 4 primary sectors and 27 subsectors of the manufacturing industry.

Table 4.5 provides information on the growth in the physical volume of production for the period 1990–2000. Among the primary sectors, the output by gold mines decreased on average by 3.3 percent per year. However, the decline in gold output has more to do with the profitability of mining ore reserves at specific price levels that became less lucrative over the past decade, than with trade liberalization.

Quite a number of sectors that fall within the ambit of light manufacturing experienced shrinking production levels (the sectors relevant to this study are shown in bold). Among these are the manufacturing of footwear, beverages, clothing, furniture, and radio and television.

At the same time, the volume of production by a number of light industries was increased between 1990 and 2000. Among these industries are the

Table 4.5 Percentage Annual Growth in Physical Volume of Production: Primary and Manufacturing Sectors (1990–2001)

Negative Growth		Positive Growth	
Sector	Growth Rates	Sector	Growth Rates
Footwear	−5.32	Glass and glass products	0.32
Gold mining	−3.98	**Textiles**	**0.57**
Professional equipment etc.	−1.87	Nonelectrical machinery	0.67
Printing and publishing	−0.95	**Processed food**	**0.72**
Nonmetallic mineral products nec	−0.70	Petroleum and petroleum products	0.81
Other transport equipment	−0.31	**Agriculture**	**1.01**
Beverages	**−0.31**	**Furniture**	**1.45**
Rubber products	−0.15	Other mining	1.66
Other manufacturing	−0.11	Metal products, excluding machinery	1.77
Radio, television, and communication apparatus	**−0.05**	Other chemical products	1.96
Clothing, excluding footwear	−0.04	Paper and paper products	2.01
		Electrical machinery	**2.54**
		Coal mining	2.62
		Basic iron and steel products	2.64
		Plastic products	**2.78**
		Motor vehicles, parts and accessories	4.38
		Industrial chemicals	4.56
		Wood and wood products	**5.15**
		Leather and leather products	**5.58**
Total manufacturing	1.88	Nonferrous metal products	9.07

Source: Annex E.

manufacturing of processed food, plastic products, furniture, and leather and leather products. The output of agriculture increased as well as that of coal mining and other mining among the primary sectors.

Export Intensity. The change in the export intensity of a sector to some extent reflects the impact of the liberalized trading environment on the performance in international trade. Available data allows the export intensity of sectors to be calculated by expressing the value of exports as a percentage of sales of domestically produced goods of that sector. Export intensities caluculated in this manner

are shown in Table 4.6 for 1990, 1995, and 2000. The last column shows the change in export intensity between 1995 and 2000 that helped in ranking the sectors and subsectors according to the change in their respective export intensities. The year 1995 signaled the advent of trade liberalization.

The trend toward a more open economy is clear from the contents of Table 4.6 in which all sectors experienced an increase in their export intensity between 1995 and 2000. (The results for the sector "Other mining" must be interpreted within the context of the activities of the Central Selling Organization for diamonds that results in a high export

Table 4.6 Exports/Sales
(percent)

Sector	1990	1995	2000	Change (1994–2000)
Other mining	87	106	106	0
Basic iron and steel products	43	49	58	18
Other transport equipment	17	77	91	18
Agriculture	11	12	14	18
Industrial chemicals	19	36	43	19
Coal mining	49	47	56	20
Nonferrous metal products	60	45	60	35
Paper and paper products	15	21	28	35
Leather and leather products	17	34	46	37
Footwear	1	4	5	38
Printing and publishing	1	2	3	39
Textiles	11	12	18	46
Processed food	9	9	13	49
Wood and wood products	7	15	24	62
Nonmetallic mineral products nec[a]	2	6	10	70
Other chemical products	5	10	20	89
Professional equipment etc.	8	35	70	99
Other manufacturing	16	15	31	101
Metal products, excluding machinery	6	6	12	113
Plastic products	2	4	9	117
Glass and glass products	8	9	19	122
Beverages	2	6	13	122
Electrical machinery	4	8	19	139
Furniture	4	18	44	146
Motor vehicles, parts and accessories	5	9	24	168
Clothing, excluding footwear	4	6	18	182
Nonelectrical machinery	5	19	62	221
Rubber products	3	8	24	222
Radio, television, and communication apparatus	2	10	39	294
Petroleum and petroleum products	1	3	28	865

Source: Calculated from information published by Statistics South Africa.
a. nec: not elsewhere classified

ratio for the sector and for exports to be higher than production in any given year as diamond sales are managed according to demand conditions.)

The sectors relevant to this study are shown in bold in Table 4.6. A common feature among them is that with the exception of the subsector "leather and leather products," their export intensities were relatively low in 1995. This is most clear for those subsectors that achieved high rates of increases between 1995 and 2000.

Furthermore, a comparison of the results of Tables 4.5 and 4.6 indicates that the increase in export intensity for footwear manufacturing, beverages, rubber products, clothing, radio and tele-vision manufacturing, and furniture was insufficient to prevent a decline in the physical volume of production. Growth in the volume of production benefited from higher export intensities with respect to agricultural production, the processing of food, and manufacture of textiles, plastic products, wood and products, and leather and leather products.

Import Intensity. The import intensities are the imports as a percentage of domestically produced goods (see Table 4.7). Except for the first four sectors, the trend toward a more open economy is clear among all sectors.

Table 4.7 Imports/Sales
(percent)

Sector	1990	1995	2000	Change (1994–2000)
Paper and paper products	11	13	11	−12.2
Other mining	4	12	11	−6.7
Leather and leather products	29	32	31	−1.4
Industrial chemicals	39	46	46	−1.1
Basic iron and steel products	6	7	7	0.6
Electrical machinery	30	44	44	0.6
Other manufacturing	12	21	22	5.0
Wood and wood products	9	12	13	7.4
Printing and publishing	10	17	20	17.9
Beverages	4	3	4	19.5
Motor vehicles, parts and accessories	34	39	47	20.3
Processed food	5	8	10	20.5
Nonelectrical machinery	83	127	156	23.0
Textiles	22	26	32	25.9
Metal products, excluding machinery	9	10	13	37.0
Other chemical products	25	32	46	44.6
Agriculture	4	4	7	52.8
Plastic products	12	13	20	57.0
Glass and glass products	14	18	29	58.7
Coal mining	1	1	2	60.2
Professional equipment etc.	279	273	455	66.8
Nonferrous metal products	11	15	27	73.7
Rubber products	16	23	40	74.9
Nonmetallic mineral products nec	9	11	23	105.0
Clothing, excluding footwear	6	8	18	112.1
Other Transport Equipment	54	99	215	116.5
Radio, Television, and communication apparatus	52	137	332	141.8
Furniture	2	4	12	163.3
Footwear	10	20	63	219.1
Petroleum and petroleum products	2	1	7	415.9

Source: Calculated from information published by Statistics South Africa.

Table 4.8 Aggregate Earnings on the Current Account Balance
(percent)

Heading	1990	1992	2001
Merchandise exports	60.9	63.3	72.6
Gold earnings	24.8	21.5	9.2
Services and investment income	14.3	15.2	18.2
Total	100.0	100.0	100.0

Source: Quarterly Bulletin June 2002, South African Reserve Bank.

In the sectors relevant to the study, the import intensities of those sectors that historically exhibited high import intensities did not rise significantly (see Table 4.7, sectors relevant to the study are in bold). This is clear in the leather and leather products and electrical machinery sectors and to a lesser extent in the textiles sector. However, the import intensity in the radio, television, and communication equipment sector rose steeply from an already high base. This can be related to the introduction of new technology, i.e., the introduction of mobile phones. Footwear manufacturing is experiencing a consistent increase in the import intensity, of as high as 63 percent of domestically produced sales in 2000. Imports are mainly sourced from low-cost producers located in the Far East.

The import intensity increased from a low base to ratios ranging between 4 and 13 percent in 2000 for the wood and wood products, beverages, processed food, agriculture, and furniture sectors. These developments are the logical outcomes of trade liberalization especially for an economy that operated in isolation for a protracted period.

Summary. Trade liberalization and globalization were adopted as one of the important policy directions of the past decade. Their impact on the growth of individual sectors can be expected to be different as the pattern of competitive advantages and disadvantages evolve compared with a preceding period characterized by protection and economic isolation. As a consequence, a number of sectors—some of which are relevant to this study—experienced negative growth and others exhibited positive growth over the past decade.

Analysis of changes in import and export intensities showed that, with few exceptions, all sectors opened up internationally with rising import and export intensities. Many of the sectors relevant to this study opened to world markets from low export and import intensiveness, an indication of a historically inward orientation.

As the markets of sophisticated, developed countries remain the main destination of exports and source of imports, the rising export and import intensities of sectors imply that South African producers had to improve the quality and standards of their products for export penetration purposes and as a defense against imports at lower protection levels.

Structure of Imports and Exports

Foreign Exchange Earnings. South Africa has three aggregate headings under which foreign exchange earnings on the current account of the balance of payments are recorded. Table 4.8 shows changes over the past decade.

The decline in the importance of the export of gold in total foreign exchange earnings is the striking feature of the past decade. This is the result of a low gold price and a decline in physical production. Real growth in total exports was

Table 4.9 Relative Shares of Expenditure
(percent)

Heading	1990	1994	2001
Merchandise imports	65.8	70.6	68.3
Services and investment payments	34.2	29.4	31.7
Total	100.0	100.0	100.0

Source: Quarterly Bulletin June 2002, South African Reserve Bank.

Table 4.10 Changing Composition of Merchandise Exports
(percent)

Heading	1990	1994	2000
Primary exports	58.5	59.1	20.0
Processed primary products	32.3	32.7	53.3
Manufactured products	9.2	17.2	26.7
Total	100.0	100.0	100.0

Source: Department of Finance 2002.

4.4 percent per year between 1990 and 2001. This is due to the expansion and diversification of merchandise exports and services receipts.

Disbursement of Foreign Exchange. The figures in Table 4.9 show that relative shares of expenditure on merchandise imports and services receipts fluctuated with about two-thirds expended on merchandise imports and one-third on services including investment-related payments. Investment-related payments became more prominent after 1994.

The Structure of Merchandise Exports

The Overall Pattern of Change in the Export Structure. The overall trend in merchandise exports is the move away from the export of primary products to processed primary products and manufactured exports (see Table 4.10).

A major reason for the decline in the share of primary exports is the decline in gold production, referred to earlier, as well as the more rapid growth rate in the export of processed primary products and merchandise exports. Except for gold, the trend in the physical level of exports tended to remain positive for the more important primary export products.

Merchandise exports are shown in Annex F expressed as values and a percentage share of total exports, classified according to chapters of the Harmonized Code. Certain deductions on structural changes in the export basket can be made with the help of this information.

Important Shifts in Exports by Sector. Table 4.11 summarizes changes in export shares by sector. Among the sectors that gained in export share, some benefited from interventionist policies especially motor vehicles and parts and aluminum

exports. The exports of a number of sectors relevant to this study also showed significant gains in export, namely radio, television, communication and electrical machinery and apparatus, plastic and articles, wood and articles, and furniture.

The share of motor vehicles and parts sector is prominent among those that gained in exports. In this sector, producers are required to comply with strict standards as laid down by the international original equipment manufacturers. South African producers are successful in this.[1] The South African Bureau of Standards (SABS), according to its ISO 9000 Registration Scheme, facilitates standards and quality compliance. These standards are recognized internationally by more than 70 countries and include

- ISO 9001 Quality Systems: Model for quality assurance in design, development, production, installation, and servicing;
- ISO 9002 Quality Systems: Model for quality assurance in production, installation, and servicing;
- ISO 14001 Environmental Management;
- QS 9000 Quality Management applicable to the motor industry; and
- VDA 6.1 Quality Management applicable to the motor industry.

Significant among the sectors that lost in export share are the precious stones and metals sectors. The decline in gold output contributed to the smaller share of the metals sector.

Furthermore, a significant development over the past decade is that the sectors that gained in their export shares became more important in the export basket than those that lost their export share.

Primary and Processed Foods. Calculations from Annex F show that the export of primary and processed foods rose consistently from 7 percent of

---

[1] See the "Automotive Sector" http://www.tisaglobal.com/auto/current_development.asp

Table 4.11 Changes in Export Shares by Sector
(percentage of total exports)

Sector	1990	1995	2001
Sectors That Gained			
Edible fruits and nuts	1.69	2.03	2.06
Wine and beverages	0.32	1.35	1.49
Mineral fuels substances and waxes	6.14	8.71	11.41
Inorganic chemicals etc	1.32	2.90	2.21
Organic chemicals	0.54	0.83	1.37
Plastics and articles	0.53	0.93	1.20
Wood and articles	0.52	0.86	1.15
Paper and paperboard	1.17	1.56	1.72
Aluminum and articles	0.91	0.83	3.19
Machinery	1.59	3.43	7.63
Radio, Television, and electrical machinery	0.64	1.43	2.36
Motor vehicles parts and machinery	1.09	2.66	7.66
Furniture and bedding	0.23	1.46	1.48
Subtotal	16.69	28.98	44.93
Sectors That Lost			
Pulp of wood, cellulose, or waste	1.37	2.18	1.18
Precious stones and metals	39.15	31.48	23.84
Iron and steel	8.66	9.57	7.86
Articles of iron and steel	1.44	1.34	1.20
Subtotal	50.62	44.57	34.08

Source: Calculated from information published by Statistics South Africa.

total exports in 1990 to 8.3 percent in 1995 and to 9 percent in 2001. Increased exports of wine, fish, tobacco, and tobacco products and edible fruits and nuts were mainly responsible for the rise in the share of primary and processed foods in total exports. However, quite a number of products with a small share in total exports also improved their shares. A loss in export shares was observed in the case of vegetables, cereals, animal and vegetable fats and oils, waste from the food industries, and animal feeds. The share of total exports for a number of products remained relatively stable over the past decade.

Other Light Industries. Exports of leather remained at 0.64 percent of total exports in 1990 and 2001 after having reached a high of 0.83 percent in 1995. Exports of leather goods increased from 0.01 percent of total exports in 1990 to 0.07 percent in 1995 before falling back to 0.05 percent in 2001. This sector is constrained by shortages in the supply of leather since South Africa became a leading supplier of leather cover seats for motorcars. Exports of the latter are classified as part of the furniture sector.

Exports of footwear increased from 0.03 percent of total exports to 0.08 percent in 1995 before receding to 0.05 percent in 2001. Exports of textiles lost ground in total exports, textiles' share declined from 2 percent in 1990 to 1.7 percent in 1995 and to 1.4 percent in 2001. However, exports of clothing and made-up textiles improved their share in total exports from 0.24 percent in 1990 to 0.53 percent in 1995 and to 0.85 percent in 2001.

Summary. The South African economy became more open over the past decade. Most of the sectors relevant to this study increased their share of total exports but for many this happened from a very low base. The important exporters among these sectors are agriculture and processed food, wood and wood products, plastics and plastic products, and radio, television, and communication equipment with the clothing exports among the textiles sector growing

Table 4.12 Selected Sectors' Share of Imports
(percent)

Sector	1990	1995	2001
Machinery	21.61	20.29	16.22
Mineral Fuels	0.52	8.63	14.80
Electrical machinery	8.28	10.68	11.66
Motor vehicles	11.74	11.71	6.38
Instrumentation including optical	3.80	3.65	3.72
Aircraft	1.02	1.84	3.08
Total	58.12	56.80	55.86

Source: Annex F.

in prominence. As a consequence, standards as an underlying facilitator of exports increased in prominence.

The Structure of Merchandise Imports

Important Shifts in Imports. South African imports historically tended to be concentrated on a small number of sectors or products (see Table 4.12). Imports of products in six sectors constitute more than 55 percent of total merchandise imports. The machinery sector lost in prominence of imports over the past decade. This trend could be attributed to a low level of fixed investment in the economy that should be reversed in the future. The share of imports of mineral fuels rose significantly since 1990. To some extent this can be ascribed to imports of oil becoming overt rather than covert in the course of

the decade (see high percentage of unclassified imports in 1990 in Annex F), while high oil prices could have blown up the import share for 2001.

Imports of electrical machinery and equipment rose due to the installation of information technology services. The development program for the motor industry is affecting imports of motor vehicles.

Imports of Sectors Relevant to the Study. The share in total imports of these sectors changed as shown in Table 4.13 during the past decade.

A general pattern of gains in import share emerged among sectors in the period up to 1995, but receded again thereafter. Sectors whose share in imports rose consistently include footwear, furniture, radio television communication. Sectors whose share in imports declined include electrical machinery and textiles.

Table 4.13 Percentage of Total Merchandise Imports
(percent)

Sector	1990	1995	2001
Agriculture and processed food	5.33	7.32	4.61
Fish	0.17	0.13	0.13
Edible fruits and nuts	0.08	0.10	0.08
Beverages	0.54	0.41	0.37
Wood and products	0.69	0.70	0.51
Leather and leather products	0.61	0.61	0.55
Footwear	0.40	0.67	0.77
Textiles	4.54	3.67	3.08
Plastic products	2.95	3.13	2.67
Furniture	0.29	0.40	0.59
Radio, television, and electrical machinery	8.28	10.68	11.66
Total	23.14	27.18	24.44

Source: Annex F.

Table 4.14 Destination of South African Exports
(percentage share)

Region	Country	1990	1995	2001
Africa (excluding SADC) total		0.80	2.27	3.85
Eastern Europe total		0.28	0.44	0.45
	Germany	4.35	4.55	7.49
	United Kingdom	4.14	8.17	9.65
EU total		23.92	29.92	34.10
	China	0.21	1.02	1.67
	Japan	5.94	5.29	5.83
Far East total		13.58	14.66	13.80
Middle East total		3.83	4.86	6.45
	United States	3.06	5.41	9.82
Northern America total		3.56	6.31	10.92
Oceania total		0.49	1.18	1.78
Other total		46.78	27.10	15.79
SADC total		5.72	11.26	11.09
South America total		0.95	1.90	1.76
Western Europe (excluding EU) total		0.09	0.11	0.02
Total		100.00	100.00	100.00

Source: Annexes G and H.

Destination of Exports

Total Exports. A summary of the destination of South African imports is shown in Table 4.14. The item "Others" constituted almost 50 percent of total exports in 1990 ("Others" includes unclassified items that were exported in the sanctions era). The proportion of exports under this item decreased to 15.8 percent in 2001 (Classification of a high proportion of exports in this item in 1990 is a remnant of the era of trade sanctions. "Other" also includes gold). However, some meaningful deductions can be made for the period 1995–2001.

It is clear from the information that the share of exports going to the traditional trading partners, the EU and United States, increased as well as exports to Africa excluding Southern African Development Community (SADC), the Middle East and Oceania. Due to the growth in exports to the Far East, SADC, and South America having been less rapid than that to other destinations, their share in total exports diminished between 1995 and 2001. It is not clear if standards issues played a role in this. China as a destination of exports increased in importance.

Destination of Exports of Sectors Relevant to This Study. Data for 1990, 1995, and 2001 are shown in Annex G according to value and percentage of exports share per sector. The comments below are derived from the information in Annex G.

Processed Food. The EU is the most important destination of processed food export but is declining in importance due to diversification of food exports to other markets. This also applies to SADC, which became the second most important destination in 1995 but then lost ground by 2001, and to the Far East, previously the third most important destination. Destinations that gained in their share of processed food exports are Africa (excluding SADC), the Middle East, North America (especially the United States), and Oceania: however, these destinations had a relatively low "starting point" (that is, they had previously received very few processed food imports), so it is not surprising that, once sanctions were removed, they gained in their shares.

Beverages. The share of beverages (wine) exports to the EU, North America, and Africa (excluding SADC) increased significantly. The export shares to SADC, Far East, and Oceania decreased greatly.

Textiles. The proportion of exports destined for SADC, North America, and Africa (excluding SADC) increased significantly, while that destined for the Far East was reduced significantly and marginally the proportion (37.6 percent of the total in 2001), that went to the EU.

Leather and Leather Products. The proportion destined for the EU is declining but still amounted to 43 percent of the total in 2001. This also applies to the Far East, the second largest market. A growing proportion of exports is going to the Americas.

Footwear. The largest proportion of footwear exports (53.8 percent in 2001) was to SADC. Gains were made to Africa excluding SADC, the Far East, Middle East, and Oceania. The share of exports to the EU diminished.

Wood and Wood Products. Exports to the Far East (mainly Japan) and North America increased, while that to the EU declined.

Plastic Products. SADC was the main destination of exports while the export share going to the EU shrunk. Gains to Africa (excluding SADC and North America) occurred.

Electrical Machinery. The EU became an important destination for exports (43.3 percent in 2001) and there were gains in export share to Africa excluding SADC, the Middle East, and North America.

The share of exports destined for SADC and South America diminished significantly.

Radio, Television, and Communication. Gains in export share were made to Africa excluding SADC, the Far East, Middle East and Oceania. The export share of the EU remains significant at a reduced level as well as the export that of SADC.

Furniture. The EU remains the single most important destination at a stable level (about 83 percent of furniture exports). Export of leather covers for automotive seats used in luxury German cars are important for this sector. Gains in export share happened in the case of the Far East and North America. Loss in export share to Africa, as well as SADC occurred.

Agriculture. The EU remains the most important destination for agricultural exports (52.2 percent in 2001). Gains in export share are made to Africa excluding SADC, North and South America, and Oceania. The percentage of exports going to the Middle East is shrinking.

Origin of Imports

Total Imports. A summary of the origin of total imports is shown in Table 4.15. The EU remains the

Table 4.15 Origin of South African Imports
(percentage share)

Region	Country	1990	1995	2001
Africa (excluding SADC) total		0.23	1.10	1.33
Eastern Europe total		0.25	0.50	0.77
	Germany	19.68	16.50	14.97
	United Kingdom	11.78	11.07	8.43
EU total		48.71	47.82	43.00
	China	0.77	1.90	4.22
	Japan	9.83	10.17	6.82
Far East total		18.09	20.74	18.97
Middle East total		2.24	9.58	15.11
	United States	11.43	11.89	11.98
Northern America total		12.65	13.14	13.04
Oceania total		0.98	1.84	3.01
Other total		13.53	1.04	0.89
SADC total		1.42	1.88	1.27
South America total		1.87	2.32	2.60
Western Europe (excluding EU) total		0.04	0.04	0.02
Total		100.00	100.00	100.00

Source: Annexes G and H.

most important source of imports but its share is marginally declining. The same can be said of the Far East but to a lesser extent. However, China's share of South African imports is growing. Many are increasing their share from a low level, namely Africa excluding SADC, Eastern Europe, the Middle East (possibly as the result of overt oil imports and higher priced oil in 2001), North America, Oceania and South America. After an increase in its share between 1990 and 1995, SADC lost ground in the period 1995–2001.

Imports of Merchandise Relevant to This Study.
Processed Food. South America and the EU are the main sources of processed food imported into South Africa, each with a share of about 25 percent. Oceania improved its share of South African imports, as have Eastern Europe and the Middle East, SADC and Africa excluding SADC. The Far East (an important supplier) lost its share of South African imports.

Beverages. Imports are predominantly from the EU (76.2 percent in 2001). North America is gaining in share as are a number of regions that have a small proportion in total imports.

Textiles. The Far East and the EU are the most important suppliers of textiles to South Africa but their respective shares in total imports are on the decline. However, China is increasing its share rapidly and so is the Middle East. The share from SADC is also on the rise as well as imports from Africa excluding SADC.

Leather and Leather Products. The EU, Far East, Middle East and South America are the most important suppliers. Among them, the Far East (China) and South America are gaining in share.

Footwear. The Far East accounted for 88.6 percent of imports in 2001. Imports from China alone accounted for 64.5 percent up from 14 percent in 1990. The share of footwear imports declined with respect to all other regions.

Wood and Wood Products. The EU and the Far East increased their significant shares of total South African imports of wood and wood products. The share of South Africa's imports held by the Middle East and North America declined.

Plastic Products. The EU continues to supply about 50 percent of South African imports of plastic products but its share is on the decline. The same applies to imports from North America (15.6 percent in 2001). The share of the Far East increased to 26.7 percent in 2001 due to rising imports from China.

Electrical Machinery. The share of the EU of South African imports of electrical machinery is on the decline but still amounted to 54 percent in 2001. The share of the Far East (that of China) is on the increase as is the share of North America in the period 1995–2001.

Radio, Television, and Communication. The share of the EU of South African imports (57 percent) in 2001 is growing, while that from the Far East (27 percent in 2001) is on decline (except for China). Imports from North America remain about 10 percent of the total.

Furniture. About 57 percent of furniture imports are sourced from the EU and 23 percent from the Far East. North America lost import share as well as SADC between 1995 and 2001.

Agriculture. Imports of agricultural products tend to fluctuate severely upsetting the establishment of set patterns. From the information in Annex H, it is clear that the EU is losing its share of South African imports. This seems to be true for imports from the Far East and North America too. Import gains are clear with respect to South America, Oceania, SADC and Africa excluding SADC.

Multilateral and Bilateral Trade Agreements

The multi- and bilateral trade agreements that are important to South Africa and those that came into existence over the past decade are dealt with below.

World Trade Organisation. South Africa is a member of the World Trade Organisation (WTO) and was a founding member of its predecessor, the General Agreement on Tariffs and Trade. As such, all relevant trade promotion activities and all negotiations that South Africa undertakes fall within WTO rules.

The tariffs that South Africa's trading partners apply to its exports are according to their Most Favoured Nations' schedules. However, South Africa has become party to a number of bilateral agreements in the past six years. These are discussed next.

Southern African Customs Union (SACU).

The Southern African Customs Union (SACU) is an agreement between South Africa, Botswana, Lesotho, Namibia and Swaziland, which sets a common trade system for the five countries. In terms of the SACU, there are no tariff barriers between member countries and all members share a common external tariff on imports into the region.

Providing for an almost unrestricted flow of goods and services among its members, the SACU collects the levies on member states' imports from the rest of the world and apportions this income among the member states according to an agreed formula.[2] Earnings from the customs and excise pool contribute substantially to the government revenues of Botswana, Lesotho, Swaziland and Namibia.

During 1994, South Africa and its partners in the SACU agreed that the 1969 Customs Union Agreement in its original form had become outdated and had to be democratized and renegotiated. This resulted in the creation of an institutional working group to negotiate and oversee the operations of the SACU and investigate issues on an ongoing basis.

SADC Free Trade Area.

South Africa became a member of the Southern African Development Community (SADC) in 1994. A trade protocol has been negotiated within SADC, which forms the basis of the Free Trade Area (FTA), which came into effect on 1 September 2000. The Protocol requires an 85 percent reduction of internal trade barriers over an eight-year period and all tariff barriers to be removed within the next four years.

The tariff phase-down schedule, which was negotiated for the FTA, requires that the SACU phase down its tariffs faster than the rest of SADC. There are also mechanisms in place for member states to apply for further time for industries that may have been adversely affected by the tariff phase-down and for infant industries to be provided with additional protection on a temporary basis.

South Africa-EU Trade, Development and Cooperation Agreement.

The implementation of the SA-EU Trade, Development and Cooperation Agreement (TDCA) on 1 January 1999 marked the end of more than three years of negotiations with the European Union toward a Trade, Development and Cooperation Agreement. This Agreement covers a comprehensive range of elements, including provisions for political dialogue, free trade in a wide range of goods, promoting trade-related issues, economic cooperation, financial assistance and development cooperation.

Some of the most important aspects of the TDCA are as follows:

SA-EU Free Trade Area.

Under the TDCA, the majority of tariffs on imports to the EU will be phased down over a ten-year period (see Annex H). The majority of tariffs on imports to South Africa will be phased down over a twelve-year period. The FTA covers the free movement of goods in all sectors as well as covering the liberalization of trade in services.

There are a number of exceptions in terms of the agreement to protect industries in the EU and in South Africa; most notably the agricultural and textiles sectors in the EU and the agricultural and automotive sectors in South Africa. Some aspects relating to the agricultural sector are still being negotiated. In all, the EU is committed to the full liberation of 95 percent of South African exports over the ten year period and South Africa is committed to the full liberalization of 86 percent of EU exports over the twelve year period. Annex H provides a summary of the tariff phase-down schedule for South African exports into the EU.

Development Cooperation.

The TDCA provides for access by South Africa to development assistance from the EU. This includes assistance aimed at integrating the South African economy into the global economy, development of sustainable private enterprises, regional cooperation, improving the delivery of social services as well as support to protection of human rights and strengthening civil society. In

---

[2] The Southern Africa Customs Union has a formula whereby revenues derived from customs duties are shared. The formula favors Botawana, Lesotho, and Swaziland at the expense of South Africa on the premise that South African industrial development benefits from tariff protection at the expense of consumers in these three countries. This is a remnant from the import replacement era and the formula is under review following the adoption of trade liberalization. For more information visit http://www.dti.org.za.

addition, development cooperation is aimed at strengthening the link between South African government and society as a whole.

Economic Cooperation. The economic cooperation aspect of the agreement includes strengthening economic links between the EU and South Africa, supporting regional economic cooperation, promoting sustainable development, promoting SMMEs, promoting economic empowerment, promoting the role of women in the economy and promoting worker and trade union rights as well as protecting and improving the environment.

African Growth and Opportunity Act. The African Growth and Opportunity Act (AGOA) represents a unilateral, nonreciprocal political gesture by the United States, aimed at assisting and elevating growth and development of sub-Saharan African countries, by extending duty-free and quota-free access into the U.S. market. AGOA provides this access for a range of products for an eight-year period, beginning 1 January 2001. South Africa, along with 33 other African countries, has been designated as an eligible country in terms of the Act.

The AGOA provides for 1800 tariff lines in addition to the approximately 4600 tariff lines under the normal GSP list. At this stage, the automotive and the textiles and clothing industries are most relevant to South Africa.

Under AGOA, various automotive components and various types of motor vehicles (including motor cars), subject to certain conditions, qualify for duty-free access into the United States. This enhances access by South African automotive industry to the U.S. market by building on the current list of products under the existing Generalized System of Preferences (GSPs). Aside from increasing the list of qualifying components, importantly, AGOA also adds motor vehicles to the list, none of which were accessible to the U.S. market duty-free.

Another important facet of AGOA is the access provided for most types of apparel to the U.S. market duty free. The Act does, however, place a limit on how much duty-free apparel can be imported in terms of the total U.S. imports, but it is likely that the African continent will only reach this limit toward the end of the eight-year life span of AGOA. Products exported to the United States from AGOA ountries must be made from local (i.e., AGOA country) inputs. A few exceptions apply.

Generalized System of Preferences. South Africa has been granted GSP facilities by a number of developed countries. These programs provide South African exports with preferential access to developed markets, through the reduction of import tariffs on predetermined products. However, the preferential access varies in terms of the extent of tariff cuts and in product coverage.

South Africa has been granted GSP facilities by the United States, the EU, Japan, Canada, Norway, Hungary, Switzerland, and the Czech Republic. The GSP facilities given by the United States and the European Union are further enhanced by the AGOA and the SA-EU TDCA, respectively. In addition to AGOA and GSPs given by the United States to South Africa, there is a US-SA Bilateral Trade Commission which is responsible for the promotion of trade and cooperation between the two countries.

Under Negotiation. South Africa is presently exploring trade accords with Mercosur as well as with individual countries, including India, Nigeria, Zimbabwe and Malawi. The United States also has given tentative indications at a bilateral trade agreement with South Africa.

Institutional Framework for Trade Negotiations

The Department of Trade and Industry is responsible for South Africa's multi- and bilateral trade relations and negotiations. The Directorate: Multilateral Trade Relations coordinates South Africa's relations and negotiations in the World Trade Organization, commissions established to deal with bilateral trade agreements and also liase with the UNCTAD, the Organisation for Economic Cooperation and Development (OECD), the SADC, and the G77.

Coordination takes place with the Department of Agriculture and the Department of Mineral and Energy Affairs, especially with regard to multilateral trade relations. Coordination with the Department of Finance and Reserve Bank relates to trade in services. The Department of Foreign Affairs usually becomes involved on the political side of agreements.

Following a pattern set at the time South Africa entered into the Uruguay Round of trade negotiations, the relevant government departments coordinate with the business sector and organized labor on these matters in the National Economic

Development and Labour Council (NEDLAC). NEDLAC is a statutory body that was established by government for purposes of deliberation among the social partners—government, business and labor—on important economic policy issues. A special subcommittee, Teselico, was established by NEDLAC to deal specifically with trade-related matters. Most of Teselico's work involves negotiations and deliberation of the contents of multi- and bilateral trade agreements.

Relevance of Standards

A number of groundbreaking World Bank studies have highlighted the potential impact of increased regulatory stringency on trade flows. In an October 2001 draft report entitled: *To Spray or Not to Spray: Pesticides, Banana Exports, and Food Safety,* Wilson and Otsuki (2001a) presented the findings of an econometric analysis of the impact of stricter pesticide residue standards in 11 OECD countries on banana exports from 19 developing nations. The report estimates that a 10 percent increase in regulatory stringency (i.e., moving from the current CODEX maximum residue level for *chlorpyrifos* to the much stricter EU level) could result in a loss of US$ 5.3 million exports per year or a decrease of 14.8 percent in banana imports.

Although it may be argued that stricter pesticide residue standards would reduce health risks and, in so doing, compensate for any direct export losses, the short- to medium-term effects on banana exporting countries would be considerable.

Similarly, in another World Bank study on the effect of drug residue limits on the beef trade Wilson, Otsuki and Majumdar (2001) argue that stricter regulations on the use of veterinary drugs can result in additional costs to livestock producers. The study, which analyzed the quantitative effect of veterinary medicine standards on trade in bovine meat between 16 exporting countries and 5 importing countries together with the entire EU, estimates that reducing the maximum residue limit on tetracycline antibiotics (one of the most commonly used veterinary medicines) by 1 percent (to the CODEX level) would result in a 0.6 percent reduction in imports from low-income countries included in the sample. This is due mainly to the fact that the United States, whose standard was less strict than the CODEX standard, had been importing most of their bovine meat.

The above examples highlight the impact that increased regulatory stringency can have on developing countries. Policymakers need to balance consumer safety, on the one hand, with sustained trade flows and market access for developing nations on the other hand. The key is, therefore, to ensure food safety without over regulating.

During the 1990s, South Africa stabilized its macroeconomic environment thereby laying the foundations for more rapid and sustainable growth. Trade liberalization played an indispensable part in this process and the economy is increasingly being drawn into the global economy while the overall economic growth rate is becoming even more dependant on export growth than ever before. The composition of the export basket changed substantially away from primary exports to processed and manufactured merchandise. While some progress was made to penetrate "new" (geographic) markets, the traditional markets of the developed countries remain particularly important. Ties with these markets are believed to have become even stronger as the result of the SA-EU TDCA and the AGOA of the United States. Deeper penetration into the more sophisticated domains of international trade, as suggested by these developments, increasingly requires South African producers to comply with applicable international standards to reap the benefits inherent in standards compliance.[3]

While South Africa built a well-established infrastructure (as is explained in the next paragraph), to deal with standards compliance, the domestic and especially the international standards environment, is particularly dynamic. This requires a matching response on the part of the South African infrastructure since standards compliance is becoming increasingly important to business to enhance the momentum in export growth and as a defense against imports.

In a recent policy document,[4] the Department of Trade and Industry (DTI) underscored the importance of quality and standards in facilitating (foreign) market access and sustainable export growth.

---

[3] Quantitative information on the proportion of exports that comply with standards is not available.

[4] The Department of Trade and Industry South Africa: *"Accelerating Growth and Development: The Contribution of an Integrated Manufacturing Strategy"* 2002.

The development of systems for Standardization, Quality Assurance, Accreditation and Metrology (SQAM) are singled out as an important platform for sustainable long-term competitiveness (page 25 of the DTI report).

Similarly, the South African Bureau of Standards (SABS) and the South African National Accreditation Systems (SANAS) are prominent among the battery of institutions at the disposal of the Department of Trade and Industry for achieving national development objectives (page 57 of the DTI report).

With respect to regulated standards, the Department of Trade and Industry is concerned with the impact of NONTARIFF BARRIERS. However, no indication is given as to possible approaches in this respect aside from the statement that: "We need to intensify our analysis of the continued constraints to significant export growth, both in terms of other barriers to trade—such as Nontariff Barriers..." (page 16 of the DTI report).

The importance of this aspect is underscored by the review of the South African experiences in dealing with the regulatory requirements in the export of the fruit industries (section entitled "Fruit Industries"); the meat and livestock industries (section entitled "Meat and Livestock Industry"); and to a lesser extent in fisheries (section entitled "Fisheries"). In the case of fisheries, South Africa seems to be among the leaders in respect to standards and their compliance.

Although compliance to standards in the regulated industries are important to each and every market on the micro level, requirements with respect to South African exports of fruit seem to be the more critical in view of the importance of the industry in the totality of exports and in the socioeconomic sphere. Furthermore, apart from the regulatory requirements, standards that are being implemented in the procurement of merchandise by large industrial country importers in the retail sector can in fact become barriers to trade as is mentioned in section entitled "Industry Review."

Because of the importance of fruit to South African exports, and the priority that government attaches to the development of agri-industries (not only for purely economic reasons but also because of the industry's favorable employment ratio), render compliance to regulatory and other standards imperative for future development.

Compliance is furthermore complicated by standards fragmentation among countries where countries tend to implement their own criteria even in the face of accepted international standards, for example CODEX (Wilson and Otsuki 2001b). Many country-based standards are more stringent than the internationally accepted ones and Wilson and Otsuki (2001b), with the application of econometric techniques, demonstrated the trade-constraining effect of these more stringent standards on international trade. Inadvertently, this practice could lead to instances where health and safety considerations can be abused for purely protective purposes. Harmonization of country standards with the internationally accepted ones thus, still has a long way to go.

Since South Africa follows a policy of compliance to standards and reaps the benefits thereof in the penetration of export markets, it remains important to build on its existing standards and compliance infrastructure especially with regard to regulatory standards. Fragmentation in a different sense, that is fragmentation of the functions of standard setting, compliance and dispute settlement, in the case of South Africa as explained in section entitled "Domestic Regulatory Structures and Policies" (internationally as described by Wilson and Otsuki 2001b) remains to be addressed.

From the foregoing it is clear that issues around standards and quality are receiving prominent attention in terms of establishing the infrastructure to deal with them and policies and standards-related incentives to promote market access by South African exporters. There is a need in South Africa for more data on the benefits of standardization. Action plan three in Table 4.19 proposes a full-fledged study to determine the economic benefits derived from standardization in South Africa. The benefits gained by these industry sectors will be assessed to obtain information on the impact of standards on

- Growth of the different industries.
- Competitiveness of South African industries.
- Empowerment of small-, micro- and medium-size enterprises.
- Regulatory enforcement.
- Regional and international trade.

Issues such as the cost of compliance to firms and other micro-level aspects are also becoming more important. The sector analysis in section entitled "Industry Review," in conjunction with the World

Bank survey on the cost of compliance and other standards-related issues, conveys the impression that businesses do not regard the cost of compliance as prohibitive. However, this view may vary among sectors. Most regard the benefits derived from compliance to be far in excess of the cost thereof, even if investment or modification of plants is involved. Nonetheless, smaller firms may find the cost involved in complying with international standards to be a deterrent as well as the effort and the managerial time spent. In these respects, it needs to be noted that compliance with regulatory standards is usually more cumbersome than in the instance of voluntary ones.

The development of SMEs in South Africa receives priority and perhaps more so than in other countries as SME development is seen as a vehicle for bringing PDIs into the main stream of the economy. Standards compliance is seen as an important step for SMEs to gain a foothold in the local market, especially in respect to government procurement and later on in export markets. In an effort to ameliorate the cost of standards compliance, the DTI introduced a number of initiatives (see section entitled "Private Sector Perspectives and Development Assistance to SMMEs") to assist SMEs to obtain standards compliance. Financial assistance is mostly on a matching grant basis. Some of these initiatives are undertaken with the help of foreign assistance, for example the World Bank in respect to the Competitiveness Fund (section entitled "DTI Incentive Schemes" (a) The Competitiveness Fund). Use of these schemes by businesses seems to enhance competitiveness and export penetration.

Standards development and compliance are dynamic in nature on the national and even more so on the international level. Businesses are well aware of the positive tradeoffs between standards compliance and the competitive benefits to be derived there from. The future export performance, as one of the single most important determinants of overall economic development, requires this awareness to become increasingly pervasive among producers.

Domestic Regulatory Structures and Policies

The South African regulatory and standards system comprises various role players. These role players perform different functions pertaining to regulations and standards setting, as well as policing and accreditation. Figure 4.1 shows the regulatory and standards landscape, as well as links between different role players in South Africa as well as internationally. Apart from providing a brief overview of the main role players, this section also sheds some light on possible problems and constraints being experienced. Issues pertaining to the functions of the different role players and details on procedures followed in respect to disease notifications, etc. are given in Annex I.

Department of Trade and Industry (DTI). As mentioned, the DTI is responsible for South Africa's multi- and bilateral trade relations and negotiations. In addition, the DTI is also responsible for trade and export promotion and oversees various development assistance programs.

It also oversees accreditation of all South African test laboratories, certification bodies and inspection bodies whether commercial or within the state, as the key to international market access (see section entitled "South African Development Assistance" for more details). DTI has also invested a significant amount of funds into the South African National Accreditation System (SANAS). In addition, the DTI has invested a significant amount of money over the past six years in upgrading the National Metrology Laboratory (NML) to ensure that South Africa's national measurement standards are at par with its trading partners. The NML, based at the Council for Science and Industrial Research (CSIR), currently receives R32 million per year (approximately US$3,154 million).[5] These measuring standards form the basis of all calibration in the economy and are vital to increased industrial competitiveness. The measurement standards also underpin South Africa's test laboratory capabilities.

The two action plans shown in Table 4.20 relate specifically to the improvement of measurement capability in South Africa and within SADC as a whole. The National Metrology Laboratory has just completed a mobile metrology unit for Mozambique (funded by UNIDO). This rugged piece of equipment, which also houses sleeping quarters, is mounted on a truck chassis, four wheel driven and designed for both on and off-road use. The truck has been tested to military specifications and can

---

[5] Exchange rate 26 May 2002: $1 = R10,145. This exchange rate is used throughout the chapter.

4.1 SA Regulatory and Standards Landscape

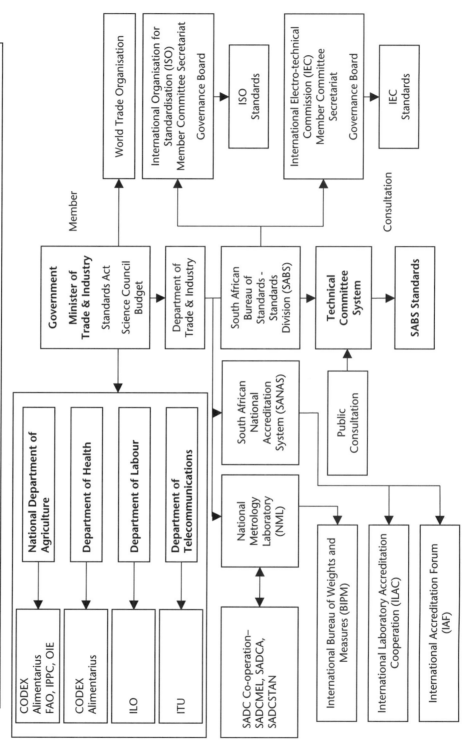

SOUTH AFRICAN STANDARDS, QUALITY, ACCREDITATION & METROLOGY LANDSCAPE

withstand almost any conditions. It can house calibration equipment for any of the main measurement disciplines such as force, mass, temperature, flow, and volume, etc. The objective of the NML's new Measurement Practice Improvement Guide is to improve measurement accuracy in SME manufacturing firms.

Both the National Physical Laboratory in the United Kingdom, as well as the Mexican Metrology Institute have used similar toolkits to assist SMEs.

National Department of Health

The South African Health System. Within the health sector, the Government of South Africa has adopted the Primary Health Care (PHC) approach through the *National Health Plan for South Africa* and the Reconstruction and Development Programme in 1994, and subsequently the *White Paper on Health: Towards a National Health System,* published in November 1996. The *White Paper* provides for the establishment of a national health system in South Africa, which will in broad terms consist of three levels (National Department of Health, Provincial Health Departments and Local Authorities) for public health service delivery with each level responsible for specific functions. The following broad functions, as determined by the *White Paper,* are the responsibility of the Department:

- Overall coordination
- Determination of policy (national norms and standards)
- Monitoring (auditing)
- Supporting the provinces
- International liaison and cooperation

On behalf of the National Department of Health, a full-time Port Health Service is rendered by the four provinces responsible for the control of most of the foodstuffs imported into South Africa, namely: Kwazulu-Natal, Eastern Cape, Western Cape and Gauteng.

The Directorate: Food Control. The Directorate: Food Control, included in the Chief Directorate:

Pharmaceutical and Food Services, is directly responsible for all matters related to food safety control at the national level and addresses this through the broad objectives as outlined in the Health Sector Strategic Framework's Ten Point Plan 2000–2005 (1999).

The primary objective of the Directorate: Food Control is to ensure an optimal nonpersonal preventive primary health care service in respect to the safety of food for the South African community based on basic needs and the right to make informed choices without being misled by means of scientifically founded legislation, auditing and information actions.

The Directorate: Food Control administers parts of the following Acts that relate to food (see Annex J for details on Acts):

- Foodstuffs, Cosmetics and Disinfectants Act, 1972 (Act No. 54 of 1972).
- The Health Act, 1977 (Act No. 63 of 1977).
- The International Health Regulations Act, 1974 (Act No. 28 of 1974).

National Department of Agriculture (NDA)

Directorate: Plant Health and Quality (DPHQ). The NDA has several functions with respect to setting and policing of regulations and standards pertaining to agricultural products. These functions are under the DPHQ,[6] which is the official National Plant Protection Organisation (NPPO) for South Africa in terms of South Africa's membership of the International Plant Protection Convention (IPPC). Table 4.16 shows the structure of the DPHQ.

The DPHQ administers parts of the following Acts that relate to plant health and quality control: (see Annex J for details on Acts)

- Agricultural Pests Act, 1983 (Act No. 36 of 1983)
- Agricultural Product Standards Act, 1990 (Act No. 119 of 1990).
- The Fertilizers, Farm Feeds, Agricultural Remedies and Stock Remedies Act (Act No. 36 of 1947)
- The Liquor Products Act, 1989 (Act No. 60 of 1989)
- The Plant Breeders' Rights Act, 1976 (Act No. 15 of 1976),

---

[6] Note that DPHQ also collaborates with the Directorate of Genetic Resources (DGR) insofar as regulatory activities are concerned pertaining to regulations and standards. The South African Customs Service participates by detaining imported goods, which do not comply with the requirements laid down by the DPHQ and DGR.

Table 4.16 Structure of the DPHQ

Subdirectorate: Quality Control	Subdirectorate: Plant and Quality Services	Subdirectorate: Plant Health
Divisions	*Divisions*	*Divisions*
Processed products	Plant Health Service	National Phytosanitary Matters
Agronomy and	Analytical Service North	Plant Health Promotion
Vegetables	Technical Maintenance	Protocols and Work Programs
Perishable Products	Support Service	Plant Health Auditing North
Liquor Products	Staff Function Support	Plant Health Auditing South
Quality Auditing North	Service	Analytical Services North
Quality Auditing South		
Quality Promotions		

Information on the functions of the different sub-directorates in DPHQ is provided in Annex I.
Source: National Department of Agriculture 2002.

- The Plant Improvement Act, 1976 (Act No. 53 of 1976)
- The Act on Genetically Modified Organisms, 1997 (Act No. 25 of 1997),

The main functions of the DPHQ in Pretoria also include auditing fruit, vegetables, grain and some other specific other products for compliance with maximum residue limits (MRLs). These are either prescribed by internationally agreed standards or are specific requirements set by individual importing countries. This regulatory analysis is in compliance to international agreements, pesticide detection is done by multiresidue analysis and the monitoring is focused on a wide spectrum of substances that includes pesticide residues from

- Registered spraying programs
- Listed in the requirements of importing countries, as well as
- Banned or illegal substances.

Directorate: Genetic Resources. The Directorate: Genetic Resources is divided into the Subdirectorate: Animal Genetic Resources and Subdirectorate: Plant Genetic Resources. Each of these subdirectorates is further divided into divisions to handle specific issues related to animals and plant genetics (see Annex I for more details).

The Subdirectorate of Animal Genetic Resources administers the following Acts on behalf of the Minister for Agriculture and Land Affairs: (see Annex J for details on Acts)

- Agricultural Pests Act, 1983 (Act No. 36 of 1983)
- The Animal Improvement Act, 1998 (Act No. 62 of 1998)
- The Livestock Brands Act, 1962 (Act No. 87 of 1962)

The Subdirectorate of Plant Genetic Resources administers the following Acts on behalf of the Minister for Agriculture and Land Affairs (see Annex J for details on Acts):

- The Plant Improvement Act, 1976 (Act No. 53 of 1976)
- The Plant Breeders' Rights Act, 1976 (Act No. 15 of 1976)
- The Genetically Modified Organisms Act, 1997 (Act No. 15 of 1997)

Directorate of Veterinary Services. Legislation in the meat industry in South Africa has for many years been based on the standards of international bodies such as the OIE and CODEX Alimentarius, as well as importing countries such as the United Kingdom, and is therefore very much in line with the requirements of the international meat trade.

The Directorate of Veterinary Services has the mandate to set legislation, policy and standards regarding all functions of Veterinary Services. The nine provincial directorates of veterinary services have the mandate to execute all regulatory functions, within their own contexts and in close cooperation with both the National Directorate and the other provincial directorates of veterinary services.

The aims of the National Directorate Veterinary Services is to ensure effective biological risk management in terms of animal diseases, food safety, as well as veterinary imports and exports. This goal is obtained by providing information, legislation, policy, standards, capacity building, certification, control and audits. The Directorate of Veterinary Services has five subdirectorates (see Annex I for more details).

The Directorate of Veterinary Services administers the following Acts on behalf of the Minister for Agriculture and Land Affairs: (see Annex J for details on Acts)

- Animal Diseases Act, 1984 (Act No. 35 of 1984).
- The Abattoir Hygiene Act, 1992 (Act No. 121 of 1992).
- Meat Safety Act, 2000 (Act No. 40 of 2000)

Directorate: Agricultural Production Inputs. This directorate is responsible for the registration of all pesticides, insecticides (including household and industrial insecticides), fungicides, herbicides, adjuvants, plant growth regulants and algaecides (also swimming pool remedies), all animal feeds and pet food, all organic and inorganic fertilizers, all pest control operators, all sterilizing units, and certain animal medicines. It also renders an inspection service and investigates criminal offences regarding aspects of the Fertilizers, Farm Feeds, Agricultural Remedies and Stock Remedies Act, 1947 (Act No. 36 of 1947) countrywide.

The Directorate: Agricultural Production Inputs administers the following Acts on behalf of the Minister for Agriculture and Land Affairs (see Annex J for details on Acts):

- The Fertilizers, Farm Feeds, Agricultural Remedies and Stock Remedies Act, 1947 (Act No. 36 of 1947);
- Pesticide Residue Trial Requirements Act (No. 36 of 1947).

South African Bureau of Standards (SABS)

Most industrial product standards are developed under the auspices of the SABS, which was established under Act 24 of 1945 (now Act 29 of 1993). That is, the SABS currently functions in terms of the Standards Act (Act No. 29 of 1993) (see Annex I for more details).

The SABS administers a large range of compulsory specifications across a wide spectrum of areas. These compulsory specifications are legal measures and requirements to ensure that products locally manufactured or imported into South Africa or exported from South Africa meet the minimum requirements for health and safety as set out in the relevant South African National Standards. Examples include the production and canning of fish (products) or the import of motor vehicles. The objective of SABS is to protect the consumer and to oblige industry to comply with the compulsory specifications.

The SABS fields a team of inspectors that visits importers, retailers and manufacturers to monitor compliance with compulsory specifications. This is funded by industry levies based on firms' import figures and manufacturers' turnover figures (see Annex M). Levies can be paid monthly, quarterly and, by prior arrangement, every six months.

South African National Accreditation System (SANAS)

The South African National Accreditation System (SANAS) was formally established in 1994 as a, nonprofit, Section 21 company. Previously it was known as the National Calibration Service (NCS) and was in operation from 1980 to 1994 under the auspices of the CSIR.

The establishment of SANAS is backed by a Cabinet Memorandum and is recognized by the South African Government through DTI as the single National Accreditation Body within its defined scope of activity. SANAS accredits Certification Bodies, Inspection Bodies, Proficiency Testing Scheme Providers and Good Laboratory Practice (GLP) test facilities as competent to carry out specific tasks. SANAS certificates are a formal recognition that an organization is competent to perform specific tasks (see Annex I for details).

Perishable Product Export Control Board (PPECB)

PPECB is the control body for exports of all the perishable products. About 90 percent of the controlled products are fruit, 5 percent are vegetables and the rest comprises maize, rice, groundnuts, dairy products, and meat. PPECB is assigned by NDA to carry out mandatory regulations and standards (see

Annex I for details). The PPECB's work pertains to two Acts, namely the PPECB Act (Act No. 9 of 1983) and the Agricultural Products Standards Act (Act No. 119 of 1990).

PPECB has well-developed infrastructure to carry out its functions and has established offices all over the country. The inspection services offered by PPECB are ISO 9001 certified. This ensures that the service offered is of a good standard and that business is conducted according to international accepted standards.

PPECB does not disseminate new standards to producers and producer organizations, because this is done by the export agents or commodity boards. Furthermore, PPECB only has an indirect influence in the standard setting procedure, but if PPECB considers it to be necessary to change certain mandatory standards and regulations, it applies to the NDA.

The PPECB receives no government funding or subsidies, and generates its entire funding from business activities (see Annex N for PPECB rates). The rates offered by PPECB are considered competitive in relation to other certification agencies involved in Hazard Analysis Critical Control Points (HACCP) and European Retailers Produce on Good Agricultural Practices (EUREPGAP), namely SABS and Societé Général de Surveillance (SGS). Regarding perishable products, these two agencies have a mandatory function relating to HACCP certification, and are more involved in system certifications. Sometimes, when required by an export agent, these bodies provide a second opinion on a PPECB decision.

The Effectiveness of the Current SQAM Landscape

The minister of Trade and Industry understands the importance of SQAM role players such as the SABS, the SANAS, and the NML. This is evidenced by the fact that these organizations have been brought into his strategic Council of Trade and Industry (COTI) forum that brings together representatives from DTI-linked organizations on a regular basis. This has certainly given these organizations an unprecedented platform on which to promote SQAM issues.

There are some idiosyncrasies in the budgeting system however. Whereas the NML and SANAS submit their budgets to the Minister of Trade and Industry for approval, the SABS is allocated its core funding by way of Parliament's Science Vote for the Science Councils. This means that the SABS is put into the unhealthy position of being forced to "compete" with research organizations (which the SABS is not), such as the Council for Science and Industrial Research (CSIR). Clearly, the SABS should be removed from this process and placed entirely on the DTI's budget.

The notification link to the WTO via SABS works well. However, there is no effective mechanism of notifying the South African industry of foreign technical regulations. This means that industry is often ignorant or late in being informed of draft regulations in other countries. This severely restricts the ability to respond to these draft regulations. As far as participating in the activities of the WTO-TBT committee are concerned, the Department of Trade and Industry has stepped up its participation. However, more can still be done to proactively build SADC, South-South, etc., alliances in respect to TBT issues.

The process of standards harmonization within SADC has been very slow. This is mainly due to the fact that delegates of member states fail to participate in technical committee meetings because of financial constraints. Travelling and subsistence costs are high and most member states have limited travel budgets. As more and more projects for harmonization are identified, the strain on resources is increased and this has slowed the pace of harmonization. This is why the first harmonization projects that were identified have taken more than three years to be finalized. The action plans contain a proposal for a regional video conferencing system to remedy this problem.

The interaction between government departments in this domain leaves a lot to be desired. There are, for example, no regular meetings between the relevant government officials to discuss issues of common interest. The DTI is busy drafting a technical regulatory framework that is aimed at harmonizing the way in which technical regulations are drafted. This should increase the transparency of the drafting process and oblige officials to use a set of common rules.

As far as the international recognition and participation of SANAS, the NML and the SABS is concerned, South Africa can boast full membership of nearly all the relevant international cooperation mechanisms. SANAS enjoys full recognition through the International Laboratory Accreditation Cooperation (ILAC) and the International Accreditation Forum (IAF) and is one of the only a handful of organizations outside the OECD to be a full member of the GLP Panel thus ensuring excellent recognition of South African certificates and test reports. The NML is represented on the BIPM Council and is a signatory to the BIPM mutual recognition arrangement. The SABS participates actively in approximately 50 percent of the ISO and IEC committees and serves as the secretariat on a number of these committees.

The problems mentioned above are also echoed by a thorough study of the South African standards, quality assurance, accreditation and metrology (SQAM) system in 2000 by the DTI. The final report, presented to DTI in April 2001, made some major recommendations in the regulatory domain. The study found that there were a number of shortcomings in the current South African regulatory system, i.e.,

- There is often confusion among regulators about responsibilities as well as a duplication of responsibilities.
- There is no way of measuring the effectiveness of technical regulations contained in legislation.
- There is a lack of transparency in technical regulations which hinders local trade, particularly in the SMME sector.
- It is difficult and time consuming to consult technical regulations contained in legislation.
- The consumer, ultimately, foots the bill for regulatory inefficiency.
- The lack of regulatory transparency hampers South Africa's ability to negotiate mutual recognition agreements.
- The lack of regulatory transparency hinders South Africa's ability to meet international obligations under the WTO Agreement on Technical Barriers to Trade (TBT).

Various issues discussed and conclusions made during a workshop on Food Safety Capacity Building, 25–26 April in Pretoria, South Africa, facilitated by a consortium[7] of research institutes from Wageningen University and Research Centre in the Nether-

lands, provided insight into the efficiency of the standards and regulations landscape. The deficiencies pointed out include the following:

- An integrated framework of government action and public-private partnership is lacking;
- Potential weaknesses are constraints in surveillance and monitoring of data, human resources due to lack of education and training, and law enforcement capacity;
- Central registration is lacking, while there is little willingness to share information;
- No "central" monitoring or surveillance database systems are available in the country;
- Roles and responsibilities of both the government and the private sector in South Africa need to be clarified; and
- Current legislation pertaining to food safety and quality matters is described as a myriad of laws and regulations, while many regulations are cross cutting over several government departments. This state of affairs leads to ineffective policing of policies, uncoordinated application of legislation and dissemination of information.

Many of the issues discussed will be further highlighted in the next section as they relate to specific industries.

Industry Review

Electro-Technical

Domestic Regulations. Electrical and electronic components are well regulated by the SABS. There are ten "compulsory specifications" in this domain (see Annex K for details). The monitoring of compliance seems to work quite well. SABS inspectors have all the relevant information about producers and product details on handheld PCs, which they use to inspect importers, retailers and manufacturers. The SABS works closely with Customs and Excise to monitor imports of electrical and electronic components and products.

The formulation of compulsory specifications can, however, be fraught with difficulties. In some cases technical expertise resides solely or largely

---

[7] The consortium is conducting a project within the World Bank program aiming at development of Guidelines to address the questions: How to assess technical, economical, and institutional issues of food safety at country level? and How to develop an action plan for capacity building on food safety to address the needs of the country?

within the corporate sector. This means that corporate competition creeps into the technical committee arena. For example, it took SABS Technical Committee TC 3350.7 more than five years to amend (with ministerial intervention) the circuit breaker compulsory specification in line with IEC circuit breaker standards (see Annex K for details). This was mainly due to the fact that the committee was composed of competing commercial interests. There is no simple solution to this problem and it is likely to resurface during technical discussions with respect to earth leakage units.

Domestic Standards. South Africa has approximately 1200 standards in the electro-technical domain. These standards cover the whole spectrum of distribution, reticulation, installation and appliances. There are, however, no performance standards for video machines, cell phones or personal computers. This is due to the fact that the technology changes too rapidly for the SABS standardization system to keep pace. However, the safety of this equipment is covered by compulsory specification VC 8055—Electrical and electronic apparatus. It must also be borne that the size of the South African electrical appliances manufacturing industry is quite small. In fact South Africa imports approximately 80 percent of its information technology and telecommunications products.

The Department of Trade and Industry's aim is to adopt international standards as far as possible. The following statistics show that this is being achieved. Sixty percent of the electro-technical standards are exactly the same as the equivalent IEC standards and 30–35 percent are based on the IEC equivalent standards but contain minor deviations to allow for local climatic conditions, consumer needs or available technology. Five percent of South Africa's standards in this domain are unique, i.e., those standards referring to wiring and installation. Obviously, foreign companies are unhappy with the unique wiring and installation standards as this often leads to re-testing and authorization of their products to South African standards and, in some cases, modifications to the products concerned. It is, however, important to point out that this is not unique to South Africa. For example, each country in Europe also has its own wiring code.

The Electrical Suppliers Liaison Committee (ESLC) has developed its own standards called National Rationalized User Specifications. The ELSC is composed of members of the electricity transmission and distribution industry, for example ESCOM, etc. An example of such a standard is NRS 041:1995 Electricity Transmission & Distribution Code of Practice for Overhead Power Lines.

The SABS standards formulating process follows the WTO Code of Good Practice for the development of standards (see Annex K for details). The process appears to work well and is aimed at eliciting inputs from all stakeholders. Although the SABS tries to disseminate standards information as widely as possible, this process is still mainly paper based, for example through its "Bulletin," etc. There is room for leveraging web-based technology, etc. to disseminate information. One major improvement would be to sell standards over the Internet.

Major Problems in Meeting Technical Requirements for Market Access. According to industry sources there is a European "ban" on the import of electronically regulated earth leakage devices. Although some European countries are in favor of reviewing this situation, Germany, France, Switzerland and Italy are clearly opposed to this.

Circuit Breaker Industries (CBI) has, for example, made substantial investments to change its production to IEC-related technology. The irony, according to CBI, is that IEC standards are not always accepted in Europe. While the Europeans clearly claim that IEC is the basis of all CENELEC standards there are often subtle critical differences. According to CBI they are obliged to test according to European standards despite complying with the relevant IEC standards. Ireland, the United Kingdom and Austria are, clearly prepared to accept IEC standards in the electrical domain.

Firms often have problems in Germany where the local firms refuse to purchase foreign electrical components, as the local labor unions do not allow their members to install these products.

The South African lights and light armature industry has been adapting to IEC standards for several years. They have made the production changes and are now ready.

Cost of Compliance. To denote compliance to South Africa's electrical standards by way of the SABS Mark Scheme, manufacturers pay the following fees to the SABS: First round audit fees of R3,000 per audit man day plus 14 percent VAT, for assessment per manufacturing premises. Once the mark has been awarded, the firm must pay annual mark fees to the SABS. The size of these fees will depend upon whether or not the firm is ISO 9000 certified. If the firm is ISO 9000 certified, the SABS will only conduct one follow-up audit per year. If, on the other hand, the firm is not ISO 9000 certified it will be audited four times per year at R3,000 per audit man day per manufacturing premises. In addition, the firm will pay R1,500 per year in respect of administration fees, sampling and testing fees that can vary from R1,500 per sample to R15,000 per sample depending on the product.

There is also a compulsory levy for electrical goods. The levy is calculated as follows: Total (quantity of commodities manufactured and/or imported) × Levy + 14 percent VAT. The tariffs for electrical products are contained in the Annex O.

According to the Electrical Cable Manufacturers Association of South Africa, local electrical cable manufacturers spend only R1.5 million per year on local cost of compliance. To put this into perspective, the industry generates average annual sales (30 percent imports and 70 percent locally produced) of R2.5 billion. Local cost of compliance is not, therefore, an issue. The Electrical Manufacturers Association shares this view.

Circuit Breaker Industries (CBI), the only South African manufacturer of earth leakage devices and circuit breakers, which employs more than 1300 people, spends approximately R4 million per year on compliance. To put this figure into perspective, CBI generated revenue of approximately R400 million in 2001. Export sales accounted for 19 percent of the manufactured products. This means that cost of compliance for CBI represents 1 percent of total revenue. This is clearly a relatively small item. According to CBI, foreign product approval and certification costs for a product range are generally 40 percent to 75 percent more expensive than in South Africa. In the case of Underwriters Laboratories (UL) conformity assessment in the United States, Canada and Mexico can be more than twice as expensive, which could be an issue when conformity assessment is required in these countries.

The electrical cable industry does not regard the domestic technical regulations as a constraint. International regulations are, however, regarded as barriers to market entry. The Association describes these as time-consuming, expensive and often challenging from a foreign language perspective. The most difficult markets to penetrate are Japan, Korea, most of Europe and the United States. The Underwriters Laboratories (UL) in the United States are insurance-based organizations that test a wide range of products. According to the Association many products are not purchased in the United States unless they bear the UL mark. This is clearly due to the risk of litigation in the case of product failure or user injury. Despite many attempts, no member of the Electrical Cable Manufacturers Association of South Africa has ever obtained the UL mark. Cost and differing specifications are cited as some of the reasons for this state of affairs. However, there is also a perception that South African cable products are, perhaps unfairly, tested over very long periods of time that makes the applicants to eventually give up hope and abandon the process.

CBI also believes that foreign requirements pose a barrier to entry. The European electrical standards are derived from IEC standards. However, each country in Europe has its own wiring code. For example, whereas IEC specifications provide for "mains power supply" and "not mains power supply" components, Germany only allows "not mains power supply" equipment to be hooked to its electricity grid. This keeps South African circuit breakers out of Germany.

Forestry

Domestic Regulations. Forestry and its products are regulated by the Department of Water Affairs and Forestry as well as the Department of Agriculture, the Department of Trade and Industry and the SABS in terms of various acts and regulations (see Annex K for details). This proliferation of regulatory responsibility is not ideal.

The minister of Water Affairs and Forestry has convened a National Forests Advisory Council. The Council is charged with establishing criteria, indicators and standards for sustainable forestry development. The National Forests Act stipulates that these criteria, indicators and standards will be legislated.

The forestry industry believes that many of the draft criteria are impractical and expensive. Industry is concerned that the resulting compliance costs could hurt smaller players and that some of the social requirements, for example community consultation, etc. are overly burdensome. As the international Forestry Stewardship Council (FSC) uses the environmental guidelines and regulations of a country as part of its certification process the above criteria, once part of the regulations and burdensome could jeopardize South African FSC certification in cases of noncompliance.

Domestics Standards. South Africa has twenty-five timber-related standards. There is one standard for wooden office furniture and a so-called CKS (Coordinating Specification) standard for wooden school furniture that was written specifically for use in government tenders. There is also a toilet paper standard. South Africa has adopted the ISO standard for Particle-Board without any modification. ISO standards in this domain specify what must be tested, but not how it must be tested. Countries are allowed the freedom to determine test methods. South Africa has, therefore, developed its own test methods to accommodate local conditions.

Although there are timber-related standards, South Africa has no specific forestry standards. The forestry industry has, therefore, developed its own "Guidelines for the Environmental Conservation of Commercial Plantations in South Africa". This dovetails closely with ISO 14001.

Major Problems in Meeting Technical Requirements for Market Access. Market forces have controlled Forestry Stewardship Council (FSC) certification. It started becoming important for South Africa in 1995 after the FSC made a big presentation to the biggest retailers in the United Kingdom. The British retailer B & Q then sent out a memorandum to its suppliers stating that it would no longer accept timber products that were not FSC certified. This was a shock for South African suppliers. At the time there were no FSC compliant forests in South Africa not to mention any FSC chain of custody.

As a result, the major timber and pulp producers such as Mondi Timber, Mondi Forest, the South African Forestry Company Ltd. and SAPPI moved rapidly to certify their forests. It is interesting to note that, at the time, SAPPI only certified the timber sawing parts of its plantations, as this was where the biggest need lay. As SAPPI relied for approximately 50 percent of its supply on smaller plantations and cooperatives, individual FSC certification of all these SMME suppliers was, in any event, too expensive at the time. However, the stringent FSC requirements posed a particular dilemma in that only a small percentage of fiber from noncertified forests was allowed in paper manufacturing. To solve the SMME dilemma, the FSC implemented a group certification scheme. This has made FSC certification much more affordable for smaller plantations. The costs are as follows:

- Documentation: R500 per file with attaching documentation.
- First year cost: R10 per planted hectare.
- Annual cost: R1,500 for the first 500 planted hectares, plus R2.50 for every hectare exceeding 500 hectare (maximum fee of R10,000).

Group certification membership now stands at 56 members, owning approximately 55,000 hectare of timber area. About 26,000 hectare is pine with the remaining 29,000 hectare being made up of wattle and eucalyptus plantations.

Although close to 200 growers have attended training workshops, only 56 of these have become certified. The main stumbling block in this process is the perception by growers that they cannot cope with the administration load of the system.

The training workshops involve introducing members to the management system and highlighting information that needs to be documented. Many members either decide that they cannot cope with the system or procrastinate and do not submit an application to be audited. A post-training workshop contact visit could, however, be offered to members to assist them with implementing the system on their farms.

Already ISO 14001 certified, SAPPI will, therefore, soon also have all its source plantations FSC certified. The FSC requires compliance with the SA forestry industry's "Guidelines for the Environmental Conservation of Commercial Plantations in South Africa" as well as any other relevant South African legislation.

In 1996 there were no FSC or ISO 14000 certified forests. By the end of 2002 the industry estimates that there will be, out of a total of 1.4 million hectares of pine, eucalyptus and wattle plantations:

- 760,000 hectares of FSC certified plantations, and
- 250,000 hectares of FSC and ISO 14001 certified plantations.

The demand for FSC certification is growing and most sawmills and woodworking companies now adhere to some form of quality or environmental management standard.

FSC certification has not come cheaply at an average of R3 to R4 per hectare. South African firms have traditionally had to rely on foreign certification bodies, accredited by the FSC, to carry out both of the above activities. There is a preliminary assessment, followed by a third party audit that has often led to corrective actions requiring substantial additional investments. SGS is still the main certifying body in South Africa. However, the SABS Timber Department (part of the SABS certification business TCS) has recently been accredited to carry out Chain of Custody certification and is now seeking accreditation for Forestry Management certification from the FSC. Hopefully this additional competition will reduce certification costs.

The next step is likely to be an international MRA. South Africa is participating through the International Forestry Industry Round Table (IFIR). The FSC supports this and the process is gaining momentum. The IFIR has been working with international stakeholders to operationalize the proposed International Mutual Recognition Framework during 2001, in order to achieve the following objectives:

- Facilitate the development of mutual recognition arrangements between credible certification systems;
- Provide assurance to customers and consumers that forest certification standards participating within the Framework produce substantially equivalent forest benefits;
- Significantly expand the availability of certified forest products in response to growing market demand;
- Encourage customers to adopt inclusive purchasing policies that recognize that different systems deliver substantially equivalent, credible outcomes; and
- Prevent unfair discrimination against any region or country by providing an open and free market for wood products from sustainable managed sources.

Apart from the certified plantations and sawmills, there are more than a dozen FSC Chain of Custody holders in the furniture industry. Half of these companies are also ISO 9000 certified.

South Africa exports a significant number of power line transmission poles. Mozambique requires that the South African Department of Agriculture certify every consignment to indicate that the poles have been treated accordingly. This is despite the fact that all the poles already bear the SABS mark.

Cost of Compliance. To denote compliance to South Africa's timber-related standards by way of the SABS Mark Scheme, manufacturers pay the following fees to the SABS: First round audit fees of R4,400 plus 14 percent VAT for assessment to a single standard. Should the firm apply for assessment to two or more standards at the same time, the audit fee for the additional standard(s) would be reduced by 50 percent, for example, for assessment to two standards the total audit fee would amount to R6,600 plus VAT, for assessment to three standards R8,800, and so forth. Once the mark has been awarded, the firm must pay annual mark fees to the SABS. These fees are usually negotiated with each permit holder individually and depend upon factors such as size, turnover, and location, etc. However, the minimum fee per company, which includes the price of follow-up audits, is R8,000 plus VAT per year.

The price charged by SGS for a main first Forestry Stewardship Council (FSC) assessment of an average plantation is approximately R100,000. The annual follow-up audit costs approximately R60,000.

According to SAFCOL, FSC certification costs approximately 8c per cubic meter. This is negligible compared to an average timber price of R130 per cubic meter. The cost of complying with legal forestry requirements in general is unknown.

Textiles

Domestic Regulations. There is a gap in directly regulating the safety of textiles. There are only two compulsory specifications, i.e., for life jackets and Child-Restraining Devices for use in Motor Vehicles (see Annex K for details). The country needs (like the EU) seat-belt regulations governing the safety of the seat-belt textile.

However, textile safety is often addressed indirectly. For example, legislation regulating the transport of hazardous substances includes safety requirements for protective clothing. The South African National Building Regulations have fire safety requirements that regulate carpets, curtains and upholstery in buildings.

Domestics Standards. South Africa has approximately 1,500 textile standards. More than half of these standards refer to test methods, the balance refer to product standards. Here again, the majority of these standards are ISO standards, which is in line with DTI's aims. The SABS has, in fact, spent much time and energy over the past five years in aligning its textile standards with ISO standards.

Major Problems in Meeting Technical Requirements for Market Access. With respect to textiles, the main problem has not been on the export side but on the import side. For example, a European firm recently exported army boots to South Africa. It used linen thread to stitch the sole to the uppers. Due to harsher climatic conditions South Africa has stringent requirements with respect to thread and its resistance to microorganisms. Although the product complied with European standards, it did not comply with South African standards, as South Africa's humidity test method is stricter. In the end the manufacturer had to treat his thread with a resin-based varnish.

A few years ago a foreign carpet manufacturer experienced problems when it set up a factory in South Africa. They neglected to put UV inhibitors in their polymers. Due to higher ultra-violet exposure in South Africa their carpets started "staining" as the white fibers faded.

Local retailers have had problems with imports from the Far East where, for example, the test sample is OK, but the consignment does not comply.

The main problem our exporters have experienced relates not to standards, quality or conformity assessment, but rather to stricter origin rules in foreign markets. South Africa does not have origin labeling requirements for textiles and clothing. Exporters find it difficult to cater to foreign markets that do have origin requirements.

Cost of Compliance. According to the Textile Federation, cost of compliance amounts to approximately 3 percent of production costs for the industry as a whole, which is negligible.

Fisheries

Domestic Regulations. This sector is extremely well regulated, mainly by the SABS, but also by the DOH, NDA and DEAT (see Annex K for details). Enforcement appears to be working well. The SABS inspectors enforce compliance with the compulsory specifications through surveillance and conformity assessment. For high risk and imported fishery products, the SABS follows what it calls a "continuous inspection" system. This means that SABS inspectors are stationed, more or less permanently, in factories and plants where they subject raw material and final products to both physical and sensory examinations. There are also announced and unannounced audits and random samples. The SABS food inspectorate has been accredited by SANAS. This has established the competence of the inspectorate.

Domestics Standards. There are no ISO standards in this sector. Like most countries, South Africa applies the international CODEX Alimentarius codes of hygienic practice, guidelines and standards as far as possible. The two main standards are SABS 587: Canned fish other than hake and SABS 585: The production of frozen fish, frozen marine mollusks and frozen products derived there from.

Major Problems in Meeting Technical Requirements for Market Access. As far as fishery exports to the United States are concerned South Africa has expressed interest in an "equivalency" MOA. According to SABS officials the USFDA is satisfied, in principle, with the South African HACCP system. It will, however, take some time before the United States is ready to negotiate an MOA with South Africa.

Spain rejected a few consignments of South African white fish in 2001 due to so-called parasite infestation. Infrequently there are problems in different countries due to differing microbiological standards. These standards have not yet been harmonized at CODEX level. During the early 1990s Italy banned imports from one or two South African suppliers due to mercury content problems.

However, South Africa experienced the most severe problems in early 1994 when France implemented *EU Council Directive 91/493/EEC,* literally overnight. This is the main EU legislation governing the health requirements of fishery products.

Developing countries were not given any opportunity to prove compliance with the requirements of the Directive and were, therefore, banned from the French market. The French government was, of course, trying to appease its fisherman who had gone on the rampage in Brittany to protest difficult economic conditions and cheaper imports.

This step came as a great shock to the South African Fishing industry. Other EU member states had given developing countries plenty of time to prove compliance with the requirements of the Directive. The French action would today fly in the face of the transparency rules contained in Annex B to the SPS agreement.

In the months that followed, South African diplomats tried desperately to get South Africa's name put on a list of countries, from which France would import fish. Every conceivable phytosanitary guarantee was provided. Finally, after nearly four months of diplomatic wrangling, South Africa appeared on the list of authorized exporting countries, on 26 April 1994.

Many developing countries were hard hit by the French action. Money was lost and, no doubt, financial ruin faced a number of smaller exporters. Although the exact financial losses suffered by the South African fishery industry were unknown, the impact on South Africa's white fish exports was undoubtedly severe.

The EU does not allow imports of South African aquaculture products. This is a problem for South Africa as the DTI has identified aquaculture as a growth industry. Aquaculture production requires a sophisticated monitoring infrastructure (water quality, regular medication and inspections, etc.) and is fairly capital intensive, therefore it remains to be seen whether South Africa can satisfy the international requirements.

The EU also does not allow imports of South African mariculture products such as bivalve or marine mollusks. However, South Africa does export mussels, oysters, abalone and shellfish to the Far East.

In June 2001, South Africa banned imports of Namibian canned fish and ordered the withdrawal of large numbers of cans from store shelves. SABS inspectors discovered corrosion in the expansion rings of cans.

The major South African fish exporters are I and J, Sea Harvest and Marine Products. Marine Products exports are mainly to the Far East and to the EU. HACCP in the EU has been the main conformity assessment issue of the past few decades. Initially this firm saw HACCP compliance as a barrier to trade. However, improvements to the fishing vessels, factory vessels and plants have paid off and the final product has improved in quality. This has enhanced the firm's reputation.

Cost of Compliance. Compliance to HACCP in the fisheries industry has been expensive. For example, Marine Products exports two lines of products, i.e., canned pilchards in tomato sauce, mainly to the United Kingdom and white fish, mainly Hake, to the EU as a whole. In the latter half of the 1990s Marine Products invested approximately R15 million in upgrading its canning plants to EU HACCP requirements. On the white fish side, the fishing trawlers and factory vessels were upgraded, over a period of two years, at a cost of between R8 and R12 million. According to industry sources, I & J and Sea Harvest spent approximately R10 million each to upgrade to EU requirements. Although no figures are available, Marine Products also spent a considerable sum on the "softer" HACCP requirements. Consultants were hired to train staff in the implementation and running of the HACCP system. Extra staff members were appointed to run the HACCP system that required detailed documenting of every single process and step in the production chain. As the HACCP chain even extends to suppliers of such inputs as salt, etc. extra staff were required to ensure compliance. Record-keeping is a full time task and data had to be built up over time to establish and demonstrate confidence in the system, for example measuring the bacteria count in fresh water over time".

To fund the administration and enforcement of the compulsory specifications in the fishery industry, the SABS charges levies every six months. These levies are reviewed and adjusted (if necessary) every year and submitted to the Ministry of Trade and Industry for approval and promulgation in terms of the Standards Act. Local producers as well as importers pay the levies at the end of every six-month period. The levy is calculated as follows: Total (quantity of commodities manufactured and/or imported) × Levy + 14 percent VAT. The tariffs for fishery products are given in the Annex P.

The South African fishery industry as a whole paid to the SABS R39 million in levies during the 2001/2002 financial year. The forecast for

265

2002/2003 is R47 million. According to budget estimates for 2002/2003 a further R15 million will be allocated to the SABS from core parliamentary funding for all regulatory activities.

The SABS also charges for its export certification. As it is the formally notified certification body for exports to the EU, exporters are obliged to seek SABS certification. The SABS inspectors charge R275 per hour and R300 per hour after hours. Each consignment certificate costs R90 and the SABS charges R1.70 per kilometer traveled.

Fruit Industries

Domestic Regulations. The exports of deciduous fruit, citrus, mangoes and avocadoes are regulated under the Agricultural Product Standards Act, 1990 (Act No. 119 of 1990). Standards and requirements regarding control of the export of these fruits are enforced by government notice no. R. 1983 of 23 August 1991. In general, it stipulates standards regarding the quality of deciduous fruit, citrus, mangoes and avocados and the requirements regarding the packing, marking and labeling thereof (see Annex K for details).

The export standards and requirements for fresh fruit were amended in conjunction with the industry to make the stating of the production unit code (farm code) on each carton compulsory to enhance traceability up to production unit (farm) level, thus satisfying local and international quality, food safety and phytosanitary requirements. The local standards are also in the process of being updated and when finalized will have the same requirement. This means that every farm producing fresh fruit for sale must be registered with the NDA. At present, fresh fruit producers without registered production unit codes cannot legally export their produce.

Of particular importance to the South African fruit industry is the issue of Maximum Residue Levels (MRLs). MRLs applicable to the South African fruit industry are regulated by export grading regulations under the Agricultural Product Standards Act, 1990 (Act No. 119 of 1990). Most countries have established MRLs for pesticides used in the control of pest and diseases not only to safeguard consumer health but also to minimize the presence of these residues in the environment. As a condition of market access products exported must comply with these residue standards.

South African export legislation furthermore requires, among other things, that

- Only chemical remedies registered in terms of The Fertilizers, Farm Feeds, Agricultural Remedies and Stock Remedies Act (Act No. 36 of 1947) be used on the specific crop;
- Crops or agricultural products exported should not exceed the maximum chemical residue limits of the importing countries; and
- Records are kept of the chemical remedies used in spray and fumigation programs and as post-harvest treatment.
- To ensure compliance with legislation monitoring samples are drawn during the quality inspections and analyzed.

The DPHQ, together with other government departments and directorates is responsible for the government-to-government coordination with regard to MRLs on export products or rejection of consignments by importing authorities.

Exporters and producers have, among other things, the responsibility to

- Comply with the requirements on the correct, approved use and application of pesticide remedies in terms of the Fertilizers, Farm Feeds, Agricultural Remedies and Stock Remedies Act (Act No. 36 of 1947);
- Keep record of the chemical remedies used in spray programs and as post-harvest treatment and to provide this information on request to the responsible authorities;
- Verify the MRLs with their importer or agent in the relevant country;
- Keep up with the registration and re-registration processes of pesticides within South Africa as well as in importing countries; and
- Inform the DPHQ of any rejections by importing country authorities due to residues.

The Citrus Growers Association (CGA) the Deciduous Fruit Producers Trust (DFPT), the Mango Growers Association (MGA), the Avocado Growers Association (AGA), etc. all are involved in the setting of export standards through collaboration with the NDA's DPHQ, other relevant government departments and industry representatives, such as Capespan. Information received from the DPHQ with respect to issues pertaining to the IPPC is circulated to relevant role players (CGA, CRI—Citrus Research International, ARC and Exporters Forums). The DPHQ then combines the inputs and submits to the IPPC. The DPHQ Market Access Team, includes, CGA, CRI, ARC, SANSOR, Exporters Forum and DFPT, who handle problems related to market access.

Domestic Standards. Most voluntary standards in place for exports are much higher than the mandatory standards set by government. New voluntary standards are submitted by agents and checked by the PPECB for compliance with the government standards and regulations stated in the Agricultural Product Standards Act (Act No. 119 of 1990).

In many markets the private sector regulates itself in conforming to international standards for exports (Botha 2002), i.e., various standards are also derived from international retailers. These standards are then conveyed to producers for compliance. With respect to such standards, PPECB has the responsibility to check for compliance, which is mandatory according to overseas retail organizations, for example "Natures Choice" from the English Retail Group TESCO. The standards for this product scheme are similar to the standards set by EUREPGAP. Many European retailers supply their own technical staff to monitor the situation in South Africa concerning conformity with certain standards, but they are tending to use local certification bodies to do the work for them to a greater extent.

Private companies, such as Capespan, play an important role in the standard setting landscape for fruit. Capespan, for example, has accreditation both with SABS and ISO 9002. It has its own Quality Assurance department that developed a set of grading and packing standards to which all fruit packed under their trademarks must conform. These standards meet and exceed minimum requirements of the importing countries such as labeling, sizing, maximum residue limits and phytosanitary measures. The Quality Assurance department works in close conjunction with the PPECB to ensure that standards are applied consistently and strictly. Interesting to note is that certain private sector role players indicated that they are unaware of the extent to which the laws, regulations and standards with regard to food safety were based on the guidelines provided by CODEX and IPPC. They did not consider this to be all that relevant to them (Botha 2002).

Ultimately the type of fruit that can be exported is the type of fruit foreign consumers and retailers are willing to buy. Not only is it important to the buyers what the final product looks and tastes like, but also the way the fruit was grown and where it was grown. In this regard buyers are now asking for descriptions of environmental circumstances in which the fruit is grown and where it is grown as well as setting standards for quality and packaging.

The Issue of Pest Risk Assessment. PRAs (Pest Risk Analyses) are conducted by the DPHQ. Industry bodies (such as CGA, CRI and DFPT) provide the majority of the input information and work closely with the DPHQ on these issues. It is believed that the strengths of the risk assessments lies in the industry's expertise, but a weakness could be that the DPHQ can be stretched at times, and so they do not operate at optimal efficiency (Hattingh 2002). This weakness is a result of a too small unit at DPHQ that has to handle a huge workload.

Conforming to HACCP, ICM, and EUREPCAP. The pressure to conform to the standards sought by the buyers takes various forms. One example is the demand by overseas supermarkets that farmers and pack houses are to follow the HACCP system or at least a slight variation of it, and attain Integrated Crop Management (ICM) accreditation. ICM accreditation is a requirement of many supermarkets in the United Kingdom. These supermarkets have installed a two-year time frame in which they would like to source fruit only from ICM accredited producers and pack houses. The focus of ICM is placed on environmental management, responsible agricultural practices, responsible use of agrochemicals, integrated quality management and socio aspects such as occupational health and safety and worker welfare (Scholtz 2001). Exporters of fruit are also more and more confronted with complying with the European Retailers Produce on Good Agricultural Practices (EUREPGAP) protocol. EUREPCAP includes a wide array of issues that need to be addressed, which increases the demand of the grower to ensure compliance. The South African fruit producers do not have say in the setting of this protocol. It is set solely by reference to the preferences of the importer.

The absence of any say in the setting of these regulations greatly distresses many South African growers and exporters (Grieb 2002). These growers feel that many of the regulations they are being forced to adhere to are out of line with domestic norms, enormously time consuming and unrelated to the core production issue—the quality of the fruit they produce. In essence, they feel the protocol serves as a major deterrent to export to their traditional markets—as if it were a deliberate attempt to bury their interest under a colossal weight of red tape. Frequently mentioned by way of example in this connection are the stringent rules relating to services provided to workers—washing facilities and portable toilets for every 600 meters in the orchard. It is unclear to them why such an issue is relevant to the citrus export exchange and they feel that this is rather a matter for resolution between them, the workers, the labor unions and the South African government (Grieb 2002).

The deciduous industry is dependant on the judicious and responsible use of plant protection products, in order to produce, high quality export deciduous fruit in South Africa. According to DFTP, one of the problems that occur in this matter is the pesticide requirements for EUREPGAP. To meet compliance with this food standard in regard to the usage of pesticides, the pesticides used have to be registered in the products' country of origin. In South Africa, a lot of pesticides are either not registered or are registered for another crop or commodity. Registering a pesticide requires two or three years of trails, which are very costly and it depends on the economical importance of the targeted crop whether this is done.

Pest/disease complexes encountered on deciduous fruit crops differ around the world with South Africa's requirements differing from those encountered in southern Europe. Consequently the range of plant protection products of importance to the South African industry differs from the requirements of the European industry. The consequence is that there may not be a call from the European deciduous industry to support Maximum Residue Levels (MRLs) for certain pesticide and crop combinations that are of importance to the South African industry. The loss of certain pesticide usage through the EU MRL review process, results in a shift in the importance of remaining crop protection options and also a loss of vital actives used as a part of the pest management resistance strategy in the deciduous fruit industry in South Africa. The continued economic viability of producing deciduous fruit of a sufficiently high quality may be seriously jeopardized by the potential loss of several important MRLs. The agricultural chemical industry may not be prepared to carry the costs of further data generation to support MRLs on deciduous fruit crops for some of these products, since many crop/active combinations are regarded as having minor crop status, therefore not justifying the financial investment to obtain registration in South Africa. According to the DFPT, this situation is resulting in growing crisis within the South Africa deciduous fruit industry and has resulted in several problems during the past export season due to the loss of certain key actives particularly regarding mite control.

Twelve actives with notified support status under EU directive 91/414/CEE, concerning the placing of plant protection products on the market, have been identified by South Africa's deciduous industry as critical priorities to acquire South African registration and EU MRLs, to address this crisis. The deciduous fruit industry is, however, not in a position to fund the generation of the required data to forward registration trials in South Africa, without external financial assistance. According to the DFTP there is intense need to remain informed of the developments within the EU on issues relating to MRLs on deciduous fruit crops.

The Issue of Traceability. The "South African Fresh Produce Traceability Guidelines" (SA FPT guidelines) comprise a collection of documents that were developed by the South African Fresh Produce Traceability Project (SA FPTP) workgroup, in conjunction with and under the guidance of EAN South Africa and other role players in the fresh produce export industry, for example the DFPT.

The SA FPT guidelines define the minimum requirements for the traceability of fresh produce. In line with international guidelines, they primarily apply to products subject to custom code nomenclature starting with the digits 07 and 08.

The aim of the guidelines is to provide a common approach to tracking and tracing of fresh produce by means of an internationally accepted numbering and bar coding system—the EAN.UCC system. The degree to which companies will implement these guidelines may vary because of differences in commercial operations. However, the use of common identification and communication standards is encouraged since it would significantly improve the accuracy and speed of access to information about the production and provenance of fresh produce. The adoption of the SA FPT guidelines is voluntary.

The SA FPT guidelines could be amended whenever deemed necessary by a committee representing the SA FPTP workgroup, after which the updated edition will be published. The SA FPT guidelines are fully consistent with commercial and intergovernmental arrangements for the identification of fresh produce where the EAN.UCC system is adopted. The use of EAN.UCC standards is subject to the "General EAN/UCC Specifications" and membership in EAN South Africa, EAN International or the Uniform Code Council, Inc.

Major Problems in Meeting Technical Requirements for Market Access. Pest risk analysis being done at present by the NPPO is carried out by a small group of personnel. The group has a large backlog of work mainly due to lack of personnel, a wide job description (regulation, pest risk analysis and surveillance) and due to the fact that PRA is time consuming. PRA is done based on the guidelines outlined by the IPPC, but is not always as detailed due to the lack of capacity. NPPO coordinates with industry and research institutions, such as the Agricultural Research Council (ARC) and universities, in South Africa especially in cases where a detailed identification of an organism has to be made before notification of the exporting country.

A major obstacle faced by South Africa in the bilateral negotiations between different NPPOs is due to cultural and language differences. For example, all the South Africa's technical or nontechnical documentation to Japan has to be translated. The translation has to be done at the Japanese mission in South Africa if it is to be accepted as an official document from the South African NPPO, yet the Japanese mission in South Africa does not have personnel with the necessary technical skills to ensure a complete translation.

South African fruit is subject to two kinds of international standard constraints. The most important kind is the quality and packing standard requirement imposed by the importers of the fruit on the exporters. For example, for most South African citrus growers, this constraint is a binding one and limits the proportion of their total crop that they may export up to about 60 percent. Second in importance is the kind of standards set by the importing country governments aimed at preventing the spread of diseases from South African citrus to other producing countries and the paperwork/procedural requirements that have to be met in order to export.

Arguably the most formidable sanitary constraint facing South African citrus exports is the limitation of citrus importing countries on fruit infected with citrus black spot (CBS). It is formidable because of the difficulty in preventing this infection in most citrus-growing areas in South Africa. In South Africa, where standards and regulations pertaining to CBS are breached, the penalties are severe. The first breach leads to the pack house being black listed and the second results in the importing country disallowing the import of fruit from that pack house again.

Motivated by Spanish citrus growing interests the European Union (EU), the EU has moved to follow the U.S. in banning the import of citrus fruit infected by CBS (Cook 2002). The citrus growers in South Africa have been highly alarmed by this development. About 70 percent of South Africa's citrus are exported to Europe and the United Kingdom.

The South African citrus industry perceive the U.S. and mooted EU CBS standard as an unfair trade barrier against the South African citrus sector, aimed at increasing its export costs and not posing any threat of infection to European Union growers. Black spot is a fungus that causes black spots on the fruit. The spots can develop at any stage, even after the fruit leaves the harbor. The spots merely detract from the appearance of the fruit and are harmless to consumers. CBS is only controlled by the spray chemicals, thereby pushing up costs of production and reducing the incentive to export (Cook 2002).

According to Schutte (2002), a plant pathologist and black spot expert, there is no basis for believing that the black spot could be transferred to the orchards of Europe. The fungus does not occur in any winter rainfall areas and has never shown up in the Western Cape's Mediterranean climate, despite fruit entering the area frequently from the North. The only citrus producing countries in the EU are the Mediterranean countries of Spain, Italy and Greece. South Africa has been exporting citrus fruit to Europe since 1925; over 70 years. Despite this, European orchards remain free of black spot. It is for all of these reasons that the South African citrus industry deduce and argue that the CBS standard, especially that proposed by the EU, is quite simply a new form of protection (Cook 2002).

There are also concerns that the EU does not always use the IEC or ISO standards to which it has agreed. For example, in 1995 the EU adopted legislation lowering the SO_2 levels in dried apples and pears from 2,000 mg/kg to 600 mg/kg. According to the EU this step was based on the health recommendations of the Joint WHO/FAO Expert Committee on food additives. However, at the time the maximum level specified by CODEX (the UN Economic Commission for Europe (UNECC) and ISO (Adopted in 1994 as ISO 7701—dried apples, ISO 7702—dried pears and ISO 7703—dried peaches) was 2,000 mg/kg. Industry commentators have also pointed that IEC standards are not always accepted in Europe. While the Europeans clearly claim that IEC is the basis of all CENELEC (European Committee for Electrotechnical Standards) standards, there are often subtle but critical differences. Companies are obliged to test according to European standards despite complying with the relevant IEC standards.

Cost of Compliance. The cost of complying with the new CBS and EUREP GAP regulations was estimated in this report based on feedback received from three different citrus companies in the Eastern Cape: Whyte Citrus in the Kirkwood region, Riverside Enterprises in the Kat River area and Patensie Citrus in the Patensie area. These costs are shown in Table 4.17. Table 4.17 shows that the cost of compliance in the sample of grower exporters selected for this analysis is about 4 percent of the revenue for CBS prevention and EUREPGAP regulations. If foregone trade opportunities are used as a basis, the percentage cost could be in the region of about 10 percent.

South African citrus exporters have to comply with two certification systems (EUREPGAP and HACCP) in order to export their produce. The costs to comply with EUREPGAP (at a Kirkwood or Hermitage pack house) has been estimated at R1 million for the new bar coding machine, R170,000 for a pack house upgrade, and R120,000 for shifting the workshop to comply with EUREPGAP (Bakker 2002). This brings the total amount to R1,290,000, and it is applicable to both pack houses at Kirkwood as well as the one in Hermitage.

Only one grower in Kirkwood has upgraded his farm to comply with the new EUREPGAP standards (although all growers will soon have to convert). The farm was already in line with the HACCP system and so it was easy to upgrade to the EUREPGAP system, because of the two systems similarity. Most farms do not even comply with the HACCP regulations, and so it would be harder for them to

Table 4.17 Estimated Costs of Compliance on Select Farms in South Africa with Select Standards Currently being Applied Externally to Citrus Exports

Costs and Other Details	Whyte Citrus	Riverside Enterprises	Patensie Citrus	Average
Tons of citrus grown (2001)	2,700	11,000	15,000	9,567
Hectares used	40	150	200	130
Revenue received per ton (2001)—rand	2,520	1,675	1,525	1,907
Per year costs of compliance per ton (2001–2002) with CBS—rand	19	68	27	38
Per year costs of compliance per ton (2001–2002) with EUREP GAP regulations—rand	37	9	47	31
Percentage of Revenue lost due to costs incurred in compliance with CBS and EUREP GAP regulations	2.2 percent	4.6 percent	4.9 percent	3.9 percent
A foregone earnings per year estimate of the cost of U.S. CBS regulations (Percentage of total revenue)	—	—	R10 million (10 percent)	—

Sources: Based on responses of Whyte (2002); Painter (2002); and Grieb (2002).

convert to the new system. Even though the farm that has converted to EUREPGAP standards found it easy, it still came at a cost of R67,000 (Stephens 2002).

Meat and Livestock Industry

Domestic Regulations. The text of legislation pertaining to the meat and livestock industry is provided in Annex K. While most of the existing legislation is based on international standards, the legislation does not always dovetail fully. An example of this is the fact that abattoirs are not responsible for residue testing, but cutting rooms are, yet many abattoirs distribute carcasses directly to the informal sector where there are no facilities for such testing. Similarly, feed imported into the country does not have to undergo testing for heavy metals, which could result in the contamination of meat. Loopholes also occur where certain tasks are delegated to Provincial Authorities.

The slow processes associated with amending legislation have led to some frustration within the industry. An example is the legislation requiring animals to be hung while they are bled. Modern abattoirs employ horizontal slaughtering systems, which are more efficient, but this is not permitted in South Africa.

Great frustration has been experienced in the meat industry due to the clear double standards in implementing legislation. The larger abattoirs appear to be targeted when it comes to the implementation of standards, while smaller rural abattoirs are ignored. This also applies to the classification of carcasses.

Domestic Standards. A number of industry standards or codes of practice have been developed by the meat industry. These include the Code for the transportation of livestock, the Code for the handling of livestock at saleyards, the feedlotting code. Guidelines for abattoir managers and guidelines for the correct use of prodders and stunning equipment. The Red Meat Abattoir Association (RMAA) and the South African Meat Industry Company (SAMIC) assisted the NDA in compiling the Hygiene Assessment System for Abattoirs. The pork industry has developed certain production norms and practices to comply with animal welfare re-

quirements. The ostrich industry participated fully in the drawing up of export standards. It is expected that the requirements of importing countries will force the pace of development of a number of industry standards.

Conforming to HACCP and ISO. Although few facilities in the meat industry are HACCP or ISO certified (see Annex R for beef case study), there is no shortage of capacity within the country to assess and audit these systems. Certification is provided by a number of domestic and international certification institutes. The most prominent of these in the meat industry is SGS of Belgium.

The Issue of Traceability. Although the Livestock Brands Act, 1962 (Act No. 87 of 1962) does not constitute a traceability system on its own, it provides the basis for such a system. This Act makes provision for the registration of identification marks, for both a tattoo for smallstock and a brand for cattle to provide a legal and uniform system of animal identification and proof of ownership. The Act is compulsory for all livestock owners, except for stud owners who have their own identification system as determined by the constitution of the specific breed association. All livestock identification marks are registered in a central Department of Agriculture database to enable traceability to the original owner and to provide easy identification of livestock, to prevent illegal animal movements and to facilitate the identification of stolen livestock. The pending new legislation, i.e., the Animal Identification Bill, will most probably replace the current Act and is intended to make the legislation more user friendly and practical. It also caters to the electronic and other forms of livestock identification, which could possibly accommodate individual livestock identification.

It is furthermore important to take cognizance of the fact that at this stage differences exist with respect to the requirements for traceability systems as far as the export and domestic (direct and feedlots)[8] markets are concerned.

Because of the above-mentioned Act together with standard record-keeping practices, livestock traceability in the beef industry from feedlot to the abattoir level is well-established, for beef destined for both the domestic and export markets. However,

---

[8] Note that approximately 60–70 percent of all cattle slaughtered in South Africa originates from feedlots.

traceability for animals destined for the domestic market is in most cases not continued after abattoir level once leaving in the form of swinging sides. Boxed primals are traceable on a batch basis per specific time interval for both the domestic and international markets.

As indicated above, South Africa has a well-developed traceability system for red meat for export. Basically, all beef exported by South Africa originates from feedlots, which in most cases have their own export abattoirs and de-boning facilities or have some investment in such facilities that comply with international or buyer determined standards. In addition to branding, cattle entering feedlots are individually identified and recorded for traceability purposes. This information will follow the animal until slaughtering takes place, during which time the information will be linked to its carcass. Carcasses are processed in batches that allow for the traceability back to the batches after the deboning process has been completed. Hence, all beef packed for export can be traced back to a specific batch and from there back to the farm level in the majority of cases.

It should, however, be noted that different feedlots and exporters currently use different traceability technology. Although these traceability systems comply with what is expected from international buyers, these systems are not necessarily compatible between exporters or nationally. This leaves a need in terms of a uniform national traceability system for beef destined for both the domestic as well as the export market. There are however discussions taking place between role players in the beef industry to adopt a more uniform traceability system. This should not be too difficult a task as the principles, guidelines, systems and procedures are already in place.

Hides and Skins. The production and processing of hides and skins are not subject to any direct legislative requirements, but are to a large extent governed by the requirements of the importing countries (such as ISO 14000) and the general legislation pertaining to industries and the environment. Certification that the hides, skins and leather is free of PCP (pentachlorophenol) is also required from most importing countries.

Environmental concerns include the containment of salt, zinc, arsenic, cadmium and chromium, all of which are associated with the tanning process.

Tanning requires at least 35 liters of water per kilogram of leather and the purification of this water presents many difficulties. The odors associated with tanneries also present a problem if the plant is situated near to settlements.

Quality control is a major problem in the South African leather industry. South African hides and skins from extensive farming operations are generally of poor quality as the animals are raised under harsh conditions and damage from seeds, parasites, and scratches from thorn bushes are common. Unfortunately, much of this damage is not clear to the human eye before the wet blue stage when considerable costs (about 60 percent of the total eventual costs) have already been incurred.

The incorrect placing of brands on the animal often reduces the size of the panel that can be cut from the leather. Standards of flaying and hide preparation at abattoirs are not always up to standard.

Major Problems in Meeting Technical Requirements for Market Access. The inputs of the South African representatives at OIE meetings tend to be reactive at present and little is being done to provide proactive inputs to the benefit of the meat industry. There is no full time dedicated official manning an OIE desk. For example, submissions requested by the OIE with regard to the Foot and Mouth disease status of South Africa were not submitted on time. Some of the Provincial Departments of Agriculture did not conduct the sampling in time, highlighting the breakdown in communication between the National and Provincial Departments.

The meat industry is not involved in the preparation of submissions to the OIE and is generally not aware of the activities of the OIE or the opportunities to influence OIE decisions. OIE requirements are communicated to the meat industry after they have come into force and this communication channel is quite effective at the industrial level, but awareness at individual farmer level is very poor.

Due to the lack of reciprocal communication and the failure of the directorate to submit the results of the required FMD sampling to the OIE on time, there is a general lack of confidence on the part of the meat industry in the ability of the department to conduct their affairs at the OIE in the best interest of the meat industry. An example of this is the failure of the directorate to lobby strongly for the limitations on the export of pork due to African

Swine Fever to be applied on a provincial basis as opposed to a national basis. This would enable the export of pork from provinces, which have not had cases of African Swine Fever for at least two years. South Africa chairs the OIE committee on African Swine Fever.

Cost of Compliance. Relatively little information on cost of compliance is available in the meat industry. Interviews with, among others, Dooley (2002) and Bruwer (2002) provided some information on the cost of compliance.

According to Dooley (2002), the cost to South African Natural Beef (see Annex Q) of implementing a quality assurance system amounted to R1.2 million for 2001 on a turnover of R40 million, or roughly 3 percent. The customer paid a premium of R1.00 per kilogram for the product, but this is passed on to the producer. Regular yield tests have indicated that the customers save R0.85 per kilogram on drip loss and throwaway, and they are prepared to absorb the extra 15c for the added consumer satisfaction associated with the South African Natural Beef Products. There is no added cost to the consumer at this stage, but it is likely that consumers will be prepared to pay more for these products.

There are a few cost savings associated with the Quality Assurance system, such as a reduction in transport insurance costs because of HACCP and reduced public liability insurance premiums.

Bruwer (2002) states that to upgrade an existing abattoir to comply with international or buyer determined standards could cost in the range of R55 to R60 million. The cost to establish a new abattoir that complies with international or buyer determined standards could range between R25 and R30 million.

Cross Cutting Issues Pertaining to Meeting Standards

The main obstacles to participate in the process of standard setting are timely notification, capacity in dealing with standards setting, language barriers, length of protocols and poor commercial understanding of those charged with negotiating on behalf of the industry. The agencies that are the national contact points for CODEX and IPPC are said to be effective in that they have a very good knowledge, but poor capacity leads to inadequate consultations (Hattingh 2002). There also appear to be problems with respect to industry contact with the national enquiry points for CODEX-, IPPC- and ISO-related matters. At times, it appears that interaction between these bodies is deficient, that is, interaction between departments within government does not appear to be very good. Notification agencies, which distribute new information to local stakeholders, are also not seem to be very efficient, but this is not always their fault because South Africa often receives late notifications through e-mails and meetings (Hattingh 2002). Limited core, personnel core, heavy workload and a high demand from clients and persistence of industry pressure groups wanting to utilize political factors in relation to technical issues, were listed by the NDA as being constraints to the above agencies.

South Africa's participation in the various international committees and working groups is greatly challenged by the voting procedure within the committees in which South Africa often disagrees with the EU. The EU dominates the representation in the food safety committees. There are also problems in terms of definitions with respect to international standards in regard to availability and participation in the standards setting process that is dominated by certain blocks or countries. South Africa does not have such an advantage, as countries with similar interests, African developing countries, cannot afford participation at all levels which developed countries can easily afford. This is more significant than lack of timely notification of proposed regulation, language barriers, lack of capacity among the developing countries.

There appears to be a naïve approach to reporting of the international regulation as required by World Trade Organisation/Technical Barriers to Trade. The reporting is simply not up to date in light of the advances that have been made in technology and communication. South Africa plans to improve its reporting database system based on the Canadian model.

CE marking[9] to EU regulatory requirements is becoming more important. However, where the

---

[9] The CE Marking is the manufacturer's declaration, showing compliance with all applicable EU directives. For most products sold in the EU, the use of the CE Marking and a Declaration of Conformity are mandatory. *Source:* Website TUV-Rheinland.

intervention of a notified body is required South African firms are have to fork out large sums of money to have the relevant conformity assessment work carried out in the EU. For example, there is an SMME company in the Cape that produces semirigid fully inflatable craft that requires the intervention of a "notified body" to get into the EU. A European company quoted euro 1,500 (approximately R15000) to carry out this activity. It is understood that the South African firm paid this fee, as there was no other way to obtain market access for their product to the EU. In another case, a European company quoted euro 10,000 (approximately R100000) to carry out this activity. A few years ago a South African SMME tried to export a wire-cutting and straightening machine to the EU but decided against this as it would have had to pay DM 50000 (approximately R225000) to a "notified body" for conformity assessment work in terms of the EU's Machinery Directive. Although South Africa has safety regulations governing the manufacture and distribution of the above-mentioned products, it is the lack of recognition by EU regulators (in the above-mentioned cases) of the local conformity assessment infrastructure (i.e., the absence of mutual recognition) that obliges exporters to test and certify overseas in foreign currency.

South African Involvement in International Standards Development

South Africa has, through the various stakeholders mentioned in this document, representation on various different international standard-setting bodies. Their involvement is also indicated in Figure 4.1 (also see Annex I). This section will focus on examples where South Africa has contributed toward the setting and changes to international standards.

Table 4.18 shows the attendance of international Codex Meetings by South African representatives. Examples where South Africa's participation in the International Codex Committee has been favorable to the South Africa include the following:

- Work on the Standard for Smoked Fish in the Codex Committee on Fish and Fishery Products: South Africa proposed that this standard should include all smoked fish and not only cold smoked fish as proposed by Denmark. The Committee accepted this proposal and South Africa was requested to draft a discussion document in this regard, which was submitted for discussion.

- South Africa further participates actively in the development of The Code of Practice for Fishery Products to ensure that the interests of the country are taken care of. The South African delegation to the Codex Committee on Fish and Fishery Products (CCFFP) was largely responsible for defusing a serious dispute within the Committee with a proposal on how to handle HACCP within the document. The dispute revolved around the differences in interest between developed and developing countries on how to handle HACCP. Also, there was a deadlock on how guidelines should be handled. One group felt that it should be on a product specific basis, whereas another group suggested generic guidelines on a product category basis. The latter approach was approved since the former would have resulted in much difficulties as far as implementation and policies is concerned. The final document is not yet finalized, but expectations are that this will happen soon.

- With regard to the food hygiene matters discussed at the Codex Committee on Food Hygiene, South Africa has on several occasions supported issues specifically affecting developing countries. For example, the proposed draft Code of Hygienic Practice for Milk and Milk Products, South Africa made proposals to changes to the title of the document (to better reflect who the code was aimed at), and South Africa further supported India in highlighting the plight of small and lesser-developed farmers. South Africa also supported India and other developing countries in preventing the proposed draft revised guidelines for the application of HACCP in small and/or less developed businesses from proceeding to Step 8 of the Procedure. The Committee on South Africa and India's intervention agreed to forward the document to Step 5 of the Procedure. This will allow developing countries more time to discuss the document and make further inputs.

- South Africa has also supported the higher levels of 15 mcg/kg of Aflatoxin in peanuts for further processing as opposed to the 4–6 mcg/kg suggested by the EU and other cooler countries (in the Codex Committee on Food Additive and Contaminants). The lower levels are not

Table 4.18 Attendance of International Codex Meetings by South African Representatives till May 2002

Committee	1994	1995	1996	1997	1998	1999	2000	2001	2002
Codex Alimentarius Commission	—	H	—	HI	—	HTAI	—	HI	—
Codex Committee on General Principles	O	—	HA	—	HA	HIA	HIA	H	O
Codex Committee on Food Hygiene	H	H	O	H	H	O	H	H	HS
Codex Committee on Food Inspection and Certification Systems	NM	NM	NM	NM	NM	NM	NM	H	HS
Codex Committee on Food Labelling	HI	—	HA	H	HI	H	HI	HI	HI
Codex Committee on Pesticide Residues	O	HA	HA	HA	HIA	HA	HA	HA	H
Codex Committee on Veterinary Drugs Residues in Foods	O	A	H	O	HA	—	HA	O	—
Codex Committee on Food Additives and Contaminants	O	H	O	O	H	H	H	H	H
Codex Committee on Fresh Fruit and Vegetables	A	—	A	A	—	A	A	—	(later this year)
Codex Committee on Fish and Fishery Products	IS	—	SI	—	SI	—	SI	—	S
Codex Committee on Nutrition and Foods for Special Dietary Uses	—	H	H	—	HI	—	HI	HI	(later this year)
Codex Committee on Meat Hygiene	NM	NM	NM	NM	NM	NM	NM	—	A
Methods of Analysis and Sampling	O	O	—	O	A	—	A	A	(later this year)
Ad hoc Task Force on Fruit and Vegetable Juices	—	—	—	—	—	—	—	—	O
Biotechnology (ad hoc Task Force)	—	—	HA	—	HA	—	H	H	H
Coordinating Committee for Africa	O	—	O	—	O	O	HA	—	(later this year)
Codex Committee on Cocoa Products and Chocolates	—	—	O	—	—	—	—	NM	NM
Codex Committee on Fats and Oils	—	—	O	—	O	—	—	NM	NM
Codex Committee on Milk and Milk Products	O	—	O	O	O	O	NM	NM	NM
Codex Committee on Processed Fruits and Vegetables	—	—	—	—	O	—	—	NM	NM
Ad hoc Task Force on Animal Feeding	—	—	AP	A	A	—	—	NM	NM
Codex Committee on Import/Export Inspection/Certification	—	A	O	A	A	HA	HA	NM	NM
Codex Committee on Mineral Waters	—	—	O	—	O	—	—	NM	NM

—: No session held
O: Session not attended
NM: Not a member

A: National Department of Agriculture
H: Department of Health
S: SA Bureau of Standards
T: Tertiary education institute

I: Industry (observer)
P: Perishable Product Export Control Board

Source: SADC SPS/Food safety Workshop, Country paper SA, 2000; Information from 2000 retrieved from Department of Health 2002)

practically feasible in countries like South Africa and a lower level would harm South African exports. Similarly, with levels of tin in canned foods, South Africa supported the higher levels. In countries with higher temperatures it is not possible to have lower levels as is the case in Europe. White fruits like pineapple and apple are canned in nonlacquered tins, which helps to keep the fruit white. Should South Africa have to change over to lacquered tins, ascorbic acid will need to be added to keep the fruit white and this will be a costly exercise. South Africa will continue supporting the higher level whenever it comes up at meetings. South Africa also supported the higher level for Patulin in apple juice (50 mcg/kg). It is not economically feasible to attain a level of 25 mcg/kg as suggested by Northern Hemisphere countries.

- South Africa has also compiled the "Consideration of elaboration of MRLs for spices" and "minor crops" documents for developing countries discussed at the Codex Committee on Pesticide Residues in Foods (CCPR). Spices are grown in and exported almost exclusively from developing countries. In 1993, developing countries accounted for 74 percent of the world's export in spices. The large importers of spices are the United States, Europe and Japan. Since no Codex MRLs and Extraneous Maximum Residue Limits are set, it causes trade disruption problems in the international spice trade. The CCPR has thus recommended that MRLs be set on monitoring data and that the Joint Meeting for Pesticide Residues (JMPR) be consulted on how to submit data. In addition to this, South Africa has also presented a paper indicating the lack of Codex, EU, and United States MRLs for tropical fruit crops (to CCPR), which is creating problems for developing countries. In many instances, the pesticide industry is not interested in supporting MRLs on these crops since the pesticide usage is minor. Developing countries can address this problem by cooperating with industry to coordinate the elaboration of the necessary MRLs. This was supported by the CCPR.
- Governments are requested to provide such data necessary for conducting acute exposure assessments of pesticide residues. This includes large portion of consumption data. Currently the database contain information from Australia, United States, United Kingdom, France, Japan and the Netherlands. However, South Africa has recently compiled such data and is the first developing country to submit data.
- South Africa's contribution with regard nutrition and labeling issues lies in the fact that it adds pressure to continue work on health claims and the demand that such type of claims be permitted on foodstuffs. Similarly, South Africa has contributed to the pressure to force the Codex Committee on Nutrition and Foods for Special Dietary Uses to at least consider a risk assessment approach versus the Recommended Dietary Allowance (RDA) approach while determining maximum levels for vitamins and minerals for nutritional supplements.
- South Africa together with Canada and the United States ensured that the issue of traceability was seriously considered by the ad hoc Task Force on Foods Derived from Biotechnology and in the process convinced a number of additional countries, and an acceptable consensus decision was reached. Traceability is warranted in specific situations, but is extremely expensive and South Africa cannot afford more increases in food prices. The same applies to the labeling of GMOs as discussed by the Codex Committee on Food Labelling (CCFL) where South Africa is strongly lobbying with Australia, United States and other countries against the proposals of the EU which will have major cost implications for South Africa.
- South Africa has also made considerable inputs into drafting standards for fresh fruit and vegetables, milk and milk products, etc. and always in the context of what would benefit South Africa as a country (economically while protecting the health of consumers). For example, South Africa will at the forthcoming Session of the Codex Committee on Fresh Fruit and Vegetables propose that the Standard for Pineapples be reopened for discussion with regard to stem length, sizing and marking requirements following the local developments. (A method was developed locally whereby pineapples can be exported by sea over a three-week period.)
- According to the NCC, other than making a contribution (and influencing decisions taken) at the various committees, the contacts made at these meetings are most valuable. South Africa now has

access to several experts in the field when information is needed during elaboration of South Africa's regulations.

South Africa has contributed to various drafts circulated by the IPPC, i.e., ISPM 5 Glossary of phytosanitary terms 2001, ISPM Publication number 17: Pest reporting. South Africa's active participation also highlighted by South Africa's insistence that there should be clarity on the place of production. For example, seed produced in Kenya under license and packed in the Netherlands should not appear on the market as seed produced in the Netherlands but as seed produced in Kenya under license and packed in the Netherlands, clearly stating the place of production. South Africa has also requested for a clearer definition of tissue culture to ensure no confusion over the term "tissue culture".

The issue of Citrus Black Spot (CBS) is very sensitive to South African Citrus producers. In this regard, following lengthy negotiations, the United States was furnished with the necessary pest risk analysis data and now accepts some areas of the Western Cape as being free of CBS.[10]

The United States was also provided with technical data with regard to *Amaryllis sp*, indigenous bulb flowers exported to the United States. The technical data provided by South Africa aided the United States authorities in setting up the necessary regulations regarding the import of *Amaryllis sp* from South Africa.

South Africa has challenged quarantine regulations on some products in some countries on some occasions. At present, South Africa is negotiating with the EU to remove CBS from its list of quarantine pests. South Africa is in the process of providing the necessary pest risk analysis to justify its claim that CBS is not a risk to the EU due to the difference in climatic conditions.

Technical data was provided to the NPPO of the South Korean government to assist them to develop the necessary regulation to govern imports of citrus products from South Africa, as there had been no trade between the two countries thus no data and it would have taken very long for South Korea to generate its own data.

The SABS is the national member body for ISO and IEC. SABS was a founder member of ISO in 1947 and it is the only standards body in SADC which is a member of IEC. As the national member body to ISO and IEC, standards adopted at ISO and IEC are adopted as national standards set by SABS. This saves the public from the huge cost associated with the purchase of an ISO standard in comparison to the purchase of a SAB standard. The SABS also acts as the official WTO/TBT enquiry point.

South Africa's participation takes place at two levels: First, South Africa has three representatives at the IEC management level. These representatives are from the National Electricity Regulator, the SABS and the Circuit Breaker Industries respectively. The President of the SABS sits on the ISO Council.

Most of the standards settings are done at the technical committees, on which South Africa is well represented. ISO has several different technical committees for standards, which are involved in different fields of standard setting and involved in different projects concerning the standards setting procedure. Similar committees on the national level are maintained in South Africa, these are referred to as National Standards Committee. The members of these committees interact closely with their international counterparts. South Africa is active in approximately 300 ISO and IEC technical committees and is an observer in approximately 150 committees. The SABS is, therefore, active in approximately 50 percent of the ISO and IEC committees and holds the secretariat for a number of them. South African energy is focused on areas where its industries participate in global trade.

- SABS holds the chair of the international ISO committee for water quality. This committee is mainly oriented toward the European Union (EU) because most members are from the EU. When the committee was setting standards for collecting water samples collecting, the majority of the members did not take into consideration that the SA situation and other developing countries was totally different from the EU situation with regard to the of distances between the water collection points and the laboratory.

---

[10] The magisterial districts included in the western Cape Pest Free Area are: Bredasdorp, Caledon, Clanwilliam, Heidelberg, Hermanus, Ladysmith, Motagu, Paarl, Picketberg, Robertson, Somerset-west, Stellenbosch, Strand, Swellendam, Wellington, and Worcester.

South Africa's representatives advocated for change and were able to influence a change in the standards for water sample collection in such a way as to make it suitable for the South Africa's situation.

- South Africa has played an influential role in some IEC technical committees, for example with respect to power line insulators and prepaid metering where South African proposals have been accepted.

An outstanding example of long-term industry participation can be found in the involvement of Mr. Viv Cohen of Circuit Breaker Industries. Mr Cohen has been representing South African industry in various IEC working groups for nearly twenty years. Mr Cohen has been active in TC 23 and SC 23E (all equipment in electrical installations); TC 17 & SC 17B (switchgear and control gear—low voltage circuit breakers) and TC 64 (wiring rules). He has also played an active role in the IEC Electro Magnetic Compatibility activities.

- South Africa, via the SABS, is very active within ISO TC 165 that deals with structural timber and, especially, the treatment of timber. South Africa is also active as a participating member in most of the other related ISO technical committees, for example fiber board, etc.

Due to limited indigenous natural forests South Africa actively developed tree plantations during the twentieth century. As a result, the country gained quite a lot of expertise in obtaining, for example, construction timber from plantations. South Africa was one of the first countries in the world to actively use "finger-jointing" in timber for use in high-risk construction projects. In fact, it is interesting to note that the South African SABS "Finger-Joint" Code of Practice that was developed in 1976 is referred to in ISO documents and was recently made available to Russia for implementation there.

However, one of the main problems with plantation forestry in South Africa is that trees grow faster (plantation trees are for example, fed fertilizer) and do not produce the same quality or grade of timber as trees of the same species in the Northern Hemisphere. These grades are based on the strength of the timber, which is determined by visual inspection, mechanical grading and testing. In the 1980s the SABS tested nearly 45000 samples of wood to determine a proper timber grading system. Approximately 15 percent of South African construction timber production is of grade 5 or 6 quality, 60 percent of production is of grade 7 quality and the balance is better than grade 7.

As a result, South Africa has spent considerable time and effort within ISO TC 165 to influence the grading of structural timber so as to allow for the inclusion of grades lower than grade 7, which is usually the lowest grade in the Northern hemisphere. South Africa was successful in getting the lower grades accepted at ISO level. Although there appears to be good cooperation within TC 165, it is often the case that there is a lack of understanding for a given tropical or subtropical technical problem among Northern Hemisphere nations. In TC 165, South Africa tends to ally itself with Australia and New Zealand who have similar problems.

South Africa was also successful in getting its test method for laminated beams accepted by ISO. On the timber treatment side South Africa was successful in getting the so-called risk categories expanded. This is important because not all timber species are suitable for specific applications in Africa. For example, American Red Cedar is susceptible to the African Termite and only two species of Pine are suitable for the manufacture of power transmission poles in South Africa. This is often an issue where international donor funded projects specify the use of say, European timber or U.S. timber that is not treated or suitable for African conditions.

SADC countries, such as Zambia, Malawi and Zimbabwe, are adopting South African timber standards. In 1994, the SABS carried out wide-ranging tests in Zimbabwe to determine timber grades. These now form the basis for the acceptance of Zimbabwean timber without further conformity assessment provided the timber bears the Zimbabwe Standards Mark.

- The SABS represents the SABS fishery interests at the international CODEX level. Usually at least three representatives from the fishery industry accompany the SABS to the international CODEX meetings. The DTI, Department of Foreign Affairs and the consumer unions are observer members. It is important to emphasize that there are no ISO international fish product standards. This is a CODEX responsibility. The SPS agreement, therefore, refers to the CODEX codes of hygienic practice, guidelines and standards.

South Africa has, as far as fishery products are concerned, played an influential role at the international CODEX level, which meets in plenary every two years. Although developing nations have traditionally been inadequately represented at CODEX, South Africa's aim is to develop alliances with other developing countries to tackle technical issues. For example, South Africa and Thailand joined forces to oppose a CODEX recommendation that fish reach a temperature of zero degrees centigrade within one to two hours of being caught. Although this is possible in the North Atlantic it is not feasible in warmer oceans and seas. South Africa and Thailand successfully proposed a compromise at a level approaching the temperature of melting ice.

• The SABS is also a member of the informal international fishery discussion forum called the International Association of Fish Inspectors (IAFI). South Africa is a founder member of IAFI and believes it serves a useful function in allowing for the informal exchange of technical information among authorities.

The SABS has an enviable international reputation when it comes to phytosanitary regulation and surveillance of fishery products. South Africa has, in the past, exported significant quantities of fish to Norway. When a Norwegian factory started experiencing problems with the seams in their cans they called in the SABS to assist them with the problem. The SABS also assisted the factory in implementing HACCP measures. In appreciation for the assistance the Norwegians awarded Mr Gideon Joubert, an SABS official, with the Norconserf award for assistance to the Norwegian fishery industry and his contributions at CODEX.

Chile, Peru and Thailand implemented South African standards so as to facilitate exports to South Africa. Two Thai firms, two Namibian firms, one Philippine firm, one Norwegian firm and one Portuguese firm are all certified to SABS 587: *Canned fish other than hake*. This means that these firms can affix the SABS mark to their product.

South Africa is a very active participating member of the textiles technical committees of the ISO, i.e., TC38 (25 participating countries) and TC219 (17 participating countries).

TC 38 (Textiles) is responsible for the standardization of fibers, yarns, threads, cords, rope, cloth and other fabricated textile materials and the relevant test methods; textile industry raw materials and the chemicals required for processing and testing as well as specifications for textile products. South Africa coordinates regularly with all of the subcommittees of TC 38 and the Textiles Fiber Technology Standards Department of the SABS hosts the secretariat for subcommittee 20: *Fabric Descriptions*.

TC 219 (Floor Coverings) is responsible for standardization in the field of textile, resilient and laminate floor coverings.

It should be noted that 90 percent of these committees' work is on test methods. Product requirements are, therefore, not that important. That is why test houses participate so actively. South Africa's main focus is, therefore, to ensure that it can test to ISO requirements.

As with other standards, the SABS circulates documents to the national mirror committee for comment, collates the responses, and sends them back to TC 38 using ISO's *Livelink* server. The SABS ensures that all interested parties are involved, for example The Textile Federation of South Africa, the Clothing and Textile Institute, The South African Wool Board, government purchasers, hospital administrators, and test houses, etc.

Active participation in TC38 and TC219 has, undoubtedly, given South Africa an ideal opportunity to influence standards development in the textile domain. For example, the idea for draft ISO standard 21863: Textile Floor Coverings—Guidelines for Maintenance and Cleaning originated in South Africa and are based, to a large extent, on SABS 0245-1993.

South Africa recently hosted a meeting of TC38's Subcommittee 20 in Cape Town to discuss ISO 3758—Textiles Care Labelling Code Using Symbols. South Africa presented 48 comments of which the majority, were accepted by TC38. Another example concerns ISO 13936—Textiles Determination of the Slippage Resistance of Yarn at a Seam in Woven Fabrics—Part 1: Fixed Seam Opening Method. South Africa made 23 comments in respect to, for example, Test Methods of Seams, where South Africa pushed for the inclusion of different cross head speeds.

SANAS is a signatory to the mutual recognition agreements of both the International Accreditation

Forum (IAF) as well as the International Laboratory Accreditation Cooperation (ILAC). The IAF agreement has provided significant international recognition to South African ISO 9000 and ISO 14000 certificates.

The Chief Executive Officer of SANAS is the chairman of ILAC. The ILAC Arrangement, which involves 37 member bodies from 28 economies means that goods tested in one country by a laboratory that is accredited under a signatory to the Arrangement, will be accepted by other signatories. The Arrangement, which entered into force on 31 January 2001, was a major step toward reducing or eliminating the need for re-testing of the goods by the importing country. This marked the first great multilateral stride in the elimination of technical barriers to trade. At the stroke of a pen South Africa obtained recognition of accredited test and calibration reports among all its major trading partners.

SANAS has also been recognized by the OECD as the GLP monitoring authority in South Africa. Two facilities have already been GLP accredited by SANAS. This will, hopefully, play an important role in making South Africa an attractive source of nonclinical trials.

South African government officials have held preliminary MRA discussions with the European Commission, the People's Republic of China and Australia. South Africa is on a list of countries with which the EU will negotiate an MRA. China has, for example, expressed interest in negotiating an MRA with South Africa along the lines of the APEC agreements in electrical goods, Foods and Food Products and Telecommunications Equipment.

Regional Involvement: Article 17 of the 1996 SADC Trade Protocol lays the foundation for the harmonization of standards among the fourteen member countries based on international standards. However, this has yet to happen, as the ground rules must still be ironed out. South Africa has been participating actively in the SADC standards, quality assurance, accreditation and metrology activities (SQAM) since 1996. There are four SQAM expert groupings (SQAMEG), i.e., SADC-STAN—composed of the SADC standards bodies, SADCMET—composing of the regional metrology bodies, SADCMEL—the legal and trade metrology forum and SADCA—regional accreditation of conformity assessment bodies. The main aim of these bodies is to harmonize product and measurement standards and to put in place a regional accredita-

tion infrastructure. SADCSTAN is tasked with harmonization of standards. The SABS hosts the SADCSTAN Secretariat. There are already many standards that are the same or similar, for example cement standards. Although there are cases where SADC countries have adopted certain South African standards this process must be handled sensitively and diplomatically so as to avoid accusations of being "big brother" in the region.

SADC has not carried out any harmonization of regulations as yet. The major fishery exporters such as Mauritius, Seychelles and Namibia have all implemented HACCP, as their export markets require this. HACCP would, therefore, form the basis of any future harmonization. The last SADC SPS discussions took place in Namibia in November 2000. The challenge, at least from a South African regulatory point of view, is how to deal with imports from those SADC countries with less well-developed phytosanitary systems within a free trade environment.

Conclusions

It is clear from the above discussion that South Africa plays an important role in the international standards forums. However, a 2001 Department of Trade and Industry commissioned study into the South African standards, quality, accreditation and metrology (SQAM) infrastructure, questioned this high level of participation in international committees, especially in cases where there were no national "mirror" committees. The report recommended that the basic driver for any participation should be the benefits to be derived for South African industry. The report also recommended a thorough review of committee participation to ensure that resources were targeted to areas of most relevance to South African Industry. It is generally recognized that private sector industry delegates with relevant technical knowledge are best suited to participation in international technical committees. However, the SQAM study found that industry participation in international committee meetings was rather limited and needed to be enhanced.

South Africa has less industry experts than first world countries and, as a result, industry participation is at a premium. However, industry interviews revealed a worrying trend regarding declining SABS financial support for industry participation in international forums. Although the SABS uses government funding to finance the participation of its own staff members, it is unclear whether it will, in future, SABS will meet the travel costs for industry participants. Companies must, in any event, foot the hotel and subsistence bills of their employees that participate in ISO or IEC meetings. It would be beneficial for South Africa, in the long run, if industry participation in ISO and IEC activities could be directly subsidized by government.

Private Sector Perspectives and Development Assistance to SMMEs

South African Development Assistance

The South African government provides significant assistance to Small, Medium, and Micro Enterprises (SMMEs) in the domain of standards, quality assurance, accreditation and metrology.

NTSIKA. The NTSIKA Enterprise Promotion Agency has a number of support programs that are tailored to SMME needs. NTSIKA is funded by the DTI. This funding amounted to R50 million in 2001 (approximately US$4.928 million). The following programs are relevant to this study:

(a) The Local Business Service Centres (LBSC)
There are currently 107 LBSCs around the country, which are funded by the government. They provide nonfinancial business expertise support to SMMEs. The LBSCs make use of preferred service providers through which special expertise is required. This includes conformity assessment services such as testing and certification, etc. NTSIKA pays commercial rates for these service providers. The LBSCs are funded through NTSIKA and received R10 million (approximately US$985707) in 2000 for its activities.
(b) The Tender Advice Centre Programme (TAC)
The TAC program focuses on SMMEs with 5 to 50 employees in the construction, manufacturing and services sectors. Participants are assisted to access tender contracts and to perform within the requirements of the tenders. Essentially NTSIKA tries to ensure that a slice of government tenders goes to SMMEs by ensuring that they can comply with the quality requirements.
(c) The Trade and Investment Development Programme (TIDP)

The TIDP is a joint program between NTSIKA and the European Union, it is run by the Local Business Service Centres. It is designed to help SMMEs to compete internationally. The TIDP program will provide R60 million (approximately US$5.9 million) over three years. The program is divided into three tracks:

- Track 1: Provides basic advice and training. An initial audit is carried out to identify areas for improvement.
- Track 2: Assistance to selected firms with product and export market development. This is more one-on-one attention where, for example, the Council for Scientific and Industrial Research (CSIR) (as a preferred service provider) may be called upon to provide a specific service. SMMEs would, for example, be referred to test laboratories and certification in this manner.
- Track 3: Facilitate local partnership between SMMEs and EU counterparts.

(d) The Technology Programs
These programs are aimed at facilitating SMME access to technology and skills transfer.

The Manufacturing Advisory Centres (MACs). The MACs were created by NTSIKA to assist SMMEs in the manufacturing sector. One of the MACs stated aims is to assist SMMEs with the implementation of quality systems. As a result the MACs are overwhelmingly in favor of ISO 9000 certification. They use government money to fund 65 to 90 percent of the costs involved in certification if the client is a MAC member. This funding is acquired through the DTI and NTSIKA. The contribution is based on Previously Disadvantaged Individuals (PDI) shareholding, turnover, and profit margin, etc. The MACs also assist SMMEs with marketing, productivity improvement and access to finance.

The MACs have spent R43 million (approximately US$4.2 million) on assistance to SMMEs over the past five years. Of this amount approximately 16 percent was spent on so-called quality systems activities that cover aspects such as testing, certification, and calibration, etc. It is interesting to note that the average cost of technical assistance is approximately R70,000 (approximately US$6,899) per firm.

The MAC industrial advisors evaluate a firm to size up its strengths and weaknesses. Once this is done the MAC advisor makes recommendations and draws up an action plan. Money is made available to fund approved service providers for certain activities, for example Implementation of an ISO 9000 quality management system.

The SABS SMME Section. The role of the SABS SMME Department is to identify suitable SMMEs, then conduct company audits and identify a series of interventions and, ultimately, provide focused technical assistance and training.

The SABS offers training in welding, brick laying, and clothing manufacture, etc. through its so-called Missing Link Programme. It also facilitates access to the following services: The SABS Mark Scheme, ISO 9000 and ISO 14000 certification, product testing, the SA Excellence Model, etc.

To qualify for SABS assistance firms need to comply with the following:

- Need to have been trading for more than a year.
- Have an annual turnover between R100000 (approximately US$9850) and R30 million (approximately US$2.95 million). (Operate in one of the following sectors: Agriculture, clothing and textiles, construction, arts and crafts, chemicals, tourism, welding, mining, IT, security, training and development, fire extinguishers, bakery and confection, medical devices or catering.
- 50 percent of the business should be owned by either people with disabilities or PDIs or be a SMME or a joint venture between PDIs and non-PDIs.

It is interesting to note this same section also advises the Government Tender Board on reference to SABS specifications in tender documents (the so-called CKS—Coordinating Specifications). The service includes the evaluation of preproduction samples for compliance, assessing applicants' capacity and capability to supply products, tender adjudication and awarding and ongoing consignment inspections if so required.

The SABS also has its own internal "Learnership Programme" that scouts for talented PDIs at tertiary institutions, to undergo a standards development course. To date nine of these people have been employed in the SABS's electrotechnical standardization section.

DTI Incentive Schemes. There are only three DTI incentive schemes that fund conformity assessment activities.

(a) The Competitiveness Fund

The Competitiveness Fund currently offers the most comprehensive support of conformity assessment activities. The fund will reimburse up to 50 percent of eligible costs up to a maximum amount of R600000 (approximately US$59000) over the three-year lifetime of the Fund. In its guidelines the following activities are listed as being eligible for grant fund assistance:

- Product Testing—the Fund covers the testing organization's fees.
- Quality Management Improvement—the Fund covers consultancy fees and expenses toward installing or improving quality management systems.
- Acquisition of Quality Standards—the Fund covers consultancy fees and expenses.
- Training in Quality Management—the Fund covers course fees and international travel costs.

(b) The Sector Partnership Fund (SPF)

The SPF supports partnerships of five or more firms and organizations in the development and execution of collaborative projects. The SPF will support the development of such partnerships through the provision of 65:35 matching grants: 65 percent from the SPF and 35 percent from the partnership. Grant support for each approved partnership is limited to a cumulative ceiling of R1 million, (excluding VAT) (approximately US$98500).

A required outcome is improved product/service quality, uniformity and reliability. Since conformity assessment is a common need, the MACs include these costs in the main SPF application when they apply on behalf of SMMEs.

(c) Export Marketing Incentive Assistance (EMIA)

Primary Market Research scheme of EMIA provides R100000 per year (approximately US$9601) to exporters for the funding of "product registration". This covers 50 percent of the costs relating to the registration of a product in a foreign market such as patents, trademarks and quality marks (for example ISO 9000 range).

Foreign Development Assistance

South Africa became a recipient of foreign assistance in 1994 under a new political dispensation. At present, foreign assistance amounts to about R800 million per year or 0.08 percent of gross domestic product (what has been the trend since 1994 —rising, falling?). The beneficiaries of foreign support are government, the nongovernmental development community and emerging businesses. The level of foreign assistance is estimated to remain at the present level of R800 million for the foreseeable future.

Foreign assistance is made up of grants to finance government projects through the Reconstruction and Development Programme, and technical and project assistance that is financed directly by foreign offices. Presently the focus in development assistance is shifting from support to policy and strategy development for delivery of services with a focus on poverty reduction.

Some of the incentives that the Department of Trade and Industry offers to producers to improve quality and standards are funded through foreign assistance, mainly from the World Bank.

The Trade and Investment Development Programme (TIDP). The TIDP is a joint program between NTSIKA and the European Union. The LBSCs run this. It is designed to help SMMEs to compete internationally.

During the period 1996 to 1999 the EU provided euro 8.9 million for the TIDP. The EU has also been funding a similar TIDP program in Namibia.

According to a 1999 report[11] there are sometimes delays in disbursement (at the EU level as well as with the transfer of money within the Government, for example from the Department of State Expenditure to the relevant organization). This sometimes obliges Government departments to prefinance EU projects. For example, the DTI had to lend money to NTSIKA to implement the TIDP, because the Department of Finance had not yet released funds.

The United States Agency for International Development (USAID). USAID funds the cost of providing technical experts to support Standardization, Quality assurance, Accreditation and Metrology (SQAM) development, for example Sanitary and Phytosanitary (SPS) support in the Southern African Developing Community (SADC). A USAID official is stationed at the regional office in Gabarone, Botswana. He is currently tasked with assisting SADC in SPS issues such as regulatory harmonization and conformance issues.

Swedish International Development Agency (SIDA). South Africa has a newly established Furniture Technologies Training Centre (Furntech) that is situated on the Port Elizabeth Technikon's Saasveld Campus at George in the Southern Cape. The Department of Trade and Industry will inject a total of R18 million (approximately US$1775 million) into Furntech over the period April 2000 to March 2005. SIDA will contribute 8 million Swedish Krone over the same period. The main objectives of Furntech are to

- Develop furniture industry employee skills;
- Develop a pool of trainers; SIDA has also seconded trainers from Sweden's Tibro Training Centre to assist South African trainers;
- Introduce new manufacturing technologies;
- Enhance industry competitiveness by teaching and entrenching quality management techniques, etc.

Past Studies

DTI study. In 1999, the DTI, together with the NTSIKA Enterprise Promotion Agency, the South African Quality Institute, the South African Bureau of Standards and the National Manufacturing Advisory Centres conducted an assessment of the quality of infrastructure in the SMME sector.

The survey was inspired by a need to identify effective methods of government SMME support and intervention in the field of standards, quality assurance, accreditation and metrology (SQAM). The survey was aimed at understanding and realizing SMME concerns, needs and awareness in respect to SQAM issues. The research team studied the 1997 UNIDO Quality and Environmental Management Systems study to refine the survey.

The study focused on the following key themes: General understanding and awareness of quality,

---

[11] Evaluation of EC Country Strategy: South Africa 1996–1999—Investment Development Consultancy, France; Development Strategies, Italy—Carlos Montes, Stefano Migliorisi & Toby Wolfe—August 1999.

customers and quality, the achievement of quality, the importance and benefits of SABS standards, ISO 9000 standards, ISO 14000 standards, environmental legislation and the South African Excellence Model. A questionnaire was used to gather data from a representative sample of the industry. 70 percent of the sample frame included firms from the manufacturing sector.

The study found that the levels of SQAM awareness among SMMEs were very low. There is also a perception that conformity assessment is unaffordable and that it is too expensive to implement a quality management system. In fact 38 percent of respondents indicated they could not afford to implement ISO 9000. There was also a worrying perception among SMMEs that local certification bodies could not guarantee international recognition of their certificates. However, all certification bodies accredited by the SANAS enjoy international recognition in terms of South Africa's membership of the International Accreditation Forum. The awareness of ISO 14000 was also particularly low. However, it was encouraging to note that 95 percent of respondents indicated that their customers would change to another supplier if the quality of their products were unsatisfactory.

The study led to the redesign and improvement of government intervention. These are discussed under the section entitled "South African Development Assistance—Provision of Development Assistance."

World Bank Survey of SMME Exporters in South Africa. During the period 2001–2002 the World Bank conducted a survey of 70 South African SMMEs active in the export market to determine what problems they experience and challenges they face. A number of the questions were aimed at eliciting information in respect to standards and technical requirements to identify problems with compliance. Some of the most salient findings are summarized below. The information has been obtained from the World Bank Standards and Trade database.

The Overall Importance of Technical Requirements to Export Success. It is clear that most of the respondents (especially i.r.o. agriculture and textiles and apparel) regard technical requirements as being either important or very important to their exports to the EU and the United States. Product quality

and performance topped the bill as the most important issues. Labeling, testing and certification were also rated as important with consumer safety being highlighted as particularly important in the United States.

Most importantly, in terms of market access, nearly 79 percent of those that responded to the relevant question indicated that their locally obtained test results and certificates were accepted in export markets. This undoubtedly contributes to market penetration and export success.

Nearly 77 percent of respondents that answered the relevant question felt that international standards were important for success in domestic and/or international sales.

ISO 9000 remains the most important quality standard and certification system. Hardly any of the respondents have ISO 14000 certification. This is likely to change as environmental pressures increase.

Cost of Compliance. The cost effect of foreign technical requirements appears to be relatively small. Most (55 percent) of the responses rated this cost, as a percentage of total investment, in the 1 to 10 percent range. However, a significant number (28 percent) of responses rated costs in the 11 to 25 percent range. Costs relating to additional plant and equipment topped the bill followed by product redesign and additional labor for production. 75 percent of the responses fell into the above three categories. It is interesting to note that additional labor for certification and testing hardly features as a cost factor at all. This points to the fact that firms are capable of handling compliance without having to appoint specialized staff to deal with these issues.

For product testing done within the firm the respondents operating in the textiles sectors reported the biggest expenditure (mean percentage of 17.5), followed by agriculture, expressed as a percentage of total production costs. Overall the mean expenditure was approximately 6 percent of total production costs.

For product testing done outside the firm, the respondents operating in the textiles sectors reported the biggest expenditure (mean percentage of 5) followed by agriculture, expressed as a percentage of total production costs. Overall the mean expenditure was approximately 5 percent of total production costs. Overall, the mean expenditure on internal and external product testing is approximately 6 percent of total production costs.

Most respondents felt there were little or no duplication of effort, and very little increase in costs, involved in testing for both domestic and foreign requirements or for multiple foreign requirements.

Few (mainly in the electrical sector) of the respondents had seen cost savings because of complying with international standards. The majority reported increased costs of between 1 percent and 24 percent i.r.o. capital outlay, labor and inspection. This was especially evident in the agricultural sector.

Apart from the textiles sector cost of compliance does not appear to be a major challenge.

Access to Information. Most of the respondents indicated that they had no difficulty in obtaining information about applicable regulations in countries.

Standards Development. It is interesting to note that most of the respondents felt that the South African government had not aligned its regulations with international requirements.

There was a fairly even split between respondents involved in international standards development and those that are not. Of those that are involved the majority attend meetings in one form or another (face-to-face or videoconference). This is fairly encouraging as it points to the involvement of smaller firms in the SABSs technical committees.

Interviews with SMME Organizations

Interviews were conducted with NTSIKA Enterprise Promotion Agency, the SABS Small Business Section and five of the Manufacturing Advisory Centres to get a sense of how important were the conformity assessment issues.

The Impact and Importance of Conformity Assessment. *General Issues.* Most respondents agreed that conformity assessment is important to win tenders and to be able to export. It must be noted that the emphasis at this level is overwhelmingly on ISO 9000 certification. A few respondents mentioned the SABS Mark Scheme as being important.

PERMAC in Port Elizabeth has, for example, helped more than 50 SMMEs to obtain ISO 9000 certification. This is probably to be expected, as many of PERMAC's clients are suppliers in the engineering and automotive sectors where big companies insist on ISO 9000, QS9000 and VDA 6 certification.

Most respondents felt that SMMEs had benefited tremendously from ISO 9000 certification, not only from a business point of view but also from a management point of view.

Winning government tenders is a major preoccupation for many South African SMMEs. That is why they are actively seeking ISO 9000 certification. However, an inability to comply with specifications is often a problem. For example, a firm recently lost a R7 million tender to produce overalls for the South African Police Service because it could not comply with the required specs.

There are a number of success stories. In Durban, Cornuseal and Woodstreet have managed to secure export orders because of ISO 9000 certification. With the SABSs assistance a firm called Africa Haute Couture succeeded in securing a tender from the Department of Correctional Services and the Department of Education after its product was tested. This has led to an increase in staff. Bell Products, a chemical manufacturer, was recently awarded government contracts based on a chemical test report. Khoi Linen and Textile won tenders from the SANDF and the SAPS based on successful conformity assessment. Thabiso Chemicals has become South Africa's first black owned chemical firm to obtain the SABS mark.

Case Studies. The following mini case studies indicate that the agencies (the SABS in this case) are having success in helping emerging black entrepreneurs to win contracts and increase their business by making use of the existing conformity assessment tools. If anything, this support should be expanded as rapidly as possible to assist other previously disadvantaged businessmen. It is interesting to note that the SABS SMME support is anchored in the *Job Creation* component of the *Presidential Imperatives Programme*.

- Case study 1: Thabiso Chemicals
  Owner: Mr Brian Nyezi
  Industry: Chemical Manufacturing & Distribution

Thabiso Chemicals was the first black owned chemicals firm in South Africa to obtain the SABS mark for its products (for example soap). Mr Nyezi estimates that this has resulted in an increase in turnover from R11 million during 2001 to a projected R18 to R20 million for 2002. The cost associated with obtaining the mark was approximately R30 000, which is negligible when compared to turnover. However, the firm wants to obtain ISO 9000 certification. This will entail improving quality control, etc. Mr Nyezi estimates that this will require some upgrading of his plant and that the total cost of the exercise (including certification that normally costs no more than R10 000) could be as high as R400 000. This would represent approximately 2 percent of the projected 2002 turnover, which is not very high. Mr Nyezi believes that ISO 9000 certification will increase his turnover even further and that he may secure export contracts as well.

- Case study 2: Khoi Linen & Textile
  Owner: Mr Kenny Modike
  Industry: Clothing and Textiles

Khoi Linen has made use of the SABS's "missing link" training program as well as product testing and consignment inspection. It is currently seeking the SABS Mark and Mr Modike is also keen to apply for ISO 9000 certification. Mr Modike estimates that he will have to upgrade his factory (new machinery, etc.) to the tune of R200 000 to R300 000 to prepare for certification. The firm's annual turnover varies between R4 million and R8 million. The ISO 9000 outlay is, therefore, unlikely to exceed 7 percent to 8 percent of turnover. Mr Modike regards this as expensive, but well worth the investment as he is keen to increase his firm's competitiveness and to produce a good quality product.

- Case study 3: Samsokol Construction
  Owner: Mr Albert Magagula
  Industry: "Breeze" Blocks Manufacturer

Mr Magagula had his blocks tested by the SABS's construction test laboratory. This resulted in his firm winning a major RDP housing project, worth R3.9 million, to supply blocks for 1500 low-cost houses. The SABS tests cost him R800 (subsidized at 50 percent), which is negligible. He did not have to invest any money in improving his production methods.

- Case study 4: Ncema Supplies
  Owner: Mrs. Zenzile Maseko
  Industry: Clothing & Textiles

Mrs. Zinzile Maseko obtained the SABS Mark for her overalls. This cost was R2,000. She did not need to upgrade her facilities. As a result she won

a contract to supply the Department of Correctional Services. This brought about a 47 percent increase in turnover, i.e., from R289,000 to R425,000. Clearly the direct cost of compliance was negligible.

Factors Inhibiting Growth.

- Most respondents did not regard affordability as a problem. This response needs to be qualified, however. As the MAC's use government funding to subsidize between 65 percent and 90 percent of the conformity assessment costs, affordability is unlikely to be a big issue. SMMEs often have difficulty paying their annual SABS Mark Scheme fees as the MAC only subsidizes the first year's fee. For example, a firm postponed ISO 9000 certification for five years because of the expense involved. It is, therefore, safe to say that most micro and many small firms would not be able to afford conformity assessment without some form of subsidy.

- Only one of the respondents was concerned about the reliability of conformity assessment. Both the MACs and NTSIKA select preferred service providers based on internal criteria. DU-MAC in Durban has, for example, selected the SABS, TuV and SGS.

- A lack of knowledge and awareness about conformity assessment and its benefits appears to be the main inhibiting factor. Many SMMEs are unaware of the benefits of conformity assessment. For example, one of GAUMAC's (in Gauteng) clients that do powder coating was completely unaware of either ISO 9000 or the SABS Mark Scheme. Clearly firms need more information in respect to technical requirements. However, the DTI is trying increase awareness through road shows etc. Although NTSIKA disseminates information to SMMEs it does not supply SQAM information.

Ways of Assisting SMMEs. Most respondents cited increasing the awareness of what conformity assessment services are available as the most useful way of assisting SMMEs. NTSIKA suggests using existing programs to disseminate information. This should be augmented by using websites, printed media, TV and radio spots, brochures distributed through the 107 Local Business Service Centres around the country. DTI road shows are also a useful way of disseminating information.

The South African Bureau of Standards uses a system called "Bridging Standards" to accommodate unsophisticated products and to make standards more accessible to previously disadvantaged communities. Only the basic and most essential components are taken from the main standard and incorporated into a Bridging Standard". For example, the SABS will shortly publish a standard for simple lamps. This will cover lamps that are made by microentrepreneurs and street vendors of basic materials such as, for example, wooden logs, with simple wiring and fittings. Action plan number two concerns the development of Bridging Standards for Crafts and Cultural artifacts in South Africa. The development of the Craft industry is a main aim of the South African Government's Integrated Manufacturing Strategy. The aim of the action plan is, therefore, to improve the quality of commercial products originating from this sector and to enhance the sustainability and survival of this industry.

Another SABS project to make standards more accessible is the use of schematic diagrams and pictures in standards to bridge language difficulties. This is aimed primarily at the craft industry in rural areas, for example basket weaving, basic joinery etc. SABS draft standard *0188—Standard Methods of Garment Measurement* is a bridging standard that uses sketches to explain the standard.

Specific Problems. As SMMEs begin penetrating export markets they start encountering foreign technical regulations. CE marking, in particular, seems to be causing difficulties. For example, there is a company in the Cape that produces semi-rigid fully inflatable craft that appears to require the intervention of a "notified body" to get into the EU. A European company has quoted a huge price in euro to carry out the activity. The MACs have not yet subsidized foreign testing and certification expenses and there are doubts whether their budgets could accommodate this on a significant scale.

Industry Perspectives

The Forestry Industry. According to the SA Lumber Miller's Association (SALMA) sawmills still cater overwhelmingly for the construction industry's demand for roof trusses as opposed to the higher quality needs of the smaller but growing furniture industry. Furniture manufacturers have,

therefore, often battled to get suitable raw materials. This is especially important to ensure that South African furniture manufacturers secure export orders. To address this situation SALMA is devising a new quality mark that will lay down moisture content levels for appearance/furniture grade timber. The South African standards will be based on US, EU, and New Zealand standards. The scheme that relies on audits is entering its testing phase and will be tried out at two sawmills in May 2002. If all goes well full rollout will follow in October 2002.

FSC certification is a requirement in the United States as is ISO 9000 and ISO 14000 certification. It is interesting to note that there is an industry perception that FSC certification is not as big an issue in the United Kingdom as seven years ago. However, the United Kingdom and the United States are still the biggest FSC supporters as far as South African firms are concerned. Although it can be argued that FSC certification offers some form of market differentiation it could also be viewed as a basic requirement for doing business in many cases.

The SABS TCS certification division offers the biggest timber certification in South Africa. The fact that the Unfair Business Practices Act requires producers to belong to the SABS Mark Scheme ensures a captive market. The other big player is Utility Pole Consultants.

In the United Kingdom the large DIY stores such as B & Q insist on FSC certification. In the United States big retailers like Home Depo also insist on FSC certification. Industry considers the U.S. market as particularly difficult to do business in. The U.S. product quality requirements are exceptionally high. For example, in terms of visual quality U.S. importers are only interested in clear timber without any knots. They also insist on sliced veneer and do not accept rotary cut veneer. This means that South African exporters only sell a relatively small number of carefully selected products into the United States. In the U.K. market, on the other hand, there is a demand for knotted timber.

There has been local industry concern for some time now about roof trusses in roof structures. The partial collapse of roof structures in two shopping centers in Pretoria has highlighted shortcomings. There are an increasing number of reports that point to the use of inferior roof trusses and poor construction methods. Various organizations and individuals have voiced concerns about the incorrect erection of nail plated roof trusses. Organizations such as the Institute for Timber Construction fear a major accident unless local authorities improve their oversight. Increased costs and additional building delays while waiting for certification are cited as reasons for not having structures inspected by a "Registered Person" as recommended by National Building Regulation A 19.

The power transmission pole industry is a good example where standards have been used by local industry to differentiate their products. The SABS mark, which denotes compliance with the relevant South African standard, clearly provides a certain cachet in the industry. It would appear that the SABS mark is slowly but surely obtaining some measure of recognition internationally, at least as far as the timber industry is concerned. There is probably no better proof of quality than a pole that has been standing for nearly sixty years. This is leading to increased export orders. Each and every manufacturer of power transmission poles has testing equipment. The SABS tests samples on a regular basis. It is interesting to note that SABS personnel recently assisted the Australians in testing their transmission poles. This illustrates the esteem in which SABS expertise is held.

The Fishery Industry. Industry sources believe the next barrier will be ecological in nature. There are already buyers in first world countries that are insisting on ecofriendly fish harvesting and processing on the part of suppliers. An international Marine Stewardship Council (MSC) has been formed. Only a few fisheries are currently (MSC) registered, for example Alaskan Salmon Fishery, Bering Sea Pollack Fishery, etc. The South African Hake fishing industry is preparing for MSC registration.

The Marine Stewardship Council is a nongovernmental organization based in Britain that aims to promote the sustainability of marine fisheries by promoting "responsible, environmentally appropriate, socially beneficial and economically viable fisheries practices".

The key MSC activities are:

- To produce and maintain a fisheries certification standard (The Marine Stewardship Council Principles and Criteria For Sustainable Fishing).
- To operate an accreditation program for third party, independent certification bodies offering certification against the MSC fisheries standard.

- To provide a logo scheme that demonstrates to the fish consumer that fish and fish products carrying that logo come from a certified sustainable source.
- To develop an education program in order to raise awareness of fisheries issues and the impact of fishing on the wider marine environment.

The MSC works with the fishing sector worldwide to promote the responsible management of the world's marine wild fisheries.

The Textile Industry. The CSIR, SABS, Wool Testing Bureau, SGS and Intertek Testing Services South Africa are active in this field. The laboratories carry out textile tests such as strength, color fastness etc. Most fabric testing work is done for the U.S. and EU export markets. Most of the required tests can be carried out in South Africa. The exception is a small number of highly specialized tests requiring very expensive testing equipment. However, these tests are rare.

It is interesting to note that the big purchasers such as GAP, Levy and Tommy Hillfigger in the United States and Jockey in Europe "accredit" the test laboratories based on their own correlation tests. The fact that South African laboratories are accredited by SANAS and accepted in terms of the International Laboratory Accreditation Cooperation's (ILAC) multilateral agreement, is not sufficient.

There is also an increasing demand among international customers for so-called social audits. These customers require reports from reputable inspection bodies that confirm that suppliers are complying with local labor laws.

The survey did not uncover any major problems in foreign markets. The Woolmark Company based in Australia owns the international Wool Mark that offers some opportunity for market differentiation. With the decline in the external value of the rand, the Woolmark annual license fees have become quite expensive in rand terms, i.e., R71 000 for 2002. The Wool Testing Bureau is the official Woolmark testing body in South Africa. The Bureau takes samples at companies every six months. There is currently ten Woolmark license holders in South Africa, nine for apparel and one for interior textiles.

Other Issues. Of all the regions in the world sub-Saharan Africa is the worst effected by the spread of the HIV/AIDS disease. This is also the region that could least afford the direct and indirect costs associated with this disease. Hence, this disease holds serious implications for the economies of this region. The impact of HIV/AIDS is not restricted to the individual infected. The impact of HIV/AIDS is much broader in that it has demographic, economic, social and developmental consequences. Most disturbing is the fact that HIV/AIDS is most prevalent among the most economically active members of the population, community and households.

In South Africa the spread of the disease is seemingly much more profound than initially expected. This only emphasizes the fact that urgent attention will have to be paid to ways and means to lessen the effect of this disease. The urgency of the state of affairs is further highlighted by the fact that South Africa is rated among the highest with respect to disparities that exist between the poor and rich. Although the disease itself does not discriminate between the poor and the rich it should be obvious that it would be much more difficult for the poor to cope with the legacies of this disease (Balyamujura, Jooste, Van Schalkwyk, Geldenhuys, Crew, Carstens, Bopape and Modiselle 2000).

The impact of HIV/AIDS on the macroeconomic environment takes two dimensions, namely the direct and indirect costs. ING BARINGS (1999) is of the opinion that one can cautiously assume that in South Africa the direct cost of treating an AIDS patient is likely to be about twice the per capita GDP. They furthermore state that with about 630 000 AIDS deaths expected in 2005 and per capita GDP at approximately R18 000 the cost of direct treatment and care could amount to R23bn over the incubation period or R2.3bn per year. The annual cost could be closer to R3bn per year if one assumes that the number of full-blown AIDS cases is about 33 percent of the number of deaths.

In respect to indirect costs, ING BARINGS (1999) analyzed the impact of HIV/AIDS on the South African economy using the WEFA annual macroeconometric modeling framework. The results obtained show that HIV/AIDS will have a negative impact on South Africa's GDP. In the period 2006 to 2010 South Africa's GDP in the AIDS scenario will be 3,1 percent lower than it would be without HIV/AIDS. This would drop further to 4,7 percent in the period 2011 to 2015. This is mainly due to the lower income assumption, thus lower disposable income and lower consumption expenditure (ING BARINGS 1999). LoveLife (2000) reports that estimates suggest that HIV/AIDS could

reduce the GDP growth rates in South Africa by an average of between 0.3 and 0.4 percent per year over the next 15 years. They are furthermore of the opinion that the impact on human and social development is expected to be much more profound than reflected in very limited indicators such as GDP or per capita GDP. Development objectives can also be compromised by this state of affairs.

ING BARINGS (1999) also endeavored to estimate the impact of HIV/AIDS on the workforce in South Africa. They state that the HIV positive rate of semi- and unskilled labor is over three times as high as that of highly skilled labor, while the HIV positive rate for skilled labor is about double that of highly skilled labor. Similar results were obtained with regard to the number of AIDS deaths by skill category. This emphasizes the possibility of skills shortages in the future. Furthermore, the cost of replacing highly skilled laborers is substantially higher than replacing semi- and unskilled laborers (ING BARINGS 1999).

Thus, although HIV/AIDS it is not a direct constraint to compliance as such it will increasingly become a constraint on production as increasing numbers of the country's workforce succumb to the disease.

The creation of a National HIV/AIDS Management Standard will provide organizations with a standardized document that will guide them in policymaking on HIV/AIDS and the implementation thereof. Organizations will report on a standardized set of system criteria, reflect their pro-active approach to managing their business risk and simultaneously address their social responsibilities. In this regard action plan 1 in Table 4.19 of great importance.

Conclusion and Action Plans

There can be no doubt that South Africa has committed itself to fully participate in the international trade arena. South Africa also possesses over the necessary institutional framework and infrastructure to participate and adhere to international regulations and standards, probably the best in Africa. The mere fact that most regulations and standards conform, or are in close conformity with international standards and regulations clearly shows the level of commitment from stakeholders. The study has also shown that there is a sincere drive to assist SMMEs to become part and parcel of, not only domestic economic activities, but also the international trade arena by providing assistance to enhance the ability to comply with regulations and standards. Cost of compliance as such does not seem to be the main obstacle to adhere to domestic and international standards. Problems are however experiences in terms of nontransparent conformity assessment requirements internationally that leads to, among others things, lengthy intervals before information is received back; the foreign cost component for SMMEs could be more of an issue than for large companies; and upgrading of facilities, for example in plant equipment, could hamper the ability of SMMEs to participate on the international market.

The study has shown that there are currently various other constraints and areas of inefficiencies that need to be addressed within the standards and regulations landscape. These include:

- There is a general lack of capacity within the NDA and its respective directorates to participate efficiently in the deliberations of international organizations such IPPC and OIE. Firstly, not all meeting are attended; secondly, there is a lack of continuity with regard to the representatives; and thirdly representatives tend to be reactive at present and little is being done to provide pro-active inputs. The lack of capacity mainly stems from the fact that too few people are responsible for too much work.

   Apart from the capacity problems experienced in terms of the number of people available to do what is required, there is also a capacity problem that relates to timely notifications and handling urgent issues. The main reason for this state of affairs is probably the fact that there exist loopholes in terms of communication between the national and provincial departments, as well as too few people to attend to urgent issues.

- The funding of activities in the supply chain to ensure safe products of a high quality that adhere to international standards and regulations need to be addressed from the highest level possible in government. The lack of funding, i.e., to maintain facilities, to pay proper salaries, to increase the number of people employed, to outsource specific research pertaining to MRLs, PRA and auditing, etc. are among the main stumbling blocks. This issue also needs serious consideration also from international institutions such as the World Bank, UN and FAO. This is not only a South African problem, but a problem experienced by most developing countries. The forma-

tion of partnerships should also be considered in order to reduce the burden of funding specific issues of common concern.

- A cross cutting issue related to the standards and regulatory environment is the fragmentation of coordination, policing, etc. There is a general need for a single food control authority/contact point to reduce the amount of duplication that is taking place between different regulatory departments and enforcing agencies (This was also a main point discussion at the Food Safety Workshop, 2002). This does not necessarily entail that stakeholders should lose their autonomy to influence standards and regulations, but rather that coordination should take place between different stakeholders to ensure that "the right hand knows what the left hand is doing". It is vital that such a body is not unnecessarily prescriptive, but rather focuses on procedures and programs to ensure that all stakeholders are served equitably and at the same time improve the efficiency of applying and policing of standards and regulations.

The action plans shown in Table 4.19 to Table 4.22 were sourced from the relevant role players mentioned in this study. The actions plans aim at addressing the various shortcomings mentioned in the study, but also relate to projects for further improvement in areas that are currently efficient as far as service delivery and assistance to SMMEs are concerned. These action plans are in close conformity to the technical regulatory reform plan currently being developed by the DTI (in consultation with other departments) that will, in the future, address the following:

- Appropriate quality control mechanisms for regulatory drafting and review at both national and provincial level.
- Carry out regulatory impact assessments that take into account SMME concerns.
- Focus on essential health and safety requirements as opposed to detailed technical requirements by cross-referencing relevant standards.
- Ensure that Technical Regulations specify outcomes, rather than conformity assessment activities.
- Gather and disseminate both local and international regulatory information in a timely and transparent manner.

Table 4.19 Action Plans Related to SABS Activities

No.	Title	Justification	Objectives	Outcomes	Budget
1.	The development of an HIV/AIDS System Management Standard for organizations.	HIV/AIDS is an epidemic that threatens to rob South Africa of its most productive human resources. Many organizations have identified HIV/AIDS as a priority issue to be addressed, but are in dire need of a guidance document to manage the crisis. Benefits to be gained from implementation of an HIV/AIDS System Management Standard are many fold: • A standardized approach to developing and implementing a policy for HIV/AIDS will assist in identifying the adequacy of an organization's infra structure, both in terms of physical and human resources support. The knowledge, perception, attitude and behavior of staff will be determined and appropriate projects implemented to address these needs. • It will influence strategic decisionmaking based on sound scientific projections. • Result in planned training, education and care projects for all. • Compliance to the UNAIDS Best-Practice model requiring effectiveness, ethical soundness, relevance, and efficiency, which can be readily determined. • It will assist the process to identify (voluntary prevalence studies) and manage the disease in its early (HIV) phase when productivity can be sustained with early intervention (empowering informed people to take decisions on their health). • Compliance will affect positively on absenteeism, and staff benefits	Specific objectives of this Technical Committee will be to: • Seek an interview with the Presidents AIDS Council. • Gauge the need for such a standard in the Industry and Public sector. • If supported, to Create a specific National Technical Committee (working group) to develop a draft standard, and thereafter a national standard. • A certification system could be developed • Embark on a national awareness campaign. • Engage the SADC role players in this effort. The target population and beneficiaries are the formal industrialized environment, its management, clients, work force and	Creation of a National HIV/AIDS Management Standard (HAMS): • Organizations would gain a standardized document which will guide them in policymaking on HIV/AIDS and the implementation thereof. • Organizations will report on their system improvements and reflect their pro-active approach to manage their Business risk and simultaneously address their social responsibility.	Duration: 18 months Estimated cost: R445 000

(continued)

Table 4.19 (Continued)

No.	Title	Justification	Objectives	Outcomes	Budget
		• It will influence the supplier chain to follow a similar approach to the benefit of all concerned (spreading the message and information on how to go about, to other companies). • It will ensure compliance to the legislative requirements and thus avoiding unfair labor practices reflect a social responsibility, which in turn will cultivate employee trust and support. • Cultivate Government support by innovative incentives to companies, such as tax benefits and recognition of HIV training for consideration as skills levies, etc. • Create incentives for voluntary disclosure and treatment, resulting in earlier intervention and a longer life expectancy and quality of life. • Lead to increased HIV/AIDS knowledge of staff and communities alike and take it beyond awareness with social outreach programs.	community. The immediate short-term focus will be South Africa and in time, the SADC region.		
2.	The development of Bridging Standards for Crafts and Cultural artifacts in South Africa.	This project ties in with the Presidential Imperatives, as it forms part of human resource development, the upliftment of rural communities, and will contribute to job creation. The indigenous arts, crafts and cultural artifacts, are an informal activity practiced by many rural people. A large number of these artifacts find its way into foreign countries as souvenirs, thereby inadvertently, achieving export status. Research and development is needed to improve the quality and safety of these products (ensuring materials used do not pose a risk in transmitting diseases). Poor quality goods and imitations could further damage the reputation of this industry.	The aim of this project is to create a national Technical Committee for indigenous Crafts and Cultural artifacts. This technical committee will have the added responsibility to: • Assist in identifying other areas in need of standards • Support a questionnaire survey to establish the needs of	• Create a TC for indigenous Arts and Cultural Artifacts • This TC will assist in executing an environmental scan on the need for standards and standardization • Once new possible projects have been identified, a working group will assist the SABS	Duration: 14 months Estimated cost: R235 000

(continued)

People need to be informed on the benefits that these standards will have on the improvement of their products. Typically standards will be developed to address aspects such as the treatment procedure for raw materials, type and durability of materials used, sustainable use of materials, etc. Indigenous craftsman and entrepreneurs will participate in this project, covering a wide range of activities. These include the physical manufacture of products, such as arts, carving, pottery, weaving, beadwork, ceramics, papermaking and production of charcoal. Natural products such as wood, grass, leather, bone, and sometimes blood and gall are used. Steel, modern textiles as well as materials such as plastics and rubber are also used frequently. Interior and exterior decorating is also practiced commercially, both in African and Western style. Nontangible, socio-cultural products such as traditional drama, and music, are more difficult areas to venture into. A Crafts and Cultural Artifacts Focus Group has been established by the SABS Standards Development Division during 2001. This focus group will provide guidance on how to proceed on these projects. Once identified, R&D projects could be executed. Benefits: The quality of commercial products originating from this sector, will be improved, and the sustainability and survival of this industry enhanced.	other indigenous crafts niches • Facilitate meetings with the main role players • Identify standardization needs and areas of support • Possible labeling of products • Once a need has been identified, Bridging Standards may be developed according to the normal standards development program The target population and beneficiaries are those in the informal sector involved in the creation of crafts and cultural artifacts.	R&D Division to research the needs and report on the viability to SABS Standards Development • Commence with the creation of new standards as identified from this program

Table 4.19 (Continued)

No.	Title	Justification	Objectives	Outcomes	Budget
3.	The economic benefits of Standardization in South Africa.	The contribution of standards to economic development is not well understood. A large number of standards are developed every year at a considerable cost to the taxpayer. According the German standards organization DIN, the overall economic benefit of standardization amounts to at least 1% of GDP in Germany. However, nobody knows what the financial benefits are resulting from standardization in South Africa. This information is vital within an environment where funds are limited and various interests compete for financial support. This study is aimed at determining the macroeconomic impact of standardization in South Africa. Information gleaned from this experiment will be of importance to: • Manufacturers • Exporters • Importers • Consumers • Government Departments • SADC and other developing economies	The aim of this study is to determine the economic benefits derived from Standardization in South Africa, and will be based on an assessment of the following Industry sectors: • Mechanical, Transportation and Civil engineering • Electronic and Electrotechnical • Chemical and Biological sector • Fiber Technology • Information Communication Technology • Systems Management Standards • Consumer sector The benefits gained by these Industry sectors will be assessed to obtain information on the impact of standards on: • Growth of the different industries. • Competitiveness of South African industries.	A sector specific database will be generated by SABS and co-workers. The DIN questionnaire will be amended to align it with the South African/SADC environment and needs. The anticipated results would highlight the value of standards and standardization in each of the Industrial sectors, and the possible holistic effect of standardization in South Africa, will be calculated and presented in monetary terms.	Duration: 12 months Estimated cost: R437 000

No.	Project	Description		Output	Estimated cost
4.	A video conference facility to facilitate the activities of SADCSTAN.	SADCSTAN's objective is to promote the coordination of standardization activities and services in SADC, with the purpose of achieving harmonization of standards and technical regulations. There are currently more than 27 standardization projects for harmonization and agreement has been reached among SADC member states to advance the first eleven projects to the final Draft Harmonized stage. However, the process of harmonization has been very slow mainly due to member states' delegates failing to participate in technical committee meetings because of financial constraints. There is a need to improve communication between SADC standards bodies. Travel and subsistence costs are very high and most member states have limited travel budgets to afford to send delegates each time to attend numerous technical committees. As more and more projects for harmonization are identified, this has put a lot of strain on member states and has slowed the pace for harmonization of standards. It's for this reason that the first harmonization projects that were identified have taken more than three years to be finalized. A regional video conferencing facility would, therefore, greatly facilitate the standards development process and speed up the harmonization of SADC standards.	• Empowerment of Small, Micro- and Medium-size enterprises. • Regulatory enforcement. • Regional and International trade. The objective is to ensure that the video conferencing facility is set up in such a way that all member states have access to the facility. This may require the installation of special ISDN lines in certain instances.	A video conferencing system that will link up all the standards bodies in SADC.	Estimated cost: R3 million This includes the cost of the initial technical survey, the cost of setting up ISDN phone lines, the cost of the equipment, training and the cost of usage and maintenance for one year.

Table 4.20 Action Plans Related to NML Activities

No.	Title	Justification	Objectives	Outcomes	Budget
1.	Measurement Practice Improvement Guide for Small & Medium Firms	The measurement of physical features is vitally important in the manufacturing industry. Measurement accuracy is based on the traceability of measurements to national standards and the competence of measurement staff. However, SMEs in particular require assistance to improve their measurement capability.	The Measurement Practice Improvement Guide is structured to lead the SME through three steps: • Assess the importance & relevance of measurement in the SME's market. • Self-assess the firm's capability against the importance of measurement in the SME's market. • Suggest actions to improve measurement capability. The objective is to improve measurement accuracy in SME manufacturing firms. Both the National Physical Laboratory in the United Kingdom as well as the Mexican Metrology Institute have used similar toolkits to assist SMEs.	The paper based Measurement Practice Improvement Guide is being rolled out in South Africa to SMEs in the manufacturing sector. However, there is a need to spread this toolkit throughout Africa. In fact SADC delegates at South Africa's recent Test & Measurement Conference in August, expressed great interest in using the toolkit in their countries.	The Average cost per country would be approx.:: Printing costs: $2 per unit $\times$ 10000 + $5000 for rollout, training & workshops, i.e., approx. $25000 per

| 2. | Mobile Metrology Unit | The National Metrology Laboratory has just completed a mobile metrology unit for Mozambique (funded by UNIDO). This rugged piece of equipment, which also houses sleeping quarters, is mounted on a truck chassis, four wheel driven and designed for both on and off-road use. The truck has been tested to military specifications and can withstand almost any conditions. It can house calibration equipment for any of the main measurement disciplines such as force, mass, temperature, flow, volume, etc.

Accurate measurement is a key component in supporting the legal system (occupational health and safety, etc.), Protecting the consumer (everyday trade weights and measures in mass and volume) and supporting fair trade and competitiveness in industry.

Nigeria has already expressed an interest in purchasing two of these mobile units while: PTB in Germany will probably fund the purchase of a unit for Ethiopia. | The objective is to provide measurement capabilities in rural and under-developed areas to SMEs that have not, traditionally had access to advanced measurement capabilities. | Ideally the entire continent should be provided with these units. | country. The mobile units cost approximately $200,000 per truck depending on the configuration. |

Table 4.21 Actions Plans Related to National Department of Agriculture Activities

No.	Title	Justification	Objectives	Outcomes	Budget
1.	Management Information System (MIS) for Regulatory Services. (Initial emphasis on NDA)	During enforcement of legislation through inspections and audits, as well as surveillance, a lot of data pertaining to plant, animal and food safety, as well as quality is generated. If the data are not managed properly the benefits/purpose of and outcomes of enforcement cannot be measured to obtain a proper risk profile on performance management. Currently inspectors spend a lot of time to complete inspection and audit reports. Data capturing is not standardized which lead to a loss of value of information. There is also a lack of proper coordination and communication between regulatory services, as well as between regulatory services and private sector due the lack of a standardized and accurate database.	The objective is to create a database with the following functionalities: • Inspectors/auditors to capture data in the field on hand-held computer technology, and in pre-established templates either inspection form or audit form. • Communication of data of each inspection and audit via landline or modem or telecoms to a central database. • Data to be recorded and managed automatically. Data collection is thus fast and consistent and the process consolidation, retrieval, analysis and communication are streamlined. • Templates of protocols or product standards to be set up according to the standards set in legislation and must be automatically updated on all systems. • Guidance notes to be added, to assist in interpretation where necessary. • Report generation to be automated. • Invoicing to be automated. • Comparison of data over time, across audits and between audits, to allow for in-depth analysis and performance monitoring. • Benchmarking and risk scoring within audits, to enable the managers to	The database will improve mechanisms for data collection, provides for data handling, analysis and dissemination between different directorates and even sections of directorates in the NDA to conduct and evaluate performance management, as well as to conduct better risk management and increase effectiveness of management of inspections and audits. Apart from the benefits to risk management the policy divisions within Regulatory Services will also be able to take policy decision that can be substantiated by data. The MIS could also be flagged over more than one government	Estimated cost: R800,000 for the MIS and R1,200,000 for hand held data capturing devices for 200 inspectors. The proposed MIS could be developed and fully operation in a period of 2 years.

				department to enhance data and information dissemination.	
2.	Improve, maintain and enhance SPS-related information to ensure sustain-able market access.		respond to changing conditions with strategies based on clear presentation of available data. • Flagging of a client to determine next audit according to monitoring program or if the client poses a risk due to low performance.		Estimated cost: R75 000 per trial.
2a.	Registration of agricultural remedies in the case of minor uses in line with GLP and EUREPGAP surveillance and	Although the South African agricultural remedy registration process do provide for the registration of minor use remedies, there is still a lack of registered remedies in the case of certain crops. Since the food safety risk of the use of agricultural remedies can only be accessed and managed properly through the use of only registered agricultural remedies according to good agricultural practices, the use of unregistered agricultural remedies need to be prevented while still addressing the producer's need for sufficient plant protection means.	Development of data by means of supervised trials and GLP (good laboratory practices) in support of the registration of agricultural remedies in the case of minor uses of agricultural remedies and generic agricultural remedies, as well as an awareness and training program to all producers with regard to good agricultural practices and food safety	The food safety and human health risk of the use of agricultural remedies in South Africa can be assessed and managed. Producers will have sufficient registered agricultural remedies to use legally in their plant protection programs to enhance market access. Producers will be informed of their role in food safety specifically with regard to the use of agricultural remedies.	The total cost of the project need to be determined during a feasi-bility study and according to the combination of the crop type X minor use or generic agricultural remedies.

Table 4.21 (Continued)

No.	Title	Justification	Objectives	Outcomes	Budget
2b.	listing of pests (imports and exports)	The process of Pest Risk Analysis (PRA) forms the basis for protecting a country against introduction of alien pests when plants and plant products are imported. Similarly, when exporting pests occurring in the country on a specific host/commodity is equally important since importing countries also require pest lists to enable them to conduct a PRA to protect their country against exotic pests. Surveillance and pest listing are therefor of cardinal importance to international trade in plants and plant products.	Pest lists are confirmed and updated to enhance international trade and to ensure sustainable market access.	South Africa will be in a position to support export industries with data to obtain import tolerances in importing countries. • RSA's NPPO compliance with IPPC standards and norms • PRA's more scientifically based • Negotiations scientifically based w.r.t. pest occurrence • International trade enhanced, specifically exports • Complete pest information available to both commercial and small farmers • Enhance management of agricultural industry in the RSA • Enhance RSA's competitiveness on international markets • Ensure sustainable market access	Estimated cost not known.

300

2c.	Surveillance of microbiological contamination of agricultural products, specifically fresh produce.	Internationally the emphasis with regard to food safety of agricultural commodities, specifically fresh produce, is no longer only on agro-chemical use, but has now also shifted toward the risk of microbiological contamination. Although numerous surveys have been carried out in many countries to determine the presence of pathogenic microorganisms on raw fruit and vegetables the detection of bacterial pathogens varied significantly. Limited South African data are available on the detection or association of bacterial, protozoa, as well as viruses in fresh produce.	Through a survey proactively determine the microbiological risk associated fresh produce manage the risk without increasing the cost of control and competitiveness of the industry.	• Information obtained through this survey will ensure that only the fresh produce of risk and areas of risk are addressed. • Prevent unnecessary monitoring and control measures but give assurances that only safe produce is exported and sold on the local market. • Scares resources can be focused on the risk areas. • The information obtained will also be used to contribute to the standardization of microbiological standards by international standardization bodies such as Codex.	Estimated cost: R1,000,000 over a period of three years. This includes the possibility of obtaining international expertise on viruses, bacteria and protozoa associated with fresh produce.
2d.	Development, evaluation and implementation of identification and mitigation techniques for organisms.	In the process of phytosanitary control of pests, the development, evaluation and implementation of identification of pests are of utmost importance. Decisionmaking then depends on the identity of the pest.	Development of new pest identification techniques to ensure a quick and accurate identification and ensure that regulatory activities do not affect the timely conveyance of cargo and cost effectiveness.	• South Africa's NPPO complying with IPPC standards and norms. • Negotiations with regard to pest identification and mitigation are based on scientific evidence.	Estimated cost not known.

(continued)

Table 4.21 (Continued)

No.	Title	Justification	Objectives	Outcomes	Budget
				• Justifiable and transparent decision-making process based on scientific evidence. • South African exports competitive and enhanced. • Assurances in place for sustainable market access. • Enhance management of South Africa's agricultural industry.	
3.	Program to ensure that meat and dairy products intended for human consumption on the local market is free from residues of antibiotics	A foreign country recently found antibiotics in chicken meat from China. The antibiotic concerned was chloramphenicol. Its use in humans results in non-dose-related development of aplastic anemia. For this reason it was banned for use in animals. The inappropriate use of antimicrobials also reduces their therapeutic value and can result in the emergence of multiresistant bacteria. Antibiotics should be available to treat specific human and animal diseases with proper accountability and oversight of the drugs used.	Initiate a program to test imported meat and dairy products for residues of antibiotics in an attempt to monitor this risk, and maintain the benefits these drugs confer on human medicine and agricultural.	Unless monitoring is implemented, we will have to rely on rumors from foreign countries to ensure that imported meat and dairy products is safe for consumption by South African citizens.	Estimated cost: R700 000 to R800 000

| 4. | National laboratory approval program to validate the competency of laboratories responsible for ensuring that meat and dairy products are safe for human consumption. | However, there is growing public concern over food safety in relation to the inappropriate use of antimicrobials in food animals. This concern threatens public confidence in animal agricultural. The meat and milk industries identified the need for a uniform system to evaluate the hygiene of production in dairy factories and slaughterhouses. Dairy factories and slaughterhouses implement monitoring programs and documented systems whereby the effectiveness of measures to control the hygiene of production can be validated and verified. Factors that have the potential to adversely affect the safety of food are rigorously monitored and controlled. The microbiological status of products is used as an indicator of the adequacy of process interventions and process hygiene. However, these programs are only as valid as the competency and reliability of the laboratory performing the analyses. | A National Laboratory Approval Program must be designed to provide a credible independent system to verify that laboratories are competent to carry out tests required to verify hygiene of production. | The strategy encompasses all aspects of a microbiological monitoring program, including the development of standardized sampling plans, sampling and transportation procedures and analytical methods, the verification of laboratory proficiency and the generation and maintenance of ongoing national microbiological databases.

A National Laboratory Approval Program will also facilitate international recognition of the equivalence of the South African hygiene programs. It will ensure continued market access for fresh meat and dairy products. | Estimated cost: R700 000 to R800 000. |

(continued)

Table 4.21 (Continued)

No.	Title	Justification	Objectives	Outcomes	Budget
5.	Program to ensure access off South African animals and animal products to foreign markets	The South African Government must prove that animals and animal products from South Africa do not pose a risk to the health of humans and animals in prospective importing countries. Bovine spongiform encephalopathy (BSE) and residues of agricultural chemicals, environmental contaminants and veterinary drugs are of particular concern. For example, South African animals and animal products will be refused access to foreign markets unless programs are instituted to prove freedom from BSE and residues. The foremost concern at present is the inappropriate use of antimicrobials in animals for therapeutic, preventive and growth promotion use that can reduce the therapeutic value of antimicrobials used in animal and human medicine, as well as the human health risk of bovine spongiform encephalopathy (BSE).	• Reception, sorting and storage of all the samples. • Ensuring that establishments that take part in the program have a sufficient supply of sampling equipment and packaging materials. • Training of personnel responsible for collecting the samples in the correct procedures to take, wrap and dispatch them. • Ensuring that establishments are regularly informed as to which samples they are required to take. • Management of all the data.	Ensuring sustainable and increased market access for red meat products on international market, while safeguarding human health.	Estimated cost: R850 000 to R950 000

Table 4.22 Actions Plans Related to National Department of Health (Directorate: Food Control) Activities

No.	Title	Justification	Objectives	Outcomes	Budget
1.	Milk Hygiene (monitoring)	Actions plans related to the Directorate: Food Control is justified due to their relevance to the protection of human health (domestically and internationally) on a sustainable basis.	A survey based on sampling of fresh milk offered for sale to the consumer analyzed for prescribed microbiological indicators	Assess the status of fresh milk in respect of compliance to national legal standards	R150 000
2.	Aviation food survey (monitoring)		A survey based on sampling of food served to passengers on international flights analyzed for specific selected microbiological indicators	Assess status of food in question in fulfilling the Department's responsibility in terms of the International Regulation Act.	R50 000
3.	Aflatoxin in Peanut Butter and Peanuts		Defining a program to reduce aflatoxin levels in peanuts and peanut butter	Meet critical need for food safety requirements of consumers	R500 000
4.	Improving participation at Codex		Investigate ways of improving participation in Codex meeting. Provision of training to government, industry, consumers and other stakeholders on Codex Alimentarius	Improved capacity to participate in the development of international standards and hence local harmonization of standards.	R225 000
5.	Food Control Display Unit		Develop and design a display unit to be used to communicate the role of the directorate with respect to setting national standards	Effectively communicate to other stakeholders the role and importance of food control	R150 000

References

Balyamujura, H. N., Jooste, A., Van Schalkwyk, H. D., Geldenhuys, F. I., Crew, M., Carstens, J., Bopape, L. E., and Modiselle, D. S. 2000. *The Impact of HIV/Aids on Agriculture*. National Department of Agriculture, Pretoria.

Benic, L. 2002. "Quality and Safety Requirements for Fruit Exports." In *Handbook of South African Produce Exports*. Fred Meintjes and Associates.

Bentley West. 2001. *SQAM Review (Final Report, South African Situation Report, SA SQAM Landscape Report, SA SQAM Country and Stakeholder Needs Report)*. NATA, CSIRO, Standards Australia, and Bentley West.

Claasen, A. 2002. *SABS Code of Practice on the Development of National Standards and other Normative Documents*. SABS.

Citrus Growers Association. 2002. www.cga.co.za/marketreports/default.htm.

Cook, L. 2002. "SA Citrus Growers Blame Spain for Ban." Business Day article from website. http://allafrica.com/publishers.html. 14 March 2002.

Deciduous Fruit Producers Trust. 2002. www.deciduous.org.

Department of Health. 2000. *Information Document: Role and Responsibility of the Public Health Sector in SA Regarding to Food Safety Control*. Directorate Food Control, Department of Health, Pretoria.

Department of Health. 2002a. *Progress Report on Efforts to Harmonize National Standards with Codex Standards*. National Codex Contact point. Department of Health, Pretoria.

Department of Health. 2002b. *Progress Report on the Establishment/Strengthening of the National Codex Contact Point and the National Codex Committee in the Region*. National Codex Contact point. Department of Health, Pretoria.

Department of Health. 2002c. www.doh.gov.za.

DTI Fund for Research into Development, Growth and Equity (FRIDGE). 2001. *Review of the South African Standards, Quality Assurance & Metrology Infrastructure*.

EVA—EU Association. 2000. *Evaluation Programme of the European Commission Aid in the Fields of Institutional Capacity Building and Economic Infrastructure—Evaluation of the Cross-Border Initiative*. Vol. 2. Country Reports and Organisational Findings. DRN, ECO, IDD, Synergie, and NCG.

Howells, G. 2000. "Food Safety: Origin Certification and Traceability." Paper presented at the XIII World Meat Congress. Belo Horizonte, Brazil, September 20, 2000.

ING BARINGS. 1999. The Demographic Impact of AIDS on the South African Economy. ING BARINGS: South African Research, Johannesburg.

ISO. 2001. *Memento*. ISO Publication.

ISO. 2001-10. ISO/TC38/SC24/DIS 13936-1. *ISO Electronic Balloting Commenting Template*.

LoveLife. 2000. *The Impending Catastrophe: A Resource Book on the Emerging HIV/AIDS Epidemic in South Africa*. Abt Associates South Africa Inc., Colorpress (Pty) Ltd.

Maasdorp, H., and Opperman, H. 2000. *An Assessment of Quality Infrastructure in the SMME Sector of South Africa*. NTSIKA Enterprise Promotion Agency.

Meyer, S. G. H. 2002. "The New Animal Health Bill/Act." Paper presented at the Livestock Health and Production Group Annual Congress 2002, Knysna.

Montes, C., Migliorisi, S., and Wolfe, T. 1999. Evaluation of EC Country Strategy: South Africa 1996–1999. Investment Development Consultancy, France; Development Strategies, Italy.

National Department of Agriculture. 2002a. *Abstract of Agricultural Statistics*. Pretoria.

National Department of Agriculture. 2002b. *RSA—Phytosanitary regulations*. Directorate Plant Health and Quality, National Department of Agriculture, Pretoria.

National Department of Agriculture. 2002c. www.nda.agric.za

Nortje, M., Crane, J., and Petersen, M. 2002. *Export Trade Directory, 2002—South Africa's Furniture and Value-Added Timber Products*. Malnor (Pty.) Ltd.

OIE. 2002. www.oie.int.

Pelser, C. 1995. *Standardisation in South Africa: The Story of the South African Bureau of Standards*. SABS.

Perishable Product Export Control Board. 2002. www.ppecb.co.za.

SABS. 1999. *SABS Bulletin*. Standards Information, SABS.

SABS. 2000. *SABS Catalogue*. Standards Information, SABS.

SABS. 2001a. *The SABS Register—2001/2002*. Malnor (Pty.) Ltd.

SABS. 2001b. *The SABS Buyers Guide—2001/2002*. Direct Line Communications.

SABS. 2002. *Consumer Protection—Guide to Food and Associated Industries*. SABS Food Standards Division.

SABS. 2000. *Position Paper on Standardisation, Quality Assurance, Accreditation and Metrology (SQAM)*. South African Bureau of Standards, Pretoria.

SADC SPS/Food Safety Workshop. 2000. *Country Paper South Africa*. Safari Court Hotel, Windhoek, Namibia.

SAMIC. 2002. www.samic.co.za

Scholtz, P. 2001. "An Analysis of Critical Operational and Marketing Factors Influencing Market Share of a Packing Entity in the Citrus Industry." Unpublished MBA dissertation, Port Elizabeth Technikon, Port Elizabeth.

Southern African Developing Community. 2002. *Website on Standardisation, Quality Assurance, Accreditation and Metrology (SQAM)*. www.sadc-sqam.org.

SQAM Review, Executive Summary, April 2001, R. Bradley, G. Harley Bentley West Management Consultants, Australia; A. Rusell, Dr. H. Liddy National Association of Testing Authorities, Australia; Dr. B. Inglis, G. Sandars CSIRO National Measurement Laboratory, Australia; J. Owen, F. Reynolds Standards Australia International Ltd.

Van de Venter, T. 2002. "Country Assessment and Development for Food Safety Capacity Building." Keynote Address, Workshop on Food Safety Capacity Building, 25–26 April 2002.

Warwick, J. 1999. *The SABS Guide to Commodities for use in Electrical Installations*. Crown Publishers CC.

Wilson, J. S., and Otsuki, T. 2001a. *To Spray or Not to Spray: Pesticides, Banana Exports, and Food Safety* Development Research Group (DECRG), The World Bank, Washington D.C.

Wilson, J. S., and Otsuki, T. 2001b. *Global Trade and Food Safety: Winners and Losers in a Fragmented System.* Development Research Group (DECRG), The World Bank, Washington D.C.

Wilson, J. S., Otsuki, T., and Majumdar, B. 2001. *Food Safety Scare or Reasonable Risk: Do Drug Residues Limits Affect International Trade in Beef?* Development Research Group (DECRG), The World Bank, Washington D.C.

World Trade Organisation. 2002. www.wto.org.

List of Interviews

Mr Pierre Badenhorst—Groupe Schneider.

Mr. D. Bakker, Administration Manager of the Sundays River Citrus Company. 15 August 2002.

Ms A Baxter and Mr. M. Holzhausen, Directorate: Plant Health and Quality, NDA.

Mr Terry Bennett—Irvin & Johnson.

Ms L. Benic, Manager Market Access Affairs, Deciduous Fruit Producers Trust.

Mr Robert Bodenhan—Department of Environmental Affairs and Tourism: Marine and Coastal Management.

Ms Magda Bolton—Dir. Plant Production, Health & Quality—National Department of Agriculture.

Mr. Manie Booysen—CEO, SAMIC.

Mr. A. Botha, Capespan Business Manager for the Eastern Cape, Port Elizabeth.

Mr Rudolf Brits—Deputy-Director: Multilateral Trade Relations: DTI.

Dr Gerrit Bruwer—Manager: Export Market Development, SAMIC.

Dr G. Campbell, Manager Food Safety, Perishable Product Export Control Board.

Mr S. Carstens, Divisional Manager Legal Metrology, SABS.

Mr Petrus Cetswayo Industrial Advisor MPUMAC.

Mr Johan Coetzer—Wool Testing Bureau.

Mr Adolf Claasen—Manager SABS Electrotechnical Standards.

Mr Viv Cohen—Circuit Breaker Industries.

Dr Tshenge Demana—Director Standards and Environment: DTI.

Mrs. Jean du Plessis—Intertek Testing Services—Laboratory Manager.

Mr David Dooley—Director—S A Natural Beef.

Mr. Peter Dooley—Managing Director, S A Natural Beef.

Dr du Toit—South African Lumber Millers Association.

Ms Aline Field—TDM (door manufacturers).

Mr Elton Geldenhuys—SABS WTO Notification.

Ms. Wilhela Gie—PERMAC.

Mr I. Grieb, Technical Manager of Patensie Citrus.

Mr Nico Grobelaar—Director Nature Conservation—Gauteng Provincial Authorities.

Mr Roger Godsmark—Forestry SA.

Ms. Mandy Govender—Industrial Advisor DUMAC.

Dr. V. Hattingh, General Manager of Citrus Research International (CRI) Pty Ltd.

Mr G. A. Holloway, Manager Chemical & Biological Standards, South African Bureau of Standards.

Mr Gideon Joubert—Technical Expert—SABS Food Standards & Inspection.

Ms M. Krause, Technical Advisor (Act No. 36/1947), Directorate Agricultural Production Inputs, NDA.

Mr Brian Langeneger, Industrial Advisor GAUMAC (East Rand office).

Mrs. Margaret McCleary—SABS Textiles Fiber Technology Standards.

Dr Siegfried Meyer—Deputy Director: Animal Health, NDA.

Mrs Nozipho Mfunzi—Industrial Acvisor CAPEMAC.

Mr Khaya Njingolo—Head: Incubation and Mentorship Unit—NTSIKA.

Mrs Ndileka Nobaxa—Manager: SMME Support at SABS.

Dr Gerhard Neethling—General Manager—Red Meat Abattoir Ass

Dr Liesa Odendaal—Sen. State Vet.: Veterinary Public Health.

Mr C. Painter. CEO of Riverside Enterprises.

Mr AW Pretorius—Directorate Food Control—Department of Health.

Mr Keith Ramsey—Registrar of Animal Improvement and Identification, NDA.

Ms. Ingrid Rousseau—SABS Enquiry Point.

Mr Rowan Scully—Moxwood (door manufacturers).

Mr. Albie Spears—Specialist Timber Auditor TCS SABS.

Mr Simon Streicher—Manager, Pork Producers Association.

Mrs. Isabella van Ghent—Wool Testing Bureau.

Mr N. Whyte. CEO of Whyte Citrus.

Mr. Alan Wright—SABS Regulatory Section: Electrotechnical.

Mr. G. Stephens. Grower in the Kirkwood Area. 15 August 2002.

Annex A Gross Value Added by Kind of Economic Activity at 1995 Prices
(rand million)

Sector	1990	1991	1992	1993	1994	1995	1996	1997	1998	1999	2000	2001
Agriculture, forestry, and fishing	23,735	24,795	18,036	22,366	24,126	19,317	23,950	24,153	22,519	23,658	25,389	24,590
Mining and quarrying	35,171	34,397	34,978	35,782	35,946	34,830	34,542	35,120	34,840	34,472	33,821	33,865
Manufacturing	10,5405	100,590	97,291	97,114	99,706	106,180	107,648	110,562	108,418	108,084	113,587	116,913
Electricity, gas, and water	15,141	15,436	15,520	16,133	17,069	17,408	19,287	20,034	20,358	20,728	20,244	20,103
Construction	17,774	16,942	15,889	14,804	15,233	15,774	16,092	16,646	17,084	16,670	17,122	17,805
Trade, catering, and accommodation	68,560	67,349	65,768	66,121	67,780	71,768	74,415	74,748	73,905	74,161	77,372	80,029
Transport, storage and communication	37,745	36,919	37,620	38,507	40,281	44,538	47,271	50,879	54,273	58,141	61,000	63,354
Financial services	74,720	75,875	76,199	76,580	79,378	82,162	87,737	91,866	96,737	104,191	110,318	114,488
General government	76,552	78,286	79,161	79,366	80,157	80,832	82,393	83,043	82,830	82,469	81,758	81,136
Other services	10,880	11,035	11,198	11,341	12,420	13,690	14,210	13,971	14,108	14,439	14,925	15,404
Other producers	13,353	13,432	13,499	13,556	13,687	13,855	14,066	14,298	14,626	14,918	15,217	15,663
Total economy	47,9036	475,056	465,159	471,670	485,783	500,354	521,611	535,320	539,698	551,931	570,753	583,350

Source: Quarterly Bulletin June 2002, South African Reserve Bank.

Annex B Gross Fixed Capital Formation at 1995 Prices
(rand million)

Sector	1990	1991	1992	1993	1994	1995	1996	1997	1998	1999	2000	2001
Agriculture, forestry, and fishing	3,229	2,655	2,246	2,612	3,158	3,293	4,011	3,545	3,092	2,751	2,743	2,867
Mining and quarrying	10,549	9,831	7,992	6,006	7,099	7,397	7,514	8,465	9,286	8,746	9,347	9,910
Manufacturing	19,183	16,948	15,938	16,567	18,099	21,820	23,257	23,971	23,516	23,585	23,974	24,712
Electricity, gas, and water	7,051	5,578	5,591	5,132	5,831	7,018	7,953	7,674	5,393	4,355	3,650	3,436
Construction	1,099	1,117	963	832	868	896	934	983	1,006	936	957	1,069
Trade, catering, and accommodation	4,565	4,749	4,860	4,846	5,079	5,269	6,187	5,881	6,019	6,988	7,226	7,157
Transport, storage, and communication	6,153	7,367	6,651	8,825	8,682	9,281	10,125	12,316	20,027	15,029	14,226	14,932
Financial services	18,332	17,310	16,823	16,865	18,601	20,022	21,940	23,571	22,994	20,698	22,128	23,066
Community, social, and personal services	12,598	11,614	11,976	10,959	11,218	12,046	12,962	13,925	14,036	14,038	13,173	13,511
Total fixed capital formation	82,759	77,169	73,040	72,644	78,635	87,042	94,883	100,331	105,369	97,126	97,424	100,660

Source: Quarterly Bulletin June 2002, South African Reserve Bank.

Annex C Expenditure on Gross Domestic Product at 1995 Prices

(rand million)

Description	1990	1991	1992	1993	1994	1995	1996	1997	1998	1999	2000	2001
Final consumption expenditure by households	311,613	310,001	305,589	311,367	323,844	343,037	358,377	370,051	375,257	380,511	392,886	403,853
Final consumption expenditure by general government	100,568	102,840	104,759	105,987	106,844	100,424	104,245	106,478	104,412	103,675	104,177	105,655
Gross fixed capital formation	83,256	77,105	73,049	72,644	78,635	87,042	94,883	100,331	105,369	97,126	97,424	100,660
Change in inventories	−9,501	−4,197	−3,389	1,847	8,637	11,517	6,015	833	−2,520	2,678	6,966	2,963
Residual item	14,621	11,764	8,183	2,878	2,997	1,303	2,365	2,774	871	−652	−1,018	−2,097
Exports of goods and services	101,757	101,700	104,276	109,163	113,879	125,869	137,063	141,669	144,266	150,173	164,859	166,740
Imports of goods and services	76,691	78,334	82,523	88,999	103,297	121,092	131,243	138,299	140,345	129,820	139,167	139,764
Expenditure on gross domestic product	525,066	519,720	508,613	514,887	531,539	548,100	571,705	586,837	591,310	603,841	624,127	638,010

Source: Quarterly Bulletin June 2002, South African Reserve Bank.

Annex D Percentage Growth in Production, Investment, and Demand

Production			
Agriculture, forestry and fishing	0.39	1.05	0.78
Mining and quarrying	0.29	−0.84	−0.37
Manufacturing	−1.52	2.34	0.73
Electricity, gas and water	2.80	2.44	2.59
Construction	−2.78	2.27	0.17
Trade, catering and accommodation	−0.06	2.43	1.39
Transport, storage and communication	1.34	6.70	4.47
Financial services	1.27	5.38	3.67
General government	1.25	0.18	0.62
Other services	3.02	3.18	3.11
Other producers	0.55	1.95	1.36
Total Economy	0.21	2.65	1.64
Investment			
Agriculture, forestry and fishing	−1.02	−0.73	−0.85
Mining and quarrying	−7.66	5.03	−0.26
Manufacturing	1.87	4.76	3.56
Electricity, gas and water	−4.07	−5.84	−5.10
Construction	−2.69	3.15	0.71
Trade, catering and accommodation	3.15	5.30	4.40
Transport, storage and communication	6.64	10.70	9.01
Financial services	−2.05	3.34	1.09
Community, social and personal services	−2.56	2.80	0.57
Total fixed capital formation	−1.39	3.75	1.61
Demand			
Final consumption expenditure by households	1.37	3.22	2.44
Final consumption expenditure by general government	1.67	−0.12	0.63
Gross fixed capital formation	−1.46	3.75	1.58
Change in inventories	−96.45	−86.67	−90.75
Residual item	−29.31	−5.58	−15.47
Exports of goods and services	2.64	5.65	4.40
Imports of goods and services	5.11	4.66	4.85
Expenditure on gross domestic product	0.20	2.65	1.63

Source: Production Annex A; Investments Annex B; Demand Annex C.

Annex E Physical Volume of Production by Subsector

(1995 = 100)

Sector	1990	1991	1992	1993	1994	1995	1996	1997	1998	1999	2000	2001
Agriculture	122.87	128.36	93.37	115.78	124.89	100.00	123.98	125.04	116.57	122.47	131.44	128.85
Coal mining	85.95	87.06	85.50	89.21	95.12	100.00	100.60	105.86	108.33	107.70	108.43	107.90
Gold mining	115.48	114.71	117.03	118.22	110.57	100.01	95.05	94.50	88.85	86.14	82.25	76.59
Other mining	94.31	91.76	90.84	93.29	94.76	99.99	100.82	103.84	106.05	104.14	105.43	108.75
Processed food	93.64	94.72	97.89	97.77	96.74	100.01	102.59	101.53	100.20	99.20	99.22	104.89
Beverages	106.52	100.74	101.04	90.02	94.30	99.99	98.26	103.50	102.30	100.76	92.64	97.15
Textiles	90.60	90.13	87.63	90.98	96.77	100.00	98.05	103.17	93.57	91.31	93.53	96.42
Clothing, excluding footwear	87.53	83.76	77.74	81.83	86.40	100.00	90.41	93.28	87.48	88.34	82.76	78.92
Leather and leather products	75.50	71.91	75.62	75.10	87.99	100.02	102.93	106.02	110.50	122.85	125.23	114.78
Footwear	105.33	107.16	94.27	94.17	94.86	100.00	85.63	84.59	74.50	69.20	65.58	53.88
Wood and wood products	77.42	76.28	75.23	76.28	88.23	99.99	103.90	113.75	107.35	114.12	119.31	120.94
Paper and paper products	86.70	83.58	84.83	82.81	89.21	100.01	89.78	92.49	93.96	98.16	105.31	103.48
Printing and publishing	94.93	97.83	92.50	100.08	102.05	99.99	99.64	99.12	93.66	93.11	87.83	83.78
Petroleum and petroleum products	93.27	92.90	99.35	108.51	101.27	100.00	95.13	99.63	100.24	106.37	104.53	104.57
Industrial chemicals	100.03	93.55	81.28	81.02	89.52	100.00	108.15	113.66	117.10	126.87	134.85	140.26
Other chemical products	87.58	87.53	88.48	90.30	93.35	100.00	102.72	106.01	103.07	103.27	101.81	105.33
Rubber products	108.03	93.93	93.71	93.10	93.53	99.98	94.26	97.23	94.40	92.78	98.69	99.26
Plastic products	68.97	69.91	74.53	78.31	91.73	100.00	98.88	93.03	90.81	86.48	89.67	97.27
Glass and glass products	99.01	93.78	78.64	76.40	91.21	100.03	94.76	95.43	89.63	85.20	88.46	98.93
Nonmetallic mineral products nec	106.75	97.10	88.35	87.89	89.81	99.99	100.74	99.61	94.21	84.97	89.96	91.28
Basic iron and steel products	95.46	84.77	80.16	80.88	86.93	100.00	95.20	101.67	97.11	96.94	116.26	113.78
Nonferrous metal products	79.30	78.63	78.38	77.62	85.57	100.01	144.15	143.54	144.53	153.29	163.43	171.97
Metal products, excluding machinery	97.93	92.38	88.27	86.99	92.76	99.98	108.54	113.91	108.69	99.12	103.40	111.07
Nonelectrical machinery	105.46	99.11	93.92	92.88	89.78	100.00	105.03	110.88	103.43	97.54	99.65	109.08
Electrical machinery	82.77	81.70	78.48	81.25	88.16	100.00	96.47	101.73	98.43	96.33	102.13	102.77
Radio, television, and communication apparatus	128.13	116.88	108.68	109.25	114.88	99.99	86.08	100.04	120.22	126.90	123.78	110.22
Professional equipment, etc.	90.24	98.58	107.93	101.42	99.26	100.01	99.73	99.47	79.14	77.90	80.92	89.46
Motor vehicles, parts and accessories	78.09	79.78	69.56	71.55	77.42	100.00	95.39	93.51	82.07	96.98	114.94	128.23
Other transport equipment	139.35	132.77	117.44	95.34	101.84	99.99	138.21	132.52	126.32	113.17	115.07	117.63
Furniture	99.09	93.75	81.78	79.38	87.38	99.98	103.60	111.45	103.44	102.68	98.93	98.53
Other manufacturing	123.33	112.28	102.73	107.33	102.50	100.01	103.88	115.08	111.99	107.74	111.56	110.64
Total manufacturing	93.14	89.88	87.17	89.22	92.42	99.99	101.49	104.33	101.10	101.35	105.97	109.62

Source: Statistics South Africa 2002.

311

Annex F South African Merchandise Exports and Imports

HS Code	Description	Exports rand million 1990	Exports rand million 1995	Exports rand million 2001	Exports percent 1990	Exports percent 1995	Exports percent 2001	Imports rand million 1990	Imports rand million 1995	Imports rand million 2001	Imports percent 1990	Imports percent 1995	Imports percent 2001
1	Live animals	9.7	22.8	100.1	0.02	0.02	0.04	5.8	19.0	55.9	0.01	0.02	0.03
2	Meat and edible meat offal	137.8	175.9	544.6	0.23	0.17	0.24	63.9	528.6	636.9	0.14	0.54	0.30
3	Fish and crustaceans	270.3	817.1	2,182.8	0.44	0.80	0.95	77.2	124.6	269.7	0.17	0.13	0.13
4	Dairy produce; birds' eggs; natural honey	60.7	169.0	259.4	0.10	0.16	0.11	30.2	133.4	256.3	0.07	0.14	0.12
5	Products of animal origin, n.e.s	14.9	28.6	73.7	0.02	0.03	0.03	47.7	133.6	188.4	0.11	0.14	0.09
6	Live trees and other plants; bulbs, flowers	62.3	131.3	247.7	0.10	0.13	0.11	9.6	22.4	34.1	0.02	0.02	0.02
7	Edible vegetables and certain roots and tubers	98.4	141.9	200.5	0.16	0.14	0.09	25.0	194.5	165.2	0.06	0.20	0.08
8	Edible fruit and nuts	1,031.6	2,078.8	4,723.0	1.69	2.03	2.06	35.5	98.5	170.1	0.08	0.10	0.08
9	Coffee, tea, mate and spices	20.2	63.2	265.2	0.03	0.06	0.12	111.9	294.0	398.6	0.25	0.30	0.19
10	Cereals	675.6	670.4	1,026.1	1.10	0.65	0.45	462.8	1,491.2	1,573.3	1.05	1.53	0.73
11	Products of the milling industry; malt; starches.	75.7	227.3	368.6	0.12	0.22	0.16	136.1	187.1	215.1	0.31	0.19	0.10
12	Oil seeds and oleaginous fruits; medical plants	69.3	142.9	490.2	0.11	0.14	0.21	70.8	312.8	290.4	0.16	0.32	0.13
13	Lac; gums, resins and other extracts	6.8	9.5	40.8	0.01	0.01	0.02	58.0	62.4	128.1	0.13	0.06	0.06
14	Vegetable plaiting materials	4.6	1.3	7.3	0.01	0.00	0.00	15.1	21.4	27.0	0.03	0.02	0.01
15	Animal or vegetable fats and oils and waxes	122.6	215.5	304.6	0.20	0.21	0.13	324.5	1,182.8	1,431.3	0.73	1.22	0.66
16	Preparations of meat, of fish or of crustaceans,	32.6	59.7	133.2	0.05	0.06	0.06	94.0	290.0	209.6	0.21	0.30	0.10
17	Sugars and sugar confectionery	772.8	654.4	2,929.7	1.26	0.64	1.28	57.2	77.8	150.9	0.13	0.08	0.07
18	Cocoa and cocoa preparations	17.5	61.5	172.8	0.03	0.06	0.08	55.9	110.2	264.3	0.13	0.11	0.12
19	Preparations of cereals, flour, starch, or milk	19.1	73.4	170.8	0.03	0.07	0.07	17.1	65.3	269.6	0.04	0.07	0.13
20	Preparations of vegetables, fruit, nuts	471.1	976.0	1,675.2	0.77	0.95	0.73	12.1	103.2	162.6	0.03	0.11	0.08

21	Miscellaneous edible preparations	31.5	114.0	471.4	0.05	0.11	0.21	49.2	235.1	573.8	0.11	0.24	0.27
22	Beverages, spirits and vinegar	194.9	1,363.8	3,410.5	0.32	1.33	1.49	237.4	400.0	798.2	0.54	0.41	0.37
23	Waste from the food industries; animal feeds	130.6	66.0	102.1	0.21	0.06	0.04	262.4	518.4	1,169.5	0.59	0.53	0.54
24	Tobacco and manufactured tobacco substitutes	44.1	214.7	1,190.5	0.07	0.21	0.52	141.2	230.2	503.9	0.32	0.24	0.23
25	Salt, sulphur, earths and stone, lime and cement	743.7	733.6	1,187.9	1.22	0.71	0.52	253.8	461.9	529.8	0.57	0.48	0.25
26	Ores, slag and ash	2,762.0	3,428.8	9,065.5	4.52	3.34	3.96	87.9	136.3	257.6	0.20	0.14	0.12
27	Mineral fuels, oils, substances; mineral waxes	3,751.4	8,937.3	26,091.7	6.14	8.71	11.41	228.6	8,389.5	31,901.2	0.52	8.63	14.80
28	Inorganic chemicals; organic or inorganic compounds of precious metals, of rare-earth metals, of radioactive elementsor of isotopes	806.4	2,972.7	5,061.9	1.32	2.90	2.21	742.5	1,289.6	3,825.9	1.68	1.33	1.78
29	Organic chemicals	331.8	852.3	3,134.3	0.54	0.83	1.37	1,635.5	3,532.6	5,218.5	3.70	3.63	2.42
30	Pharmaceutical products	108.3	188.3	552.2	0.18	0.18	0.24	556.1	1,610.2	5,381.1	1.26	1.66	2.50
31	Fertilizers	147.8	580.3	1,077.6	0.24	0.57	0.47	77.8	179.7	808.1	0.18	0.18	0.38
32	Tanning or dyeing extracts, dyes, paint, inks, etc	133.2	785.8	808.0	0.22	0.28	0.35	345.9	773.8	1,649.3	0.78	0.80	0.77
33	Essential oils, perfumery, cosmetics, toilet preps	38.6	174.1	681.1	0.06	0.17	0.30	174.7	359.9	1,142.1	0.40	0.37	0.53
34	Soap, washing preparations, lubricating, polishes artificial waxes, prepared waxes, candles, dental waxes and dental preparais of plaster	46.6	172.7	601.9	0.08	0.17	0.26	130.8	259.2	648.6	0.30	0.27	0.30
35	Albuminoidal substances; modified starches; glues; enzymes	22.5	40.9	111.2	0.04	0.04	0.05	96.5	222.4	537.3	0.22	0.23	0.25
36	Explosives; pyrotechnic products; matches; combustible preparations	62.0	104.5	262.3	0.10	0.10	0.11	12.7	58.1	135.1	0.03	0.06	0.06
37	Photographic or cinematographic goods	8.1	37.9	111.7	0.01	0.04	0.05	257.7	459.2	651.6	0.58	0.47	0.30
38	Miscellaneous chemical products	190.9	805.4	2,286.5	0.31	0.78	1.00	747.2	1,625.2	3,410.1	1.69	1.67	1.58

Annex F (Continued)

HS Code	Description	Exports (rand million)			Exports (percent)			Imports (rand million)			Imports (percent)		
		1990	1995	2001	1990	1995	2001	1990	1995	2001	1990	1995	2001
39	Plastics and articles thereof	321.3	952.9	2,737.5	0.53	0.93	1.20	1,303.2	3,042.2	5,759.3	2.95	3.13	2.67
40	Rubber and articles thereof	84.2	435.0	1,387.8	0.14	0.42	0.61	589.9	1,435.3	2,500.2	1.33	1.48	1.16
41	Raw hides and skins (excluding furskins) and leather	392.5	855.0	1,461.1	0.64	0.83	0.64	197.9	405.4	773.5	0.45	0.42	0.36
42	Articles of leather; saddlery, travel goods	8.6	70.2	112.1	0.01	0.07	0.05	70.9	186.3	412.7	0.16	0.19	0.19
43	Furskins and artificial fur; manufactures thereof	6.4	7.7	18.0	0.01	0.01	0.01	0.9	1.4	0.8	0.00	0.00	0.00
44	Wood and articles of wood; wood charcoal	318.6	884.1	2,623.5	0.52	0.86	1.15	304.0	683.3	1,095.0	0.69	0.70	0.51
45	Cork and articles of cork	0.3	4.3	11.2	0.00	0.00	0.00	28.5	58.5	167.6	0.06	0.06	0.08
46	Manufactures of straw, basketware and wicker	0.6	0.5	9.6	0.00	0.00	0.00	4.7	8.6	34.8	0.01	0.01	0.02
47	Pulp of wood, cellulosic waste paper and board	840.2	2,232.7	2,697.8	1.37	2.18	1.18	63.5	192.6	223.9	0.14	0.20	0.10
48	Paper and paperboard; articles thereof	716.3	1,601.2	3,925.5	1.17	1.56	1.72	863.5	1,935.3	2,723.1	1.95	1.99	1.26
49	Printed books, newspapers, other printed products	34.1	149.7	272.5	0.06	0.15	0.12	322.7	644.4	1,210.0	0.73	0.66	0.56
50	Silk	0.5	2.2	3.2	0.00	0.00	0.00	3.7	11.9	28.3	0.01	0.01	0.01
51	Wool, animal hair; horsehair yarn and woven fabric	944.8	898.1	1,252.6	1.55	0.87	0.55	40.2	95.7	121.8	0.09	0.10	0.06
52	Cotton	119.1	116.3	339.2	0.19	0.11	0.15	222.6	566.5	999.8	0.50	0.58	0.46
53	Other vegetable fibers; paper yarn and wovens	12.5	3.0	2.3	0.02	0.00	0.00	30.0	214.3	60.3	0.07	0.22	0.03
54	Man-made filaments	137.9	335.5	648.7	0.23	0.33	0.28	391.0	567.6	1,303.3	0.88	0.58	0.60
55	Man-made staple fibers	64.0	208.1	269.5	0.10	0.20	0.12	594.3	838.8	943.2	1.34	0.86	0.44
56	Wadding, felt and nonwovens; special yarns; twine, cordage, ropes and cables, and articles thereof	12.8	30.0	106.2	0.02	0.03	0.05	57.6	136.6	234.0	0.13	0.14	0.11

57	Carpets and other textile floor coverings	33.6	64.5	142.4	0.05	0.06	0.06	38.1	62.7	154.9	0.09	0.06	0.07
58	Special woven fabrics; tufted textile fabrics; lace tapestries; trimmings; embroidery	13.8	42.7	128.9	0.02	0.04	0.06	52.1	207.9	159.5	0.12	0.21	0.07
59	Impregnated, coated, covered or laminated textile fabrics; textile articles suitable for industrial use	16.7	32.8	126.2	0.03	0.03	0.06	145.3	276.8	499.7	0.33	0.28	0.23
60	Knitted or crocheted fabrics	38.7	50.9	53.8	0.06	0.05	0.02	98.6	195.4	381.4	0.22	0.20	0.18
61	Articles of apparel and clothing accessories, knitted or crocheted	84.2	144.8	1,087.0	0.14	0.14	0.48	116.9	186.2	600.4	0.26	0.19	0.28
62	Articles of apparel and clothing accessories, not knitted or crocheted	125.5	397.8	841.3	0.21	0.39	0.37	130.4	225.7	856.6	0.30	0.23	0.40
63	Other made up textile articles; sets; worn clothing and worn textile articles; rags	17.0	68.9	231.7	0.03	0.07	0.10	87.9	187.1	305.0	0.20	0.19	0.14
64	Footwear, gaiters and the like and parts	16.4	85.6	111.3	0.03	0.08	0.05	175.3	649.8	1,664.9	0.40	0.67	0.77
65	Headgear and parts thereof	4.3	15.3	47.0	0.01	0.01	0.02	8.9	45.8	94.4	0.02	0.05	0.04
66	Umbrellas, sun umbrellas, walking-sticks, whips	3.8	11.2	49.9	0.01	0.01	0.02	8.7	16.0	24.4	0.02	0.02	0.01
67	Feathers and down and articles, human hair	0.8	6.8	27.1	0.00	0.01	0.01	6.4	12.2	54.3	0.01	0.01	0.03
68	Articles of stone, plaster, cement, asbestos, mica	75.9	303.7	657.3	0.12	0.30	0.29	86.9	194.0	532.4	0.20	0.20	0.25
69	Ceramic products	44.0	90.7	209.1	0.07	0.09	0.09	299.6	616.4	1,715.4	0.68	0.63	0.80
70	Glass and glassware	133.7	161.9	497.3	0.22	0.16	0.22	229.4	448.8	719.2	0.52	0.46	0.33
71	Natural or cultured pearls, precious or semi-precious stones, precious metals, metals clad with precious metal, and articles thereof; imitation jewelry; coin	23,937.9	32,309.5	54,534.7	39.15	31.48	23.84	469.4	1,262.0	3,957.9	1.06	1.30	1.84
72	Iron and steel	5,295.2	9,818.7	17,983.4	8.66	9.57	7.86	463.7	1,095.4	1,901.4	1.05	1.13	0.88

(continued)

Annex F (Continued)

HS Code	Description	Exports						Imports					
		rand million			percent			rand million			percent		
		1990	1995	2001	1990	1995	2001	1990	1995	2001	1990	1995	2001
73	Articles of iron or steel	883.4	1,375.9	2,746.9	1.44	1.34	1.20	807.5	1,353.5	2,519.7	1.83	1.39	1.17
74	Copper and articles thereof	1,190.0	1,381.7	1,402.4	1.95	1.35	0.61	97.2	260.5	390.8	0.22	0.27	0.18
75	Nickel and articles thereof	807.2	751.8	543.2	1.32	0.73	0.24	76.6	408.3	223.6	0.17	0.42	0.10
76	Aluminum and articles thereof	558.7	855.1	7,305.3	0.91	0.83	3.19	173.6	480.9	657.3	0.39	0.49	0.31
77	(blank)	—	—	—	—	—	—	—	—	—	—	—	—
78	Lead and articles thereof	5.5	3.4	35.0	0.01	0.00	0.02	6.6	24.0	63.4	0.01	0.02	0.03
79	Zinc and articles thereof	15.0	52.9	214.9	0.02	0.05	0.09	26.9	35.9	47.3	0.06	0.04	0.02
80	Tin and articles thereof	9.0	4.5	65.2	0.01	0.00	0.03	3.4	59.1	88.3	0.01	0.06	0.04
81	Other base metals; cermets: articles thereof	157.2	236.9	203.9	0.26	0.23	0.09	48.1	118.8	237.7	0.11	0.12	0.11
82	Tools, implements, cutlery, spoons and forks	99.7	260.5	645.5	0.16	0.25	0.28	341.1	643.5	1,399.4	0.77	0.66	0.65
83	Miscellaneous articles of base metal	34.1	71.7	183.8	0.06	0.07	0.08	178.7	381.5	689.3	0.40	0.39	0.32
84	Nuclear reactors, boilers, machinery and mechanical appliances; parts thereof.	973.2	3,521.1	17,444.5	1.59	3.43	7.63	9,552.5	19,727.6	34,947.4	21.61	20.29	16.22
85	Electrical machinery and equipment and parts thereof; sound recorders and reproducers, television image and sound recorders and reproducers, and parts and accessories of such articles	389.5	1,467.6	5,399.6	0.64	1.43	2.36	3,659.9	10,384.2	25,131.0	8.28	10.68	11.66
86	Railway or tramway locomotives, rolling-stock and parts thereof; railway or tramway track fixtures and fittings and parts thereof; mechanical (including electromechanical) traffic signaling equipment of all kinds	304.5	708.3	871.0	0.50	0.69	0.38	34.8	63.7	169.9	0.08	0.07	0.08

87	Motor vehicles and parts and accessories thereof	668.4	2,728.0	17,528.4	1.09	2.66	7.66	5,187.5	11,384.0	13,755.9	11.74	11.71	6.38
88	Aircraft, spacecraft and parts thereof	85.0	420.4	1,842.9	0.14	0.41	0.81	449.4	1,789.8	6,631.8	1.02	1.84	3.08
89	Ships, boats and floating structures	91.1	99.9	292.3	0.15	0.10	0.13	21.0	91.0	290.5	0.05	0.09	0.13
90	Optical, photographic, cinematographic, measuring, checking, precision, medical or surgical instruments and apparatus: parts and accessories	131.4	400.4	1,162.0	0.21	0.39	0.51	1,679.3	3,545.9	8,016.6	3.80	3.65	3.72
91	Clocks and watches and parts thereof	1.8	9.6	19.5	0.00	0.01	0.01	114.4	169.7	303.7	0.26	0.17	0.14
92	Musical instruments; parts and accessories	4.5	20.5	24.3	0.01	0.02	0.01	25.5	37.9	57.9	0.06	0.04	0.03
93	Arms and ammunition; parts and accessories			332.5	—	—	0.15	—	—	97.9	—	—	0.05
94	Furniture; bedding, mattresses, mattress supports, cushions and similar stuffed furnishings; lamps and lighting fittings, not elsewhere specified or included; illuminated signs, illuminated name-plates and the like; prefabricated buildings	139.9	1,496.9	3,392.0	0.23	1.46	1.48	128.9	389.0	1,273.5	0.29	0.40	0.59
95	Toys, games and sports requisites	16.2	38.9	113.6	0.03	0.04	0.05	213.7	411.8	1,156.6	0.48	0.42	0.54
96	Miscellaneous manufactured articles	14.4	44.0	74.1	0.02	0.04	0.03	143.7	307.8	553.4	0.33	0.32	0.26
97	Works of art, collectors' pieces and antiques	23.6	56.9	133.7	0.04	0.06	0.06	31.3	60.1	110.2	0.07	0.06	0.05
98	Special classifications provisions	—	11.8	27.4	—	0.01	0.01	—	2,209.1	18,412.9	—	2.27	8.55
99	Other unclassified goods	7,158.9	6,445.6	—	11.71	6.28	—	5,938.9	−11.2	—	13.44	−0.01	—
	Total	61,146	102,650	228,735	100	100	100	44,195	97,227	215,478	100	100	100

Source: Customs and Excise 2002.

Annex G Destination of Exports and Origin of Imports

Sector	Continent	Country	Destination of Exports			Origin of Imports		
			1990	1995	2001	1990	1995	2001
Processed food	Africa (excluding SADC) total		72.7	140.3	664.4	23.4	52.7	98.6
	Eastern Europe total		2.1	17.1	106.1	2.4	32.8	88.2
		Germany	239.2	205.5	206.9	63.6	144.0	197.9
		United Kingdom	223.2	254.1	242.8	63.7	227.7	247.3
	EU total		1,086.3	1,327.5	2,375.7	327.0	1,031.6	1,558.0
		China	8.8	1.8	18.8	2.3	23.8	175.8
		Japan	346.3	447.8	742.9	14.5	2.5	19.2
	Far East total		650.7	751.2	1,860.2	284.1	789.6	1,226.2
	Middle East total		233.6	214.4	1,031.9	32.5	110.4	326.7
		United States	15.0	165.5	492.9	147.1	374.3	401.6
	Northern America total		32.1	234.1	629.5	157.9	513.6	492.2
	Oceania total		5.9	56.2	247.1	49.3	368.2	644.6
	Other total		5.3	13.3	25.8	11.1	10.6	27.1
	SADC total		315.4	956.9	2,073.2	63.8	158.0	190.3
	South America total		10.2	42.4	80.2	356.2	957.1	1,704.7
	Western Europe (excluding EU) total		0.5	1.9	4.6	1.8	2.9	3.0
	Total		2,414.7	3,755.4	9,098.7	1,309.6	4,027.4	6,359.5
Beverages	Africa (excluding SADC) total		8.4	43.3	253.8	0.0	0.2	0.0
	Eastern Europe total		7.0	8.7	9.0	0.1	0.8	0.5
		Germany	8.4	48.7	181.7	15.5	17.0	22.2
		United Kingdom	11.1	198.4	793.7	242.4	338.3	465.6
	EU total		53.7	423.2	1,866.3	324.4	461.5	712.7
		China	—	1.0	0.9	0.0	0.0	0.6
		Japan	6.1	8.7	30.6	0.2	0.1	0.1

Far East total	8.8	24.6	104.0	0.2	0.3	1.2
Middle East total	9.3	29.8	180.8	0.8	2.8	8.2
United States	0.1	15.9	227.7	2.3	19.8	43.2
Northern America total	0.3	35.1	324.7	19.0	53.2	188.4
Oceania total	0.1	6.0	24.5	0.0	0.7	5.1
Other total	6.4	232.3	33.5	0.1	1.6	11.8
SADC total	99.0	344.6	577.8	3.2	13.3	6.8
South America total	1.5	223.0	29.3	0.7	2.5	0.7
Western Europe (excluding EU) total	0.0	—	0.9	0.0	1.3	0.0
Total	194.5	1,370.6	3,404.5	348.5	538.1	935.4
Textiles Africa (excluding SADC) total	1.8	12.1	39.3	0.1	9.4	20.0
Eastern Europe total	0.0	1.2	8.2	2.9	15.2	22.8
Germany	66.2	69.5	137.6	131.1	163.3	241.0
United Kingdom	76.7	135.6	208.9	101.9	126.6	161.7
EU total	280.7	403.3	792.5	443.3	602.9	888.4
China	0.3	18.4	131.5	47.1	136.6	455.2
Japan	93.2	68.2	41.7	66.1	44.5	19.3
Far East total	250.9	293.3	303.9	627.6	1,091.4	1,541.1
Middle East total	5.6	48.8	92.0	74.9	325.8	550.3
United States	0.6	43.4	187.2	51.6	121.1	183.3
Northern America total	19.0	68.5	230.1	60.8	136.8	217.4
Oceania total	18.2	49.4	62.1	10.3	25.3	37.7
Other total	0.5	2.6	8.6	2.0	3.1	9.5
SADC total	109.0	170.4	520.8	40.2	77.3	154.6
South America total	3.0	24.6	47.4	13.1	7.5	25.4
Western Europe (excluding EU) total	0.3	0.1	0.7	0.4	0.8	0.2
Total	689.0	1,074.2	2,105.8	1,275.7	2,295.4	3,467.6

(continued)

Annex G (Continued)

Sector	Continent	Country	Destination of Exports			Origin of Imports		
			1990	1995	2001	1990	1995	2001
Leather and leather products	Africa (excluding SADC) total		0.0	0.7	3.7	0.1	0.7	16.7
	Eastern Europe total		—	0.0	0.4	0.2	0.8	2.2
		Germany	11.3	25.6	37.9	29.4	8.4	27.7
		United Kingdom	12.3	20.1	22.0	26.5	23.9	16.9
	EU total		113.4	265.1	456.9	128.4	110.3	205.4
		China	—	1.1	2.0	9.4	51.5	158.7
		Japan	22.7	123.8	144.7	5.7	1.2	1.0
	Far East total		27.7	169.3	302.0	49.5	130.0	245.4
	Middle East total		0.9	24.5	27.6	42.4	140.8	189.6
		United States	6.2	90.0	172.5	7.5	13.1	79.3
	Northern America total		6.9	92.0	221.0	7.6	13.8	80.2
	Oceania total		0.5	5.4	2.8	0.5	48.3	7.4
	Other total		0.0	0.1	12.0	0.3	1.1	12.2
	SADC total		2.3	5.4	14.8	15.1	31.5	20.6
	South America total		0.2	0.4	19.1	8.2	29.0	87.2
	Western Europe (excluding EU) total		—	0.1	—	0.0	0.0	0.0
	Total		151.9	562.9	1,060.4	252.3	506.3	867.0
Footwear	Africa (excluding SADC) total		0.8	5.2	8.0	0.0	1.7	0.1
	Eastern Europe total		—	0.5	0.0	0.1	0.9	1.1
		Germany	1.0	4.8	0.1	1.6	4.3	3.3
		United Kingdom	5.1	26.9	12.2	7.0	17.3	16.8
	EU total		7.8	46.2	15.6	36.3	88.7	65.4
		China	—	0.1	0.6	24.7	231.5	764.2
		Japan	—	0.5	0.1	0.8	0.3	0.0
	Far East total		0.3	2.9	2.8	106.2	456.6	1,049.2
	Middle East total		0.2	2.8	5.1	8.2	22.3	20.3

Wood and wood products	United States	0.0	2.5	1.4	6.3	26.7	16.9
	Northern America total	0.2	2.5	1.7	6.4	27.1	19.5
	Oceania total	0.0	1.3	2.9	0.0	1.1	2.0
	Other total	0.1	0.1	0.2	0.7	1.1	0.9
	SADC total	7.0	23.8	43.3	11.9	43.2	20.2
	South America total	0.0	0.2	0.8	5.3	7.0	5.8
	Western Europe (excluding EU) total	—	0.0	—	0.0	0.1	0.0
	Total	16.4	85.6	80.4	175.3	649.8	1,184.5
	Africa (excluding SADC) total	10.1	30.5	54.8	5.8	15.7	62.1
	Eastern Europe total	0.0	0.7	2.3	5.4	2.8	8.6
	Germany	18.8	58.0	123.6	11.6	11.7	47.0
	United Kingdom	68.5	74.9	317.3	9.8	14.3	22.8
	EU total	158.4	172.9	548.1	66.9	154.0	400.6
	China	1.1	0.7	11.8	2.8	8.7	44.8
	Japan	16.8	412.7	1,439.2	0.5	2.6	0.3
	Far East total	37.1	488.2	1,508.2	70.6	157.2	304.2
	Middle East total	6.5	30.6	25.7	67.2	107.3	44.4
	United States	3.8	32.5	132.8	46.3	119.2	156.4
	Northern America total	3.8	33.0	136.6	54.9	139.1	195.7
	Oceania total	1.2	1.7	16.6	0.3	1.5	6.7
	Other total	0.1	0.2	5.2	0.4	0.5	13.2
	SADC total	16.3	100.4	135.0	29.2	106.6	117.8
	South America total	0.5	3.2	10.8	21.5	35.7	53.1
	Western Europe (excluding EU) total	0.1	0.1	0.1	0.2	0.0	0.0
	Total	234.1	861.5	2,443.3	322.3	720.3	1,206.4
Plastic products	Africa (excluding SADC) total	1.8	26.0	108.4	0.1	0.3	1.2
	Eastern Europe total	0.0	2.0	3.5	0.0	1.8	24.1
	Germany	2.4	29.3	104.3	82.4	180.9	374.5

(continued)

321

Annex G (Continued)

Sector	Continent	Country	Destination of Exports			Origin of Imports		
			1990	1995	2001	1990	1995	2001
	EU total	United Kingdom	16.1	62.5	106.8	76.8	130.0	233.7
	EU total		27.6	150.0	302.9	295.3	622.3	1,238.4
		China	0.1	0.0	1.0	3.5	33.7	242.2
		Japan	0.3	0.6	1.5	32.1	74.8	100.6
	Far East total		2.0	11.4	16.6	90.0	273.1	663.0
	Middle East total		1.1	13.8	32.9	11.1	48.6	123.9
	Northern America total	United States	3.1	10.6	84.3	85.6	158.6	374.2
	Northern America total		3.8	11.9	88.2	88.9	167.4	387.9
	Oceania total		2.6	8.4	26.6	1.3	12.5	18.9
	Other total		0.4	1.8	2.5	0.8	1.1	12.3
	SADC total		44.0	151.5	408.0	2.2	4.2	1.8
	South America total		1.4	11.9	16.0	3.6	3.1	10.7
	Western Europe (excluding EU) total		0.0	0.1	1.0	1.6	0.8	0.3
	Total		84.7	388.7	1,006.6	495.0	1,135.1	2,482.6
Electrical machinery	Africa (excluding SADC) total		0.9	58.8	211.1	0.1	2.8	7.6
	Eastern Europe total		0.2	5.5	11.4	4.3	34.1	98.4
	EU total	Germany	17.0	221.6	514.5	440.9	900.6	1,306.1
		United Kingdom	22.6	128.9	284.5	335.9	422.3	544.4
	EU total		60.7	442.7	1,172.8	1,158.7	2,475.3	3,572.2
		China	0.0	0.2	13.2	7.2	54.6	428.4
		Japan	0.8	0.3	7.1	172.0	276.7	426.0
	Far East total		8.0	47.8	102.4	294.2	670.1	1,430.7
	Middle East total		6.1	29.6	197.1	21.7	106.3	184.5
		United States	7.0	18.9	141.5	185.7	411.1	876.8

Commodity	Region / Country					
	Northern America total	7.7	21.2	192.3	198.1	442.3	987.3
	Oceania total	6.0	16.2	51.4	4.1	20.0	117.6
	Other total	0.4	2.3	5.3	3.6	9.7	48.5
	SADC total	138.1	292.1	757.0	17.2	28.6	51.1
	South America total	58.4	9.0	10.8	11.6	52.5	117.5
	Western Europe (excluding EU) total	0.3	0.8	0.2	1.2	1.8	2.7
	Total	286.7	926.0	2,712.0	1,714.8	3,843.5	6,618.0
Radio, television and communication apparatus	Africa (excluding SADC) total	0.0	26.9	439.0	0.2	1.0	14.2
	Eastern Europe total	0.0	34.8	23.7	6.0	14.9	49.2
	Germany	29.8	39.0	193.0	217.0	974.0	1,901.8
	United Kingdom	7.3	42.4	182.9	126.6	811.7	1,823.8
	EU total	56.7	148.1	677.0	573.0	2,789.6	8,414.6
	China	—	0.6	22.2	17.9	110.1	810.1
	Japan	0.4	2.0	0.8	239.7	467.1	662.6
	Far East total	5.6	24.4	285.0	540.1	1,367.5	4,019.4
	Middle East total	1.2	5.9	121.3	63.3	337.8	606.7
	United States	3.0	19.9	86.2	129.3	452.6	1,324.6
	Northern America total	5.3	21.3	93.5	133.3	473.6	1,605.5
	Oceania total	0.5	6.5	112.7	3.3	84.0	90.9
	Other total	0.2	0.5	5.4	3.1	13.9	54.8
	SADC total	16.2	132.5	362.4	2.5	5.7	15.4
	South America total	0.6	12.1	4.3	1.6	2.2	20.0
	Western Europe (excluding EU) total	—	1.2	2.1	0.1	1.7	6.2
	Total	86.4	414.2	2,126.4	1,326.4	5,091.8	14,897.0
Furniture	Africa (excluding SADC) total	8.9	31.1	63.1	0.0	0.2	16.5
	Eastern Europe total	—	0.0	4.9	0.1	2.4	43.4
	Germany	10.6	1,036.9	1,968.1	14.6	33.0	337.6
	United Kingdom	50.5	172.7	484.5	5.5	22.2	27.9

(continued)

Annex G (Continued)

Sector	Continent	Country	Destination of Exports			Origin of Imports		
			1990	1995	2001	1990	1995	2001
	EU total		82.0	1,254.3	2,659.1	41.2	116.9	547.8
		China	—	0.1	2.8	0.3	5.4	81.4
		Japan	0.1	3.1	115.9	0.5	1.3	9.4
	Far East total		1.5	11.7	139.2	17.1	42.9	223.2
	Middle East total		0.2	12.9	36.1	2.2	7.5	15.2
		United States	1.2	29.8	71.3	4.9	11.0	36.9
	Northern America total		1.6	33.5	82.0	5.3	11.1	37.6
	Oceania total		1.0	6.5	20.2	0.0	2.0	0.8
	Other total		0.2	0.6	0.6	0.6	0.5	5.0
	SADC total		20.8	75.7	198.8	7.1	41.8	64.6
	South America total		0.0	1.4	1.7	0.1	0.0	6.8
	Western Europe (excluding EU) total		—	0.1	0.1	0.0	0.0	0.5
	Total		116.1	1,427.9	3,205.9	73.7	225.4	961.5
Agriculture	Africa (excluding SADC) total		21.4	60.5	203.4	28.0	289.5	141.1
	Eastern Europe total		13.9	25.2	199.6	8.4	10.1	31.1
		Germany	313.0	284.5	387.5	47.2	110.4	50.7
		United Kingdom	563.6	452.0	1,134.4	20.6	43.5	40.5
	EU total		1,573.7	2,221.9	4,632.7	110.5	303.2	322.3
		China	12.0	48.1	134.8	14.3	129.0	73.9
		Japan	466.6	168.0	1,010.3	2.3	3.9	6.7
	Far East total		614.3	562.6	1,639.1	137.2	483.1	436.9
	Middle East total		246.2	360.6	565.9	97.9	196.7	253.4
		United States	5.3	100.8	451.8	84.2	640.6	206.7
	Northern America total		38.5	161.4	600.1	248.1	830.6	284.5
	Oceania total		1.2	7.3	50.7	14.4	85.6	246.3

	Col 1	Col 2	Col 3	Col 4	Col 5	Col 6
Other total	0.7	50.6	10.5	5.5	17.2	21.5
SADC total	113.7	349.7	923.5	196.8	394.1	866.2
South America total	5.4	4.7	45.9	32.8	294.7	492.3
Western Europe (excluding EU) total	0.1	1.1	3.0	0.0	1.3	1.1
Total	2,629.0	3,805.6	8,874.5	879.7	2,906.1	3,096.6
Africa (excluding SADC) total	490.7	2,327.6	8,809.5	101.0	1,071.4	2,868.3
Eastern Europe total	173.1	450.3	1,029.0	112.3	487.6	1,654.2
Germany	2,659.1	4,669.8	17,141.6	8,696.0	16,038.5	32,265.5
United Kingdom	2,531.2	8,385.6	22,077.4	5,204.4	10,766.4	18,168.2
EU total	14,626.7	30,714.4	77,997.5	21,527.7	46,493.7	92,649.7
China	130.8	1,049.0	3,825.7	338.6	1,848.7	9,087.9
Japan	3,630.4	5,431.0	13,331.3	4,342.7	9,886.5	14,685.3
Far East total	8,305.9	15,043.8	31,576.3	7,995.7	20,165.9	40,870.4
Middle East total	2,341.5	4,987.5	14,746.6	991.6	9,315.7	32,555.0
United States	1,873.7	5,555.3	22,465.4	5,051.2	11,556.0	25,814.2
Northern America total	2,176.4	6,473.2	24,976.2	5,589.1	12,775.1	28,104.0
Oceania total	300.9	1,213.1	1,075.1	431.0	1,785.3	6,477.0
Other total	28,602.9	27,822.4	36,110.4	5,978.3	1,012.7	1,910.0
SADC total	3,496.1	11,558.8	25,358.2	627.0	1,824.9	2,745.5
South America total	578.7	1,947.0	4,018.7	825.5	2,258.3	5,591.8
Western Europe (excluding, EU) total	53.5	112.3	37.7	16.0	37.3	53.0
Total	61,146.5	102,650.4	228,735.2	44,195.2	97,227.8	215,478.9

Annex H Summary of EU Tariff Phase-Down Schedule (Percent) According to Chapters of the Harmonized Code

HS2	Description	2000	2001	2002	2003	2004	2005	2006	2007	2008	2009	2010	2011	2012
01	Live animals	22	22	22	22	22	22	22	22	22	22	22	22	22
02	Meat and edible meat offal	22	22	22	22	22	20	19	17	15	14	12	12	12
03	Fish and crustaceans, mollusks and other aquatic invertebrates	10	10	10	10	10	10	10	10	10	10	10	10	10
04	Dairy produce; birds' eggs; natural honey; edible products of animal origin, not elsewhere specified or included	7	7	7	7	7	6	6	5	4	4	3	3	3
05	Products of animal origin, not elsewhere specified or included	—	—	—	—	—	—	—	—	—	—	—	—	—
06	Live trees and other plants; bulbs, roots and the like; cut flowers and ornamental foliage	8	7	6	4	4	4	4	4	4	4	4	4	4
07	Edible vegetables and certain roots and tubers	12	12	12	10	10	8	6	5	3	2	0	0	0
08	Edible fruit and nuts; peel of citrus fruit or melons	16	16	16	15	14	13	12	11	10	8	7	7	7
09	Coffee, tea, mate and spices	2	1	1	0	0	0	0	0	0	0	—	—	—
10	Cereals	15	15	15	15	15	15	14	14	13	13	12	12	12
11	Products of the milling industry; malt; starches; inulin; wheat gluten	8	8	8	8	8	8	7	7	6	6	5	5	5
12	Oil seeds and oleaginous fruits; miscellaneous grains, seeds and fruit; industrial or medical plants	0	0	0	—	—	—	—	—	—	—	—	—	—
13	Lac, gums, resins and other vegetable saps and extracts	2	2	2	2	2	2	2	2	2	2	2	2	2
14	Vegetable plaiting materials; vegetable products not elsewhere specified or included	—	—	—	—	—	—	—	—	—	—	—	—	—

15	Animal or vegetable fats and oils and their cleavage products; edible fats; animal or vegetable waxes	5	4	3	1	1	1	1	1	1	0	0	0
16	Preparations of meat, of fish or of crustaceans, mollusks or other aquatic invertebrates	15	15	15	15	14	14	13	12	11	10	10	10
17	Sugars and sugar confectionery	15	15	15	15	15	15	15	15	15	15	15	15
18	Cocoa and cocoa preparations	19	19	19	18	18	18	18	18	18	18	18	18
19	Preparations of cereals, flour, starch, or milk; pastrycooks products	27	27	27	27	27	27	27	27	27	27	27	27
20	Preparations of vegetables, fruit, nuts or other parts of plants	27	26	25	23	22	20	17	15	13	10	8	8
21	Miscellaneous edible preparations	12	12	11	10	10	10	10	10	10	10	10	10
22	Beverages, spirits and vinegar	4	4	4	4	3	3	3	3	3	2	2	2
23	Residues and waste from the food industries; prepared animal fodder	3	2	2	2	2	2	2	2	2	2	2	2
24	Tobacco and manufactured tobacco substitutes	22	16	9	3	3	2	2	2	2	2	2	2
25	Salt, sulfur, earths and stone, plastering materials, lime and cement	—	—	—	1	1	1	0	—	—	—	—	—
26	Ores, slag and ash	1	—	0	0	0	0	0	0	0	—	—	—
27	Mineral fuels, oils and products of their distillation; bituminous substances; mineral waxes	—	—	—	—	—	—	—	—	—	—	—	—
28	Inorganic chemicals; organic or inorganic compounds of precious metals, of rare-earth metals, of radioactive elements or of isotopes	—	—	—	—	—	—	—	—	—	—	—	—
29	Organic chemicals	2	2	1	0	0	0	0	0	0	0	0	0
30	Pharmaceutical products	—	—	—	—	—	—	—	—	—	—	—	—
31	Fertilizers	3	2	1	1	—	—	—	—	—	—	—	—

(continued)

HS2	Description	2000	2001	2002	2003	2004	2005	2006	2007	2008	2009	2010	2011	2012
32	Tanning or dyeing extracts, tannins and their derivatives; dyes, pigments and other coloring matter; paints and varnishes; putty and other mastics; inks	1	1	0	—	—	—	—	—	—	—	—	—	—
33	Essential oils and resinoids; perfumery, cosmetic or toilet preparations	1	1	1	1	1	1	1	1	1	1	1	1	1
34	Soap, organic surface-active agents, washing preparations, lubricating preparations, artificial waxes, prepared waxes, polishing or scouring preparations, candles and similar articles, modeling pastes, dental waxes and dental preparais of plaster	—	—	—	—	—	—	—	—	—	—	—	—	—
35	Albuminoidal substances; modified starches; glues; enzymes	6	5	5	4	4	4	4	4	4	4	4	4	4
36	Explosives; pyrotechnic products; matches; pyrophoric alloys: certain combustible preparations	—	—	—	—	—	—	—	—	—	—	—	—	—
37	Photographic or cinematographic goods	—	—	—	—	—	—	—	—	—	—	—	—	—
38	Miscellaneous chemical products	2	2	2	2	2	2	2	2	2	2	2	2	2
39	Plastics and articles thereof	2	1	1	—	—	—	—	—	—	—	—	—	—
40	Rubber and articles thereof	0	0	0	—	—	—	—	—	—	—	—	—	—
41	Raw hides and skins (excluding furskins) and leather	1	1	1	—	—	—	—	—	—	—	—	—	—
42	Articles of leather; saddlery and harness; travel goods, handbags and similar containers; articles of animal gut (excluding silk-worm gut)	1	1	0	—	—	—	—	—	—	—	—	—	—
43	Furskins and artificial fur; manufactures thereof	—	—	—	—	—	—	—	—	—	—	—	—	—

(continued)

HS	Description														
44	Wood and articles of wood; wood charcoal	—	—	—	—	—	—	—	—	—	—	—	0	1	1
45	Cork and articles of cork	—	—	—	—	—	—	—	—	—	—	—	0	1	1
46	Manufactures of straw, of esparto or of other plaiting materials; basketware and wickerwork	—	—	—	—	—	—	—	—	—	—	—	0	0	1
47	Pulp of wood or of other fibrous cellulosic material; waste and scrap of paper or paperboard	—	—	—	—	—	—	—	—	—	—	—	—	0	1
48	Paper and paperboard; articles of paper pulp, of paper or of paperboard	—	—	—	—	—	—	—	—	—	—	—	—	0	0
49	Printed books, newspapers, pictures and other products of the printing industry; manuscripts, typescripts and plans	—	—	—	—	—	—	—	—	—	—	—	0	1	1
50	Silk	—	—	—	—	—	—	—	—	—	—	—	0	1	1
51	Wool, fine or coarse animal hair; horsehair yarn and woven fabric	—	—	—	—	—	—	—	—	—	1	2	3	3	5
52	Cotton	—	—	—	—	—	—	—	—	2	3	3	4	6	6
53	Other vegetable textile fibers; paper yarn and woven fabrics of paper yarn	—	—	—	—	—	—	—	—	—	—	1	1	2	3
54	Man-made filaments	—	—	—	—	—	—	—	—	—	1	2	2	4	7
55	Man-made staple fibers	—	—	—	—	—	—	—	—	1	2	2	4	6	8
56	Wadding, felt and nonwovens; special yarns; twine, cordage, ropes and cables and articles thereof	—	—	—	—	—	—	—	—	—	—	2	3	5	6
57	Carpets and other textile floor coverings	—	—	—	—	—	—	—	—	—	—	4	5	7	8
58	Special woven fabrics; tufted textile fabrics; lace tapestries; trimmings; embroidery	—	—	—	—	—	—	—	—	—	—	—	2	5	7
59	Impregnated, coated, covered or laminated textile fabrics; textile articles of a kind suitable for industrial use	—	—	—	—	—	—	—	—	—	—	—	2	3	5

Annex H (Continued)

HS2	Description	2000	2001	2002	2003	2004	2005	2006	2007	2008	2009	2010	2011	2012
60	Knitted or crocheted fabrics	9	7	5	4	2	1	—	—	—	—	—	—	—
61	Articles of apparel and clothing accessories, knitted or crocheted	10	7	5	2	1	1	—	—	—	—	—	—	—
62	Articles of apparel and clothing accessories, not knitted or crocheted	10	8	5	3	2	1	—	—	—	—	—	—	—
63	Other made up textile articles; sets; worn clothing and worn textile articles; rags	8	7	4	2	2	1	—	—	—	—	—	—	—
64	Footwear, gaiters and the like; parts of such articles	8	5	3	—	—	—	—	—	—	—	—	—	—
65	Headgear and parts thereof	—	—	—	—	—	—	—	—	—	—	—	—	—
66	Umbrellas, sun umbrellas, walking-sticks, seat sticks, whips, riding-crops and parts thereof	—	—	—	—	—	—	—	—	—	—	—	—	—
67	Prepared feathers and down and articles made of feathers or of down; artificial flowers; articles of human hair	—	—	—	—	—	—	—	—	—	—	—	—	—
68	Articles of stone, plaster, cement, asbestos, mica or similar materials	—	—	—	—	—	—	—	—	—	—	—	—	—
69	Ceramic products	3	2	1	2	1	1	—	—	—	—	—	—	—
70	Glass and glassware	2	1	1	3	2	1	—	—	—	—	—	—	—
71	Natural or cultured pearls, precious or semi-precious stones, precious metals, metals clad with precious metal, and articles thereof; imitation jewelry; coin	0	0	0	—	—	—	—	—	—	—	—	—	—
72	Iron and steel	2	2	2	2	1	1	—	—	—	—	—	—	—
73	Articles of iron or steel	3	3	3	3	2	1	—	—	—	—	—	—	—
74	Copper and articles thereof	3	2	1	—	—	—	—	—	—	—	—	—	—
75	Nickel and articles thereof	—	—	—	—	—	—	—	—	—	—	—	—	—
76	Aluminum and articles thereof	5	4	2	1	1	1	1	1	1	1	1	1	1

78	Lead and articles thereof	1	0	0	—	—	—	—	—	—	—	—	—	—
79	Zinc and articles thereof	1	1	1	1	1	1	1	1	1	1	1	1	1
80	Tin and articles thereof	—	—	—	—	—	—	—	—	—	—	—	—	—
81	Other base metals; cermets: articles thereof	2	1	1	—	—	—	—	—	—	—	—	—	—
82	Tools, implements, cutlery, spoons and forks, of base metal; parts thereof of base metal	—	—	—	—	—	—	—	—	—	—	—	—	—
83	Miscellaneous articles of base metal	—	—	—	—	—	—	—	—	—	—	—	—	—
84	Nuclear reactors, boilers, machinery and mechanical appliances; parts thereof	0	0	0	—	—	—	—	—	—	—	—	—	—
85	Electrical machinery and equipment and parts thereof; sound recorders and reproducers, television image and sound recorders and reproducers, and parts and accessories of such articles	1	1	0	—	—	—	—	—	—	—	—	—	—
86	Railway or tramway locomotives, rolling stock and parts thereof; railway or tramway track fixtures and fittings and parts thereof; mechanical (including electromechanical) traffic signaling equipment of all kinds	—	—	—	—	—	—	—	—	—	—	—	—	—
87	Vehicles (excluding railway or tramway rolling-stock) and parts and accessories thereof	5	4	4	3	2	2	1	1	1	1	1	1	1
88	Aircraft, spacecraft and parts thereof	—	—	—	—	—	—	—	—	—	—	—	—	—
89	Ships, boats and floating structures	—	—	—	—	—	—	—	—	—	—	—	—	—
90	Optical, photographic, cinematographic, measuring, checking, precision, medical or surgical instruments and apparatus: parts and accessories thereof	0	0	0	—	—	—	—	—	—	—	—	—	—

(continued)

Annex H (Continued)

HS2	Description	2000	2001	2002	2003	2004	2005	2006	2007	2008	2009	2010	2011	2012
91	Clocks and watches and parts thereof	1	1	0	—	—	—	—	—	—	—	—	—	—
92	Musical instruments; parts and accessories of such articles	0	0	0	—	—	—	—	—	—	—	—	—	—
93	Arms and ammunition; parts and accessories thereof	2	2	1	—	—	—	—	—	—	—	—	—	—
94	Furniture; bedding, mattresses, mattress supports, cushions and similar stuffed furnishings; lamps and lighting fittings, not elsewhere specified or included; illuminated signs, illuminated name-plates and the like; prefabricated buildings				—	—	—	—	—	—	—	—	—	—
95	Toys, games and sports requisites; parts and accessories thereof	2	1	1	—	—	—	—	—	—	—	—	—	—
96	Miscellaneous manufactured articles	1 / 1	1 / 0	0 / 0	— / —	— / —	— / —	— / —	— / —	— / —	— / —	— / —	— / —	— / —
97	Works of art, collectors' pieces and antiques	—	—	—	—	—	—	—	—	—	—	—	—	—

332

Annex I Overview of Different Government Departments and their Functions

Directorate: Food Control (National Department of Health)

This directorate's main functions, among other things, include:

- To administer, compile, and publish legislation relating to food safety, food labeling, and related matters.
- To initiate, coordinate, and evaluate general as well as more specific food monitoring programs.
- To audit and support provinces and local authorities with food law enforcement.
- To inform, educate, and communicate (IEC) food safety and related matters to stakeholders such as industry, consumers, and other departments.
- To act as the national contact point for the joint FAO/WHO Codex Alimentarius Commission.
- To evaluate agricultural remedies and chemicals and food produced by means of biotechnology.

Directorate DPHQ (National Department of Agriculture)

Subdirectorate: Plant Health. The aim of the Subdirectorate: Plant Health is to prevent the import, export, and spread of agricultural and forestry pests and diseases, thereby protecting both national and international agriculture and the environment in general.

The Division: National Phytosanitary Matters (NPM) is responsible for administering and making revisions to the Agricultural Pests Act, 1983 (Act No. 36 of 1983). The measures contained in this Act are in accordance with the objectives of the International Plant Protection Convention (IPPC) of which South Africa is a member.

NPM is also responsible for import control to prevent the introduction of foreign pests and diseases into South Africa. An import permit is not necessary for those plants and plant products listed in the Government Notice No. R1013 of 26 May 1989, but published conditions must be complied with in terms of a declaration on a phytosanitary certificate issued by the NPPO of the exporting country. In respect of plants and plant products not published in the Government Notice, prospective importers have to apply for an import permit. A

pest risk assessment (PRA), based on scientific data, is conducted and specific conditions are set according to the phytosanitary risk(s) involved. These conditions are then stipulated in their permit issued to the importer. Depending on the risk(s), the following categories can be established concerning the importation of organisms, plants and plant products:

- Prohibited material: Plants and plant products with an extremely high phytosanitary risk for which authorization will not be granted.
- Post-entry quarantine: Bio-control agents and plant species constituting a high phytosanitary risk are evaluated at a quarantine facility of the NPPO, an approved facility or the premises of the importer, depending on the PRA outcome.
- Specific phytosanitary conditions: Phytosanitary conditions on the import permit determined by a PRA must be endorsed on the phytosanitary certificate as an additional declaration.
- Open phytosanitary certificate: Plants and plant products visually inspected and found free from quarantine pests and practically free from other harmful pests.
- No phytosanitary certificate: Inspection of plants and plant products in the exporting country is not compulsory.

NPM is also responsible for the eradication of potential alien pests and control measures of agricultural pests. In respect of the former the following actions are taken:

- Conducting a survey to determine the distribution of the organism.
- Drafting an eradication program.
- Coordinating with other departments, specialists, research institutes, and the respective industries.
- Coordinating and participating in the eradication program.

With respect to the latter measures taken to prevent or combat the spread of harmful organism(s) to other areas in the country, include the following:

- A national policy which prohibits the transportation of plant material from an infested or infected area to areas free from the specific organism and infested and/or infected material from a specific producer or area.

- Testing samples to determine the specific pest status of the organism.
- Monitoring the specific pest.
- Coordinate on national level with all relevant institutes, industries and specialists.

Finally, NPM is also responsible for ensuring that the exported South African agricultural products comply with the import conditions of a specific country or group of countries by issuing phytosanitary certificates. In this regard this responsibility entail the following:

- Maintaining a database on the import conditions and procedures of various countries and the occurrence of harmful organisms within South Africa
- Rendering advisory and identification services.
- Conducting laboratory tests as requested by the importing country.
- Carrying out of field inspections.

The Division: Plant Health Auditing (PHA) is responsible for inspections of imported material to minimize the risk of importing alien organisms with the ability to spread and become established in South Africa. This division is also responsible for inspection, evaluation, and certification of consignments of plants and plant products intended for exports.

The Division: Protocols and Work Programmes (PWP) is responsible for

- Notifying exporting countries of South Africa's import conditions;
- Coordinating with the FAO and the NPPOs of the other countries to ensure that South Africa's import conditions are complied with;
- Notifying an exporting country of any alien organisms(s) intercepted on imported controlled goods; and
- Reporting to the IPPC on all organisms newly established in South Africa. The PWP is also responsible for coordinating with the NPPOs of the importing countries to establish a phytosanitary export program, as well as ensuring that the requirements of the export program and phytosanitary regulations are complied with.

The Division: Plant Health Promotion (PHP) is responsible for revising, establishing, and maintaining awareness program to inform the travelling public, importers, community members, exporters, and producers, including subsistence farmers, regarding phytosanitary risks involved in the import or export of controlled goods.

Subdirectorate: Quality Control. The Subdirectorate: Quality Control is responsible for standardization of quality norms for agricultural and related products by establishing the criteria for such norms and distributing the information to all interested parties. These criteria may include the quality, packaging, marking, and labeling, as well as the chemical composition and microbiological contaminants of products. These norms are validated by publication in the Government Gazette under the Agricultural Product Standards Act, 1990 (Act No. 119 of 1990).

The directorate carries out its own inspections but may on occasion appoint assignees to undertake inspections at the point of sale, manufacture, packing, or export to ensure that the set standards and requirements are maintained and that the benefits of classification, grading, and marking reach the consumer. The case where assignees are appointed the directorate carries out audit inspections to verify that the set standards are applied correctly. The following assignees are currently appointed:

- The Perishable Export Control Board (PPECB)

  - Handles all agricultural products intended for export except dried fruit.

- The South African Meat Industry Company (SAMIC)

  - Handles all meat carcasses intended for sale on the local market.

- PROKON

  - Handles all potatoes intended for sale on the local market.

Routine analysis of various agricultural products helps to determine the composition, microbiological contamination, and pesticide residue levels in food products. Chemical residue analyses and the detection of harmful organisms are of particular importance for products marketed internationally.

As with the Directorate: Plant Health, this directorate also has several divisions. The Division: Perishable Products and Flowers is responsible for determining product norms and standards for perishable products (deciduous, citrus, and subtropical fruit) and flowers. The Division: Agronomy and Vegetables is responsible for determining product norms and standards for agronomy and vegetable products, while the Division: Animal and Processed Products is responsible for determining product norms and standards for animal and processed products. The same applies to the Division: Liquor Products for liquor products. The following roles of these divisions can be summarized and also follow for both imports and exports:

- Evaluate, compile, and amend, in consultation with the industry and consumers, as well as in accordance with national and international developments, standards with regard to composition, packaging, marking, labeling, and inspection/control/monitoring of agriculture and liquor products destined for local sale and export, also taking into account the legal, marketing, international, and economic aspects that may have an influence on or be influenced by this standards.
- Evaluate, compile, and amend, in consultation with the industry and in accordance with national and international developments, guidelines for management control systems including food safety aspects.

- Interpretation of national and international standards guidelines to ensure uniformity of application and inform international counterparts of acceptable terms of international developments.

A list of the products covered by the Subdirectorate is shown in Table 4.23.

The Division: Quality Promotion has the responsibility to participate in the development of quality education programs and to facilitate the implementation of quality education and awareness programs.

In terms of the Division: Auditing, it is responsible for the auditing the quality of exported/imported/local products in terms of the Agricultural Product Standard Act and the Liquor Products Act. Auditing of agricultural products intended for export, except dried fruit, is for example handled by PPECB as an assignee of the NPPO. In cases where disputes may arise about the outcome of inspections done by PPECB this division also serve on appeal boards to resolve such disputes.

Directorate Genetic Resources (National Department of Agriculture)

Subdirectorate: Animal Genetic Resources. The Division: Animal Improvement is responsible for the regulation of imports and exports of genetic material, the registration of reproduction operators, collection centers, and donor animals, the evaluation of new breeds and the regulation of the activities of breed societies and registration authorities.

Table 4.23 Products Covered by the Subdirectorate: Quality Control

Animal and Processed Products	Perishable Products and Flowers	Vegetables and Grain
Dairy and Imitation Dairy Products, Red Meat, Poultry Meat, Eggs, Fruit Juice and Drink, Vinegar, Druid Fruit, Honey, Dehydrated Vegetables, Mohair, Apricot and Peach Kernels, Fat Spreads, Jam, Jelly, Marmalade, Canned fruit and Vegetables, Frozen Fruit and Vegetables, Mayonnaise and Salad Dressings, Rooibos Tea	Apples, Avocados, Citrus Fruit, Cut Flowers, Mangoes, Strawberries, Pears, Melons, Papayas, Grapes, Plums and prunes, Pineapples, Apricots, Fruit (excluding deciduous fruit and citrus), Cherries, Peaches, Litchis, KiwiFruit	Buckwheat, Dry beans, Grass seeds, Groundnuts, Sorghum, Wheat, Wheat products, Maize, Maize products, Oil seeds, Leguminous seeds, Tobacco, Feed products, Vegetables, Potatoes, Tomatoes, Onions

Source: NDA 2002.

The Division: Animal Improvement is responsible for

- The regulation of imports and exports of animal genetic material and the activities of breed societies and registration authorities.
- Facilitating programs to promote the sustainable use of farm animal genetic resources with special reference to indigenous and locally developed breeds.
- The registration of reproduction operators, collection centers, and donor animals.
- Maintaining an animal identification system to register owner identification marks.
- The evaluation of new breeds and the regulation of the activities of breed societies and registration authorities.

Subdirectorate: Plant Genetic Resources. Figure 4.2 shows the structure of the Subdirectorate: Plant Genetic Resources. The Division: Seed Quality Con-

4.2 Structure Directorate Genetic Resources

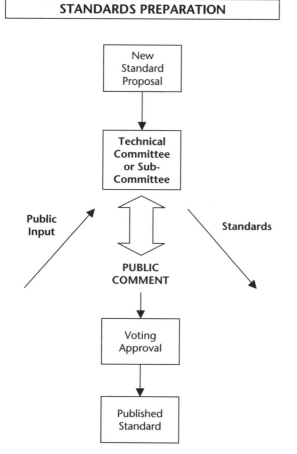

trol aims at ensuring that physical and physiological quality of seed which is grown locally, imported or exported meets determined international norms and standards before being traded or propagated by farmers. The Division: Genetic Control coordinates activities relating to the conservation and sustainable use of plant genetic resources for food and agriculture which include management of the national gene bank as well as determination and management of norms and standards for genetically modified organisms to reduce environmental impact.

The Division: Variety Control is involved in evaluation of new varieties of plants and propagating material to ensure genetic authenticity as comprehensively described in accordance with internationally accepted guidelines for registration of new varieties. The Division: Plant Genetic Auditing is responsible for deployment of auditing officers or inspectors to enforce the requirements as stipulated in the Acts administering plant genetic resources to pursue optimal utilization of agricultural resources. The Division: Plant Genetic Promotion facilitates education, awareness, and outreach programs in conservation and sustainable use of plant genetic resources for food and agriculture, particularly to rural communities through extension and other agencies.

Directorate of Veterinary Services (National Department of Agriculture)

The National Director of Veterinary Services takes responsibility for controlling the veterinary services, setting norms and standards, and import control as well as other international aspects.

The Directorate of Veterinary Services has five subdirectorates:

- Subdirectorate: Animal Disease Control administers the Animal Disease Act, 1984, and exercises border control.
- Subdirectorate: Veterinary Hygiene administers the Abattoir Hygiene Act, 1992, and associated standards and norms.
- Subdirectorate: Import Control controls veterinary import permits and ports of entry.
- Subdirectorate: Export Control controls export abattoirs and certification.
- Subdirectorate: Epidemology is responsible for disease surveillance, reporting, data collection, training, and liaison.

If a noticeable disease is identified, it is reported to the state veterinarian. If it is foot and mouth disease, African swine fever, or any abnormal outbreaks of African horse sickness, anthrax, Newcastle disease or Rift Valley fever, or any disease that has never occurred in South Africa or has been eradicated from South Africa, then the disease is reported immediately (by state veterinarian) to the Provincial Director of Veterinary Services. The Provincial Director then immediately reports to the National Director of Animal Production and Health (CVO). This disease outbreak is then reported immediately to the OIE, as well as to neighboring countries and any other interested parties. If the disease is an OIE List B or List C disease, it is reported to the National Director of Animal Production and Health at monthly intervals, and is then reported to the OIE annually or monthly, depending on the disease.

Directorate: Agricultural Production Inputs (National Department of Agriculture)

Any application for the registration of an agricultural remedy[12] or the annual renewal thereof is submitted to the Registrar, Act No. 36 of 1947. The regulations require that prior to the commencement of any trials the Registrar must be informed in writing of the intention to conduct such trials in order that the Registrar may inspect their performance. Furthermore, the Act makes provision for the Registrar to call for any further information in order to determine whether the remedy is acceptable in the context of public interest, suitability, and biological efficacy. Field data are provided by the applicant, while some data are generated by the Agricultural Research Council (ARC) institutes in field trials and the SABS in the case of wood. A committee INDAC (Inter Departmental Advisory Committee) comprising representatives from Labor, Health, Water affairs, ARC, Environmental affairs, and selected outsiders provides advice for the safeguard of man against poison.

Before an agricultural remedy containing a new active ingredient may be registered in South Africa, approval must first be obtained from the Department of Health. The Department of Health evaluates the data and prepares a risk assessment using human health and environmental safety criteria. If the risk assessment is favorable, permission is then given to the NDA to proceed with the registration. Cognizance should also be taken of the "International Code of Conduct on the Distribution and use of Pesticides" and 'Guidelines for the Registration and Control of Pesticides" issued by the Food and Agriculture Organisation of the United Nations (FAO), as well as the "GCPF Position Paper on Intellectual Property" issued by the Global Crop Protection Federation.

South Africa recognizes the registration authorities of the United States of America, Germany, the United Kingdom, and France. Under certain circumstances conditional registration may be granted in South Africa if the active ingredient and formulation in question has already been registered by one of the authorities mentioned. Instances where the granting of such conditional registrations may be considered are the following:

- Remedies not intended for use on food crops or food animals
- Remedies which will not adversely affect the environment
- Remedies for use on food products if it can be shown that residues cannot be detected on the particular crop or food (when applied according to good agricultural practice).
- Agricultural remedies for "minor use."

Recommendations and requirements on agrochemical container labels are based on current registrations of plant protection products used in the South African deciduous fruit industry, and in terms of the Fertilizers, Farm Feeds, Agricultural Remedies, and Stock Remedies Act, 1947 (Act No. 36 of 1947) and good agricultural practice (GAP)

---

[12] An agricultural remedy is defined by the Fertilizers, Farm Feeds, Agricultural Remedies and Stock Remedies Act as any chemical substance or biological remedy, or any mixture or combination of any substance or remedy intended or offered to be used for the destruction, control, repelling, attraction, or prevention of any undesired microbe, alga, nematode, fungus, insect, plant, vertebrate, invertebrate, or any product thereof but excluding any chemical substance, biological remedy or other remedy in so far as it is controlled under the Medicines and Related Substances Control Act, 1965 (Act No. 101 of 1965), or the Hazardous Substances Act, 1973 (Act No. 15 of 1973; or as plant growth regulator, defoliant, desiccant or legume inoculant, and anything else which the minister has be notice in the Gazette declared an agricultural remedy for the purposes of this Act

must be adhered to at all times. The label has to conform to the requirements of the *"Guidelines for the RSA Classification Code of Agricultural and Stock Remedies and Associated Labelling Practices."*

Certain living modified organisms (LMOs) resulting from modern biotechnology will find their application in the field of plant protection and pest control. Although these LMOs are controlled by the Genetically Modified Organisms Act (Act No. 15 of 1997), some will also be controlled by Act No. 36 of 1947. These will include organisms genetically modified to express certain toxins. Excluded will be crops that have been genetically altered to be resistant to certain insect species, plant pathogens, or herbicides as these will be controlled exclusively by the Genetically Modified Organisms Act.

No agricultural remedy derived from a recombinant DNA organism may be released (trial release and general release) unless a risk assessment to evaluate the risk posed by the genetically modified organism to human health and the environment has been carried out and the necessary permits have been obtained. An evaluation of the risk to the environment should cover all issues required by the Environmental Impact Reports in terms of the Environmental Conservation Act. The risk assessment should be done by a biological safety committee appointed by the organization concerned. SAGENE is available to provide advice when required. Cognizance should also be taken of the United Nations Environment Programme (UNEP) Technical Guidelines on Safety in Biotechnology.

The Pesticide Residue Trial Requirements Act (No. 36 of 1947) is also the responsibility of this directorate. The object of carrying out residue trials is to determine the range of residue levels on or in a commodity that can be expected when the commodity is treated with a pesticide according to its registered use. To set realistic maximum residue limits (MRLs), which are toxicologically acceptable, and to ensure that withholding periods is based on good agricultural practice, various requirements have to be adhered to for generating residue data, that is, residue trial requirements, required trials, presentation of residue data, etc.

SABS

The SABS, as a statutory body, is funded from the Science Council's budget by way of a parliamentary grant. Funding is channeled via the DTI to the SABS. Its commercial conformity assessment activities operate in the competitive domain and are self-funding. The SABS is governed by the SABS Council, which is appointed by the minister of Trade and Industry from nominations received from industry, consumer bodies, NGOs, etc. The Council consists of six members, the Chairperson as well as the CEO of the SABS in an ex officio capacity.

Section 3 of the Standards Act sets out the SABS's objectives as follows:

- To obtain membership of foreign or international bodies having any objectives similar to an object of the SABS.
- To obtain the cooperation of State Departments, local authorities, other public bodies representatives of any branch of commerce and industry, and other persons.
- To test precision measuring instruments, gauges and scientific apparatus in order to determine their accuracy and to calibrate them.
- To examine, test, and analyze articles, materials, and substances.
- To supply reference materials for specific purposes.
- To furnish reports and issue certificates in connection with examinations, tests, analysis, calibration, and assessments carried out by the SABS, subject to conditions it may consider expedient.
- To supply information and guidance.
- To compile and issue recommended practices as a supplement to a relevant standard.
- To issue as a national standard a specification, code of practice, or standard method, and to administer schemes based thereon.
- To control the use of distinctive marks, certification marks of proof and marks of authenticity.
- To assist the person or state department in the preparation and framing of any document which embodies characteristics similar to those of a standard.
- To perform, insofar as is not repugnant to or inconsistent with any Act of Parliament, such functions as the Minister might assign to the SABS.

There are five areas of Regulatory Management:

- Food and Fisheries Products (Food Safety);
- Automotive;

- Human, health, and the Environment;
- Electrotechnical, Electrical, and Gaming; and
- Management of the Trade Metrology Act.

The SABS's regulatory services carry out the following activities[13]:

- Administration of Compulsory Specifications.
- Approvals of products covered by Compulsory Specifications.
- Surveillance of markets and products covered by Compulsory Specifications.
- Sanctioning of noncomplying products. Restraining the circulation and availability of noncomplying products in the Regulatory Environment through official procedures and legal actions.
- Risk assessment reporting.
- Informing concerned and affected parties about Compulsory Specifications.
- Surveillance of the regulatory environment for products covered by focus areas, that is, floatation aids, respiratory equipment, breathing apparatus, safety helmets, child restraining devices, fire arms, and biological safety.
- Cabinets, coal burning appliances, brake and clutch fluid, disinfectants and detergents, products affecting human health and environmental safety
- Compliance monitoring of products covered and affected by focus areas through inspections and tests.

SABS Standards Setting System. The SABS standards development process in South Africa mirrors what happens internationally. The process is depicted in the Figure 4.3. Compulsory specifications are developed in a similar way. The SABS has almost 450 technical committees and subcommittees. The process follows the WTO Code of Good Practice for the development of standards and is part of the SABS's *Code of Practice on the Development of National Standards and Other Normative Documents.*

The SABS must ensure that South African standards have market relevance. To achieve this the SABS tries to involve all valid interest groups in the

technical committees, subcommittees, and working groups. The draft standards are, of course, submitted to the public for scrutiny once the technical committees have reached consensus. The principle of consensus is paramount and is sought either in formal meetings or by correspondence. There is an appeal procedure for the resolution of disputes. Besides standards the SABS also publishes National and Sectoral Technical Agreements, which can be developed further into standards.

The committees are constituted to be representative, as far as possible, of valid national interests in the standardization of products or processes. Membership is usually open to organizations, associations, and forum representatives as opposed to individuals. Organizations normally invited to serve on committees include government bodies, industry associations, consumer organizations or associations, NGOs, organized labor and professional, technical, and trade organizations. Experts may be invited to serve on committees in an advisory capacity. P-members participate actively whilst O-members follow the work as observers. Committees may set up working groups to undertake specific, short-term tasks, such as the preparation of working drafts, etc. Committee chairpersons (preferably non-SABS) are appointed for a maximum term of three years.

New work may be requested in writing by any person or organization. The proposal is considered by the responsible technical committee and the Standards Approval Committee. On acceptance of the committee draft, a draft South African standard is made available for public comment both nationally and internationally. There is a comment period of 60 days. Comments are reviewed by the technical committee and further drafting may be required. Finally the standard is forwarded to the Standards Approval Committee for ratification.

Every South African standard is reviewed periodically. The SABS has published approximately 4,500 standards. The SABS uses its website to disseminate standards information. It must be noted that the SABS does not yet sell its standards over the Internet. The SABS is busy expanding its website to allow for greater transparency. Committee members will soon be able to access the following

---

[13] The SABS standards and regulatory division was recently renamed the South African National Standards Organization (SANSO). The acronym "SABS" has been retained by the now separated commercial arm of the organization.

4.3 Standards Preparation Process

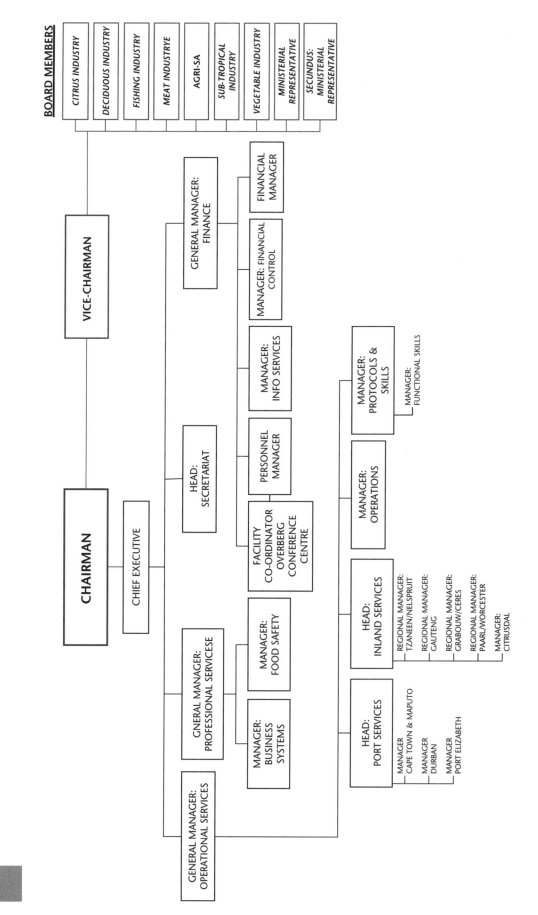

standardization information by technical sector: Technical committee information (processes and work programs) and working documents (for committee members). The Standards Information Centre's website will allow the public to access the titles of standards.

The SABS also publishes its "Bulletin: Technical Journal of the South African Bureau of Standards" eight times every year. This journal is circulated to any interested party and covers the entire spectrum of SABS activities, that is

1. All standards that are new, revised, amended, reaffirmed, withdrawn, new standardization projects approved, standardization projects cancelled, drafts for comment and WTO notifications.

2. New ISO and IEC standards issued.

3. New CEN/CENELEC (European) standards issued.

4. SABS Mark Scheme permits issued during a given period (the first SABS product certification mark denoting compliance with a standard dates back to 1946. The current scheme provides for various categories of compliance, for example that the article is safe for use according to specifications; certification mark denoting compliance with a standard dates back to 1946. The current scheme provides for various categories of compliance, for example that the article's approved performance is according to specifications; environmental friendliness; that the article's packaging conforms to spec; etc. The basic certification mark is used only on articles of precious metals to certify the purity of the metal).

5. List of suppliers whose quality systems comply with SABS ISO 9000—Summary of additions/cancellations/amendments.

6. List of suppliers whose quality systems comply with QS 9000—Summary of additions/cancellations/amendments.

7. The SABS ISO 9000 registration scheme advisory committee update—Summary of additions/cancellations/amendments.

8. List of suppliers whose environmental management systems comply with SABS ISO 14000—Summary of additions/cancellations/amendments.

9. List of suppliers with registration schemes other than SABS ISO 9000 or SABS 14000—Summary of additions/cancellations/amendments.

The SABS can provide global standards information at its Information Centre at its head office in Pretoria. The SABS is also the national WTO/TBT Enquiry Point. It is linked to the International Perinorm database that contains global standards information.

SANAS

SANAS is responsible for the accreditation of Certification bodies to ISO/IEC Guide 62, 65, and 66 (and the IAF interpretation thereof), and laboratories (testing and calibration) to ISO/IEC 17025. Inspection Bodies are accredited to ISO/IEC/17020 standards. GLP facilities are inspected for compliance to OECD GLP principles.

Currently accredited are: 92 test laboratories; 137 calibration laboratories; 95 medical laboratories; 19 legal metrology labs (this will be augmented in the near future by as many as 120 additional laboratories because, as of 1 April 2002, the function of accreditation of verification laboratories has been transferred to SANAS from the SABS Trade Metrology Division); 49 inspection bodies; 7 certification bodies; 1 Proficiency Testing laboratory; and 2 GLP facilities at the SABS.

SANAS is currently studying the entire national regulatory framework to establish government's short, medium, and long-term accreditation needs. Inspection activities are a priority of this research. The ultimate aim is to accredit all of the national and provincial governments' conformity assessment activities so as to ensure a transparent and objective measure of competence. This study should be complete by August 2003."

PPECB

Figure 4.4 shows the organizational structure of PPECB. The food safety auditing done by the PPECB comprise EUREPGAP, HACCP, Good Manufacturing Practise (GMP), and Good Agricultural Practise (GAP). For some high-risk commodities, such as fresh plums, the PPECB also issues health certificates for biological contamination. Most Arab nations demand these certificates. To monitor food quality control the PPECB draws samples to be sampled for MRLs by the laboratories of the Department of Health, Council for Scientific and Industrial Research (CSIR), or SABS. The percentage of rejections lies between 4 and 8 percent,

4.4 Organizational Structure of the PPECB

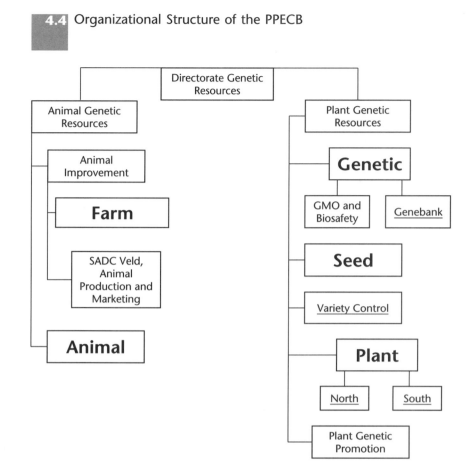

depending on the weather conditions of the growing season.

Functions of PPECB related to the PPECB Act (Act 9 of 1983):

- Control export shipments of perishable products from South Africa;
- Determine vessel suitability and assign products to class of accommodation required;
- Determine various products' export volumes and related particulars;
- Determine shipping capacities, service opportunities, and sailing schedules of shipping lines;
- Arrange provision of port facilities and shipping space as required;
- Research and make recommendations regarding handling, conveyance, and cold storage procedures for perishable products;
- Promote uniform freight rates as prescribed by regulation; and
- Temperature management

The PPECB also has functions related to the Agricultural Products Standards Act (Act 119 of 1990).

The functions of the PPECB pertaining to the Agricultural Product Standard Act is to act as assignee of government and to execute the Act with regard to export of certain perishable export products, that is:

- Control over sale of products;
- Control over export products;
- Control description of products;
- Investigation and sampling;
- Appeals; and
- Regulations.

ISO 9001 certification ensures that business is conducted in a certain manner. This is achieved by uniformity regarding standards for procedures and instructions. The inspectors conducting inspections and working for PPECB are continuously tested in respect of their capacity to do inspections. In this respect the so-called Koffer-test is used widely, and entails, among others, that inspectors must be able to identify pest and diseases, identify different classes of fruit, etc. Certain inspectors also receive further training in inspection and auditing or Hazard Analysis Critical Control Points (HACCP).

Annex J Acts Administered by Different Government Departments

Foodstuffs, Cosmetics, and Disinfectants Act, 1972 (Act No. 54 of 1972)

This Act addresses the manufacture, sale, and importation of foodstuffs. Authorized local authorities in their areas of jurisdiction enforce it. Food import control is conducted by the Port Health Services of the Provincial Health Departments on behalf of the national Department of Health. The Act does not require the issuing of food import permits by South Africa or of certification by exporting countries. Food is detained by Customs and Excise for clearance by port health and may be inspected, sampled, and analyzed. Entry into the country can be denied if the food is not in compliance with the requirements of the Act. See Annex L for a list of regulations related to this Act.

The Health Act, 1977 (Act No. 63 of 1977)

Regulations related to the hygienic handling of food and the inspection of, among other things, food premises published under this Act are also enforced by local authorities in their areas of jurisdiction. This Act oversees the following regulations:

- Milking sheds and the transport of milk (R. 1256 OF 27/6/1986)
- Inspections and investigations (R. 1128 OF 24/5/1991)
- Regulations governing general hygiene requirements for food premises and the transport of food (R. 918 OF 30/7/1999)

The International Health Regulations Act, 1974 (Act No. 28 of 1974)

This Act provides for the approval by the Department of Health of the source of food for consumption at ports, airports, on vessels, and on aircraft, as well as for the inspection of such premises and the sampling of food by local authorities. The provincial health departments currently approve premises on behalf of the National Department of Health.

Agricultural Pests Act, 1983 (Act No. 36 of 1983)

The Act regulates the import of controlled goods, among other things, plants, plant products, exotic animals, insects and pathogens, honey, and used apiary equipment. It is administered and enforced by the DPQC.

Agricultural Product Standards Act, 1990 (Act No. 119 of 1990)

This Act covers mandatory standards for 220 different commodities. It controls and promotes specific product standards (for example, meat, dairy products, cereals, certain canned products, fruit, and vegetables) for local as well as export purposes. Furthermore, the Act sets compositional, as well as, quality, packaging, labeling chemical, and microbiological standards in respect of a variety of other foodstuffs such as fruit, fruit juices, vegetables, cereals, and eggs. The norms are based on the specific needs of the South African market and are usually harmonized with international standards. The Act is administered and enforced by the DPHQ. Various assignees such as the Perishable Products Export Control Board (PPECB) are however also appointed and authorized to do the physical inspections in terms of this Act.

The Liquor Products Act, 1989 (Act 60 of 1989)

This Act addresses wine and spirits. It is also administered and enforced by the DPHQ.

Genetically Modified Organisms Act (Act 15 of 1997)

This Act provides for measures to promote the responsible development, production, use, and application of genetically modified organisms; to ensure that all activities involving the use of genetically modified organisms (including import, production, release, and distribution) shall be carried out in such a way as to limit possible harmful consequences to the environment; to give attention to the prevention of accidents and the effective management of waste; to establish common measures for the evaluation and reduction of the potential risks arising out of activities involving the use of genetically modified organisms; to lay down the necessary requirements and criteria for risk assessments; to establish a council for genetically modified organisms; to ensure that genetically modified organisms are appropriate and do not present a hazard to the environment; and to establish appropriate procedures for the notification of specific activities involving the use of genetically modified organisms; and to provide for matters connected therewith.

The Animal Improvement Act, 1998 (Act No. 62 of 1998)

This Act makes provision for the registration of semen collectors, inseminators, embryo collectors, embryo transferors, import agents, centers, donor animals, animal breeder's societies, and registering authorities; the registration requirements for the above-mentioned operators, centers, or breeder's societies; the restriction of certain actions in respect to animal genetic material; the restriction on the sale or import of genetic material; and the restriction of certain actions with reference to stud book animals.

Enforcement of the Act is done through a system of registration and permits, with a number of inspectors ensuring that the registered operators comply with these requirements. All sales of genetic material require a certificate of guarantee. There is a move toward the self-regulation of the industry through bodies such as the Animal Genetics Traders Association, the South African Veterinary Semen and Embryo Group, and the Artificial Insemination Committee. The South African Poultry Association is already self-regulating.

The Livestock Brands Act, 1962 (Act No. 87 of 1962)

This Act makes provision for the registration of identification marks for animals to provide a legal and uniform system of animal identification and proof of ownership. This Act ties in with the Stock Theft Act, and policing is done by the Stock Theft Unit of the South African Police Service (SAPS). All animals entering the country, animals presented for sale or being transported must be marked according to the requirements of the Act. The SAPS is in the process of clamping down on people not complying with the Act.

The Animal Diseases Act, 1984 (Act 35 of 1984)

It is administered by the Directorate: Animal Health of the NDA and enforced by the provincial departments, except for import control, which is a national responsibility. This act emphasizes the fact that infectious animal diseases and parasites pose a threat to the agricultural sector in South Africa. It therefore provides for the control of this disease, the measures to promote animal health and matters connected therewith. Various areas in South Africa have been declared permanent controlled

areas and are promulgated in this Act. Thus, this Act deters the spread of a disease from controlled areas (African swine fever, Corridor disease, Rabies, and Foot and mouth disease). It also deters the spread of diseases to a controlled area, that is, African horse sickness.

This Act, however, is under review to bring it in line with the Constitution and to clarify provincial and national responsibilities. The purpose of the proposed new Animal Health Bill is to promote production of animals and their products. The Bill further aims to promote the elimination of exposure to zoonotic diseases by humans and to ensure unhindered trade in agriculture, if an acceptable disease control system is maintained in South Africa. This is accomplished by (Meyer 2002)

- preventing the introduction of exotic animal diseases into the Republic via import.
- controlling the spread of existing animal diseases within the Republic.
- preventing the spread of existing animal diseases or parasites to humans.
- promote animal health in the national herd.

The Bill retains the following valuable provisions contained in the Animal Diseases Act (Act 35 of 1984):

- Principles of disease control measures as these measures are according to international norms and standards, for example OIE.
- Establishment of quarantine stations.
- Import control aimed to prevent the introduction of exotic animal diseases into the Republic.
- Establishment of animal health schemes to eradicate certain diseases in the Republic.
- Services rendered by the State to the animal owner.
- Compensation for anything that has been destroyed or disposed of pursuant to any control measure.
- To declare certain animal diseases, that have a detrimental effect on the national animal herd or on the livestock and game industry, "controlled diseases." They are then controlled on a country-wide basis.
- To declare certain areas in the Republic, where controlled animal diseases pose a constant threat, or areas that are free of diseases, as controlled areas in which strict control measures are applied

to prevent the spread of disease from such area or to such areas, as the case may be.

In additions thereto the following new provisions are included in the Bill:

- To clarify the division of functions between the national and provincial spheres of governance.
- The designation of an official veterinarian in the department as a national executive officer who will exercise the powers and perform the duties conferred or imposed upon him or her under the Bill.
- The designation of an official veterinarian in each province by the Member of the Executive Council (MEC) concerned as the provincial executive officer for the implementation of certain clauses of the Bill on a provincial level.
- Provide for trade in terms of international agreements and makes provision for restriction on export.
- Human rights are included in the implementation of the proposed Bill. In all cases of entering a premise the need for a warrant is required. Only under certain circumstances powers of entry and investigation will be without the prior authority of a warrant.
- Assignment of executive authority to provinces and organizations/assignees with regard to the implementation of certain clauses of the Bill.

The Abattoir Hygiene Act, 1992 (Act 121 of 1992)

The Act is administered by the Directorate: Veterinary Public Health of the NDA. It addresses food safety in red meat and poultry abattoirs and sets hygiene standards for abattoirs. These regulations are enforced mainly by the provincial agriculture departments. The import of unprocessed meat is also controlled by the Act. This aspect is enforced by the NDA.

Meat Safety Act (Act 40 of 2000)

The Act is administered by the Directorate: Veterinary Public Health of the NDA. It provides for measures to promote meat safety and the safety of animal products; to establish and maintain essential national standards in respect to abattoirs; to regulate the import and export of meat; to establish meat safety schemes; and to provide for matters connected therewith.

The Fertilizers, Farm Feeds, Agricultural Remedies, and Stock Remedies Act, 1947 (Act 36 of 1947)

It is administered and enforced by the Directorate: Agriculture Production Inputs of the NDA. Animal feeds, stock remedies, and agricultural remedies (pesticides, etc.) are registered in terms of this Act.

Annex K Details on Regulations per Industry

Electrotechnical

The Occupational Health and Safety Act makes compulsory the SABS Code of Practice 0142:1993—The Wiring of Premises. The Wiring Code requires that each item or defined system of electrical equipment used in an electrical installation shall comply with the relevant technical requirements or be authorized.

An electrical installation is defined as any machinery used for the transmission of electrical energy, including any article that forms part of such an installation. These are typically cables, circuit breakers, switches, transformers, distribution boards, socket outlets, transformers, etc.

All equipment and techniques that do not fall within the scope of existing standards, or that do not fully comply with the relevant standards, but that are considered not to lower the safety of the installation, or to influence the safety of the product, are to be authorized for use in an electrical installation in South Africa by SANSO's Electrotechnical Regulatory Services.

An application together with a full test report, a sample and a product brochure must be submitted to SANSO's surveillance auditors.

There are ten compulsory specifications in this domain, which have been drafted by SABS's technical committees and promulgated by the Minister of Trade and Industry. These compulsory specifications have been amended a number of times during the past decades. The dates refer, therefore, to the latest versions:

- VC 8003—Manually operated switches for fixed installations—1998;
- VC 8006—Safety of flexible cords for electrial appliances—1995;
- VC 8008—Plugs, socket outlets and socket outlet adapters—1998;

345

- VC 8011—Lamp holders—1999;
- VC 8029—Cord sets and cord extension sets—1998;
- VC 8035—Earth leakage protection units—1987;
- VC 8036—Circuit-Breakers—1999;
- VC 8039—The safety of starters for tubular fluorescent lamps—1989;
- VC 8043—The safety of incandescent lamps—1990;
- VC 8055—Electrical and electronic apparatus—1996.

Most of the above regulations are based on IEC standards with the exception of the following compulsory specifications that are not based entirely on IEC standards: VC 8008—Plugs, socket outlets, and socket outlet adapters; VC 8036—Circuit-Breakers and VC 8035—Earth leakage protection units.[14]

Forestry

The Department of Water Affairs and Forestry, the DTI, the SABS, and the Department of Agriculture regulate the forestry industry in South Africa.

First, at the plantation level, which is covered by the National Forests Act (No. 84 of 1998) and the National Veldt and Forest Fire Act (No. 101 of 1998) under the auspices of the Department of Water Affairs and Forestry.

Second, timber processing and treatment is dealt with under the Unfair Business Practices Act (Act 21 of 2001) and the National Building Regulations under the auspices of the Department of Trade and Industry and the SABS. The National Building Regulations are mandatory and must be enforced by local authorities together with the provisions of the National Building Regulations and Building Standards Act, 1977 (Act 103 of 1977) as amended. In terms of the Unfair Business Practices Act any timber (excluding timber for construction) processed and treated in South Africa must comply with the relevant national standards. All producers must subscribe to the SABS mark scheme. The SABS plans to include construction timber within the gamut of the above-mentioned Act in the near future. Currently the National Building Regulations cover construction timber, that is SABS 0400, stipulates that all timber used in construction shall either comply with the relevant national standard or be certified by a structural engineer. The constructor must, therefore, prove that the timber used complies with requirements. SABS 05 requires that all timber used for construction at the coast, must be pretreated for such use.

Third, every consignment of raw timber (that is with bark) that comes into the country must be certified free of pests and insects by inspectors from the NDA. Customs and Excise will not allow a consignment into the country unless such a certificate accompanies it.

The Ministry of Water Affairs and Forestry has convened National Forests Advisory Council. The Council is charged with establishing criteria, indicators, and standards for sustainable forestry development. The National Forests Act stipulates that these criteria, indicators and standards will be legislated. The Institute for Natural Resources at the University of Natal has been tasked to draft the criteria, indicators, and standards. There are currently 92 draft criteria.

---

[14] VC 8036 makes compulsory the safety aspects of the South African circuit breaker standard SABS 0156. The old SABS 0156 standard was written to suit hydraulic-magnetic circuit breaker technology perfected by Circuit Breakers Industries (CBI), the only South African manufacturer of circuit breakers. The other members of the technical committee represent international corporations. As a result it proved impossible to achieve a consensus within technical committee 3350.7 in respect to the choice of a new molded case circuit breaker standard. In the end a majority (but not all) of the participants supported a compromise based on international standard IEC 60647-2, albeit with two minor deviations in respect to the voltage level and power factor. The voltage at which tests are performed had to be raised to +10 percent to cater for the wide voltage tolerance in South African Supply Voltage Regulations. This is vital since the national electricity supplier, ESCOM cannot guarantee constant supply voltages in the country. The voltage fluctuates from the nominal voltage of 240V to as high as 270V. This necessitates a 10 percent margin over the nominal rate. Circuit breakers must therefore be able to withstand the voltage varieties, i.e., it must accommodate a 10 percent margin instead of the 5 percent margin catered for in IEC 60947-2. The minister of Trade and Industry authorized the compromise. The technical committee for VC 8035 concerning earth leakage units is basically composed of the same participants as above. It is, therefore, unlikely that a consensus on amendments to this compulsory specification will be reached soon.

Textiles

The only compulsory specifications in this domain are

- VC 8032 (1982)—Personal Flotation Aids which covers the compulsory safety requirements for life jackets and
- VC 8033 (1997)—Compulsory specification for Child-Restraining Devices for use in Motor Vehicles.

There are no other car seat belt regulations. In contrast, the EU for example, requires by law seat belts are to be tested every five years.

However, textile safety is often addressed indirectly. For example, legislation regulating the transport of hazardous substances includes safety requirements for protective clothing. The South African National Building Regulations include fire safety requirements that regulate carpets, curtains, and upholstery in buildings.

On the textile labeling side, two SABS 1992 Codes of Practice were made compulsory in 2001. These Codes of Practice were made compulsory by the Minister of Trade and Industry in terms of the Merchandise Marks Act (Act 17 of 1941) and gazetted in Government Gazette 2410 of 2000. The resulting fiber content labeling makes provision for the U.S., EU, and Australian test methods and cross references SABS ISO 1833 and SABS ISO 5088 as well as EU Directive 96/74 of 16 December 1996 on Textile Names:

- 0235 (1992)—Code of Practice—Fiber Content, Labeling of Textiles, and Textile Products and
- 011 (1992)—Code of Practice—Care Labeling of Textiles and Clothing.

Fishery Regulations

SABS Compulsory Specifications. The Minister of Trade and Industry appointed the SABS in the 1950s to regulate frozen and canned fish, canned marine mollusks, canned meat, and shellfish by way of so-called compulsory specifications. There are six SABS fishery compulsory specifications promulgated in terms of the Standards Act, i.e.,

- VC 8014 (1972) The manufacture, production, processing, or treatment of canned fish, canned fish products, and canned marine mollusks.

- VC 8015 (1972) The manufacture, production, processing, or treatment of canned crustaceans.
- VC 8021 (1974) Smoked Snoek.
- VC 8019 (1980) The manufacture, production, processing, or treatment of canned meat products.
- VC 8017 (1999) Frozen fish, frozen marine mollusks, and frozen products derived there from.
- VC 8020 (1999) Frozen Lobster and frozen lobster products.

Most of the above regulations are based on CODEX Alimentarius. Although the entire industry must comply with the SABS compulsory specifications and other regulations, not all the firms comply with HACCP requirements because all of them do not export. Half of the white fish processors are HACCP compliant while only a third of (i.e., two) canning factories are HACCP compliant. It is likely, however, that HACCP will be legislated throughout the food producing, retailing, and vending industries in the future.

Customs officials refer all imported fishery products falling under the compulsory specifications for clearance to provincial port health authorities. Health authorities will transfer the import documents to the nearest SABS office. The SABS will inspect and test representative samples of the imported consignments and will release it to importers and health authorities if the product complies with the compulsory specification. However, if the products do not comply, the SABS coordinates with the importer to decide whether the product should be re-exported or destroyed under supervision.

SABS inspectors are appointed in terms of the Standards Act and the Foodstuffs, Cosmetics, and Disinfectants Act. Tests are conducted in either state laboratories or private sector laboratories accredited by the South African National Accreditation System (SANAS). The food inspection divisions of the SABS are accredited to ISO/IEC 17020: 1998 (for the operation of various types of inspections) by SANAS. These are

- SABS—Food and Associated Industries Division—Durban Fish and Fish Products.
- SABS—Food and Associated Industries Division—Hermanus Fish and Fish Products.
- SABS—Food and Associated Industries Division—Port Elizabeth Fish and Fish Products.

- SABS—Food and Associated Industries Division—Pretoria Fish and Fish Products.
- SABS—Food and Associated Industries Division—West Coast Fish and Fish Products.
- SABS—Food and Associated Industries Division—Western Cape Fish and Fish Products.

Accredited Food Laboratories. The following laboratories are accredited by SANAS to ISO/IEC 17025 for food testing:

- Micron Laboratories Cape Town—Cape Province Microbiology and Fish testing.
- Agricultural Research Council (ARC-ANPI)—Irene Centurion—Pretoria Chemical, Microbiological, Food Testing.
- CSIR—Food, Biological, and Chemical Technology, BioChemtek Cape Town—Cape Province Chemical, Biochemical, Food Analysis.
- Plant Pathology Laboratories—Testing Food Safety, Biological Control, Postharvest Pathology.
- Woolworths Food Laboratory Cape Town—Cape Province Chemical, Microbiological, and Food Analysis.

EU Fish Export Certification. The SABS is also the competent certifying authority for exports of frozen and canned fish to the EU. It is important to note that South African exporters of frozen and canned fish to the EU are required to comply with the relevant EU Directives. This entails the implementation of HACCP rules on board fishing vessels and in factories. The SABS is also the competent authority for Namibian fishery exports to the EU. HACCP is the relevant international phytosanitary requirement in the fishing industry and is audited by SABS. The SABS performs an HACCP audit twice a year, the EU once every five years through its Veterinary and Food Inspection Office, and the United States three years through its Food and Drugs Agency (FDA).

Department of Health. The Department of Health's Food Control Directorate regulates domestic and imported chilled fish in terms of the Act on Foodstuffs, Cosmetics and Disinfectants (Act No. 54 of 1972). However, the monitoring and surveillance is the responsibility of the provincial and local authorities. The nine Provincial Health Departments must also enforce Regulation R 918 of 1999/07/29 governing the general hygiene of food

premises so as to ensure that fishery products are sold to the public in a hygienic environment.

National Department of Agriculture. The NDA regulates the import of live freshwater fish and tropical fish in terms of the Pest Act (Act 36 of 1983). Prior to import importers must obtain an import permit from the NDA. Only fish on the NDA's approved list is allowed into South Africa. Each consignment shall be accompanied by a health certificate issued by a veterinarian who is a full-time employee of the Government of the exporting country stating that the fish is free from diseases and parasites with special reference to the following diseases: Infectious haematopoletic necrosis; Epizootic haematopoletic necrosis; Oncorhynchus masou virus disease, Viral haemorrhagic septiceamia, and Spring viraemia of carp.

When the consignment arrives at the port of entry in South Africa it is detained for so-called plant inspection. Plant inspectors of the NDA carry out a visual inspection of the fish and, if acceptable they are sent to a State Veterinary quarantine station for the required period. Accompanying water is disposed of under surveillance or disinfected. There is a curious overlap between the NDA and the different provincial authorities. When importing live freshwater fish one is obliged to obtain a permit from the provincial authorities, as the fish is "moving across provincial borders." The provincial authorities check their list of so-called wanted and unwanted fish to establish whether the species may enter the province. The provincial veterinarians assess the risk based on ecological considerations, water contamination issues, etc. It is interesting to note that they do not evaluate whether or not the fish is free of disease. Furthermore, not all the provincial authorities are equally strict in enforcing the permit requirements. Retailers and importers often approach the less efficient provincial authorities to obtain permits that then allows for nationwide distribution.

The NDA's Directorate: Agricultural Resource Conservation selects sites for aquaculture development in terms of the Conservation of Agriculture Resources Act (Act 43 of 1983).

Department of Environmental Affairs and Tourism. The Department of Environmental Affairs' Marine and Coastal Management section issues permits for all import and export consignments of fishery products. This is done in terms of Regulation 27(e) and (f) of the Marine Living Resources Act.

Fruit Industries

Regulations for deciduous fruit are specific with regards to the following:

- General standards and requirements for deciduous fruit,
- Standards and requirements for deciduous fruit, excluding deciduous fruit intended for industrial processing,
- Standards and requirements for deciduous fruit intended for industrial processing and illustrated quality factors.

Table 4.24 shows the different amendments and annexes related to the Agricultural Product Standards Act, 1990 (Act No. 119 of 1990) pertaining to specific deciduous crops.

The standards regulations regarding citrus are divided into.

general standards and requirements for citrus fruit and

specific standards and requirements for citrus fruit.

See Table 4.25 for different standards and requirements, as well as annexes applicable to citrus exports.

The avocado regulations consist of requirements for approval, quality standards, containers, packing requirements, marking requirements, sampling procedures, methods of inspection and chemical treatment.

The mango regulations consist of: general standards and requirements for mangoes (definitions, scope and requirements for approval), standards and requirements for mangoes excluding mangoes intended for industrial processing (quality standards, containers, packing requirements, marking requirements, sampling procedures, methods of inspection and chemical treatment) and standards and requirements for mangoes intended for industrial processing (quality standards, containers, packing requirements, marking requirements, sampling procedures, and chemical treatment).

For amendments and annexes to standards regulations applicable to avocados and mangoes see Table 4.26.

Meat and Livestock Industry

With few exceptions, meat and livestock industry are subject to the same requirements as far as legislation and quality are concerned. There are a number of Acts applicable to the meat and livestock industry:

- The Health Act (Act 63 of 1977)
- The Foodstuffs, Cosmetics and Disinfectants Act (Act 54 of 1972)
- The Meat Safety Act (Act 40 of 2000)
- The Animal Improvement Act (Act 62 of 1998)
- The Livestock Brands Act (Act 87 of 1962)
- The Fertilizers, Farm Feeds, Agricultural Remedies and Stock Remedies Act (Act 36 of 1947)

Table 4.24 Annexes to Standards Regulations and Amendments Related to
Specific Deciduous Crops

Crop	Amendments	Annex
Apples	No. R. 2480 of 19 November 1999 (1998–02) No. R. 6798 of 22 December 2000 (1998–03) No. R. 2371 of 14 December 2001 (1998–04)	Permissible cultivars; Quality Standards; Maximum permissible deviations by number; Maximum residue limits for permissible chemicals (all classes); Over ripeness standard (all classes); Minimum ripeness: pip color (all classes); Minimum ripeness: the iodine test (all classes); Quality standards applicable to apples intended for industrial processing; Maximum permissible deviations by number applicable to apples intended for industrial processing.
Pears	No. R. 1288 of 29 October 1999 (1998–02) No. R. 4634 of 17 November 2000 (1998–03) No. R. 2053 of 21 September 2001 (1998–04)	Permissible cultivars (all classes); Quality standards; Maximum permissible deviations by number; Average minimum and maximum pressure readings in kilogram; Maximum residue limits for permissible chemicals (all classes); Quality standards applicable to pears intended for industrial processing; Maximum permissible deviations by number applicableto pears intended for industrial processing.
Peaches	No. R. 19873 of 1 April 1999 (1998–02) No. R. 1244 of 22 October 1999 (1998–03) No. R. 4214 of 10 November 2000 (1998–04) No. R. 2026 of 21 September 2001 (1998–05)	Permissible cultivars (All classes); Quality standards; Maturity indices; Maximum permissible deviations by number; diameter groups and diameter codes (All classes); Maximum residue limits for permissible chemicals (All classes); Illustrations applicable to peaches and nectarines: Extra Class; Illustrations applicable to peaches and nectarines: Class 1; Illustrations applicable to peaches and nectarines: Class 2.
Table Grapes	No. R. 1242 of 22 October 1999 (1998–02) No. R. 4174 of 3 November 2000 (1998–03) No. R. 1884 of 24 August 2001 (1998–04)	Permissible cultivars (All classes); Quality standards; Size of berries; Maturity indices; Maximum permissible deviations by number; Maximum permissible deviations by number per bunch; Temperature correction table where the refractometer is used at temperatures other than 20°C; Maximum residue limits for permissible chemicals (All classes); Illustrations applicable to table grapes: Extra Class; Illustrations applicable to table grapes: Class 1; Illustrations applicable to table grapes: Class 2.

Source: NDA 2002.

Table 4.25 Standards and Requirements for Citrus Fruits

Crop	Standards and Requirements	Annexes
All citrus	Definitions, scope, requirements for approval, and chemical treatment	Blemish standards
Grapefruit and Pummelos	Quality standards, Containers, Packing requirements, Marking requirements, Sampling procedures, Methods of inspection.	Quality standards, Maximum permissible deviations by number, Limits for scale, Limits for seed content, Flesh diameter, Size references and diameter, Cultivar indication on containers, Brix-hydrometer reading-correction tables, Temperature correction table—Refractometer, Illustrations only applicable to grapefruit and pummelos.
Kumquats	Quality standards, Containers, Packing requirements, Marking requirements, Sampling procedures, Methods of inspection.	Quality standards, Maximum permissible deviations by number.
Lemons	Quality standards, Containers, Packing requirements, Marking requirements, Sampling procedures, Methods of inspection.	Quality standards, Maximum permissible deviations by number, Limits for scale, Limits for seed content, Size references and diameter requirements. Illustrations only applicable to lemons.
Oranges and Seville oranges	Quality standards, Containers, Packing requirements, Marking requirements, Sampling procedures, Methods of inspection.	Quality standards, Maximum permissible deviations by number, Limits for scale, Limits for seed content, Cultivar indication on containers, Brix-hydrometer reading-correction tables, Temperature correction table—Refractometer, Illustrations only applicable to oranges and Seville oranges.
Soft citrus	Quality standards, Containers, Packing requirements, Marking requirements, Sampling procedures, Methods of inspection.	Quality standards, Maximum permissible deviations by number, Limits for scale, Limits for seed content, Cultivar indication on containers, Brix-hydrometer reading-correction tables, Temperature correction table—Refractometer, Illustrations only applicable to soft citrus.
Citrus for industrial processing	Quality standards, Containers, Packing requirements, Marking requirements, Sampling procedures.	Quality standards applicable for citrus intended for industrial processing, Maximum permissible deviations by number applicable to citrus fruit intended for industrial processing.

Note: Amendment No. R. 1209 of 5 May 2000 (1999–2002) is applicable to all citrus.
Source: Website NDA, Subdirectorate: Quality Control (2002).

Table 4.26 Annexes to Standards Regulations and Amendments Related to Specific Avocados and Mangoes

Crop	Amendments	Annexes
Avocados	No. R. 530 of 9 April 1999 (1998–02) No. R. 91 of 4 February 2000 (1998–03) No. R. 114 of 12 January 2001 (1998–04) No. R. 2380 of 21 December 2001 (1998–05)	Permissible cultivars, Quality standards, Maximum permissible deviations by number, Mass range and size code, Maximum residue limits for permissible chemicals
Mangoes	No. R. 2686 of 17 December 1999 (1997–02) No. R. 21733 of 17 November 2000 (1997–03) No. R. 2217 of 2 November 2001 (1997–04)	Mangoes not intended for industrial processing: permissible cultivars, quality standards, maximum permissible deviations by number, mass range and size code, maximum residue limits for permissible chemicals. Mangoes for industrial processing: quality standards, maximum permissible deviations by number.

Source: Website NDA, Subdirectorate: Quality Control (2002).

Annex L Foodstuffs, Cosmetics and Disinfectants Act, 1972 (Act 54 of 1972)

List of Regulations

- No. R. 2627—12 December 1986
  Regulations: jam, conserve, marmalade and jelly
- No. R. 2527—13 November 1987
  Regulations: governing emulsifiers, stabilizers and thickeners and the amounts thereof that foodstuffs may contain
- No. R. 313—16 February 1990
  Regulations: governing tolerances for fungus-produced toxins in foodstuffs
- No. R. 952—6 August 1999
  Regulations: relating to perishable foodstuffs
  Definition: declaration of certain perishable foodstuffs
- No. R. 1931—17 August 1990
  Regulations: governing radio activity in foodstuffs
  Table
- No. R. 2486—26 October 1990
  Regulations: relating to baking powder and chemical leavening substances
- No. R. 2718—23 November 1990
  Regulations: governing the composition and labeling of raw boerewors, raw species sausage and raw mixed species sausage
- No. R. 2554—25 October 1991
  Regulations: prohibiting guargum as a foodstuff

- No. R. 3128—20 December 1991
  Regulations: relating to the use of sweeteners in foodstuffs
- No. R. 1809—3 July 1992
  Regulations: governing the maximum limits for veterinary medicine and stock remedy residues that may be present in foodstuffs
- No. R. 1468—13 August 1993
  Regulations: relating to herbs and spices
- No. R. 2034—29 October 1993
  Regulations: governing the labeling and advertising of foodstuffs
- No. R. 246—11 February 1994
  Regulations: governing the maximum limits for pesticide residues that may be present in foodstuffs
- No. R. 1518—9 September 1994
  Regulations: relating to metals in foodstuffs
- No. R. 996—7 July 1995
  Regulations: relating to salt
- No. R. 382—8 March 1996
  Regulations: enforcement by local authorities
- No. R. 1008—21 June 1996
  Regulations: relating to food colorants
- No. R. 1316—16 August 1996
  Regulations: relating to edible fats and oils
- No. R. 692—16 May 1997
  Regulations: governing microbiological standards for Foodstuffs and related matters
- No. R. 2507/1982
  Regulations: anti-caking agents—amounts that may be used in foodstuffs

- No. R. 965/1977
  Regulations: preservatives and antioxidants
- No. R. 1600/1983
  Regulations: irradiated foodstuffs
- No. R. 2162/1973
  Regulations: duties of inspectors and analysts
- No. R. 1769/1985
  Regulations: soft drinks
- No. R. 92/1986
  Regulations: mayonnaise and other salad dressings
- No. R. 1555/1997
  Regulations: milk and dairy products
- No. R. 2839/1979
  Regulations: enrichment of maize meal
- No. R. 230/1977
  Regulations: mineral hydrocarbons in foodstuffs
- NO. R. 2064/1973
  Regulations: sea food
- No. R. 1466/1987
  Regulations: tolerances for certain seeds in certain agricultural products

- No. R. 2417/1987
  Regulations: use of certain food additives in certain wheaten and rye products
- No. R. 2870/1981
  Regulations: substances in wine, other fermented beverages and spirits—additives, amounts and tolerances
- No. R. 115/1986
  Regulations: acids, bases and salts—the amounts thereof that foodstuffs may contain
- No. R. 219/1975
  Regulations: restriction on the sale of food additives containing nitrite and/or nitrate and other substances
- No. R. 2037/1975
  Regulations: manufactured or processed meat products
- No. R. 1130/1984
  Regulations: foodstuffs for infants, young children and children
- No. 575—28 March 1930
  Regulations under the food, drugs and disinfectants act No. 13 of 1929.

Annex M SABS Levies

Table 4.27 Inspection Fees at Acknowledged Inspection Point

Kind of Product	Inspection Fees
Apples	30c per container in a consignment
Apricots	25c per container in a consignment
Avocados	25c per container in a consignment
Buckwheat	15c per 100 kilogram or part thereof in a consignment
Butter/Botter	15c per kilogram or part thereof in a consignment
Canned foods	50c per 100 kilogram or part thereof, in a consignment, with a minimum of 50c per inspection
Canned fruit	50c per 100 kilogram or part thereof, in a consignment, with a minimum of 50c per inspection
Canned mushrooms	50c per 100 kilogram or part thereof, in a consignment, with a minimum of 50c per inspection
Canned vegetables	50c per 100 kilogram or part thereof, in a consignment, with a minimum of 50c per inspection
Canned pasta	50c per 100 kilogram or part thereof, in a consignment, with a minimum of 50c per inspection
Cheese	15c per kilogram or part thereof in a consignment
Cherries	25c per container in a consignment
Citrus fruit	20c per container in a consignment
Citrus fruit for inland inspections	30c per container in a consignment
Dry beans	15c per kilogram or part thereof in a consignment
Dairy products	15c per 100 kilogram or part thereof in a consignment
Dried fruit	R1.30 per 100 kilogram or part thereof in a consignment, with a minimum of 95c per inspection
Eggs	15c per kilogram or part thereof in a consignment
Feed products	15c per 100 kilogram or part thereof in a consignment
Fresh cut flowers and ornamental foliage	15c per kilogram or part thereof in a consignment
Frozen fruit and vegetables	80c per 100 kilogram or part thereof in a consignment
Fruit, excluding citrus fruit, and certain deciduous fruit (as defined in the regulations promulgated under section 4 of the Act)	25c per container in a consignment
Grapes	25c per container in a consignment
Grass seed	15c per 100 kilogram or part thereof in a consignment
Groundnuts	R3.30 per 100 kilogram or part thereof in a consignment
Kernels: Apricot and peach kernels	25c per 10 kilogram or part thereof in a consignment
Kiwifruit	25c per container in a consignment
Leguminous seeds	15c per 100 kilogram or part thereof in a consignment
Lesser known types of maize	15c per 100 kilogram or part thereof in a consignment
Litchis	15c per kilogram or part thereof in a consignment
Maize	15c per 100 kilogram or part thereof in a consignment
Maize products	15c per 100 kilogram or part thereof in a consignment
Mangoes	25c per container in a consignment

(continued)

Table 4.27 (Continued)

Kind of Product	Inspection Fees
Meat	
(a) Beef:	
(i) Carcasses	25c per kilogram or part thereof in a consignment
(ii) Cuts not packed in containers	25c per kilogram or part thereof in a consignment
(iii) Cuts packed in containers	25c per kilogram or part thereof in a consignment
(b) Veal, mutton, lamb, goat, and kid's meat	
(i) Carcasses	25c per kilogram or part thereof in a consignment
(ii) Cuts not packed in containers	25c per kilogram or part thereof in a consignment
(iii) Cuts packed in containers	25c per kilogram or part thereof in a consignment
(c) Pork	
(i) Carcasses	25c per kilogram or part thereof in a consignment
(ii) Cuts not packed in containers	25c per kilogram or part thereof in a consignment
(iii) Whole baconer sides or middles	25c per kilogram or part thereof in a consignment
(iv) Cuts packed in containers	25c per kilogram or part thereof in a consignment
Melons	25c per container in a consignment
Mohair	20c per bale, case or carton in a consignment
Oil seeds	15c per 100 kilogram or part thereof in a consignment
Onions	25c per 10 kilogram or part thereof in a consignment
Pears	30c per container in a consignment
Peaches and nectarines	25c per container in a consignment
Pineapples	35c per container in a consignment
Plums and prunes	25c per container in a consignment
Potatoes	20c per 10 kilogram or part thereof in a consignment
Poultry meat	25c per kilogram or part thereof in a consignment
Sorghum	15c per 100 kilogram or part thereof in a consignment
Strawberries	25c per container in a consignment
Tea/Tee: Honeybush and Rooibos	
(a) Presented for visual inspection and laboratory analysis	R20.00 per 100 kilogram or part thereof in a consignment
(b) Presented for visual inspection only	R2.00 per 100 kilogram or part thereof in a consignment
Tobacco/Tabak	20c per bale, case or carton in a consignment
Vegetables (excluding onions and potatoes)	20c per 10 kilogram or part thereof in a consignment
Watermelons	25c per container or part thereof in a consignment
Wheat	15c per 100 kilogram or part thereof in a consignment

Source: SABS.

Table 4.28 Other Inspection Fees

Function	Fees Payable
Inspection for export at a place other than an acknowledged inspection point and an inspection on request	(a) R60.00 per half hour or part thereof, including travelling time, spent on the inspection concerned by each inspector; and (b) R35.00 per half hour or part thereof, including travelling time, spent on the inspection concerned by each assistant of an inspector referred to in subparagraph (a)
Inspection certificate and certification of grape juice and concentrated must for export	(a) R45.00 per application; plus/R45.00 per aansoek; plus (b) R15.00 per hectoliter or part thereof, up to the first 100 hectoliter; plus (c) R20.00 per certificate

Table 4.29 Laboratory Fees [Reg. 3]

Laboratory Analysis	Fees Payable
Residue analysis	R270.00 per sample
Sulfur dioxide analysis	R95.00 per sample
Mycotoxins	R195.00 per sample
Diverse analysis	R190.00 per hour

Microbiological inspection	(a) Qualitative inspection: R40.00 per sample
	(b) Serological verification of microorganisms:
	    (i) *Salmonela:* R80.00 per verification
	    (ii) *E. Coli:* R70.00 per verification
	    (iii) Total bacterial count: R40.00 per sample

Table 4.30 Appeal Fees: Export [Reg. 4]

Kind of Product	Fees Payable
Apples	R140.00 per consignment
Apricots	R140.00 per consignment
Avocados	R120.00 per consignment
Buckwheat	R120.00 per consignment
Butter	R230.00 for the first production lot and R40,00 for each subsequent production lot in the same consignment
Canned food	R140.00 per consignment or production group
Canned fruit	R140.00 per consignment or production group
Canned mushrooms	R140.00 per consignment or production group
Canned vegetables	R140.00 per consignment or production group
Canned pasta	R140.00 per consignment or production group
Cheese	R230.00 for the first production lot and R40,00 for each subsequent production lot in the same consignment
Cherries	R170.00 per consignment
Citrus fruit/Sitrusvrugte	(a) R330.00 per consignment in respect to separate consignments; or (b) R330.00 for the first consignment plus R155,00 for each additional consignment in respect to a group of consignments which were consigned on the same day
Dairy products (excluding butter and cheese)	R140.00 per consignment
Dried fruit	R215.00 per consignment or production group
Dry beans	R120.00 per consignment
Eggs	R120.00 per consignment
Feed products	R120.00 per consignment
Fresh cut flowers and ornamental foliage	R120.00 per consignment
Frozen fruit and vegetables	R140.00 per consignment or production group
Fruit, excluding citrus fruit and certain deciduous fruit (as defined in the regulations promulgated under section 4 of the Act)	R120.00 per consignment
Grapes	R230.00 per consignment
Grass seed	R120.00 per consignment
Groundnuts	R120.00 per consignment
Kernels: Apricot and peach kernels	R110.00 per consignment
Kiwi fruit	R120.00 per consignment
Leguminous seeds	R120.00 per consignment
Lesser known types of maize	R120.00 per consignment
Litchis	R120.00 per consignment
Maize	R120.00 per consignment
Maize products	R120.00 per consignment
Mangoes	R120.00 per consignment

(continued)

Table 4.30 (Continued)

Kind of Product	Fees Payable
Meat/Vleis:	
(a) Beef	
(i) Carcasses	R120.00 for the first carcass or part thereof, plus R45,00 for each additional carcass or part thereof
(ii) Cuts not packed in containers	R25.00 for each separate cut, with a minimum of R170,00
(iii) Cuts packed in containers	R25.00 per container, with a minimum of R170,00
(b) Veal, mutton, lamb, goat and kid's meat	
(i) Carcasses	R60.00 for the first carcass plus R30,00 for each additional carcass
(ii) Cuts not packed in containers	R25.00 per kilogram with a minimum of R170,00
(iii) Cuts packed in containers	R25.00 per container, with a minimum of R170,00
(b) Pork	
(i) Carcasses	R95.00 for the first carcass plus R40,00 for each additional carcass
(ii) Cuts not packed in containers	R25.00 for each separate cut with a minimum of R170,00
(iii) Whole baconer sides or middles	R25.00 for each whole baconer side or middle, with a minimum of R170,00
(iv) Cuts packed in containers	R25.00 per container, with a minimum of R170,00
Melons	R120.00 per consignment
Oil Seeds	R120.00 per consignment
Onions	R120.00 per consignment
Pears	R140.00 per consignment
Peaches and nectarines	R140.00 per consignment
Pineapples	R110.00 per consignment
Plums and prunes	R140.00 per consignment
Potatoes	R140.00 per consignment
Poultry meat	R140.00 per consignment
Rooibos tea	R80.00 per consignment
Sorghum	R120.00 per consignment
Strawberries	R110.00 per consignment
Tea/Tee: Honeybush	R80.00 per consignment
Tobacco	R155.00 per consignment
Vegetables (excluding potatoes and onions)	R120.00 per consignment
Watermelons	R120.00 per consignment
Wheat	R120.00 per consignment

Source: SABS.

Annex N PPECB Levies

PPECB—Imposition of Levies on Perishable Products

In terms of section 17(i) of the Perishable Products Export Control Act, 1983 (Act No. 9 of 1983), the Board imposes the following levies, in respect to each of the under-mentioned perishable products, as defined in section 1 (i) of the above mentioned Act, which may be exported from the Republic of South Africa. These levies will be valid from 1 January 2002 until further notice.

Product	Levy	Unit
Avocados	R14.80	per pallet
Citrus (conventional)	R 5.75	per pallet
Citrus (containerized)*	R 6.80	per pallet
Citrus (containerized inland)	R 8.90	per pallet
Deciduous (conventional)	R 5.25	per pallet
Deciduous (containerized)*	R 6.30	per pallet
Deciduous (containerized inland)	R 8.40	per pallet
Litchis	R16.10	per pallet
Mangoes	R16.10	per pallet
Prickly pears	R16.10	per pallet
Melons	R14.30	per pallet
Pineapples	R15,00	per pallet
Other fresh fruit	R0,0560	per carton

* Rate will apply to all pallets containerized within a radius of 20 kilometers from one of the three export harbors in the Republic of South Africa, namely Durban, Port Elizabeth, and Cape Town.
All levies by pallet will be based on the standard ISO pallet size.
All above levies are exempt from VAT.

	6M Container	12M Container	Conventional (per kilogram)
Concentrates	R200.00	R265.00	R0.0106
Dairy products	R140.00	R200.00	R0.0166
Fresh vegetables	R170.00	R265.00	R0.0133
Frozen fruit and Vegetables	R140.00	R200.00	R0.0122
Flowers and proteas	R 80.00	R160.00	R0.0222
Maize and grain	R110.00	R160.00	R0.0085
Meat	R130.00	R190.00	R0.0085
Marine	R130.00	R150.00	R0.0082
Chocolate	R 80.00	R160.00	R0.0044
All other products	R140.00	R200.00	R0.0085
All perishable products exported by air			R0.0085

All levies by kilogram will be based on gross weight.
All above levies are exempt from VAT.

Container Inspection Fees

The fees listed below exclude any travelling, kilometer, and incidental costs, which will be charged separately for all services rendered outside a radius of 20 kilometers from a PPECB port (harbor) office.

	Week days (per unit)	Weekends/Public Holidays (per unit)
Integral containers:		
Cleanliness inspection	R7.00	R14.00
Technical inspection	R7.00	R14.00
Ducted containers:		
Special callouts	R7.65	R15.30
Hour and or kilometer rates as listed below.		

All above levies are subject to 14 percent VAT.

Other Fees

The fees listed below exclude any travelling and incidental costs, which will be charged for separately.

Conventional shipments under Cold Treatment Protocols:	R5.80 per pallet in addition to normal PPECB levy
Containerized shipments under Cold Treatment Protocols:	Hourly rate as listed below
Calibration of vessel temperature recording equipment:	R6 350.00 per vessel (depending on the number of cooling compartments).
Inspection and registration of Refrigerated Road Motor Transport:	R265.00 per vehicle inspected (depending on structure of vehicle).
Stuffing report:	R115.00 per request
Redo of special shipment documentation	R250.00 per request
Inspection and registration of Cold Storage Facilities	Hourly rate as listed below
Calibration of onboard container data loggers and portable data loggers for use in sterilization shipments	R35.00 per calibration

All above levies are subject to 14 percent VAT.

Agricultural Product Standards

In terms of section 17(i) of the Perishable Products Export Control Act, 1983 (Act No. 9 of 1983), and by virtue of the Board's appointment as Assignee in terms of Regulation 1978 of the Agricultural Products Standards Act, 1990 (Act No. 119 of 1990), the Board hereby imposes the following levies and tariffs in respect to each of the products specified in the tables, which may be exported from the Republic of South Africa. These levies will be valid from 1 January 2002 until further notice.

Inspection Fees (Agricultural Product Standards):

Products	Inspection Fee
All canned products	0.51c per kilogram or part thereof in a consignment
All dairy products	6.5c per kilogram or part thereof in a consignment
All flowers	10.7c per kilogram or part thereof in a consignment
All fresh vegetables (excluding asparagus)	1.88c per kilogram or part thereof in a consignment
All frozen fruit and vegetables	0.85c per kilogram or part thereof in a consignment
All grain and grain products (excluding maize)	0.11c per kilogram or part thereof in a consignment
All red meat	2.20c per kilogram or part thereof in a consignment
All other meat	2.20c per kilogram or part thereof in a consignment
Avocados	18.6c per container in a consignment
Citrus fruit*	17.6c per container in a consignment
Citrus fruit (small cartons less than 5 kilograms)*	7.4c per container in a consignment
Citrus fruit (small cartons less than 5 kilograms) for inland inspection	10.6c per container in a consignment
Citrus fruit for inland inspection	27.0c per container in a consignment
Citrus fruit in bulk bins*	17.6c per 15.2 kilograms or part thereof
Citrus fruit in bulk bins for inland inspection	27.0c per 15.2 kilograms or part thereof
Egg products	5.2c per kilogram or part thereof in a consignment
Grapes	23.5c per container in a consignment
Litchis	7.0c per kilogram or part thereof in a consignment
Mangoes	22.2c per container in a consignment
Pineapples	25.4c per container in a consignment
Pome fruit	24.8c per container in a consignment
Pome fruit in bulk bins	24.8c per 12.5 kilograms or part thereof
Stone fruit	21.2c per container in a consignment
All other fresh fruit	24.4c per container in a consignment
All other products	2.44c per kilogram or part thereof in a consignment
Red tea	2.76c per kilogram or part thereof in a consignment
Maize (bulk loading at harbors)	0.08c per kilogram or part thereof in a consignment
Maize	0.11c per kilogram or part thereof in a consignment
Concentrates	0.73c per kilogram or part thereof in a consignment
Melons	24.0c per container in a consignment
Onions	1.88c per kilogram or part thereof in a consignment
Potatoes	1.88c per kilogram or part thereof in a consignment
Groundnuts	R28.60 per metric ton in a consignment

* Rate will apply to all inspections done within a radius of 20 kilometers from one of the three export harbors in the Republic of South Africa, namely Durban, Port Elizabeth, and Cape Town.
All above levies are subject to 14 percent VAT.

Inspections on request	Published inspection levy or hour rate (dependent on the site of inspection) plus R2.25 per kilometer
Kilometer rate	R2.25 per kilometer
Hour rates	Rate per hour
Normal Time (8 am to 5 pm weekdays)	R190.00 per hour
Normal Overtime	R212.00 per hour
Sundays and Public holidays	R232.00 per hour

In all instances where a service is delivered, the PPECB will retain the right to, at its discretion, charge the hourly rates above and or the kilometer rate, instead of the published fees above. For administrative purposes these hourly and kilometer rates may be adapted to an equivalent tariff per unit.

Where hourly rates are charged, a minimum fee for a one-hour call out will be charged. Thereafter time will be charged in half-hour segments that is R95 per half hour or part thereof. The same principle will be applied to overtime and Sunday time.

All above levies are subject to 14 percent VAT.

Compositional quality (dairy products and oilseeds)	R505.00 per analysis (or less, depending on the complexity of the analysis) plus VAT
Pesticide residue analysis	The relevant fees as published by the State laboratories. All courier and transport costs relating to getting the samples to the respective State Laboratories, will be borne by the party requesting the inspection.

Source: Gazette number 22980 dated 31 December 2001.

Annex O Electrical Goods Levies

Description of Commodity	Unit	Tariff
Portable television antennae	Item	R0.09
TVs, Hi-Fi systems, VCRs, radio, and audio-visual equipment, etc.	Item	R0.09
Lighting appliances, for example fluorescent, fixed, portable, band-held lamps, lighting chains, flood lights, Christmas tree lighting sets, etc.	item	R0.09
Lamp-holders	100 items	R1.89
Starters for tubular fluorescent lamps	1000 items	R9.79
Incandescent lamps (globes)	1000 items	R14.40
Plugs	100 items	R0.73
Socket outlets	100 items	R3.90
Socket outlet adaptors including "Janus" couplers	100 items	R2.16
Switches for fixed installations	100 items	R3.75
Switches for appliances	100 items	R3.75
Cord sets with plug and appliance coupler	Unit	R0.18
Cord extension sets—without switches	Unit	R0.36
Cord extension sets—with switches	Unit	R0.50
Cord extension sets—with switches and MCB	Unit	R1.28
Cord extension sets—with switches and ELPU	Unit	R3.49
Flexible cords	100 meter	R0.83
Molded case circuit-breakers: Single pole	Item	R0.81
Molded case circuit-breakers: Double pole	Item	R3.00
Molded case circuit-breakers: Triple pole	Item	R1.58
Molded case circuit-breakers: Four pole	Item	R1.58
Electric tools (hand-held power tools, lathes, saws, grinders, Compressors, etc.), welding machines, electric gardening and Agricultural equipment	Item	R0.09
Earth leakage protection units: Single phase	Item	R4.80
Earth leakage protection units: Multi phase	Item	R7.40
Appliance couplers	100 items	R3.20
Appliances: (for example, vacuum cleaners, heaters, electric irons, heated blankets, fans, Hairdryers, cooling appliances, kettles, refrigerators, stoves, Dishwashers, washing machines, air-condition units, motor-operated Appliances, catering equipment, geysers, instantaneous water hearers, Microwave ovens, soldering irons, battery chargers, etc.)	Item	R0.09
Information technology equipment (for example computers, monitors, printers, copiers, fax machines, scanners, battery chargers for I.T.E. telephones, PABX, modems, power supplies, ACIDC adaptors, Electric amplifiers, etc.)	Item	R0.09

Source: SABS Regulatory Division.

Annex P Fishery Levies

Table 4.31 Fishery levies

Description of Fishery Commodity	Unit	Tariff
Canned crustaceans—imports	1000 kilogram	R230.00
Canned fish and canned fish products (other than fish paste)—imports	1000 kilogram	Sliding scale D
Canned fish and canned fish products (other than fish paste)—RSA	1000 kilogram	Sliding scale D
Canned marine mollusks (other than abalone)—imports	1000 kilogram	R230.00
Canned marine mollusks (other than abalone)—RSA	1000 kilogram	R230.00
Fish paste—imports	1000 kilogram	R49.00
Fish paste—RSA	1000 kilogram	R49.00
Frozen fish and frozen fish products—imports	1000 kilogram	Sliding scale B
Frozen fish and frozen fish products—RSA	1000 kilogram	Sliding scale B
Frozen unpacked (loose) fish—RSA	1000 kilogram	Sliding scale C
Frozen marine mollusks and frozen marine mollusk products—imports	1000 kilogram	R235.00
Frozen marine mollusks and frozen marine mollusk products—RSA	1000 kilogram	R235.00
Frozen rock lobster tails—imports	10 kilogram	Sliding scale G
Frozen rock lobster tails, leg, and breast meat—RSA	10 kilogram	Sliding scale G
Frozen whole rock lobster, cooked and uncooked—imports	30 kilogram	Sliding scale G
Frozen whole rock lobster, cooked and uncooked—RSA	30 kilogram	Sliding scale G
Smoked snoek—RSA	1000 kilogram	R68.70
Frozen shrimps, prawns, and langoustines—imports	1000 kilogram	Sliding scale E
Frozen shrimps, prawns and langoustines—RSA	1000 kilogram	Sliding scale E
Frozen crabs—imports	1000 kilogram	R45.75
Frozen crabs—RSA	1000 kilogram	R45.75
Frozen cephalopods—imports	1000 kilogram	Sliding scale F
Frozen cephalopods—RSA	1000 kilogram	Sliding scale F
Frozen mussels—imports	1000 kilogram	Sliding scale H
Frozen mussels—RSA	1000 kilogram	Sliding scale H
Cannes abalone—imports	1000 kilogram	R325.00
Cannes abalone—RSA	1000 kilogram	R325.00

Source: SABS Food Standards Section, Pretoria.

Table 4.32 Fishery Sliding Scale—Tariffs Per Unit (1000 kilogram)
(1 Unit = 10 kilogram or 30 kilogram)

Sliding Scale A	Sliding Scale B
R330.00 per unit for first two units	R330.00 per unit for 1st two units
R279.00 per unit for 3rd to 12th unit	R260.00 per unit for 3rd to 12th unit
R77.00 per unit for 13th to 62nd unit	R54.50 per unit for 13th to 62nd unit
R69.00 per unit for 63rd to 1000th unit	R13.60 per unit for 63rd to 562nd unit
R37.50 per unit for 1001st to 3000th unit	R8.45 per unit for 563rd to 2,562nd unit
R21.80 per unit for each subsequent unit	R6.00 per unit for 2,563rd to 7,562nd unit
	R2.85 per unit for each subsequent unit

Sliding Scale C	Sliding Scale D
R198.00 per unit for 1st two units	R330.00 per unit for 1st two units
R156.00 per unit for 3rd to 12th unit	R275.00 per unit for 3rd to 12th unit
R32.70 per unit for 13th to 62nd unit	R110.00 per unit for 13th to 62nd unit
R8.16 per unit for 63rd to 562nd unit	R30.00 per unit for 63rd to 562nd unit
R5.07 per unit for 563rd to 5,562nd unit	R20.70 per unit for 563rd to 5,562nd unit
R3.60 per unit for 5,563rd to 20,562nd unit	R17.75 per unit for 5,563rd to 20,562nd unit
R1.70 per unit for each subsequent unit.	R9.53 per unit for each subsequent unit

Sliding Scale E	Sliding Scale F
R385.00 per unit for 1st two units	R330.00 per unit for 1st two units
R327.00 per unit for 3rd to 12th unit	R260.00 per unit for 3rd to 12th unit
R82.80 per unit for each subsequent unit	R48.50 per unit for 13th to 62nd unit
	R27.80 per unit for each subsequent unit

Sliding Scale G	Sliding Scale H
R110.00 per unit for 1st ten units	R223.00 per unit for 1st twenty units
R4.40 per unit for each subsequent unit	R87.00 per unit for 21st to 50th units
	R38.00 per unit for each subsequent unit

Source: SABS Food Standards Section, Pretoria.

Annex Q Red Meat Case Study

Company Profile

South African Natural Beef can be regarded as a pioneer in the field of quality assurance from the farm to the consumer or client through its "Country-Reared" program. It was the first company in the meat industry to gain ISO 9002 and HACCP certification and applies HACCP requirements to each of the suppliers of raw products to the company.

The company is totally committed to the Quality Assurance Program to ensure that all products supplied by the company conform to a strict set of quality criteria. All employees and all suppliers are held accountable and responsible in their specific areas of competence to ensure that the quality criteria are adhered to.

Scope of the System

The South African Natural Beef Quality Management System covers the production, slaughtering, maturing and processing of fresh meat. The company ensures that this policy is understood, implemented and maintained at all levels of the company's operations.

The system includes procedures to trace livestock from birth until slaughter as well as to provide suitable identification and traceability of products during all stages of production, usage and delivery.

Process Control

The South African Natural Beef management system identifies and plans the production, handling, marketing and transport processes which directly affect quality and ensures that these processes are carried out under controlled conditions which include:

- Documented procedures defining the manner of production, where the absence of such procedures could adversely affect product quality.
- Use of suitable production equipment and a suitable working environment.
- Compliance with industry standards or codes, quality plans and documented procedures.
- Monitoring and control of suitable process parameters and product characteristics.
- The approval of processes and equipment as appropriate.
- Criteria for staff to carry out procedures.
- Suitable maintenance of equipment.

Inspection and Testing

South African Natural Beef has established documented inspection and testing procedures to ensure that all products conform to customer requirements. Documented procedures are in place for feeding, grazing, introduced livestock, chemical use, the use of hormones and antibiotics, pathogens, soil, water, receiving, maturing and delivery. Records are kept of all inspections and tests.

The Practical Implications of Quality Control

South African Natural beef began the implementation of its quality control system in 1996, and rapidly developed as the market leader in terms of complete quality control from conception to the retailer. The concept is in a constant state of development and milestones include the first ISO 9002 certification for a South African meat plant in 1999 and the first HACCP certification for a South African meat plant in 2001.

The road has not been smooth in terms of overcoming resistance both within the meat industry and with the authorities, and the outbreaks of Foot and Mouth disease have prevented exploitation of international marketing opportunities. Creating a culture of compliance with the highest standards in the industry has been a difficult task and has led to some conflict.

Problems with Competent Authorities

The South African Natural Beef facility has been approved for export to the European Union, and both the HACCP and ISO certificates have been issued by SGS of Belgium. There is strong demand for the product from the EU, and a contract has been signed but due to the problems experienced with the Veterinary Authorities, who, for various reasons are not prepared to certify the consignments, these deliveries have not been made. A considerable premium will be paid by the importers, and the volumes of meat processed by the plant can be increased dramatically if the authorities give the go-ahead for exports.

There is evidently a lack of communication between the National Department of Agriculture and the Provincial Department of Agriculture as far as the implementation of Veterinary requirements is concerned. The National Department of Agriculture is the Competent Authority, but inspection at abattoirs and certification of consignments is done by the Provincial Department of Agriculture. There is also no clear and concise guideline stating the requirements for approval of exports of beef to the EU. Guidelines have only been drawn up for the export of ostrich and game products.

The Provincial authorities do not have a thorough knowledge of the requirements of the importing countries and are not attuned to the requirements of the exporters.

South African Natural Beef has somewhat of a problem with the Hygiene Assessment System for Red Meat Abattoirs (HAS) as they claim that there is no system to disqualify abattoirs which do not conform to certain critical requirements such as the total absence of sterilizers for instance, which would only result in a 15 point deduction where an overall score of 65 percent is required. This could lead to a serious fall-off of quality without immediate remedial action being taken.

The Cold Chain

The HAS also allows for the chilling of meat to a deep bone temperature of 10°C, yet the Health Act which applies to cutting and boning halls which are not situated on the abattoir premises, requires that the temperature may not exceed 7 degrees C. International requirements are considerably lower at between 1 and 4 degrees C.

Because the South African Natural Beef HACCP system requires meat to be delivered at 7°C (in accordance with the relevant legislation) and meat from the abattoir only has to be chilled to 10°C, a number of consignments have been turned away, causing a great deal of animosity and a loss of income for all parties.

Culture of Quality

There is not an entrenched culture of quality among retailers or consumers in the domestic market. Consignments of meat which have been refused by South African Natural Beef for reasons of quality or hygiene have been accepted by retailers claiming to adhere to high standards. This undermines the image of high-quality meat and results in financial losses for companies committed to high standards.

Regulations do not dovetail sufficiently to allow the effective implementation of HACCP as there is a number of loopholes allowing for the lowering of standards and the ineffective implementation of the legislation allows unacceptable practices to take place. According to Mr. Spencer Watson, Vice Chairman of the South African Feedlot Association, inspection disciplines at some of the abattoirs are questionable. The industry is fragmented and does not have the courage of their convictions to support HACCP and other quality assurance systems. This makes management commitment very difficult and expensive.

Control of the Raw Product

Control of the raw product in feeds poses a problem. Recently there was a problem of mercury contamination in fish meal imported from Japan which resulted in a number of carcasses from a South African Natural Beef producer being rejected due to high mercury levels. All the control measures are on the end product and not on the raw products, which means that the producer had very little protection against such a loss. The Foodstuffs, Cosmetics and Disinfectants Act is only applicable to final products and the Farm Feeds Act does not cover residues in feed.

Conclusion

It is clear that South African Natural Beef, as a pioneer in the field of quality assurance in the meat industry in South Africa, is identifying most of the problems within the legislation and the state departments dealing with standards and quality assurance. It is also clear that the economic well-being of this enterprise will depend to a large extent on exporting their high-quality products to international niche markets where they will enjoy a premium for their unique qualities. As South Africa responds to the challenge of exporting increasing volumes of meat, these shortcomings must be addressed and rectified and the capacity must be created within state departments or the functions should be outsourced to institutions which have the capacity to provide solutions to the problems.

Annex R Veterinary Laboratories

Name	Province	Capabilities
Allerton Regional Veterinary Laboratory	Kwazulu-Natal Province	Bacteriology Serology PCR Parasitology Biochemistry Histopathology Virology Mineral Analysis Toxicology Mycology Haematology
Bloemfontein Veterinary Laboratory	Free State Province	Bacteriology Mastitis control Parasitology Post Mortems Simple Haematology Serology Toxicology
Stellenbosch Veterinary Laboratory in the Western Cape Province	Western Cape	Routine Bacteriology Virology (poultry) Serology PCR Histopathology Chemistry Biochemistry Monitoring of imported meat Abattoir monitoring Haematology
Ellisras Veterinary Laboratory	Northern Province	Post mortems Blood smears, brain smears etc
Potgietersrus Veterinary Laboratory	Northern Province	Simple bacteriology Serology Helminthology Histopathology Simple Haematology Post Mortems
Potchefstroom Veterinary Laboratory	North West Province	Serology Bacteriology Post Mortems Histopathology Parasitology

(continued)

Annex R (Continued)

Name	Province	Capabilities
Kroonstad Veterinary Laboratory	Free State Province	Serology Bacteriology Histopathology Chemistry Biochemistry Parasitology Simple haematology Post Mortems
Grahamstown Veterinary Laboratory	Eastern Cape Province	Bacteriology Serology Simple haematology Limited Biochemistry
Vryheid Veterinary Laboratory	Kwazulu Natal Province	Bacteriology Limited serology Post Mortems Parasitology
Vryburg Veterinary Laboratory	Northern Cape Province	Bacteriology Serology Histopathology Post Mortems Parasitology
Ermelo Provincial Veterinary Laboratory	Mpumalanga Province	Serology (Brucellosis) Bacteriology Parasitology Post Mortems Histopathology
Louis Trichardt Veterinary Laboratory	Northern Province	Serology Bacteriology Helminthology Reproduction Parasitology Post Mortems
Queenstown Veterinary Laboratory	Eastern Cape Province	Bacteriology Serology Parasitology Mastitis control Toxicology (limited) Post Mortems
Beaufort West Veterinary Laboratory	Western Cape Province	Fertility testing Bacteriology Limited serology Post Mortems

(continued)

Annex R (Continued)

Name	Province	Capabilities
Middleburg (Cape) Veterinary Laboratory	Eastern Cape	Serology Bacteriology Virology Sheep Reproduction Chemical Pathology Parasitology Histopathology Toxicology Haematology Post Mortems
Skukuza Veterinary Laboratory	Northern Province	Blood smears, brain smears Preparation of serological samples Post Mortems
Upington Veterinary Laboratory	Northern Cape Province	Bacteriology Parasitology Serology Post Mortems
Sibasa Veterinary Laboratory	Northern Province	Serology Bacteriology Helminthology Reproduction Parasitology Post Mortems

Source: Website NDA, Directorate of Veterinary Services.

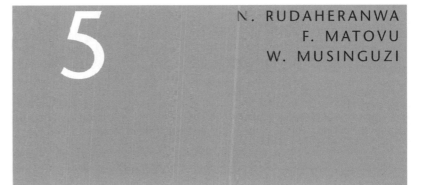

N. RUDAHERANWA
F. MATOVU
W. MUSINGUZI

ENHANCING UGANDA'S ACCESS TO INTERNATIONAL MARKETS

A Focus on Quality

THE UGANDAN ECONOMY IS HEAVILY RELIANT ON AGRICULTURE AND ASSOCIATED activities. The agricultural sector is a major employer and foreign exchange earner and is likely to remain so in the foreseeable future. Considerable progress has been made regarding macroeconomic policies but considerable efforts are still needed at the micro-level.

Most of the country's exports are destined for European markets and quality requirements (standards) in these markets are becoming more restrictive, combined with increased competition as more policy-induced barriers (such as tariffs, quotas, and so on) are reduced or eliminated. Therefore, Ugandan producers and exporters will need strong institutional and infrastructural support to improve the competitiveness of their products in export markets. Standards and technical regulations can raise or lower economic efficiency, promote or block competitiveness, facilitate or constrain international trade, and enable or exclude the participation of the poor from export-oriented economic activities. The fundamental purpose of standardization, however, is to promote fair trade between countries; eliminate technical barriers to trade; and protect health, safety, and environmental aspects. Whereas compliance with standards and technical regulations may be beneficial in a number of ways, it can have serious consequence for small exporting developing countries such as Uganda which have limited capacity (in both human and financial resources) to comply with such standards. The ban on Uganda's fish exports for the period between April and August 1999 alone, for example, led to huge losses in terms of export earnings and loss of employment. This scenario suggests that the impact could be even worse if such standards-related restrictions were applied to the major sectors of the economy such as coffee, horticulture, flowers, and so on that provide a major share of Uganda's export earnings and provide employment for the most of the country's population. This has implications for efforts to fight poverty in Uganda.

In the recent years Ugandan exporters are faced with a number of challenges while complying with the stringent standards and technical regulations. This is of particular significance as importing is part of the Uganda's sources of foreign exchange needed to finance debt and import expenditures. Though Uganda has implemented a range of trade policy reforms since 1987 which resulted in a substantial reduction of policy-oriented constraints to trade, the role of infrastructural and institutional constraints is of increasing significance in influencing external trade. Much as the infrastructural and institutional constraints are important factors in limiting external trade, the current analysis focuses on the role and impact of standards and technical regulations on the competitiveness of Ugandan exports.

An Overview of the Ugandan Economy

Nature and Composition of GDP

Uganda is mainly an agricultural country with the sector dominating the exports sector, GDP, employment, and so on. The agricultural sector employs (directly or indirectly) more than 80 percent of the population, accounting for more than 42 percent of GDP in 2001, a share that declined from over 55 percent in 1992. By 2001, agricultural exports were accounting for more than 80 percent of the country's export revenue. Agricultural output comes almost exclusively from about 2.5 million smallholders, about 80 percent of who have less than two hectares of land each. Only tea and sugar cane are grown on large estates. Most of the agricultural farms therefore use traditional production methods. There are a few modern farms especially in tea, sugarcane, flowers, and fruits. The predominance of smallholder farms and the traditional production techniques used have significant implications for complying with standards set by the international institutions.

Food crop production dominates the agricultural sector, accounting for about 50 percent of the agricultural GDP on average while the cash crop production is, on average, 16 percent of the agricultural GDP for the last ten years. The fisheries sector accounted for 8 percent and the forestry sector was only 4 percent of the agricultural GDP (The Republic of Uganda, various issues). Only a third of the food crop production is marketed and this explains the significance of the nonmonetary GDP. Most of the agricultural output is therefore subsistence.

Overall, the economy is still predominantly an agricultural economy but the other sectors such as manufacturing and the service sectors, are steadily expanding. For example, the share of the manufacturing sector in the GDP rose from 5.6 percent in 1991 to 7.5 percent in 1995 and to just less than 10 percent in 2001 (The Republic of Uganda, various issues).[1] The contribution of other sectors to GDP is low with the community services contributing most (of just over 15 percent of the GDP since 1995) to the GDP.

Composition of Uganda's External Trade

The composition and direction of commodity trade in Uganda has not changed much since the colonial days. Ugandan exports can be grouped into traditional exports (TE) and nontraditional exports (NTE). The country's exports (both volume and value) are dominated by traditional agricultural commodity exports, mainly coffee, cotton, and tea, that have contributed over 70 percent[2] of total exports by 2000. The share of traditional agricultural exports, which used to be more than 80 percent until 1990, was reduced to just over 60 percent in the late 1990s following the policy to diversify the country's economic activities and was reduced to just less than 40 percent in 2001 due to a decline in coffee prices in the export market.

NTE are dominated by agricultural products that include low-value staples, (for example, maize, cereals, beans and animal products, and spices), high-value export crops (namely vanilla, fish, chilies, ginger, silk, oil seeds, vegetables and pineapples), and floricultural exports (such as roses and plant cuttings). NTE also include timber and wood products. High-value NTE products (for example, fish, flowers, vanilla, and so on) are mainly sold in overseas markets since the value they fetch can offset the high storage and transport costs. However, low-value NTE (such as maize, beans, and so on) are mainly sold in regional markets.

Economic diversification strategies, initiated in the early 1990s, have raised the share of NTE products from about 14 percent in 1990 to just less than 30 percent by 1995 and to about 47 percent in 2000 (see Appendix C). Figure 5.1 shows that the traditional export commodities still dominate the exports sector but the nontraditional exports have been performing relatively well with a remarkable improvement in their share. The significant increase in the share of NTE products for the years 2000 and 2001 can be explained by a continuous fall in international prices of coffee. Thus, the composition of Ugandan exports is sensitive to changes in the world coffee prices.

---

[1] See Appendix D.

[2] Even these traditional agricultural exports have been traditionally dominated by coffee exports, which contribute over 80 percent.

5.1 Composition of Uganda's Exports: 1990–2001

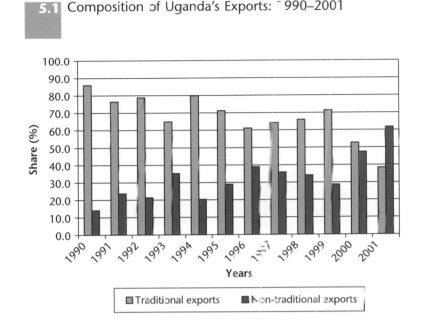

The sharp increase in the percentage share of non-traditional exports indicates a shift from export commodity concentration to a more diversified export basket. The country needs market access and policies that will move it away from traditional agricultural exports, whose contribution has been declining recently mainly due to the declining terms of trade. Since the contribution of the manufacturing sector is still small but has the potential to improve, policies to encourage light manufacturing and probably food processing would be important. Uganda's manufacturing sector provides goods mainly for the domestic market and relies heavily on imported inputs. The manufacturing sector could maintain profitability and production efficiency by sourcing a large share of its input from the domestic market or selling a larger share of its output in the export market. The manufacturing sector contributes well less than one percent of the total export revenue (The Republic of Uganda, various issues).

The trade liberalization and diversification policies initiated in the 1990s have generally improved export earnings (with fluctuations in some years because of unstable prices, particularly for coffee). However, import expenditures have been rising (Figure 5.2) mainly because of the needed essential

5.2 External Trade Performance: 1990–99

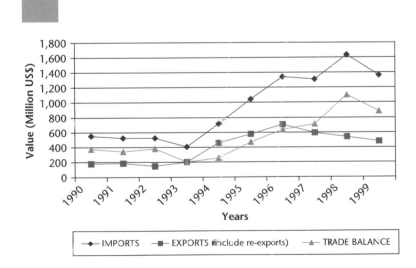

Table 5.1 Uganda's Exports by Region of Destination, 1995–99
(percent)

Region	1995	1996	1997	1998	1999
COMESA	20.4	26.0	18.1	16.5	18.9
Other Africa	0.4	0.2	0.8	1.1	5.5
European Union	38.9	35.4	53.9	50.9	59.3
Other Europe	33.6	29.2	11.0	11.9	9.7
North America	0.1	0.5	0.5	2.2	0.3
Middle East	0.6	1.3	0.9	2.2	0.6
Asia	1.8	6.2	4.3	4.6	3.6
South America	0.0	0.0	0.1	0.0	0.0
Rest of the world	4.1	1.2	10.4	10.7	2.0
Total	100	100	100	100	100

Source: Own compilation using data from The Republic of Uganda (various issues).

inputs that are not available locally.[3] As a result, the Ugandan economy has continued to experience balance of trade deficits. For example, the trade deficit in 1995 stood at US$471 million, which more than doubled to about US$1.2 billion in 2001 (The Republic of Uganda 2002). This suggests that some import expenditures are financed from sources (for example, loans) other than the country's own export earnings with implications for the external debt position. For example, the ratio of debt servicing to export of goods and services (which measures the amount of foreign exchange earnings foregone in servicing the country's debt) increased from 19 percent in 1996 to 25 percent in 2001. Financing import expenditure by external loans is not sustainable. Therefore, there is a need to promote export earnings through improving the competitiveness of the country's exports.

To increase the competitiveness of the country's commodity exports would require improving the quality (and the quantity) of export products to acceptable international standards. A small exporting country like Uganda may find it difficult to influence conditions in the export market. However, export earnings may be increased by improving the quality of exports. With globalization, most of the tariffs and some nontariff barriers to market entry in industrial countries have reduced substantially. However, the compliance with standards and technical barriers (TBT) in such markets has been shown to be a major constraint to the country's export competitiveness, as in the case of fish exports to the European Union (EU) in the late 1990s. The EU is a very important market for Uganda's exports; therefore, standards and technical regulations in such markets are bound to have serious economic consequences to the country's export performance. Thus commodity standards and technical barriers that either constrain or facilitate trade and how these influence the country's export trade need to be analyzed so as to identify the gaps and the way forward.

The Direction of Ugandan Exports

There is limited formal trade activity between Uganda and the neighboring countries in the region, except for imports from Kenya and Tanzania. Uganda's major trading partners are the European Union and COMESA (Common Market for Eastern and Southern Africa) member countries (Table 5.1). The share of the country's exports to the EU has been high and rising in recent years; for example, this share rose from about 39 percent in 1995 to about 59 percent in 1999. However, the share of exports to COMESA has experienced a downward trend, from 26 percent in 1996 to about 19 percent in 1999 (Ugandan Statistical Abstract 2000). This is surprising given that attempts have been made to reduce tariff barriers to trade in the region and there is no evidence to suggest that the adoption of standards is related to the increased trade to the EU, which is

---

[3] In 1999 only 22 percent of the Ugandan imports originate from the COMESA region while about 19 percent is from the industrial countries and 20 percent from Asia, the balance being contributed by countries in the Middle East, and other developing countries (see Appendix A).

a traditional market for Ugandan exports.[4] Furthermore, a number of investors (particularly in coffee, flowers, and fish sectors) are subsidiaries with mother companies in Europe and poor transport infrastructure is constraining regional trade than that destined for Europe.

The kind of trade structure given in Table 5.1 suggests that the EU market is one of the major destinations for Ugandan exports and therefore any form of restrictions (such as commodity standards and quality requirements) to entry in this market may greatly affect the country's export performance. It is therefore important to identify constraints and challenges that explain why Uganda is slow in diversifying the market destination of its commodity exports.

The Trade Policy Framework in Uganda

For the period from 1970 to the mid-1980s, Ugandan trade policies were characterized by a high degree of controls of external trade (export taxes, high tariffs, quotas, and so on), foreign exchange market (allocation of foreign exchange, fixed exchange rate system), internal pricing, and so forth. The economy was characterized by a low tax base with high government expenditures leading to fiscal deficits that were being financed by monetary accommodation. Low export earnings (mainly from coffee exports), accompanied by high import expenditures, resulted in trade deficits. The infrastructure (roads, transport, and so on) deteriorated further, making it difficult to collect agricultural produce from, or deliver inputs to, rural areas. This was compounded by the political turmoil of the early 1980s, further undermining the fiscal discipline and economic growth. The Ugandan economy therefore performed poorly in the early to mid-1980s. For example, inflation went up to three digits, the exchange rate was overvalued, and the debt to GDP ratio increased. However, policy makers responded to this crisis by introducing more controls of trade, foreign exchange market, and of internal pricing system until 1987 when the SAP was effectively implemented under the Economic Recovery Program (ERP).

Economic Recovery Program in Uganda since 1987. Structural Adjustment Programs (SAP) in Uganda were first introduced in 1981 and involved reforms in fiscal and monetary policies including control of inflation, exchange rate and interest rate re-alignment, liberalization of the marketing system (that is, reduced price controls), and the return of expropriated properties to their owners (mainly Asians). This initiative, however, failed in 1984 when donors froze the credit support to the reforms since the government could not restrain the defense budget because of pressure to finance the war.

A comprehensive Economic Recovery Program (ERP) was launched in 1987 which aimed at sustaining economic growth at around 5 percent per year, restoring fiscal and monetary discipline, reducing inflation and the balance of payments (BOP) deficits, and generating surplus of foreign reserves in excess of four months of imports and rehabilitating the major economic sectors (Morrissey and Rudaheranwa 1998). The government embarked on trade policy reforms with the aim of promoting the exports sector in terms of increased volume and diversity of exports (to reduce the dominance of traditional exports in the exports sector). This was to be achieved by improving the productive efficiency, liberalizing commodity markets, and eliminating all forms of anti-export bias. The type and sequencing of the trade policy reforms is given in Annex G. These policies were a reaction to the macroeconomic imbalances that arose from fiscal deficits, poor terms of trade for major traditional export commodities, and the oil shock of the 1970s, which left the economy in an increasingly vulnerable position in terms of debts relative to export earnings. These reforms were, therefore, geared toward improving Uganda's export competitiveness (mainly in terms of price competitiveness).

Quantitative restrictions were abolished or converted into tariff equivalents and a number of goods on the negative list were reduced significantly. As already noted, the country has been very active in promoting export growth and diversification. The foreign exchange market was initially liberalized in 1990 when forex bureaus were licensed and was fully liberalized in 1993 when the auctioning of foreign exchange by the Bank of Uganda was phased out. In

---

[4] It should be noted that countries in the COMESA region have more or less similar consumption and production patterns, and high-valued, nontraditional agricultural exports. which increased substantially in the 1990s, and are destined for overseas markets.

1991, Uganda Revenue Authority (URA) was established to rationalize the tax and revenue systems. A new law, "the Investment Code" was passed that led to the creation of the Uganda Investment Authority (a one-stop center for investors in the country).

Since the early 1990s, export taxes in Uganda have been implicit rather than explicit (Rudaheranwa 1999). The tax on coffee exports was abolished in 1992 but temporarily reintroduced between 1994 and 1996 mainly to limit the appreciation of the exchange rate as a result of the coffee boom. The coffee boom substantially increased the inflow of foreign exchange leading to appreciation of the exchange rate and thus making other (mainly nontraditional) exports less profitable and less competitive.

In summary, the trade policy regime in the 1990s revolved around liberalization as the central theme for export promotion. Trade liberalization was expected to increase productivity, foster export competitiveness, and improve resource allocation. Increased export earnings could promote investments and growth, and ease the balance of payments constraints and the debt burden. Attempts have been made to improve compliance with standards and technical regulations through enactment of statutes and acts since the 1960s and amendments of others in the 1990s, but, because of limited capacity (both human and financial resources) and institutional weaknesses, the enforcement of these regulations has been weak. The role of standards and technical regulations in improving Ugandan export competitiveness has been minimal until the late 1990s when it gained prominence (particularly in enforcement) following the fish ban.

Despite a range of trade policy reforms indicated above, Ugandan producers and exporters still face a number constraints that include high costs of utilities, transport and information-related costs, costs of compliance with commodity standards and quality assurance, and so on. The subsequent analysis shifts the focus to issues related to standards and technical regulations in Uganda, that is, the nature, development, and extent of compliance to standards in Uganda and how standards promote or hinder export competitiveness.

Institutions and Related Projects

Institutions and Associations

To take into consideration the views of stakeholders and policy makers, the research team worked closely with various producer associations and government institutions that facilitate and promote production and trade. The associations contacted included the Uganda Coffee Trade Federation (UCTF) for coffee exports, the Uganda Flower Exporters' Association (UFEA), the Horticultural Exporters' Association (HORTEXA), the Uganda Fish Processors' and Exporters' Association (UFPEA), Uganda Honey Association (UHA) and the Uganda Manufacturers' Association (UMA).

Private institutions involved in standards-related issues contacted included the Total Quality Management (TQM) that provides training services to producers and organizations in quality management; and the SGS, which is an independent private institution operating in a number countries to monitor, inspect, and certify compliance with standards as may be specified by importers. Public institutions contacted included the Uganda Export Promotion Board (UEPB), the Uganda Coffee Development Authority (UCDA), Ministry of Tourism, Trade and Industry (MTTI), the World Trade Organization (WTO) desk in the MTTI, the Uganda National Bureau of Standards (UNBS), the National Environment Authority (NEMA), and the Private Sector Foundation (PSF). Both public and private institutions helped the research team by providing information regarding constraints relating to compliance with standards in the subsectors considered in the study.

Related Projects

A number of donor-funded projects of relevance to this study either have been completed or are in progress. The Competitive Private Enterprises and Trade Expansion (COMPETE), a USAID-funded project is designed to improve the country's export competitiveness of the private enterprises in international markets so as to increase foreign exchange earnings, and boost domestic economic activity and employment. The project focuses on the fish, coffee, and cotton subsectors. The Support for the Private Enterprise Expansion and Development (SPEED) project, also funded by USAID, focuses on the accessibility to finance and business skills development by small and medium enterprises.

The Investment in Developing Export Agriculture (IDEA), a USAID/Uganda government joint funded project, focuses on the expansion of production and export of both low-value food crops (maize, beans) and high-value produce (for example, flowers, fish, cocoa, vanilla, and so on). There is also a Trade Policy Capacity Building project that is designed to enable Uganda's private and public sectors to address current and upcoming trade policy issues such as those arising from WTO and regional trade agreements. This is done through the provision of training, technical assistance, and research. The Joint Integrated Technical Assistance Program (JITAP) facilitates the country's full integration into the multilateral system within the framework or rules provided for in the WTO agreements. This is done through the enhancement of the country's ability to take advantage of trade opportunities arising from improved market access conditions. Furthermore, the PSF/World Bank study (2001) examined the existing policy, legal and regulatory framework for the coffee sector of Uganda and the respective mandates, roles, and functions of various regulatory institutions in the country.

Justification of the Subsectors

A number of sectors have been considered. However, emphasis has been placed on flowers, horticultural exports, fish and coffee exports, and light manufacturing products, specifically clothing and textiles. These sectors were selected mainly because of their importance in terms of foreign exchange earnings to the country (see Appendix C), employment creation, and, therefore, income generation. Specifically, the flower and horticultural subsectors were selected because of a number of factors. First, this is in line with the government policy to diversify the country's exports. Second, as is seen from the structure of Ugandan exports (commodity composition, Appendix C and destination Table 5.1), these products have had considerable growth in recent years. For instance, horticultural exports increased by about 27 percent between 1998 and 2001 while flower exports increased by 13 percent over the same period (IDEA 2002). Third, they are labor-intensive activities and, therefore, a source of employment. Fourth, the production processes in these sectors tend to use a lot of chemicals. Fifth, they are relatively small, new players in the export market and therefore need special attention, as transaction costs of exporting are likely to be high. Finally, the country's soils and climate are favorable to the production of these agricultural products and the government singled out some of these products (coffee, fish, and horticultural commodities) as Uganda's strategic exports.[5]

The coffee subsector has been selected mainly because it is still the country's major contributor to export earnings. The fish sector was selected for two reasons: (a) Its share in total exports has increased significantly, from 5.6 percent in 1995 to 17.3 percent in 2001; and (b) It is one of the sectors that suffered from a series of bans (because of noncompliance with required standards) in export markets. This makes it a good case study to learn from based upon the experiences of how standards affected the sector and the measures put in place to comply with standards.

Regulatory and Institutional Framework in Uganda

There are a number of institutions in Uganda entrusted with the responsibility of the setting, inspection, monitoring, auditing, and enforcement of commodity and process standards. They include, for example, the Uganda National Bureau of Standards (UNBS), different departments in the Ministry of Agriculture Animal Industry and Fisheries (MAAIF), private organizations such as SGS, ACE and TQM, and producers/exporters' associations in different sectors with voluntary standards as specified in various codes of practice, and so on. The institutional framework for public institutions responsible for standards in various sectors is given in Appendix H.

The responsibility of setting and enforcing standards in Uganda falls under different ministries as summarized in Appendix H. For example, the implementation of sanitary and phytosanitary requirements is the responsibility of the Crop Protection Department at Kawanda Agricultural Research Institute (KARI) and the Fisheries Department under the MAAIF, while those in the manufacturing sector are implemented by the UNBS. We have focused on Sanitary and Phytosanitary Inspection Service (SPIS) and the Uganda National Bureau of Standards (UNBS) as public agencies and TQM

---

[5] Horticultural, fish and coffee commodities (among others) are referred to as strategic exports because they are thought to stimulate indigenous investment, have multiplier effects on the whole economy, and help in poverty reduction given that they form a large source of employment

(U) Limited, a private agency, to get an insight into the procedures and problems encountered in enforcing standards in Uganda.

Public and Private Institutions

The Sanitary and Phytosanitary Inspection Services (SPIS). The SPIS, a department in the MAAIF based at KARI, is mandated by the Plant Protection Act of 1962 to regulate and inspect plant products for import and export. The plant products inspected include imports of planting materials (vegetation), and relief items such as maize grain and seeds. Exports, which are given phytosanitary certificates, are flowers, fruits and vegetables, grains, coffee, tea, tobacco, and so on.

There are 28 government-gazetted custom entry points that are supposed to have inspection units in Uganda but presently SPIS serves only 11 points. Before the government policy of decentralization took effect in 1993, district agricultural officers were supposed to conduct plant inspection and issue plant import permits at these custom entry points. The local government decentralization system views inspection services as the responsibility of the central government. Therefore, the SPIS department has to negotiate with the local government to assign staff for the inspection work that has not yet been done.

The staffing of the SPIS department is very inadequate especially in light of the growing size of the exports sector. For example, 10 members of staff are meant for Kampala and Entebbe zone but the available staff is only three (one based at the airport, one at the UCDA, and the other at Kawanda). The understaffing is partly attributable to the civil service system's lengthy recruiting process.

The infrastructure facilities are also a problem. For example, there should be a laboratory to conduct some basic tests at the border entry points but only a visual inspection is conducted at these points. DANIDA has provided the department with some basic equipment but there is a need for laboratory space to accommodate them. DANIDA has committed itself to the construction of a modern laboratory to enable SPIS to conduct more complex tests. The DANIDA assistance did not include human resource development, insisting that the government should be responsible to train its own manpower.

The SPIS faces some challenges particularly in the horticultural sector, which is a fast-growing but relatively new sector in export markets and is still poorly organized. The horticultural sector comprises small, scattered, and poorly financed producers and exporters. Thus, it is difficult to organize and regularize their standards on quality assurance, and pest and sanitary control at the farm or firm level. Export market opportunities under the AGOA require stringent measures on quality performance. For example, the USA market requires SPIS to undertake a pest risk analysis (PRA) that involves listing all the pests attacking the fruits and vegetables per region in the country before opening its market to Ugandan produce. Conducting a PRA is a huge exercise requiring a lot of resources that the SPIS does not have.

The SPIS works in collaboration with the customs officials and police to enforce their mandate. Any consignment with plant material meant for export or import is supposed to be cleared by the SPIS before leaving customs. However, according to an official in the SPIS department, there have been allegations of cases where consignments have left the country without clearance or contravening recommendations from the SPIS. This signifies a laxity (or lack of capacity) in the coordination and enforcement of the SPIS mandate. In addition, publicizing the activities and importance of the SPIS is still a problem.

Uganda National Bureau of Standards (UNBS). The UNBS is a statutory body under the MTTI mandated to promote standardization in health and safety activities, determination, review, monitoring, modification or amending standards. The UNBS Act of 1983 provides for a national framework for developing and implementing national standards. The UNBS is an apex body for standardization activities in the country. It undertakes what is called integrated standardization, that is, the development and enforcement of standards. UNBS is structured into five divisions (see Annex K). The UNBS is empowered to carry out a number of functions (Annex H) regarding the development and maintenance of standards in the country. In performing its functions, the UNBS collaborates with other bodies having similar functions relating to industrial or commercial standards. The UNBS performs the function of ensuring compliance with international standards both for imports and exports. However, UNBS does not have permanent enforcement or monitoring units and facilities at district and lower levels. This creates a communication gap between UNBS and producers, consumers and other stakeholders.

Total Quality Management (U) Limited. Total Quality Management (U) Ltd. (TQM), which started operations in 1988, is affiliated with International Quality Media AS (a Norwegian Company).[6] The main activity of the TQM is to train corporate bodies and other organizations in the Total Quality Management concept per ISO certification standards. ISO orientates companies to perform to internationally accepted standards. It is based in Geneva and is subscribed by all national standards organizations in the world.

The training is done in a group of about 10 organizations. Each organization appoints a person, normally a mid-level manager, to train and transfer the skills to the subordinates. One- or two-day seminars are organized every month for the training and TQM staff make a follow-up study of the implementation process in the individual organizations.

The first requirement in the training program is to develop an organizational quality policy. This is evolved and evaluated by all the staff with the guidance of TQM. Secondly, management commits to providing all of the resources and cooperation needed for the implementation. Following the training course, the company can apply for certification, which is done by independent, high profile, and accredited institutions such as Bureau Veritus Quality Internationale (BVQI), a French company, and NEMCO Certified, a Norwegian company. The quality management system is re-evaluated every year through a surveillance audit and the company has to be certified every three years. One of the benefits is that the company can use the certification logo as a marketing tool.

The cost of training and certification tends to be prohibitive to small business establishments. Certification costs are about US$3,000 and training costs average US$7,000, which is done every three years. There are projects providing financial assistance to organizations to train for compliance with ISO standards. For example, the BUDS-SSE project under PSF that assisted about 40 organizations, the USAID-funded SPEED project that is presently assisting the fish industry and will move to other sectors, and the European Union project EBAS based in Nairobi.

Other institutions such as the UNBS, UMA, and UCDA carry out training on issues relating to standards. We use the UNBS to highlight the nature and cost of the training services offered. UNBS provides monthly training services on standards and quality to companies at a fee ranging from Ushs 50,000 to Ushs 75,000 per participant (2001 rates) for a one-day training workshop.[7] The technical staff at the UNBS sometimes get training at a fee of about US$500 per person.

Regulatory Framework

Standards Development in Uganda. The legal basis on the preparation and issuance of standards in Uganda is based on articles 7 and 14 of the Uganda National Bureau of Standards Act of 1983. In this act, the rules of procedure on preparation and issuance of Uganda Standards are issued by the National Standards Council (NSC), which is a governing body for UNBS. The rules of procedure on preparation and issuance of standards are based both on the "ISO Manual for Development of National Standards" and on surveys and studies made by UNBS on the standardization needs of the country in respect to different sectors of the economy, on export and import products, and on available standards documents regarding international standards, regional standards and foreign standards.

During the development of standards, UNBS prepares a discussion document and convenes appropriate technical committee (TC) meetings to discuss the contents of the document after which it prepares a draft standard for public comment. The TCs are a representation of interested stakeholders such as industrial exporters, producers, academia and research institutions, consumers, importers, and so on. UNBS has about seven operational committees with a TC on each of the following areas: basic standards, food and agricultural products, building and construction, mechanical engineering and metrology, chemical and environment, electrical technology, and textiles.

Draft standards are circulated for wide public comment (including other countries such as trading

---

[6] TQM can be accessed at www.TQMAfrica.com.

[7] The exchange rate in 2001 was Ushs 1750 per one US$.

partners) so as to avoid creating technical barriers to trade. A 60-day period is provided for such comments and the TC convenes after such comments have been received to ensure that relevant concerns are considered. Draft standards are then submitted to the National Standards Council (NSC) for approval. UNBS with the approval of the minister responsible for trade, declares which standards are mandatory (mandatory standards apply to products whose low quality is likely to affect the health and safety of consumers). Standards that are compulsory (mandatory[8]) in this respect become technical regulations in the context of WTO agreements. Approved standards are published in newspapers as well as in the *Government Gazette*.

UNBS, which works closely with other international bodies entrusted with standardization, is the national enquiry point notified to the WTO. It runs an information and documentation center that provides information on the standards of other countries on request through its networks.[9] UNBS publishes annually a catalog of Uganda standards (both mandatory and voluntary) with about 49 standards that are still in draft form. The standards in the catalog cover a wide range of sectors including environmental protection, and quality management and assurance in agricultural, manufacturing, and service sectors. However, given continuous changes in production patterns and market conditions, there is a need for their review.

With the US$3 million assistance from the UNDP/UNIDO, the UNBS set up a microbiology laboratory and upgraded two other laboratories. The microbiology laboratory has been accredited by the South African National Accreditation System (SANAS) at a fee of US$20,000. The preparation for accreditation including international consultancy services cost a total of US$82,000. The remaining four laboratories (located at Nakawa in Kampala) are yet to get international recognition. The constraints to accreditation are mainly both the lack of equipment to increase the capacity of these laboratories and the financial resources to begin the accreditation process. Specifically, the chemistry laboratory needs to be accredited so as to carry out heavy metal contaminants and pesticides residue analysis that are of increasing prominence in food control and safety standards globally. The metrology laboratory needs assistance to acquire temperature, pressure, force, and optics equipment. The overall estimated cost of restructuring the four laboratories for accreditation is US$12 million. In addition, UNBS lacks their own permanent home and, according to the UNBS official, about US$11.4 million is required to put up the structure. More detailed information about the UNBS laboratories can be obtained from the UNBS at www.unbs.org.

UNBS has developed and currently issues a quality mark known as the Uganda Standards Certification Mark, which indicates that the manufacturer certified is capable of consistently manufacturing a safe and quality product in accordance with Uganda- or internationally-accepted standards. By the end of 2001, about 28 manufacturing companies had benefited from the certification mark and about 12 more were expected to benefit from the certification mark soon. By year 2002, 35 firms had received UNBS certification (for details, see Appendix J). The accreditation of the remaining four laboratories will make the certification more accessible and less costly. For example, costs related to shipment of samples for testing abroad would be reduced by about US$2,000, as demonstrated in the case of fish (see section entitled "Impact of the Fish Ban").

The UNBS does not enforce the ISO standards. These standards are voluntarily undertaken by organizations to enhance their competitiveness and managerial competence. That is, they are market-driven since market sanctions exist especially in the export business that compel organizations to undertake the ISO certification. Environmental standards are moving toward legal enforcement as the government adopts a cleaner production environment policy.

---

[8] For compulsory (mandatory) standards, the intention of declaring them compulsory is first published by the minister for trade in the newspapers as well as in the *Government Gazette*. A period of 60 days is given for comments and reactions from the affected parties. After 60 days, if no comments are received, the standards are declared mandatory by the statutory instrument.

[9] UNBS runs information and documentation center with information on Ugandan standards, British standards, and international standards such as ISO. Uganda is a former British protectorate and some laws and standards have been inherited from the British system.

UNBS still faces considerable constraints mainly regarding human capacity and infrastructure requirement to fulfill its obligations, that is, inspection, monitoring, and enforcement of the compliance with the standards. It lacks equipment, sufficient technical staff, and financial resources. UNBS requires about 130 technical staff but only 50 are in place. The five laboratories (microbiology, chemistry, mechanical and building materials, electrical cable and appliance testing, and metrology), each of which requires about a technical staff of five, have only two members. The monitoring and enforcement of standards to ensure health and safety requirements are inadequate, and inspection of existing facilities such as testing laboratories is rare (World Trade Organization 2001). Sanitary conditions, particularly in food processing are inadequate and the UNBS lacks adequate funding. Only those in the fish sector have improved recently mainly due to a series of fish bans.

Uganda's Participation in the FAO/WHO Codex Alimentarius Commission. The Codex Alimentarius Commission (CAC) is a worldwide food standardizing body based in Rome, Italy. UNBS is the Codex contact point in Uganda and it coordinates all Codex activities. UNBS as a Codex contact point serves a number of roles. First, it is a custodian of Codex documents in the country, that is, it receives Codex documents and publications, and maintains a library of Codex standards. Information on standards and TBT is available in hard copy form but the library still lacks the electronic means of obtaining and disseminating information. UNBS has a duty to disseminate Codex documents to all interested parties for comments and information. Secondly, it communicates the government position in elaboration of Codex standards. Finally, UNBS participates in the work of the Codex Coordinating Committee for Africa (CCA) by deliberating on specific standards which are unique to the region, for example, standards on produce such as millet, cassava, and so on.

National Codex Committee. In Uganda there exists a National Codex Committee (NCC) that cuts across sectors. The aim of setting up the NCC is to establish an effective mechanism for considering the government's National Food Control requirements in relation to the work of the CAC Food Standards Program. The function of the National Codex Committee is to consider technical issues on food standards and then advise the government on the application of various food standardization and food safety issues arising out of the work of CAC and its subsidiary bodies.

Uganda's Participation in International Standardization Development. The formulation of national standards or adoption of foreign and international standards as Ugandan standards is important for the competitiveness and profitability of Ugandan products. As of September 2001, UNBS[10] had developed, promulgated, and gazetted about 253 Ugandan standards in the field of food and agriculture, building materials, electrical items, and chemicals (World Trade Organization 2001; UNBS 2001). UNBS also participated in the development of about 207 East African harmonized standards (in various areas) to facilitate the regional trade (see Appendix E). Thus the UNBS has made efforts to formulate and integrate national standards with international standards.

UNBS has developed 67 food standards, 46 of which were Codex-based. The National Codex Committee has developed the Draft National Food Law based on the FAO/WHO food law model. The Ugandan and East African Standards on labeling of prepackaged foods are based on the corresponding Codex Standards and UNBS is a corresponding member of ISO in the country. Among others, it attends ISO meetings as an observer but contributes to the work of ISO in the form of providing comments on draft ISO/IEC standards and trains on the ISO/IEC standards. UNBS is a contact point for ISO publications, adopts/adapts ISO standards, and attends ISO general meetings.

Regarding the negotiations in respect of TBT and SPS agreements, the Ministerial Paper for Uganda presented to the Nov/Dec 1999 Seattle Conference raised two basic issues. The first was the review of both TBT and SPS agreements by their respective committees at WTO to determine the difficulties in implementation of these agreements by developing countries. The second was the procedure to prevent the illegal use of SPS and TBT measures by industrial importing countries on agricultural products originating from developing countries.

[10] Discussion in this section is based on information obtained from the UNBS Documentation and Information Center.

TBT and SPS Agreements in Uganda

The SPS agreement encourages WTO members to create and maintain sanitary and phytosanitary (SPS) measures based on SPS standards established by the Codex Alimentarius Commission, the Internal Plant Protection Convention (IPPC), and the International Office of Epizootics (OIE). Uganda, a founding member of WTO, like other WTO member countries, is required to ensure that national laws and technical regulations are in line with the provisions of SPS and TBT agreements. It is also required to adopt international standards and to establish transparent processes for standards development. National measures based on risk assessment and SPS measures should be communicated to WTO members. In Uganda's case the following has been done. First, UNBS was designated a National Enquiry Point (NEP) in 1997 for TBT and SPS. Second, as a requirement in Annex B of SPS and Annex 3 of TBT agreements, the Code of Good Practice for preparation, adoption, and application of standards was accepted by UNBS and WTO was notified. The standardization programs and national standards in preparation and application have been communicated to WTO. East African harmonization of standards and technical programs has been communicated to WTO. Finally, compulsory national standards (technical regulations in accordance with definitions of WTO terms) have been communicated to WTO members, who were given with sufficient time to answer queries from other member states.

Equivalence Principle toward Market Access in Uganda

Uganda as an exporting country of fish and fishery products to the European Union (EU) and other countries, has implemented a program to harmonize standards in the processing and exporting of fish that are equivalent to the European Directive Technical Regulation, EC No. 91/493/EEC (that is, "The laying down the health conditions for production and placing on the market of fishery products") and other related decisions and directives of the EU. To that end, Uganda is now enlisted under category one since May 2001 (Waniala 2001), which means full compliance with the EU Technical Regulations on directives, related to export of fishery products to the EU.

Technical Regulations in Some Selected Sectors

A number of regulations exist in Uganda in the form of acts and statutes purposely for monitoring health and safety. However, most regulations date back to the 1960s but efforts have been made to update them to match the changing production patterns and market conditions. A summary of statutes is given in Table 5.2 on next page (for details, see Annex I). Various regulations have been in place but their enforcement has been weak.

East Africa Regional Standardization Program

In the postIndependence period, Kenya, Tanzania, and Uganda continued to form a regional trading block called the East African Community (EAC) with improved and harmonized services including infrastructure such as roads, communication systems, trade and commerce, and so on. In 1977 the community collapsed because of economic and political problems among other factors. The trading arrangement was, however, revived in 1998 and subsequently, the East African Community Treaty was signed in 1999.

Among other cooperation programs established with the revival of EAC, "Standardization, Quality Assurance, Metrology and Testing" (SQMT) was also provided for in the treaty for (a) the facilitation of sustainable modernization in areas of SQMT; (b) the undertaking to evolve and apply a common policy to standardization, quality assurance, and testing of goods and services produced and traded in the region; and (c) an agreement to conclude a protocol on SQMT that was signed on 15 January 2001 by the three states.

The SQMT protocol provides for (a) the application of uniform standards on all products whether manufactured, produced, or packaged within the community; (b) quality standards on products imported in the region; and (c) services offered in the manufacture, production, handling, packaging, or delivery of products traded in the EAC. The SQMT also provides for the evolution and application of a common policy on (a) the standardization, quality assurance, metrology, and testing of products produced and traded in the region; (b) the relationship of the standardization Bureau (bodies) with regional, international and other organizations and institutions concerned with standardization and quality assurance; and (c) the development of activities in

Table 5.2 Technical Regulations in Selected Sectors

Statute	Purpose/Objective	Competent Authority	Comment
The Agricultural Seeds and Plant Protection Statute, 1994	Provides for national seed certification, plant breeding and registration of breeders, seed testing, sanitary and phytosanitary standards and product multiplications and licensing of seeds and other planting material.	National Seed Industry Authority, KARI	Lack of resources to conduct effective testing and certification
Fish Quality Assurance Rules 1998 as supplement to the Fish and Crocodile Act 1964	Provides for quality management and inspection function, i.e., compliance in hygiene and sanitation concerns, fish handling, processing, transportation and marketing.	Department of Fisheries Resources	Need for more accredited local testing institutions like Chemiphar (U) Ltd.
The Uganda Coffee Development Statute 1991	To regulate, promote, and monitor the development, improvement and marketing of coffee and the coffee sector in Uganda. To issue grade and quality certificates and register all organizations in the coffee sector.	Uganda Coffee Development Authority (UCDA)	Has limited mandate to enforce quality requirements at the farm and primary processing levels
The Cotton Development Statute, 1994	Creates zones for cultivation and restriction of the movement of cotton into and out of the zones. The promotion and creation of institutional linkages from the farm level to marketing.	Cotton Development Organization (CDO)	There is a restriction on the sourcing of inputs by the farmers and the lack of an organized market system as it was in the case of cooperative that leads to exploitation of the farmers in pricing
The Dairy Industry Act 1998	Promotes the production, processing and marketing of milk and dairy products.	Dairy Development Authority (DDA)	Insufficient capacity to monitor local processors on hygiene standards
The National Environmental Statute 1995	Provides for the sustainable management of the environment and enforcement of standards including air, water pollution and control	National Environment Management Authority (NEMA)	Insufficient capacity to police and manage all environmental concerns in the country
The Agricultural Chemicals Regulations 1993	Regulation and control of manufacture import and use of agricultural chemicals, fumigators or commercial applicators, testing of Agricultural chemicals. Publishing of acceptable labeling, packaging and transportation of chemicals.	Agricultural Chemicals Board	
The Public Health Act, 1964 Food Act, 1964			The Public Health and Food Acts need updating to reflect current situation, e.g., maximum chemical residues requirements
National Drug Policy Statute	Establishment of technical regulations of drugs, inspection and monitoring the production, import, sale and dispensing of drugs in the country.	National Drug Authority (NDA)	Insufficient capacity to police the indiscriminate use and sale of drugs

Source: Modified from Foodnet (2002).

Table 5.3 Other Provisions of SQMT

Application of uniform rules and procedures for the formulation of national standards for each member state.
Development of a program for harmonization of national standards so as to develop East African Standards.
Adoption and implementation of East African Standards as National Standards.
Application of uniform rules and procedures for formulation of national standards of each member state.
Application of the principle of reference to standards in their (member states) National legislation so as to facilitate the harmonization of their technical regulations.
Harmonization of procedures for inspection, sampling and testing of products traded in the Region that is Conformity Assessment.
Development and encouragement on use of harmonized documentation for evaluation of quality of goods produced in the Region.
Adoption and application of a harmonized scheme for certification of products traded, produced in the region and also the same with Accreditation of testing and calibration laboratories, certification bodies, etc.

standardization, quality assurance, metrology, and testing. Other provisions in the SQMT protocol are summarized in Table 5.3.

Since the advent of the revival of the East African Community, a lot of progress has been attained in standardization programs. First, the private sector has been involved in the standard committees for harmonization of standards in the region to ensure fast and easy implementation of the standards. Second, the process of the establishment of the Regional Training Institute for legal metrology has been initiated. Third, to harmonize the conformity assessment procedures, the idea of the regional inter-laboratory testing comparisons was initiated. To this end, the assessment procedure is under way, for example, in steel bars, soap, mattresses, cooking oil, mineral water, and edible salt. Fourth, the work on harmonization of laws regarding legal metrology has started. Training needs in standardization, quality assurance, metrology, and testing have been identified but need funding. About 207 standards for goods and some codes of practice have been harmonized and notification of harmonized standards to WTO has been made. Fifth, the idea of establishment of the East African Accreditation Body for Quality Systems has been decided against and con-

sumer organization in the region is slated to participate in the development of regional standards.

As a result of the SQMT protocol, over 200 product standards have been harmonized for application and implementation in the region and the standardization programs for the region are being continuously communicated to WTO as required by the provisions of TBT and SPS agreements.

Standards in Selected Sectors

This section analyzes standards in selected sectors taking into account product characteristics, existing regulations, actors, and institutions involved, as well as, the risks at stake for particular commodities. Only the coffee sector, fish industry, floriculture, horticulture sectors, and light manufacturing are analyzed.

Standards in the Coffee Industry

The coffee industry plays an important role in the economy[11] since it contributes about 33.6 percent of the monetary GDP, employs over 5 million people (UCTF 2001), and contributed about 59 percent to export earnings in 1999 but declined to just over 30 percent in 2001 (The Republic of

---

[11] Over 2.5 million people in Uganda directly depend on coffee growing and trading for their livelihood. Coffee traditionally contributes more than 60 percent of the country's export earnings (except for the last two years). Thus, standards that constrain the operations in the coffee sector and blocks the Uganda's coffee exports, for example, would heavily affect the economy. Standards regarding chemical residue limits on Uganda agricultural export products to Europe Union are to came into force in February 2003 and may have had similar effects as those in the fish sector.

Uganda 2002).[12] Two main types of coffee, namely Arabic (10 percent) and Robusta (90 percent) have been grown in Uganda. But Clonal coffee was introduced in the 1990s as a high-yield, pest-resistant improvement of existing varieties.

Constraints affecting the coffee industry in Uganda include aged coffee trees, pests and diseases (for example, coffee wilt), oversupply on the international market with relatively inelastic demand leading to low prices and poor postharvest handling methods at farm and primary processing levels, which compromise quality. The low prices act as a disincentive for farmers to invest in better crop husbandry leading to low yields and low quality coffee. Uganda has limited influence over coffee prices in the export market and coffee buyers tend to be more selective (particularly on quality) where there is a surplus. Under these circumstances, a viable alternative is for Uganda to strengthen the quality standards of their coffee exports. A number of regulations have been put in place over time to enforce compliance and improve the quality standards in the coffee sector.

The regulation of the coffee industry dates back to 1929 when the colonial government established the Coffee Board mainly to advise on the quality of coffee exported. In 1943 the Coffee Industry Board (CIB) was established to buy all the crop (except Bugisu coffees) from smallholders and to export it. The 1953 Coffee Act increased the mandate of CIB to regulate the marketing of the coffee output by recommending prices payable to producers and processing factories. The responsibility of the CIB changed to solely grading and selling processed coffee by a new legislation in 1959. In 1963 the Coffee Act was amended leading to the formation of the Coffee Marketing Board (CMB) with powers to control the coffee industry, that is, to purchase and export all dry processed coffee. The washed and pulped coffee processors would directly export their own output with license from CMB. The CMB was given full monopoly to export all Ugandan coffee by the Coffee Marketing Act of 1969.

The coffee industry remained under the state-controlled monopoly of CMB until the early 1990s when the Uganda Coffee Development Authority (UCDA) statute (1991) repealed the Coffee Marketing Act (1969). The statute provided for the entry of private exporters and by 2001 about 200 licenses had been issued to coffee exporters (PSF/World Bank 2001).

Coffee Regulations enacted in 1994 give detailed guidelines and requirements for licensing coffee processing at export level. They also stipulate the required standards and grades for the Ugandan coffee. The Coffee Regulations enforced by UCDA are complemented by the Code-of-Practice developed by the Uganda Coffee Trade Federation (UCTF).

The liberalization of the coffee industry had an overriding policy objective of improving the producers' share of the world market price, which increased to over 75 percent of the free-on-rail/track export price offered in Kampala (PSF/World Bank 2001). However, the liberalization of the coffee industry also led to undesirable outcomes. First, increased competition and lack of experience among the new exporters led to malpractices that impinged on the quality of coffee, particularly at the farm and primary processing levels. Second, the prevalence of unfair trading practices with unscrupulous players resulted in failure to conform to acceptable standards and practices in the coffee industry. This has necessitated the UCDA to increase the monitoring and enforcement of quality standards in the coffee sector.

In ensuring and enforcing quality measures, the UCDA requires all coffee exporters to permit entry of UCDA inspectors into their premises at any time (failure of which is an offence) to carry out inspection of the processing and handling procedures. The UCDA may take samples of coffee found in the store or processing plant for testing. The UCDA gives advice and directions to ensure that the store or processing facility complies with the required standards. In extreme circumstances, the UCDA may prohibit the use of any store or the operation of any part of the processing facility until the authority is satisfied that the required standards are complied with.

UCDA works closely with UCTF (whose membership is open to all players in the coffee industry, including exporters, processors, coffee roasters, traders, and associations that render services to the coffee industry) in enforcing standards. Concerns of quality matters are the responsibility of the Marketing, Quality and Standards Committee of UCTF, which ensures that members conform to the quality standards for coffee as stipulated in the *Coffee Regulations of 1994*. The UCTF expects members to maintain quality standards as given in the Code-of-Practice that may change from time to time in response to the international standards, market demand and other

---

[12] This sharp decline is partly due to diversification of exports and decline in international coffee prices.

requirements. For example, the Code of Conduct of UCTF requires every coffee roaster and exporter to employ or acquire the services of a certified quality controller registered with the UCTF Secretariat. The certification of the quality controller is essentially the responsibility of the UCDA. Minimum requirements and qualifications of quality controllers are agreed upon both by UCDA and the UCTF.

All agents involved in the coffee industry are required to take adequate pest control measures to avoid infestation of the coffee, thereby preserving the quality of coffee output. All coffee for export should be fumigated using such conventional and accepted methods as set by the UCTF or determined by the contract for the sale of such coffee, or other internationally acceptable standards. Coffee for export must meet a maximum moisture content of 12.5 percent for dry processed Robusta coffee, and 13 percent for wet processed Robusta coffee. All exportable Arabic coffee must not exceed 12 percent moisture content. All coffee output (by all operators) is supposed to be kept in stores and warehouses per the *Coffee Regulations 1994* specifications. Exporters are required to cooperate in maintaining high standards of quality, aimed at projecting a positive image of Ugandan coffee in the world market, and should discourage any acts that would compromise the quality of Uganda's coffee.

All operators are required to ensure that coffee in transit is safeguarded from contamination arising from rain, water, or mixture with other produce which may lead to cross-infestation, or other forms of contamination. For example, coffee should not be transported in containers used for petroleum products with pungent odors.

The UCTF makes recommendations on the licensing of coffee exporters (to the UCDA) and any other operators directly involved in the marketing of coffee in Uganda. Any coffee trader who is found to consistently breach the code-of-practice is not recommended for renewal of their operating license until they comply with quality requirements specified in the code. Any member who is issued a second warning on a similar misconduct, is required to pay such fine(s) as determined by the Board of UCTF, a schedule of which is made available at the Federation's office, and communicated to members accordingly. The Federation keeps an up-to-date register of its members who have subscribed to the code of conduct, and makes the list available to coffee associations in importing countries. This creates an incentive for all coffee processors and exporters to become members of the UCTF.

The UCDA has statutory powers to regulate the coffee industry at the processing and export level. However, most of the activities affecting the quality of coffee take place at the grassroots level where the UCDA does not have much presence. The UCDA does not have the authority and the capacity to enforce compliance with quality standards at production and primary processing levels. Powers to enforce quality standards lie with local authorities who may have other priorities over enforcement of quality requirements. There have been occasions where local authorities have issued rules or regulations regarding the trading of coffee in their localities, some of which have been found to introduce bottlenecks to the coffee industry (UCTF 2001; CFC 2001). There is a need for decentralizing the coffee quality monitoring in the countryside to local authorities. This requires a new statute clearly stating the roles of various players in the coffee industry, including local authorities, the coffee research institutions, the private sector, and the coffee authority. This would reduce conflict resulting from unclear mandates that currently exists in the coffee industry.

Phytosanitary services are provided by Kawanda Agricultural Research Institute while the certification of quality is done by UCDA, SGS, Audit Control and Expertise (ACE), while weights are inspected and certified by SGS and ACE.[13] All these regulations and certification requirements are mandatory, and clients requiring the service bear the costs associated with these services.

The implementation of the coffee code-of-practice is voluntary and even if a member is dismissed from the federation he or she can continue to operate since membership is voluntary. The UCTF does not have powers to enforce quality requirements among nonmembers, nor does it have powers and the capacity to monitor and enforce quality requirements at the farm and primary processing levels. Furthermore, the liberalization of the coffee industry has had implications for the quality of coffee (CFC 2001). First, a number of unscrupulous and inexperienced coffee buyers (middlemen) who are more concerned with

---

[13] Importers are said to rely more on private firms as regards quality certification because of low confidence in public agencies but certification from these public agencies is a requirement by custom officials.

the quantity (and less with quality) have joined the coffee industry. Second, farmers realized that their coffee output could be sold even when the coffee beans are harvested unripe.

The current incentives and penalties for compliance with quality standards in the coffee industry are not adequate. For example, a penalty for poor quality coffee is only 2 kilograms per every 70 kilograms bag of coffee. This penalty is smaller relative to investment costs required to ensure the quality required. The following example illustrates costs of quality assurance and incentives of avoiding adherence to quality requirements of the coffee output. We assume two categories of coffee producers, that is, farmer A who invests in quality control facilities, and farmer B, who ignores the need for quality measures.

Coffee prices are known for high fluctuations. A range of Shs 250 to Shs 900 per kilogram was assumed. Assuming a total coffee output per hectare of 3,000 kilograms, the quality assurance costs per

kilogram of coffee, which is equivalent to total quality control costs divided by the total output per hectare, is Shs 84 per kilogram using tarpaulin and Shs 57 using papyrus mat and zero costs when no effort is made to care for quality measures. Papyrus mats are more attractive compared to tarpaulin as they are affordable and are thought to be environmental friendly.

It was assumed that Farmer B dries his or her coffee on bare ground and does not care so much about quality requirements, that is, he or she does not dry the coffee to the recommended 12 percent moisture content. This is a very common practice with smallholder coffee farmers in rural Uganda. However, farmer B gets the same price as farmer A, the difference being only 2 kilograms of coffee deducted (per every 70-kilogram bag) by coffee processors/exporters for poorly dried coffee with moisture above the 12 percent level. As Table 5.4 shows the quality assurance cost per kilogram is Shs 57 (using papyrus mat for drying), which is higher than Ushs 26, the

Table 5.4 Comparative Costs of Quality Assurance at Farm Level

Item	Quality Measures Taken (A) (Ushs)	Zero Quality Control (B) (Ushs)
1. Labor		
Harvesting	180,000	108,000
Drying	45,000	15,000
Sub total	225,000	123,000
2. Equipment		
Scissors	4,000	
Tarpaulins (or papyrus mat)	123,000 (43,000)	
Gunny bags	25,000	3,000
Sub total	152,000 (109,000)	3,000
Total costs (1 + 2)	377,000 (297,000)	126,000
Quality control costs (Tarpaulin)	377,000 − 126,000 = 251,000	
Quality control costs (papyrus mat)	297,000 − 126,000 = 171,000	
Quality costs/kg (tarpaulin)	251,000/3000 = 84	
Quality costs/kg (papyrus mat)	171,000/3000 = 57	
Price of coffee (range)	250 to 900	
Revenue for poor quality (per 70 kg bag)		250 (70 − 2) = Shs 17,000 to 900 (70 − 2) = Shs 61,200
Unit revenue with fine		17,000/70 = Shs 243 to 61,200/70 = Shs 874
Unit revenue without fine	250 to 900	

Source: Own computation-using information from CFC (2001).

premium lost by not complying with quality in the case of the highest price and Ushs 7 in the case of the lowest price. The situation worsens when a tarpaulin is used for drying instead of a papyrus mat.

The example above suggests that a price premium between Shs 31 and Shs 50 per kilogram of coffee (using papyrus) and Ushs 58 and Ushs 77 (when using tarpaulin) is an important incentive for any farmer to invest in producing good quality coffee. Without this incentive, farmers are less likely to invest in producing good quality coffee—in effect, many farmers produce poor quality coffee. This leads to extra expenses for exporters and processors, who must meet international standards or face high costs (due to higher rejection rates for poor coffee).[14]

The quality of coffee has to be controlled and managed from production to consumption. Once the quality has been compromised at the lower levels of the production chain, it becomes difficult to achieve the required quality or to avoid quality-related losses at subsequent stages. At the very best, it results in higher rates of low grade coffee beans (for example, broken, hand-picked, sun-dried Arabic) that are sold to local processors at lower prices. Thus, considerable resources may be saved by ensuring the quality of the coffee produce throughout the entire production and distribution process.

Standards in the Flower Industry

The flower industry, dominated by roses and plant cuttings, has experienced considerable improvement over the last ten years. The value of flower exports rose from US$2.3 million in 1995 to about US$16 million in 2001 (IDEA 2002). The flower industry uses a considerable amount of chemicals in the production process with implications to human and animal health, and the environment. The flower industry faces challenges of adhering to standards regarding a maximum chemical residues requirement that comes into force early in 2003. In addition, flower products require special postharvest handling measures (for example, grading, refrigerated storage, transport and handling facilities, and so forth) since they are perishable products. Hence, standards are important in the flower industry.

Adoption and adherence to standards in the flower industry is principally motivated by benefits associated with good quality produce. Failure to stick to standards implies that the exporter finds it difficult to access the export market or receives a lower price. This is also expressed by the most of the members in the Uganda Flowers Exporters Association (UFEA).

Standards and other guidelines to the production and delivery of flower output are contained in the National Code-of-Practice for the flower subsector. This code-of-practice was developed in 1998 jointly by UFEA and HORTEXA, with technical and financial assistance from the IDEA project. It has since been updated in line with changing conditions. However, the UNBS had a limited role in its development, only advising on the contents of the code.

The main aim of the Code-of-Practice is to provide guidelines to growers of flowers on how to achieve and conform to international standards. The code lays out requirements for ensuring the protection of health and welfare of all human beings directly or indirectly involved in the flower industry, and the protection of the environment (see Annex F). UFEA has a committee on standards and ethics that ensures that the standards and requirements set in the code are consistent with international standards and those in the region.

UFEA organizes and contracts a medical doctor to test and monitor the effects of chemical use on the health, and safety of workers in the flower production environment. However, an independent and internationally recognized and reputable organization to undertake the monitoring, inspection, and certifying for compliance with standards is still lacking. The cost of testing by the local doctor is borne by firms being inspected, which is an indication of the importance attached to quality standards by the exporters.

The awareness of quality standards and requirements is well-rooted at the managerial level and information on quality requirements is channeled through (a) the inspection by the Kawanda Agricultural Research Institute and (b) the training on the use chemicals and other health risky inputs by UFEA. There is a monthly newsletter through which communication is made, and regular field visits act as an opportunity to guide and advise flower producers on the importance and process of maintaining quality standards. UFEA also holds

---

[14] Price premium on good quality indeed exists but export traders are told not to pass part of it on to producers and processors of coffee (observation during the field visits, 2002).

regular seminars on production and processing of flower exports at the UFEA headquarters.

The flower industry however still faces challenges. At the level of unskilled workers, the awareness or education regarding good practice of workers' health and the environment is still low. Some workers do not adhere to the advice provided. There is no certification in place at the moment to distinguish between those strictly complying with quality assurance and those who do not. Maintaining standards require costly investments that should be rewarded in the form of price premiums and recognition. The UNBS does not render inspection and certification services, probably because of low capacity of the institution. The lack of certification acts as a disincentive for investing in infrastructure that would ensure high quality standards.

There are regular farm visits for inspection, monitoring, evaluation, and certification by authorities from Kawanda Crop Protection Department under MAAIF to ensure compliance with quality standards as laid out in the Code-of-Practice. These visits occur once a month, which is not adequate for effective monitoring and certification. UFEA officials feel that the farm visits should occur twice a month but because of limited capacity (personnel and transport logistics, and so on), this is not possible. The inspection and certification of any flower export consignment is supposed to be done (in principle) at the point of exit (Entebbe airport) but officials from Kawanda rarely do it because of lack of facilitation (testing equipment, transport). Internationally recognized quality assurance auditors to undertake inspection and certification are nonexistent in the flower subsector, yet such a reputable independent third party is crucial in convincing consumers and importers that the commodity and process standards have been complied with from production to export.

The infrastructure system and facilities designed to monitor and certify compliance with standards requirements are severely inadequate. UFEA officials explained that the testing of chemical residuals on flowering plants is done by observing the physical appearance of leaves, but the actual amount of chemicals within plants themselves is difficult to determine due to lack of appropriate equipment and personnel.

Currently, only roses and cuttings are being exported but there are about 52 flower varieties on trial at the research laboratory center at UFEA headquarters. There is even greater potential for other flower products to be exported, for example, potted plants and papyrus reeds. However, these are not being exported at the moment because of the substantial costs involved to airfreight them to overseas markets. As a measure of going around the transport cost problem, UFEA is currently proposing to grow potted plants and export them as cuttings.

Technical assistance from IDEA has enabled the flower industry to achieve better temperature management and general improvement in the market-arrival quality of flower products. There are now far fewer temperature-related losses and exporters now understand the importance of quality management and monitoring at all stages. The compliance with standards in the flower industry is mainly market-driven. The general awareness among low skilled staff requires strengthening. In addition, the capacity of the complementary public institutions (for example, UNBS) concerned with the development, enforcement, and monitoring of standards needs to be strengthened.

Standards in the Honey Sector

The Uganda Honey Beekeepers Association (UHA) is a national apex body in apiculture sector formed in 1995 with headquarters at Nalukolongo, Kampala. The association is supported by a 13-member executive board, five of whom are full-time staff. The basic aim of the association is to promote the development of beekeeping in Uganda by promoting affordable, appropriate, and sustainable beekeeping technology, and secondly, to help people gain income and protect their habitat. The association comprises over eighty primary societies and community groups with a membership of over 70,000 beekeepers.

The association is involved in the production, processing, and marketing of honey products. The association performs a number of functions at the production level. First, it trains beekeepers in good practices in beekeeping and provides materials and resources such as beehives, protective gear, collecting cans, and so on. By 2001, 1900 items of protective gear had been distributed to farmers but this is inadequate. About 52,000 beekeepers have so far received training in traditional beekeeping, harvesting, and extraction through the training programs of the association. The trainees are given handouts containing information on quality control and best practices in apiculture. A training and resource center has been established at Nakasongola with funding from

NORAD.[15] There are currently 757,262 traditional hives and 11,871 top bar hives all of which have been colonized. A total of about 16,000 metric tons (MT) of honey is produced per year (that is, each beehive produces an average of 10 kilograms per season and there are two seasons a year).

At the processing stage, honey from upcountry collection centers is transported in airtight cans to the headquarters for processing and packaging. However, there are transportation constraints since trucks used are not refrigerated and are rented, not owned. The appropriate trucks need to be temperature-regulated at about 25 °C, but such trucks have not yet been acquired due to lack of funds. To ensure compliance with international standards, it requires a laboratory to carry out sample testing at each processing stage, a heating system to control room temperature inside the refinery, and a bigger storage room to handle exportable capacity. The infrastructure available at the processing center includes a settling tank, centrifugal cylinder, sumtank, and a honey fractometer (for moisture testing). However UHA officials indicate that they have plans to double the current operational capacity that would require about US$130,000.

Current Market Potential for Honey. Currently, the biggest outlet for honey is the local market. Some of the honey is exported to Kenya (about 40 MT each year) since the Kenyan market does not pose very stringent standard requirements, unlike the other markets. For example, the EU Directive 74/409/EEC places a number of strict quality requirements on honey imports, such as certificate confirming the health of the bee population and changes in health or conditions of the bees. However, there is great potential market for Ugandan honey as demonstrated by contacts made with countries including Italy (300 MT per year), Norway (900 MT per year), Sweden (300 MT), Germany (21 MT), and the United States. However, the quality of Ugandan honey will have to be further improved to penetrate and effectively compete in international markets, given the stringent standards and regulations, for example, including the labeling of nutrient ingredients in a given quantity of honey. There is considerable economic benefit to the people in the industry given this market potential and potential revenues; for example, the current farmgate price for honey is US$0.60 per kilogram. For illustrative purposes, a farmer with 20 beehives (which is the economically viable production level) each yielding 20 kilograms per year would earn US$240 per year. Compared to the returns in the coffee sector, the average income of a coffee farmer was US$200 per year in 1997 when the coffee prices were five times higher than the current prices, which suggests that a honey farmer is better-off in terms of income than a coffee farmer, on average.

Standards and Regulations in the Honey Sector. International standards on production and processing of honey exist but there is little awareness about it among association members. According to UHA officials, there are no established Ugandan standards, regulations, or policies for the honey sector. Initial efforts in 1998 by the Uganda National Bureau of Standards (UNBS) to develop standards for the honey sector (which were more or less a replication of the EU standards) were not successful, because there was no consultation with stakeholders (beekeeper association and exporters).

The Ministry of Agriculture, Animal Industry, and Fisheries, and UNBS are jointly developing guidelines (standards) and a policy for the sector. The draft Food Law is yet to be enacted by the parliament. With assistance (technical and financial) from UNIDO, the UHA has developed a proposal toward establishing national standards for the sector as an input to the national policy, standards, and regulation formulation process. The UHA has sent samples of honey to Germany for testing the product parameters, after which accredited institutions (particularly Chemiphar (U) Ltd.) could provide certification to honey exporters. The UHA took the initiative in sending honey samples for testing directly to Germany rather than relying on the UNBS because of the slow and bureaucratic process, and lack of technical capacity to carry out the testing at the UNBS.

The regional and international linkages with UHA include Tehan Company of Norway (for testing and sharing information, and so on); Really Raw Honey of the United States for marketing; International Center for Insect Physiology and Ecology, based in Nairobi; International Bee Research Association (Cardiff, U.K.); and Barak Agricultural College in Kenya. These existing linkages are a clear indication of the increasing interest in the honey sector in

---

[15] The Naksongola resource center has just been completed and officially opened in October 2002. The UHA general secretary could not ascertain the amount involved since it was a turnkey project.

Uganda. The challenge that remains is to develop and comply with national standards as well as to develop a product that meets international market standards.

Challenges and the Way Forward. It has been observed that the existing regulatory framework by UNBS regarding the food industry, and honey, in particular is weak and is under review. The suggestion by UHA is to come up with generally acceptable standards, and for the association to be party to the formulation and enforcement of the standards. There is also a need to develop a national policy for the sector spelling out future participation and the role of the government, exporter associations, farmers, and honey producers in the production and marketing of honey and other bee products. Developing and adhering to quality standards is seen as beneficial to the beekeepers and honey exporters in two respects. First, it would reduce dumping of low quality products on the domestic market that would frustrate domestic producers, and secondly it would promote effective competition in external markets, fetching better prices to the sector.

The basic challenges beyond developing national policy guidelines and setting standards and regulations, is the training of farmers, processors, and laboratory technicians in quality control practices, and acquiring necessary equipment at the farm and processing-export level. The other challenge is the monitoring of residues in honey. There should be an action plan for monitoring of residues in honey by (a) building capacity (physical infrastructure and personnel) in the national laboratories to analyze residues and to begin implementing quality management systems together with UHA and (b) recognition/accreditation of national laboratories for analysis of residues in food products. The honey processing plant, owned by UHA at Nalukolongo in Kampala, needs to be upgraded to conform to the food-safety ISO standards. A feasibility study has been done in this respect, and about Ushs 300 million (about US$170,000) is required for the construction and purchasing of equipment.

Standards in the Fish Industry

The contribution of the fish industry in exports increased substantially in the 1990s except for the period when fish exports were under ban to EU markets. For example, fish and fishery products in total exports rose from 0.7 percent in 1990 to 5 percent in 1996 and just less than 8 percent in 2000 and was projected to 17 percent in 2001 after the ban was lifted (The Republic of Uganda 2002).[16] Over 15,000 tons of factory-processed fish were exported generating more than US$30 million in 2000 while 23,000 tons exported in 2001 generated more than US$70 million (Foodnet 2002).

The fish product is an important source of protein and the fish industry employs (and is a source of income to) over 500,000 people involved in various activities including fishermen, fishmongers, fish transporters, and boat builders. The fish industry in Uganda comprises private operators including fishermen, transporters, and fish processors/exporters. The first processing plants began production in 1989 and by 2002 about 11 companies were involved in processing and exporting of fish and fishery products (UFPEA 2002). The total investment in the fish sector in Uganda is about US$60 million. Fish are exported, fresh or frozen, to the European Union, Japan, Hong Kong, Singapore, Australia, Dubai, Israel, and the United States since 1989.

Regulatory System in the Fish Sector. Fish and fishery products are highly susceptible to contamination throughout the distribution chain. The distribution chain comprises fish harvesting from the lake followed by delivery of fish to landing sites, some of which are then purchased and delivered to processing firms for export. A number of players are involved in the distribution chain and therefore the processing and handling of fish requires stringent quality measures, which requires adequate and suitable infrastructure and a strong regulatory body.

The inspection, certification, and control of fish and fish products is the responsibility of the Department of Fisheries Resources (DFR) in the Ministry of Agriculture, Animal Industry, and Fisheries (MAAIF). DFR is the competent authority responsible for the certification of fish and fishery products intended for export and local consumption. DFR inspectors carry out inspection of factory premises, processing lines, landing sites, fish transport means, and exit ports for adherence to safety and

---

[16] There were two bans on exports of fish and fishery products to the European Union from Lake Victoria in 1997 and 1999. However, Uganda fish got access to the U.S. markets, whose only requirement for fish factories was the use of approved HACCP systems (Waniala 2001).

quality requirements and give remedial advice where necessary. DFR is the authority that issues health certificates that accompany export consignments. The certificates are required at the customs exit point, before export of fish products is allowed to proceed.

The Fish Act of 1964 provides for the control of fishing and fish conservation; the purchase, sale, marketing, and processing of fish; and related matters. It is supported by the subsidiary legislation "Fish (Quality Assurance) Rules, 1998". This set of rules was gazetted in accordance with the provision in Section 43 of the Fish Act (The Republic of Uganda 2000b). It describes the powers of fish inspectors, the modalities of issuing sanitary certificates, and offences and penalties. It also prescribes the hygienic conditions including HACCP-based systems required for the placing of fish on the market, for landing sites and establishments on land, in cold stores, during transportation and the general requirements for distribution and monitoring of water in the fish establishments.

European Bans on Ugandan Fish Exports. The fish industry experienced three bans of fish exports in the late 1990s on health grounds expressed by consumers in the European market (Waniala 2001; Dijkstra 2001; Foodnet 2002). European countries, notably Spain and Italy, detected high levels of bacteria contamination including *salmonella* in fish products from Lake Victoria in 1997, after which, they requested EU to impose a ban on fish exports from that lake. Following the fish ban, the EU missions of veterinary inspectors carried four inspections to assess the health control and monitoring of production conditions to comply with the EC directive 91/493/EEC. The first inspections were conducted in March 1997 and December 1997 for overall hygiene standards while the second inspection was conducted in November 1998 for harmonization of Ugandan standards with the EU directive regarding the ban following which Uganda was put on List II and Tanzania on List I. The third mission was in March 1999 for guarantees regarding absence of pesticide residues in fish. The fourth was in October 2000 for harmonization and guarantees regarding pesticide residues.

These missions identified a number of problems faced by the fish industry. The structure of competent authority was not well streamlined to meet quality standards as required by the EU directives. First, there was lack of a clear line of command since two bodies, namely, the Uganda National Bureau of Standards (UNBS) under the Ministry of Tourism, Trade, and Industry and fish inspection services in the Department of Fisheries Resources (DFR) under MAAIF were involved at different stages but lacked coordination (Annex N). Second, inspectors from the DFR were unable to perform their duties as they did not have clear guidelines and standard operating practices, especially with regard to inspecting batches of landed fish, hygiene conditions at landing sites, sampling procedure records of their own activities and documents required for traceability of origin and transportation of fish.

Third, suitable laboratories for pesticide residues, which was the key concern, were nonexistent. The performance and capacity of the government chemist in charge of performing pesticides residual analysis in fish products were found to be inadequate. Fourth, district fisheries officers were not answerable to UNBS and hence were not following the instructions regarding hygiene and handling of fish as required by the EU regulations. Fifth, most public landing sites had not been upgraded and their facilities did not meet EU requirements and therefore fish was poorly handled throughout the distribution chain.

Therefore, fish exports, which had grown tremendously since 1989, suffered from import bans imposed by the European Union in January 1998 and March 1999 (Commission decisions 97/0878/EC, 98/0084/EC and 99/253/EC). The first ban was caused by the failure by fish factories to meet EU food safety and quality assurance standards. A second ban was imposed due to the outbreak of cholera in Uganda, Kenya, Tanzania, and Mozambique in January 1998 by the Commission decision 98/0084/EC in accordance with article 19(1) of the directive 90/685/EEC to protect public health.[17] The third and longest ban was imposed in April 1999 for pesticide residues following the

---

[17] Indeed the Commission decision 98/116/EC of 4 February 1998 also adopted special measures for the import of fruits and vegetables from Uganda, Kenya, Tanzania, and Mozambique by arguing that the infectious agent *Vibrio cholera* survives on foodstuffs imported from these countries (Jha 2001). The EU ruled that samples covering at least 19 percent of consignments of foodstuffs from these countries be subjected to microbiological tests. The World Health Organization advised that the health risk from these products would not be justified if it takes more than ten days to ship the fruits and vegetables from the producing countries to consumers. So only those products shipped by air were a potential health risk. The sampling at the point of entry revealed a very low incidence of contamination of *Vibrio cholera*.

Table 5.5 The Impact of EU ban on Uganda's fish exports

	Effect/Group	Loss
	Export earnings	US$36,900,000
Income of fishermen community (US$850,000 per month) due to reduced prices and fish activities		US$4,250,000
	Factories that closed down	3 out of 11
	Factories that reduced their labor force (2/3)	8 out of 11
	Jobs lost in fish factories (1/3)	2,000
	Jobs lost in fishing activities (1/3)	32,000
	Persons that lost 2/3 of their income	68,000
	Affected family members and relatives living on the same income	300,000

Source: UNIDO available at www.unido.org, accessed September 2002.

notification to the EU by UNBS that it could no longer guarantee the safety of its fish exports. The EU demanded a comprehensive monitoring program that would determine levels of chlorine pesticides, organophosphate pesticides, and their trace elements in fish, water, and sedimentation in the lake.

Quality standards in the fish industry have been developed based on EU regulatory requirements such as EU directive 91/493/EEC and Codex Alimentarius standards. Standards in the fish industry cover areas of microbiology levels, pesticide residues, heavy metals, effluents, good manufacturing practices, and HACCP. With the assistance of USAID-funded Support for Private Enterprises Expansion and Development (SPEED) project, all UFPEA[18] members are expected to be ISO 9001 or ISO 9002 compliant by 2003 (UFPEA 2002). The SPEED provides financial assistance to fish processors for training (currently by TQM) in quality control as part of the process for ISO certification. The ban on fish was officially lifted in 2000 and fish exports to EU resumed on a bilateral basis, that is, Uganda was placed on List II until May 2001 before which Uganda was placed on List I (Waniala 2001). The ban was lifted after the European Commission inspection team verified that the Department of Fisheries Resources had the capacity to monitor and enforce standards regarding fishing, handling, processing, and marketing

of fish and fish products that are compliant with EU standards.

Impact of the Fish Ban. The effects of the EU ban on fish exports have been both at micro- and macro-levels (see Table 5.5).[19] At the macroeconomic level, fish exports declined with consequent reductions in revenue from fish exports. The loss to Uganda in terms of reduced returns as a result of the fish ban from March to July 1999 is estimated at about US$36.9 million while the loss to fishing communities on account of reduced prices and less fishing is thought to be US$1 million per month. Out of 11 factories that were operational before the ban, three closed down and the remaining were operating at 20 percent capacity (Waniala 2001). The decline in production resulted in about 60 percent to 70 percent of the directly employed people being out of employment. About 35,000 people involved in fish-related activities (for example, fishermen, fishmongers, and transporters) became jobless. Other indirectly employed people earned less than one-third of their pre-ban earnings. Families and dependants of the directly and indirectly employed people were also adversely affected. Other related industries such as packaging, transporting and the economy in general were directly affected and all the people involved suffered direct consequences because of the EU ban on Ugandan fish exports.

---

[18] UFPEA refers to Uganda Fish Processors and Exporters Association and, with the assistance of SPEED, UFPEA developed and launched a website (www.ufpea.co.ug) at the end of June 2002.

[19] Out of 100,000 people involved in various fishing activities, 32,000 lost their jobs, others earned less than one third of their normal income while families and other dependants (about 300,000 people) of the directly employed were also affected by the ban on Uganda's fish exports in 1999 (available at www.unido.org, accessed September, 2002).

Individual firms have had to take additional investments to comply with quality requirements. For example, over the last three years, additional cost in equipment has ranged between US$12,000 and US$13,500 across the four firms visited during the data collection exercise, while the training of personnel on fish processing and handling cost between US$2,500 and US$5,000. The initial cost of certification was US$15,000 for each individual firm, while the hired testing and certification services ranged between US$2,000 and US$4,000 over the same period. These costs were borne by firms themselves apart from the training from developing agencies such as UNIDO and the World Bank. These additional requirements to improve standards obviously increased production costs. However, returns on these investments to individual firms are difficult to ascertain because of the reluctance of firms to reveal information, but the investments were beneficial since they played an important role in getting the ban lifted and increasing fish exports. For example, fish exports increased from 14,075 tons before the ban to 28,119 tons after the ban. This increase is partly attributed to the compliance with standards that enabled Ugandan fish and fishery products to upgrade from List II to List I.[20]

However, the fish ban was not entirely negative. There are some positive developments associated with the three bans on Ugandan fish exports to the EU. The fish ban made authorities pay more attention to the problems of the fish subsector; for example, the government solicited support from UNIDO that facilitated a private laboratory (Chemiphar (U) Ltd.). This was approved by the EU inspectors for pesticides residue analysis (Waniala 2001). The availability of such internationally recognized laboratory services in Uganda greatly facilitates exports of other products and reduces the costs of laboratory analysis that used to be undertaken abroad. Before the ban, samples were flown to Belgium for testing at an estimated cost of US$66,000 per year (personal communication with UNBS officials 2002) which has since reduced.[21]

Because of the fish ban, Uganda got access to U.S. markets, which demanded only that the fish factories use Hazard Critical Control Points (HACCP) systems (rather than the full scale establishments as demanded by the EU). The restructuring of the fish industry to comply with EU standards did not result in extra market opportunities in the United States, since, for the U.S. market, the quality assurance arrangements are between fish exporters and importers, as opposed to EU which places the responsibility of quality assurance on government agencies. The UNBS microbiology laboratory has been fully equipped and technical assistance was provided by UNDP. The government has invested about US$ 180,000 for a period of two years in a monitoring program on Lake Victoria and recruited 10 inspectors to supervise fish production at processing plants.

In summary, the fish industry was restructured over the last three to five years to comply with health and safety standards and other quality requirements. The monitoring and enforcement of standards in the fish industry is the responsibility of the Department of Fisheries Resources under MAAIF. This restructuring of the industry has made possible for Ugandan fish products to be exported to the EU under List I. The need to restructure the industry arose from the conditions of import markets, but other sectors can learn from this experience the impact of a ban on exports, and put in place measures to comply with standards before bans are put in place. This is important in the case of floriculture and horticulture sectors where maximum chemical residual level requirements are coming into force in February 2003 and potential exports to the United States under AGOA will require requirement of pest risk analysis (PRA). These actions, however, require strengthening the institutions concerned in terms of developing both technical personnel training and equipping laboratories.

Standards in the Manufacturing Sector

The manufacturing sector in Uganda is dominated by light manufacturing basically in textiles, food

---

[20] List I permits a country to export directly to any country in the EU.

[21] There are 14 sites on Lake Victoria where samples are obtained on a quarterly basis for testing at TNO Nutrition and Food Research (Holland) and Chemiphar (U) Ltd., which are contracted by the DFR. The cost of testing the samples is about US$85 both at each of the testing center but samples are shipped to Holland for verification. This results in an extra freight of about US$1950 per year that could be saved if local firms were upgraded and accredited to international standards-setting bodies. The UNBS has an accredited microbiology laboratory but Chemiphar (U) Ltd. can perform both microbiology and chemical residue tests and is therefore preferred.

processing, and beverages. The share of the manufacturing in the GDP is still small but has increased from 7 percent in 1995 to 10 percent in 2001. The Uganda Manufacturing Association (UMA), established in the 1960s and revived in 1988 after a long period of dormancy is the apex body to promote and coordinate manufacturing activities in Uganda. The current membership of UMA is over 700 that comprises large, medium, and small manufacturing firms mainly from the private sector. UMA initiates and facilitates the discussion and exchange of information on industrial issues among members. It disseminates information to members and the general public through a bi-weekly bulletin, a quarterly manufacturer journal, and a weekly *Economic Desk* TV program. Furthermore, it is in the process of setting up an Internet information training center that is expected to offer sensitization and skills training to members. These activities are largely funded from UMA's own sources (membership contribution, revenue from consultancy services, and so on) and other contributors, for example, the Uganda government. It prepares and hosts international trade fairs with the intentions of improving the quality and promoting competitiveness of products both within domestic and export markets.

UMA has set up an ISO 9000 certification program to improve the quality and competitiveness of products for member companies. Most of the quality standards in the sector have been harmonized with the EAC and COMESA standards (consult UNBS at www.unbs.org for details). The UMA encourages association members to adapt to standards so as to improve the competitiveness of their products. The standards adapted are expected to be consistent with those designed by international standard-setting bodies such as WTO and ISO.

There are still a number of constraints to the manufacturing sector as regards the development and compliance with standards. First, the awareness of the need and importance of process and product standards is still lacking among stakeholders. Hence, the application of standards in the manufacturing sector is limited except for those exporting their produce to overseas markets. Second, the UMA officials recognize and appreciate that the macroeconomic environment is conducive to the country's manufacturing activities, but at the micro-level, considerable

improvement is required to facilitate better performance of the manufacturing sector. UMA officials believed that government needs to assist producers, particularly small and medium scale firms (in terms of fiscal incentives, and so on), in developing an infrastructure system[22] that complements the development and implementation of standards and associated regulations. Where such infrastructure exists, the government could assist manufacturers in the undertaking of major improvements. The development of such an infrastructure system is currently the sole responsibility of the individual manufacturing firms.

Third, UMA officials feel that a communication gap exits between producers and consumers in the market (especially export markets). Consumers in export are thought to be more aware of health and, of the safety consequences associated with poor quality products and are more organized into stronger associations with considerable influence on policy makers. Hence such organized consumers are capable of influencing the quality requirements of commodities that must meet compliance before such products are placed on the market. However, the communication gaps are being addressed through international trade fairs.

Fourth, there is a poor enforcement system in the country regarding compliance with the established standards. The UNBS has succeeded in areas of labeling manufactured products with the manufacture and expiration dates for some products, but the enforcement of the ingredient proportions for a given product and bar coding has not been successful.

Fifth, the enforcement of standards and associated sanctions for defaulters is still weak and the UNBS does not have sufficient capacity (both personnel and financial resources) to undertake the enforcement of sanctions of those firms compromising with established standards. UNBS has often collaborated with other government agencies, such as the Uganda Revenue Authority (URA) and individual firms, affected by the standards in monitoring and enforcement of quality standards. Finally, there is hardly any price premium for products that comply with quality standards over those which do not. This has greatly hindered the standards compliance in the sector.

UMA participates in the development of standards and it is represented on some of the UNBS technical committees. UMA has a committee on

---

[22] Such infrastructure would include preparation for certification to compliance with standards such as the training of personnel and setting up laboratories, and so on.

ethics and in-house structure to monitor and certify the standards compliance.

UMA officials view quality requirements throughout the production chain as beneficial to members because they enhance the competitiveness of the sectors' products and promote environmental-friendly production systems. However, to comply with quality standards, producers in Uganda (especially, small- and medium-scale firms) would need assistance to establish the necessary infrastructure systems that enable the development and implementation of quality requirements in different markets.

The analysis focused on the textile industry to get an insight of the existing standards and how they affect the export of textile products. There are about four textile factories (including Tri-Star, Phenix Logistics (U) Limited, and Nytil Picfare (U) Limited) mainly targeting the domestic market. However, with the AGOA initiative, preparations are in progress to exploit opportunities that exists in the USA and other export markets. We use Phenix Logistics (U) Limited as a case study to illustrate the issue of standards and the level of development of the textile industry in Uganda.

The Case of Phenix Logistics (U) Ltd. Phenix Logistics (U) Ltd., formerly Uganda Garment Industries Limited (UGIL), is one of the four textile and garment manufacturers in Uganda. UGIL was established in 1965 as a joint venture between the Uganda government, Yamato of Japan, Malbeni of Japan, and a garment firm in India. At the time, UGIL specialized in the manufacture of shirts using imported materials. In 1973, a knitting line was introduced, and Ugandan cotton yarn brought in from NYTIL and Lira spinning Mills started being used for knitwear instead of imports from abroad. In 1988, a spinning line was introduced, initially with a capacity of 18 tons per year, and expanded to 54 tons per year in the early 1990s.

As a result of the general mismanagement that affected state-owned enterprises, the company became a loss-making venture and was closed in 1994 pending privatization. UGIL was finally sold off to private investors (a joint venture between Japanese, Ugandan, and Singaporean business partners) in 2000, and was incorporated as Phenix Logistics (U) Limited. Operations resumed in August 2001 using imported materials and production has since been restored to 4000 dozen of T-shirts and 2000 dozen shirts per month. Currently, cotton yarn for knitwear (underwear and T-shirts) is locally obtained, while all materials for woven textiles (school uniforms, and casual wear) are still being imported from China and other countries.

Market Analysis and Outlets. Phenix Logistics (U) Ltd. (Phenix) has concentrated on the domestic market since 2001 for two reasons: first, to get back into the market and capture domestic market share; and second, the firm has not been operating long enough to raise output to export capacity and improve quality to required standards in external markets. There are, however, efforts to explore trade opportunities in the EU and other markets abroad such as the U.S. market under the AGOA arrangement.

Whereas there is greater focus on the domestic market, there is still low demand for textile products. This is attributed to reliance on cheaper second hand (used) clothes from abroad, which are more affordable to the majority of consumers. In addition, the cost of production in terms of transport costs for imported inputs and cost of utilities, particularly electricity, have rendered textile products less competitive, both in domestic and external markets. According to the factory manager, current efforts to export have involved sending out samples of manufactured products to potential buyers in the EU, the United States, Hong Kong, and so on who have responded by providing information on the minimum required quality standards. The basic sources of information about product and quality specifications are buyers in targeted markets. Product quality specifications range from knot-free yarn and texture finishing to organic-only cotton products.

To comply with quality requirements, the firm is upgrading production technology from the current mechanical to electronic technology. Even with the mechanical methods of production currently used, investment is being made into the yarn specification machine (Wooster Tester), which is able to detect and provide information on yarn specification that can then be attached to the finished product. The other investment is in a machine that can detect knots and folds in the yarn, and produce knot-free and fold-free yarn. However, Phenix officials were reluctant to provide specific information on international standards and the nature of investment required.

Whereas Phenix has taken initiatives to improve the quality standards, there has been limited interaction with UNBS in terms of obtaining information about quality requirements in external markets. Likewise, there is no specific endeavors being made through the Uganda Textile and Garment Association, regarding the promotion of standards in the industry though the activities of the Association itself are limited. As such, all efforts to improve and comply with quality standards are being done at firm-level.

Although compliance with commodity standards is a major constraint for accessing external markets, there is a wide range of other factors that make Ugandan textile less competitive. Transport costs and delays in delivery of the imported materials increase production costs. For example, transporting a container from Hong Kong to Mombassa costs an average of US$2,000, and another US$3,000 between Mombassa and Kampala. The customs documentation process is also causing further delays and warehouse costs. The other constraint is the cost associated with the availability and reliability of utilities, particularly power tariffs.

The analysis above indicates that the textile industry is still in the early stages of development and faces a number of constraints in producing and marketing its products. Concerted efforts are therefore needed in areas of improving quality requirements and compliance with standards as required by different markets, and in lowering costs of utilities. Current initiatives taken by the firm need to be complemented by the government agencies such as the UNBS in complying with standards. It should be noted that all firms in the textile industry are more or less at the same level of development hence the case generally applies.

The Horticultural Sector

The Horticultural Exporters Association of Uganda (HORTEXA) was established in 1990 with the aim of promoting horticultural exports in Uganda by encouraging high-quality exportable produce, market research, and training of the association members (farmers and exporters) in production systems, harvesting and postharvesting handling, and pricing. It disseminates information regarding the pricing and market requirements for fresh produce to exporters and producers.

Membership is open to all farmers and exporters of fruits and vegetables. HORTEXA is run by an executive body comprising the Chairman, General Secretary, Treasurer, and Technical Advisor. HORTEXA has a number of objectives. First, it aims to promote agricultural exports in Uganda by encouraging high-quality exportable produce, market research and training. Second, it encourages standardized and high quality packaging of fruits and vegetables. Third, HORTEXA provides technical assistance to the association members (farmers and exporters) in production systems, harvesting and postharvesting handling, and pricing. Fourth, it disseminates information regarding fresh produce to government, exporters, and producers, for planning purposes. HORTEXA currently operates in six districts, namely Mpigi, Mukono, Kayunga, Luweero, Masaka, and Mubende and currently there are about 600 registered members (both farmers and exporters).

There are over 25 different products produced by the different members of the Association. These include plantains such as *Matooke, Bogoya,* and *Ndizi*; fresh and dried fruits such as pineapple; passion fruits; jackfruits; and pawpaw. Other produce includes cereals (peas, ground nuts, and so on); hot peppers; and chilies. Most of the produce is exported to European (particularly Belgium, U.K., and the Netherlands) and American markets, and a few fruits to the Middle East. Between 150 and 230 metric tons of the total produce is exported each month, varying according to seasonal changes (HORTEXA database).

According to HORTEXA officials, markets for most of the produce are available but basic challenges that remain include maintaining a steady supply for some of the produce, and meeting the required quality standards to become competitive in external markets. Given that most of the Ugandan farmers use an organic farming system (limited use of chemicals and fertilizers), it makes Uganda's produce desirable to consumers, but quality control in handling and packaging remains a big challenge. A number of measures are being undertaken to address this problem, as illustrated in the following discussion.

Standards and Regulations in the Horticultural Sector. Standards in the horticultural sector include a maximum chemical-residue level; grading to size, color, and texture of products; maximum moisture and sugar and fiber contents, and so on. HORTEXA exporters are provided with information by importers about quality requirements in respect to postharvest handling and packaging. However, most farmers are not well aware of the international standards. HORTEXA is now placing greater emphasis on quality through obtaining information on

397

quality requirements in potential markets for horticultural products and sensitize farmers on recommended chemical use, organic farming, and postharvest handling through field visits and demonstrations. Assistance to HORTEXA could be in the form of support to the training programs, sourcing, and speeding up the flows of information on market opportunities and, quality requirements.

Enforcement and monitoring of standards is done at two levels, that is, farm and export. At the farm level, all of the farmers in the association are coded and the code number is attached to the consignments (boxes) from a particular farmer. This way, it becomes easy to identify which farmer has not met required standards if the produce for a given code gets rejected in the market. Likewise, it makes it possible to identify those farmers with good quality produce. The coding system provides an incentive for each farmer to adhere to quality requirements so as to attract a good price or market share. Similarly, corrective measures can easily and quickly be undertaken in cases where poor quality is supplied by a given farmer. The coding system, which makes it easy to monitor quality requirements, can easily apply to other sectors. The enforcement becomes hard for those exporters/farmers who do not belong to the association. Therefore, for the coding system to be effective, membership should be mandatory and the cost of coding should be borne by individual exporters but funded preferably through the respective associations. The second level of quality enforcement and monitoring is at pre-shipment stage, which is done by SGS. However, the quality requirement comprised at stage one is difficult to be rectified at this stage and chances are high that the substandard produce will find its way to the market but at a lower unit return.

In the recent past, rejecting produce that was considered below quality used to be common, but this has been reduced through the sensitization workshops and farm visits being undertaken. Access to some markets is still limited because of stringent standards requirements. Desired quality standards by external markets for some of the produce is very costly to meet. For instance, there is a requirement for specific size, color, and weight per box that may be prescribed by the customer. This implies that grading and packaging has to be done in accordance with stated specifications, for example, five avocados per box of 2 kilograms. The exporter or farmer therefore has to do the grading and packaging to meet such a requirement. Lack of equipment, such as an automated grader makes grading to particular specifications laborious, costly and also increases postharvest losses. However, through the on-going training programs (at US$280 per participant per year) both for the farmers and exporters, it will become easier to meet required standards and eventually access these markets, but acquiring the necessary equipment for grading and packaging remains challenging. Farmers are being encouraged to form groups, which can jointly export the produce directly, instead of relying on middlemen. This will further improve quality and the quality-monitoring system, since the association has direct contact with the farmer unlike the middlemen.

Challenges to Improving the Competitiveness of Uganda's Horticultural Exports. There is an opportunity to expand the market, especially with the enactment of, and publicity given to, AGOA. However, this translates into new and more challenges to improving the competitiveness of the exports, especially regarding the quality of the products to be exported.

As already pointed out, horticultural exporters are loosely organized under the Horticultural Exporters' Association (HORTEXA), with the office in Kampala. HORTEXA coordinates with the Uganda Export Promotion Board (UEPB) in a bid to promote compliance with standards so as to boost horticultural exports.

However, both HORTEXA and UEPB do not have adequate funds to carry out activities aimed at promoting compliance with standards and giving information on products available for exports (information on, for example, the quantities available, the prices, and quality of the products) to potential customers. For example HORTEXA has no website, which would be useful in informing importers about Ugandan horticultural products. HORTEXA uses the website of UEPB, but the information given here was described by HORTEXA members as "too brief" to attract many potential customers. However, exporters of horticultural products from other countries (that is, competitors with HORTEXA members) carry out a lot of publicity, especially on the Internet, with their websites giving details on quality, quantity available, and price quotations. Potential customers get all the information at the "click of a button." To counter this (by giving information on their products) individual firms have to fax or make telephone calls to their customers to give details of their products. This increases their marketing costs and may translate into higher prices, further eroding the competitiveness of Uganda's horticultural exports.

Further, this communication problem constrains the individual firms from attracting new customers as they (firms) call up only their already established customers, and vice versa (that is, customers make telephone calls only to firms they have dealt with before).

One of the standard requirements for export of horticultural products is that they must be damage-free and clean. Given the state of transport infrastructure within the country, exporting firms have found it difficult to satisfy this requirement without incurring losses.

Problems in Implementation of Standards in the Horticulture Sector. There are still a number of constraints facing the horticulture sector in enforcing quality standards. First, most of the farmers are small and scattered, which makes it difficult to provide information regarding quality control in a coordinated manner. Second, the HORTEXA lacks finance to support outreach programs. Currently, the association is being supported by the IDEA Project to carry out field visits and training programs but this funding is not sufficient to support all activities. Third, farmers are constrained by limited capital to adopt better farming systems. The commercial loans attract a fairly high interest rate that is considered too high for the farmers to afford, given the risks involved in the sector. Finally, there is insufficient technical staff at the UNBS to provide supervisory services prior to harvesting. The only supervision currently available is at pre-shipment-level, which does not address the real quality concerns at farm-level. This service is considered more of a deterrent than a supportive service.

It must be noted that most horticultural exporting firms do not produce on their own, but instead buy products from farmers located in different parts of the country. In the process of transporting these products from upcountry to Kampala for packaging before export, some of the products get damaged. The damaged products become ineligible for export markets, which is one of the challenges to improving the competitiveness of Uganda's horticultural exports. Some exporting firms revealed that they do not export directly to certain markets

(for example, Germany) because they cannot meet the standards requirements (for example, weight, size, and texture specifications) in those markets.

Inadequate cooling facilities reduce the shelf life of perishable products. Since it is a requirement that horticultural products be exported while fresh, exporting firms have to pick and package the export products a day or two before the flight. This reduces the quantity available for export. This has constrained horticultural exporters from penetrating the larger markets.

Most of Uganda's competitors are not landlocked and export their products by sea transport, a cheaper transport mode—unlike Uganda, which mostly relies on air transport. Airfreight charges are high and often involve flight cancellation. Flight canceling and rescheduling negatively affects firms involved in exporting horticultural products by air, given the inadequate cold-storage facilities. Thus the products packaged for export fail to meet the standard requirement.

There is a loose link between HORTEXA and horticultural farmers, and individual exporters deal with specific farmers to ease monitoring of quality compliance, which increases the operating costs of the export firms. Consequently, the need to comply with standards may translate into lower profit margins for Ugandan products compared to those of competitors.

The technical advisor and general secretary of HORTEXA suggested a number of interventions to address the key constraints in the sector. First, there is a need to improve capacity of UNBS to provide technical assistance in liaison with HORTEXA. Second, the government should show more commitment to the sector as representing one of the promising export sectors in the country. The government should provide "soft loans" to the farmers in coordination with HORTEXA.

Despite these constraints, some factors that help to foster the competitiveness of Uganda's horticultural exports are also in place. For example, horticultural exports are free from taxation; and the exporters' association provides members with information on technical standards and regulations in the different markets. HORTEXA has, in collaboration with the IDEA project of USAID, facilitated several standards-related training sessions for its members. However, the impact of such training may be minimal given that HORTEXA does not cover all horticultural exporters.

Horticultural exporters still incur a lot of expenses in order to get their products to conform to standard requirements, for example, sorting and grading. Efforts toward ensuring conforming to standards right from farm-level should be stepped up to ensure reduced expenses by the exporters, probably higher prices to farmers, and conformity to international standards requirements. Cold storage facilities need to be improved if Uganda is to comply with commodity standards requirements and benefit from the expanding horticultural market.

The marketing strategy should be enhanced through supporting farmers and encouraging them to exhibit their products in international trade promotions, and bazaars. The Ugandan embassies and high commissions abroad should have a technical person to provide information to potential buyers, and provide market opportunities to Ugandan farmers and exporters. This will also promote other export products as well. Finally, HORTEXA should be given more recognition by the government as a key stakeholder in the development of the sector. Designing of a strategic plan, the national code of conduct for the sector, and disbursement of any form of assistance to the sector should be done with the consultation and participation of the association.

Specialty Products in Uganda: The Case of Organic Coffee

Organic products are those that are grown from an organically certified chain of production, which excludes all forms of synthetic materials such as chemicals in pests and disease control. Organic products provide with economic, social and environmental advantages (ITC/UEPB 2000). First, consumers tend to pay relatively higher prices for organic food products compared to conventional products because organic products are thought to result in healthier and safer foods. Second, avoiding or minimizing the use of synthetics tends to improve the natural environment resulting in the sustainable use of soils and the maintaining of soil fertility.

Organic production and exports in Uganda include coffee, cotton, sesame, cocoa, vanilla, and horticultural products. Most traditional techniques of agricultural production in Uganda are said to be consistent with rules of organic production and most of the land is said to be free from chemicals but the certification services are still limited and costly. For example, organic farmers sold less than

20 percent of the organic cotton and sesame as certified organic products in 2000/2001 season, the rest being sold as conventional products (Waniala 2001). Price premiums for organic products tend to be high. Waniala (2001) reports that the price premiums received for organic over conventional products were 20 percent in the case of coffee, 15 percent for cotton and about 120 percent in the case of organically produced horticultural products (with growers of pineapples, apple banana, passion fruit and ginger receiving a price premium ranging from 40 to 80 percent). Unlike conventional products, the prices of organic products tend to be stable.

The challenging factors in the production and marketing of organic products include high costs of monitoring, inspection and certification, identification of markets, and promotion. Production of organics in Uganda is small-scale and the amount exported is dependent on the producers' ability to meet costs of certification. The limited use of chemicals (and availability of cheap labor) suggests that conversion to organic production could easily be accomplished among small-scale producers but certification costs need to be reduced. The conversion period takes about one and a half years if the soils were not contaminated by chemicals and about three years if the fields were already contaminated. The production and distribution of organics require inspection and certification by a competent and internationally accredited firm or agency (Vossenaar and Jha 2001; Waniala 2001). A number of options for reducing the costs of certification are suggested that include (a) the creation of a locally certifying body; (b) group certification particularly for small-scale and scattered producers[23], (c) reduce the costs of obtaining international accreditation for certifiers in the country, and (d) promoting and facilitating the creation of local and regional certification bodies.

Markets for organic products have grown rapidly over the past few years, estimated at US$13 billion by 1998 and is predicted to grow to US$40 billion by 2004 (UCTF 2001). Uganda first entered the market for certified organic products in 1994 when Lango Cooperative Union exported certified organic cotton followed by exports of certified sesame. Exports of organic products in Uganda increased considerably from about 100 metric tons to 1000 metric tons between 1998 and 2001 (UCTF 2001). While

---

[23] This is the current system being used in Uganda for monitoring, inspection, and certification.

there is a considerable increase in the quantity of organic products, the market for organic products is comparatively small relative to conventional markets and organic products which tend to face considerable production and processing costs.

The production, marketing and promotion of organic products in Uganda is primarily a private sector initiative under NOGAMU, which is an agricultural movement aiming at fostering good health and environment by promoting organic farming practices. NOGAMU, officially launched in 2001, comprises farmers, researchers, exporters, and traders, works with government institutions such as UIA and NEMA. According to the NOGAMU secretariat, the current membership comprises 65 individuals, mainly farmers and 30 organizations. NOGAMU is affiliated with the International Federation of Organic Agricultural Movement (IFOAM) and is supported in terms of infrastructure (such as office space) by KULIKA Trust, a local NGO supported by Norway and Sweden.

The services offered by NOGAMU include training in organic farming, creating market linkages and assisting members to get certified, sensitization, advocacy, and promoting organic farming in Uganda. The training of farmers in organic farming methods includes (a) soil control methods such as the use of cow dung to improve soil fertility and the use of terraces in controlling soil erosion, (b) methods of pest control using biological means such as banana weevil control using cow's urine, cotton stainers using repellants such as marigold flower and natural predators such as black ants, and (c) postharvest control measures such as controlling weevils and pests.

Currently, the certification is done by internationally renowned firms such as IMO (a German and Swiss firm), KRAAV (a Swedish firm), and ECO-CERT (a French firm), all accredited to the IFOAM. They have local consultants who carry out the training and inspection in Uganda. The cost of training normally ranges between US$5,000 and US$6,000 for a group of farmers and thereafter an annual inspection fee of US$3,000. These costs are normally met by the exporters, some of whom have received assistance from SIDA (a Swedish grant agency) through the Export Promotion of Organic Products from Africa (EPOPA) initiative. Others, such as Tropical Ecological Foods Uganda (TEFU) have exporter-importer linkages where the importer covers the certification costs but for a lower premium.

The enforcement of compliance is normally done through group solidarity with the knowledge that if one member defaults, all farmers lose when their certificate is withdrawn. Routine audits are carried out by the inspectors to ensure that standards are kept and random testing is done on the products, testing their chemical residue levels.

Conclusion

The Ugandan economy is heavily reliant on agriculture and associated activities. The agricultural sector is a major employer and foreign exchange earner and is likely to remain so in the foreseeable future. Considerable progress has been made regarding macroeconomic policies but considerable efforts are still needed at the micro-level. Recent attempts to diversify the country's economic activities has concentrated efforts in diversifying the commodity composition but the diversification in terms of market destination is still not adequate. Most of the country's exports are destined for European markets and quality requirements (standards) in these markets are becoming more restrictive, combined with increased competition as more policy-induced barriers (such as tariffs, quotas, and so on) are reduced or eliminated. Therefore, Ugandan producers and exporters will need strong institutional and infrastructural support to improve the competitiveness of their products in export markets.

Overall, there is considerable appreciation (both by public and private producers) of the need to develop and comply with standards, but major problems in the setting, monitoring, and enforcement of standards remain:

- There are limited resource (both technical personnel and infrastructure) in most institutions responsible for the setting, monitoring, and enforcement of standards in the country. There are some efforts under way to harmonize standards across the region, mainly in the East African community (EAC) and COMESA, which may reduce costs of enforcement of compliance with standards.
- The compliance with standards requirements is largely being spearheaded by producers mainly for export markets, and therefore applies to a small proportion of production. This limits producers from taking advantage of economies of scale and scope in terms of standards development and compliance that would be the case if

standards requirements were uniformly applied to output irrespective of the market.

- There is limited awareness of the nature and existence of standards (at varying levels[24]) among producers particularly regarding international standards. However, some sectors have attempted to develop and enforce standards in the form of codes of practice that demonstrate the willingness to comply with standards and appreciation of the importance of standards by producers and exporters.

- The enforcement of standards is more at the export level, yet the standards or quality control should start right from the first point of production through the production chain and distribution system.

- The inspection, monitoring, and certification of local firms with international recognition are limited and acquiring these services from foreign firms is very expensive for most producers. There are considerable cost savings if local firms are accredited for certification to the level of other international standards-setting bodies. UNBS and other government agencies responsible for developing and enforcing standards are inadequately funded and understaffed; therefore, they do not perform to expectation.

- Incentives for compliance with standards are still weak in some sectors such as coffee but strong in other sectors, for example, in fish and flowers where no sales can be made without meeting the standards.

Action Plan

Increasing the competitiveness of the country's exports—that is, maintaining and improving an export's market share—require a number of innovative initiatives so as to maintain and even improve the market share. However, this would entail improving compliance with standards and other market requirements. In turn, this requires setting up strong institutions and an infrastructure network that would enable compliance with such standards. Compliance with standards and other quality requirements is essential throughout the production and distribution chain. The following are recommended areas for intervention or action: (a) the capacity building in terms of human resources; (b) capacity building in terms of equipment, particularly laboratories to facilitate the monitoring, testing, and enforcement of compliance with standards; (c) accreditation to international standards of the established or upgraded institutions responsible for the certifying, monitoring, and enforcement of compliance with standards; and (d) sensitization of various stakeholders to the needs and measures to comply with standards, and the benefits associated with conforming to standards; assistance to various categories for participating in the trade fairs (local and international) and in developing standards (also see Appendix E).

Capacity Building

Actions regarding capacity building are of two categories, that is, the training of technical staff for developing, monitoring, and enforcement of standards; and developing the infrastructure, such as laboratories, necessary for testing. Recommendations regarding each are provided below.

Capacity Building (Training). Institutions responsible for setting, monitoring, enforcement and issuing of standards in Uganda are understaffed relative to the enormous work expected to be done. For example, Kawanda Agricultural Research Institute (KARI), responsible for enforcing and issuing certificates relating to sanitary and phytosanitary issues has a technical staffs of five; there are about 24 entry points to attend to, and five people cannot but attend to all these points. Under the AGOA trade arrangements, the United States has asked Uganda to carry out a pest risk analysis but KARI, who is responsible for this exercise, lacks both equipment and technical staff. The UNBS has a technical staff of about 50, which falls short of the desired level of 130 needed to provide good quality and efficient services. Each of the five laboratories has a technical staff of two but the desirable number is said to be five, that is, two analysts, two technical staff members[25] and one coordinator. To effectively monitor and enforce standards, an adequate technical team is required at the ports of entry/exit, in laboratories at

---

[24] For example, the level of awareness about standard requirements is greater in the case of the fish sector compared with the horticultural sector.

[25] At least two analysts are needed for a number of reasons, for example, one analyst to countercheck the analysis made by the other. Equal arguments are made for the two technical staff members.

the UNBS headquarters, in the field, providing guidance to producers and exporters; and another team is required in the market, to constantly monitor developments in spheres of standards and technical regulations. Currently teams at entry points and in the markets are nonexistent.

UNBS has benefited from a US$3 million UNDP grant for establishing national metrological and electrical laboratories and upgrading of the microbiology laboratory. The chemistry and building material laboratories still require some form of upgrading. The donation from UNDP did not cover the personnel training and required the government to get accommodation for the UNBS and increase recruitment from the earlier 22 to 50 technical staff members. Thus, an area of intervention is to increase the technical staff and update the technical capacity of the current technical staff.

Training services can be provided within the country or outside the country. The within-country training would involve inviting qualified and experienced personnel into the country to provide training services, taking into account the local environment and equipment on-ground. Unlike training outside the country, the within-country training would increase the number trained since this would avoid the cost of flying few individuals abroad. It is hoped that with increased technical staff, the monitoring and enforcement will be more effective, and the testing and certification will take relatively short time and more products will be covered. If standards are consistently monitored and enforced, the reputation of institutions responsible for standards and the image of the country's export will be improved. Issues of standards and technical regulations are complex and operate in dynamic conditions (new standards and technology must constantly be incorporated), and therefore capacity-building in the form of updating technical staff is essential.

Capacity Building (Infrastructure/Equipment). Effective monitoring and enforcement of standards would need modern laboratories to carry out the necessary testing. It is recommended that appropriate laboratories be set up or existing laboratories be upgraded. It is estimated that the overall cost of restructuring the laboratories for accreditations at UNBS amounts to US$12 million. It will require a further US$11.4 million to set up a permanent home for UNBS. Where equipment exists in the country but outside institutions designed to deal with standards issues, they can be put to use. For example, UNBS often contracts the Department of Chemistry at Makerere University to carry out the testing of some samples. This increases efficiency and optimizes resource use. Where this is not a viable option, assistance would be needed to establish these facilities. A case in point is the pest risk analysis required under the AGOA that requires Kawanda Agricultural Research Institute to have equipment to undertake the exercise.

Sensitization

It has been made apparent in all sectors considered in this study, that standards and quality requirements are compromised right from the production and primary processing levels where production and other operations are on a small scale with limited financial capital. For example in the case of coffee, unripe cherries are harvested and recommended drying conditions are often ignored because the incentive for investing in the infrastructure that ensures compliance with quality requirements is nonexistent and the penalty for compromising coffee standards is weak. Premium for good quality coffee (for example, specialty coffees) exists but the awareness for the need to comply and associated benefits is lacking. Furthermore, even if farmers are aware of the price premiums, they may not be aware of the measures needed to be taken to achieve the desired quality. Thus the sensitization of producers through different channels such as radio and TV programs, newsletters, and so on is required. These initiatives that have been in existence need to be strengthened and mobile demonstration services (mobile van) should be used to complement radio and others programs. A mobile demonstration van can move from location to location at different times of the year and could easily benefit other sectors in the economy.

The awareness schemes should include assisting sectors (preferably at the producers' association level) in acquiring information technology that is essential in the current era of electronic commerce. An USAID-funded project (SPEED) assisted the UFPEA in launching a website in June 2002 regarding activities in the fish sector. The success of this innovation is difficult to assess as of now but stakeholders in the fish industry expect improvement in their activities. The parallel initiative can be undertaken in other sectors. The use of the Internet reduces costs of providing information and the opportunities available in the market can be on and accessed from the website.

Accreditation of Firms for Certification

One of the problems faced by Ugandan producers is the certification problem (particularly the specialty products such as organic products, wet processed coffee, and so on) by UCDA, UNBS, KARI, and some private firm agencies. Certificates issued by these statutory bodies are essential for any shipment to be allowed by custom officials. A number of exporters contacted during the fieldwork informed us that importers of Ugandan products tend to engage an independent certifying body (for example, SGS and ACE). Importers are said to have had some experience in the past where the information claimed on certificates were not consistent with samples obtained from actual shipment. Exporters of organic products have had to use foreign firms to get their produce monitored, inspected, and certified as organic products. Local institutions can be accredited at the international level if they demonstrate the capacity (qualified technical personnel and infrastructure) to undertake an effective monitoring and testing process that is credible to guarantee compliance with standards. The monitoring and testing that is locally provided would be relatively cheaper in terms of financial costs and delays. Benefits go beyond reduction in costs of certification since the countries get a good reputation for having the capability to undertake effective certification, that is, there are economies of scope as other products can be confidently demanded by importers.

Promotion of Specialty Products

Ugandan products can benefit from upcoming and specialized markets of organic, environmental-friendly products when accompanied with high quality standards. The quality standards tend to be more stringent when there is surplus in the market but there are premiums on high quality products. One product that has suffered in this respect is the coffee export and suggestions have been made to improve the quality of coffee through wet processing. The wet processing requires some additional investments in pulping equipment and extra care in handling. The COMPETE project has initiated this process and in June 2002 about 10 farmers were sent to Brazil for training in the wet processing of coffee.

Under the same program, ten electric/diesel coffee hullers are to be installed at a cost ranging from US$25,000 to US$28,000 each. However, ten hullers are not adequate to efficiently serve all coffee growing areas. For example, the catchment area for some coffee hullers will have to be over 200-kilometer radius. The delivery of coffee cherries for wet processing (which is supposed to be within 48 hours of picking) is not financially feasible for smallholding farmers who would have to travel long distances to the coffee hullers. Therefore, it is recommended that hand pulp coffee hullers, which cost about US$750 each, would be more suitable, given the coffee production structure of small and scattered holdings. In light of this it would be better if hand pulp equipment are made available to coffee producers to facilitate the wet processing. Hand pulp equipment has a number of advantages including its affordability for one farmer. Also a group of farmers—within, for example, a 5-kilometer radius—could be formed to buy and utilize one hand pulp.

Reference

Abdel-Latif, A. M., and F. B. Nudgent. 1996. "Transaction Cost Impairments to International Trade: Lessons from Egypt." *Contemporary Economic Policy* 14 :1–14.

ADC. 2000. "National Code of Practice for the Horticultural Sector." IDEA Project.

CFC. 2001. "Quality Assurance and Certification (for coffee) Coffee and Cotton Development and Trade Promotion." USAID Sponsored Project, Kamplala, Uganda.

Charnovitz, S. 2000. "The Supervision of Health and Bio Safety Regulation by World Trade Rules." *Tulane Environmental Law Journal* 13 :271.

COMPETE (Competitive Private Enterprises and Trade Expansion). 2001. "The Path Forward in Uganda's Coffee Sector." The presidential conference on Export Competitiveness, Kampala, Uganda.

Dijkstra, T. 2001. "Export Diversification in Uganda: Developments in Nontraditional Agricultural Exports in Uganda." ASC Working Paper no. 47.

EPRC. 2001. "Review of the Trade Policy Regime and Policy Making Process in Uganda." Paper submitted to the IDRC.

Foodnet. 2002. *Transaction Costs Analysis*. A final report for the Modernization of Agriculture prepared by The Natural Resources Institute and the International Institute of Tropical Agriculture, Kampala.

Gandal, N. 2000. "Quantifying the Trade Impact of Compatibility Standards and Barriers—An Industrial Organization Perspective." Tel Aviv University.

Giovannucci, D. 2001. "Sustainable Coffee Survey of the North American Specialty Coffee Industry."

North American Commission for Environmental Cooperation.

Henson, S, A. Brouder, and W. Mitullah. 2000. "Food Safety Requirements and Food Exports from Developing Countries: The Case Study of Fish Exports from Kenya to the European Union." *American Journal of Agricultural Economics* 85 (5) :1159–69.

Grote, U., and S. Kirchhoff. 2001. Environmental and Food Safety standards in the Context of Trade Liberalization: Issues and Options. Discussion Papers on Development Policy, June 2001.

IDEA. 2002. *Fourteenth Semi-Annual and Seventh Annual Progress Report.* A USAID funded project. Kampala, Uganda.

ITC/UNACTD/WTO. 2000. "Multilateral Trading System Impact on National Economy and External Trade Policy Adaptation of Uganda." JITAP.

Jha, V. 2001. "Strengthening Developing Countries' Capacities to Respond to Health, Sanitary and Environmental Requirements." Scoping Paper for South East Asia presented at the African Workshop on Standards and Trade, September 2001, Kampala, Uganda.

Morrissey, O., and N. Rudaheranwa. 1998. "Uganda Trade Policy and Export Performance." Credit Discussion Paper 6. School of Economics, University of Nottingham.

Ndaba, M. 2001. "The Impact of SPS on Fish and Horticultural Products from EAC: The Case of Tanzania." Paper presented at the African Workshop on Standards and Trade, Kampala, Uganda, September 2001.

Nnam. 2002. "Economic Partnership Agreements (EPAS) Status of Negotiations." Paper presented at PSF/Trade Policy Capacity Building National Conference, Kampala, Uganda.

Ntoyai, R. 2001. "Impact of SPS Requirements on Exports (Kenya)." Paper presented at the African Workshop on Standards and Trade, Kampala, Uganda, September 2001.

Private Sector Foundation/World Bank. 2001. "Modernization of Coffee Farm to Market Chains—Legal and Regulatory Frame Work Study for Uganda." Draft Report prepared by Barugahare & Co. Advocates, Advocates and Legal Consultants.

Rothery, B. 1998. "Standards and Certification." In D. Lock, ed. *The Gower Handbook of Management.* 4th Edn. England: Gower Publishing Company, Chapter 15.

Rudaheranwa, N. 1999. "Transport Costs and Export Trade of Landlocked Countries: Evidence from Uganda." Ph.D. Thesis. University of Nottingham.

———. 2000. "Transport Costs and protection for Uganda Industry." In H. Jililian, M. Tribe, and J. Weiss, eds. *Industrial Development and Policy: Issues of De-industrialization and Development Strategy.* U.K.: Edward Elgar.

SADC. 2002. "SADC SPS and Food Safety Issues: An Agenda for Action." Proceedings of the Windhoek Workshop on SPS Food safety, November 2000.

Ssemmogerere, G. 1997. "Trade Liberalization Policies and Economic Development in Uganda 1965–1995: A Sample Survey of Enterprises Manufacturing Tradeables." Department of Economics, Makerere University.

The Republic of Uganda. 2000. "Manufacturing of Standards Operating Procedures for Operating Procedures for Fish Inspection and Quality Assurance." Ministry of Agriculture, Animal, Industry and Fisheries, June 2000.

———. 2000b. *Manual of Standards Operating Procedures for Fish Inspection and Quality Assurance.* Ministry of Agriculture, Animal Industry and Fisheries, Kampala, Uganda.

———. (various issues). *Background to the Budget.* Ministry of Finance, Planning and Economic Development, Kampala.

———. 2002. *The Budget Speech.* Ministry of Finance, Planning and Economic Development, Kampala, Uganda.

UCTF (Uganda Coffee Trade Federation). 2001. *The Coffee Year Books 1998/99 and 2000.* Kampala, Uganda.

UEPB (Uganda Export Promotion Board). 2000. *Trade Secrets. The Export Answer Book for Small and Medium Sized Exporters.* International Trade Center.

UFPEA. 2002. www.ufpea.co.ug.

Uganda Coffee Development Authority. 1992. *Wet Coffee Processing in Uganda.* Consultancy for the Coffee Processing Technology.

Uganda Law Reform Commission. 2000. "The Legal Implementation of the WTO Agreements in East Africa." Document presented in a Workshop held at Imperial Botanical Beach Hotel, Entebbe, Uganda.

UNBS (Uganda National Bureau of Standards). 2000/2001. *Catalogue of Uganda Standards.* Uganda National Bureau of Standards, Kampala.

UNCTAD/WTO. 2000. *Uganda Matrix of Export Product and Markets.* JITAP Report no. ITC/DTCC/JITAP/UGA/11/04.

UNDP/World Bank. *Uganda: An Agenda for Trade Liberalization.* UNDP-World Bank Trade Expansion Program, Country Report no. 6.

Vossenaar, R., and V. Jha. 2001. "Trade Opportunities for Organic Food Products from Developing Countries." Paper presented at the workshop, Dar es Salaam, April 2001.

Waniala, N. 2001. "Impact of SPS Measures on Uganda Fish Exports." Paper presented at the UNCTAD sponsored workshop on Standards and Trade, Kampala.

Wilson, J. S., and T. Otsuki. 2001. *To Spray or not to Spray Banana Exports and Food Safety.* Development Research Group, the World Bank

World Bank. 1993. *Uganda's Agricultural Sector.* A World Bank Country Study.

———.1996s. *Uganda: The Challenge of Growth and Poverty Reduction.* The World Bank

World Trade Organization. 1995 and 2001. *Trade Policy Review Uganda.* Reports by the Secretariat, WT/PR/S/93, Geneva.

Annex A Ugandan Imports by Origin
(percentage)

Region	1990	1991	1992	1993	1994	1995	1996	1997	1998	1999
COMESA		19.3	26.8	24.0	30.1	22.8	16.1	14.4	14.5	21.6
Other Africa		0.6	0.2	0.1	1.0	3.0	1.9	2.6	4.4	3.8
EU		36.8	28.3	35.4	29.1	31.7	20.7	17.5	17.3	17.5
Other Europe		4.8	3.2	2.1	1.2	1.0	1.3	1.9	2.2	1.1
Asia		24.1	24.8	25.6	22.1	27.8	16.9	15.8	15.9	20.4
North America		3.7	7.1	7.5	6.3	4.2	2.7	3.3	3.2	5.1
Middle East		10.4	9.2	4.7	9.6	6.4	10.7	12.0	9.7	4.7
Rest of the World		0.3	0.5	0.5	0.6	3.1	29.7	32.5	32.9	25.8
Total imports		100.0	100.0	100.0	100.0	100.0	100.0	100.0	100.0	100.0

Source: Computed using data from Republic of Uganda (various issues).

Annex B Exports by Destination
(percentage)

Region	1990[a]	1991	1992	1995	1996	1997	1998	1999
PTA/COMESA	7.1	10.8	13.1	20.4	26.0	17.5	16.5	18.9
Other Africa	0.6	1.2	1.7	0.4	0.2	0.8	1.1	5.5
EU	71.1	66.1	63.8	38.9	35.4	52.1	50.9	59.3
Other Europe	3.9	2.9	6.1	33.6	29.2	14.0	11.9	9.7
Asia	3.3	5.2	2.6	1.8	6.2	4.1	4.6	3.6
North America	10.7	10.9	9.1	0.1	0.5	0.4	2.2	0.3
Middle East	0.8	0.6	0.4	0.6	1.4	0.9	2.2	0.6
Rest of the World	0.0	0.1	0.2	4.1	1.2	10.1	10.7	2.0
Not specified (1)	2.4	2.2	3.0	0.0	0.0	0.1	0.0	0.0
Total exports	100	100	100	100	100	100	100	100

Source: The Republic of Uganda (various issues).
a. 1990–92 figures include re-exports.

Annex C Domestic Exports by Value: 1990–2001
(percentage)

Commodity	1990	1991	1992	1993	1994	1995	1996	1997	1998	1999	2000	2001
Traditional exports												
Coffee	79.0	63.8	65.0	53.1	74.6	66.9	55.8	52.0	55.1	60.1	31.2	21.6
Cotton	3.3	6.4	5.6	2.7	0.8	1.7	2.2	4.9	1.4	3.6	5.5	3.0
Tea	2.0	3.7	5.3	5.5	2.6	1.2	2.2	5.1	5.3	4.5	9.4	6.7
Tobacco	1.7	2.5	2.9	3.5	1.8	1.3	1.0	2.1	4.2	3.1	6.7	7.1
nontraditional exports												
Maize	1.9	2.3	2.7	11.6	6.2	4.0	2.6	2.5	1.7	1.1	0.6	4.1
Beans and other legumes	2.3	2.3	1.9	6.3	2.8	2.8	2.3	2.0	1.2	1.8	1.1	0.5
Fish and fish products	0.8	2.9	4.4	4.4	2.3	5.6	6.5	4.7	7.4	5.2	7.7	17.3
Cattle hides	2.3	1.8	2.3	2.6	2.3	1.8	1.1	1.7	1.1	0.6	3.2	5.7
Sesame seeds	2.9	5.7	4.4	1.4	0.3	1.0	1.3	0.2	0.0	0.3	0.2	0.2
Soya beans	0.0	0.3	0.0	1.0	0.2	0.3	0.4	0.0	0.0	0.0	0.0	0.0
Soap	0.0	0.0	0.0	0.6	0.4	0.5	0.3	0.4	0.3	0.4	0.4	0.6
Electric current	0.7	0.5	1.0	0.4	0.5	0.4	0.6	2.0	2.2	2.8	4.6	2.3
Cocoa beans	0.3	0.2	0.2	0.4	0.1	0.1	0.2	0.2	0.3	0.3	0.4	0.4
Goat and sheep skins	1.2	0.5	0.5	0.3	0.1	0.0	0.0	0.0	0.0	0.0	0.0	0.0
Hoes and hand tools	0.1	0.2	0.3	0.2	0.2	0.3	0.1	0.0	0.0	0.1	0.1	0.1
Pepper	0.0	0.1	0.1	0.2	0.1	0.0	0.0	0.0	0.0	0.1	0.1	0.1
Vanilla	0.0	0.1	0.0	0.2	0.1	0.0	0.1	0.0	0.2	0.0	0.0	
Live animals	0.1	0.0	0.0	0.1	0.0	0.0	0.0	0.0	0.0	0.0	0.0	0.0
Fruits	0.0	0.0	0.0	0.1	0.1	0.0	0.0	0.1	0.1	0.0	0.2	0.0
Groundnuts	0.0	0.1	0.0	0.1	0.1	0.1	0.0	0.0	0.0	0.0	0.0	0.0
Bananas	0.0	0.1	0.1	0.1	0.1	0.1	0.1	0.0	0.0	0.1	0.2	0.2
Roses and cut flowers	0.0	0.0	0.0	0.1	0.1	0.1	0.4	0.6	1.4	1.5	2.5	3.3
Ginger	0.0	0.1	0.1	0.1	0.0	0.0	0.0	0.0	0.0	0.0	0.0	
Gold and gold compounds	0.0	5.2	0.0	0.0	0.0	4.7	9.2	13.6	3.6	7.0	10.8	10.9
Other precious compounds	0.0	0.0	0.0	0.0	0.0	0.0	0.0	0.0	0.0	0.6	2.7	2.8
Other products (1)	1.6	1.3	3.2	5.0	4.1	6.9	13.7	7.8	14.3	6.7	12.7	10.5
Traditional exports	85.9	76.4	78.7	64.8	79.8	71.1	61.1	64.2	65.9	71.3	52.6	38.3
nontraditional exports	14.1	23.6	21.3	35.2	20.2	28.9	38.9	35.8	34.1	28.7	47.4	61.7
Total	100	100	100	100	100	100	100	100	100	100	100	100

Source: Own computation using data from The Republic of Uganda (various issues).

Annex D Composition of GDP at Factor Cost at Constant (1991) Prices 1990–2001

(percentage)

Industry Group	1990	1991	1992	1993	1994	1995	1996	1997	1998	1999	2000	2001
Monetary												
Agriculture	24.5	24.5	24.6	24.7	24.3	23.7	23.3	22.7	23.0	22.8	23.0	23.0
Cash crops	3.3	3.4	3.3	3.1	3.3	3.2	3.8	4.0	3.5	3.9	3.8	4.5
Food crops	11.6	11.6	12.0	12.4	12.6	12.4	11.4	10.6	11.7	11.3	11.7	12.4
Livestock	6.2	6.2	6.0	5.9	5.4	5.1	5.2	5.2	4.9	4.8	4.8	3.4
Forestry	1.0	1.0	1.1	1.1	1.0	1.0	1.0	1.0	1.0	1.0	1.1	0.7
Fishing	2.3	2.3	2.3	2.2	2.0	1.9	1.9	1.9	1.9	1.7	1.7	2.1
									0.0	0.0		
Mining and quarrying	0.2	0.3	0.3	0.3	0.3	0.3	0.5	0.7	0.7	0.6	0.7	0.6
Manufacturing	5.5	5.9	6.1	6.4	6.9	7.5	8.2	9.0	9.5	9.9	9.1	9.9
Coffee, cotton, sugar	0.6	0.7	0.7	0.7	0.8	0.7	1.0	1.0	0.9	1.1	1.1	0.0
Manufactured food	0.7	0.8	0.8	0.8	0.9	1.0	1.1	1.2	1.1	1.1	1.2	0.0
Miscellaneous	4.2	4.4	4.5	4.9	5.2	5.8	6.1	6.9	7.5	7.7	6.9	0.0
									0.0	0.0		
Electricity/water	0.8	0.8	0.9	0.8	0.9	0.9	0.9	1.0	0.9	1.0	1.0	1.5
Construction	5.0	5.1	5.1	5.3	6.0	6.6	7.3	7.6	7.5	7.6	7.8	6.5
Wholesale and retail trade	11.1	11.4	11.3	11.3	12.2	9.5	13.0	12.8	13.0	13.2	12.8	10.1
Hotels and restaurants	1.1	1.3	1.4	1.5	1.7	1.8	1.9	1.9	1.8	1.8	1.7	1.9
Transport and communication	4.1	4.2	4.2	4.3	4.4	4.7	4.9	5.2	5.1	5.3	5.5	4.7
Road	3.1	3.2	3.2	3.2	3.2	3.3	3.4	3.7	3.7	3.8	3.7	3.4
Rail	0.3	0.3	0.2	0.2	0.3	0.4	0.3	0.2	0.2	0.2	0.2	0.2
Air & support services	0.3	0.4	0.4	0.4	0.5	0.6	0.6	0.7	0.7	0.7	0.6	0.3
Communications	0.4	0.4	0.4	0.4	0.4	0.5	0.5	0.5	0.5	0.6	0.9	0.7
									0.0	0.0		
Community services	14.7	15.2	15.8	15.9	15.4	15.2	15.3	15.5	15.2	15.2	15.7	19.8
General government	3.4	3.6	3.7	3.7	3.5	3.4	3.4	3.4	3.3	3.3	3.3	4.1
Education	3.7	3.6	3.6	3.5	3.3	3.3	3.3	3.4	3.3	3.4	3.7	5.6
Health	1.4	1.5	1.5	1.5	1.4	1.3	1.3	1.3	1.3	1.3	1.3	2.1

Rents	2.9	3.1	3.3	3.4	3.3	3.4	3.5	3.5	3.5	3.5	3.5	3.9
Miscellaneous	3.3	3.5	3.8	3.9	3.9	3.8	3.8	3.9	3.8	3.7	3.9	4.0
	0.0	0.0	0.0	0.0	0.0	0.0	0.0	0.0	0.0	0.0	0.0	0.0
Total monetary	67.2	68.6	69.7	70.6	72.0	73.7	75.2	76.4	76.8	77.4	77.3	77.9
nonmonetary									0.0	0.0		
Agriculture	29.0	27.6	26.6	25.8	24.5	22.9	21.3	20.1	19.6	19.1	19.0	18.0
Food crops	24.9	23.5	22.6	21.9	20.9	19.5	17.8	16.6	16.3	15.8	15.8	14.8
Livestock	2.8	2.7	2.7	2.6	2.5	2.3	2.4	2.4	2.3	2.3	2.3	1.8
Forestry	1.0	1.0	1.0	1.0	0.9	0.9	0.8	0.8	0.8	0.8	0.7	1.1
Fishing	0.3	0.3	0.3	0.3	0.2	0.2	0.2	0.2	0.2	0.2	0.2	0.3
									0.0	0.0		
Construction	0.8	0.8	0.7	0.7	0.7	0.6	0.6	0.6	0.6	0.6	0.6	0.5
Owner-occ.dwellings	3.1	3.0	3.0	2.9	2.8	2.8	2.9	3.0	2.9	3.0	3.1	3.6
									0.0	0.0		
Total nonmonetary	32.8	31.4	30.3	29.4	28.0	26.3	24.8	23.6	23.3	22.6	22.7	22.1
Total GDP	100.0	100.0	100.0	100.0	100.0	100.0	100.0	100.0	100.0	100.0	100.0	100.0
Per capita GDP (Shs)	120849	123534	124698	128445	137154	144233	147109	150840	158053	161785	164597	377847

Annex E The Nature and Status of Standards in Uganda

Year	Name	Purpose	Standard Harmonized with	Status
1999	Drinking water	Water that is packaged for drinking		Compulsory
1999	Drinking water	Testing bottled water		Compulsory
1994	Drinking water	Standards for potable D/water		Compulsory
2000	Clothes	Standards for baby napkins	EAS 154	Compulsory
2000	Food	Specification for mayonnaise		Compulsory
2000	Food	Specification for low fat mayonnaise		Compulsory
1993	Maize cereals	Preparation of maize for consumption		Compulsory
1993	Maize cereals	Specification for degermed maize meal		Compulsory
1993	Pulses (including beans)	Standard for pulses intended for D/consumption		Compulsory
1993	Sorghum grains	Standards for sorghum for D/consumption		Compulsory
1993	Maize cereals	Standard for maize packaged for consumption		Compulsory
1993	Wheat flour	Standard for wheatflour for human consumption		Compulsory
2000	Pasta	Standard for methods of testing pasta	EAS 173	Compulsory
1992	Fruits and derived products	Specification for fresh pineapples		Compulsory
1992	Fruits and derived products	Specification for fresh avocados		Compulsory
2000	Fruits and derived products	Specification for papain powder		Compulsory
1999	Fruits and derived products	Specification for jam and jellies		Compulsory
1999	Fruits and derived products	Specification for citrus marmalade		Compulsory
1999	Fruits and derived products	Specification for tomato ketchup		Compulsory
1999	Fruits and derived products	Specification for tomato sauce		Compulsory
1993	Milk and milk products	Specification for whole and skimmed milk		Compulsory
1993	Milk and milk products	Specification for butter and whey butter		Compulsory
1993	Ice cream and confectionary	Specification for yorghut		Compulsory
1993	Ice cream and confectionary	Specification for flavoured yorghut		Compulsory
1993	Meat and meat products	Specification of luncheon meat		Compulsory
1993	Meat and meat products	Specification for canned corned beef		Compulsory
1999	Fish and fish products	Code of practise in handling fish for market		Compulsory
1993	Tea	Specification for instant tea in solid form	ISO	Compulsory
1999	Alchoholic beverages	Specification for gins		Compulsory
2000	Alchoholic beverages	Specification for brandy	EAS 143	Compulsory
2000	Alchoholic beverages	Specification for rum	EAS 142	Compulsory

410

Year	Product/Subject	Description	Code	Status
1999	Quality management and assuarance	Clarifies the quality concepts	ISO 9000/1	Voluntary
1999	Enviromental management system	Standard requirements for ems	ISO 14001	Voluntary
1999	Enviromental audit	Standards in enviromental audit	ISO 14010	Voluntary
1999	Food	Hazard analysis critical control points		Voluntary
1999	Fish and fish products	Determination of concentration of TVBN		Voluntary
2000	Milk and milk products	Hygenic conditions of handling milk		Voluntary
2000	Fruits and vegetables	Determination of mineral impurities content	ISO 762	Voluntary
2000	Fruits and vegetables	Determination of ash insoluble hydrochloric acid	ISO 763	Voluntary
2000	Fruits and vegetables	Determination of titrable acidity	ISO 750	Voluntary
2000	Fruits and vegetables	Determination of essential oils content	ISO 1955	Voluntary
2000	Fruit juice	Determination of solid content	ISO 2172	Voluntary
2000	Fruits and vegetables	Determination of tin content in products	ISO 2447	Voluntary
2000	Fruits and vegetables	Determination of ethanol content	ISO 2448	Voluntary
2000	Fruits and vegetables	Determination of copper in products	ISO 3094	Voluntary
2000	Fruits and vegetables	Determination of iron content in the products	ISO 5517	Voluntary
2000	Fruits and vegetables	Determination of sulpurdioxide content	ISO 5523	Voluntary
2000	Fruits and vegetables	Determination of volatile acidity	ISO 6632	Voluntary
2000	Fruits and vegetables	Determination of lead content	ISO 6633	Voluntary
2000	Fruits and vegetables	Determination of arsenic content	ISO 6634	Voluntary
2000	Fruits and vegetables	Determination of zinc content	ISO 6636/3	Voluntary
2000	Fruits and vegetables	Determination of the mercury content	ISO 6637	Voluntary
2000	Fruits and vegetables	Sampling and test methods	EAS 41-0	Voluntary
2000	Fruits and vegetables	Determination of benzoic acid content	EAS 41-7	Voluntary
2000	Fruits and vegetables	Determination of water insoluble solids	EAS 41-2	Voluntary
2000	Fruits and vegetables	Determination of soluble solids content	EAS 41-9	Voluntary
2000	Fruits and vegetables	Determination of ascorbic acid	EAS 41-11	Voluntary
2000	Fruits and vegetables	Determination of the PH	EAS 41-4	Voluntary
2000	Fruits and derived products	Specification for mango chutney		Voluntary
2000	Milk and milk products	Determination of phosphatase activity	EAS 160	Voluntary
2000	Milk and milk products	Sampling—inspection by attributes	EAS 161	Voluntary
2000	Milk and milk products	Sampling—inspection by variables	EAS 165	Voluntary
2000	Milk and milk products	Determination of total solid content	EAS 162	Voluntary
2000	Milk and milk products	Determination of freezing point	EAS 163	Voluntary
2000	Milk and milk products	Determination of fat content	EAS 164	Voluntary

Annex F Uganda Code of Practice for Horticultural Export

Principle	S/N	Criterion	S/N	Indicators	S/N	Implementation
To ensure the welfare of workers and out growers	1.4	Fair purchasing policy for growers and producers is ensured	1.42	All producers/outgrowers shall be paid cash or under a mutually accepted mode of payment		
			1.43	There will be an agreement written or oral between the producer and exporter covering product volumes, frequencies, and pricing		
Consumer health shall be safe guarded	3.1	Due delligence in crop production and pesticide use	3.11	Crop production areas should be located away from enviromental threats		Fields used for crop production should not be sited in areas con-taminated from air, water, or soil etc.
			3.12	Fields should be free from feacal and other contamination		In areas close to human habitation, access to fields should control human waste
			3.13	All crops are grown according to good agricultural practice following ICMS		Exporters conform to requirements of pesticide use detailed in the enviromental criteria
			3.14	Harvested products should be traceable from the farm source		Harvested products must be traceble back to the individual field level
			3.15	Product samples are analyzed for pesticide residues by an accredited laboratory		In most cases this is done by the country of import by arrangement with the importer
			3.16	Risk contamination by irrigation water is controlled		Guidelines on the assessment of risk of contamination by irrigation water, e.g. analysis of microbial, chemical, and mineral pollutants
	3.2	Production and equipment safe guard product from contamination	3.21	Location of production facilities to avoid potential sources of contamination		Facilities should be located away from environmentally polluted areas, e.g. flooding and wastes
			3.22	Building and interior facilities permit good food hygiene		Follow guidelines on packhouse design and construction

3.3	Hazards to products in postharvest handling are identified and controlled	3.29	Materials used for cleaning are approved for food use	Guidelines on acceptable food grade cleaning materials and recommended methods of use
		3.31	Process controls are in place determined by HACCP	Guidelines required on HACCP, product specifications, and record keeping
		3.32	Field products and packed or prepared products are kept separately	Separation is done either physically or by time provided areas are cleaned before commencing handling of packed products
		3.33	Access to production areas is restricted	e.g., access should be via a changing or hand washing facility
		3.34	Managers and supervisors have sufficient knowledge of hygiene	They should be able monitor and judge potential risk and take corrective action
		3.35	Stock is maintained and traceability of all products is maintained through the dispatch	e.g., lot marking at goods receipt and stock records maintained
		3.36	Fresh produce is protected from contamination by pests or by physical or chemical contaminants	Handling procedures and techniques must avoid contamination by foreign bodies such as glass
3.4	Personal hygiene of produce handlers	3.41	All staff should have the necessary knowledge of personal hygiene to avoid contamination	Basic induction training in personal hygiene should be conducted
		3.42	Hand sanitation facilities and procedures in place	Hand washing and drying facilities (bactericidal soap is recommended.)
		3.44	All staff involved in packing and dispatch should wear clean clothing	Protective clothing be issued to all staff involved in final preparation of the product
3.6	Packaging and other materials in contact with the product do not cause contamination	3.61	All packaging materials should be food grade	They should conform to the food grade standards

(continued)

Annex F (Continued)

Principle	S/N	Criterion	S/N	Indicators	Implementation
			3.62	Raw materials container should be clean	Raw materials container should be suitably durable and easy to clean
			3.63	Storage and stock control facilities should be clean and ensure hygiene	Packaging and storage facilities must prevent contamination by pests
			3.64	All surfaces and finishes in contact with the product are food safe and easily cleaned or disinfected	Surfaces include tabletops, cutting boards, knives, and finishes include paint
To control and reduce environmental degradation resulting from agrochemical use	4.1	Quantity and hazard level of chemical usage is reduced	4.11	Integrated crop management practices shall be promoted to reduce agrochemical use	Varieties must be suited to the local conditions and must be chosen for their seed quality and weed resistance to keep chemical treatment low
			4.12	Internationally by and nationally banned chemicals shall not be used	Growers must use only accepted chemicals
	4.2	Application of pesticides is safe and appropriate	4.21	Spraying mixing and application must be carried out by trained personnel	All operators must be trained in the proper handling of equipment
			4.25	Pesticides are not applied during wind or heavy rain and over-head irrigation	The safest conditions to spray are when there is a steady force (light breeze)
			4.26	Procedures and measures in case of emergencies should be developed	A written contingency plan should be written detailing the procedures to be followed in an emergency
			4.27	An incident record for all accidents involving pesticides shall be kept	In addition to recording accidents, corrective action should be recorded
To ensure general conservation of the	5.1	Water resources are managed	5.11	A water reservoir with adequate capacity is used	

Annex G Trade Policy Reforms in Uganda Since 1987

Year	Policy Reform
1987	Dual trade licensing system introduced
	Duty exemption on raw materials and capital goods suspended
1988	Some protective tariffs (sugar, soap) raised
	Open General License (OGL) scheme implemented
1989	Retention Account scheme for export earnings
	Special Import Program (SIP)
	Duty exemption on raw material
1990	Export licensing system replaced with the certificate system
	Forex bureau/parallel foreign exchange market legalized
	Coffee Marketing Boards monopoly removed
1991	Import licensing replaced by certification system
	Investment Code introduced
	Creation of Uganda Investment Authority
	Creation of Uganda Revenue Authority
	Duty draw back scheme introduced
	The Uganda Coffee Development Authority statute enacted
1992	Foreign exchange auction market created
	Tariff structure rationalized
	Several duties on raw materials abolished
	Tax on coffee exports abolished
1993	Unified inter-bank foreign exchange market/floating exchange rate
	Surrender of coffee receipts waived, special import surcharges on Kenyan imports imposed
	Harmonized commodity coding system for imports introduced
	System of trade documentation reformed
	Pre-shipment requirements introduced
	Cross Border Initiatives (CBI) introduced
1994	The Cotton Development Statute enacted
	The Agricultural Seeds and Plant Statute enacted
	Further rationalization of the tariff structure
	Import duties on some of the materials suspended
	Tax on coffee exports reintroduced
	Coffee regulations introduced
1995	The National Environment Statute enacted
	Coffee tax reduced
	Narrow range of products on the negative list of imports
	Reduced exemption of duties on raw materials and intermediate inputs
1996	Coffee tax abolished
	Further rationalization of tariffs
	Introduction of VAT
	The Uganda Export promotion statute enacted
1997	Reduction of tariff rates of 0, 5, 10, and 20 percent
1998	Sodas, beer, car batteries removed from the negative list
	The Diary Industry Act enacted
1999	The fish industry restructured to comply with EU standards
2002	Taxes on computers and accessories abolished
	Taxes on imported second hand clothes raised by 5 percent

Source: Updated from Rudaheranwa (1999).

Annex H Functions Expected of the UNBS

It formulates national standards specifications for commodities and codes of practices.

It promotes standardization in commerce, industry, health, safety, and social welfare.

It determines, reviews, modifies, or amends standard specifications and codes of practice as may be required from time to time.

It endorses or adopts any international or other country's specification with or without any modification as suitable for use in Uganda.

It requires certain products to comply with certain standards in manufacture, composition, treatment, or performance and prohibit substandard goods where necessary.

It enforces standards in protection of the public against harmful ingredients, dangerous components, shoddy material, and poor performance.

It promotes trade among African countries and the world-at-large through the harmonization of standard specifications demanded in various countries.

It provides for the testing of locally manufactured and imported commodities with a view to determining whether such commodities conform to the standard specification.

It makes arrangements (or provides facilities) for the examination, testing, or analysis of commodities and any material or substance used to manufacture, produce, process, or treat those commodities.

It makes arrangements or provides facilities for the testing, and calibration of precision instruments, gauges, and scientific apparatus for determining their degree of accuracy by comparing with the devices approved by the Ministry of MTTI on the recommendation of the Council and for the issue of certificates thereto.

It assists the government, a local administration unit, a statutory corporation, a company, or any other person in the preparation or framing of any internal or company standard specification or in the preparation or framing of any internal or company code of practice.

It provides for cooperation with the government representatives of any industry, commercial organization, local administration, statutory corporation, or any other person with a view to securing the adoption and practical application of standards.

It encourages or undertakes educational work in connection with standardization.

It procures the recognition of the Bureau by any other country.

It seeks membership of any international organization connected with standardization.

It develops and maintains a collection of materials relating to standardization and related matters.

It verifies Weights and Measures instruments used in trade and for carrying out industrial calibration.

Source: UNBS Documentation and Information Division.

Annex I Technical Regulations in Some Selected Sectors

Technical Regulations of Seeds

The regulation of seeds (agriculture, forestry, and horticulture plants intended for sowing or planting purposes) is undertaken by the National Seed Industry Authority under the provisions of the Agricultural Seeds and Plant Statute of 1994. The statute has provisions for national seed certification service, plant breeding and registration of breeders, seed testing, phytosanitary standards and practices, multiplication, and licensing among other functions. For effective administration and regulation under this legislation, there is an established Variety Release Committee that reviews and maintains the national varieties and approves new varieties of seeds, reviews the history and performance records of selected varieties of seeds under the same. The National Seed Certification Services is also established as a unit under this statute, responsible for design, establishment, and enforcement of Certificate Standards, Methods, and Procedures.

Technical Regulations on Fish and Fishery Products

The Control and Regulation of Fish and Fishery products is undertaken by the Fisheries Department under the Ministry of Agriculture, Animal Industry and Fisheries, and complemented by other government bodies such as UNBS and other related organizations. The technical regulations have provisions for control of fishery products called "The Fish (Quality Assurance) Rules of 1998," which were made under the provisions of the Fish and Crocodile Act of 1964.

The Fish (Quality Assurance) Rules of 1998, were made to ensure that the fish and fishery products exported from Uganda conform to the International Standards and due consideration was made in regard to Export Market Technical Regulations globally. One examples of Export Regulation was the European Union 91/493/EEC Directive. "Health conditions on placing of Fish and Fishery products in the EU and other Related Technical Directives and Decisions of the EU." The Fish (Quality Assurance) Rules have put in place a structure to implement internationally recognized quality systems such as "Hazard Analysis of Critical Control Point" (HACCP) concept and implementation of ISO 9000 Quality Management Systems in the fish production chain.

These rules have provisions for fish inspectorate (administration and control), issuance of Fish Sanitary Certificates to operators/stakeholders in the production chain, conditions for placing the fish products on the market, requirements for exportation and importation (Sanitary Standard requirements), inspection of fish for export, approval of fish establishments, approval of official landing sites, inspection, and monitoring.

In addition to the above, the rules provide for quality and self tests: submission of Quality Management Programmes by stakeholders to Fisheries Department regularly, mandatory implementation of HACCP in the fish processing establishment and for action in case of health risk. The rules provide schedules for mandatory formats of documentation in fish processing for the ease of traceability and risk assessment.

Technical Regulations for Dairy Products

After trade in Uganda was liberalized, the government established the Dairy Development Authority, a statutory organization under the Ministry of Agriculture, Animal Industries and Fisheries, in 1998. The Dairy Industry Act 1998 was repealed to replace the Dairy Industry Act of 1967 to harmonize with policies of liberalization. The Dairy Industry Act 1998 provides for the structure and functions of the Dairy Development Authority (DDA) to provide for the promotion and control of the production, processing and marketing of milk and dairy products and generally to facilitate the development of the dairy industry.

To achieve the above-stated functions, the DDA controls and regulates dairy and dairy-related import and export activities in conformity with other legislations such as the External Trade Act (responsible for restrictions on import and export of goods in case of substandard goods) and Animal Disease Act. It implements government policy designed to promote the development of the dairy sector. It supports various dairy development activities, such as dairy extension, dairy breeding, dairy research, training, dairy products development, and general market promotion. DDA enforces Technical Mandatory Standards formulated by Uganda National Bureau of Standards. There exist currently a number of product and process National Standards enforced by DDA.

417

Regulations on Environment and Environmental Standards

Given the global concerns on environment, the Uganda established National Environment Management Authority (NEMA) in 1995 under the provisions of "The National Environment Statute of 1995." The statute provides for sustainable management of the environment and established NEMA as the coordinating, monitoring, and supervisory body for that purpose. Under this statute, one important function of NEMA is developing, implementing, and enforcing environmental standards. The scope of standards is wide and includes air quality standards, water quality standards, standards for discharge of effluents into water, standards for the control of noxious smells, soil quality standards, standards for minimization of radiation, and other standards.

There are a number of regulations under the National Environmental Statute of 1995. First, there are regulations meant to protect the depletion of wetlands in the country, that is, the National Environment (Wetlands, River Banks, and Lake Shores Management) Regulations of 2000. Second, according to the Environmental Impact Assessment (EIA) Regulations of 1998, every project must undergo an assesment of its impact on the environment. These regulations have provisions for Control and Approval of Environment Impact Assessment studies/reports of projects be agricultural or industrial before they are effected. Third, the National Environment (Standards for Discharge of Effluent into Water or On Land) Regulations of 1999 provides for issuance of guidelines on method of treatment of effluent for industries or establishments so as to ensure assimilation by the wetland into which the effluent is discharged. The regulations provide standards for discharge of effluent or water waste (mainly chemical maximum permissible limits). These regulations have implications for producers of, for example, flowers and horticultural export commodities that use considerable amount of chemicals.

Regulations on Agricultural Chemicals, Public Health, and Food

In the MAAIF, there exists an Agricultural Chemicals Board responsible for registration and control of manufacture, import, and use of agricultural chemicals. The Agricultural Chemicals (Registration and Control) Regulations of 1993 provide for the regulation on stakeholders such as workers, operators, fumigators or commercial applicators, registration of agricultural chemicals, testing of agricultural chemicals, publishing of acceptable agricultural chemicals in trade, labeling, packaging, and transportation of chemicals. The Board coordinates with other relevant government bodies such as UNBS, National Drugs Authority (NDA), and so on, to implement its functions.

Public Health and Food Safety generally is regulated by old laws (that is, the Public Health Act of 1964 and the Food Act of 1964, respectively), which are currently under review to make them WTO compliant. These laws are implemented by departments under the Ministry of Health. There are also a number of regulations made under these acts to undertake food control from production, street vending, eating-houses, and manufacturing.

Regulation of Veterinary Drugs

Veterinary and Human drugs in Uganda are regulated by a statutory body called National Drugs Authority (NDA) under the Ministry of Health. NDA is established under provisions of the National Drugs Policy Statute. The statute provides for establishing technical regulations concerning veterinary drugs. It also provides for publishing Essential Veterinary Drugs List of Uganda, which stipulates drug specifications and recommended dosages for administration in animals. There is a 2001 Essential Veterinary Drug List of Uganda (EVDLU 2001) that identifies those drugs deemed necessary and appropriate for the treatment and prevention of common animal diseases in Uganda. Due attention was put on prevalence and incidences of various diseases in Uganda to safety, efficacy, and the cost effectiveness of the medicine used in treatment and prevention of these diseases.

Uganda is an agricultural country mainly dealing in food processing with great potential for contamination at various stages of processing. In addition to the challenges of complying with these regulations, there are challenges that cover the whole food production chain. First, there is an indiscriminate use of chemicals, pesticides, and veterinary drugs in the production that may lead to food products containing higher than acceptable maximum residual limits, and acceptable daily intakes. Second, poor or inadequate infrastructure in production and processing of food (improper drying and storage, especially of grain) may result in the formation of aflotoxin and other mycotoxins that lead to toxity on consumption and postharvest losses. Third, the transportation both of animals and plants is inadequate.

Fourth, there is still an element of inadequate hygiene such as proper toilet and hand washing facilities or protective clothing in most of food processing industries. The fish processing industry, which was inspected by the EU team, in the late 1990s gives an example of inadequate infrastructure including unhygienic landing facilities but this has improved since then. Laboratory facilities (human capacity) for routine quality control of products and the use of firms' standards for production and processing are not adequate. Poorly trained personnel are employed in the processing and quality assurance matters and as a result there is inadequate processing of waste effluents from processing plants before disposal. Finally, a number of food factories were not built according to the hygienic layout of a food factory, which makes cross-contamination of raw and processed products possible. Furthermore, the absence of a consolidated modern food law in the country makes the coordination of enforcement efforts more difficult.

Annex J Firms Certified by UNBS

Permit No.	Holding Company	Certified Products	Relevant Uganda Standards
0001	Victoria Pumps Ltd.	U_2, U_2/U_3 and extra deep well hand pumps	US 403, 404, 405 & 406: 1995
0002	RECO Industries Ltd.	Refined papain	US 40: 2000
0003	RECO Industries Ltd.	Food products, honey, tomato ketchup, and chilli sauce	US 7, 18 & 28: 1993, US 32, 38, 39: 1999
0004	RECO Industries Ltd.	Polyurethane foam products	US 202: 1994
0005	Gulu Foam Industries	Polyurethane foam products	US 202: 1994
0006	Vitafoam Uganda Ltd.	Polyurethane foam products	US 202: 1994
0007	Cable Corporation Ltd.	Aluminum stranded conductors & aluminum stranded conductors—steel reinforced	US 611: 1995
0008	Cable Corporation Ltd.	Domestic and building cables	US 602: 1995
0009	Cable Corporation Ltd.	Flexible cables	US 605: 1995
0010	Cable Corporation Ltd.	Underground cables	US 601: 1995
0011	Steel Rolling Mills Ltd.	Steel bars for reinforcement of concrete	US 155: 1995
0012	Hima Cement Ltd.	Ordinary portland cement	US 108: 1993
0013	Uganda Millers Ltd.	Wheat flour	US 24: 1995
0014	Tororo Cement Ind. Ltd.	Ordinary portland cement	US 108: 1993
0015	Tororo Cement Ind. Ltd.	Galvanized plain and corrugated iron sheets	US 301: 1993
0016	Roofings Limited	Galvanized plain and corrugated iron sheets	US 301: 1993
0017	Hwan Sung Ltd.	Ice mix	US 33: 1993
0018	A. K. Oils & Fats (U) Ltd.	Edible oil	US 168: 2000
0019	A. K. Oils & Fats (U) Ltd.	Edible fat	US 168: 2000
0020	Mukwano Industries Ltd.	Laundry soap	US 53: 2000
CERT/0001	Chemiphar (U) Limited	Laboratory testing services	ISO/IEC Guide 25
CERT/0002	SGS (Uganda) Limited	Laboratory testing services	ISO/IEC Guide 25
0021	Tororo Cement Ind. Ltd.	Portland Pozzolana cement	US 63: 1999
0022	Hima Cement Limited	Portland Pozzolana cement	US 63: 1999
0023	Uganda Baati Limited	Galvanized plain and corrugatzed iron sheets	US 301: 1993
0024	Hitech Metal Industries Ltd.	Domestic and building cables	US 602: 1995
0025	Hitech Metal Industries Ltd.	Flexible cables	US 605: 1995
0026	Hitech Metal Industries Ltd.	Underground cables	US 601: 1995
0027	A. K. Detergents (U) Ltd.	Detergent powder	US 55: 1999
0028	A. K. Detergents (U) Ltd.	Domestic liquid detergent	US 54: 2000
0029	A. K. Oils & Fats (U) Ltd.	Margarine	US 27: 1993
0030	A. K. Detergents (U) Ltd.	Scouring powder	US 326: 2001
0031	Shumuk Enterprises Ltd.	Domestic aluminum cooking pots and lids (Sufurias)	US 153: 2000
0032	Revoline Lubricants (U) Ltd.	Engine oil	US 249: 1999

Annex K Operational Structure within UNBS

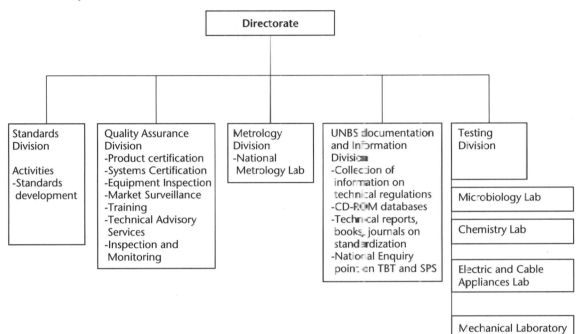

Annex L Summary of Action Plan at Sectoral Level

No.	Title	Justification	Objectives	Media	Activities	Coverage/ Frequency	Estimated unit cost (Ushs)
1	Sensitization of the public and stakeholders	Quality assurance starts right from the production level throughout the distribution channel to the market.	Promote awareness among the people specifically those in the sector	Radio	Radio programs (30 minutes each)	5 major languages	550,000
					Radio adverts (30 seconds each)	Twice a week	50,000
				Posters and brochures			
		There are price premiums on good quality products, which farmers may not be aware of.	Promote visual awareness and demonstration	Television	Sponsoring popular programs (30 minutes each)	Once a week	600,000
					TV commercials (30 seconds each)	Each day for two week per 3 months	180,000
		Some farmers are not aware of methods to use to obtain good quality produce.			TV documentary (30 minutes each)	Once in two months	1,200,000
		In case of an export ban (e.g., the case of fish see Table 5.5 in main text), there would be a great loss of income to community and the economy.	Promote awareness among the people	Newspaper	Supplements (a full page)	Once in six months	2,340,000
					Adverts (per full page)	Once in 3 months	2,340,000
					Insertion (pull-out)	Once in 3 months	1,177,000
			Reach out to areas that are remote	Mobile van	Publicizing up-coming activities		
					Demonstrations using videos (one day)	Covering major growing areas	1,288,000

No.	Activity	Justification/Assumptions	Output	Means	Coverage/Frequency	Cost (US$)
2	Promotion of specialty products	There are price premiums to reap.	Promote organic and eco-friendly, high-premium products	Radio program	5 major languages (once a week)	550,000
		There is a continuous decline in prices of some conventional products (e.g., coffee).		TV program		
		Soils and climatic conditions in Uganda are favorable for promoting specialty products, e.g. organics.		Demonstration units	In each subcounty of the growing regions	NA
				Processing equipment	In each subcounty of the growing regions	Varying with product

Notes: Promotion of specialty products applies to organic and eco-friendly products in coffee, flowers, and horticulture. The exchange rate is assumed to be Ushs 1800 per US$.

Annex M Action Plan Summary-Institutional Level

No.	Title	Justification	Objectives	Lead Agency	Outcomes	Budget Estimate
1	Capacity Building in Human Resources	KARI currently has only 5 technical staff member for SPS but it requires about 50 to be effective (40 for the 24 entry points and 10 at KARI headquarters). In 3 to 5 years, the desirable number would be 144 technical staff members. There are new demands, e.g., Pest Risk Analysis to be undertaken, etc.	To strengthen the technical capability to develop, monitor, promote, and enforce standardization, quality requirements, and related activities in Uganda.	KARI	Over 140 trained technical staff members in the next 5 years. Pest Risk Analysis done. Increased frequency in inspection	US$500 unit cost of training =US$70,000
		UNBS requires three teams (one at entry points, one at the headquarters, and another for surveying the market and production). These teams would require about 130 technical staff members but UNBS currently has 50.	To equip and strengthen the skills of the technical staff that represent Uganda in regional and international negotiations regarding standards, SPS, and TBT, etc.	UNBS	About 130 trained technical staff members in the next 5 years. Competent technical team for standards development and negotiations	US$500 unit cost of training =US$65,000
		DFR technical staff require further training on issues regarding quality assurance in the processing of fish and measure up to new demands, e.g., maximum chemical residue limits requirements.		DFR	About 150 trained technical staff members in the next 5 years	US$500 unit cost of training =US$75,000
2	Capacity Building in Infrastructure	UNBS has only one accredited laboratory out of the 5 existing laboratories. There will be cost savings (e.g., US$ 2000 per year is spent in shipping fish samples to Holland).	To develop the infrastructure for effective monitoring and enforcing standards and quality requirements in Uganda.	UNBS	Four upgraded laboratories. Permanent home secured	US$3 million for accreditation each laboratory =US$12 million

UNBS has no permanent home and spends about US$ 1,700 per month in rent.			US$4 million for first phase and US$5 for second phase.
KARI lacks a well-equipped laboratory at the headquarter and mobile laboratory units to perform all required tests	KARI	Well-equipped main laboratory and mobile laboratory units for simple tests secured	US$3.2 million for laboratories
DFR lacks well-equipped laboratory and currently contracts other testing firms for microbiology and chemical residue tests.	DFR	Well-equipped accredited laboratories to perform the necessary tests secured	US$3 million for each laboratory

Note: Costs of establishing and upgrading laboratories are assumed to be equivalent to US$ 3 million incurred on UNBS microbiology laboratory. The costs of accreditation are assumed to be the same across all units and are based on those incurred on the UNBS microbiology laboratory as outlined below. The accreditation of, for example, the UNBS would involve the following:

(a) Preparation for four divisions of UNBS is about US$50,000;
(b) International consultancy on accreditation for two missions (each at US$16,000) is about US$32,000;
(c) Accreditation charges for four laboratories (each at US$20,000) is about US$80,000;
(d) Training specialized products is about US$10,000;
(e) Orientation for the four heads of divisions (each at US$10,000) is about US$30,000. These figures are largely based on previous experiences in the UNBS.

Annex N The Business Chain in the Fish Sector

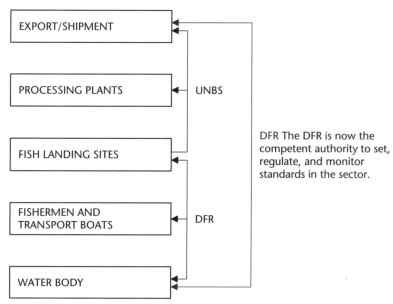

Note: DFR is under the MAAIF, whereas UNBS is under MMTI. Therefore, they had different mandates which made coordination on quality standards in the fish sector difficult. As a way of streamlining the enforcement of standards, the entire business chain in the fish sector is currently under DFR.

Index

A

AAK. *See* Agrochemicals Association of Kenya (AAK)

Abattoir Hygiene Act, South Africa, 345

ABLH. *See* Association of Better Land Husbandry (ABLH)

ACM. *See* Mozambique Commercial Association (ACM)

ACP-EU. *See* African Caribbean, Pacific–European Union (ACP-EU)

AEC. *See* African Economic Community (AEC)

AFIPEK. *See* Kenya Fish Processors and Exporters Association (AFIPEK)

African Caribbean, Pacific–European Union (ACP-EU), 11: Cotonou Economic Partnership Agreement, 175; Lome Agreement, 1, 9, 84, 174

African Economic Community (AEC), 174

African Growth Opportunity Act (AGOA), 84, 89, 94, 175, 216, 250

African Regional Industrial Property Organization (ARIPO), 85

African Regional Standardization Organization (ARSO), 14, 126

African Union (AU), 67

AGOA. *See* African Growth Opportunity Act (AGOA)

Agricultural Pests Act, South Africa, 343

Agricultural Product Standards Act, South Africa, 343

Agricultural Research Council (ARC), South Africa, 269

Agrochemicals Association of Kenya (AAK), 28

AICAJU. *See* Cashew Industrial Association (AICAJU)

AIDS. *See* HIV/AIDS

AIMO. *See* Mozambique Industrial Association (AIMO)

AMAPIC. *See* Mozambican Association of Industrial Prawn Fisheries (AMAPIC)

Animal Diseases Act, South Africa, 344–45

Animal Improvement Act, South Africa, 344

APAMO. *See* Mozambican Association of Sugar Producers (APAMO)

ARC. *See* Agricultural Research Council (ARC)

ARIPO. *See* African Regional Industrial Property Organization (ARIPO)

ARSO. *See* African Regional Standardization Organization (ARSO)

ASARECA. *See* Association of Agricultural Research for Central and Eastern Africa (ASARECA)

Association of Agricultural Research for Central and Eastern Africa (ASARECA), 25

Association of Better Land Husbandry (ABLH), 29–30, 31t, 56

AU. *See* African Union (AU)

B

best manufacturing practice (BMP), 186

BMP. *See* best manufacturing practice (BMP)

C

CAC. *See* Codex Alimetarius Commission (CAC)

Capespan, 267

cashew, Mozambique export: barriers, 86–87, 96–97; disease control, 97, facilitation recommendations, 98; grading, 98; Institute for the Promotion of Cashew, 96–97, 111; marketing, 97; processing, 95; production trends, 96t; tree distribution, 95

Cashew Industrial Association (AICAJU), 96

CBI. *See* Circuit Breaker Industries (CBI)

CBK. *See* Central bank of Kenya (CBK); Coffee Board of Kenya (CBK); Cotton Board of Kenya (CBK)

CBS. *See* citrus black spot (CBS)

CCA. *See* Codex Coordinating Committee for Africa (CCA)

CCFL. *See* Codex Committee on Food Labeling (CCFL)

CCFP. *See* Codex Committee on Fish and Fishery Products (CCFP)

CCM. *See* Mozambique Chamber of Commerce (CCM)

CCP. *See* Codex contact point (CCP)

CCPR. *See* Codex Committee on Pesticide Residues in Foods (CCPR)

CCT. *See* Labor Consultative Council (CCT)

Center for Environmental Health and Medical Examinations (CHAEM), Mozambique, 109

Central bank of Kenya (CBK), 5

CGA. *See* Citrus Growers Association (CGA)

CHAEM. *See* Center for Environmental Health and Medical Examinations (CHAEM)

CIB. *See* Coffee Industry Board (CIB)

Circuit Breaker Industries (CBI), 260–61

CISS. *See* Comprehensive Import Supervision Scheme (CISS)

citrus black spot (CBS), 269, 277

Citrus Growers Association (CGA), South Africa, 266

CLMSB. *See* Cotton Lint and Seed Marketing Board (CLMSB)

CMB. *See* Coffee Marketing Board (CMB)

cocoa, Nigeria export, 209–10

Codex Alimetarius Commission (CAC), 12–14, 57, 130, 160, 165, 176–78, 180–81, 251, 381

Codex Committee on Fish and Fishery Products (CCFP), 274

Codex Committee on Food Additives and Contaminants, 274

Codex Committee on Food Hygiene, 274

Codex Committe on Food Labeling (CCFL), 276

Codex Committe on Pesticide Residues in Foods (CCPR), 276

Codex contact point (CCP), Nigeria, 165, 176, 176–78, 180–81, 188–89, 191

Codex Coordinating Committee for Africa (CCA), 381

coffee, Kenya export: commodity support programs, 60; costs of production, 33t, 58; grading, 32–33; husbandry practices, 33; industry concerns, 34–35; milling, 34; processing, 33–34; production, 32; standards implementation, 34, 58

coffee, Uganda export: barriers, 385; costs of quality assurance, 387t, 388; market size, 384–85; organic coffee, 400–1; prices, 387–88; regulations, 385–87; wet processing, 404

Coffee Board of Kenya (CBK), 34–35

Coffee Industry Board (CIB), Uganda, 385

Coffee Marketing Board (CMB), Uganda, 385

COMESA. See Common Market for Eastern and Southern Africa (COMESA)

Common Market for Eastern and Southern Africa (COMESA), 8, 11

Community of Countries with Portuguese as the Official Language (CPLP), 129–30

COMPETE. See Competitive Private Enterprises and Trade Expansion (COMPETE)

Competitive Private Enterprises and Trade Expansion (COMPETE), 376, 404

Competitiveness Fund, South Africa, 282

Comprehensive Import Supervision Scheme (CISS), Nigeria, 193

Confederation of Business Associations of Mozambique (CTA), 132–33

cotton, Kenya export: commodity support programs, 59–60; costs of production, 49t; ginning, 49–50; industry needs, 50–51, 58; marketing, 48–49; production, 47–48; standards, 49–50, 58–59; textiles manufacturing, 50

cotton, Mozambique export: action plan for facilitation, 103; barriers, 87, 101; grading, 101–2; lint classification, 102; Mozambique Cotton Institute, 111; producers, 99, 100t; production trends, 100t; regulation, 102

Cotton Board of Kenya (CBK), 48, 50

Cotton Lint and Seed Marketing Board (CLMSB), 47

Council for Scientific and Industrial Research (CSIR), South Africa, 281

CPI. See Investment Promotion Centre (CPI)

CPLP. See Community of Countries with Portuguese as the Official Language (CPLP)

CSIR. See Council for Scientific and Industrial Research (CSIR)

CSTA. See Higher Technical Council for Customs (CSTA)

CTA. See Confederation of Business Associations of Mozambique (CTA)

D

Dairy Development Authority (DDA), Uganda, 417

DDA. See Dairy Development Authority (DDA)

Deciduous Fruit Producers Trust (DFPT), South Africa, 266

DECOM, Mozambique, 125

Department of Environmental Health (DHA), Mozambique, 108, 125

Department of External Trade (DET), Kenya, 11

Department of Fisheries Resources (DFR), Uganda, 391–92

Department of Plant Health (DSV), Mozambique, 109, 125

Department of Trade and Industry (DTI), South Africa, 251–53, 259–60, 264–65, 282–84

Department of Veterinary Services (DVS), Kenya, 12–13, 17–19, 22

DET. See Department of External Trade (DET)

DFPT. See Deciduous Fruit Producers Trust (DFPT)

DFR. See Department of Fisheries Resources (DFR)

DHA. See Department of Environmental Health (DHA)

DINAP. See National Directorate of Livestock (DINAP)

DIP. See Fisheries Inspection Department (DIP)

DNFFB. See National Directorate of Forestry and Wildlife (DNFFB)

DSV. See Department of Plant Health (DSV)

DTI. See Department of Trade and Industry (DTI)

DVS. See Department of Veterinary Services (DVS)

E

EAC. See East African Community (EAC)

East African Community (EAC), 11, 382

Economic Community of Western African States (ECOWAS), 174, 211–12

Economic Recovery Program (ERP), Uganda, 375–76

ECOWAS. See Economic Community of Western African States (ECOWAS)

EID. See Establishment Inspection Division (EID)

Electrical Suppliers Liason Committee (ESLC), 260

electronics, South Africa export: barriers, 260; compliance costs, 260–61; domestic regulations, 259–60; domestic standards, 260; levies, 363t; regulations, 345–46

EMIA. See Export Marketing Incentive Assistance (EMIA)

ENPEE Industries, 211–12

EPOPA. See Export Promotion of Organic Products from Africa (EPOPA)

EPZ. See Export Processing Zone (EPZ)

ERP. See Economic Recovery Program (ERP)

ESLC. See Electrical Suppliers Liason Committee (ESLC)

Establishment Inspection Division (EID), 191

EU Council Directive 91/414/CEE, 268

EU Council Directive 91/493/EEC, 264, 382

EUREPGAP. See European Retailers Produce on Good Agricultural Practices (EUREPGAP)

European Retailers Produce on Good Agricultural Practices (EUREPGAP), 267–68, 270

Export Marketing Incentive Assistance (EMIA), South Africa, 282

Export Processing Zone (EPZ), 48

Export Promotion Institute (IPEX), 83

Export Promotion of Organic Products from Africa (EPOPA), 401

External Market Task Force, Mozambique trade promotion, 84

F

Famine Early Warning System (FEWS), 72

FAO. See Food and Agriculture Organization (FAO)

FDI. See foreign direct investment (FDI)

FDIC. See Food and Drug Information Center (FDIC)

FDRPAC. See Food, Drug, and Related Products Approval Committee (FDRPAC)

Federal Ministry of Commerce (FMC), Nigeria, 175–76, 187, 216

Federal Produce Inspection Unit (FPIS), Nigeria, 216–17

FEWS. See Famine Early Warning System (FEWS)

fish, Kenya export: bans on African fish imports, 52–53; commodity support programs, 59; costs of production, 47t; industry concerns, 47, 58; marketing, 44; markets, 44–45; production, 44; sanitary and health requirements, 45; standards before and after export ban, 45–46; standards compliance costs, 46–47, 58

fish, Mozambique export: action plan for facilitation, 119–20; catch by type, 116t; legislation, 158; regulation, 117–19; shrimp production and export, 116, 117t

fish, Nigeria export, 213–15

fish, South Africa export: barriers, 264–65; compliance costs, 265–66; domestic regulations, 264; domestic standards, 264; industry perspectives on standards, 288; levies, 364t; regulations, 347–49; tariffs, 365t

fish, Uganda export: business chain, 426f; economic loss following ban, 393t; European bans, 392–94; market, 391; regulation, 391–92, 417; standards, 391

Fisheries Inspection Department (DIP), Mozambique, 117–18

Fisheries Research Institute (IIP), Mozambique, 118

Flower Label Program (FLP), 20

flowers, Kenya export: commodity support programs, 59; costs of production, 41, 42t; differentiation of products, 55; industry concerns, 44; marketing, 42–43; production, 40–42; standards, 43; standards compliance costs, 43–44, 58

flowers, Nigeria export, 205–7

flowers, Uganda export: barriers, 389; market size, 388; standards, 388–89, 412–14t

FLP. See Flower Label Program (FLP)

FMC. See Federal Ministry of Commerce (FMC)

Food and Agriculture Organization (FAO), 337

Food and Drug Information Center (FDIC), Nigeria, 191

Food, Drug, and Related Products Approval Committee (FDRPAC), Nigeria, 191

food products, Nigeria export, 207–9

food products, South Africa export: destinations, 246; trends, 243–44

Foodstuffs, Cosmetics, and Disinfectants Act, South Africa, 343, 352–53

foreign direct investment (FDI): Kenya, 5, 8; Mozambique, 74, 77

Forestry Stewardship Council (FSC), 262–63, 287

FPEAK. See Fresh Produce Association of Kenya (FPEAK)

FPIS. See Federal Produce Inspection Unit (FPIS)

Fresh Produce Association of Kenya (FPEAK), 20, 28, 31t, 36, 37b

FRUITISUL, 90

fruits and vegetables, Kenya export: commodity support programs, 59; costs of production, 33t; differentiation of products, 55; industry concerns, 39–40; market-driven standards, 39; marketing, 36–38; production, 32t, 33; standards compliance costs, 39, 40t, 58; technical standards, 38; value-added exports issues, 53–54

fruits and vegetables, Mozambique export: action plan for facilitation, 94–95; banana, 93; citrus, 90–92; coconut, 92–93; distribution of production, 93–94; fruit production, 88t; government regulation, 89–90; mango, 92; pineapple, 92; processing plants, 88–89; types, 87–88; wild fruits, 93

fruits and vegetables, Nigeria export, 205–7

fruits and vegetables, South Africa export: barriers, 259–70; compliance costs, 270–71; domestic regulations, 266–67;

domestic standards, 267–69; pest risk assessment, 267; regulations, 349, 350t, 351t, 352t; South African Fresh Produce Traceability Guidelines, 268–69

fruits and vegetables, Uganda export: challenges, 397–99; organic production, 400; products, 397; seed regulations, 417; standards and regulations, 397–400

FRUTIMEL, 90

FSC. See Forestry Stewardship Council (FSC)

G

GAP. See Good Agricultural Codes of Practice (GAP)

GDP. See gross domestic product (GDP)

Generalized System of Preferences (GSP), 84, 175, 250

Genetically Modified Organisms Act, South Africa, 338, 343

Geographic information system (GIS), 73

GIS. See Geographic information system (GIS)

Global System of Trade Preferences (GSTP), 174

Good Agricultural Codes of Practice (GAP), 41

good manufacturing practice, 215

GPSCA. See Office for the Promotion of Commercial Farming (GPSCA)

gross domestic product (GDP): Kenya, 3, 4t; Mozambique, 68–69; Nigeria trends, 166, 226t; South Africa trends, 236t, 237t, 309t; Uganda, 372, 408–9t

GSP. See Generalized System of Preferences (GSP)

GSTP. See Global System of Trade Preferences (GSTP)

H

HACCP. See Hazard Analysis Critical Control Point (HACCP)

Hazard Analysis Critical Control Point (HACCP): Kenya adoption, 14, 29, 37–39, 46; Mozambique adoption, 119–20, 137; Nigeria adoption, 187, 191, 198–99, 220, 224; South Africa compliance, 265, 267, 270–71, 273, 280, 347–48, 366–67; Uganda compliance, 394, 417

HCDA. See Horticultural Crops Development Authority (HCDA)

HDI. See Human Development Index (HDI)

Higher Technical Council for Customs (CSTA), Mozambique, 107

HIV/AIDS, 288–89

honey, Uganda export: action plan for promotion, 391; barriers, 391; market potential, 390; standards and regulations, 389–91

HORTEXA. See Horticultural Exporters' Association (HORTEXA)

Horticultural Crops Development Authority (HCDA), 22, 27, 31t, 35–36

Horticultural Exporters' Association (HORTEXA), Uganda, 376, 388, 397–400

Human Development Index (HDI), 68

I

IAEA. See International Atomic Energy Agency (IAEA)

IAF. See International Accreditation Forum (IAF)

IAM. See Mozambique Cotton Institute (IAM)

ICM. See Integrated Crop Management (ICM)

ICUMSA. See International Commission for Unified Methods of Sugar Analysis (ICUMSA)

IDEA. See Investment in Developing Export Agriculture (IDEA)

IDEAA. See Initiative for Development and Equity in African Agriculture (IDEAA)

IDF. See Import declaration fee (IDF)

IDPPE. See Small-Scale Fisheries Development Institute (IDPPE)

IFIR. *See* International Forest Industry Round Table (IFIR)

IFOAM. *See* International Federation of Organic Agriculture Movements (IFOAM)

IIP. *See* Fisheries Research Institute (IIP)

ILAC. *See* International Laboratory Accreditation Cooperation (ILAC)

ILO. *See* International Labor Organization (ILO)

Import declaration fee (IDF), Kenya, 10–11

INA. *See* National Sugar Institute (INA)

INCAJU. *See* Institute for the Promotion of Cashew (INCAJU)

Indian Ocean Rim Association for Regional Cooperation, 130

INIVE. *See* National Veterinary Research Institute (INIVE)

INNOQ. *See* National Institute for Standardization and Quality (INNOQ)

Institute for Public Analysts of Nigeria (IPAN), 190, 193

Institute for the Promotion of Cashew (INCAJU), 96–97, 111

Integrated Crop Management (ICM), 267

Intellectual property, Mozambique protection, 85

International Accreditation Forum (IAF), 259, 279–80

International Atomic Energy Agency (IAEA), 196

International Commission for Unified Methods of Sugar Analysis (ICUMSA), 22

International Federation of Organic Agricultural Movement (IFOAM), 55, 401

International Forest Industry Round Table (IFIR), 263

International Health Regulations Act, South Africa, 343

International Labor Organization (ILO), 25, 55

International Laboratory Accreditation Cooperation (ILAC), 259, 280

International Organization of Legal Metrology (OIML), 131

International Organization for Standardization (ISO): functions, 160; Mozambique involvement, 130–31; Nigeria adoption of ISO 9000, 198–99, 224; South Africa compliance, 264, 270–71, 277–78, 284–87, 366; Uganda compliance, 380–81, 395

International Plant Protection Convention (IPPC), 12–13, 130, 160, 189

Intitiative for Development and Equity in African Agriculture (IDEAA), 83–84

Investment in Developing Export Agriculture (IDEA), 376–77, 399

Investment Promotion Centre (CPI), 77

IPA. *See* Livestock Production Institute (IPA)

IPAN. *See* Institute for Public Analysts of Nigeria (IPAN)

IPEX. *See* Export Promotion Institute (IPEX)

IPPC. *See* International Plant Protection Convention (IPPC)

ISO. *See* International Organization for Standardization (ISO)

J

JECFA. *See* Joint Export Committee on Food Additives and Contamination (JECFA)

JITAP. *See* Joint Integrated Technical Assistance Program (JITAP)

JMPR. *See* Joint Meeting on Pesticide Residues (JMPR)

Joint Export Committee on Food Additives and Contamination (JECFA), 189

Joint Integrated Technical Assistance Program (JITAP), 377

Joint Meeting on Pesticide Residues (JMPR), 189

K

KAM. *See* Kenya Association of Manufacturers (KAM)

KARI. *See* Kawanda Agricultural Research Institute (KARI)

Kawanda Agricultural Research Institute (KARI), 377, 402, 404

KEBS. *See* Kenya Bureau of Standards (KEBS)

Kenya: animal product certification, 17b; balance of payments, 6–7t; capacity-building efforts for standards and regulations, 30, 31t, 32; coffee standards, 32–35, 58; commodity support programs, 59–60; cotton standards, 47–51, 58–59; differentiation of products, 55; economic indicators, 4t; economy structure and performance, 3, 5; exports, 9, 12, 62t, 64t; fish standards, 44–47, 58; flower standards, 40–44, 58; food safety procedures, 19b; foreign direct investments, 5, 8; fruit and vegetable standards, 35–40, 58; geography, 1; importation standards, 22–24; imports, 9–10, 14, 63t; international industry and commodity organization participation, 20; international standard comparison with Kenyan standards, 23b; international standards and participation, 12–13, 51, 57–58; labor laws and international norms, 24–25; macroeconomy and standards, 12; Mauritius chick import ban, 54b; organic farming and products, 55–56; plant material certification, 16b; population, 3; private sector involvement in standards setting, 20–21, 28–30, 60; regional standards, 25; research and biotechnology imports, 26; seeds and chemicals standards, 25–26; social indicators, 2t; standards adoption impact on poor, 51–52; standards development and implementation, 13–21, 27–28, 56–60; standards legislation, 21–22; standards notification of WTO, 20; standards setting procedure, 13b; tariffs, 10; trade policy bureaucracy, 11, 18–20, 60; trade volume, 8, 64t; value-added exports issues, 53–54; WTO agreements and administrative structure, 11–12

Kenya Association of Manufacturers (KAM), 29, 50

Kenya Bureau of Standards (KEBS), 11–15, 18–22, 31t, 57

Kenya Fish Processors and Exporters Association (AFIPEK), 29, 46–47

Kenya Flower Council (KFC), 21, 28–29, 31t, 41b, 42

Kenya Institute of Organic Farming (KIOF), 30, 56

Kenya Plant Health Inspectorate Services (KEPHIS), 12–13, 15–16, 18–20, 22, 25, 31t, 40, 42–43, 57

Kenya Planters Cooperative Union (KPCU), 35

KEPHIS. *See* Kenya Plant Health Inspectorate Services (KEPHIS)

KFC. *See* Kenya Flower Council (KFC)

Khoi Linen & Textile, 286

KIOF. *See* Kenya Institute of Organic Farming (KIOF)

KPCU. *See* Kenya Planters Cooperative Union (KPCU)

L

Labor Consultative Council (CCT), Mozambique, 107

labor laws, Kenya, 24–25

LBSC. *See* Local Business Service Centres (LBSC)

leather, South Africa export: destinations, 247; domestic standards, 272; trends, 244

Liquor Products Act, South Africa, 343

Livestock Brands Act, South Africa, 344

Livestock Production Institute (IPA), Mozambique, 111–12

LNHAA. *See* National Laboratory for Water and Food Hygiene (LNHAA)

Local Business Service Centres (LBSC), South Africa, 281

LOMACO, 93–94

LOUMAR Industries, 91

M

MAAIF. *See* Ministry of Agriculture Animal Industry and Fisheries (MAAIF)

MACs. See Manufacturing Advisory Centres (MACs)

MADER. See Ministry of Agriculture and Rural Development (MADER)

maize: Kenya import standards, 23–24; Mozambique export barriers, 87; quality specifications, 23b

MAN. See Manufacturing Association of Nigeria (MAN)

Mango Growers Association (MGA), South Africa, 266

Manufacturing Advisory Centres (MACs), South Africa, 281–82

Manufacturing Association of Nigeria (MAN), 176, 217–18, 222

Manufacturing under Bond (MUB), 48

MA&RD. See Ministry of Agriculture and Rural Development (MA&RD)

Marine Stewardship Council (MSC), 288

Maximum Residue Levels (MRLs), 266, 268, 276, 338

meat, South Africa export: barriers, 272–73; compliance costs, 273; domestic regulations, 271; domestic standards, 271–72; regulations, 349

Meat Safety Act, South Africa, 345

Memorandum of Understanding (MOU), 127, 162–63

MFN. See Most Favored Nation (MFN)

MGA. See Mango Growers Association (MGA)

MIC. See Ministry of Industry and Trade (MIC)

Ministerial diplomas, Mozambique, 107–8

Ministry of Agriculture Animal Industry and Fisheries (MAAIF), Uganda, 377, 391–92, 418

Ministry of Agriculture and Rural Development (MA&RD), Kenya, 12, 15, 17, 19, 27–28

Ministry of Agriculture and Rural Development (MADER), Mozambique, 72, 82–84, 89–90, 105, 109–12, 125

Ministry of Fisheries, Mozambique, 112, 117–18

Ministry of Health (MISAU), Mozambique, 108–1

Ministry of Health (MoH), Kenya, 18–19

Ministry of Industry and Trade (MIC), Mozambique, 112–13

Ministry of Tourism, Trade, and Industry (MTTI), Uganda, 376

Ministry of Trade and Industry (MTI), Kenya, 11, 18, 31t, 32, 50

MISAU. See Ministry of Health (MISAU)

MoH. See Ministry of Health (MoH)

Most Favored Nation (MFN), Kenya, 11

MOU. See Memorandum of Understanding (MOU)

MOZAL, 74, 77, 134, 138

Mozambican Association of Industrial Prawn Fisheries (AMAPIC), 118

Mozambican Association of Sugar Producers (APAMO), 99

Mozambique: agricultural production and trade, 70, 71t, 72–73, 85, 86t, 87, 136; balance of payments, 74, 75–76t; capital flows and borrowing, 77; cotton exports, 99–103; customs and tariffs, 113, 158–59; development assistance provisions, 80–83; directives for trade facilitation, 138; domestic standards setting agencies, 120–26; economically active population, 67; export promotion, 83; export value by country, 67t; fishery legislation, 157–58; food production, 73–74; foreign direct investment, 74, 77; forestry and agricultural production legislation, 155–57; fruit and vegetable exports, 87–98; geography, 65–67; health legislation, 153–55; imports, 89; industrial development strategy, 79–80; institutions and legislation, internal market barriers, 107–20; livestock production, 73t; metrology, 121–22; natural disasters, 67; peanut exports, 103–4; phytosanitary inspection legislation, 157; poverty reduction, government programs, 78–80; poverty status, 68; private sector perspectives, 132–35; public finance

and fiscal policies, 78; rail system, 77–78; regional and international standards development involvement, 126–32, 146t; regulatory system development action plan, 139–40t; salt export, 113–16; Sanitary and Phytosanitary agreement conformity, 65–66, 135, 147–48t; seed exports, 104–7; standard setting system development action plan, 140–45t; study design, 66; sugar exports, 98–99; Technical Barriers to Trade agreement conformity, 65–66, 135–36, 147t; trade barriers, 85–87; trade facilitation, 84–85; trade organization membership, 67; value-added output and demand growth, 68–70

Mozambique Chamber of Commerce (CCM), 133

Mozambique Commercial Association (ACM), 133

Mozambique Cotton Institute (IAM), 100, 111

Mozambique Industrial Association (AIMO), 133

MRLs. See Maximum Residue Levels (MRLs)

MSC. See Marine Stewardship Council (MSC)

MTI. See Ministry of Trade and Industry (MTI)

MTTI. See Ministry of Tourism, Trade, and Industry (MTTI)

MUB. See Manufacturing under Bond (MUB)

N

NACCIMA. See National Association of Chamber of Commerce, Industry, Manufacturing, and Agriculture (NACCIMA)

NAFDAC. See National Agency for Food, Drugs Administration, and Control (NAFDAC)

National Agency for Food, Drugs Administration, and Control (NAFDAC), 176–77, 182–83, 185–94, 196–99, 214–20, 221t, 222

National Association of Chamber of Commerce, Industry, Manufacturing, and Agriculture (NACCIMA), Nigeria, 222

National Cereals Produce Board (NCPB), Kenya, 23–24

National Codex Committee (NCC): Nigeria, 165, 176, 176–78, 180–81, 187–89, 191–92; Uganda, 381

National Committee on World Trade Organization (NCWTO), 11, 18, 26

National Council for Science and Technology (NCST), 26

National Department of Agriculture (NDA), South Africa: action plan, 290; Directorate: Agricultural Production Inputs, 257, 337–38; Directorate: Genetic Resources, 256, 335–36; Directorate: Plant Health and Quality, 255–56, 266–77, 333–34; Directorate of Veterinary Services, 256–57, 336–37; Division: National Phytosanitary Matters, 333–34; Division: Plant Health Auditing, 334; fishery regulation, 348

National Department of Health, South Africa, 255, 305t, 333

National Directorate of Forestry and Wildlife (DNFFB), Mozambique, 110–11

National Directorate of Livestock (DINAP), Mozambique, 73, 110, 125

National Drugs Authority (NDA), Uganda, 418

National Economic Development and Labor Council (NEDLAC), South Africa, 250–51

National Enquiry Point (NEP), 382

National Environment Management Authority (NEMA), Uganda, 376, 418

National Institute for Food Science and Technology (NIFST), Nigeria, 177

National Institute for Standardization and Quality (INNOQ): adequacy, 120–21, 134; conformity assessment, 122; functions, 123–25; Mozambique development assistance, 80–81, 90, 98

National Laboratory for Water and Food Hygiene (LNHAA), Mozambique, 109

National Metrology Laboratory (NML), South Africa, 253, 255, 258–59, 290, 296–304t

National Seed Service (SNS), Mozambique, 109–10

National Standards Council (NSC), Uganda, 380

National Sugar Institute (INA), Mozambique, 112

National Veterinary Research Institute (INIVE), Mozambique, 112

NCC. *See* National Codex Committee (NCC)

Ncema Supplies, 286

NCPB. *See* National Cereals Produce Board (NCPB)

NCS. *See* Nigerian Customs Service (NCS)

NCST. *See* National Council for Science and Technology (NCST)

NCWTO. *See* National Committee on World Trade Organization (NCWTO)

NDA. *See* National Department of Agriculture (NDA); National Drugs Authority (NDA)

NECA. *See* Nigerian Employers' Consultative Association (NECA)

NEDLAC. *See* National Economic Development and Labor Council (NEDLAC)

NEMA. *See* National Environment Management Authority (NEMA)

NEP. *See* National Enquery Point (NEP)

NEPC. *See* Nigerian Export Promotion Council (NEPC)

NIFST. *See* National Institute for Food Science and Technology (NIFST)

Nigeria: action plan for standards compliance, 218–22, 224–25; animal health regulation, 184; awareness of international standards, 197–98, 219; capacity building for standards and regulations development, 194–97; cocoa exports, 209–13; Codex Alimetarius Commission participation and conformity, 165, 176–78, 180–81, 188–89, 191–92; compliance costs for international standards, 220; destination of exports, 170, 232t; donor-supported programs for standards capacity, 195t, 196t, 197t; enforcement of international norms, 186, 219–20; exports, 169–70, 231t; fiscal deficits, 167, 227t; fish exports, 213–15; food and beverage exports, 207–9; food safety regulation, 183–84; gross domestic product trends, 166, 226t, 223; Hazard Analysis Critical Control Point adoption, 187, 191, 198–99, 220, 224; horticulture exports, 205–7; import bans, 201, 203t, 204; imports, 170, 230t, 233t; income sectors, 168, 169t, 229t; inflation, 167; international standards development participation, 176–82; ISO 9000 adoption, 198–99, 224; light manufacturing regulation, 185–86; macroeconomic performance, 166–67; manufacturing capacity utilization, 167, 226t; ongoing public and private initiatives related to regulatory standards, 216–18; plant protection regulation, 184; product differentiation for export, 204; regional standards development, 181–82; Sanitary and Phytosanitary agreement conformity, 176, 186–94, 201, 204–5, 220, 223; tariff structure in importing countries, 170–73, 223; Technical Barriers to Trade agreement conformity, 201, 204, 220, 223; trade agreements, 173–75; trade legislation and regulation, 184–85; trade performance, 167–68, 228t; United Kingdom plant interception notices, 199, 200t, 201; United States refusal of exports, 201, 202t; World Trade Organization interacting agencies, 175–76

Nigerian Customs Service (NCS), 218

Nigerian Employers' Consultative Association (NECA), 217

Nigerian Export Promotion Council (NEPC), 214

Nigerian Industrial Standard (NIS), 191

Nigerian Marketing Association (NIMARK), 217

Nigerian Textile Mills (NTM), 211–13

NIMARK. *See* Nigerian Marketing Association (NIMARK)

NIS. *See* Nigerian Industrial Standard (NIS)

NML. *See* National Metrology Laboratory (NML)

NOGAMU, 401

NSC. *See* National Standards Council (NSC)

NTM. *See* Nigerian Textile Mills (NTM)

NTSIKA Enterprise Promotion Agency, 281, 285–86

O

OECD. *See* Organization for Economic Cooperation and Development (OECD)

Office for the Promotion of Commercial Farming (GPSCA), 72, 84, 90

Office International des Epizooties (OIE), 12–13, 110, 130, 160–61, 189, 272–73

OIE. *See* Office International des Epizooties (OIE)

OIML. *See* International Organization of Legal Metrology (OIML)

OPEC. *See* Organization of Petroleum Exporting Countries (OPEC)

OPS. *See* Organized Private Sector (OPS)

organic farming: Kenya, 55–56; Uganda, 400–1, 404, 423t

Organization for Economic Cooperation and Development (OECD), 250, 280

Organization of Petroleum Exporting Countries (OPEC), 175

Organized Private Sector (OPS), Nigeria, 176, 217

P

Patent Cooperation Treaty (PCT), 85

PCPB. *See* Pest Control Products Board (PCPB)

PCT. *See* Patent Cooperation Treaty (PCT)

peanut, Mozambique export, 103–4

Perishable Product Export Control Board (PPECB), South Africa, 257–58, 267, 334–35, 341–42, 359t, 360t

Pest Control Products Board (PCPB), Kenya, 22, 25, 27

pest risk analysis (PRA), 54–55, 394

Pesticide Initiative Program (PIP), 38

Pesticide Residue Trial Requirements Act, 338

Pesticides, Kenya certification, 25–26

Phenix Logistics Ltd., 396–97

PID. *See* Ports Inspection Division (PID)

PIP. *See* Pesticide Initiative Program (PIP)

Plan of Action for the Reduction of Absolute Poverty (PARPA), Mozambique, 79

Plant Protection Act, 15

Plant Quarantine Service (PQS): Kenya, 16; Nigeria, 187, 198–99, 204, 217

PODE, Mozambique development assistance, 81

Ports Inspection Division (PID), Nigeria, 191

PPECB. *See* Perishable Product Export Control Board (PPECB)

PQS. *See* Plant Quarantine Service (PQS)

PRA. *See* pest risk analysis (PRA)

Private Sector Foundation (PSF), Uganda, 376

PROAGRI, Mozambique development assistance, 82–83, 105

PROCONSUMERS, Mozambique, 125

PSF. *See* Private Sector Foundation (PSF)

R

RDA. *See* Recommended Dietary Allowance (RDA)

Recommended Dietary Allowance (RDA), 276

Red Meat Abbattoir Association (RMAA), South Africa, 271

Registration and Regulations Directorate, 191

RMAA. *See* Red Meat Abbattoir Association (RMAA)

S

SABS. *See* South African Bureau of Standards (SABS)

SACU. *See* Southern Africa Customs Unit (SACU)

SADC. *See* Southern African Development Community (SADC)

SALMA. *See* South Africa Lumber Miller's Association (SALMA)

salt, Mozambique trade: facilitation, 115; harmonization of standards and regulations, 115; import, 115t; national program of salt iodination, 115–16; production, 114t

SAMIC. *See* South African Meat Industry Company (SAMIC)

Samsokol Construction, 286

SANAS. *See* South African National Accreditation System (SANAS)

Sanitary and Phytosanitary (SPS) agreement: Kenya conformity, 1, 11–12, 15, 20, 26, 30, 54–56; Mozambique conformity, 65–66, 135, 147–48t; Nigeria conformity, 176, 186–94, 201, 204–5, 220, 223; Southern African Development Community activities, 129; Uganda conformity, 381–82

Sanitary and Phytosanitary Inspection Services (SPIS), Uganda, 377–78

SAP. *See* Structural Adjustment Program (SAP)

seafood. *See* fish

Sector Partnership Fund (SPF), South Africa, 282

seed, Kenya certification, 25

seed, Mozambique export: National Seed Service, 109–10; regulation, 104–5; studies related to legislation, 106–7

SGS International, 30

SIC. *See* Standards Industrial Council (SIC)

SIDA. *See* Swedish International Development Agency (SIDA)

Small, Medium, and Micro Enterprises (SMMEs), South Africa, 235, 253, 262, 274, 281–87

Small-Scale Fisheries Development Institute (IDPPE), Mozambique, 118

SMMEs. *See* Small, Medium, and Micro Enterprises (SMMEs)

SNS. *See* National Seed Service (SNS)

SOMOPAL, 92

SON. *See* Standards Organization of Nigeria (SON)

South Africa: appeal fees, 357–58t; Codex standard compliance, 251–52, 273–74, 275t, 278–81, 347; cross cutting issues pertaining to standards compliance, 273–74, 290; destination of exports, 246–47, 318–25t; electro-technical exports, 259–61; export intensity and composition, 239, 240t, 241, 243t; fish exports, 246–66; foreign development assistance, 283; foreign exchange earnings and disbursement, 242–43; forestry exports, 261–63; fruit exports, 266–71; gross domestic product trends, 236t, 237t, 309t; growth in aggregate demand, 238t, 309t, 310t; Hazard Analysis Critical Control Point compliance, 265, 267, 270–71, 273, 280, 347–48, 366–67; HIV/AIDS impact on trade, 288–89; import intensity, 241t, 242; import origins, 247–48, 318–25t; inspection fees, 354–55t, 356t, 361–62t; International Organization for Standardization compliance, 264, 270–71, 277–78, 284–87, 366; international standards development participation, 274, 275t, 276–81; investment

in fixed assets, 238t, 308t; laboratory fees, 356t; legislation and enforcement, 343–45; levies, 359t, 363t, 364t; macroeconomic conditions, 235–37; meat exports, 271–73; National Department of Health action plan, 255, 305t; National Metrology Laboratory action plan, 290, 296–304t; private sector development assistance, 281–83; production growth in manufacturing, 239t, 308t, 310t; regulatory structures and policies, 253, 254f, 255–59, 333–39, 341–42; sectors of economy, 237–39; shifts in exports by sector, 243–45, 311t, 312–18t; shifts in imports by sector, 245; South African Bureau of Standards action plan, 290, 291–95t; standards preparation process, 339, 340f, 341; textile exports, 244, 246–47, 263–64; trade agreements, 248–50; trade negotiation institutions, 250–51; veterinary laboratories, 368–70t

South Africa–European Union Trade, Development and Cooperation Agreement; development cooperation, 249–50; economic cooperation, 250; free trade area, 249

South Africa Lumber Miller's Association (SALMA), 287

South African Bureau of Standards (SABS), 252, 257–61, 263–66, 277–82, 285–88, 291–95t, 338–39, 340f, 341, 345–49, 354–55t

South African Meat Industry Company (SAMIC), 271, 334

South African National Accreditation System (SANAS), 252–53, 257–59, 279–80, 288, 341, 347, 380

South African Natural Beef, 366–67

Southern Africa Customs Unit (SACU), 249

Southern African Development Community (SADC), 67, 80: aims, 161; Cooperation in Accreditation, 128–29, 164; Cooperation in Legal Metrology, 127–28, 163; Cooperation in Measurement Traceability, 127, 163; Cooperation in Standardization, 128, 164; formation, 161; membership, 164; Mozambique involvement, 126–27; Sanitary and Phytosanitary agreement activities, 129; South Africa involvement, 249, 279–80; SQAM Expert Group, 127, 163; sugar agreements, 99; Trade Protocol, 85, 127, 132, 135, 161–62

SOVIN, 91

SPEED. *See* Support for the Private Enterprise Expansion and Development (SPEED)

SPF. *See* Sector Partnership Fund (SPF)

SPIS. *See* Sanitary and Phytosanitary Inspection Services (SPIS)

SPS agreement. *See* Sanitary and Phytosanitary (SPS) agreement

SQAM. *See* Standardization, Quality Assurance, Accreditation, and Metrology (SQAM)

Standardization, Quality Assurance, Accreditation, and Metrology (SQAM), 127, 131, 162–63, 252, 258–59, 280, 283–84, 382, 384

Standards Industrial Council (SIC), Kenya, 13b

Standards Organization of Nigeria (SON), 185–90, 192–99, 204, 218–20, 222

Structural Adjustment Program (SAP): Nigeria, 165, 175, 184, 209, 223; Uganda, 375–76

sugar, Kenya import standards, 22–23

sugar, Mozambique export: factories, 98–99; production trends, 86t, 99

SUMOVIT, 91

Support for the Private Enterprise Expansion and Development (SPEED), 376, 393, 403

Swedish International Development Agency (SIDA), 80–81, 283

T

TAC. *See* Tender Advice Centre Programme (TAC)

tariffs: European Union, 172–73, 174t, 326–32t; Mozambique, 113; United States, 171–72

TBT agreement. *See* Technical Barriers to Trade (TBT) agreement

Technical Barriers to Trade (TBT) agreement: Kenya conformity, 11, 15, 20, 26, 30, 56; Mozambique conformity, 65–66, 135–36, 147t; Nigeria conformity, 201, 204, 220, 223; Uganda conformity, 381–82

TEFU. *See* Tropical Ecological Foods Uganda (TEFU)

Tender Advice Centre Programme (TAC), South Africa, 281

textiles, Kenya export: commodity support programs, 59–60; costs of production, 49t; ginning, 49–50; industry needs, 50–51, 58; marketing, 48–49; production, 47–48; standards, 49–50, 58–59; textiles manufacturing, 50

textiles, Nigeria export, 210–13

textiles, South Africa export: barriers, 264; compliance costs, 264; destinations, 246–47; domestic regulations, 263–64; domestic standards, 264; industry perspectives on standards, 288; regulations, 347; trends, 244

textiles, Uganda export: barriers, 395; Phenix Logistics Ltd. case study, 396–97; standards, 394–96

Thabisco Chemicals, 285–86

TIDP. *See* Trade and Investment Development Programme (TIDP)

timber, South Africa export: barriers, 262–63; compliance costs, 263; domestic regulations, 261–62; domestic standards, 262; industry perspectives on standards, 287–88; regulations, 346

Total Quality Management (TQM), Uganda, 376, 379

TPRM. *See* Trade Policy Review Mechanism (TPRM)

TQM. *See* Total Quality Management (TQM)

Trade and Investment Development Programme (TIDP), South Africa, 281, 283

Trade Policy Review Mechanism (TPRM), 187–88

Tropical Ecological Foods Uganda (TEFU), 401

U

UCDA. *See* Uganda Coffee Development Authority (UCDA)

UCTF. *See* Uganda Coffee Trade Federation (UCTF)

UEPB. *See* Uganda Export Promotion Board (UEPB)

UFEA. *See* Uganda Flower Exporters' Association (UFEA)

UFPEA. *See* Uganda Fish Processors' and Exporters' Association (UFPEA)

Uganda: accreditation of firms for certification, 404; barriers to trade, 401–2; capacity building for standards promotion, 402–3, 424–25t; coffee exports, 384–88, 400–1; destination of exports, 374–75, 406t; Economic Recovery Program, 375–76; exports, 372, 373f, 374, 406t, 407t; fish exports, 391–94; flower exports, 388–89; fruit and vegetable exports, 397–400; gross domestic product, 372, 408–9t; Hazard Critical Control Point compliance, 394, 417; honey exports, 389–91; horticultural export code of practice, 412–14t; imports, 406t; International Organization for Standardization compliance, 380–81, 395; international standard development participation, 381–82, 384; overview of trade, 371–72;

reforms in trade policy, 415t; regulatory and institutional framework, 376–82, 383t, 384; sensitization of stakeholders to standards, 403–4, 422t; specialty product promotion, 404, 423t; standards development, 379–81; standards types and status, 410–11t; technical regulations by sector, 417–19; textile exports, 394–97

Uganda Coffee Development Authority (UCDA), 376, 385–86

Uganda Coffee Trade Federation (UCTF), 376, 385–86

Uganda Export Promotion Board (UEPB), 376, 398

Uganda Fish Processors' and Exporters' Association (UFPEA), 376, 403

Uganda Flower Exporters' Association (UFEA), 376, 388–89

Uganda Garment Industries Limited (UGIL), 396

Uganda Honey Association (UHA), 376, 389–91

Uganda Manufacturers' Association (UMA), 376, 395–96

Uganda National Bureau of Standards (UNBS), 376–81, 390, 394–97, 399, 402–4, 416t, 421f

Uganda Revenue Authority (URA), 376, 395

UGIL. *See* Uganda Garment Industries Limited (UGIL)

UHA. *See* Uganda Honey Association (UHA)

UL. *See* Underwriters Laboratories (UL)

UMA. *See* Uganda Manufacturers' Association (UMA)

UNBS. *See* Uganda National Bureau of Standards (UNBS)

Underwriters Laboratories (UL), 261

UNDP. *See* United Nations Development Program (UNDP)

UNEP. *See* United Nations Environment Program (UNEP)

UNIDO, 80–82, 394

United Nations Development Program (UNDP), 196

United Nations Environment Program (UNEP), 338

United States Agency for International Development (USAID), 283, 376

URA. *See* Uganda Revenue Authority (URA); Uruguay Round Agreement (URA)

Uruguay Round Agreement (URA), 165, 222

USAID. *See* United States Agency for International Development (USAID)

V

value added tax (VAT): Mozambique, 78, 116; South Africa, 263, 265

VAM. *See* Vulnerability Assessment and Mapping (VAM)

VAT. *See* value added tax (VAT)

vegetables. *See* fruits and vegetables

Vulnerability Assessment and Mapping (VAM), 72

W

wheat: Kenya import standards, 24; quality specifications, 24b

WIPO. *See* World Industrial Property Organization (WIPO)

World Industrial Property Organization (WIPO), 85

World Trade Organization (WTO): creation, 135, 222; South Africa agreements, 248–49. *See also specific agreements*

WTO. *See* World Trade Organization (WTO)

Z

Zambia, Malawi, Mozambique Growth Triangle (ZMM-GT), 84–85

ZMM-GT. *See* Zambia, Malawi, Mozambique Growth Triangle

Standards and Global Trade: A Voice for Africa provides information and guidance for policymakers, the development community, and others in the critical area of "behind the border" barriers to trade. With a view to promoting efforts to strengthen Africa's capacity to meet trade standards and comply with technical regulations, the volume examines the link between those standards and regulations and export success in case studies of five countries: Kenya, Mozambique, Nigeria, South Africa, and Uganda.

Each chapter describes the economic context of trade standards in a country and examines the mechanisms by which standards and regulations are established and revised at the local and international levels. The authors — local experts in the region — review existing trade regulations and determine the extent to which they are consistent with international practices. They also analyze each country's physical infrastructure, organizational capacities, and current standard implementation process and consider the probable impact of new standards, regulations, and related production/marketing practices in key industries.

The first comprehensive assessment of the relationship between trade standards and development priorities in Sub-Saharan Africa, this volume offers concrete action plans for supporting African firms and farmers in their efforts to improve product quality and reach international markets in key commodity sectors.

THE WORLD BANK

15473

9 780821 354735

0-8213-5473-6